YEARBOOK ON INTERNATIONAL INVESTMENT LAW & POLICY 2017

YEARBOOK ON INTERNATIONAL INVESTMENT LAW & POLICY
LISA E. SACHS, Editor
Director, Columbia Center on Sustainable Investment, New York City
LISE J. JOHNSON, Editor
Head, Investment Law and Policy, Columbia Center on Sustainable Investment, New York City
JESSE COLEMAN, Editor
Legal Researcher, Columbia Center on Sustainable Investment, New York City
ROMAIN LAUGIER, Managing Editor
Alumnus, University Paris I Panthéon-Sorbonne and College of Europe

ADVISORY BOARD

JOSÉ E. ALVAREZ
New York University School of Law, New York City

RUDOLF DOLZER
University of Bonn

EMMANUEL GAILLARD
Shearman & Sterling LLP, Paris

GABRIELLE KAUFMANN-KOHLER
University of Geneva Law School

PETROS C. MAVROIDIS
Columbia Law School, New York City

JAN PAULSSON
Three Crowns, LLP, Washington, D.C.

DANIEL M. PRICE
Rock Creek Global Advisors LLC, Washington, D.C.

FRANCISCO ORREGO VICUÑA
Heidelberg Center, Santiago

LOUIS T. WELLS
Harvard Business School, Boston

MANFRED SCHEKULIN
Austrian Federal Ministry of Economy, Family and Youth, Vienna

GEORGE A. BERMANN
Columbia Law School, New York City

AHMED S. EL KOSHERI
Kosheri, Rashed and Riad, Cairo

MICHAEL HWANG, SC
Barrister & Arbitrator, Singapore

CAROLYN B. LAMM
White & Case LLP, Washington, D.C.

THEODORE H. MORAN
Georgetown School of Foreign Service, Washington, D.C.

W. MICHAEL REISMAN
Yale Law School, New Haven

CHRISTOPH SCHREUER
Of Counsel at Zeiler Partners, Vienna

MUTHUCUMARASWAMY SORNARAJAH
National University Singapore Law School

STEPHEN M. SCHWEBEL
Independent Arbitrator and Counsel Washington, D.C.

KARL P. SAUVANT, Founding Editor of the Yearbook
Columbia Center on Sustainable Investment, New York City

EDITORIAL COMMITTEE

N. JANSEN CALAMITA
National University of Singapore, Centre for International Law

MARK FELDMAN
Peking University School of Transnational Law, Shenzen

PETER MUCHLINSKI
School of Oriental and African Studies School of Law, London

LUKE NOTTAGE
Sydney Law School

UCHEORA ONWUAMAEGBU
Arent Fox, LLP, Washington, D.C.

FEDERICO ORTINO
King's College London School of Law

AUGUST REINISCH
University of Vienna

CATHARINE TITI
French National Centre for Scientific Research (CNRS) & CERSA, University Paris II Panthéon-Assas

EDITORIAL STAFF

EMMA LEONORE A. DE KOSTER
Columbia Law School, New York City

NICCOLÒ PIETRO CASTAGNO
Legal Counsel

NATHAN LOBEL
Columbia Center on Sustainable Investment, New York City

ISABELLA REYNOSO
Columbia Law School, New York City

ARTURO SÁNCHEZ BROWN
Columbia Law School, New York City

TINGLIANG WANG
New York University School of Law

RISHIKEESH WIJAYA
Columbia Law School, New York City

YEARBOOK ON INTERNATIONAL INVESTMENT LAW & POLICY 2017

Editors
LISA E. SACHS
LISE J. JOHNSON
JESSE COLEMAN

UNIVERSITY PRESS

Great Clarendon Street, Oxford, OX2 6DP,
United Kingdom

Oxford University Press is a department of the University of Oxford.
It furthers the University's objective of excellence in research, scholarship,
and education by publishing worldwide. Oxford is a registered trade mark of
Oxford University Press in the UK and in certain other countries

© Oxford University Press 2019

The moral rights of the authors have been asserted

First Edition published in 2019

Impression: 1

All rights reserved. No part of this publication may be reproduced, stored in
a retrieval system, or transmitted, in any form or by any means, without the
prior permission in writing of Oxford University Press, or as expressly permitted
by law, by licence or under terms agreed with the appropriate reprographics
rights organization. Enquiries concerning reproduction outside the scope of the
above should be sent to the Rights Department, Oxford University Press, at the
address above

You must not circulate this work in any other form
and you must impose this same condition on any acquirer

Crown copyright material is reproduced under Class Licence
Number C01P0000148 with the permission of OPSI
and the Queen's Printer for Scotland

Published in the United States of America by Oxford University Press
198 Madison Avenue, New York, NY 10016, United States of America

British Library Cataloguing in Publication Data
Data available

ISBN 978–0–19–883038–2

Printed and bound by
CPI Group (UK) Ltd, Croydon, CR0 4YY

Links to third party websites are provided by Oxford in good faith and
for information only. Oxford disclaims any responsibility for the materials
contained in any third party website referenced in this work.

COLUMBIA CENTER ON SUSTAINABLE INVESTMENT

The Columbia Center on Sustainable Investment (CCSI) is a leading applied research center and forum for the study, practice, and discussion of sustainable international investment. CCSI focuses on analysing important topical policy-oriented issues and constructing and implementing an investment framework that promotes sustainable development and the mutual trust needed for long-term investments that can be practically adopted by governments, companies, and civil society. The Center undertakes its mission through interdisciplinary research, advisory projects, multi-stakeholder dialogue, educational programmes, and the development of resources and tools. The Center's website is found at http://ccsi.columbia.edu/.

SUBMISSION POLICY

The *Investment Yearbook* is an annual publication published by Oxford University Press in association with the Columbia Center on Sustainable Investment. It draws on the guidance of a distinguished Advisory Board, ongoing engagement by an Editorial Committee consisting of leading academics in the field of investment law and policy, and skilful work by an Editorial Staff of students from Columbia Law School.

The *Investment Yearbook* addresses legal and policy issues in the area of international investment—from national, regional, and international perspectives. The Editorial Committee invites for publication manuscripts that are of outstanding quality in terms of academic rigour, quality of the argument, originality, and contribution to the field of international investment law and policy. The *Investment Yearbook* will not consider a manuscript that has been published previously. Every manuscript that is considered for publication will be assessed through an external double-blind peer-review process. The style of the manuscripts should be in accordance with the OSCOLA guidelines, as adapted to the *Yearbook* (available from the Editorial Committee).

The Editorial Committee welcomes the submission of manuscripts to the *Investment Yearbook*. Manuscripts should be electronically sent to the Columbia Center on Sustainable Investment, ccsi@law.columbia.edu.

PEER REVIEWERS

The Editorial Committee of the Investment Yearbook thanks all those who helped in the preparation of this publication and especially the peer reviewers, who include:

Axel Berger
Nathalie Bernasconi-Osterwalder
Ernesto Bonafé
Lee M. Caplan
Damien Charlotin
Manjiao (Cliff) Chi
Kaitlin Y. Cordes
Aaron Cosbey
Julia Cortez da Cuhna Cruz
Rahul Donde
Kabir Duggal
Tomaso Ferrando
John Gaffney
Alejandro M. Garro
David Gaukrodger
Katia Fach Gómez
Sarah McGrath
Gus Van Harten
Jarrod Hepburn
Matthew Hodgson
Ursula Kriebaum
Hannes Lenk
Miguel Pérez Ludeña
Alexandra A. K. Meise

Kate Miles
Suzy H. Nikièma
Pietro Ortolani
Nicolás Marcelo Perrone
Matthew C. Porterfield
Theodore R. Posner
Anthea Roberts
Andrea Saldarriaga
Mavluda Sattorova
Harm Schepel
Wouter P. F. Schmit Jongbloed
Thomas Schultz
Eloise Scotford
Jeremy K. Sharpe
Elizabeth Sheargold
Susan Sell
Elisabeth Tuerk
Anthony Vanduzer
Jorge E. Viñuales
Markus Wagner
Heng Wang
JoAnn Kamuf Ward
Elizabeth Whitsett
Katia Yannaca-Small

FOREWORD

It is a privilege to write a foreword for a yearbook, as it allows one to take a pause, to think back and ponder about the year that has passed. And it is particularly gratifying to prepare a foreword for a yearbook on international investment law when every year comes with a host of new developments. Unlike international trade law which has crystallized over decades and consolidated with the 1995 Marrakesh Agreements establishing the WTO, issues in investment law continue to unfold, bringing with them calls for a more unified development, for more consistency, especially against the background of over 3,000 underlying treaties. At the same time, the system devised to settle disputes arising under international investment laws, treaties, and conventions in the 1960s has come under scrutiny and strong criticism not only by the users of the investment dispute settlement system—states, private investors, and practitioners—but also, and most importantly, in several regions, by civil society, parliaments, and political decision-makers.

The recurrent question for over a decade now has been about how to revisit the investment arbitration system, how to assess whether it still serves the purposes for which it had been originally designed, and whether it needs to be reformed. Not surprisingly, different views have been expressed over the years about relying on the international arbitration community to correct deficiencies encountered with the arbitration system, to deal with inconsistency in outcomes, to give meaning to broad concepts by developing jurisprudence, and to decide on procedural innovations drawing upon arbitral practice in commercial cases. Some have suggested that institutions in charge of administering investment arbitration should be able to adapt the rules and the practice to an evolving international context. At the same time, states have begun to modify their model treaties and to conclude new generation treaties where they clarify the meaning of core protection standards, express what they do not agree to, protect their right to regulate not only through positive wording but also through procedural safeguards in investor-state dispute settlement (ISDS), and enhance predictability of the arbitration process by including detailed dispute settlement procedures into the treaties themselves. But while doing so, going forward, very little has been done with respect to the existing network of over 3,000 treaties that cover an important part of the investment flows across the globe.

The latest wave of discontent and suspicion with the ISDS system has been more powerful than previous ones, or possibly it has gathered power from the previous ones. The view expressed by the former Solicitor General of Singapore, Mr

Sundaresh Menon, that it was up to the states, the masters of investment promotion and protection treaties, to take up the reform of the system they themselves had set up, reflects the state of mind of the delegations participating in the 50th UNCITRAL Commission in July of 2017.

The Commission had heard about the challenges posed by investment treaty arbitration already in the context of the negotiation of the Transparency Rules and the Mauritius Convention in 2010 onwards. It had seen proposals for reform that were being considered by a number of other organizations, including the European Union proposal to replace the existing ISDS system with international investment courts. In 2016, it considered mechanisms for states to incorporate reform options into the investment treaty negotiation process. Then, in 2017, after consultations with a wide variety of stakeholders, the Commission gave UNCITRAL's Working Group III a mandate to work on ISDS reform.

In its mandate, the Commission requested the Working Group to: (i) first, identify and consider concerns regarding ISDS; (ii) second, consider whether reform was desirable in light of any identified concerns; and (iii) third, if the Working Group were to conclude that reform was desirable, develop any relevant solutions to be recommended to the Commission. The Working Group was requested to ensure that the deliberations would be government-led with high-level input from all governments while benefiting from the widest possible breadth of available expertise from all stakeholders, consensus-based and fully transparent.

Emphasis is put in the mandate on 'high-level' input from governments, in light of the importance of the broader policy messages and implications but also because complex issues of public international law are involved.

It is gratifying to note that at the same time the UNCITRAL Commission is embarking on this reform agenda, efforts are under way also in a multilateral context in the ICSID Secretariat to revise and refine the arbitration rules and further address shortcomings and concerns with the existing ISDS system. The process at ICSID also takes a broad and inclusive approach, involving many stakeholders and ultimately turning to the member states of the ICSID Convention for a revision of the rules underlying the system.

While the pendulum of international relations keeps swinging, from unilateralism to bilateralism, regionalism to multilateralism and back, it is rewarding to consider that when it comes to reforming an important component of international economic law, the multilateral route has been preferred over other avenues for reform.

UNCITRAL, drawing on the global convening power of the United Nations, is the most multilateral forum available to deliberate such issues. UNCITRAL has a reputation for serious and substantive legal work with both developing and developed countries. It is our shared responsibility to live up to the expectations of our states (members and non-members) and numerous stakeholders and ensure in the year to come that the UNCITRAL forum indeed provides the platform for constructive and effective deliberations on the reform of ISDS.

Beyond the interesting exercise of taking a big picture approach to the foreword of the *Yearbook*, it is the *Yearbook* and its many chapters that are really the important contribution to international investment law. The *Yearbook* for 2017, like the previous editions, constitutes the valuable stocktaking of steps and stages in the development of international law. It will inform generations of researchers and practitioners about what today's actors had in mind and how from the contractions and convulsions of international deliberations and negotiations, a body of law has taken shape.

Anna Joubin-Bret
June 2018

CONTENTS—SUMMARY

Author Biographies   xxxi

Part I YEAR IN REVIEW

A. DEVELOPMENTS IN FOREIGN INVESTMENT

1. Trends in Global FDI Flows and Policy Implications — 5
   James X Zhan

2. Blended Finance in 2017: Advancing Financing for Development but Not a Panacea — 15
   Brooke Skartvedt Güven

3. Institutional Developments in Investment Law and Policy — 36
   Taylor St John

4. 2017 Developments in Home and Host State Policy Responses to Foreign Direct Investment — 49
   Olabisi D Akinkugbe and Sara L Seck

5. Investment Facilitation Agreement in the WTO: Where is it Headed? — 65
   Reji K Joseph

6. Trends and Developments in the Credit and Political Risk Insurance Market in 2017 — 77
   Julie A Martin, Stephen J Kay, and Mark van der Does

B. DEVELOPMENTS IN TREATIES AND TREATY POLICY

7. International Investment Agreement, 2017: A Review of Trends and New Approaches — 99
   Jesse Coleman, Lise J Johnson, Lisa E Sachs, and Nathan Lobel

C. DEVELOPMENTS IN INVESTOR-STATE ARBITRATION

8. Recent Developments in ISDS: Jurisdiction and Admissibility—Procedure and Conduct — 133
   Catharine Titi

Contents—Summary

9. 2017 Developments in Investment Treaty Arbitration 150
   Jarrod Hepburn

D. INVESTMENT AND...

10. Human Rights in International Investment Law: Recent Trends in Arbitration and Treaty-Making Practice 177
    Markus Krajewski

11. Developments in International Investment Law in Relation to Intellectual Property in 2017 194
    Carlos M Correa

12. Investor–State Arbitration in the Extractive Industries 206
    Zoe Phillips Williams

13. Farmland in International Investment Law and Dispute Settlement: Developments in 2017 218
    Lorenzo Cotula and Thierry Berger

E. REGION REPORTS

14. International Investment Law and Policy: 2017 Developments in Africa 231
    Mouhamadou Madana Kane

15. Expanding ISDS, Active National Courts, and Concluding Mega-Regional Treaties: 2017 Developments in International Investment Law in Asia 247
    Diane A Desierto

16. Developments in International Investment Law and Policy in the European Union 260
    Catharine Titi

17. Recent Trends in Investment Law and Policy in Latin America 273
    Facundo Pérez-Aznar

18. North America Investment Law and Policy: 2017 289
    David Schneiderman

Part II GENERAL ARTICLES

19. Importing WTO General Exceptions into International Investment Agreements: Proportionality, Myths, and Risks 305
    Andrew D Mitchell, James Munro, and Tania Voon

Contents—Summary

20. The FET Standard under CETA: A Missed Opportunity to Restore the Balance between Private and Public Interests in the EU Investment Treaty Landscape? 356
    Antonin Sobek

21. The Notion of Investor under the Energy Charter Treaty: The Latest Developments in the Spanish Solar Disputes 389
    Crina Baltag

22. Policy Coherence and the Promotion of Foreign Direct Investment in the Renewable Energy Sector: Lessons from Europe 409
    Avidan Kent

23. Integrating Civil Liability Principles into International Investment Law: A Solution to Environmental Damage Caused by Foreign Investors? 446
    Alessandra Mistura

24. Unanticipated Consequences: The Human Rights Implications of Bringing Sovereign Debt Disputes within Investment Treaty Arbitration 492
    Juan Pablo Bohoslavksy and Edward Guntrip

25. Has ISDS Gone Rogue for Australia and New Zealand? CPTPP (C-3PO), RCEP (RD-D2), and Beyond 536
    Amokura Kawharu and Luke Nottage

26. India's 2015 Model BIT Against the Backdrop of Global ISDS reforms 570
    Aveek Chakravarty

CONTENTS—DETAILED

Author Biographies   xxxi

Part I YEAR IN REVIEW

A. DEVELOPMENTS IN FOREIGN INVESTMENT

1. Trends in Global FDI Flows and Policy Implications
James X Zhan

A.	Introduction	1.01
B.	Global Investment Trends and Prospects	1.02
	1. Trends: low level and weak recovery	1.02
	2. Prospects: fragile growth with high uncertainty	1.05
	3. Impact: lacklustre for GVCs and productivity	1.08
C.	Global Investment Policy Developments	1.15
	1. Dynamics in policymaking	1.16
	2. Dichotomy in regulatory direction	1.19
	3. Divergence in the approach to IIAs	1.21
	4. Dilemmas in pursuing sustainable development objectives	1.24
D.	Concluding Remarks	1.29

2. Blended Finance in 2017: Advancing Financing for Development but Not a Panacea
Brooke Skartvedt Güven

A.	Introduction: Blended Finance in 2017	2.01
B.	Development Finance Flows: Significant Gaps Persisted in 2017	2.04
	1. Domestic resource mobilization	2.05
	2. Private finance	2.08
	3. Official development assistance	2.10
C.	Blended Finance: Notable 2017 Developments at the G20, the World Bank, and the OECD	2.13
	1. The G20	2.14
	2. The World Bank Group	2.16
	3. The OECD	2.18

D.	Blended Finance: Not a Panacea?	2.20
	1. The financial and/or development additionality of blended finance is not always clear	2.25
	2. Blended finance does not necessarily support pro-poor activities and often focuses on middle-income countries	2.26
	3. Blended finance may give preferential treatment to donor-countries' own private outward investors	2.30
	4. Blended projects may not involve sufficient country ownership and may not align with country development plans	2.32
	5. Blended finance may fail to satisfactorily incorporate transparency, accountability, and stakeholder participation in project design and implementation	2.33
	6. Risks of infrastructure as an asset class are insufficiently considered	2.35
	7. The role of China	2.36
E.	Conclusion	2.37

3. Institutional Developments in Investment Law and Policy
Taylor St John

A.	Introduction	3.01
B.	Unprecedented Deliberations: UNCITRAL	3.05
C.	Amending and Appointing: Developments at Arbitral Institutions	3.14
D.	Exchanging and Updating: OECD and UNCTAD	3.18

4. 2017 Developments in Home and Host State Policy Responses to Foreign Direct Investment
Olabisi D Akinkugbe and Sara L Seck

A.	Introduction	4.01
B.	Business and Human Rights—Europe and Canada	4.03
C.	Continental, Regional, and National FDI Developments in Africa	4.14
	1. The Continental Pan-African Investment Code	4.16
	2. Regulatory developments at the regional level	4.19
	3. Regulatory developments at the national level	4.24
D.	Conclusions	4.29

5. Investment Facilitation Agreement in the WTO: Where is it Headed?
Reji K Joseph

A.	Introduction	5.01
B.	Submissions in the WTO	5.02

C.	Major Elements of an IFA	5.05
D.	Discussion on Investment Facilitation during the Buenos Aires Ministerial Meeting	5.07
E.	Later Developments	5.10
F.	A New Dynamic in the WTO	5.16
	1. Emergence of a new group of capital exporting countries	5.17
	2. Need for developing countries and LDCs to attract FDI and to integrate with global trade	5.20
G.	Limitations of an IFA	5.22
H.	Concluding Remarks	5.25

6. Trends and Developments in the Credit and Political Risk Insurance Market in 2017
Julie A Martin, Stephen J Kay, and Mark van der Does

A.	Introduction	6.01
B.	Industry Statistics	6.04
C.	Size and Growth	6.06
D.	Trends and Developments in the Private Market	6.07
	1. Private market trends and developments	6.07
	2. Private CPRI market trends and developments	6.10
E.	Market Trends and Developments: Focus on Public Sector	6.26
	1. OPIC	6.26
	2. MIGA	6.28
	3. African Trade Insurance Agency (ATI)	6.30
	4. Other Agencies	6.31
F.	Conclusion	6.32

B. DEVELOPMENTS IN TREATIES AND TREATY POLICY

7. International Investment Agreements, 2017: A Review of Trends and New Approaches
Jesse Coleman, Lise J Johnson, Lisa E Sachs, and Nathan Lobel

A.	Introduction	7.01
B.	Covered Investors and Investments	7.09
C.	Substantive Obligations: Focus on Fair and Equitable Treatment	7.20
	1. (How) does FET relate to the customary international law minimum standard of treatment?	7.23
	2. What is the content of 'FET' and how is a breach established?	7.26
	3. A note on other substantive standards	7.34

D. Protecting Public Interest Objectives?		7.36
1. Sustainable development and the public interest		7.37
2. Climate change and environmental measures		7.42
3. Human rights and investor obligations		7.51
E. Conclusion		7.59

C. DEVELOPMENTS IN INVESTOR–STATE ARBITRATION

8. Recent Developments in ISDS: Jurisdiction and Admissibility—Procedure and Conduct
Catharine Titi

A. Jurisdiction and Admissibility	8.01
1. Existence of covered investment	8.01
2. Nationality and foreign control	8.02
3. Umbrella clause and most-favoured-nation treatment	8.05
4. Scope of arbitration clause in Chinese BITs	8.09
5. Intra-EU BITs	8.10
6. Counterclaims	8.11
7. Energy Charter Treaty claims against Russia	8.12
8. Denunciation of the ICSID Convention	8.13
9. Corruption and other illegality	8.17
10. Abuse of right	8.18
11. Jurisdictional objections in the merits phase	8.19
B. Procedure and Conduct	8.20
1. Arbitrator challenges	8.20
2. Bifurcation	8.23
3. Privilege	8.24
4. Power to reconsider pre-award decisions under the ICSID Convention	8.25
5. Power of ICSID tribunals to seek assistance from domestic courts	8.28
C. Conclusions	8.29

9. 2017 Developments in Investment Treaty Arbitration
Jarrod Hepburn

A. Introduction	9.01
B. Merits	9.02
1. 'Investment and …'—human rights, social and environmental issues in investment treaty case law	9.03
2. Domestic judicial conduct and investment treaties: *Eli Lilly v Canada*	9.17
3. Venezuela and the investment treaty regime	9.20
4. Investment treaty regulation of solar power incentives	9.25
5. Domestic delays in administrative or judicial conduct	9.28
6. Proportionality in investment treaty case law	9.29
C. Provisional Measures	9.32

D.	Remedies and Settlements	9.42
E.	Annulment and Set-Aside	9.51

d. INVESTMENT AND ...

10. Human Rights in International Investment Law: Recent Trends in Arbitration and Treaty-Making Practice
Markus Krajewski

A.	Introduction	10.01
B.	Neither Foes nor Friends? Investment Law and International Human Rights	10.03
C.	Recent Developments in Investment Law	10.09
	1. Investor–state dispute settlement cases	10.09
	2. Human rights obligations for investors in investment treaties	10.23
D.	Recent Developments in Human Rights Law-making	10.28
	1. Treaty on business and human rights	10.29
	2. General Comment No 24 of the Social, Economic and Cultural Rights Committee	10.34
E.	Conclusion	10.38

11. Developments in International Investment Law in Relation to Intellectual Property in 2017
Carlos M Correa

A.	Introduction	11.01
B.	Intellectual Property Rights as Investment	11.02
C.	Arbitral Award: *Eli Lilly v Canada*	11.11
	1. The revoked patents: an example of 'evergreening'	11.12
	2. Patents as a protected investment	11.17
	3. NAFTA safeguards	11.21
D.	Final Remarks	11.25

12. Investor–State Arbitration in the Extractive Industries
Zoe Phillips Williams

A.	Introduction	12.01
B.	New Cases	12.07
	1. Acacia Mining and AngloGold Ashanti v Tanzania	12.07
	2. Kingsgate v Thailand	12.12
	3. Rockhopper v Italy	12.17

C.	Concluded Cases	12.21
	1. Bear Creek v Peru	12.21
	2. Burlington Resources v Ecuador	12.33
D.	Conclusion	12.38

13. Farmland in International Investment Law and Dispute Settlement: Developments in 2017
Lorenzo Cotula and Thierry Berger

A.	Introduction	13.01
B.	Policy Developments	13.05
C.	Developments in Investment Disputes	13.12
D.	Future Outlook	13.17

E. REGION REPORTS

14. International Investment Law and Policy: 2017 Developments in Africa
Mouhamadou Madana Kane

A.	Introduction	14.01
B.	Investment Treaty Practice: Overview of Trends and Lessons Learned	14.04
	1. International investment agreements: negotiation, signature and ratification	14.05
	2. Investor–state disputes	14.09
C.	Investment Treaty Policy: The Positives, the Negatives, and the *Rendez-Vous Manqués*	14.16
	1. The positives	14.17
	2. The negatives and the *rendez-vous manqués*	14.30
D.	Conclusion	14.33

15. Expanding ISDS, Active National Courts, and Concluding Mega-Regional Treaties: 2017 Developments in International Investment Law in Asia
Diane A Desierto

A.	Introduction	15.01
B.	Contested Gateway Issues over Jurisdiction and Admissibility	15.03
	1. Unsuccessful public policy or regulatory defences	15.11

C.	Active National Courts on Investor–State Arbitration	15.13
	1. New models of mega-regional or regional investment treaties and Asian arbitral rules reform	15.16
D.	Conclusion	15.19

16. Developments in International Investment Law and Policy in the European Union
Catharine Titi

A.	Introduction	16.01
B.	State-of-play of EU Negotiations and Investment Agreements	16.02
C.	Division of Competences between the EU and its Member States	16.04
D.	International Investment Court and Multilateral Reform of ISDS	16.08
E.	Compatibility with EU Law: Investment Court and Intra-EU BITs	16.12
F.	Conclusions	16.18

17. Recent Trends in Investment Law and Policy in Latin America
Facundo Pérez-Aznar

A.	Introduction	17.01
B.	Trends in the Conclusion of Bilateral Agreements and in the Enactment of Legislation Related to Foreign Investments	17.07
C.	Trends at the Regional Level and their Implications for Multilateral Forums	17.22
D.	Conclusion	17.36

18. North America Investment Law and Policy: 2017
David Schneiderman

A.	Introduction	18.01
B.	Jurisprudence	18.02
	1. Judicial misconduct	18.04
	2. Legitimate expectations	18.06
	3. Arbitrariness	18.09
C.	Investment Treaty Policy	18.11
	1. Gender	18.11
	2. Investment court	18.14
	3. TPP	18.17

Contents—Detailed

D.	NAFTA Renegotiation	18.21
	1. US ISDS proposal	18.21
	2. Two amigos respond	18.25
	3. Gender and indigenous chapters	18.27

Part II GENERAL ARTICLES

19. Importing WTO General Exceptions into International Investment Agreements: Proportionality, Myths and Risks
Andrew D Mitchell, James Munro, and Tania Voon

A.	Introduction	19.01
B.	Comparing Policy Space under Investment Protections and WTO General Exceptions	19.10
	1. Proportionality requirements in substantive investment obligations	19.10
	2. Hidden policy space in GATT Article XX and GATS Article XIV	19.30
C.	Impact of General Exceptions on the Interpretation of Investment Protections	19.60
	1. Interpreting general exceptions in IIAs pursuant to customary rules of interpretation	19.61
	2. Relevance of general exceptions in interpreting obligations	19.71
	3. Relevance of WTO jurisprudence in interpreting IIAs	19.76
D.	General Exceptions and Clarifications in Modern Investment Treaty Practice	19.81
	1. Canada's 2004 model IIA: early use of WTO-style general exceptions	19.82
	2. General exceptions without clarifications to investment obligations	19.86
	3. General exceptions to selected investment obligations or with clarifications	19.93
	4. Clarifications to investment obligations without general exceptions	19.103
E.	Conclusion	19.111

20. The FET Standard under CETA: A Missed Opportunity to Restore the Balance between Private and Public Interests in the EU Investment Treaty Landscape?
Antonin Sobek

A.	Introduction	20.01
B.	The FET Standard and the Right to Regulate in Europe: From the Need to Safeguard States' Regulatory Freedom towards CETA	20.09

		1. An expansive interpretation of the FET standard as a starting point for the debate on regulatory freedom	20.10
		2. A process of redefinition of the European investment landscape	20.13
		3. The importance of CETA for the EU investment practice of tomorrow	20.15

C. The FET Standard under CETA: A Missed Opportunity to Restore the Balance between Private and Public Interests? 20.17
  1. The new approach to FET as a mere codification of past arbitral awards 20.18
  2. The consecration of legitimate expectations as a new Pandora's box 20.27
  3. The tribunal's interpretative power and an important room for discretion 20.34
  4. The reaffirmation of the right to regulate and the risk of tautologies 20.41
  5. Implications for the balance between private and public interests within the EU investment treaty landscape 20.52

D. A Call for a Further Reconsideration of the Scope and Place of the FET Standard in the European Investment Treaty Practice 20.54
  1. A case for removing the FET standard from the EU investment treaty practice 20.55
  2. An alternative approach: suggestions for further refinements 20.62

E. Conclusion 20.69

Appendix I: Examples of FET Clauses in BITs of EU Member States

Appendix II: The CETA Article on the FET Obligation

Appendix III: The CETA Article on the Applicable Law and Interpretation

Appendix IV: Extracts from the CETA Preamble

Appendix V: The CETA Article on the Right to Regulate

21. The Notion of Investor under the Energy Charter Treaty: The Latest Developments in the Spanish Solar Disputes
Crina Baltag

A. Introduction 21.01

B. Article 1(7)(a)(ii) of the ECT and the Meaning of 'Investor' 21.06

C. Lifting the Corporate Veil under the Provisions of the ECT 21.19

D.	The Spanish Solar Disputes and the Notion of 'Investor'	21.24
	1. *Isolux*	21.25
	2. *Charanne*	21.29
	3. *RREEF*	21.33
E.	Concluding Remarks	21.35

22. Policy Coherence and the Promotion of Foreign Direct Investment in the Renewable Energy Sector: Lessons from Europe
Avidan Kent

A.	Introduction	22.01
B.	Policy Coherence for Development: An Emerging Trend	22.07
	1. Policy coherence for development: background	22.08
	2. Development, PCD, and RE-related FDI	22.10
C.	Home Country Measures (HCMs) and the promotion of RE-related FDI	22.14
	1. HCMs: background	22.15
	2. International law HCMs	22.22
	3. International investment agreements (IIA)	22.49
	4. Trade treaties	22.68
	5. International cooperation and development agreements	22.82
	6. MIGA	22.96
	7. The Kyoto Protocol's flexible mechanisms	22.107
D.	Concluding Remarks	22.113

23. Integrating Civil Liability Principles into International Investment Law: A Solution to Environmental Damage Caused By Foreign Investors?
Alessandra Mistura

A.	Introduction	23.01
B.	Overview of Civil Liability Regimes	23.09
	1. Civil liability regimes: legal foundation and policy objectives	23.14
	2. Common features of civil liability regimes	23.29
	3. Assessment of the Effectiveness of Civil Liability Regimes	23.82
	4. TNCs and international civil liability	23.97
C.	International Investment Law and Civil Liability Regimes: Options for Reforms	23.101
	1. The limitations of international investment law and the need for reform	23.102
	2. The integration between international investment law and international civil liability	23.109
D.	Conclusions	23.149

24. Unanticipated Consequences: The Human Rights Implications of Bringing Sovereign Debt Disputes within Investment Treaty Arbitration
Juan Pablo Bohoslavksy and Edward Guntrip

A.	Introduction	24.01
B.	The Definition of 'Investment' and Sovereign Debt	24.10
	1. The foundations of IIL	24.11
	2. The definition of 'investment'	24.14
	3. Sovereign debt as an investment	24.17
	4. Excluding sovereign debt from the definition of investment	24.23
	5. Preliminary conclusions	24.24
C.	Sovereign Debt Disputes in Investment Treaty Arbitration	24.25
	1. Investment arbitrators as epistemic and interpretative communities	24.26
	2. Investment awards addressing sovereign debt	24.28
	3. Sovereign debt restructuring	24.38
	4. Reforming investment treaty arbitration to reflect the nature of sovereign debt	24.42
	5. Preliminary conclusions	24.44
D.	Human Rights Implications	24.46
	1. Sovereign debt and human rights	24.47
	2. International investment law and human rights	24.51
	3. Ensuring human rights compliance during sovereign debt restructuring	24.57
	4. Preliminary conclusions	24.62
E.	Conclusion	24.63

25. Has ISDS Gone Rogue for Australia and New Zealand? CPTPP (C-3PO), RCEP (R2-D2), and Beyond
Amokura Kawharu and Luke Nottage

A.	Introduction	25.01
B.	Dual-Track ISDS Reforms	25.04
C.	New Zealand's Renunciation of ISDS: Déjà Vu	25.13
D.	Low-profile Treaty (Re)Negotiations	25.28
	1. PACER-Plus	25.29
	2. New Zealand's renegotiations with Singapore and China	25.34
	3. Australia's renegotiations with Singapore and Uruguay	25.36
	4. Negotiations with the EU, India, Indonesia, and others	25.48
E.	Conclusions: C-3PO, R2-D2, and Beyond	25.58

26. India's 2015 Model BIT against the Backdrop of Global ISDS Reforms
Aveek Chakravarty

A.	Introduction	26.01
B.	ISDS Reform and the Role of States	26.07
	1. Criticism and calls for reform of ISDS	26.07
	2. State responses towards ISDS reform	26.10
C.	ISDS in India's BITs	26.13
	1. Overview of India's BIT programme	26.13
	2. Features of ISDS provisions in existing BITs	26.19
D.	India's 2015 Model BIT	26.33
	1. Background	26.34
	2. ISDS under the 2015 Model BIT	26.40
E.	Conclusions	26.81

AUTHOR BIOGRAPHIES

Olabisi D Akinkugbe is an Assistant Professor with the Schulich School of Law, Dalhousie University, Canada. He holds a PhD in law from the Faculty of Law, University of Ottawa. He is a member of the Society of International Economic Law, and the African International Economic Law group of the society. His research interests cut across African Regional Economic Integration, Transnational Law, International Law & Development, and Business Law.

Crina Baltag is a Senior Lecturer in Law at the University of Bedfordshire, UK, teaching the courses on International Commercial Arbitration, Investment Treaty Arbitration, and International Commercial Litigation. Crina received her PhD from the School of International Arbitration, Queen Mary University of London. She holds an LLM in International Commercial Arbitration from Stockholm University and an MSc in International Business from the Academy of Economic Studies, Romania. Crina is a graduate of the Faculty of Law, University of Bucharest and a qualified attorney-at-law, registered with the Romanian Bar Association. Crina was associated with law firms from Romania, Austria, and the UK and she lectured at Queen Mary University of London; FGV Law, Rio de Janeiro; and Stockholm University. Crina was the Secretary General of the Amcham Brazil Arbitration and Mediation Center. She is the acting editor of the Kluwer Arbitration Blog and she regularly publishes on international commercial and investment arbitration and sits as an arbitrator in international and domestic arbitrations. Crina is member of the Academic Council of the CAILAW—ITA Institute for Transnational Arbitration and the Thought Leadership Chair of Young ITA. Her latest book, *ICSID Convention after 50 Years: Unsettled Issues* (ed) was released by Wolters Kluwer in 2017.

Thierry Berger is a qualified solicitor and an associate at the International Institute for Environment and Development (IIED), where his work focuses on law and sustainable development. Prior to his collaboration with IIED, Thierry worked for global law firms for ten years specializing in international arbitration.

Juan Pablo Bohoslavsky is the United Nations Independent Expert on Foreign Debt and Human Rights. He previously worked at the United Nations Conference on Trade and Development (UNCTAD) and as a consultant for the United Nations Economic Commission for Latin America and the Caribbean (ECLAC) and the Argentinean State. A doctor of law with wide experience in international relations and litigation, he is the author of numerous books and articles on finance and human rights.

Author Biographies

Aveek Chakravarty is a Marie-Curie research scholar and PhD candidate in law at the University of Turin, Italy. He is admitted to practice in India and has specialised in matters pertaining to consumer law, commercial law and infrastructure arbitration. Aveek previously obtained his Master's degree in international trade law, contracts and dispute settlement from the University of Turin. His current research is focussed on the interplay of investor and State interests on issues of compensation and liability under investment treaties.

Jesse Coleman is a legal researcher for the Columbia Center on Sustainable Investment (CCSI). Her work at CCSI focuses on investment law and policy, natural resources, and the intersection between human rights and sustainable development. She received her Bachelor of Arts in Political Science and Bachelor of Laws from Trinity College Dublin, and holds a Master of Law from the University of Cambridge, where she specialized in international law. Her research while at Cambridge focused on the interplay between international human rights law and land-based investment.

Carlos Maria Correa is the Executive Director of the South Centre. He has been the Director of the Center for Interdisciplinary Studies on Industrial Property and Economics, University of Buenos Aires, a visiting professor in post-graduate courses of several universities, and consultant to UNCTAD, UNIDO, UNDP, WHO, FAO, IDB, INTAL, World Bank, SELA, ECLA, and other regional and international organizations.

Lorenzo Cotula is a Principal Researcher in Law and Sustainable Development at IIED and a Visiting Professor at the Law School of the University of Strathclyde. Lorenzo conducts research and policy work on issues spanning investment law, human rights, and natural resource governance. He also steers IIED's Legal Tools for Citizen Empowerment programme—an initiative to support local groups in investment processes.

Diane Desierto (JSD, Yale) is Tenured Associate Professor of Human Rights Law and Global Affairs at the Keough School of Global Affairs (concurrent with Law School) at the University of Notre Dame (Indiana, USA), where she teaches human rights-based courses on trade, investment, development, international law, sustainability in the global commons, and economic, social, and cultural rights. She also holds honorary appointments as Professor of International Law and Human Rights at the Philippine Judicial Academy of the Supreme Court of the Philippines; External Faculty Fellow, WSD Handa Center for Human Rights and International Justice, Stanford Global Studies, Stanford University; External Executive Director, University of the Philippines College of Law Graduate Program at the Bonifacio Global City (BGC) campus; and is a Partner at her family's twenty-year-old law firm in Ortigas Centre, Metro Manila, Philippines. Among her global appointments, Professor Desierto is SAB Member of the *European Journal of International Law* and Editor of *EJIL:Talk!*; Academic Council Member of the Institute of Transnational Arbitration; Co-Chair of the Oxford Investment

Claims Summer Academy and Advisory Board Member of Oxford Investment Claims; Drafting Team Member, Hague Rules on Business and Human Rights Arbitration; Affiliate, International Criminal Court Bar Association; Resource Expert for the ASEAN Secretariat and the ASEAN Coordinating Committee on Investment, the Asian Development Bank, the US Agency for International Development, and the European Union External Action Service; former Director of Studies and current Faculty of the Hague Academy of International Law. Professor Desierto has taught as visiting/tenure-track/tenured professor at law faculties in Paris, China, Manila, Hawaii, and the Hague; served senior fellowships in Berlin, Heidelberg, Singapore, Honolulu, and Michigan; authored four books (three more forthcoming) and around a hundred law review articles, essays, and book chapters in her fields of expertise; and is repeatedly recognized as one of the world's 'Future Leaders of Arbitration' by *Who's Who Legal*.

Edward Guntrip is a Lecturer in Law at the University of Sussex. Edward worked as a legal practitioner before completing his PhD at Brunel University in 2014. His research focuses on how public international law governs economic activities undertaken in foreign jurisdictions. He has a particular interest in the intersection of international investment law and international human rights law, and he has written various articles on this topic.

Brooke Skartvedt Guven is a legal researcher at the Columbia Center on Sustainable Investment. Her work focuses on analysing the contracts, domestic frameworks, and international legal arrangements governing cross-border investments and the impacts that these frameworks have on sustainable development objectives. Prior to joining CCSI, she was a finance lawyer specializing in cross-border transactions at an international law firm, and also worked as a legal advisor with the Liberian Ministry of Health and Social Welfare. She has an LLM from New York University School of Law, where she was a Human Rights Scholar, a JD and MA from the University of Wisconsin, and a BA in Economics and Political Science from Northwestern University.

Jarrod Hepburn is a Senior Lecturer at Melbourne Law School, Australia. Jarrod is the author of *Domestic Law in International Investment Arbitration* (Oxford University Press 2017). His other work, largely in the areas of international economic law and general international law, has been published in journals including the *American Journal of International Law, the International and Comparative Law Quarterly, the Journal of International Dispute Settlement, and the Journal of World Investment and Trade*. Jarrod holds the degrees of DPhil, MPhil, and BCL from Balliol College, University of Oxford, as well as first-class honours undergraduate degrees in both law and software engineering from the University of Melbourne. He has been a visiting researcher at the Max Planck Institute for Comparative and International Private Law in Hamburg. Jarrod is admitted to practice law in Australian federal and state jurisdictions, and has experience in the Competition group of a major Australian commercial law firm. He is also a regular contributor to a specialized news service, *Investment Arbitration Reporter*, providing coverage and analysis of foreign investment disputes.

Lise J Johnson is the Investment Law and Policy Head at the Columbia Center on Sustainable Investment (CCSI). Her work at CCSI centres on analysing investment treaties and treaty-based investor–state arbitrations, and examining the implications those instruments and cases have for host countries' domestic policies and sustainable development strategies. In addition, she concentrates on key institutional and procedural aspects of the investment law framework, including efforts to increase transparency in and legitimacy of investor–state dispute settlement. She has a BA from Yale University, a JD from University of Arizona, an LLM from Columbia Law School, and is admitted to the bar in California.

Reji K Joseph is Associate Professor at Institute for Studies in Industrial Development, New Delhi, India. His research interests are in the areas of foreign investment and development; patents and access to medicines; innovation; and development cooperation. He has to his credit several papers on trade policymaking, WTO TRIPS Agreement and access to medicines, patents and innovation, international investment agreements, and a book on the Indian pharmaceutical industry.

Mouhamadou Madana Kane is an experienced development practitioner and international lawyer specializing in international investment law, investment treaty arbitration, and project finance. He currently serves as Lead Legal counsel with the Islamic Development Bank where he has been jointly appointed by the Bank and the General Secretariat of the Organization of Islamic Cooperation (OIC) to lead the project of modernizing the OIC Investment Treaty, including establishing a permanent mechanism for the settlement of investment disputes arising thereunder. In this capacity, Dr. Kane's role includes managing the process for amending the Treaty, leading the technical consultations with OIC Member States and institutions, and preparing the relevant documentation for the approval of the OIC Council of Foreign Ministers. Dr. Kane is also the founder of the African Center of International Law Practice (ACILP), which is an international law think tank whose mandate is to bridge the gap between international law and public policy in Africa. Dr. Kane holds a Ph.D in Public International Law/International Investment Law & Arbitration, and is a member of leading international law professional associations. He has authored/co-authored several publications in the field of international investment law and policy, including the recent book entitled *Rethinking International Investment Governance: Principles for the 21st Century*.

Amokura Kawharu (BA, LLB Hons Auckland, LLM Cambridge) is an Associate Professor at the Auckland University Law Faculty, which she joined in 2005 after working in law firms in Auckland and Sydney for a number of years. Her research interests include arbitration, international trade and investment law, and international dispute resolution. She has published widely in these fields, and is a frequent speaker at international law and dispute resolution events in New Zealand

and overseas. As the leading academic in New Zealand writing on arbitration, she contributes regular reviews on dispute settlement for the New Zealand Law Review and co-authored the principal New Zealand text on arbitration law, *Williams & Kawharu on Arbitration* (recently published in its second edition, LexisNexis 2017).

Stephen J Kay is Managing Director in Marsh's Credit Specialties Practice, whose main function is to represent clients seeking to transfer risk via political risk insurance or non-payment insurance. He joined Marsh in 2009, leading the US political risk practice until 2018. Prior to Marsh, he held positions in underwriting political risk insurance at AIG, Citigroup, and Export Development Canada, as well as banking at Royal Bank of Canada.

Avidan Kent is a Senior Lecturer at the University of East Anglia and a Fellow with the Centre for International Sustainable Development Law (CISDL). Avidan's research interests include the fields of Public International Law, International Economic Law, International Dispute Resolution, and International Environmental Law. Avidan holds an LLM from McGill University, and a PhD from the University of Cambridge.

Markus Krajewski is Professor of Public International Law at the University of Erlangen-Nurnberg (Germany). He co-directs the MA programme in Human Rights and chairs the Interdisciplinary Research Centre for Human Rights Erlangen-Nurnberg (CHREN). His fields of research are human rights, international trade and investment law, and EU external relations law.

Nathan Lobel is Special Assistant to the Director at the Columbia Center on Sustainable Investment, where he focuses on climate change law and policy. He holds a Bachelor of Arts with high honors in Political Science from Yale University.

Julie A Martin is Managing Director in Marsh's Credit Specialties Practice, whose main function is to represent clients seeking to transfer risk via political risk insurance or non-payment insurance. She joined Marsh in 2001 after twenty years of experience in the political risk business at the Overseas Private Investment Corporation, the US government agency charged with promoting US investment in emerging markets.

Alessandra Mistura obtained her JD in 2013, graduating with honours from the University of Parma (Italy), and completed her LLM at Columbia Law School in 2017, specializing in Sustainable Development and International Investment Law. She is currently a Ph.D. candidate at the Graduate Institute of International and Development Studies.

Andrew Mitchell is Professor at Melbourne Law School, Australian Research Council Future Fellow, Director of the Global Economic Law Network, a member of the Indicative List of Panelists to hear WTO disputes, and a member of the Energy Charter Roster of Panelists. He has previously practised law with Allens Arthur Robinson (now Allens Linklaters) and consults for states, international organizations, and the private sector. Andrew has taught law in Australia, Canada, Singapore, and the US and is the recipient of four major grants from the Australian Research Council and the Australian National Preventive Health Agency. He has published over 140 academic books and journal articles and is a Series Editor of the Oxford University Press International Economic Law Series, an Editorial Board Member of the *Journal of International Economic Law*, and a General Editor of the *Journal of International Dispute Settlement*. He has law degrees from Melbourne, Harvard, and Cambridge and is a Barrister and Solicitor of the Supreme Court of Victoria.

James Munro has worked as a lawyer at the World Trade Organization on international trade litigation at both the panel and appellate stages. James has also practised in the fields of international trade and investment law for the Australian government, including advising on domestic compliance with international economic law, free trade agreements, trade remedies investigations, and serving as negotiator and legal counsel on various trade and environment treaties. James has published a number of book chapters and journal articles on subjects relating to international trade and investment law, and holds a PhD from the University of Melbourne in this field. The present contribution does not necessarily reflect the views of any current or former employer.

Luke Nottage (BCA, LLB, PhD *VUW*, LLM Kyoto) specializes in international arbitration, contract law, consumer product safety law, and corporate governance, with a particular interest in the Asia-Pacific region. He is Professor of Comparative and Transnational Business Law at Sydney Law School and Associate Director of the Centre for Asian and Pacific Law at the University of Sydney. Luke's fifteen books include *International Investment Treaties and Arbitration Across Asia* (with Chaisse, Brill 2018), *Foreign Investment and Dispute Resolution Law and Practice in Asia* (with Bath, Routledge 2011), and *International Arbitration in Australia* (with Garnett, Federation Press 2010). Luke is on the ILA's Committee for the International Protection of Consumers, is an ACICA Special Associate and Rules committee member, and on the panel of arbitrators for the BAC, JCAA, KCAB, KLRCA, SCIA, and TAI. Luke has consulted for law firms world-wide, ASEAN, the EC, OECD, UNCTAD, UNDP, and the Japanese government.

Facundo Pérez-Aznar is senior researcher at the Geneva Center for International Dispute Settlement (CIDS) and Adjoin Professor of International Economic Law in the Master in International Relations at the University of Buenos Aires. He worked for several years as legal counsel in the Department of International Affairs at the General Attorney's Office of Argentina, which is in charge of handling the interest of Argentina in international disputes (mostly ICSID and UNCITRAL arbitrations) and previously as legal officer in the Directorate of Latin American Economic Integration at the Ministry of Foreign Affairs of Argentina. He holds a law degree from the National University of La Plata, Argentina, and a Master degree and a PhD in international law from the Graduate Institute of International and Development Studies, Geneva.

Author Biographies

Lisa E Sachs is the Director of the Columbia Center on Sustainable Investment (CCSI), where she oversees the three areas of focus for CCSI: investments in extractive industries, investments in land and agriculture, and investment law and policy. She also lectures at Columbia Law School and the School on International and Public Affairs at Columbia University. She received a BA in Economics from Harvard University, and earned her JD and an MA in International Affairs from Columbia University, where she was a James Kent Scholar and recipient of the Parker School Certificate in International and Comparative Law.

David Schneiderman is Professor of Law and Political Science (courtesy) at the University of Toronto where he teaches international investment law in addition to Canadian and US constitutional law. He is the author of over eighty articles and book chapters and, in addition, the author or editor of twelve books, including *Constitutionalizing Economic Globalization: Investment Rules and Democracy's Promise* (Cambridge 2008) and *Resisting Economic Globalization: Critical Theory and International Investment Law* (Macmillan 2013).

Sara L Seck is an Associate Professor with the Schulich School of Law and Marine & Environmental Law Institute, Dalhousie University, Canada, and a Senior Fellow with the Centre for International Governance Innovation's International Law Research Program. She is a member of the editorial board of the Business and Human Rights Journal, and a member of the International Law Association's Business and Human Rights study group. Recent publications include the 2018 co-edited book, *Global Environmental Change and Innovation in International Law*.

Antonin Sobek is a student at the Paris Bar School (EFB), and an arbitration trainee lawyer at Wilmer Cutler Pickering Hale and Dorr LLP in London. He is also a founder and former President of the International Arbitration Society at the London School of Economics. In the past, he served as a research assistant in international investment law at Columbia University and University of Cambridge, and worked for the ICC International Court of Arbitration and the Vienna International Arbitral Centre. He holds an LLM degree in Commercial and Corporate Law from the London School of Economics, and a Master degree in Global Business Law and Governance from Sciences Po Paris (in partnership with Columbia University and University of Paris 1 Panthéon-Sorbonne).

Taylor St John is a Lecturer (Assistant Professor) in International Relations at the University of St Andrews and a Senior Research Associate at the Global Economic Governance Programme, University of Oxford. She was previously a Postdoctoral Research Fellow at PluriCourts, University of Oslo, and holds an MSc and DPhil from the University of Oxford. Her monograph, *The Rise of Investor-State Arbitration: Politics, Law, and Unintended Consequences*, was published in 2018.

Catharine Titi is a Research Associate Professor (tenured) at the French National Centre for Scientific Research (CNRS)–CERSA, University Paris II Panthéon-Assas, France. She is Co-Chair of the ESIL Interest Group on International Economic

Law, Member of the Steering Committee of the Academic Forum on ISDS; and Member of the International Law Association (ILA) Committee on Rule of Law and International Investment Law. She co-directs the research project *The impact of international investment agreements on FDI flows* funded by the French Ministry of Justice (2017–2019). Catharine holds a PhD from the University of Siegen in Germany (*Summa cum laude*) and she has previously been a consultant at the United Nations Conference on Trade and Development (UNCTAD). In 2016, Catharine was awarded the prestigious Smit-Lowenfeld Prize of the International Arbitration Club of New York for the best article published in the field of international arbitration.

Mark van der Does is a broker in Marsh's Credit Specialties Practice. He joined Marsh in 2015 after working in the political risk underwriting practice at CV Starr, and previously with another credit and political risks insurance broker.

Tania Voon is Professor at Melbourne Law School and was previously Associate Dean (Research). She is a former Legal Officer of the WTO Appellate Body Secretariat and has practised with King & Wood Mallesons and the Australian Government Solicitor and taught at the National University of Singapore, Georgetown University, the University of Western Ontario, the University of British Columbia, and several Australian universities. Tania undertook her LLM at Harvard Law School and her PhD at the University of Cambridge. She is a member of the Energy Charter Treaty's Roster of Panelists and the WTO's Indicative List of Governmental and Non-Governmental Panelists.

Zoe Phillips Williams is a Fellow in International Political Economy at the London School of Economics and Political Science. She holds a PhD in International Relations from the Hertie School of Governance in Berlin. Her current work focuses on the impact of democratic politics and policymaking on investor–state disputes and has appeared in Global Environmental Politics.

James Zhan is senior director of Investment and Enterprise at UNCTAD. He is also editor-in-chief of the *UN World Investment Report*, and the *Transnational Corporations Journal*. He has directed extensive research on key issues, facilitated the formulation of outcomes at various summits, and provided technical assistance to governments (including cabinets and parliaments) in over 160 countries. Dr Zhan led the formulation of global guidelines for a new generation of investment policies, which have been used by more than 100 countries. He is chair of the Governing Board of the UN Sustainable Stock Exchanges Initiative (which count all major stock exchanges worldwide as members). He initiated the establishment of the UNCTAD World Investment Forum. Dr Zhan is Trade and Investment Council member of the World Economic Forum and chief strategist for the World Association of Investment Promotion Agencies. He has held a number of advisory positions with academic institutions, including Cambridge University, Columbia University, Oxford University, and the University of Geneva. He has published extensively on trade and investment-related economic and legal issues.

Part I

YEAR IN REVIEW

A. DEVELOPMENTS IN FOREIGN INVESTMENT

1

TRENDS IN GLOBAL FDI FLOWS AND POLICY IMPLICATIONS

James X Zhan

A. Introduction	1.01	C. Global Investment Policy Developments	1.15
B. Global Investment Trends and Prospects	1.02	D. Concluding Remarks	1.29

A. Introduction

In what has become a perennially tough environment, growth prospects for global foreign direct investment (FDI) remain steeped in gloom. Moreover, the global distribution of FDI is expected to be shaken up after tax reforms adopted by the United States at the end of 2017—as much as $2 trillion of US multinationals' retained earnings could be repatriated. This would significantly affect the inward stock positions of countries in which US multinationals are heavily invested and, concomitantly, the US outward FDI stock position. **1.01**

B. Global Investment Trends and Prospects

1. Trends: low level and weak recovery

Contrary to expectations, global FDI lost ground again in 2017, decreasing by 23 per cent to $1.43 trillion—a level well below the peak in 2007 (Figure 1.1). This is in stark contrast to other macroeconomic variables, such as gross domestic product (GDP), which saw improvements in 2017. **1.02**

United Nations Conference on Trade and Development (UNCTAD) data for the full year show the loss was propelled by developed countries, where more than a third was shaved off FDI inflows last year. Flows to North America were as much as 40 per cent below the previous year's flows, while Europe lost 26%. **1.03**

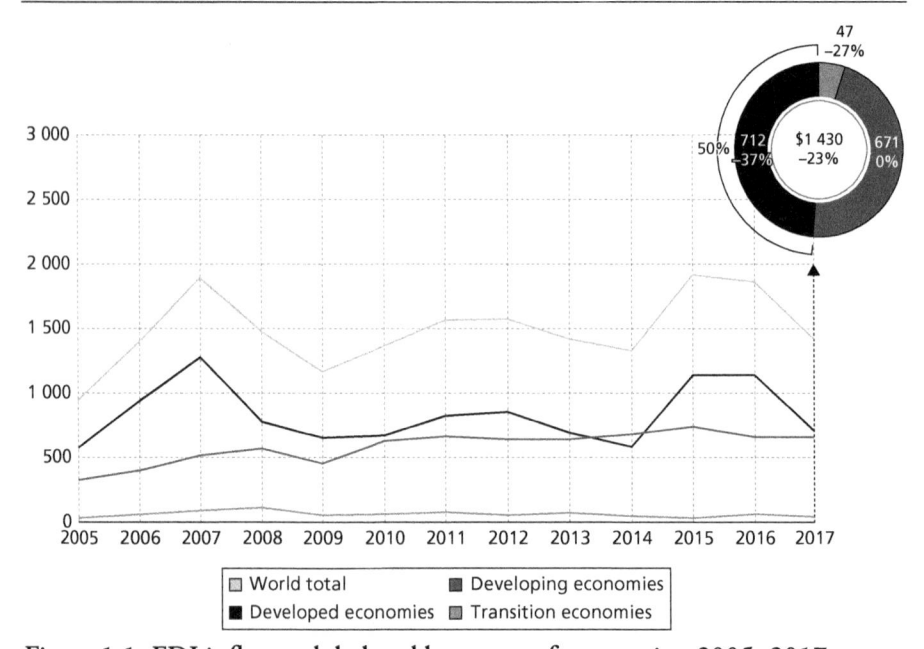

Figure 1.1 FDI inflows: global and by group of economies, 2005–2017

Adapted with permission from: UNCTAD, 'World Investment Report 2018: Investment and New Industrial Policies' (United Nations, 2018).

1.04 Flows to developing countries held steady, at $671 billion, even rising marginally in developing Asia and Latin America and the Caribbean. As a result, developing economies accounted for a growing share of global FDI inflows in 2017, absorbing 47 per cent of the total, compared with 36 per cent in 2016. Developing Asia regained its position as the largest FDI recipient region in the world, followed by the European Union and North America.

2. Prospects: fragile growth with high uncertainty

1.05 Higher economic growth projections, trade volumes, and commodity prices would normally point to a potential increase in global FDI in 2018. However, geopolitical risks and policy uncertainty can dampen the prospects for recovery. UNCTAD forecasts flows may further decline in 2018. FDI flows are also likely to be affected by the tax reforms adopted by the United States at the end of 2017 which are likely to significantly affect the investment decisions by US multinationals, with consequences for global FDI stock positions.

1.06 Key objectives of the US's Tax Cuts and Jobs Act are to stimulate investment and create jobs in the United States. To that end, the Bill contains measures seeking to encourage multinationals to repatriate overseas funds and to reduce the incentive to locate assets and activities abroad. One of these measures is the shift to a territorial tax regime for multinationals, which means earnings abroad will no longer be taxed when repatriated. A one-off tax on accumulated foreign earnings

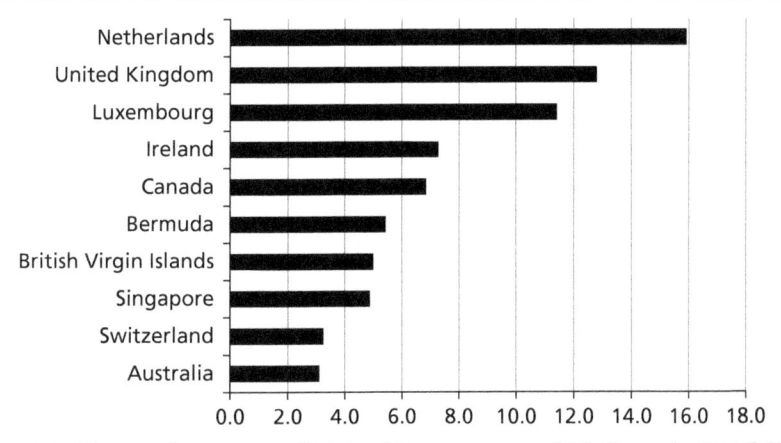

Figure 1.2 Top ten locations of United States outward FDI stock, 2016 (%)
Adapted with permission from: ©UNCTAD, IIA Navigator (United Nations, 2018).
Note: Excludes Caribbean offshore financial centres.

is set to encourage the repatriation of funds deliberately kept abroad to avoid tax. UNCTAD estimates that as much as $2 trillion of the $3.2 trillion of overseas retained earnings could be brought back to US shores, which will materially alter FDI stock positions in countries where US funds are predominantly held (Figure 1.2). It is anticipated that the reform package as a whole will have significant implications for global FDI patterns in the coming years, given that almost half of all global FDI stock is either located in the United States or owned by US multinationals.

1.07 Other current indeterminates may also undermine a recovery in FDI in 2018 and 2019.[1] These include:

- Uncertainty about the policy implications from changes to some major trade relationships may further defer investment flows, notably the United Kingdom's impending exit from the European Union, as well as the renegotiation of North American Free Trade Agreement (NAFTA).[2]
- The rise of trade and investment tensions among major trading partners may dissuade new FDI.
- For emerging and developing economies, a protracted period of developed-country investor uncertainty could hamper the recovery of investment flows to these countries.

---

[1] UNCTAD, 'Investment Trends Monitor, January 2018: Issue 28' (UNCTAD 22 January 2018) <http://unctad.org/en/PublicationsLibrary/diaeia2018d1_en.pdf> accessed 23 June 2018.
[2] North American Free Trade Agreement (signed 17 December 1992, entered into force 1 January 1994) (NAFTA).

3. Impact: lacklustre for GVCs and productivity

1.08 High volatility and low levels of global FDI flows have seriously affected the expansion of global value chains (GVCs), the growth of global trade, and the growth of productivity worldwide.

1.09 While overall FDI outflows in 2017 largely held steady, flows from developed countries have remained weak over the past few years. The character and quality of these investment flows are also important. Since the global financial crisis, for those years when global FDI increased, the increase was mainly driven by cross-border mergers and acquisitions (M&As), a large proportion of which was due to corporate restructuring or inversion. Last year was the first time in three successive years that M&As declined—down by 29 per cent to $694 billion. That said, M&A activity remained intense.

1.10 Of greater concern, however, was another contraction in greenfield projects—the kind of investment associated with job creation and an indicator of future trends. In 2017, the value of greenfield announcements shrunk by 14 per cent to $720 billion. By sector, services saw a 25 per cent decline while projects in the primary sector slumped by 61 per cent. Although activity in manufacturing industries picked up by 14 per cent, overall greenfield announcements in the sector remained relatively depressed across all developing regions from a longer-term point of view. Moreover, developing countries have seen a steep decline in greenfield projects between 2013 and 2017, compared to the prior five-year period. This does not bode well for progress on multiple sustainable development objectives under the globally agreed Agenda 2030 for Sustainable Development.

1.11 International production by foreign affiliates of multinational enterprises (MNEs) (GVC activity) is still expanding, but the rate has slowed in recent years. The average annual growth rates over the last five years of foreign affiliate sales (7.3 per cent), value added (4.9 per cent), and employment (4.9 per cent) were all lower than the rates in the five-year period between 2006 and 2010 (at 9.7 per cent, 10.7 per cent, and 7.6 per cent, respectively).

1.12 Slower growth in international production contributed to lacklustre global trade expansion. This is mainly because two-thirds of global trade is accounted for by the global value chain activities of MNEs.

1.13 Productivity is a key determinant of economic growth. Productivity increases can be fostered broadly through innovation and catch up, and FDI can play a key role, since MNEs are more innovative than most companies. This means that with advanced knowledge, technology, and skills, MNEs can support the upgrading of productive capacity in host economies. The expectation of a beneficial impact from FDI on host economies is also supported by empirical evidence at the macro level, which finds a positive relation between productivity growth and FDI.

How to restore growth has therefore taken centre stage in international fora, with productivity as a primary consideration. For developing countries to achieve elevated levels of growth to deliver the ambitions of the Sustainable Development Goals under Agenda 2030, this will require significant increases in capital and productive investment.[3]

1.14

C. Global Investment Policy Developments

On the investment policy side, three overriding factors determine policymaking at the national, regional, and global level: sustainable development objectives, trade and investment protectionism, and new industrial transformation drives. Four characterizing strands mark current investment policymaking processes: dynamics, dichotomy, divergence, and dilemma.

1.15

1. Dynamics in policymaking

Investment policymaking has been extremely dynamic. The policy environment for cross-border investment is subject to constant change. In particular, the overall share of restrictive or regulatory investment policy measures has significantly increased in recent months and some countries have become more critical of foreign takeovers.

1.16

At the national level, governments continue to adopt investment policies at an annual rate of around 100 (as measured over the past decade). In 2017, 65 countries adopted 126 policy measures. This is the highest number of countries to pursue measures over the past decade, as well as the highest number of policy changes. This continues the upward trend and compares with 2016, when 58 countries and economies adopted some 124 investment regulations and policy measures which had been the highest number since 2006 (Figure 1.3). This is accompanied by countless broader measures taken every year that influence the overall business environment for investors.

1.17

Until recently, also dynamics at the international level were also fluid, with new investment agreements concluded at the rate of one every fortnight over the past few years. As of December 2017, more than 100 countries were involved in negotiating over 50 investment treaties, of which several are mega-regional agreements. And at the level of 'soft law', the universe of codes and standards that govern investment and corporate behaviour have also mushroomed.

1.18

---

[3] See UNCTAD, 'World Investment Report 2018: Investment and New Industrial Policies' (United Nations 2018) < http://unctad.org/en/PublicationsLibrary/wir2018_en.pdf> accessed 23 June 2018.

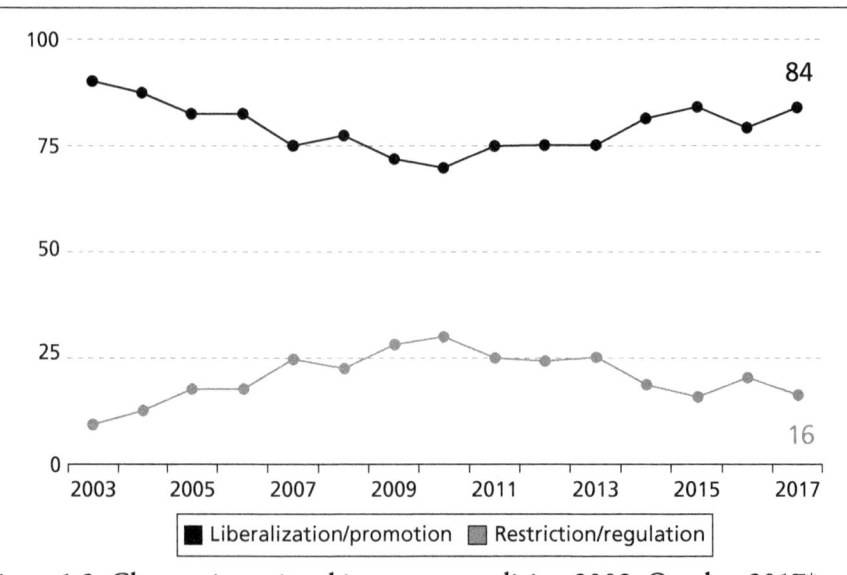

Figure 1.3 Changes in national investment policies, 2002–October 2017*

Adapted with permission from: ©UNCTAD, 'World Investment Report 2018: Investment and New Industrial Policies' (United Nations, 2018)

* The data in the figure do not include measures related to the general business climate, such as corporate taxation, environmental, or labour legislation.

2. Dichotomy in regulatory direction

1.19 There is a dichotomy in national investment policymaking with simultaneous moves to liberalize and promote investment on the one hand, and to increasingly regulate and restrict it on the other. While the bulk of national investment policy measures adopted in recent years leans towards investment liberalization and promotion, the overall share of regulatory or restrictive measures has been on the rise (from an average of 5 per cent in the early 2000s to an average of 27 per cent in the five years between 2012 and 2016).

1.20 Furthermore, governments are increasingly making use of industrial policies, tightening screening and monitoring procedures, and closely scrutinizing cross-border M&As. Restrictive measures, particularly at the administrative level, are often applied to strategic sectors, such as extractive industries and infrastructure, or are based on national security considerations. There are concerns that some of these measures are taken for protectionist purposes. It should be noted that what is seen as 'protectionism' might indeed be a result of political capture or other objectionable objectives, but may also stem from regulations to harness investment for sustainable development (eg protecting small agricultural producers for poverty reduction and food security issues, increasing local content, etc). In the case of the latter type, these are not distinct from policies in pursuit of sustainable development objectives.

Trends in Global FDI Flows

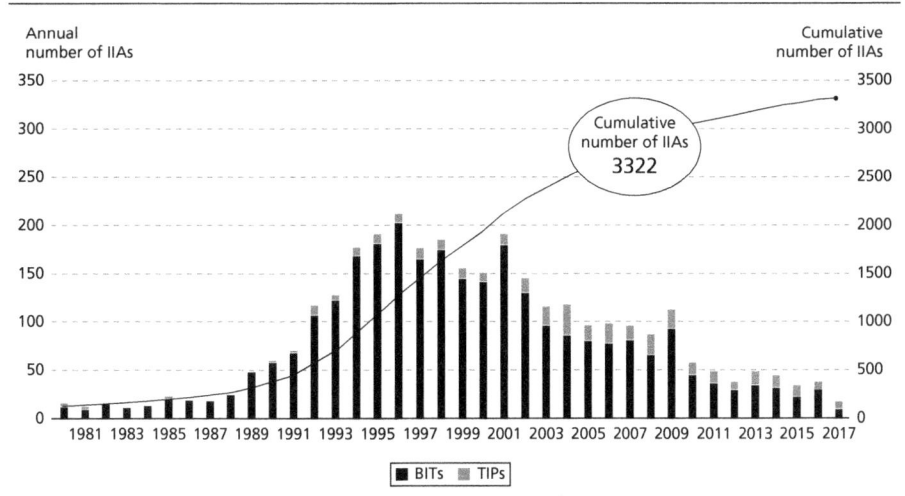

Figure 1.4 Trends in IIAs signed, 1980–2017
Adapted with permission from: ©UNCTAD, IIA Navigator (United Nations, 2018).
Note: 3,322 is the cumulative number of all signed IIAs, independently of their entry into force. Terminated IIAs, for which termination has entered into effect, are not included.

3. Divergence in the approach to IIAs

At the international level, the universe of international investment agreements (IIAs) continues to grow amid divergent approaches and systemic complexity. Some countries have been intensifying their efforts to conclude new IIAs but overall treaty-making in 2017 slowed to its tardiest pace since 1983, with only eighteen IIAs concluded. This brings the total number of IIAs to 3,322 (Figure 1.4). For the first time, the number of treaty terminations outpaced the number of new IIAs concluded, with at least twenty-two terminations taking effect; India was particularly active in terminating treaties, with seventeen treaties terminated. Ecuador had issued notices of termination of bilateral investment treaties (BITs) with sixteen countries.[4]

1.21

Governments that terminated treaties have decided to recalibrate their approach to investment policy. Furthermore, many countries have, or are in the process of, reviewing and revising their IIA networks and treaty models. All of this reflects governments' broader re-adjustments of their international investment policy engagements. Ongoing efforts to update the current (and outdated) generation of treaties can lead to *systemic divergence*. At best, the continuing proliferation of bilateral and regional investment treaties adds to the fragmentation of the global investment regime. The 3,322 IIAs in existence were concluded at different periods of time, following different approaches, and with partner countries at diverse levels of development. There is even significant divergence and inconsistency within the

1.22

---

[4] ibid.

treaty networks of individual countries. For example, Canada and Mexico, in their respective arrangements with the EU, have committed to support a multilateral initiative for the establishment of an investment court to replace the traditional investor–State dispute settlement mechanism. By contrast, Canada and Mexico in the recently concluded Comprehensive and Progressive Agreement for Trans-Pacific Partnership (CPTPP) agreed to maintain a more traditional investor–State dispute settlement mechanism. And finally, in NAFTA renegotiations, the parties have considered a number of proposals since the start of 2018, among them to remove investor–State dispute settlement by inserting an opt-out provision and providing for binding arbitration for Canada and Mexico only.

1.23 Indeed, the current international investment regime is multi-layered and multi-faceted, and overlap is rife. For example, six mega-regionals overlap with 140 existing agreements (95 BITs and 45 bilateral and regional other IIAs). To date, negotiating parties have opted for a grandfathering approach, which means older treaties coexist with new ones, compounding the complexity and potential inconsistency.

4. Dilemmas in pursuing sustainable development objectives

1.24 Efforts to boost investment in sustainable development are hampered by policy dilemmas. Financing the UN's Sustainable Development Goals, for example, will require mobilizing and channelling a vast share of private investment into relevant sectors, including most basic infrastructure industries. Many of these sectors are sensitive or have a public services nature. This gives rise to several policy dilemmas. Policymakers need to find the right balance between creating a climate conducive to investment and removing barriers to investment on the one hand, and protecting public interests through regulation on the other. They need to find mechanisms to facilitate sufficiently attractive returns to private investors while guaranteeing the accessibility and affordability of services for all. The push for more private investment must be complementary to the parallel push for more public investment and continued public sector service responsibility. Fundamentally, the entry and protection of private (including foreign) investment should be improved in sectors that are key for sustainable development, which are precisely those where most restrictions tend to apply in both national and international investment policies.

1.25 A set of common principles can help policymakers deal with these four challenges—namely, the policy dynamics, dichotomy, divergence, and dilemmas—to ensure greater policy coherence and support a conducive environment for investment in sustainable development.

1.26 In 2016, the G20 formulated a set of Guiding Principles for Global Investment Policymaking with the facilitation of UNCTAD, based on UNCTAD's Investment Policy Framework for Sustainable Development. The non-binding G20 Principles represent something approaching multilateral consensus on investment matters, as they encompass an agreement among a varied group of developed, developing, and transition economies that account for over two-thirds of global outward FDI. More recently, UNCTAD also assisted the African Caribbean Pacific (ACP) group and the Organisation of Islamic Cooperation (OIC) in the formulation of Guiding Principles for Investment Policymaking—similarly based on UNCTAD's Investment Policy Framework for Sustainable Development. The Principles are expected to guide investment policymaking in ACP and OIC member States and inform negotiations of new international investment arrangements with other countries and regions.

The adoption of the principles by a large number of countries from around the world presents a soft approach to foster an open, transparent, and conducive global policy environment for investment, and promote investment for growth and sustainable development. Among the effects, the application of the principles could boost global investment policy coherence and help roll back protectionism against international investment. 1.27

In parallel, the reform of the international investment regime has made considerable progress. Consolidating phase 1 of IIA reform, most new treaties follow *UNCTAD's Road Map for IIA Regime Reform* (as elaborated in the World Investment Report 2016),[5] which sets out five action areas: safeguarding the right to regulate, while providing protection; reforming investment dispute settlement; promoting and facilitating investment; ensuring responsible investment; and enhancing systemic consistency. Investment facilitation has also become an area of increased interest, and UNCTAD's Global Action Menu for Investment Facilitation has obtained strong support from all investment and development stakeholders. 1.28

D. Concluding Remarks

Global investment continues to face headwinds. Investment suffers from a slow pace of flows and is below the pre-crisis peak (2017's $1.43 trillion versus 2007's $1.83 trillion). It is not expected that the recovery will be smooth. Furthermore, there has been a lack of substantial investment in GVCs, hence the support for trade growth remaining slack. Investment may decline further in 2018 and but it is expected to remain below the pre-crisis peak. 1.29

---

[5] See UNCTAD, 'World Investment Report 2016: Investor Nationality: Policy Challenges' (United Nations 2016) < http://unctad.org/en/PublicationsLibrary/wir2016_en.pdf> accessed 29 June 2018; see also 'UNCTAD's Reform Package for the International Investment Regime' <http://investmentpolicyhub.unctad.org/Upload/Documents/Reform_Package_web.pdf> accessed 23 June 2018.

1.30 Investment policymaking is becoming more complex, divergent, and uncertain. The policy environment is marked by rising trade and investment protectionism and complicated by a lack of significant impetus in the multilateral trading system, the absence of a formal global investment governance system, a rise in regionalism in investment rule-making, and an overall lack of coherence in trade and investment policies. Sustainable development considerations make investment policymaking more challenging and multifaceted. The Sustainable Development Goals (SDGs) provide a framework around which different stakeholders can engage and understand future government directions, consumer expectations, and investor demands, among others.

1.31 Policymaking is also becoming more divergent, reflecting the variety of approaches with which governments respond to the effects of globalization. This, together with more government interventions, has also reduced the predictability of the investment environment for investors.

1.32 A rules-based investment regime that is credible, has broad international support, and seeks to support sustainability and inclusiveness can help reduce uncertainty and improve the stability of investment relations. At a time of pressing social and environmental challenges, harnessing economic growth for sustainable development is more important than ever. Investment is the primary driver of such growth. Mobilizing investment and ensuring that it contributes to sustainable development is therefore a priority for all countries.

2

BLENDED FINANCE IN 2017

Advancing Financing for Development but Not a Panacea

Brooke Skartvedt Güven

A. Introduction: Blended Finance in 2017	2.01	C. Blended Finance: Notable 2017 Developments at the G20, the World Bank, and the OECD	2.13
B. Development Finance Flows: Significant Gaps Persisted in 2017	2.04	D. Blended Finance: Not a Panacea?	2.20
		E. Conclusion	2.37

A. Introduction: Blended Finance in 2017

The world faces a pressing need to scale up financing for development (FfD), **2.01** and 2017 saw potentially transformative steps taken towards this objective. Historically, both public and private finance have played important roles in financing development objectives. However, amounts available from traditional sources are vastly insufficient for the world's needs as articulated in the 2030 Agenda for Sustainable Development, including its Sustainable Development Goals (SDGs). Without a fundamental change in the way development finance is provided and applied, achievement of the SDGs will be impossible.[1]

The use of 'blended finance', particularly since the 2015 Third International **2.02** Conference on Financing for Development in Addis Ababa, which resulted in the Addis Ababa Action Agenda (Addis Agenda),[2] has leapt to a prominent position

---

[1] United Nations, 'The Sustainable Development Goals Report 2017' (2017) <https://unstats.un.org/sdgs/files/report/2017/TheSustainableDevelopmentGoalsReport2017.pdf> accessed 15 June 2018.
[2] United Nations, 'Addis Adaba Action Agenda of the Third International Conference on Financing for Development' (27 July 2015) <http://www.un.org/esa/ffd/wp-content/uploads/2015/08/AAAA_Outcome.pdf> accessed 15 June 2018. The Agenda was endorsed by the United Nations General Assembly (UNGA), UNGA Res 69/313 (27 July 2015) UN Doc A/RES/69/313.

in development finance discussions and planning. Blended finance, applied through grants, loans, insurance, equity, or other mechanisms including technical assistance,[3] is intended to help tackle a wide range of investment barriers by using concessional finance to affect the perceived risk/return profile of a specific investment in order to either attract additional finance to the project, or to increase the development impact of the project.[4] Projects that are the target of blended finance may be public or, more commonly, private sector investments in developing countries. Donors often use pooled investment vehicles, such as facilities or funds, to channel official development assistance (ODA) through blended finance structures.[5] These vehicles will either pool both public and private resources at the capital structure level or will provide finance to intermediaries to do so.[6] However, as of 2017, private sector investors, while participating in select deals, were still not participating at scale in blended facilities.[7]

2.03 In 2017, the Group of 20 (G20) and the World Bank Group (WBG) took significant steps to facilitate the increased use of blended finance as a development tool, with the objective of fundamentally transforming the way in which finance for development purposes is harnessed and applied. The Organization for Economic

---

[3] One study analysed four types of blending instruments: (1) junior/subordinate capital; (2) guarantees and risk-insurance mechanisms; (3) donor-funded technical assistance facilities; and (4) design or preparation grant-funding. It found that 73 per cent of blended finance deals deploy either (1) and (3), or a combination, and that 50 per cent of deals involve (3). Only 12 per cent of deals leverage (2). Business & Sustainable Development Commission and Convergence, 'The State of Blended Finance' (July 2017) <http://s3.amazonaws.com/aws-bsdc/BSDC_and_Convergence__The_State_of_Blended_Finance__July_2017.pdf > accessed 1 June 2018, 7–8.

[4] Javier Pereira, 'Blended Finance: What it Is, How it Works and How it Is Used' (Oxfam International, February 2017) <https://d1tn3vj7xz9fdh.cloudfront.net/s3fs-public/file_attachments/rr-blended-finance-130217-en.pdf> accessed 28 May 2018, Section 1.2; Javier Pereira, 'Blended Finance for Development: Background paper prepared for the Intergovernmental Group of Experts on Financing for Development, 1st Session, 8–10 November 2017' (October 2017) <http://unctad.org/meetings/en/SessionalDocuments/tdb_efd1_bp_JP_en.pdf> accessed 1 July 2018, 1.1; Blended Finance Taskforce, 'Better Finance, Better World: Consultation Paper of the Blended Finance Taskforce' <http://s3.amazonaws.com/aws-bsdc/BFT_BetterFinance_final_01192018.pdf> accessed 15 June 2018, 11.

[5] The OECD's Development Cooperation Directorate provides a definition of official development assistance that has become the key measure used in practically all aid targets and assessments of aid performance. See OECD, 'Official Development Assistance—Definition and Coverage' <http://www.oecd.org/dac/stats/officialdevelopmentassistancedefinitionandcoverage.htm> accessed 27 June 2018. The ability of donors to participate in blending facilities at scale is limited by multiple barriers including (1) staff who have a limited understanding of investing rather than grant-making; (2) limited instruments that are flexible to blended finance participation; (3) lack of investment in project preparation; and (4) lack of effective metrics for evaluating additionality. Business & Sustainable Development Commission and Convergence, 'The State of Blended Finance' (n 3) 17.

[6] United Nations, 'Report of the Inter-agency Task Force on Financing for Development: Financing for Development: Progress and Prospects 2018' (2018) <https://developmentfinance.un.org/sites/developmentfinance.un.org/files/Report_IATF_2018.pdf> accessed 15 June 2018, 103; Business & Sustainable Development Commission and Convergence, 'The State of Blended Finance' (n 3) 7.

[7] Business & Sustainable Development Commission and Convergence, 'The State of Blended Finance' (n 3) 1. This paper provides an analysis of all known blended deals as of 2017, and it also considers the policy issues, and roles of various stakeholders.

Cooperation and Development (OECD) has advanced its analysis and technical standards relating to the use of blended finance. In response, other stakeholders increasingly raised concerns surrounding unintended consequences that may result from rapidly scaling up and expanding its use. This chapter sets forth the state of blended finance in 2017.

B. Development Finance Flows: Significant Gaps Persisted in 2017

2.04 The combination of public and private economic activity required for robust sustainable economic development has historically been undersupplied in developing countries.

1. Domestic resource mobilization

2.05 As recognized in the Addis Agenda, while continued mobilization and effective use of public domestic resources remain essential to and will compose the fast majority of funding devoted to achieving the SDGs, significant hurdles to increased mobilization of domestic resources, particularly for developing and least developed countries (LDCs) remain.[8] Despite improved policy frameworks, economic weaknesses, medium-term risks, and multi-dimensional inequalities persisted through 2017 and continue to put achievement of Agenda 2030 and the SDGs at risk.[9]

2.06 The reasons for which available domestic resources remain limited are many and stem from institutional constraints, insufficient tax capacity, and under-resourced domestic banking systems, among others. In many cases, constraints experienced by developing countries originate from and are in many ways perpetuated by international rules, institutions, and global financial flows.[10] Parallel reform of domestic tax systems and international tax cooperation, along with efforts to tackle illicit financial flows and strengthen domestic banking systems, among other efforts, are being advanced in order to boost domestic resources, but results will take time and the extent of reform is uncertain.

---

[8] United Nations, 'Addis Adaba Action Agenda of the Third International Conference on Financing for Development' (n 2) para 8; United Nations, 'Report of the Inter-agency Task Force on Financing for Development' (n 6) Chapter III.A.

[9] United Nations, 'Report of the Inter-agency Task Force on Financing for Development' (n 6) 1; United Nations, 'Addis Adaba Action Agenda of the Third International Conference on Financing for Development' (n 2) para 4.

[10] See Jesse Griffiths, 'The Sustainable Development Goals Won't Happen without a Radical Economic Rethink' (Devex, 1 November 2017) <https://www.devex.com/news/opinion-the-sustainable-development-goals-won-t-happen-without-a-radical-economic-rethink-91418> accessed 28 June 2018.

2.07 Domestic borrowing is another option that can assist countries to leverage additional capital for development purposes, but current debt service indicators suggest that many countries are constrained by growing risks of sovereign debt crises, and in 2017 many particularly low-income countries were already experiencing situations of debt distress.[11] A 2017 assessment of twenty-six low-income countries found that existing fiscal space was likely insufficient to undertake the spending needed to achieve the SDGs.[12] As such financing development by adding to the domestic debt of many countries in the current economic environment remains challenging.

2. Private finance

2.08 In addition to domestic resource mobilization, private capital flows in and to developing countries have played a remarkable part in poverty reduction in recent years. However, when left to market forces these financial flows are uneven and do not flow in sufficient amounts to critical SDG sectors, such as infrastructure (SDG 9), or to countries most in need. For example, foreign direct investment (FDI) to LDCs in 2017 amounted to about 2 per cent of global FDI flows and remained heavily concentrated in a few countries and in the extractive industries, often providing few forward and backward productive linkages within the economy, and thus perpetuating pre-existing conditions that make SDG achievement, both within host countries and globally, particularly difficult.[13]

2.09 At the same time, investment in infrastructure is critical to SDG achievement but faces an astronomical global funding gap of US$2–3 trillion every year through 2030, with more than 70 per cent of this need in emerging and developing economies.[14] Private investors perceive risks and limitations, including corruption,

---

[11] United Nations, 'Report of the Inter-agency Task Force on Financing for Development' (n 6) Chapter III.E (*Debt and Debt Sustainability*). Furthermore, in the current economic cycle, the nature of public debt in these countries has shifted in favour of both private and non-Paris Club creditors which heightens the risk that debt sustainability concerns will be exacerbated by tightening global financial conditions, and also leads to uncertainty of the conditions of potential debt restructuring. ibid 129. There are some indications that in some regions debt service indicators may be improving. United Nations Conference on Trade and Development (UNCTAD), 'World Investment Report 2018: Investment and New Industrial Policies' (2018) http://unctad.org/en/pages/PublicationWebflyer.aspx?publicationid=2130 accessed 1 July 2018, 40. The Report notes that harmful lingering macroeconomic effects from the commodity bust continue to weigh on sub-Saharan African economies, although debt levels, foreign currency shortages, and inflation appear to be improving.

[12] Anja Baum, Andrew Hodge, Aiko Mineshima, Marialuz Moreno Badia, and René Tapsoba, 'Can They Do It All? Fiscal Space in Low-Income Countries' (2017) IMF Working Paper WP/17/110.

[13] United Nations, 'Report of the Inter-agency Task Force on Financing for Development' (n 6) 63.

[14] Hendrik du Toit, Aniket Shah, and Mark Wilson, 'Ideas for Action for a Long-Term and Sustainable Financial System' (Business Commission on Sustainable Development, January 2017) <https://s3.amazonaws.com/aws-bsdc/BSDC_SustainableFinanceSystem.pdf> accessed 1 July 2018.

unstable revenue models, concerns that governments may wish to renegotiate tariffs,[15] high costs to mitigate foreign exchange risk, and other social and economic risks that limit infrastructure investments into developing economies.[16] Larger structural impediments further limit institutional investment, including capital regulations that discourage or prohibit activity in sub-investment grade or illiquid assets (which is often the case in developing country infrastructure), mark-to-market and other accounting measures, and shortcomings in project preparation.[17] Furthermore, the long-term private capital commitments that could be a source of finance for long-term, slow-return development projects on a large scale would rely on the existence of a class of liquid assets requiring standardization of project documents and regulations.[18]

3. Official development assistance

2.10 In order to fill public and private financing gaps in developing countries, ODA plays a critical role.[19] In 2017, some forms of development financial flows increased,[20] although available data is indeterminate with respect to whether ODA increased or decreased over 2016 amounts.[21] However, preliminary data available

---

[15] Notably, some evidence indicates that governments are less likely than the investor to attempt to change the terms of concessions. In a study of roughly 1000 concession contracts awarded in Latin America and the Caribbean between the mid-1980s and 2000, researchers found renegotiations occurred in 55 per cent of transportation concessions, and 74 per cent of water and sanitation contracts. Of these, 57 per cent of the transportation concession renegotiations were initiated by the investor alone (27 per cent by the government alone and 16 per cent by both the government and the operator); and, 66 per cent of the water and sanitation contract renegotiations were initiated by the operator (24 per cent by the government and 10 per cent by both the government and the operator). J. Luis Guasch, 'Granting and Renegotiating Infrastructure Concessions: Doing it right' (The World Bank, 2004) <http://documents.worldbank.org/curated/en/678041468765605224/pdf/288160PAPER0Granting010renegotiating.pdf> accessed 1 July 2018; see also J. Luis Guasch and Stéphane Straub, 'Infrastructure Concessions in Latin America' (October 2005) World Bank Policy Research Working Paper 3749.

[16] Blended Finance Taskforce, 'Better Finance, Better World' (n 4) 25; Pereira, 'Blended Finance: What it Is, How it Works and How it Is Used' (n 4) 64–65 (noting that some analysts argue that foreign investors' perception of risk is much greater than actual risk, which may be based on their inability to analyse intricate political and other risks, such as currency risks, across developing countries).

[17] du Toit, Shah, and Wilson (n 14).

[18] ibid.

[19] See Jesse Griffiths, 'Financing for Development: Current Issues for International Development Cooperation' (October 2017) <http://unctad.org/meetings/en/SessionalDocuments/tdb_efd1_bp_JG_en.pdf> accessed 1 July 2018.

[20] United Nations, 'Report of the Inter-agency Task Force on Financing for Development' (n 6) 1.

[21] The OECD has determined that ODA increased by 1.1 per cent over 2016 in real terms, based on preliminary data. OECD, 'Development Aid Stable in 2017 with More Sent to Poorest Countries' (9 April 2018) <http://www.oecd.org/newsroom/development-aid-stable-in-2017-with-more-sent-to-poorest-countries.htm> accessed 15 June 2018. Note that this was calculated without inclusion of in-country refugee costs. UNCTAD found that ODA decreased by 0.6 per cent over 2016 based on preliminary data. UNCTAD, 'World Investment Report 2018' (n 11) 12.

shows that bilateral aid to LDCs, which rely on ODA for two-thirds of external financing, increased by 4 per cent in real terms to US$ 26 billion in 2017, reversing several years of decline.[22]

2.11 Notably, certain substantive shifts in ODA were present in 2017. While most ODA continued to be in the form of grants, the volume of loans composing ODA to developing countries rose by 13 per cent in 2017, and for some specific donors, concessional loans accounted for over 25 per cent of bilateral ODA.[23] At the same time, as grants have decreased, overall concessional disbursements going to the countries most in need have stagnated.[24] Moreover, the share of ODA going to certain sectors, including health, water, sanitation, and hygiene (WASH), and education, continued downward trends (in real terms) in 2017.[25] Donor focus has shifted to support for economic sectors including transportation and energy.[26] While it is likely that a variety of factors are causing these shifts in ODA, including adaptations to the broader scope of the SDGs as compared with the Millennium Development Goals, a more fundamental shift in development policies and priorities of individual governments and multinational institutions, as will be discussed, may be partially responsible.

2.12 At the macro level, while 2017 ODA increased year-on-year, ODA from the OECD's Development Assistance Committee (DAC) was equivalent to only 0.31 per cent of DAC members' combined gross national income (GNI), down from 0.32 per cent in 2016, and below the United Nations target of 0.7 per cent of donor GNI, with 0.15 per cent to 0.20 per cent of GNI directed to LDCs.[27] Thus, most donor countries' contribution to ODA is persistently below committed levels, let alone levels necessary to achieve the objectives of Agenda 2030 and the SDGs, and 2017 saw no improvement in this deficiency.

---

[22] OECD, 'Development Aid Stable in 2017 with More Sent to Poorest Countries' (n 21); United Nations, 'Report of the Inter-agency Task Force on Financing for Development' (n 6). See also UNCTAD, 'World Investment Report 2018' (n 11) 12 (noting that ODA into developing countries is the most significant source of external finance composing 36 per cent of external finance versus 21 per cent for FDI, whereas FDI composes the largest source of external finance for developing countries at 39 per cent).

[23] OECD, 'Development Aid Stable in 2017 with More Sent to Poorest Countries' (n 21). Notably, most of Chinese outward investment relating to the Belt and Road Initiative is in the form of loans, not grants. Anja Manuel, 'China is Quietly Reshaping the World' (The Atlantic, 17 October 2017) <https://www.theatlantic.com/international/archive/2017/10/china-belt-and-road/542667/> accessed 21 June 2018.

[24] United Nations, 'Report of the Inter-agency Task Force on Financing for Development' (n 6).

[25] ibid 26 and 91.

[26] ibid 91.

[27] OECD, 'Development Aid Stable in 2017 with More Sent to Poorest Countries' (n 21).

C. Blended Finance: Notable 2017 Developments at the G20, the World Bank, and the OECD

2.13 In order to address these funding gaps, the Addis Agenda supports a role for the private sector. In 2017 'blended finance' remained a centrepiece of development finance discussions for its potential to bridge sources of financing and drive increased amounts of capital into certain critical development sectors. Notably, discussions in multinational fora since the 2015 Addis Agenda through 2017 rapidly shifted from considering whether blended finance should be used for development to how to most effectively deploy this tool.[28] The year 2017 saw significant steps taken, particularly among the G20, the WBG, and the OECD to develop, deploy, and advance analysis, understanding, and application of blended funds and structures.

1. The G20

2.14 In April 2017, the G20 Eminent Persons Group (EPG) on Global Financial Governance was formally established with a purpose to recommend, in a final report due in the autumn of 2018, practical reforms of the global financial architecture and governance.[29] The G20 EPG will consider, among other things, the optimal role of the international financial institutions, including the WBG and International Monetary Fund, and their capacity to catalyse private capital flows and domestic resources.[30] These institutions can play a critical role to bridge public and private funds given their expertise in, and mandate to support, development-oriented programmes as well as their ability to mobilize longer-term capital. The G20 EPG recommendations will be an important loadstar for future financing for development objectives and policies.

2.15 Following the establishment of the G20 EPG, the G20 finance ministers, in July 2017, endorsed a set of 'Principles of MDBs: strategy for crowding-in Private Sector Finance for growth and sustainable development' that give the WBG and other multilateral development banks (MDBs) a framework for increasing private investment to support development objectives.[31]

---

[28] Jorge Moreira da Silva, 'Blending is Trending but it's Time for International Policy Standards' (Development Finance, 1 December 2017) <https://www.devfinance.net/blending-trending-time-international-policy-standards/> accessed 15 June 2018.

[29] 'Terms of Reference: G20 Eminent Persons Group on Global Financial Governance' (31 May 2017) <http://www.iai.it/sites/default/files/g20-epg-terms-of-reference.pdf> accessed 10 June 2018.

[30] ibid.

[31] See G20—IFA WG, 'Principles of MDBs' Strategy for Crowding-in Private Sector Finance for Growth and Sustainable Development' (April 2017) <http://www.bundesfinanzministerium.de/Content/EN/Standardartikel/Topics/Featured/G20/G20-Documents/principles-on-crowding-in-private-sector-finance-april-20.pdf?__blob=publicationFile&v=2> accessed 24 June 2018.

2. The World Bank Group

2.16 During the course of 2017 the World Bank continued in its distinct pivot to 'crowd in' the private sector in development finance.[32] Alongside the G20's work and in response to the G20 Principles of MDBs, and building on its 2015 'Billions to Trillions' approach to development finance,[33] the WBG introduced in March 2017 the 'Cascade Approach' to leverage the private sector for growth and sustainable development,[34] and in July 2017 the 'Maximizing Finance for Development: Leveraging the Private Sector for Growth and Sustainable Development' agenda (MFD).[35] At their core, these policies seek to use WBG expertise to crowd in the private sector to meet development goals by creating markets and leveraging greater private participation in investments, including through blended facilities.[36] To that end, the WBG's International Development

---

[32] See Landon Thomas Jr, 'The World Bank is Remaking Itself as a Creature of Wall Street' *The New York Times* (25 January 2018) <https://www.nytimes.com/2018/01/25/business/world-bank-jim-yong-kim.html> accessed 24 June 2018. Some of the WBG policies are aimed at helping the WBG to better solve development problems by helping to overcome internal WBG capital constraints. Its intentionally conservative approach means that it (like other long-established MDBs) is constrained in its ability to exponentially scale up the amount of financing required for SDG purposes. The World Bank took steps in 2017 towards increasing its capital base but solutions remain incremental. World Bank Group, 'World Bank/IMF Annual Meetings 2017: Development Committee Communiqué' (4 October 2017) <http://www.worldbank.org/en/news/press-release/2017/10/14/world-bankimf-annual-meetings-2017-development-committee-communique> accessed 10 June 2018, para 13. MDBs and other stakeholders continue to explore capital base increases and increases in the quantum of lending. See Ricardo Gottschalk and Daniel Poon, 'Scaling up Finance for the Sustainable Development Goals: Experimenting with Models of Multilateral Development Banking' (UNCTAD December 2017) <http://unctad.org/en/PublicationsLibrary/gdsecidc2017d4_en.pdf> accessed 5 June 2018; Waqas Munir and Kevin P Gallagher, 'Scaling up Lending at the Multi-Lateral Development Banks: Benefits and Costs of Expanding and Optimizing MDB Balance Sheets' (2018) GEGI Working Paper 013 <http://www.bu.edu/gdp/files/2018/04/Munir_Gallagher_2018-1.pdf> accessed 15 June 2018.

[33] World Bank and IMF Development Committee, 'From Billions to Trillions: Transforming Development Finance' (2 April 2015) <http://pubdocs.worldbank.org/en/622841485963735448/DC2015-0002-E-FinancingforDevelopment.pdf> accessed 17 June 2018.

[34] World Bank and IMF Development Committee, 'Forward Look A Vision for the World Bank Group in 2030—Progress and Challenges' (24 March 2017) <http://siteresources.worldbank.org/DEVCOMMINT/Documentation/23745169/DC2017-0002.pdf> accessed 17 June 2018.

[35] See Joint Ministerial Committee of the Boards of Governors of the Bank and the Fund on the Transfer of Real Resources to Developing Counties, 'Maximizing Finance for Development: Leveraging the Private Sector for Growth and Sustainable Development' (19 September 2017) <http://siteresources.worldbank.org/DEVCOMMINT/Documentation/23758671/DC2017-0009_Maximizing_8-19.pdf> accessed 19 June 2018. For more information on Maximizing Finance for Development see The World Bank, 'Maximizing Finance for Development (MFD)' <http://www.worldbank.org/en/about/partners/maximizing-finance-for-development> accessed 19 June 2018.

[36] For more information on Maximizing Finance for Development see The World Bank, 'Maximizing Finance for Development (MFD)' (n 35). For a discussion of the role of MDBs and DFIs in blended finance, see Nancy Lee, 'Billions to Trillions? Issues on the Role of Development Banks in Mobilizing Private Finance' (Center for Global Development, 17 November 2017) <https://www.cgdev.org/sites/default/files/billions-trillions-issues-role-development-banks-mobilizing-private-finance.pdf> accessed 16 June 2018.

Association, which provides concessional lending to poor countries, established in April 2017 a private sector window (PSW) pursuant to which donors will provide US$ 2.5 billion to be implemented by the WBG's International Finance Corporation and Multilateral Investment Guarantee Agency through four funds.[37] Under these approaches, only where market solutions are not possible will official public resources be applied.[38] While these approaches will target infrastructure, energy, and financial services, ultimately they could also apply at greater scale to education, health, housing, and agribusiness.[39]

Notably, the WBG and other MDBs and national development finance institutions (DFIs) have been called upon by supporters of blended finance to play a larger role in facilitating blended finance mechanisms,[40] although the role that they should play is often insufficiently addressed.[41] The Blended Finance Taskforce, established in 2017 by the Business and Sustainable Development Commission,[42] has called on MDBs to more than double capital mobilization ratios (currently 1:1 (private to public)) over the next decade in order to even approach SDG

2.17

---

[37] More information on the PSW is available at IDA, 'IDA18 Private Sector Window' https://ida.worldbank.org/financing/ida18-private-sector-window> accessed 11 June 2018; see also Business & Sustainable Development Commission and Convergence, 'The State of Blended Finance' (n 3) 11; Nancy Lee, 'IDA Gets a Private Sector Window' (Center for Global Development, 26 April 2017) <https://www.cgdev.org/publication/ida-gets-private-sector-window> accessed 16 June 2018 (commending the WBG on a well-conceived, careful, yet bold creation but expressing caution is warranted (for reasons expressed elsewhere in this paper)).

[38] World Bank and IMF Development Committee, 'Forward Look A Vision for the World Bank Group in 2030—Progress and Challenges' (n 34) para 21. See also 'Remarks by Mr Joaquim Levy, Managing Director and World Bank Group Chief Financial Officer, at the Third World Bank Development Finance Forum in Accra' <https://www.modernghana.com/news/780489/world-banks-new-cascade-to-systematically-connect-private-f.html> accessed 18 June 2018 ('In the most simple terms this approach prescribes that we first consider private investments for projects; then public private partnerships; and if the first two are not available then, only then, consider public finance.').

[39] World Bank and IMF Development Committee, 'Forward Look A Vision for the World Bank Group in 2030—Progress and Challenges' (n 34); see also Business & Sustainable Development Commission and Convergence, 'The State of Blended Finance' (n 3) 5 (analysing blended finance deals by sector).

[40] Blended Finance Taskforce, 'Better Finance, Better World' (n 4) 5. Notably, the consultation paper, published after the OECD definition was published, drew heavily on the OECD's definition but did not adopt the OECD definition for analysis and discussion purposes. ibid 22. For a discussion of DFIs' activities in blended finance through 2017 see Business & Sustainable Development Commission and Convergence, 'The State of Blended Finance' (n 3) 13. Several DFIs participated in the DFI Working Group on Blended Concessional Finance for Private Sector Projects, which issued a Summary Report in October 2017, considering the role of DFIs in establishing principles and guidance, collecting DFI data on blended transactions and sharing best practices, see 'DFI Working Group on Blended Concessional Finance for Private Sector Projects: Summary Report' (October 2017) <https://www.edfi.eu/wp/wp-content/uploads/2017/10/DFI-Blended-Concessional-Finance-for-Private-Sector-Operations_Summary-R....pdf> accessed 16 June 2018.

[41] See Lee, 'Billions to Trillions? Issues on the Role of Development Banks in Mobilizing Private Finance' (n 36).

[42] Blended Finance Taskforce, 'Better Finance, Better World' (n 4) 5.

financing targets,⁴³ and on DFIs and MDBs to significantly increase their share of private sector activities.⁴⁴

3. The OECD

2.18 In 2017 the OECD progressed its existing work analysing and providing standards surrounding the use of blended finance in order to assist the development cooperation community to formulate approaches that are evidence based, informed by best practices, and backed by policy guidance.⁴⁵ The October adoption of the OECD DAC Blended Finance Principles for Unlocking Commercial Finance for the SDGs (OECD DAC Principles), both set forth a clear definition of blended finance,⁴⁶ and provided a five-point checklist to help ensure that blended finance meets accepted quality standards and achieves impact, based on DAC development rationales.⁴⁷ Noting that, based on self-reporting, seventeen of the thirty DAC members already carry out blended finance activities and that more are looking to enter the field, the OECD DAC Principles recognize that if blended finance is to work towards the SDGs, agreement among stakeholders on acceptable quality standards and impact is fundamental. 'The rise in popularity of blended finance' noted Jorge Moreira da Silva, director of the OECD development co-operation directorate 'warrants an urgent need for international policy co-ordination to ensure blending supports developing countries' SDG plans.'⁴⁸

2.19 The OECD is progressing, through the Total Official Support for Sustainable Development (TOSSD) process, its work on developing a metric to measure aid flows beyond ODA that would include blended finance.⁴⁹ While TOSSD is ongoing, it has been criticized both for its lack of transparency and stakeholder involvement, as well as substantively, as the original TOSSD proposal included perceived flaws that could have negatively impacted ODA because, among other

---

⁴³ ibid 7 and 18; Business & Sustainable Development Commission and Convergence, 'The State of Blended Finance' (n 3) 12.

⁴⁴ Blended Finance Taskforce, 'Better Finance, Better World' (n 4) 6–7.

⁴⁵ See OECD, 'Blended Finance for Development: Bridging the Sustainable Development Finance Gap' <https://www.oecd.org/dac/Blended%20Finance%20flyer%20DAC%20HLM%202017.pdf> accessed 14 June 2018.

⁴⁶ The OECD DAC defines blended finance as 'the strategic use of development finance for the mobilization of additional finance towards sustainable development in developing countries, with 'additional finance' referring primarily to commercial finance'.

⁴⁷ OECD, 'OECD DAC Blended Finance Principles for Unlocking Commercial Finance for the Sustainable Development Goals' (January 2018)<https://www.oecd.org/dac/financing-sustainable-development/development-finance-topics/OECD-Blended-Finance-Principles.pdf> accessed 5 June 2018.

⁴⁸ Moreira da Silva (n 28).

⁴⁹ See OECD, 'What is Total Official Support for Sustainable Development (TOSSD)?' <http://www.oecd.org/dac/financing-sustainable-development/tossd.htm> accessed 5 June 2018.

issues, the manner in which it would have included measurements of private financial flows that were mobilized by ODA.[50]

D. Blended Finance: Not a Panacea?

2.20 The year 2017 saw a growing number of stakeholders who, while acknowledging the theoretical potential of blended finance, were concerned about the rapid scale up and expansion of its use while there remains a general lack of consensus on a definition of blended finance (potentially mitigated by the OECD's contribution), what it means in practice, in what contexts it can work best, and in what contexts it should be applied with extreme caution or not at all. Importantly, the lack of consensus on these basic parameters represented critical gaps that could impact the effectiveness of blended finance to achieve the SDGs.[51]

2.21 For example, without an agreed definition of what blending encompasses, studies looking at blending result in considerable uncertainty as to how much ODA is being used for blending purposes, as well as how much finance is mobilized as a result of blending.[52] From a policy perspective, how and where ODA is being directed is critically important, and to the extent blended finance policies are developed based on empirical evidence, such evidence must be accurate. The OECD definition, to the extent used in discussion, analysis, and reporting of blended finance, should usefully advance understanding of the value of blended finance as a policy tool.

2.22 Beyond definitions, there were concerns, echoing the caution expressed in the Addis Agenda,[53] that rapidly scaling up the use of blended finance before its impacts and effects are properly understood could have serious unintended consequences.

---

[50] DAC CSO Reference Group, 'TOSSD—Submission for the Second Task Force Meeting' <https://www.oecd.org/dac/financing-sustainable-development/development-finance-standards/DAC-CSO-Reference-Group.pdf> accessed 5 June 2018; Griffiths, 'Financing for Development: Current Issues for International Development Cooperation' (n 19) 11–12.

[51] Javier Pereira, 'Blended Finance for Development: Background paper prepared for the Intergovernmental Group of Experts on Financing for Development, 1st Session, 8–10 November 2017' (n 4) 17.

[52] Javier Pereira, 'Blended Finance: What it Is, How it Works and How it Is Used' (n 4) 13–14.

[53] While the Addis Agenda welcomes consideration of blended finance as one instrument that has the potential to improve sustainable development outcomes, it also hints at its risks, noting that careful consideration should be given to the appropriate structure and use of this tool, and that projects involving blended finance, including public-private partnerships, should share risks and rewards fairly, should include clear accountability mechanisms, and should meet social and environmental standards. United Nations, 'Addis Adaba Action Agenda of the Third International Conference on Financing for Development' (n 2) para 48.

2.23 Various 2017 reports and policy papers focused on the use of blended finance in developing countries. While acknowledging the economic and development rationale for blending as well as the important role that it could play in opening up new markets for development purposes,[54] these reports have highlighted important gaps that can affect the development impact of blended finance as well as its alignment with important development effectiveness principles.

2.24 Risks of blended finance highlighted in 2017 include that: (1) financial and/or development additionality is not always clear; (2) it does not necessarily support pro-poor activities and often focuses on middle-income countries; (3) it may give preferential treatment to donor-countries' own private outward investors; (4) projects may not involve sufficient country ownership and may not align with country development plans; (5) it often fails to satisfactorily incorporate transparency, accountability, and stakeholder participation in project design and implementation; and (6) risks of developing infrastructure as an asset class are insufficiently considered. Furthermore, the role of China in financing developing creates enormous potential, but many stakeholders expressed reservations as to whether Chinese investment will further the SDGs in a holistic manner, particularly with respect to environmental and social objectives.

1. The financial and/or development additionality of blended finance is not always clear

2.25 When ODA is used for blending purposes one of the most critical assessments is to determine whether a project in question actually requires some form of ODA-based subsidy in order to proceed, and if so, what amount and form of subsidy is most appropriate to achieve the development objectives of the host-country. Blended finance can help overcome these hurdles by providing financial and developmental 'additionality'.[55] Evaluations of blended finance have found that donors frequently assume additionality. However, a closer examination demonstrates that measuring the added value of blended financial products is difficult at best, and even where evaluations are conducted, methodologies tend to focus more on considering financial additionality (whether blended finance is necessary to ensuring a project obtains financing and moves forward) than development additionality (whether blended finance helps the project achieve better development results).[56] The UN Inter-agency Taskforce on Financing for Development

---

[54] Pereira, 'Blended Finance: What it Is, How it Works and How it Is Used' (n 4) 43.
[55] See Pereira, 'Blended Finance: What it Is, How it Works and How it Is Used' (n 4) 14–16; United Nations, 'Report of the Inter-agency Task Force on Financing for Development' (n 6) 104.
[56] Pereira, 'Blended Finance: What it Is, How it Works and How it Is Used' (n 4) 14–16; Polly Meeks, 'Mixed Messages: The Rhetoric and the Reality of Using Blended Finance to "leave no-one behind"' (Eurodad, November 2017) <http://www.eurodad.org/blended-finance-briefing> accessed 17 June 2018; Business & Sustainable Development Commission and Convergence, 'The State of Blended Finance' (n 3) 17.

(Inter-agency Task Force) highlighted these concerns, noting that '[d]evelopment additionality in particular has proven to be a source of concern in existing projects, due to limited availability of reliable evidence on the sustainable development impact of blending.'[57]

2. Blended finance does not necessarily support pro-poor activities and often focuses on middle-income countries

2.26 While blended finance is intended to affect project risk-profiles, blended facilities and funds, by their nature, target SDG investments where there is a clear business case.[58] An analysis of existing blending facilities demonstrates a high concentration (85 per cent of all projects) in energy,[59] transport, water and sanitation, and private sector development projects concentrated in middle-income countries.[60] It is particularly attractive for its potential in the clean energy and infrastructure sectors.[61] Thus far, however, blended finance is largely eschewing the world's poorest countries. One study found that as of 2017, approximately 40 per cent of blended finance deals had been in Sub-Saharan Africa, but because of the smaller deal size these projects represented only 28 per cent of mobilized capital, raising questions as to the scalability of blended finance deals in developing regions.[62] Only 7 per cent of private finance has been mobilized for projects in LDCs,[63] while middle-income countries receive 70 per cent of capital flows (although low- and lower-middle income account for 66 per cent of capital flows).[64] This may be partially due to financial sustainability requirements in blending facilities, or that many facilities are structured without a pro-poor

---

[57] United Nations, 'Report of the Inter-agency Task Force on Financing for Development' (n 6) 104.

[58] ibid 103.

[59] Of fifty blended funds created since 2014 through 2017, at least 40 per cent focus on clean energy or energy efficiency. Blended Finance Taskforce, 'Better Finance, Better World' (n 4) 7 and 21.

[60] Pereira, 'Blended Finance: What it Is, How it Works and How it Is Used' (n 4) 25. Sectors that reflect high levels of public good, such as ecosystems, or development factors that are difficult to monetize, such as healthcare and education, see blending currently playing a much smaller role and public finance often remains the most effective financing option. United Nations, 'Report of the Inter-agency Task Force on Financing for Development' (n 6) 103.

[61] Business & Sustainable Development Commission and Convergence, 'The State of Blended Finance' (n 3) 6. See e.g. Asian Development Bank, 'Catalysing Green Finance: A Concept for Leveraging Blended Finance for Green Development' (2017) <https://www.adb.org/sites/default/files/publication/357156/catalyzing-green-finance.pdf> accessed 14 June 2018.

[62] Business & Sustainable Development Commission and Convergence, 'The State of Blended Finance' (n 3) 4. The authors note that this percentage may reflect limitations of African markets to attract and support large-scale blended finance deals.

[63] United Nations, 'Report of the Inter-agency Task Force on Financing for Development' (n 6) 103. In 2016, MDBs mobilized $7.1 billion in co-financing for infrastructure, but only 2 per cent of co-financing was mobilized for low-income and least-developed countries where infrastructure gaps are greatest. Pereira, 'Blended Finance: What it Is, How it Works and How it Is Used' (n 4) Section 2.

[64] Business & Sustainable Development Commission and Convergence, 'The State of Blended Finance' (n 3) 5.

objective, which can result in a focus on countries and sectors with the lowest risk profile.[65] It may also be a result of blending facilities, in isolation, failing to address certain hurdles to investment in these countries. In any event, these findings are not necessarily unexpected; the Blended Finance Taskforce, in calling for increased private-sector lending from MDBs, notes that doing so 'will likely shift portfolios more toward infrastructure investment and toward more stable middle-income countries. But it could also free up additional development capital for frontier, low-income countries and high additionality projects'.[66] The Business & Sustainable Development Commission has suggested a graduation approach where intermediaries would share risks with private sector investors, philanthropic investors, and public investors at graduated amounts depending on the development level of the country and sector.[67] Analysis of the challenges and risks of using blended finance vehicles in the LDC context is ongoing, including through the WBG's PSW.[68]

2.27 While blended finance investments will naturally advance some SDGs, such as infrastructure, more than others, such as ecosystems or rural roads, in the absence of increased ODA concerns arise over the tradeoff that results from a shift in ODA towards blended products and away from traditional aid modalities. Profit-making projects, while an important element of SDG achievement, are vastly insufficient to end extreme poverty or achieve the whole of the SDGs. They currently are not, and will not necessarily, channel money to developing countries in an inclusive manner, including to micro and smaller enterprises, women, the disabled, the poor, and other underserved segments of society.[69] The Inter-agency Task Force noted that as blended finance becomes an increasingly common modality of ODA provision, concerted steps will need to be taken to ensure that LDCs and other vulnerable countries do not see a fall in their overall share of development finance.[70]

---

[65] Pereira, 'Blended Finance: What it Is, How it Works and How it Is Used' (n 4) 43. World Bank Group funds were an exception.
[66] Blended Finance Taskforce, 'Better Finance, Better World' (n 4) 7.
[67] Business & Sustainable Development Commission and Convergence, 'The State of Blended Finance' (n 3) 17–18.
[68] United Nations, 'Report of the Inter-agency Task Force on Financing for Development' (n 6).
[69] ibid; Meeks, 'Mixed Messages: The Rhetoric and the Reality of Using Blended Finance to "leave no-one behind"' (n 56).
[70] United Nations, 'Report of the Inter-agency Task Force on Financing for Development' (n 6) 88 and 103. Notably the lack of consensus on key issues surrounding blended finance may itself incentivize the shift in ODA. For example, in the absence of an agreed methodology on ODA reporting of loans, equity, mezzanine finance, and guarantees to private sector entities in developing countries, donors have started reporting these instruments as ODA. ibid. The OECD DAC is working on methodologies to ensure consistent reporting of ODA in the context of blended finance, and changes were to be implemented in the reporting systems beginning in 2017. See OECD, 'Modernisation of the DAC Statistical System' <http://www.oecd.org/dac/financing-sustainable-development/modernisation-dac-statistical-system.htm> accessed 5 June 2018.

Furthermore, the risk-shifting that is itself the cornerstone of blended finance 2.28 facilities has been criticized.[71] Some note that the risk involved in an investment does not simply disappear, but is transferred from private investors to other parties such as governments and other stakeholders, including host-state taxpayers and consumers.[72] As such, absent extreme caution in its use and application, risk-shifting may undermine rather than advance the SDGs.

One area that is highlighted by concerned stakeholders is the monitoring and 2.29 evaluation systems used by intermediary institutions involved in project management of blended facilities.[73] Using blended funds for SDG purposes requires robust project planning, monitoring, and evaluating geared towards the achievement of development objectives. Many intermediaries may be less equipped to SDG analysis, including pro-poor or gender aspects of projects.[74] Further, to the extent intermediaries do not incorporate SDG targets into the structuring of a blended facility and development impact is instead analysed ex-post, such funds may mobilize finance but may have a more limited impact on poverty.[75] The Inter-agency Task Force notes that '[m]any blending projects have not monitored development impacts, and evaluations are not routinely made publicly available'.[76] It thus appears that in order to make a significant difference in pro-poor and gender equality outcomes of projects, these objectives must be integrated into the structuring of a blending facility through both its purpose and incentives, but as a general matter how to achieve these SDG targets through blending remains under-researched.[77] There is concern that rapidly expanding the scope of blended

---

[71] At the 2017 World Bank Group and IMF annual meetings 152 organizations from 45 countries launched a Public-Private Partnership Global Campaign Manifesto calling for an end to the prioritization of public-private partnerships (PPPs) over traditional public borrowing to finance social and economic infrastructure and services, focusing on how using blending to support PPPs can have a negative impact on human and environmental rights. While PPPs and blended finance are distinct and present distinct risks and challenges, PPPs are often included in discussions on blended finance because PPPs can be a form of blended finance. 'Public-Private Partnerships Global Campaign Manifesto'<http://eurodad.org/files/pdf/1546821-world-bank-must-stop-promoting-dangerous-public-private-partnerships-1510908938.pdf> accessed 18 June 2018; Meeks, 'Mixed Messages: The Rhetoric and the Reality of Using Blended Finance to "leave no-one behind"' (n 56).

[72] Nancy Alexander, 'Beware the Cascade—World Bank to the Future' (Just Governance, 23 May 2017) <http://justgovernance.boellblog.org/2017/05/23/beware-the-cascade-world-banck-to-the-future/> accessed 5 June 2018.

[73] According to one study, as of 2017 IFC was the largest public investor, followed by FMO, EIB, KfW, OPIC, PROPARCO, BIO, CDC, and USAID. Business & Sustainable Development Commission and Convergence, 'The State of Blended Finance' (n 3) 6.

[74] Pereira, 'Blended Finance: What it Is, How it Works and How it Is Used' (n 4) 40 (discussing findings relating to EU and Dutch facilities).

[75] ibid 41. The WBG facility that Pereira analysed was an exception to this finding and was structured in a way that incentivized development targets. See also United Nations, 'Report of the Inter-agency Task Force on Financing for Development' (n 6) 104.

[76] United Nations, 'Report of the Inter-agency Task Force on Financing for Development' (n 6) 104.

[77] Pereira, 'Blended Finance: What it Is, How it Works and How it Is Used' (n 4) 41.

finance products before these institutional mechanisms are established and outcomes understood may be highly problematic.

3. Blended finance may give preferential treatment to donor-countries' own private outward investors

2.30 'Tied aid', or aid that can only be used to procure goods or services from the donor country (as opposed to, for example, locally in the recipient country) can undermine development effectiveness in several ways. First, as Meeks has noted, tied aid is frequently more expensive than untied aid, in some cases up to 15–30 per cent more.[78] Because a dollar of tied aid goes less far than a comparable dollar of untied aid it decreases the amount of potential aid had the tied money been spent in a different way.[79] Relatedly, tied aid undermines the 'double dividend' that can occur when ODA involves local procurement, which can increase demand from local providers and build up the local economy.[80] Furthermore, as Meeks also highlights, tied aid undermines national ownership of development projects and plans because in cases of tied aid the donor retains significant input in how and where the money is spent.[81] It deprives aid recipients of the ability to make their own purchasing decisions that are appropriate for their own priorities and may result in them purchasing goods and services that are less well suited to local contexts.[82] While the share of tied aid has decreased in recent years (22 per cent of ODA in 2015; 19 per cent of ODA in 2016), progress is uneven and more work needs to be done.[83]

2.31 Absent more stringent definitional and reporting standards relating to blended finance, levels of 'tied' ODA may actually be higher than reported, and exacerbated by blending techniques.[84] For example, one concern surrounding the increased use of blended finance is that blended finance intermediaries, in particular DFIs, may have a bias in favour of the donor-country economic interests and businesses.[85] DFIs could tie aid to further these economic interests but current ODA accounting methodologies may not recognize the aid as tied. As such, the growing

---

[78] Polly Meeks, 'Unraveling Tied Aid' <http://www.eurodad.org/files/pdf/1546810-unravelling-tied-aid-1516803666.pdf> accessed 5 June 2018.
[79] ibid.
[80] ibid.
[81] ibid.
[82] ibid.
[83] United Nations, 'Report of the Inter-agency Task Force on Financing for Development' (n 6) 106.
[84] Griffiths, 'Financing for Development: Current Issues for International Development Cooperation' (n 19); Pereira, 'Blended Finance: What it Is, How it Works and How it Is Used' (n 4) 36–37.
[85] ibid.

role of blended finance increases the importance of ensuring that aid is fully untied and thus also effective.[86]

4. Blended projects may not involve sufficient country ownership and may not align with country development plans

Sustainable and long-term development impact depends on national ownership of projects such that they are aligned with national priorities, and national actors are involved in planning, decision-making, and implementation.[87] In many cases, blending facilities involve donors transferring responsibility, including for project selection, design, and management, to other actors, such as DFIs, who may have a different mandate than the donor.[88] In one empirical analysis of three existing blending facilities, Pereira found that participation and consultation of developing-country stakeholders in the decision-making and consultation process that occurred as the project was being developed was often lacking.[89] With respect to a Dutch blending facility, for example, projects were initiated by private companies and there was no requirement to consult developing countries or other stakeholders in the design process.[90] Overall, and particularly outside of public sector projects, host-country involvement in blended finance projects is low.[91] In some cases, where developing country governments have been consulted in designing and setting priorities for an individual blending facility, these government representatives do not sit on the board of the facility nor participate in operational decisions.[92] To the extent blended finance moves towards a direction of multi-country funds and product standardization, it may exacerbate concerns surrounding country involvement and ownership at the project level.[93]

2.32

---

[86] United Nations, 'Report of the Inter-agency Task Force on Financing for Development' (n 6) 106.

[87] ibid; see Polly Meeks, 'Mixed Messages: The Rhetoric and the Reality of Using Blended Finance to "leave no-one behind"' (n 56).

[88] For a discussion of DFIs activities in blended finance through 2017 see Business & Sustainable Development Commission and Convergence, 'The State of Blended Finance' (n 3) 13. Several DFIs participate in the DFI Working Group on Blended Concessional Finance for Private Sector Projects, which issued a Summary Report in October 2017, considering the role of DFIs in establishing principles and guidance, collecting DFI data on blended transactions and sharing best practices <https://www.edfi.eu/wp/wp-content/uploads/2017/10/DFI-Blended-Concessional-Finance-for-Private-Sector-Operations_Summary-R....pdf> accessed 7 June 2018; see also Pereira, 'Blended Finance: What it Is, How it Works and How it Is Used' (n 4) 20–21.

[89] Pereira, 'Blended Finance: What it Is, How it Works and How it Is Used' (n 4) 35–39 (noting that consultation regarding WBG facilities was held to the WBG's internal (higher) standards).

[90] ibid.

[91] United Nations, 'Report of the Inter-agency Task Force on Financing for Development' (n 6).

[92] Pereira, 'Blended Finance: What it Is, How it Works and How it Is Used' (n 4) 36.

[93] For example, the Blended Finance Taskforce has expressly called upon asset managers and project developers to work alongside MDBs and DFIs to put together ambitious multi-billion-dollar blended funds that would potentially allow for multi-country, diversified portfolios to emerge, which would have the additional benefit of helping to drive product standardization. Blended Finance Taskforce, 'Better Finance, Better World' (n 4) 16.

5. Blended finance may fail to satisfactorily incorporate transparency, accountability, and stakeholder participation in project design and implementation

2.33 Empirical evidence indicates that transparency and accountability are more limited when blended finance is involved in development assistance.[94] When intermediaries—entities that may have more limited transparency and/or accountability policies and practices than donors—are responsible for structuring and deploying blended products, transparency regarding basic information about projects, such as the objectives of the project, which entities are supporting the project, or availability of any stakeholder complaint mechanism, is often limited or unavailable.[95] This lack of transparency in projects involving blended funds can impact the ability of project-affected stakeholders to both understand and raise concerns about a project.[96]

2.34 Most MDBs and DFIs incorporate environmental and social safeguards into their investment policies. However, the robustness of these safeguards varies significantly by development bank, and the outsourcing of blended finance projects to intermediaries can significantly impact the implementation and monitoring of environmental, social, and governance policies.[97] Ray, Gallagher, and Sandborn, for example, found that MDBs based in the global North (including the WBG) condition loans on harmonized global standards regardless of the varying national standards that may apply in the borrowing country.[98] On the other hand, developing country DFIs (notably Chinese DFIs) tend to recognize the standards used by the borrowing country and do not condition finance on that country's ability to meet the DFI's own standard, nor do they offer the borrowers assistance in meeting those standards.[99] With that said, a separate report looking at actual implementation of the WBG's International Finance Corporation (IFC) Performance Standards alleged that IFC, in five case studies, failed to sufficiently incorporate and enforce its safeguards in situations in which it participated, through DFIs and private banks, in blended projects,[100] suggesting that in practice even global

---

[94] Pereira, 'Blended Finance: What it Is, How it Works and How it Is Used' (n 4) 37.
[95] ibid. While a WBG facility presented relatively higher levels of transparency, the blended finance aspect of the project was not always easy to identify in the World Bank's project database.
[96] ibid.
[97] Rebecca Ray, Kevin Gallagher, and Cynthia Sandborn, 'Standardizing Sustainable Development? Development Banks in the Andean Amazon' (Boston University Global Development Policy Center, 2018) <https://www.bu.edu/gdp/2018/04/16/standardizing-sustainable-development-development-banks-in-the-andean-amazon/> accessed 27 May 2018.
[98] ibid 9.
[99] ibid.
[100] Inclusive Development International, et. al, 'Outsourcing Development: Lifting the Veil on the World Bank Group's Lending Through Financial Intermediaries' (Part 3, March 2017) <http://www.inclusivedevelopment.net/wp-content/uploads/2017/03/Outsourcing-Development-Part-3-1.pdf> accessed 10 June 2018.

North institutions may struggle with safeguard implementation in the blended finance context.[101] Pereira notes that thus far, little analysis has been done as to the impact of blending facilities on the guidelines and policy frameworks of the institutions managing them, such as whether they should be reasonably expected to implement the same standards as donor agencies, and if not, what a reasonable minimum might be.[102]

6. Risks of infrastructure as an asset class are insufficiently considered

Long-term institutional investment in blended finance projects will necessarily require standardization of project terms and documents, the creation of bankable project pipelines, and the creation of infrastructure as an asset class.[103] For example, the World Bank's work on public-private partnerships (PPPs), ongoing through 2017, seeks improved standardization to this end.[104] In addition to concerns expressed previously in this chapter regarding intermediaries' implementation of safeguard policies, national ownership, and transparency and accountability mechanisms, which could be exacerbated in this context, the creation of liquid investment instruments out of illiquid assets must be done with extreme care as it has the potential to create short-term bubbles that could impede rather than promote long-term sustainable development.[105]

2.35

7. The role of China

The Belt and Road Initiative (BRI) is a critical part of development finance discussions, not least because the amount of financing coming out of China overshadows that of the WBG and the rest of the world. In recent decades China has been incredibly successful in reducing poverty and building quality infrastructure, both key components of the SDGs, and is now attempting to internationalize its development model through supporting roads, rails, airports, seaports, energy pipelines, among other infrastructure, that will further the political, social, and cultural linkages among over sixty countries and support China's growing consumption patterns.[106] To the extent BRI can further the

2.36

---

[101] IFC's Blended Finance work is described on its website <https://www.ifc.org/wps/wcm/connect/CORP_EXT_Content/IFC_External_Corporate_Site/Solutions/Products+and+Services/Blended-Finance> accessed 11 June 2018.
[102] Pereira, 'Blended Finance: What it Is, How it Works and How it Is Used' (n 4) 20–21.
[103] du Toit, Shah, and Wilson, 'Ideas for Action for a Long-Term and Sustainable Financial System' (n 14).
[104] See World Bank, 'Infrastructure and Public-Private Partnerships', <http://www.worldbank.org/en/topic/publicprivatepartnerships> accessed 13 June 2018. While PPPs and blended finance are distinct and present distinct risks and challenges, PPPs are often included in discussions on blended finance because PPPs can be a form of blended finance.
[105] Pereira, 'Blended Finance: What it Is, How it Works and How it Is Used' (n 4).
[106] Aniket Shah, 'Building a Sustainable 'Belt and Road'' (CIRSD Horizons, 2016) <https://www.cirsd.org/en/horizons/horizons-spring-2016--issue-no-7/building-a-sustainable-%E2%80%98belt-and-road-> accessed 24 June 2018.

SDGs, it could form the basis of a new form of multilateralism aimed at solving the world's most pressing development challenges. However, experience with BRI raises some serious concerns. For example, the environmental sustainability of Chinese infrastructure investment is questionable. China is the world's largest carbon dioxide emitter and suffers from high amounts of pollution.[107] It remains unclear what environmental, social, and governance standards China is using for BRI infrastructure projects, but, as noted, Chinese DFIs tend to recognize the standards used by the borrowing country and do not condition finance on that country's ability to meet the DFI's own standard, nor do they offer the borrowers assistance in meeting those standards, raising questions as to whether these projects may be not supporting, or worse, undermining, SDG achievement.[108] Furthermore, China's commitment to untied aid also is unclear, as BRI projects often require recipient countries to use Chinese firms for projects.[109] Moreover, of greater concern for trends in development assistance that are seeing shifts towards blended finance and economic sectors and away from traditional ODA, which remains critical for SDG achievement, most of Chinese BRI funding is in the form of loans in infrastructure sectors in which Chinese state-owned companies invest. While this kind of collateral security makes perfect sense in private-sector transactions when ODA is involved questions as to its impact on the SDGs arise.[110]

E. Conclusion

2.37 In 2017, significant steps at the highest political and economic levels were taken to fundamentally transform the way that finance for development purposes is harnessed and applied and to make achievement of Agenda 2030 and the SDGs possible. While blended finance has great potential to unleash transformational change in global development, whether it can ultimately mobilize at scale the amounts of funding necessary to achieve the SDGs has yet to be determined. Moreover, stakeholders are increasingly voicing concerns about the rapid deployment of blended funds and facilities without first having a greater understanding of its impacts on development objectives as the fear, if misapplied, blended finance could actually undermine SDG achievement. Nonetheless the use of blended finance appears to be on an upward trajectory that will continue through 2018. The G20 EPG report due in the autumn of 2018 is likely to

---

[107] ibid.
[108] Ray, Gallagher, and Sandborn (n 97) 9.
[109] Manuel (n 23).
[110] ibid. For example, the use of loans as opposed to grants means that countries may and do experience situations of default, giving China leverage over the investment, the borrower (which may or not be the government), the government (in some cases), and potentially the right to own and/or operate critical infrastructure in partner countries.

reinforce the G20 and WBG's pivot towards the private sector. The BRI and China will continue to form a new paradigm of development finance and infrastructure investment. Criticisms as to whether practices and policies that are ostensibly being deployed to achieve the SDGs may in reality be undermining them will increase.

3

INSTITUTIONAL DEVELOPMENTS IN INVESTMENT LAW AND POLICY

Taylor St John

A. Introduction	3.01	C. Amending and Appointing: Developments at Arbitral Institutions	3.14
B. Unprecedented Deliberations: UNCITRAL	3.05	D. Exchanging and Updating: OECD and UNCTAD	3.18

A. Introduction

3.01 The dynamism of investment law was channelled through international institutions to a greater extent in 2017 than ever before. For decades, investment law has been defined by its decentralization—by the absence of an institutional hub for multilateral deliberations—and by the difficulty of accessing information about investment treaty negotiations or investor–state arbitrations. As institutions led the way towards more deliberation and increased transparency, the slow-moving redefinition of investment law continued in 2017. While the outcomes of this redefinition are not yet clear (and it remains to be seen if this redefinition will lead to more inclusive and institutionalized multilateral cooperation in investment law), what is clear is that institutions are players, and fields of play, to watch.

3.02 This survey will begin with developments in the United Nations Commission on International Trade Law (UNCITRAL or the Commission) Working Group III. At the UNCITRAL meetings held in November–December 2017, government officials engaged in substantive, multilateral discussions about investor–state dispute settlement (ISDS). This meeting featured frank deliberations in the plenary sessions, which were recorded and released to the public in six languages. The autumn 2017 UNCITRAL meetings kicked off a process that will likely last for several years and may lead to major reform of ISDS. Also in 2017, an earlier UNCITRAL process reached a milestone on the long road towards transparency becoming a default norm when the Mauritius Convention on Transparency came into force.[1]

3.03 This survey then turns to developments at arbitral institutions. Several arbitral institutions updated or began updating their institutional rules in 2017. While this updating is easy to underestimate as routine, these rules matter—they define the everyday practice of investment law, including on controversial topics such as third-party funding. Arbitral institutions are both venues and actors in their own right; as actors, many institutions supported the Equal Representation in Arbitration pledge and other initiatives that draw attention to gender diversity in arbitration. While arbitral institutions cooperated on some initiatives in 2017, other decisions taken by these institutions suggest that one underlying logic of their interaction is a competition for cases.

3.04 Finally, this survey turns to continuing developments at the Organisation for Economic Co-operation and Development (OECD) and the United Nations Conference on Trade and Development (UNCTAD). These two international organizations continued to serve as important hubs for intergovernmental discussions and continued their research and advisory work to help governments keep up with developments in investment law and update their existing treaties and practice in 2017.

B. Unprecedented Deliberations: UNCITRAL

3.05 In July 2017, UNCITRAL entrusted Working Group III with a broad mandate to work on possible reform of ISDS. The mandate had three (3) parts: '(i) first, identify and consider concerns regarding ISDS; (ii) second, consider whether reform was desirable in light of any identified concerns; and (iii) third, if the Working Group were to conclude that reform was desirable, develop any relevant solutions to be recommended to the Commission.'[2] This mandate followed 'a formal request from a number of countries, including the European Union and its Member States, to examine this issue'.[3] It also built on UNCITRAL's earlier involvement with the Mauritius Convention drafting and the UNCITRAL Secretariat's study

---

[1] As discussed, the Mauritius Convention had been ratified by only three states, and signed by twenty-two, at the end of 2017. UNCITRAL, 'Status: 'United Nations Convention on Transparency in Treaty-based Investor-State Arbitration (New York, 2014)' <http://www.uncitral.org/uncitral/en/uncitral_texts/arbitration/2014Transparency_Convention_status.html> accessed 1 January 2018.

[2] UNCITRAL, 'Report of Working Group III (Investor-State Dispute Settlement Reform) on the Work of its Thirty-fourth Session, Vienna, 27 November–1 December 2017' (2017) A/CN.9/930, 3.

[3] European Commission Factsheet, 'UN Agrees to Start Work on Multilateral Reform of Investment Dispute Settlement' (10 July 2017) <http://trade.ec.europa.eu/doclib/docs/2017/july/tradoc_155744.pdf> accessed 1 January 2018.

of possible paths for ISDS reform and consultations with stakeholders, which had been underway since 2015. By July 2017, the Secretariat had prepared notes on concurrent proceedings,[4] ethics,[5] and reforms of ISDS,[6] and it had received comments from states and international organizations on ISDS.[7]

3.06 The UNCITRAL Secretariat prepared a paper in advance of Working Group III's first meeting to discuss possible reform of ISDS. The paper identified and discussed concerns with ISDS in clear language, focusing on seven 'commonly expressed' concerns that 'have been said to undermine the legitimacy of the ISDS regime and its democratic accountability': '(i) inconsistency in arbitral decisions, (ii) limited mechanisms to ensure the correctness of arbitral decisions, (iii) lack of predictability, (iv) appointment of arbitrators by parties ("party-appointment"), (v) the impact of party-appointment on the impartiality and independence of arbitrators, (vi) lack of transparency, and (vii) increasing duration and costs of the procedure'.[8] These concerns seem to prioritize procedural reforms, but procedural and substantive issues can be difficult to disentangle. For instance, governments seeking to ensure their right to regulate may address this through both procedural and substantive reforms. Reform tools can also blend procedure and substance, as procedural provisions that enable binding joint interpretations on substantive matters do.[9] In 2017, discussion on possible reform of ISDS at UNCITRAL focused on two categories: concerns with the arbitral process and outcomes, and concerns with arbitrators.

3.07 The setup for the first meeting held in Vienna in November 2017 differed from the setup of previous discussions in three ways. First and most importantly, these discussions were government-led, with arbitration practitioners playing a smaller role than in previous discussions.[10] Government leadership is so central to this UNCITRAL process that it was mentioned alongside the Working Group's mandate: 'Working Group III would, in discharging that mandate, ensure that the

---

[4] UNCITRAL, 'Possible Future Work in the Field of Dispute Settlement: Concurrent Proceedings in International Arbitration' (2017) Sales No A/CN.9/915.

[5] UNCITRAL, 'Possible Future Work in the Field of Dispute Settlement: Ethics in International Arbitration' (2017) Sales No A/CN.9/916.

[6] UNCITRAL, 'Possible Future Work in the Field of Dispute Settlement: Reforms of Investor-State Dispute Settlement (ISDS)' (2017) Sales No A/CN.9/917.

[7] UNCITRAL, 'Investor-State Dispute Settlement Framework: Compilation of Comments, Note by the Secretariat' (2017) Sales No A/CN.9/918; UNCITRAL, 'Investor-State Dispute Settlement Framework: Compilation of Comments' (2017) Sales No A/CN.9/918.Add1–Add9.

[8] UNCITRAL, 'Possible Reform of Investor-State Dispute Settlement, Note by the Secretariat for Working Group III (Investor-State Dispute Settlement Reform) on the Work of its Thirty-fourth Session, Vienna, 27 November–1 December 2017' (2017) A/CN.9/WG.III/WP.142, 6.

[9] I am grateful to Lise Johnson for bringing these points about the procedure and substance distinction to my attention.

[10] While there was more government leadership, several delegations (including Chile, Mauritius, Switzerland, and the United States) included arbitration practitioners, some of whom spoke on behalf of those governments. Some practitioners have long been part of their national delegations: James Castello, an American citizen in private practice, has been part of the American delegation since 2001. Alison Ross, 'UNCITRAL Celebrates 50th after Tense Talks on ISDS Reform'

deliberations, while benefiting from the widest possible breadth of available expertise from all stakeholders, would be government-led with high-level input from all governments.'[11] This wording strikes a careful balance between officials and experts, gently encouraging governments to send officials from national capitals and discouraging the practice of experts (arbitration practitioners) leading UNCITRAL delegations.[12] When it comes to experts, the key issue is if these external actors speak *for* the government, a practice that raises questions about who or what is being represented and can have ramifications for national and international policies. External actors speaking for governments runs through the history of ISDS: even for the drafting of the Convention on the Settlement of Investment Disputes between States and Nationals of Other States (ICSID Convention), governments were instructed to designate experts. All experts-designate attended in a personal capacity, not as representatives of the government that sent them, and some were not even employed by the governments that sent them.[13]

3.08 The UNCITRAL reforms in 2017 departed from this practice: this time, the aim was to have a process led by officials from capital, representing their governments formally, who work inside the government on investment policymaking.[14] This departure from previous practice is likely to impact reform outcomes—concerns with arbitrators were one of the two main categories of work, and it is reasonable to expect government officials to view concerns with arbitrators differently than arbitrators themselves. This move to emphasize participation from government officials was interpreted as an important change; arbitrator Charles Brower used several public speeches in 2017 to criticize the leadership from government officials, the move to Working Group III (which he interpreted as a symbolic break from past practitioner-led work), and to call UNCITRAL 'the biggest enemy'.[15] Yet the new balance between officials and experts held, and the autumn 2017

Global Arbitration Review (11 December 2017) <https://globalarbitrationreview.com/article/1151617/uncitral-celebrates-50th-after-tense-talks-on-isds-reform> accessed 10 March 2018.

[11] UNCITRAL, 'Report of Working Group III (Investor-State Dispute Settlement Reform) on the Work of its Thirty-fourth Session, Vienna, 27 November-1 December 2017' (n 2) 2.

[12] When assessing government participation, it is important to ascertain if the officials are generalists from the closest embassy or specialists from the national capital.

[13] Taylor St John, *The Rise of Investor-State Arbitration: Politics, Law, and Unintended Consequences* (OUP 2018) 137–38.

[14] Anthea Roberts, 'UNCITRAL and ISDS Reform: Not Business as Usual' *EJILTalk!* (11 December 2017).

[15] 'Keynote Speech by the Hon. Charles N. Brower: Canada's Embrace of the EU-Inspired "Investment Court System": Foresight or Folly?' Canadian Council on International Law, Forty-sixth Annual Conference (2–3 November 2017) <http://docs.wixstatic.com/ugd/1092ea_21cecc2ffcc649b3a54fdd34bd4f910f.pdf> accessed 1 January 2018; 'Hon. Charles N. Brower Delivers Keynote Address at International Arbitration Conference' Fordham Conference on International Arbitration and Mediation (17 November 2017) <https://news.law.fordham.edu/blog/2017/11/27/hon-charles-n-brower-delivers-keynote-address-international-arbitration-conference/> accessed 1 January 2018; 'Keynote Speech by the Honorable Charles N. Brower: Why the EU Investment Court is Destined to Fail Foreign Investors and Host States Alike?' EFILA Annual Conference

meeting was 'conspicuously' government-led, as Investment Arbitration Reporter noted.[16]

3.09 The second way in which the setup for UNCITRAL's autumn 2017 meeting differed from most previous discussions of ISDS was its formally inclusive, multilateral structure. Each UNCITRAL Working Group has a rotating membership of sixty states, drawn from the entire membership of the General Assembly, while other states may participate as observers. This is a profoundly different context than bilateral or plurilateral treaty negotiations, leading some to view this UNCITRAL process as the first step in a return to foreign investment rulemaking at the multilateral level.[17] This may be optimistic, but underlines that more state parties are invited to participate in the UNCITRAL process than recent multilateral negotiations with ISDS, and this matters. The Trans-Pacific Partnership negotiations included more states than most recent negotiations, yet at their most inclusive, they were a discussion among twelve governments, and low-income neighbours such as Cambodia, Indonesia, or Laos were not in the room. At UNCITRAL, low-income governments are invited, and in theory, open deliberations and multilateral procedures can bring innumerable benefits for low-income and low-capacity states. Yet the extent to which low-income countries will be able to participate in this UNCITRAL process remains questionable: in the autumn 2017 meeting, eleven out of sixty member states did not attend, likely because of resource or capacity constraints.[18] Even for states that were able to send someone, these individuals may not have had the time, resources, and qualifications to come prepared to speak. This UNCITRAL process will likely have many more meetings in the future, and many governments may have to send someone from the nearest embassy, who likely covers many issues and has little familiarity with ISDS; reforming ISDS may not be a sufficiently high priority to justify the costs of sending a well-qualified official from the capital for several weeks every year. Resource and capacity constraints are an enduring challenge, which prevent robust participation from some countries, even in systems with a formally multilateral structure, such as the World Trade

---

(5 February 2018) <http://efila.org/wp-content/uploads/2017/11/EFILA-Annual-Conference-booklet-2018_24012018_DEFb.pdf> accessed 10 February 2018

[16] Luke Eric Peterson, 'UNCITRAL Meetings on ISDS Reform Get Off to Bumpy Start, as Delegations Can't Come to Consensus on Who Should Chair Sensitive Process—Entailing a Rare Vote' *Investment Arbitration Reporter* (9 December 2017).

[17] Maria Gwynn, 'UNCITRAL and the Possibility of Returning to the Multilateral Regulation of Foreign Investments' in 'Modernizing International Trade Law to Support Innovation and Sustainable Development, Proceedings of the Congress of the United Nations Commission on International Trade Law, Vienna, 4–6 July 2017'.

[18] Burundi, Kenya, Lebanon, Lesotho, Liberia, Libya, Mauritania, Namibia, Sierra Leone, Sri Lanka, and Zambia were members of Working Group III but did not participate. UNCITRAL, 'Report of Working Group III (Investor-State Dispute Settlement Reform) on the Work of its Thirty-fourth Session, Vienna, 27 November–1 December 2017' (n 2) 3. Jansen Calamita brought this point to my attention.

Organization (WTO).¹⁹ In summary, UNCITRAL's inclusive structure is meaningful: it creates a possibility that the concerns from a variety of states will be raised and enhances the likelihood of multilateral, opt-in solutions which will be easier for low-capacity countries to implement than renegotiating or terminating dozens of bilateral treaties. In addition, a proposal for an advisory centre in investment law, to operate like the Advisory Centre on WTO Law, for instance, may gain ground as deliberations increasingly coalesce around central institutional hubs. Multilateral deliberations are a start, but capacity challenges remain an important topic for future institutional developments in investment law.

3.10 The third way in which the setup for UNCITRAL's autumn 2017 meeting differed from recent plurilateral or bilateral negotiations was its transparency. Documents prepared by the Secretariat as well as comments submitted by states were translated and made publicly accessible.²⁰ Not all documents or submissions by states were made public, however, and a key aspect of the agenda-setting process remains murky: one outside organization was commissioned to write agenda-setting papers (which then became part of the official UNCITRAL record and available on the UNCITRAL website), while it is not clear how other stakeholders could submit papers or proposals. The transparency of the UNCITRAL process is selective: with regard to agenda-setting or observer status, there is room for improvement, but with regard to disclosing deliberations, the transparency is commendable. In addition to a written summary, sound recordings of the plenary sessions were made available in the six languages of the United Nations.²¹ The speed and thoroughness of this disclosure is remarkable when compared with recent plurilateral negotiations, where substantive disclosures often took the form of unauthorized leaks or texts were posted only after the negotiations were completed or stalled.²²

3.11 From the beginning, it was clear that the UNCITRAL meeting was 'not business as usual'.²³ The multilateral, deliberative structure and call for officials to represent their governments set the stage for substantive, informed disagreements to be put out in the open; in other words, for real discussion and possible rancour. While

---

¹⁹ Marc Busch, Eric Reinhardt, and Gregory Shaffer 'Does Legal Capacity Matter? A Survey of WTO Members' (2009) 8 World Trade Review 559.
²⁰ UNCITRAL, 'Investor-State Dispute Settlement Framework: Compilation of Comments, Note by the Secretariat' (n 7); UNCITRAL, 'Investor-State Dispute Settlement Framework: Compilation of Comments' (n 7).
²¹ UNCITRAL, 'Digital Recordings, Working Group III (Investor-State Dispute Settlement Reform), 34th Session' <http://www.uncitral.org/uncitral/audio/meetings.jsp> accessed 1 January 2018
²² Panagiotis Delimatsis, 'TTIP, CETA, and TiSA Behind Closed Doors: Transparency in EU Trade Policy' in Stefan Griller, Walter Obwexer, and Erich Vranes (eds), *Mega-Regional Trade Agreements: CETA, TTIP, and TiSA: New Orientations for EU External Economic Relations* (OUP 2017) 216–45.
²³ Anthea Roberts, 'UNCITRAL and ISDS Reform: Not Business as Usual' (n 14).

the chairs of UNCITRAL meetings are usually elected by consensus, this time a secret ballot was required after a day and a half of deadlock over who should chair the Group's work.[24] Two candidates appeared on the ballot, and although neither was formally linked with a particular set of proposals, participants had a clear sense of the competing agendas they represented.[25] One was a Canadian government lawyer who had been closely involved with the Mauritius Convention and was considered a likely proponent of an opt-in multilateral investment court.[26] The other was a Singaporean government lawyer, considered more sceptical about an opt-in multilateral investment court, given Singapore's position in the Mauritius Convention discussions that states were limited in their ability to use a successive treaty to modify ISDS in their existing treaties. The chair election was a proxy battle in the larger struggle to define ISDS reform, and the ballot results, twenty-four to seventeen (in favour of the Canadian official), illustrate that articulating a shared vision for reform or reaching compromise on multilateral reform proposals will not be easy. Anthea Roberts cautions against seeing ISDS reform as a dichotomous choice, emphasizing that the likeliest outcome is a plural one in which a court, arbitration, and possibly other solutions, all exist simultaneously.[27]

3.12 The UNCITRAL process illustrates how institutional developments can build on each other, and how developments that appear inconsequential to some observers can lay the groundwork for larger proposals or can be catalysed by later developments to have more impact on investment law. The ISDS reform discussions build on the 2008–2014 discussions on transparency within a different UNCITRAL Working Group that led to the Mauritius Convention—the multilateral opt-in structure of the Mauritius Convention is viewed as the model for broader reform of investor–state arbitration.[28] The vision of an opt-in multilateral investment court was first discussed outside UNCITRAL: the European Union

---

[24] Peterson, 'UNCITRAL Meetings on ISDS Reform Get Off to Bumpy Start' (n 16).
[25] Roberts vividly observes that 'different solutions lurked in the room like elephants, often seeming to inform the positions taken by various delegations on whether particular issues (such as inconsistency) amounted to problems.' Anthea Roberts, 'UNCITRAL and ISDS Reform: Pluralism and the Plurilateral Investment Court' EJILTalk! (12 December 2017)
[26] Peterson, 'UNCITRAL Meetings on ISDS Reform Get Off to Bumpy Start' (n 16).
[27] Anthea Roberts, 'UNCITRAL and ISDS Reform: Pluralism and the Plurilateral Investment Court' (n 25).
[28] UNCITRAL Secretariat, 'The Mauritius Convention on Transparency—A Model for Further Reforms of Investor-State Dispute Settlement' (2016) E15 Initiative Think Piece <http://e15initiative.org/wp-content/uploads/2015/09/E15-Investment-Policy-UNCITRAL-Secretariat-FINAL.pdf > accessed 1 January 2018; Gabrielle Kaufmann-Kohler and Michele Potestà, 'Can the Mauritius Convention Serve as a Model for the Reform of Investor-State Arbitration in Connection with the Introduction of a Permanent Investment Tribunal or an Appeal Mechanism? Analysis and Road Map' (2016) CIDS Working Paper <http://www.uncitral.org/pdf/english/CIDS_Research_Paper_Mauritius.pdf> accessed 1 January 2018; Gabrielle Kaufmann-Kohler and Michele Potestà, 'The Composition of a Multilateral Investment Court and of an Appeal Mechanism for Investment Awards' (2017) CIDS Supplemental Report <http://www.uncitral.org/pdf/english/workinggroups/wg_3/CIDS_Supplemental_Report.pdf> accessed 1 January 2018.

and Canada co-hosted a meeting in December 2016 attended by dozens of countries to discuss a multilateral investment court.[29] Then the European Union and others formally requested UNCITRAL to take up ISDS reform, which has led many to see the court proposal as the animating force of UNCITRAL's discussions.[30] Yet even if an opt-in multilateral court is developed, this process will occur alongside other reform processes, many of which could be affected by or coordinated through UNCITRAL. For instance, since many governments seem to prepare more carefully for multilateral settings where they also learn from the experiences of other states, multilateral deliberations may make them more likely to address problems that they have not addressed in their bilateral treaties.[31] It is also possible that the UNCITRAL process will generate multiple tools for reforming ISDS and states can select which tools they wish to use when. For instance, other UNCITRAL working groups have generated Model Laws, such as the UNCITRAL Model Law on International Commercial Arbitration, which countries can use as a basis for domestic legislation.[32] Decentralized reform tools like the Model Laws have been effective at generating substantial impact in specific technical areas while creating little political resistance. Even if the process of change is slow and appears unremarkable at any one point in time, it may be transformative over time.

The most notable example of slow but transformative change in investment law is the UNCITRAL-led Mauritius Convention, which came into force on October 2017, six months after the third state ratified it.[33] For ratifying states, the Mauritius Convention updates the procedural rules governing investor–state arbitrations under all of their treaties negotiated before 2014, 3.13

---

[29] European Commission and Government of Canada, 'Discussion Paper: Establishment of a Multilateral Investment Dispute Settlement System' (Expert meeting, 13–14 December 2016) <http://trade.ec.europa.eu/doclib/docs/2017/january/tradoc_155267.12.12%20With%20date_%20Discussion%20paper_Establishment%20of%20a%20multilateral%20investment%20Geneva.pdf> accessed 1 January 2018; Luke Eric Peterson, 'Analysis: EU and Canada Convene Dozens of Countries to Discuss Informally a Multilateral Investment Court, While Institutional "Ownership" of Negotiations Remains Unclear' *Investment Arbitration Reporter* (13 December 2016).

[30] European Commission, 'Investment in TTIP and Beyond—The Path for Reform, Enhancing the Right to Regulate and Moving from Current ad hoc Arbitration Towards an Investment Court' (May 2015) 11 <http://trade.ec.europa.eu/doclib/docs/2015/may/tradoc_153408.PDF> accessed 1 January 2018; European Commission and Government of Canada, 'Discussion Paper: Establishment of a Multilateral Investment Dispute Settlement System' (n 29).

[31] IAReporter gives the interesting illustration of states at the UNCITRAL meeting lamenting that investors don't pay costs orders against them, but virtually no state have inserted clauses that require 'security for costs' orders in their treaties. Luke Eric Peterson, 'Analysis: What Did Governments Agree (and Disagree) on at Recent UNCITRAL Meetings on Investor-State Dispute Settlement Reform?' *Investment Arbitration Reporter* (4 January 2018).

[32] South Africa, for instance, passed a law in 2017 incorporating the UNCITRAL Model Law into domestic legislation. International Arbitration Bill B10-2017 (Republic of South Africa).

[33] UNCITRAL, 'Status: United Nations Convention on Transparency in Treaty-based Investor-State Arbitration (New York, 2014)' <http://www.uncitral.org/uncitral/en/uncitral_texts/arbitration/2014Transparency_Convention_status.html> accessed 1 January 2018.

effectively implementing the UNCITRAL Transparency Rules.[34] Sceptics pointed out that since only Canada, Mauritius, and Switzerland have ratified it, the Mauritius Convention only applies to arbitrations held under one investment treaty (Mauritius–Switzerland).[35] However, it is short-sighted to call the Mauritius Convention a failure: treaty ratifications often take time to accumulate and new norms take time to spread. The ICSID Convention has been open for ratification for over fifty years, and states are still signing it;[36] many institutions, such as ICSID, looked like failures for years before being rediscovered or repurposed. The Mauritius Convention is also a symbol of the growing transparency norm in investment law.[37] Increasing transparency is not always easy: in 2017, a gap between rhetoric and practice emerged as governments who are outspoken advocates of more transparency in investment law refused to release information as respondents.[38] Changing norms is often slow, hard, and starts with selective or strategic modifications in behaviour, however. In the long view, the transparency of investment law increased in 2017, albeit unevenly and slowly.

C. Amending and Appointing: Developments at Arbitral Institutions

3.14 Several arbitral institutions updated their rules of procedure in 2017. On 1 January 2017, new rules came into force at the Stockholm Chamber of Commerce (SCC).[39] The China International Economic and Trade Arbitration Commission (CIETAC) published its first set of arbitration rules tailored to investor–state disputes, which came into force in October 2017.[40] Also in October 2017, the London Court of International Arbitration (LCIA) adopted changes to its Notes

---

[34] Lise Johnson, 'The Mauritius Convention on Transparency: Comments on the Treaty and its Role in Increasing Transparency of Investor-State Arbitration' (2014) Columbia Center on Sustainable Investment Policy Paper <http://ccsi.columbia.edu/files/2013/08/Mauritius-Convention-Transparency-Paper-formatted-FINAL.pdf > accessed 1 January 2018.

[35] Erica Duffy, 'The Mauritius Convention's Entry into Force: High Hopes with Little Impact?' *Groningen Journal of International Law Blog* (18 May 2017).

[36] Mexico, for instance, signed the ICSID Convention in January 2018.

[37] The Mauritius Convention illustrates how UNCITRAL processes can lead to different, but reinforcing instruments. The Transparency Rules came first, helping to establish the transparency norm and effectively operating as guidelines for existing treaties; then the Convention made the Rules binding.

[38] Luke Eric Peterson, 'Germany Faces at Least Two Investment Treaty Disputes apart from Vattenfall Matter' *Investment Arbitration Reporter* (13 December 2017).

[39] Arbitration Institute of the SCC, 'New SCC Rules 1 January 2017' <http://www.sccinstitute.com/about-the-scc/news/2017/new-scc-rules-1-january-2017/> accessed 1 January 2018.

[40] CIETAC, 'CEITAC Released China International Economic and Trade Arbitration Commission Arbitration Rules on International Investment Disputes and Annual Report on International Commercial Arbitration in China' <http://www.cietac.org/index.php?m=Article&a=show&id=14473&l=en> accessed 1 January 2018.

for Arbitrators and opened discussions about revising its rules.[41] The process of amending the ICSID Arbitration Rules continued in 2017, with the ICSID Secretariat inviting public suggestions for amendments in January 2017. In a nod to the growing transparency norm, the ICSID Secretariat made these submissions public. The Secretariat also invited member states to make suggestions, which were not made public. The Secretariat will promulgate new Rules in 2018 and then submit them to the Administrative Council, where two-thirds of ICSID's contracting states must approve them.[42]

3.15 These rule updates do not often feature in reform debates, but they matter. These rules determine the everyday conduct of arbitrations and can have implications for substantive outcomes. They are often one of the first places where controversial or emerging issues are dealt with, and there is a lot of discretion in how arbitration rules deal with new topics. For instance, ICSID can be viewed as static and relatively constrained with regard to reform, since the ICSID Convention requires unanimity for amendment. This view underestimates the room for manoeuvre that exists within the rules, however. In fact, Aron Broches, chief architect of the ICSID Convention, intentionally reserved certain issues to the rules, which he believed would be subject to less scrutiny and would be easier to adapt.[43] Rule updates in 2017 addressed issues including the role of secretaries[44] and third-party funding.[45] Many other issues can be addressed within the framework of Rules of Procedure, or even through a change in practice.[46]

3.16 While arbitral institutions did update their practices and amend their rules in 2017, they did not emerge as key proponents for, or venues of, reform. Framed in the loyalist, reformist, and revolutionary terms set out by Anthea Roberts, arbitral institutions have an interest in undertaking 'loyalist' updates, in considering 'reformist' actions individually, and in remaining distant from 'revolutionary' proposals. The ability of arbitral institutions to lead or coordinate reform appears to be limited by their need to compete for cases.

---

[41] LCIA Implements Changes to Tribunal Secretary Processes, 26 October 2017 <http://www.lcia.org//News/lcia-implements-changes-to-tribunal-secretary-processes.aspx>.
[42] ICSID, 'Amendment of ICSID's Rules and Regulations' <https://icsid.worldbank.org/en/Pages/about/Amendment-of-ICSID-Rules-and-Regulations.aspx> accessed 1 January 2018.
[43] St John (n 13) 143.
[44] The LCIA, for instance, provide a list of tribunal secretary tasks in their Notes for Arbitrators that tribunals 'may wish to propose'—the list is 'a starting point for the discussion between tribunals and parties—parties must expressly consent to the tasks proposed'. LCIA, 'LCIA Implements Changes to Tribunal Secretary Processes, 26 October 2017' <http://www.lcia.org//News/lcia-implements-changes-to-tribunal-secretary-processes.aspx>.
[45] The ICSID Secretariat is canvassing on third-party funding. ICSID, 'The ICSID Rules Amendment Process' 2 https://icsid.worldbank.org/en/Documents/about/ICSID%20Rules%20Amendment%20Process-ENG.pdf accessed 1 January 2018.
[46] ibid 4.

While this may change in the future, in 2017, the structure of arbitration created many instances in which institutions could compete to administer cases or serve as appointing authority. The observation here is not necessarily that institutions took decisions with this competition in mind, rather that it is possible to interpret decisions made by institutions in light of how these decisions affected their likelihood of attracting more business. For instance, the Secretary-General of the Permanent Court of Arbitration (PCA) designated an appointing authority in a case brought against Libya under the Organisation for Islamic Cooperation (OIC) investment agreement.[47] This decision required a novel extension of the PCA's ability to designate. A likely consequence of this decision is to draw more requests to the PCA to designate an appointing authority and administer cases against Libya, many of which had been going to arbitration at the International Chamber of Commerce (ICC) in Paris.[48]

3.17 Arbitral institutions also cooperated on several initiatives in 2017. One notable initiative which many arbitral institutions and other organizations embraced in 2017 was the Equal Representation in Arbitration (ERA) pledge. The visibility of gender representation in arbitration increased in 2017, with many events to publicize the ERA pledge held around the world and continued work from groups such as ArbitralWomen.[49] When the Chairman of the ICSID Administrative Council made designations to the ICSID Panel of Arbitrators, the relevant ICSID Newsletter noted the gender parity of the designations, as well as the representation of various legal systems.[50]

D. Exchanging and Updating: OECD and UNCTAD

3.18 The OECD and UNCTAD, which have long provided valuable fora in which governments and other stakeholders can exchange experiences and gather technical expertise, continued their work on investment law in 2017. The OECD held its twenty-sixth Freedom of Investment Roundtable in March 2017. Fifty-seven governments were invited to participate in the Roundtable, as well as representatives

---

[47] Luke Eric Peterson, 'After Organisation for Islamic Cooperation Fails to Nominate an Arbitrator to Sit in Investor-State Case, PCA Breaks Stalemate by Designating an Appointing Authority' *Investment Arbitration Reporter* (31 March 2017).

[48] Luke Eric Peterson, 'Investigation: As Fight Continues over $1bil Award, Libya Facing at Least a Dozen Investment Treaty Arbitrations—Possibly More—in Aftermath of Arab Spring' *Investment Arbitration Reporter* (31 March 2017).

[49] Equal Representation in Arbitration 'Events' <http://www.arbitrationpledge.com/events> accessed 1 January 2018.

[50] ICSID 'ICSID Newsletter January 2018: Updates to ICSID's Panel of Arbitrators' <https://icsid.worldbank.org/en/Pages/resources/ICSID%20NewsLetter/2018-Issue1/ICSID-Newsletter-2018-Issue.aspx> accessed 1 February 2018.

from ICSID and UNCITRAL.[51] Anthea Roberts, the invited expert, highlighted four areas for governments to consider: rethinking appointment procedures, in particular finding a better way to align adjudicators with the intentions of treaty negotiators; reconsidering state–state dispute settlement; addressing the asymmetry of investment treaties, so that investors have obligations as well as rights; and reforming the remedies available, so that policy change could be a remedy instead of compensation.[52] Governments present at the Roundtable also discussed a paper on adjudicator compensation prepared by the OECD Secretariat.[53] The paper surveyed historical practice in arbitration and practices in national judicial systems, opening up several potential options for reform. Earlier in the year, the OECD Secretariat released other papers on investment treaty topics of interest to member governments.[54] With these papers and this Roundtable, the OECD Secretariat further developed a reputation for identifying emerging issues, providing well-researched analysis, and bringing experts to speak with government officials in 2017. The OECD Roundtables are a unique environment in which member governments can share experiences and learn technical information in a cordial setting.

3.19 UNCTAD held its annual high-level International Investment Agreements conference in October 2017. The conference focused on updating existing investment treaties, a topic of crucial importance for many UNCTAD member states. In advance of the conference, UNCTAD released a list of ten reform options for governments seeking to update their existing treaties: jointly interpreting treaty provisions; amending treaty provisions; replacing outdated treaties; consolidating the IIA network; managing relationships between coexisting treaties; referencing global standards; engaging multilaterally; abandoning unratified old treaties; terminating existing old treaties; and withdrawing from multilateral treaties.[55] In another testament to the growing transparency norm, presentations and other documents were available on the UNCTAD website quickly—underlining the important role that UNCTAD has played and continues to play in disseminating

---

[51] OECD, 'Freedom of Investment Roundtable: Summary of Discussions at FOI Roundtable 26, 8 March 2017' 2 (2017) DAF/INV/WD(2017)7/FINAL.

[52] ibid 3–8.

[53] David Gaukrodger, 'Adjudicator Compensation Systems and Investor-State Dispute Settlement' (2017) OECD Working Papers on International Investment <http://dx.doi.org/10.1787/c2890bd5-en> accessed 1 January 2018.

[54] David Gaukrodger, 'The Balance between Investor Protection and the Right to Regulate in Investment Treaties: A Scoping Paper' (2017) OECD Working Paper on International Investment <http://dx.doi.org/10.1787/82786801-en> accessed 1 January 2018; David Gaukrodger, 'Addressing the Balance of Interests in Investment Treaties' (2017) OECD Working Paper on International Investment <http://dx.doi.org/10.1787/0a62034b-en> accessed 1 January 2018.

[55] UNCTAD, 'Phase 2 of IIA Reform: Modernizing the Existing Stock of Old-Generation Treaties' (2017) IIA Issues Note <http://unctad.org/en/PublicationsLibrary/diaepcb2017d3_en.pdf> accessed 1 January 2018.

information.[56] In 2017, UNCTAD continued to provide global overviews of changes in national investment policies (analysing both national laws and investment treaties), as well as global aggregate statistics on the publicly available ISDS caseload.[57]

3.20 In conclusion, many interesting developments occurred in 2017 across a variety of different institutions. Frank and open multilateral deliberations at UNCITRAL heralded an exciting start to a long-term reform process. Meanwhile, arbitral institutions updated their practices and amended their rules, shaping the current practice of investor–state arbitration while intergovernmental fora such as the OECD and UNCTAD continued to help governments refine their existing investment law commitments and learn about their options for reform.

---

[56] UNCTAD, '2017 Edition of UNCTAD's High-level Annual IIA Conference: Phase 2 of IIA Reform' <http://investmentpolicyhub.unctad.org/Pages/2017-edition-of-unctad-s-high-level-annual-iia-conference-phase-2-of-iia-reform> accessed 1 January 2018.

[57] UNCTAD, 'Investment Policy Monitor' (2017) <http://unctad.org/en/PublicationsLibrary/webdiaepcb2017d9_en.pdf> accessed 1 March 2018; UNCTAD, 'Special Update on Investor-State Dispute Settlement: Facts and Figures' (2017) IIA Issues Note <http://unctad.org/en/PublicationsLibrary/diaepcb2017d7_en.pdf> accessed 1 March 2018.

4

2017 DEVELOPMENTS IN HOME AND HOST STATE POLICY RESPONSES TO FOREIGN DIRECT INVESTMENT

Olabisi D Akinkugbe and Sara L Seck

A. Introduction	4.01	C. Continental, Regional, and National FDI Developments in Africa	4.14
B. Business and Human Rights—Europe and Canada	4.03	D. Conclusions	4.29

A. Introduction

In this chapter, we provide a broad overview of some notable foreign direct investment (FDI) policy developments by both home and host states. The overview is divided into two parts and three geographical regions. The first part draws attention to developments in implementation of business and human rights norms with a focus on select European countries and Canada. The second part highlights some developments that are noteworthy in the African context both at the regional and national levels. **4.01**

The underpinning question that guides the analysis in both parts is to what extent do these legislative reforms, norms, and policy changes encourage or limit responsible FDI, including respect for human rights. Although the overview is primarily concerned with the developments in 2017, we have also noted, where relevant, specific updates to legislative reforms or policy changes that have carried on from 2016 or have been announced in early 2018. **4.02**

B. Business and Human Rights—Europe and Canada

This section considers developments in implementation of business and human rights norms in select countries that either adopted National Action Plans (NAPs) **4.03** on business and human rights in 2017, or were subject to the scrutiny of the United Nations Human Rights Council's Working Group on Business and Human Rights in 2017. The key question here is whether these countries approached implementation of business and human rights norms from the perspective of a host state, or from the perspective of a home state—that is, whether these countries took the position that business and human rights norms were relevant only to business conduct within the state, or only to outbound FDI, or to both. The conclusions will consider the implications of these developments for FDI.

4.04 In 2011, the United Nations Human Rights Council unanimously endorsed the Guiding Principles for Business and Human Rights (UNGPs),[1] and at the same time established a Working Group on Business and Human Rights, tasked with promoting the effective implementation of the UNGPs.[2] Among other initiatives, the Working Group has strongly encouraged all states to adopt NAPs on business and human rights.[3] In 2017, a number of states launched NAPs for the first time, including Ireland,[4] the Czech Republic,[5] Spain,[6] Poland,[7] Belgium,[8] Chile,[9] and France.[10] Over twenty other states are either in the

---

[1] UN OHCHR, 'Guiding Principles on Business and Human Rights: Implementing the "Protect, Respect, and Remedy" Framework' (2011)<http://www.ohchr.org/Documents/Publications/GuidingPrinciplesBusinessHR_EN.pdf> accessed 25 June 2018 (UN OHCHR Guiding Principles on Business and Human Rights).

[2] UN OHCHR, 'Working Group on the Issue of Human Rights and Transnational Corporations and other Business Enterprises' <http://www.ohchr.org/EN/Issues/Business/Pages/WGHRandtransnationalcorporationsandotherbusiness.aspx> accessed 25 June 2018.

[3] UN OHCHR, 'State National Action Plans' <http://www.ohchr.org/EN/Issues/Business/Pages/NationalActionPlans.aspx> accessed 25 June 2018. Note that the European Union has also been actively encouraging member states to adopt NAPs on business and human rights. (See further below the discussion on the Poland NAP, Government of Poland, 'Polish National Action Plan for the Implementation of the United Nations Guiding Principles on Business and Human Rights 2017–2020' (29 May 2017) <http://www.ohchr.org/Documents/Issues/Business/NationalPlans/PolandNationalPland_BHR.pdf> accessed 25 June 2018 (Polish NAP).)

[4] Government of Ireland, 'National Plan on Business and Human Rights 2017–2020'<https://www.dfa.ie/media/dfa/alldfawebsitemedia/National-Plan-on-Business-and-Human-Rights-2017-2020.pdf> accessed 25 June 2018 (Irish NAP).

[5] Government of Czech Republic, 'National Action Plan for Business and Human Rights 2017–2020'<http://www.ohchr.org/Documents/Issues/Business/NationalPlans/NationalActionPlanCzechRepublic.pdf> accessed 25 June 2018 (Czech Republic NAP).

[6] Government of Spain, 'Plan de acciónnacional de empresas y derechoshumanos' (2017) <http://www.exteriores.gob.es/Portal/es/PoliticaExteriorCooperacion/DerechosHumanos/Documents/170714%20PAN%20Empresas%20y%20Derechos%20Humanos.pdf> accessed 25 June 2018 (Spanish NAP).

[7] Polish NAP (n 3).

[8] Government of Belgium, 'Plan d'action national Entreprises et Droits de l'Homme' (23 June 2017)<https://www.sdgs.be/sites/default/files/publication/attachments/20170720_plan_bs_hr_fr.pdf> accessed 25 June 2018 (Belgian NAP).

[9] Government of Chile, 'Plan de Acción Nacional de Derechos Humanos y Empresas de Chile' (2017)<https://businesshumanrights.org/sites/default/files/documents/plan_de_accio__n_nacional_de_derechos_humanos_y_empresas.pdf> accessed 25 June 2018 (Chilean NAP).

[10] Government of France, 'National Action Plan for the Implementation of the United Nations Guiding Principles on Business and Human Rights' (2017) <https://www.diplomatie.gouv.fr/

process of developing a NAP, or have committed to doing so, including a wide range of developing countries.[11] For example, in 2017, Kenya published the 'National Baseline Assessment for Business and Human Rights' as a precursor to its NAP.[12] While concerns have been raised about the potential for NAPs to lead to meaningful change, nevertheless, they provide a useful source of information on policy approaches.[13]

4.05 A lot of attention has focused upon the state duty to protect human rights, and how this duty applies to home states of transnational corporations engaged in FDI in developing countries. The 2017 General Comment No 24 regarding 'State obligations under the Covenant on Economic, Social and Cultural Rights in the context of business activities' considers both state obligations to protect, respect, and fulfil rights within host states, and the extraterritorial obligations of states to protect, respect, and fulfil human rights in relation to outbound FDI.[14] For example, the state's 'extraterritorial obligation to respect' is described as including a requirement that in the negotiation of trade and investment or tax or financial treaties, a state party must ensure it does not obstruct another state party's compliance with its own obligations.[15] With regard to the 'extraterritorial obligation to fulfil', General Comment No 24 suggests that states parties have an obligation to 'contribute to creating an international environment that enables the fulfilment of the Covenant rights', and thus necessary legislative and policy steps must be taken to influence and encourage business actors not to undermine state efforts.[16] The 'extraterritorial obligation to protect' receives the most attention, and is described as requiring:

> States parties to take steps to prevent and redress infringements of Covenant rights that occur outside their territories due to the activities of business entities over which they can exercise control, especially in cases where the remedies available to

---

en/french-foreign-policy/human-rights/business-and-human-rights/> accessed 25 June 2018 (French NAP).

[11] Countries listed on the Working Group website include Guatemala, Kenya, Malaysia, Mexico, Thailand, and Uganda. See UN OHCHR, 'State National Action Plans' <http://www.ohchr.org/EN/Issues/Business/Pages/NationalActionPlans.aspx> accessed 25 June 2018.

[12] Government of Kenya, 'Kenya National Baseline Assessment on Business and Human Rights' (2017) <http://nap.knchr.org/Portals/0/Reports/Kenya%20NBA%20Final.pdf> accessed 25 June 2018 (Kenyan NAP).

[13] ICAR, 'Assessments of Existing National Action Plans (NAPS) on Business and Human Rights' (August 2017 Update) <https://www.icar.ngo/s/NAP-Assessment-Aug-2017-FINAL-e2ly.pdf> accessed 25 June 2018; Claire Methven O'Brien, Amol Mehra, Sara Blackwell, and Catherine Bloch Poulsen-Hansen, 'National Action Plans: Current Status and Future Prospects for a New Business and Human Rights Governance Tool' (2016) 1(1) Business and Human Rights Journal 117. doi:10.1017/bhj.2015.14.

[14] CESCR, 'General Comment No 24 on State obligations under the Covenant on Economic, Social and Cultural Rights in the Context of Business Activities' (10 August 2017) E/C.12/GC/24 (General Comment No 24).

[15] ibid para 29.

[16] ibid paras 36–37.

victims before domestic courts of the State where the harm occurs are unavailable or ineffective.[17]

4.06 It is notable that many of the NAPs consider business and human rights issues from the perspective of both the host state as well as in relation to outbound FDI. For example, the Irish NAP refers to workers' rights, equality, and environment in relation to Ireland as a host state, while it considers anti-corruption, supply chain, and procurement through the lens of Ireland as a home state. Other issues are explicitly identified as concerns from both a host and home state perspective, such as anti-trafficking.[18] Similarly, the Polish NAP considers regulation of labour rights, equality, children's rights, freedom of association, and occupational health and safety primarily as from the perspective of a host state, yet also considers the responsibilities of its export credit agency.[19]

4.07 France's NAP is largely focused upon its role as a home state of transnational corporations engaged in FDI globally, and considers a wide range of issues from trade and investment agreements to export credit and development agencies, to judicial and non-judicial remedy mechanisms.[20] There is some attention given to the exclusively national framework within France including constitutional guarantees.[21] Most notably, however, was the promulgation of a Duty of Vigilance Act in March 2017 that requires parent and outsourcing companies employing over 5,000 employees within France, or, over 10,000 employees both within and outside of France, to draft and implement plans to undertake due diligence.[22] The Duty of Vigilance Act is outlined in a short paragraph in France's NAP, where the contents of the due diligence plans are described as requiring:

> reasonable measures to identify risks and prevent serious abuse of human rights, fundamental freedoms, health, personal safety and the environment, arising as a result of the operations of the company, of companies under its direct or indirect control, or of subcontractors and suppliers with which it has well-established commercial relationships.[23]

Commentators have described the French duty of vigilance law as a 'major milestone towards improving respect for human rights and the environment' and are

---

[17] ibid para 30 and see further paras 31–35.
[18] Irish NAP (n 4) 13–15. The focus of the Irish NAP has been upon supporting and generating awareness of these norms. See Shane Darcy, 'Irish Government Misses First Key Target of National Business and Human Rights Plan' *Business and Human Rights in Ireland Blog* (23 February 2018) <https://businesshumanrightsireland.wordpress.com/2018/02/23/irish-government-misses-first-key-target-of-national-business-and-human-rights-plan/> accessed 25 June 2018.
[19] Poland NAP (n 3) 8–15 and 32–33.
[20] France NAP (n 10) 19–22, 27–30, and 49–55.
[21] ibid 22–23.
[22] France NAP (n 10) 24 ; Loi no 2017-399 du 27 Mars 2017 relative au devoir de vigilance des sociétés mères et des entreprises donneuses d'ordre <https://www.legifrance.gouv.fr/eli/loi/2017/3/27/2017-399/jo/texte> accessed 27 June 2018.
[23] France NAP (n 10) 24.

hopeful that this model will be adopted elsewhere.²⁴ Indeed, in 2017, Switzerland was considering proposals to mandate human rights due diligence through an amendment to the Swiss constitution, which would be applicable to Swiss-based companies.²⁵

The Working Group on Business and Human Rights has sought to highlight the impacts of outward FDI as well as impacts within states in its country visit reports.²⁶ For example, in its final report on its 2017 country visit to Canada, the Working Group noted that Canada's efforts in the area of business and human rights at the federal level have focused on Canadian extractive companies operating internationally, integrated within its promotion of corporate social responsibility standards.²⁷ However, during the country visit, the Working Group heard testimony about extractive industry impacts *within* Canada on human rights and the environment, including the rights of Indigenous peoples.²⁸ This report draws specific attention to the criminalization of protest both within and outside of Canada,²⁹ the rights of women, including those impacted by extractive operations and the scarcity of women as members of boards of directors of extractive companies,³⁰ and the concerns of Indigenous peoples within Canada over a lack of respect for their rights to free, prior, and informed consent.³¹ The Working Group

4.08

---

²⁴ Sandra Cossart, Jérôme Chaplier, and Tiphaine Beau de Lomenie, 'The French Law on Duty of Care: A Historic Step Towards Making Globalization Work for All' (2017) 2(2) Business and Human Rights Journal 317.

²⁵ Julianne Hughes-Jennett, Peter Hood, and Marie Davoise, 'Switzerland: The Next Frontier for Mandatory Human Rights Due Diligence?' *Hogan Lovells Blog* (1 December 2017)<https://www.lexology.com/library/detail.aspx?g=079d752d-728e-4e8d-a920-e33910a7f81f> accessed 25 June 2018; Information Platform human rights.ch, 'The Responsible Business Initiative in brief' (Update 13 September 2017)<https://www.humanrights.ch/en/switzerland/foreign-affairs/foreign-trade/kovi/responsible-business-initiative> accessed 25 June 2018. Switzerland had adopted a NAP for business and human rights in 2016, which was heavily criticized by civil society groups. See Information Platform humanrights.ch, 'Critical Feedback on the Swiss National Action Plan on Business and Human Rights' (18 January 2017)<https://www.humanrights.ch/en/switzerland/foreign-affairs/foreign-trade/transnational/critical-feedback-swiss-national-action-plan-business-human-rights> accessed 25 June 2018.

²⁶ UN OHCHR, 'Country Visits of the Working Group on the Issue of Human Rights and Transnational Corporations and Other Business Enterprises' <http://www.ohchr.org/EN/Issues/Business/Pages/WGCountryVisits.aspx> accessed 25 June 2018; UN OHCHR, 'Statement at the End of Visit to Canada by the United Nations Working Group on Business and Human Rights' (1 June 2017)<http://www.ohchr.org/EN/NewsEvents/Pages/DisplayNews.aspx?NewsID=21680&LangID=E> accessed 25 June 2018.

²⁷ Mission to Canada, 'Report of the Working Group on the Issue of Human Rights and Transnational Corporations and Other Business Enterprises' (23 April 2018) A/HRC/38/48/Add.1 paras 19–24 <http://ap.ohchr.org/documents/dpage_e.aspx?si=A/HRC/38/48/Add.1> accessed 25 June 2018 (Report Mission to Canada). For a history of such initiatives, see Sara L Seck, 'Canadian Mining Internationally and the UN Guiding Principles for Business and Human Rights' (2011) 49 Canadian Yearbook of International Law 51.

²⁸ Report Mission to Canada (n 27) paras 17–18. See also paras 49–55.

²⁹ ibid paras 44–48.

³⁰ ibid paras 42–43.

³¹ ibid paras 49–55.

also undertook a country visit to Peru in 2017, and the report on Peru similarly draws attention to the importance of public participation in environmental decision-making in relation to proposed activities by extractive companies, as well as the rights of Indigenous peoples, although the focus was very much on Peru as a host state.[32] Both countries were encouraged to develop NAPs.

4.09 While there is no indication as of yet that Canada will implement a NAP on business and human rights, Global Affairs Canada announced early in 2018 that it will create a Canadian Ombudsperson for Responsible Enterprise (CORE) to strengthen responsible business conduct abroad,[33] a move that was recommended in the Working Group's final report.[34] It remains to be seen whether a similar ombudsperson mechanism may be established to focus on business and human rights problems within Canada, as has been suggested by some.[35] In this light, it is interesting to see an inclusive approach emerging from Canada's National Contact Point (NCP) for the OECD Guidelines for Multinational Enterprises, as will be discussed, even as the structure of the mechanism has been the subject of criticism.[36]

4.10 The theme of meaningful stakeholder engagement by extractive industries, including engagement that is respectful of the rights of Indigenous peoples and the rights of women, was the subject of new OECD guidance, the final version of which was officially published in 2017.[37] This guidance, together with other sector-specific initiatives, was produced by the OECD as part of its work on responsible business conduct under the OECD Guidelines for Multinational Enterprises.[38] Entitled 'OECD Due Diligence Guidance for Meaningful Stakeholder Engagement in the Extractive Sector', this comprehensive guidance is described as 'not legally binding', yet a reflection of the 'common position and

---

[32] UN OHCHR, 'Statement at the End of Visit to Peru by the United Nations Working Group on Business and Human Rights' (19 July 2017) <http://www.ohchr.org/EN/NewsEvents/Pages/DisplayNews.aspx?NewsID=21888&LangID=E> accessed 25 June 2018. Indeed, many Canadian-based mining companies are active foreign investors in Peru.

[33] Global Affairs Canada News Release, 'Government of Canada Brings Leadership to Responsible Business Conduct Abroad' (17 January 2018) <https://www.canada.ca/en/global-affairs/news/2018/01/the_government_ofcanadabringsleadershiptoresponsiblebusinesscond.html> accessed 25 June 2018.

[34] Report Mission to Canada (n 27) paras 64–66.

[35] ibid paras 18 and 72.

[36] ibid paras 67–68 and 79(c).

[37] OECD, 'OECD Due Diligence Guidance for Meaningful Stakeholder Engagement in the Extractive Sector' (2017) <http://dx.doi.org/10.1787/9789264252462-en> accessed 25 June 2018 (OECD Guidance Extractive Sector). This Guidance was adopted by the OECD Council in July 2016, but the final text officially published in February 2017.

[38] See generally OECD, 'Responsible Business Conduct, Sectoral Guidance' <http://mneguidelines.oecd.org/sectors/> accessed 25 June 2018; OECD, 'OECD Guidelines for Multinational Enterprises' (2011) <http://dx.doi.org/10.1787/9789264115415-en> accessed 25 June 2018. The OECD also adopted the 'OECD Due Diligence Guidance for Responsible Supply Chains in the Garment and Footwear Sector' (2017) in 2017.

political commitment of OECD members and non-member adherents'.³⁹ Annex B is dedicated to engaging with Indigenous peoples, while Annex C considers engaging with women.⁴⁰ The Guidance as a whole adopts a human rights approach, distinguishing between rights-holders and stakeholders.⁴¹

4.11 Until recently, almost all of the specific instances brought before Canada's OECD NCP have raised concerns over the operations of Canadian-based companies operating internationally.⁴² However, in a final statement on Seabridge Gold and the Southeast Alaska Conservation Council, in which concerns were raised by an Alaskan community with regard to a mining project within Canadian borders, the NCP explicitly states:

> The Guidelines and this associated due diligence guidance are relevant and applicable to all mining companies and in all countries, not just developing countries. In particular, the NCP wishes to clarify with the Company that the Guidelines apply to Canadian companies regarding their Canadian projects or operations, and not just their activities in foreign countries.⁴³

The NCP specifically suggests that the company in question consider the recent Stakeholder Engagement Guidance for extractive companies.

4.12 This statement suggests, in case there was any doubt, that business and human rights issues are relevant to foreign investors wherever they operate, not just when engaging in FDI in developing countries. This aligns with the business responsibility to respect human rights which is described in the Commentary to Principle 11 of the UNGPs as 'existing independently of States' abilities and/or willingness to fulfil their own human rights obligations'.⁴⁴ Nowhere do the UNGPs suggest that the business responsibility is not equally applicable within states of the global North and South.

4.13 The extent to which any of the business and human rights developments described in this section will encourage or limit FDI will depend on many factors. The hope is that increased attention to business and human rights issues will lead to more human rights-respecting FDI, whether due to the preparation of

---

³⁹ OECD Guidance Extractive Sector (n 37) 4.
⁴⁰ ibid 92 and 100.
⁴¹ Sara Seck, 'Indigenous Rights, Environmental Rights, or Stakeholder Engagement? Comparing IFC and OECD Approaches to Implementation of the Business Responsibility to Respect Human Rights' (2016) 12(1) McGill International Journal of Sustainable Development Law and Policy 53.
⁴² Government of Canada, 'Closed National Contact Point Specific Instances' <http://www.international.gc.ca/trade-agreements-accords-commerciaux/ncp-pcn/closed-fermer.aspx?lang=eng> accessed 25 June 2018.
⁴³ Global Affairs Canada, 'Canada's National Contact Point's Final Statement—Seabridge Gold and Southeast Alaska Conservation Council' (13 November 2017) <http://www.international.gc.ca/trade-agreements-accords-commerciaux/ncp-pcn/final_stat-seabridge-comm_finale.aspx?lang=eng> accessed 25 June 2018, para 33. See further also paras 31–33.
⁴⁴ UN OHCHR Guiding Principles on Business and Human Rights (n 1) Principle 11.

mandatory due diligence plans under the new French law, or through improved mediation and non-judicial remedies available through other mechanisms such as the proposed Canadian ombudsperson mechanism. This would ideally lead to fewer instances in which individuals and communities would need to seek legal accountability from foreign investors who they allege have violated their rights, whether in host state or home state courts.[45] A common lesson from this overview may be that foreign investors should be vigilant and anticipate the need to be respectful of human rights irrespective of where in the world they choose to operate.

C. Continental, Regional, and National FDI Developments in Africa

4.14 In this section, we examine the regulatory, legislative, and policy-oriented FDI developments at the continental, regional, and nation level in Africa.[46] The objective is to provide a broad overview of these developments. At the continental level, we examine updates to the Pan-African Investment Code (PAIC) which represents the region's effort to consolidate investment regulation.[47] The PAIC provides a unique opportunity for African countries to achieve some coherence if measured against the staggered efforts at the regional level by the regional economic communities. Unlike their historical primary concern with regional integration through trade, in recent years, African regional economic organizations have also devoted significant effort to the regulation of investment. Whereas some regional trade agreements incorporate specific provisions on investment, others have taken more bold actions by adopting model investment laws. The Protocol on Finance and Investment in the Southern African Development Community (SADC);[48] the Supplementary Act on the Common Investment Rules in the Economic Community of West African States (ECOWAS);[49] the Investment Agreement for the Common Investment Area in the Common Market for Eastern and Southern

---

[45] For two 2017 decisions that allow lawsuits against foreign investors in Africa (Eritrea and Zambia) to proceed in home state courts (Canada and England), see *Araya v Nevsun Resources Ltd* 2017 BCCA 401 and *Lungowe v Vedanta Resources plc* [2017] EWCA Civ 1528.

[46] Developments regarding the African region are also explored in Chapter 14.

[47] United Nations Economic Commission for Africa, 'Draft Pan-African Investment Code' (March 2016) <https://www.tralac.org/images/docs/11444/draft-pan-african-investment-code-february-2017.pdf> accessed 25 June 2018 (the Code or PAIC).

[48] Southern African Development Community, 'Protocol on Finance and Investment' (18 August 2006) <https://www.sadc.int/files/4213/5332/6872/Protocol_on_Finance__Investment2006.pdf> accessed 25 June 2018 (FIP or Protocol on Finance and Investment).

[49] Economic Community of West African States, 'Supplementary Act Adopting Community Rules on Investment and the Modalities for their Implementation' (19 November 2008) A/SA.3/12/08 <http://investmentpolicyhub.unctad.org/Download/TreatyFile/3266> accessed 25 June 2018 (*ECOWAS Supplementary Act on Investments*).

Africa (COMESA);⁵⁰ and the East African Model Investment Code in the East African Community (EAC)⁵¹ are examples of these recent developments that we examine in this section of the chapter. As discussed in the ensuing sections of this chapter, a common trend in these regional initiatives is that while on the one hand, they aim to promote the rights of investors, on the other hand, they call for the harmonization of national investment regimes of the member states of the respective regional economic communities. At the national level, whereas some African governments have taken regulatory measures aimed at restructuring the existing investment agreements in favour of a more equal set of agreements with the overall objective of increasing revenue generation, others have taken measures aimed at the relaxation of certain legal standards as host states with a view to attracting increased FDI.

4.15 Notwithstanding these regulatory measures, in 2017, African countries experienced a sharp drop in the flow of FDI into the continent.⁵² The reason for the sharp decline though appears to have been more a function of the global challenges in relation to oil pricing than simply legislative or regulatory investment measures.⁵³

1. The Pan-African Investment Code

4.16 In 2008, the African Union initiated the process for the harmonization of the investment regulatory regime in the continent. Described as the Pan-African Investment Code (PAIC), the Code is aimed at providing a pathway and strategy to guide African Union member states in the negotiation and development of a new breed of African-centred international investment agreements.⁵⁴ The PAIC aspires to balance an effective and substantive protection of investors and investments, while preserving the right of the host state to maintain its public interests

---

⁵⁰ Common Market for Eastern and Southern Africa, 'Investment Agreement for the COMESA Common Investment Area' (23 May 2007) <http://investmentpolicyhub.unctad.org/IIA/treaty/3225> accessed 25 June 2018 (COMESA Investment Agreement).

⁵¹ East African Community, 'East African Model Investment Code' (2006) (EAC Model Investment Code).

⁵² UNCTAD, 'World Investment Report 2018—Investment and New Industrial Policies' (2018) <http://unctad.org/en/PublicationsLibrary/wir2018_en.pdf> accessed 25 June 2018, 40 (WIR 2018).

⁵³ According to UNCTAD, 'weak oil prices and harmful ongoing macroeconomic effects from the commodity bust saw flows contract in Egypt, Mozambique, the Congo, Nigeria and Angola . . ., foreign investment to South Africa continued to underperform [while] FDI inflows to diversified exporters, including Ethiopia and Morocco, were more resilient'. WIR 2018, 40.

⁵⁴ PAIC (n 47) art 1 (Objective); for an analysis of the potential of the Code, see Makane Moise Mbengue and Stefanie Schacherer, 'The "Africanization" of International Investment Law: The Pan-African Investment Code and the Reform of the International Investment Regime' (2017) 18 Journal of World Investment & Trade, 414; Mouhamadou Madana Kane, 'The Pan-African Investment Code: a Good First Step, but More is Needed' (15 January 2018) Columbia FDI Perspectives, No 217 <http://ccsi.columbia.edu/files/2016/10/No-217-Kane-FINAL.pdf> accessed 25 June 2018.

in achieving its goals of sustainable development.[55] Billed as a significant contribution to the broader call for reimagining international investment law, the PAIC remains a potentially important example of continental reform in relation to FDI in Africa.[56]

4.17 Flexibility is an important factor embedded in the PAIC. For example, in terms of its relationship with existing investment laws or chapters in regional trade agreements, the PAIC provides African Union member states the choice of going with the provisions of the Code or the intra-African trade agreement concerned.[57] Further, in the event of conflict between the Code and any intra-African bilateral investment treaty (BIT), investment chapter in an intra-African agreement, or regional investment arrangements, member states also have the discretion to elect which agreement takes precedence.[58] To attract investments to their countries as host states, member states are encouraged to introduce measures such as: financial incentives (in particular investment insurance, grants, or loans at concessionary rates); fiscal incentives (including tax holidays, pioneer status and reduced tax rates, subsidized infrastructure or service, market preferences, development-centred incentives); investment guarantees and incentives for technical assistance; and technology transfer.[59] Pursuant to the provisions of Article 6(2), member states 'may harmonize incentives for investments that are of strategic interest to the Member States or as prescribed by the relevant African Union bodies'. The PAIC also contains traditional provisions relating to National Treatment, Most-Favoured-Nation, Expropriation and Compensation, and Dispute Mechanism among others.

4.18 The significant value of the PAIC remains its potential to foster coherence and harmonization of investment regulation in the continent, especially against the complex background of investment chapters contained in several regional economic community treaties. Yet, significant challenges lie ahead for this attempt to shape international investment law from an African perspective. Negotiations towards the adoption of the Code continued in 2017. In the next section, we examine the recent developments with respect to investment regulation at the regional level.

---

[55] Dr Amr Hedar, 'The Legal Nature of the Draft Pan-African Investment Code and its Relationship with International Investment Agreements' (July 2017) South Centre investment Policy Brief No 9, 1–4.

[56] Guillaume Long, Stephen Fietta, Makane Mbengue, and Emilie Gonin, 'Investment Treaties: A Debate over Sovereignty, Trade, Development and Human Rights' (11 October 2017) Chatham House International Law programme Meeting Summary <https://www.chathamhouse.org/sites/files/chathamhouse/publications/research/Meeting%20Summary%20-%20Investment%20Treaties.pdf> accessed 25 June 2018. It is important to note however that the extent to which PAIC reforms the existing rules remain debatable. See, Kane 'The PAIC' (n 54).

[57] PAIC (n 47) art 3(2).

[58] ibid art 3(4).

[59] ibid art 6.

2. Regulatory developments at the regional level

a. *The Amendment of Annex 1 (Co-operation on Investment) of the Southern African Development Community (SADC) Protocol on Finance and Investment*

4.19 One of the key developments relates to the ratification of the Amendment of Annex 1 (Co-operation on Investment) of the Southern African Development Community (SADC) Protocol on Finance and Investment (Annex1).[60] Although the amendment was completed in 2016, it was not signed until 17 May 2017.[61]

4.20 The original Annex 1 mandates all host states in the SADC to facilitate and create favourable conditions to attract investment in their territory through the adoption of suitable administrative measures and expeditious clearance of authorizations.[62] It encourages SADC member states to support the development of local and regional entrepreneurs and enhance regional productive capacity.[63] The Protocol provides for the protection of investment against nationalization or expropriation on a discriminatory basis,[64] and also recognizes that parties may settle investor–state disputes by reference to international arbitration.[65] Criticisms of the Protocol in its original form emerged.[66] These criticisms highlighted that some provisions were unfairly skewed in favour of the protection of investors and failed to balance the regulatory autonomy of the host states, and that the Protocol incorporates investment protection standards that are contrary to the recommendations in the 2012 SADC Model Bilateral Treaty Template.[67]

4.21 The amendment to Annex 1 was undertaken in part in response to the critiques from the regions. First, although the amendment to Annex 1 provides similar investment protection to investors as found in some BITs, it now applies to a

---

[60] Protocol on Finance and Investment (n 48). The Protocol on Finance and Investment was signed by SADC member states in 2006 (except for Seychelles) and entered into force in 2010. It is binding to all SADC member states. Also see Stephan W Schill, 'Editorial: The New (African) Regionalism in International Investment Law' (2017) 18 Journal of World Trade Investment & Law 367.

[61] Talkmore Chidede, 'Amendments of Annex 1 to the SADC Finance and Investment Protocol: Are they in force yet?' (13 July 2017) TRALAC <https://www.tralac.org/discussions/article/11875-amendments-of-annex-1-to-the-sadc-finance-and-investment-protocol-are-they-in-force-yet.html> accessed 25 June 2018 (Amendments of Annex 1 to SADC FIP).

[62] Protocol on Finance and Investment (n 48) art 2 (Promotion and Admission of Investments).

[63] ibid art 3 (Promotion of local and regional entrepreneurs).

[64] ibid art 5 (Investment Protection). However, where expropriation is executed for a public purpose and due process of law, the provision requires the payment of fair and adequate compensation.

[65] ibid art 28 (Settlement of Investment Disputes).

[66] See generally Fola Adeleke, *International Investment Law and Policy in Africa: Exploring a Human Rights Based Approach to Investment Regulation and Dispute Settlement* (Taylor & Francis Ltd—Routledge Research in International Economic Law Series 2017); Sangwani Patrick Ng'ambi, *Resource Nationalism in International Investment Law* (Taylor & Francis Ltd—Routledge Publishing 2015).

[67] SADC, Model Bilateral Investment Treaty Template with Commentary (2012) <http://www.iisd.org/itn/wp-content/uploads/2012/10/SADC-Model-BIT-Template-Final.pdf> accessed 25 June 2018.

narrower scope of investors: a natural or juridical person of a state party making an investment in another state party and in compliance with the laws and regulations of the state party in which the investment is made.[68] Second, the amendment to Annex 1 replaces the requirement for fair and equitable treatment under Article 6 with a national treatment standard.[69] Thirdly, the amendment also removed the reference to the investor–state arbitration as a mechanism for the settlement of disputes. With respect to implementation, it is unclear whether the amendment to Annex 1 has entered into force.[70]

b. Revised COMESA Common Investment Agreement

4.22 In 2007, COMESA adopted a new investment agreement with the primary goal of establishing a COMESA Common Investment Area (CCIA).[71] The overarching aim of the CCIA was to enable the region to attract greater and sustainable levels of investment from within and outside the region by nurturing investor confidence and improving the ease of doing business in the region in such a way that would make it easier for investors to operate in more than one country in the region. Although the agreement was celebrated at the time it was adopted,[72] to date, the agreement has not entered into force.

4.23 In 2017, member states of Common Market for Eastern and Southern Africa[73] (COMESA) initiated the process for the revision of the CCIA.[74] Certain aspects of the original agreement have however raised various problems among the member states, particularly, those relating to the dispute settlement mechanism.[75] While the process for the overall revision of the CCIA did not start in 2017, the

---

[68] Protocol on Finance and Investment (n 48) Annex 1 (Definitions). Whereas in the original Annex 'investor' means 'a person that has been admitted to make or has made an investment', in Amendment Annex, it means 'a natural or a juridical person of a State Party making an investment in another State Party, in accordance with the laws and regulations of the State Party in which the investment is made'.

[69] Indeed, a comparison of the sub-heading of both arts 6 of the original (Investors of the Third State) and amendment (Non-Discrimination) Annexes signal an important shift and clarification in their provisions.

[70] Amendments of Annex 1 to SADC FIP (n 61).

[71] COMESA Investment Agreement (n 50).

[72] The COMESA Investment Agreement contained provisions such as National Treatment, Most Favoured Nation Treatment, Protection, Emergency Safeguard Measures, Dispute Settlement, and General Obligations as well as international investment rules.

[73] Chapter 26 of the COMESA Investment Agreement is dedicated to 'Investment Promotion and Protection'. See COMESA Investment Agreement (n 50) ch 26.

[74] Phillip Kambafwile, 'Revised COMESA Common Investment Agreement tabled before Legal Affairs Committee' (26 September 2017) <http://www.comesa.int/revised-comesa-common-investment-agreement-tabled-before-legal-affairs-committee/> accessed 25 June 2018; Schill (n 60) 367–69.

[75] Peter Muchlinski, 'The COMESA Common Investment Area: Substantive Standards and Procedural Problems in Dispute Settlement' (2010) SOAS School of Law Legal Studies Research Paper Series No 11 <http://eprints.soas.ac.uk/22042/1/Muchlinski_22042.pdf> accessed 25 June 2018, 1–34.

presentation of the revision before the Legal Affairs Committee is an important step in finalizing the process that we hope opens the region to more investment.[76] Although the working draft of the amendment to the CCIA has not been made public, we wonder whether the innovative provisions in the original agreement will be retained, improved, or even completely discarded.

3. Regulatory developments at the national level

4.24 In 2017, many African countries kept up the desire to attract, facilitate, and retain foreign investment. Countries ranging from the Middle East and North Africa (MENA) region to West Africa introduced various statutes and legal instruments that were aimed at relaxing FDI restrictions. For example, at the national level, Nigeria, Egypt,[77] and Tunisia[78] adopted new investment laws in 2017 or completed the processes towards restructuring their international investment regime in cases where it in fact had begun in 2016. In addition, while some countries took measures that were aimed at addressing trade restrictions, others also generally took measures that were aimed at investment facilitation and promotion.[79]

a. Egypt

4.25 The new Egyptian Investment Law No 72 repeals the Investment Guarantees and Incentives Law No 8 of 1997.[80] With the primary goal[81] of setting a benchmark for procedural facilitation of and ease of doing business in Egypt, the new law aims at the promotion of FDIs by offering incentives, reduction of bureaucracy, simplification, and overall enhancement of the procedures.[82] The law complements existing benefits and tax exemptions and privileges.[83] Some of the core FDI

---

[76] Osemo Ndalila, 'Experts Discuss Revised CCIA' (30 August 2016) <http://www.comesa.int/experts-discuss-revised-ccia/> accessed 25 June 2018.

[77] Egypt, 'Investment Law No 72 of 2017' (published 31 May 2017 and entry into force 1 June 2017) (Egypt Investment Law 2017). Also see Arab Republic of Egypt, Ministry of Investment and International Cooperation <<http://www.miic.gov.eg/english/pages/default.aspx> accessed 25 June 2018 with an unofficial translation available in UNCTAD Compendium of Investment Laws <http://investmentpolicyhub.unctad.org/InvestmentLaws/laws/167> accessed 25 June 2018.

[78] Tunisia, 'Investment Law 2016' (30 September 2016) Law n° 71-2016 accessed 25 June 2018—with an unofficial English translation <http://www.investintunisia.tn/Fr/upload/ang-nv_loi_sur_investissement-1476280259.pdf> accessed 25 June 2018 (Tunisia Investment Law 2016).

[79] For example, Mauritius and Algeria introduced new tax incentives that are geared towards enhancing investments in their countries.

[80] Egypt Investment Law 2017 (n 77) art VIII, stating that' The Law of Investment Guarantees and incentives promulgated by Law No 8 of 1997 shall hereby be repealed, and any provision which contradicts the provisions of this Law and the annexed Law shall hereby be repealed.'

[81] Egypt Investment Law 2017 (n 77) ch (2) 'Investment Goals and Principles'.

[82] Arab Republic of Egypt Ministry of Investment and International Cooperation, 'A Practical Guide to Doing Business in Egypt' (16 May 2017) <http://www.miic.gov.eg/English/Resources/Publications/NonPeriodical/DOCUMENTS/INVESTOR'S%20GUIDE%20TO%20EGYPT_16_05_2017.PDF> accessed 25 June 2018.

[83] Eversheds LLP, 'Investing in Renewable Energies: A Guide to Investment Treaty Protections Available to Investors in the Arab Republic of Egypt' <https://www.eversheds-sutherland.com/documents/sectors/energy/Guide-investing-Egypt.pdf> assessed 27 June 2018.

enhancing principles codified in the new law include: fair and equitable treatment to both foreign and Egyptian investors, prevention of monopolistic practices, the guarantee of the right to repatriate profit and/or receive international finance without restrictions, the application of a unified custom duty for items of temporary usage in Egypt as well as the provision of stable and consistent investment policies to boost FDI.[84]

b. Tunisia

4.26 Similarly, in September 2016, the Tunisian Parliament passed a new Investment Law that came into effect on 1 April 2017.[85] Article 1 of the Tunisia Investment Law states the aim of the law: to promote investment and encourage the creation of enterprises and their development in accordance with economic national priorities in particular through but not limited to the achievement of a sustainable development, job creation, and improvement of human resources competences, achievement of an integrated and equal regional development. The Investment Law reorganizes the governance of investments by establishing new institutions and incentive bonuses.[86] Several articles in the law include expansive new provisions on market access, investor guarantees and obligations, investment governance, grants and incentives, and dispute settlement.[87] To encourage effective regulation of FDI, the law provides for the creation of three major institutions for the governance of investment: The High Council for Investment, the Tunisian Investment Authority, and the Tunisian Investment Fund.[88] The new law eases some of the restrictions of the old Labour Code in Tunisia on the hiring or bringing in of foreign workers in Tunisia.[89]

---

[84] See generally Egypt Investment Law 2017 (n 77) ch (2) 'Investment Incentives'. Whereas art 9 provides that all Investment Projects shall enjoy the general incentives in Chapter (2), art 10 provides that the Investment Projects are exempted from the stamp tax, fees for notarization, and registration of the Memoranda of Incorporation of the companies and establishments and the credit facility and pledge contracts associated with their business for five years from the date of registration in the Commercial Register. Similarly, art 6 provides that 'the State shall allow the availability of all cash remittance operations associated with the foreign investment freely and without delay to and from the State, using a free transferable currency. The State shall also permit the conversion of the local currency into a freely usable currency without delay.'

[85] Tunisia Investment Law 2016 (n 78).

[86] ibid arts 11–19.

[87] ibid arts 7–10, and 11–19.

[88] See generally, Tunisia Investment Law 2016 (n 78) ch IV—Investment Governance. The chapter is divided respectively into: The High Council for Investment (arts 11–12), the Tunisian Investment Authority (arts 13–15), and the Tunisian Investment Fund (arts 16–18).

[89] Art 6 of the Tunisia Investment Law 2016 provides that:

Any enterprise is allowed to recruit foreign management up to 30% of the total number of the management staff till the end of the third year following the legal constitution of the enterprise or starting from the date of its entry into effective production according to the enterprise's choice. This limit is obligatory reduced to 10 % starting from the fourth year from that date. In all cases, the enterprise is allowed to recruit up to four foreign management staff.

c. Nigeria

In the West African sub-region, Nigeria also took procedural steps towards improving the ease of doing business in 2017.[90] The Executive Order (EO1) pursuant to which the steps were taken contained far-reaching measures with direct benefits for the ease of investment and doing business in Nigeria.[91] The five focus areas of the EO1 include: transparency, default approvals, single government agency for investors to deal with, port operations, and entry experience of travellers and visitors.[92]

From the foregoing, first, a big challenge that the African countries will have to contend with and resolve quickly is the likely puzzle and potential conflict that may arise from the various agreements at the continental, regional, and national levels. While a significant level of flexibility is embedded in the PAIC, this may also pose a huge challenge for member states if they believe that the aspirations of the PAIC do not mesh with their contemporary economic realities. Second, when juxtaposed against the WIR 2018,[93] it is clear that regulatory measures—either at the continental, regional, and national levels in Africa generally aimed at facilitating the flow of inward FDI and creating some coherence or harmonization of policies—are simply not enough to alter the direction of the investment in the continent. More than these regulatory measures, African countries are players in a global economy where fluctuations impact both the volume and type of investments.

D. Conclusions

Our overview straddles both normative and regulatory FDI-oriented developments from different regions of the world. While significant FDI flows are vertical in nature from developed to developing countries, we observe that developed and developing countries alike are equally confronted with the internal regulatory and

---

Beyond the percentage or the limit mentioned in the previous paragraph, the recruitment of foreign management is subject to Ministry in charge of employment approval in accordance with the Labour Code.

The recruitment of foreign management staff procedures are subject to labour Code provisions, except paragraphs 2, 3, 4, 5 of Article 258-2 of the said Code.

[90] Presidential Enabling Business Environment Council (PEBEC), 'Ease of Doing Business Executive Order (EO1) Executive Order No 001 of 2017' (18 May 2017) <http://pebec.gov.ng/wp-content/uploads/2017/03/Ease-of-doing-business-executive-order-E01.pdf> accessed 25 June 2018 (PEBEC EO1).

[91] ibid.

[92] Presidential Enabling Business Environment Council (PEBEC), '60-Day National Action Plan of the Federal Republic of Nigeria on Ease of Doing Business in Nigeria' (2017) <http://pebec.gov.ng/wp-content/uploads/2017/03/report-card.pdf> accessed 25 June 2018.

[93] WIR 2018 (n 52).

other challenges that derive from FDI. From the analysis in the first section on business and human rights, there appears to be an increasing alignment of normative expectations irrespective of where in the world FDI takes place. The hope is that the FDI that will be encouraged will be more human rights-respecting, whether it flows into or out of developed or developing countries.

4.30 In the context of African states, we highlighted some new and ongoing updates to various regulatory measures at the continental, regional, and national levels. While there appears to be some movement towards relaxing or improving regulatory measures, these actions have not necessarily translated into more FDI. Our view is that the optimism that accompanies the amendment to laws and introduction of regulations at the continental and regional level must be analysed with some nuance in relation to the actual practices of African host states at the national level.[94] Similarly, we note that the continuing difficulty in achieving coherence at the regional and national levels should not be read in isolation, particularly in view of the turbulent historical evolution of regional trade agreements in the continent.

---

[94] David Pilling, 'African Governments Take a Tough Stand against Foreign Investors' *The Financial Times* (7 March 2018) <https://www.ft.com/content/1e83ea0c-212f-11e8-a895-1ba1f72c2c11> accessed 25 June 2018.

5

INVESTMENT FACILITATION AGREEMENT IN THE WTO
Where is it Headed?

Reji K Joseph

A. Introduction	5.01	E. Later Developments	5.10
B. Submissions in the WTO	5.02	F. A New Dynamic in the WTO	5.16
C. Major Elements of an IFA	5.05	G. Limitations of an IFA	5.22
D. Discussion on Investment Facilitation during the Buenos Aires Ministerial Meeting	5.07	H. Concluding Remarks	5.25

A. Introduction

The efforts to establish a multilateral agreement on foreign investment in the World Trade Organization (WTO) have been laid to rest since the collapse of Cancun Ministerial Meeting in 2003. The endeavours resurfaced with a new dynamic in 2017 when fifteen members made submissions to the WTO, calling for discussions on an investment facilitation agreement (IFA) in the WTO.[1] The proposal for an IFA came up as an offshoot of separate initiatives at the G-20 and United National Conference on Trade and Development (UNCTAD). During the Chinese Presidency of G-20, the Hangzhou Summit endorsed the nine guiding principles for global investment policymaking and constituted a Trade and Investment Working Group (TIWG) with a mandate to facilitate cooperation on trade and investment issues of common interest to G-20 members. In the same year, UNCTAD proposed its Global Action Menu for Investment Facilitation to bridge the annual Sustainable Development Goals (SDGs) investment gap of

5.01

---

[1] The fifteen countries are Argentina, Australia, Brazil, Chile, China, Columbia, Hong Kong, Indonesia, Kazakhstan, Mexico, Nigeria, Pakistan, Republic of Korea (South Korea), Russian Federation, and Turkey.

$2.5 trillion facing developing countries.[2] The UNCTAD proposal was built on its 2012 Investment Policy Framework and 2014 SDG Investment Action Plan.[3] The Global Action Menu provides a list of ten actions, which the countries could adopt to facilitate investment. Although the action menu calls for international cooperation on investment promotion for development, UNCTAD did not suggest the establishment of a global regime, whether within the WTO or outside, to oversee its implementation. During the Hamburg Summit of the G-20 in 2017, Germany pushed investment facilitation as one of the key priorities in the area of trade and investment. This proposal could not, however, make headway in the G-20 due to United States, Indian, and South African opposition. Nevertheless, investment received much attention in 2017 when nine members of the G-20 and six other members of the WTO submitted to initiate deliberations at the WTO on an IFA to place it on the agenda of the eleventh Ministerial Meeting, which was held at Buenos Aires, Argentina, in December 2017.

B. Submissions in the WTO

5.02 During March–April 2017, fifteen members of the WTO initiated an informal discussion on an IFA in the WTO. There were five submissions from these countries to the WTO General Council, justifying the need for an IFA and pointing out the key elements of an IFA. Two of the submissions were collective ones: one from 'Friends of Investment Facilitation for Development' (FIFD)[4] and the other from Mexico, Indonesia, South Korea, Turkey, and Australia (MIKTA).[5] The submission by FIFD highlights the 'increasing inter-linkages between trade and investment' and 'their mutually reinforcing role in fostering global development'.[6] It points out that the aim of the submission is to initiate an open-ended and

---

[2] United Nations Conference on Trade and Development (UNCTAD), 'Global Action Menu for Investment Facilitation' (2016) <http://unctad.org/meetings/en/SessionalDocuments/tdb63crp2_en.pdf> accessed 3 July 2018.

[3] UNCTAD, 'Global Action Menu for Investment Facilitation' (May 2017) <http://investmentpolicyhub.unctad.org/Upload/Action%20Menu%2023-05-2017_7pm_print.pdf> accessed 3 July 2018.

[4] Friends of Investment Facilitation for Development, 'Proposal for a WTO Informal Dialogue on Investment Facilitation for Development' WTO JOB/GC/122 (21 April 2017) <https://docs.wto.org/dol2fe/Pages/FE_Search/FE_S_S009-DP.aspx?Language=E&CatalogueIdList=236954,236782,236668,236429,236189,236149,235960,235961,235962,235526&CurrentCatalogueIdIndex=6&FullTextHash=371857150> accessed 3 July 2018.

[5] Delegations of Mexico, Indonesia, South Korea, Turkey, and Australia (MIKTA) to the World Trade Organisation (WTO), 'MIKTA Investment Workshop Reflections' WTO JOB/GC/121 (6 April 2017) <https://docs.wto.org/dol2fe/Pages/FE_Search/FE_S_S009-DP.aspx?language=E&CatalogueIdList=236414,236189,236149,235996,235960,235961,235962,235526,235438&CurrentCatalogueIdIndex=7&FullTextHash=&HasEnglishRecord=True&HasFrenchRecord=True&HasSpanishRecord=True> accessed 3 July 2018.

[6] Friends of Investment Facilitation for Development (n 4) 1.

informal dialogue in the WTO on 'investment facilitation for development'[7] in which all members of the WTO are encouraged to participate. The dialogue is expected to examine possible elements of an IFA in the areas of 'improving regulatory transparency and predictability, streamlining and speeding up of administrative procedures, enhancing international cooperation and addressing the needs of developing members'.[8] The proposal clarifies that an IFA will not address controversial issues such as market access, investment protection, and dispute settlement clauses including, in particular, investor–state dispute settlement (ISDS).

5.03 The submission by MIKTA, like the one by FIFD, suggests that sensitive issues such as ISDS and investment protection be avoided in the IFA. It highlights that existing WTO agreements like the General Agreement on Trade in Services (GATS), the Agreement on Trade-Related Investment Measures (TRIMS), and the Agreement on Subsidies and Countervailing Measures and Agreement on Government Procurement (a plurilateral agreement) already cover investment, albeit in a piecemeal manner. Both the collective proposals, however, do not shed much light into what key features the IFA *will* cover.

5.04 The other three submissions were from Argentina and Brazil jointly,[9] as well as from Russia[10] and China[11] each individually. These three submissions, and those by Russia and Argentina–Brazil in particular, provide more details of key elements of the proposed IFA. The Argentina–Brazil submission, which provides an interpretation of investment facilitation, states that 'investment facilitation encompasses the set of policy measures and activities aimed at making it easier for investors to establish, maintain and expand their investment in host countries as well as to conduct their day to day business'.[12] The submission by Russia clarifies that the objective of an IFA is 'the creation of a transparent, stable and predictable regulatory and administrative framework for investors, without questioning the rights of the Members to regulate and without interfering with their policies of

---

[7] ibid.

[8] ibid.

[9] Delegations of Argentina and Brazil to the WTO, 'Communication from Argentina and Brazil on Possible Elements of a WTO Instrument on Investment Facilitation' WTO JOB/GC/124 (24 April 2017) <https://docs.wto.org/dol2fe/Pages/FE_Search/FE_S_S009-DP.aspx?Language=E&CatalogueIdList=236954,236782,236668,236429,236189,236149,235960,235961,235962,235526&CurrentCatalogueIdIndex=8&FullTextHash=371857150> accessed 3 July 2018.

[10] Delegation of the Russian Federation to the WTO, 'Communication from the Russian Federation to the Investment Policy Discussion Group' WTO JOB/GC/120 (30 March 2017) 3 July 2018 <https://docs.wto.org/dol2fe/Pages/SS/directdoc.aspx?filename=q:/Jobs/GC/120.pdf> accessed 3 July 2018.

[11] Delegation of China to the WTO, 'Communication from China on Possible Elements of Investment Facilitation' WTO JOB/GC/123 (21 April 2017) <https://docs.wto.org/dol2fe/Pages/FE_Search/FE_S_S009-DP.aspx?Language=E&CatalogueIdList=236954,236782,236668,236429,236189,236149,235960,235961,235962,235526&CurrentCatalogueIdIndex=7&FullTextHash=371857150> accessed 3 July 2018.

[12] Delegations of Argentina and Brazil to the WTO (n 9) 1.

protection of investments, including issues of nationalization, expropriation and compensation for losses'.[13]

C. Major Elements of an IFA

5.05 The main elements of an IFA emerging from the three individual submissions are the following:

1. Scope of the IFA: It covers investment in the production of goods and supply of services.
2. Transparency: In order to have transparent laws and regulations regarding investment matters, WTO members are required to report to WTO all laws relating to investment policy. They are also called on to provide, wherever possible, an opportunity for investors and other stakeholders to comment on measures related to investment.
3. Processing of applications: In order to establish a stable, predictable, and efficient framework for investors, a common set of principles for processing and screening of investment proposals would be established.
4. Single electronic window: Access to competent authorities by investors in the host countries would be through a Single Electronic Window (SEW) system.
5. National focal points: National focal points or ombudspersons would be established. They would provide information and clarify doubts on investment policies and other related issues; seek to address complaints of investors; and assist investors in resolving specific government-related difficulties to the extent possible and without prejudice to the competence of concerned national agencies. Cooperation between national focal points of different countries would help in preventing disputes between members.
6. Fees and charges: Fees and other expenses that investors incur while processing their applications are to be made publicly available and be commensurate with the actual cost of services extended by the concerned authorities.
7. Investors' principles and standards: Members are encouraged to advocate for the adoption by investors of principles and standards for responsible business conduct. Adoption of such principles and standards, however, shall be voluntary for investors.
8. Special and differential treatment: Developing countries and least developed countries (LDCs) would be permitted special provisions given their special economic and development needs. LDCs would be encouraged, but not required, to implement any obligations arising out of an IFA.

---

[13] Delegation of the Russian Federation to the WTO (n 10) 1.

9. Technical assistance: Technical assistance would be provided to developing countries and LDCs to strengthen their institutional and regulatory capacities to facilitate investment.
10. Regulatory space: Rules for the facilitation of investment would ensure the right of the members to regulate.

However, the submissions do not have a common position in the area of investment protection. While FIFD, MIKTA, and Argentina–Brazil have adopted the view that sensitive issues like investment protection would not be addressed in the IFA, China's submission contains a provision for the protection of outward investment to developing countries and LDCs. As an option for responding to the needs of developing countries and LDCs, China proposes 'appropriate policy support for outward investment, including investment insurance and guarantees, political risk coverage and investment promotion services'.[14]

D. Discussion on Investment Facilitation during the Buenos Aires Ministerial Meeting

A number of WTO members extended support to the proposal for an IFA in the WTO. A High-Level Trade and Investment Facilitation Forum for Development was organized by the government of Nigeria and Commission of the Economic Community for West African States (ECOWAS) in partnership with FIFD in Abuja, Nigeria on 2–3 November 2017. This forum came out with a statement (Abuja Statement), later circulated during the eleventh Ministerial Meeting of the WTO at Buenos Aires.[15] One of the main objectives of the forum was to examine how the WTO could contribute to facilitating investment and trade by 'developing multilateral approaches to improving transparency, cutting red tape, streamlining procedures, and strengthening international co-operation, with the aim of expanding sustainable and pro-development investment'.[16] The Abuja Statement states that 'trade and investment are inseparable and remain inseparable twin engines for economic growth, modernisation and development in Africa as well as in the wider global economy'.[17] During this meeting, a number of African countries expressed their willingness to join FIFD to support an IFA at the WTO.

---

[14] Delegation of China to the WTO (n 11) 2.
[15] Delegation of Nigeria to the WTO, 'Deepening Africa's Integration in the Global Economy through Trade and Investment Facilitation for Development, Abuja Statement' WT/MIN(17)/4—WT/GC/1867 (November 2017) <https://docs.wto.org/dol2fe/Pages/SS/directdoc.aspx?filename=q:/WT/MIN17/4.pdf> accessed 3 July 2018.
[16] ibid 1.
[17] ibid.

5.08 In the WTO, several members including the EU, Norway, Japan, and Switzerland supported the incorporation of investment facilitation into the agenda of the eleventh Ministerial Meeting. However, investment facilitation never made it onto the WTO agenda due to objections from the United States, India, Ecuador, Bolivia, and Uganda. The United States had made its stance clear during the Hamburg G-20 Summit that issues on investment should be 'on the agenda of separate bilateral, plurilateral, and multilateral negotiations' and policy actions in certain areas of investment, that is facilitation of investment, should not be prioritized over other areas of investment.[18] India argued that investment facilitation does not come under the mandate of the WTO and that pending issues in the WTO should be resolved before the WTO takes up any new issue. It also held that issues like investment facilitation is best to be dealt with bilaterally and should not be subjected to multilateral disciplines.

5.09 While the Buenos Aires Ministerial Meeting could not hold formal deliberations on an IFA due to this opposition, forty-two members of WTO, including members from advanced countries, developing countries, economies in transition and LDCs, issued a Joint Ministerial Statement on Investment Facilitation for Development calling for initiation of focused discussions to develop a multilateral framework on investment facilitation.[19] The Statement mentions that the elements of the multilateral framework will 'improve the transparency and predictability of investment measures; streamline and speed up administrative procedures; and enhance international cooperation, information sharing, the exchange of best practices, and relations with relevant stakeholders, including dispute prevention'.[20] It states that facilitating a greater role for developing and least developed members in global investment flows would be a core objective of the framework.

E. Later Developments

5.10 As a follow up of the Joint Ministerial Statement, Brazil submitted a draft text of an IFA to the WTO General Council on 1 February 2018 to initiate the structured

---

[18] D Ravi Kanth, 'US Opposed to Investment Facilitation Discussion at G20' (*Third World Network*, 18 April 2017) <https://www.twn.my/title2/finance/2017/fi170401.htm> accessed 18 June 2018.
[19] Delegations of Argentina; Australia; Benin; Brazil; Cambodia; Canada; Chile; China; Colombia; Costa Rica; El Salvador; European Union; Guatemala; Guinea; Honduras; Hong Kong, China; Japan; Kazakhstan; Korea, Republic of; Kuwait, the State of; Kyrgyz Republic; Lao People's Democratic Republic; Liberia; Macao, China; Malaysia; Mexico; Moldova, Republic of; Montenegro; Myanmar; New Zealand; Nicaragua; Nigeria; Pakistan; Panama; Paraguay; Qatar; Russian Federation; Singapore; Switzerland; Tajikistan; Togo; and Uruguay to the WTO, 'Joint Ministerial Statement on Investment Facilitation for Development' (WT/MIN(17)/59, 13 December 2017) <https://worldtradescanner.com/Investment%20Facilitation%20for%20Development.pdf> accessed 3 July 2018.
[20] ibid 1.

discussions.[21] This document puts together the key elements of the IFA, which were scattered across different submissions made earlier by individual members, in the form of a draft treaty. While it reiterates the key features of an IFA, which have been compiled in Section C of this article, it provides details of the electronic governance mechanism of SEW system, special and differential (S&D) treatment, and corporate social responsibility (CSR).

5.11 It clarifies the view expressed in earlier submissions that the IFA would not cover sensitive issues by stating that the IFA would not address the issues of market access, right to establish, and investment protection. It also clarifies that the IFA will not modify members' obligations and commitments under the GATS. Interestingly, the preamble of the draft IFA states: 'wishing to establish a multilateral framework of principles and rules for facilitating "sustainable investment" flows as a means of promoting the economic growth of all trading partners and the development of developing countries'. Sustainable investment is a concept that was not there in the earlier submissions. Sustainable investment refers to investments contributing to sustainable development.[22] Using the terms 'sustainable investment' in the preamble of the draft treaty may be due to the influence of some developing countries, especially African countries, who have been emphasizing the investment–sustainable development linkage.

5.12 The draft text of the treaty mentions that members are free to 'establish criteria for the admission, establishment, acquisition and expansion of investments in services and non-services sectors according to their national policies and to modify such criteria at any time …'.[23] Once the criteria are established, the competent authority shall process the investment applications in an expeditious manner and inform the decision to the applicants. In case of rejection, the competent authority shall inform the applicant the reasons for rejection. Members are required to establish a mechanism, administrative and/or judicial, for appeal and review of the decisions of the competent authority. The website of SEW will provide all the information regarding policy, laws, and regulations relating to the admission, establishment, acquisition, and expansion of investments. Investors will submit all documents through the SEW system.

5.13 LDCs are exempted from implementing provisions of Section III (dealing with SEW), Section IV (procedures for processing applications), and Section V

---

[21] Delegation of Brazil to the WTO, 'Communication from Brazil on Structured Discussion on Investment Facilitation' JOB/GC/169 (1 February 2017) <https://docs.wto.org/dol2fe/Pages/FE_Search/FE_S_S009-DP.aspx?language=E&CatalogueIdList=241891&CurrentCatalogueIdIndex=0&FullTextHash=371857150&HasEnglishRecord=True&HasFrenchRecord=False&HasSpanishRecord=False> accessed 3 July 2018.
[22] See, UNCTAD Secretariat, 'Promoting Foreign Investment in the Sustainable Development Goals' UN Doc TD/B/C.II/35 (25 September 2017) 6 <http://unctad.org/meetings/en/SessionalDocuments/ciid35_EN.pdf> accessed 3 July 2018.
[23] Delegation of Brazil to the WTO (n 21) art 10.

(publishing of laws and regulations affecting investments/investors and providing opportunity to comment on proposed regulations) of the treaty. Developing countries are given four years to implement Sections IV and V, and eight years for the implementation of Section III.

5.14 Investors are obliged to 'strive to achieve the highest possible level of contribution to the sustainable development of the host Member and the local community, through the adoption of a high degree of socially responsible practices, based on the voluntary principles and standards …'.[24] It spells out a detailed list of voluntary principles of CSR which includes respecting the protection of the environment and sustainable development, upholding human rights, stimulating the strengthening of local capacities, and incentivizing formation of human capital, among others.[25]

5.15 The first dialogue based on the draft IFA was held on 13 March 2018, which was reportedly attended by eighty-six delegates.[26] Media reports suggest that some of the countries like India that had opposed the IFA are reviewing their stance in favour of participating in the deliberations on the IFA.[27]

F. A New Dynamic in the WTO

5.16 Until the discussions in the WTO for an IFA, all deliberations in the WTO on investment were led by the advanced countries and often opposed by the other members. But the discussions on an IFA reveal a new dynamic with regard to investment matters in the WTO; developing countries, economies in transition, and LDCs are leading the most recent deliberations. The following discussion attempts to offer an explanation for this new dynamic.

1. Emergence of a new group of capital exporting countries

5.17 Out of the fifteen countries that originally proposed an IFA, six countries—Russia, Brazil, China, Hong Kong, South Korea, and Mexico—constitute a new group of net capital exporting countries from developing countries and economies in transition. Their combined share in the global outward foreign direct investment (OFDI) stock has increased from 2.8 per cent in 1990 to 14.4 per cent in

---

[24] ibid art 18.
[25] ibid.
[26] Axel Berger 'What's Next for the Investment Facilitation Agenda?' Columbia FDI Perspectives, No 224 (23 April 2018) <http://ccsi.columbia.edu/files/2016/10/No-224-Berger-FINAL.pdf> accessed 3 July 2018.
[27] Asit Ranjan Mishra, 'WTO: India May Drop Opposition to Investment Facilitation Treaty' (*Livemint*, 21 February 2018) <https://www.livemint.com/Politics/rlXUVoVh7lRUypYqfHZlxJ/WTO-India-may-drop-opposition-to-investment-facilitation-tr.html> last accessed 18 June 2018.

2016.²⁸ China alone (along with Hong Kong) accounted for about two-thirds (62.3 per cent) of OFDI stock from this group in 2016. For these countries, a multilateral regime to facilitate investment is hoped to smooth their export of capital.

5.18 China initiated the work towards an agreement on investment facilitation by the constitution of the TIWG. Eighty per cent of OFDI from China is destined for developing countries in Africa, Asia, and Latin America.²⁹ Between 2010 and 2015, Chinese foreign direct investment (FDI) stock in LDCs tripled to reach $31 billion, making it the largest investor of FDI in LDCs.³⁰ China is also expected to make huge investments abroad (in about sixty countries) to the tune of $1 trillion in infrastructure on account of its Belt and Road Initiative.³¹

5.19 Investment facilitation, therefore, is in the interest of this group of countries, especially China. It also benefits advanced countries that have OFDI flows to developing countries and LDCs, which likewise explains their support for an IFA.

2. Need for developing countries and LDCs to attract FDI and to integrate with global trade

5.20 Many developing countries and LDCs are looking to integrate with global trade and investment to help address their pressing development challenges, including with respect to job creation and economic growth.³² The view that investment and trade policies are inseparable and that the WTO is the appropriate forum to host an IFA, coming from some developing countries and LDCs, is a new development in the WTO. Developing countries and LDCs had opposed the incorporation of investment as part of the Singapore round of WTO negotiations by arguing that they are yet to grasp the implications of an investment agreement in

---

²⁸ The figures in this paragraph are computed using the data on OFDI stock provided in the annex tables of World Investment Report 2017 of UNCTAD. <http://unctad.org/en/Pages/DIAE/World%20Investment%20Report/Annex-Tables.aspx> accessed 3 July 2018.

²⁹ This figure is computed from the data on 'overseas direct investment by countries or region' supplied by the government of China <http://www.stats.gov.cn/tjsj/ndsj/2016/html/1119EN.jpg> accessed 3 July 2018.

³⁰ Between 2010 and 2015, more than a third of China's investment went to Cambodia, Lao PDR, and Myanmar. UN-OHRLLS, 'State of the Least Developed Countries 2017' (2017) <http://unohrlls.org/custom-content/uploads/2017/09/Flagship_Report_FINAL_V2.pdf> accessed 3 July 2018.

³¹ Jane Perlez and Yufan Huang, 'Behind China's $1Tn Plan to Shake Up the Economic Order' *The New York Times* (13 May 2017) <https://www.nytimes.com/2017/05/13/business/china-railway-one-belt-one-road-1-trillion-plan.html> accessed 3 July 2018.

³² Ambassador Chiedu Osakwe, Director General and Chief Negotiator of the Nigerian Office for Trade Negotiations, argued that integration with trade and investment will facilitate job creation, that trade and investment are interdependent, and that investment facilitation must be pursued alongside trade for success. Conference on Facilitating Investment for Sustainable Development, ICTSD, Geneva, 6 October 2017 <https://www.youtube.com/watch?v=AGk_v8sKn2Q> accessed 3 July 2018.

the WTO.³³ They also held that trade and investment are separate issues, which led to the establishment of a Working Group of Trade and Investment in the WTO in 1996.³⁴ This change in approach of some developing and LDC members on trade-investment relationship and the desirability of investment issues at the WTO indicates that the criticisms mentioned above are waning.³⁵ This perception is likely to alter the WTO dynamic on investment matters.

5.21 All the leading countries in terms of GDP growth in 2017 were developing countries. Some of these countries have driven their growth through huge public investments using borrowed funds. This has raised the public debt in many countries. Ethiopia, for example, registered the highest GDP growth globally for the past few years in part through massive infrastructure investments,³⁶ raising public debt from 40 per cent of GDP in 2014 to 50 per cent of GDP in 2016.³⁷ It is possible that such countries may be looking for FDI as a means to sustain investments by facilitating non-debt-creating investments.

G. Limitations of an IFA

5.22 Although the proposal for the IFA came from an understanding of the positive relationship between FDI and development, the discussions so far have not addressed the policy measures that host countries need to adopt in order to screen, select, and regulate FDI for development outcomes to materialize. The entire focus of the IFA is on investment facilitation. The binding provisions of this treaty are all related to facilitating investment flows.

---

[33] Martin Khor, 'The Singapore Issues in WTO: Evolution and Implications for Developing Countries' (TWN Trade & Development Series 33, *Third World Network*, Penang, 2007) <https://www.twn.my/title2/t&d/tnd33.pdf> accessed 3 July 2018.

[34] A communication from India to WTO on 'Working Group on the Relationship between Trade and Investment' clarifies that it is not only the developing countries but in fact some advanced countries that expressed the view that the available information on the relationship is inadequate and there is a need to study the relationship in greater detail <http://commerce.gov.in/international_nextDetail_WTO.aspx?LinkID=31&id=116> accessed 3 July 2018. Khor (n 33) provides a detailed description of the division among WTO members on the relationship between trade and investment.

[35] According to Nigeria's chief negotiating officer (n 30) which took the initiative in organizing the High-Level Trade and Investment Facilitation Forum for Development in Abuja, the WTO is the most appropriate forum to host an IFA, view expressed during the Conference on Facilitating Investment for Sustainable Development, ICTSD, Geneva, 6 October 2017 <https://www.youtube.com/watch?v=AGk_v8sKn2Q> accessed 3 July 2018. The 'Abuja Statement' affirms that trade and investment are inseparable issues.

[36] World Bank, 'Global Economic Prospects: Broad Based upturn, but for How Long?' (Washington DC, January 2018).

[37] World Economic Forum, 'These are the World's Fastest Growing Economies in 2017' (2017) <https://www.weforum.org/agenda/2017/06/these-are-the-world-s-fastest-growing-economies-in-2017-2/> accessed 3 July 2018.

5.23 Experiences of countries, however, show that benefits from FDI are not automatic. Advanced countries, newly industrialized countries, and emerging economies have used various policy measures to channel FDI into desired development outcomes. The policies of host countries to influence decisions of investors and stimulate local linkages of FDI are critical in using FDI for development. A World Bank study points out:

> Indeed, the extent to which countries regulate investment and devise other policies affecting spillovers can have a direct impact on the economic, environmental and social effects of FDI. Thus, the importance of governments is to obtain the 'right mix' of policies to properly manage different types of FDI. Historically, inadequate design and/or lack of implementation of appropriate policies may, on many occasions, have prevented developing countries not only from attracting, retaining and linking FDI within the domestic economy, but also from maximizing FDI benefits.[38]

5.24 Although the draft treaty provides for technical assistance or capacity building, it is limited to the measures aimed at facilitating investment. No provision has been made to assist those countries that need to develop appropriate policies to channel FDI for their desired development. The Abuja Statement highlights the pro-sustainable development linkage of FDI. However, the discussion on the IFA so far has not paid attention to qualitative aspects of FDI, that is those investments that translate to sustainable development. Sauvant points out that sustainable investment support measures should include, on the one hand, a commitment from host countries to facilitate investment and, on the other hand, a requirement on multinational corporations (MNCs) to adhere to sustainable development measures.[39] Sauvant and Mann elaborate the economic, environmental, and social factors that could be part of sustainable investment measures.[40] Such measures could include elements such as employment, local linkages, community development, biodiversity protection, pollution control, renewable energy, skills development, public health, and fair wages, among others. The draft IFA as available imposes binding obligations on members to adopt measures to facilitate investment but is very lenient on investors in their commitment to sustainable development; nothing is being made binding on them.

---

[38] Roberto Echandi, Jana Krajcovocova, and CZ Qiang, 'The Impact of Investment Policy in a Changing Global Economy: A Review of the Literature' World Bank Group, Policy Research Working Paper 7437 (2015) <http://documents.worldbank.org/curated/en/664491467994693599/pdf/WPS7437.pdf> accessed 3 July 2018.

[39] KP Sauvant, 'The Evolving International Investment Law and Policy Regine: Ways Forward' E15 Task Force on Investment Policy Options paper, E15 Initiative, ICTSD and WEF (2016) <http://e15initiative.org/publications/evolving-international-investment-law-policy-regime-ways-forward/> accessed 3 July 2018.

[40] KP Sauvant and Howard Mann, 'Facilitating Investment for Sustainable Development' (ICTSD Conference on Facilitating Investment for Sustainable Development, Geneva, 6 October 2017) <https://www.youtube.com/watch?v=AGk_v8sKn2Q> accessed 3 July 2018.

H. Concluding Remarks

5.25 The IFA is yet to figure in the agenda of the WTO to initiate formal deliberations. Current trends suggest that it may end up as a plurilateral agreement of the WTO. But one cannot rule out the probability of the IFA transforming into a full-fledged investment agreement to include issues of market access, investment protection, etc. The new dynamics in the WTO have brought about a fundamental change in the position of many members from developing countries on the relationship between trade and investment. This shift in the position may make it easier for advanced countries to push an agreement on investment in the WTO, if they decide to do so.

6

TRENDS AND DEVELOPMENTS IN THE CREDIT AND POLITICAL RISK INSURANCE MARKET IN 2017

Julie A Martin, Stephen J Kay, and Mark van der Does

A. Introduction	6.01	E. Market Trends and Developments: Focus on Public Sector	6.26
B. Industry Statistics	6.04		
C. Size and Growth	6.06		
D. Trends and Developments in the Private Market	6.07	F. Conclusion	6.32

A. Introduction

6.01 While this chapter is about trends in political risk insurance (PRI) in 2017, it behoves us to start with some background to provide context.[1] Providers of political risk insurance include public agencies such as the US government agency Overseas Private Investment Corporation (OPIC) and the Multilateral Investment Guarantee Agency (MIGA), an affiliate of the World Bank. The private PRI market comprises Lloyd's of London insurance syndicates such as Beazley, Talbot, Chaucer, and others, plus large multi-line property and casualty insurers (AIG, Zurich, AXA XL, Chubb, Liberty, etc.) and monoline credit/political risk insurers (eg Euler Hermes, Atradius, and the Foreign Credit Insurance Association).

6.02 Political risk insurance is a 'named peril' policy form, meaning that one of the criteria for any claim made under the insurance policy to be valid is that the

---

[1] We will also be making reference to related forms of insurance covering *credit risks*, the market of which is very closely intertwined with PRI by way of common providers, underwriting teams, and reinsurers, such that the two subjects are virtually inseparable.

proximate cause of loss needs to fall within the scope of the specific coverages granted, which fall into four basic categories:[2]

- Inconvertibility/non-transfer of currency: applies to offshore remittances (dividends, interest, etc.);
- Expropriation: applies to investments and assets;
- Political violence: refers to physical damage to, or loss of assets (and related loss of income and extra expenses incurred) caused by war, civil war, terrorism, etc.;
- Breach of contract: refers to frustration of project agreements by governmental bodies.

PRI can be used to protect, among other transactions, a foreign investor's assets and operations (investment insurance) and cross-border trade contracts (contract frustration insurance) as well as bank loans (structured credit insurance).

6.03 Structured credit insurance, offered by the traditional PRI market, has grown rapidly in the last decade and continues to do so as more banks seek insurance partners to transfer credit risk and obtain regulatory capital relief. Structured credit insurance protects against defaults on principal (and interest) caused by almost any event, whether it be commercial, credit, or political, and is used to insure loans to private borrowers. The PRI market initially started offering cover for trade-related loans about twenty-five years ago but has expanded, with some underwriters now offering to insure project finance and other more exotic structures. Figure 6.1 shows how private market capacity declines the further away the transaction is from traditional trade or investment, as not all markets offer cover for these longer tenor or more exotic structures.

The majority of insurance companies and insurance brokers that operate in the credit and political risk insurance (CPRI) market, as it has become known, underwrite or broker both political risk and structured credit insurance within a single team, while a separate team will manage trade credit insurance.[3] For this reason, as well as the fact that political risk can be used to reference a form of credit coverage involving default by a sovereign or sub-sovereign entity, market participants will sometimes refer to both classes of business as simply 'political risk' when discussing

---

[2] The attached Appendix gives brief definitions of these coverages. Non-payment (sometimes called 'non-honoring of a guarantee' or simply 'non-honoring') by a sovereign or sub-sovereign is also typically classified as 'political risk' although it is a form of credit coverage.

[3] Trade Credit Insurance ("TCI") comprises credit coverage for corporate insureds for their short-term trade receivables (accounts receivable insurance). While there is some overlap with the CPRI market (which offers various forms of medium- and long-term credit coverage to banks), there is enough separation that we will not be referencing the TCI market going forward.

Non-payment insurance capacity
Different types of insurable risk

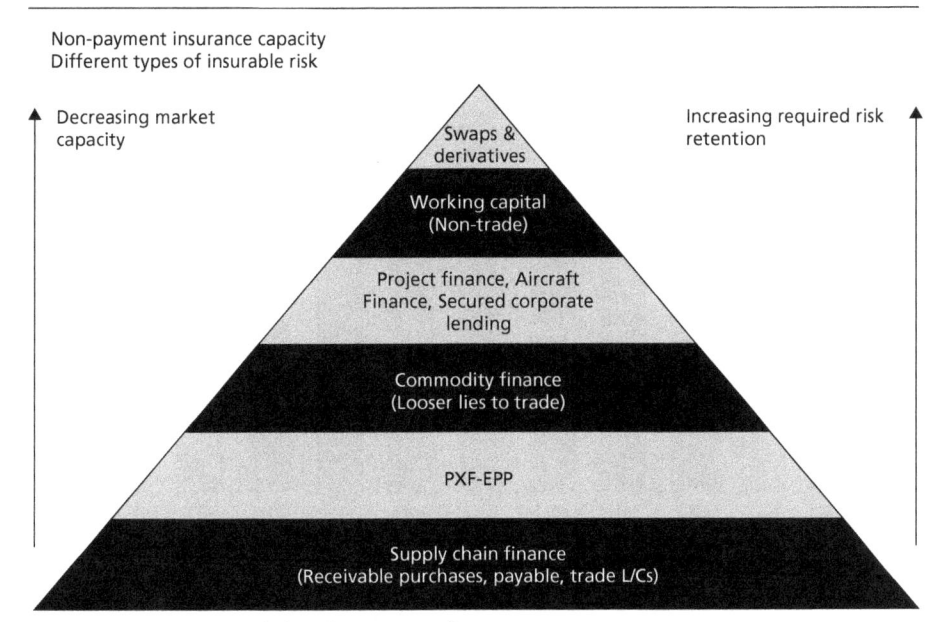

↑ Decreasing market capacity

- Swaps & derivatives
- Working capital (Non-trade)
- Project finance, Aircraft Finance, Secured corporate lending
- Commodity finance (Looser lies to trade)
- PXF-EPP
- Supply chain finance (Receivable purchases, payable, trade L/Cs)

↑ Increasing required risk retention

Figure 6.1 Historical development of non-payment insurance capacity per obligor 2003–2017

Reproduced with permission from Marsh USA.

their risk appetite, product capability, and the types of exposure in their risk portfolios. Furthermore, for many insurers, their book is now dominated by structured credit, which may represent approximately 80 per cent of their overall exposure and is the reason we include information on this portion of the market in this chapter.

B. Industry Statistics

Although the Berne Union[4] produces statistics related to three categories of cover: short-term (ST) credit, medium and long-term (MLT), and credit and

6.04

---

[4] The Berne Union is an international not-for-profit trade association representing the global export credit and investment insurance industry. The eighty-five members from seventy-three countries include government-backed export credit agencies, private credit and political risk insurers, and multilateral institutions from across the globe that provide insurance products, guarantees, and, in some cases, types of direct financing in the support of cross-border trade, therefore providing a vital link in the flow of goods, services, and investment capital world-wide. More information about the Berne Union can be found at www.BerneUnion.org. Not all private sector insurance providers (such as many Lloyd's syndicates) are members of the Berne Union, so their statistics do not capture the full universe of transactions. However, they have the most comprehensive market statistics.

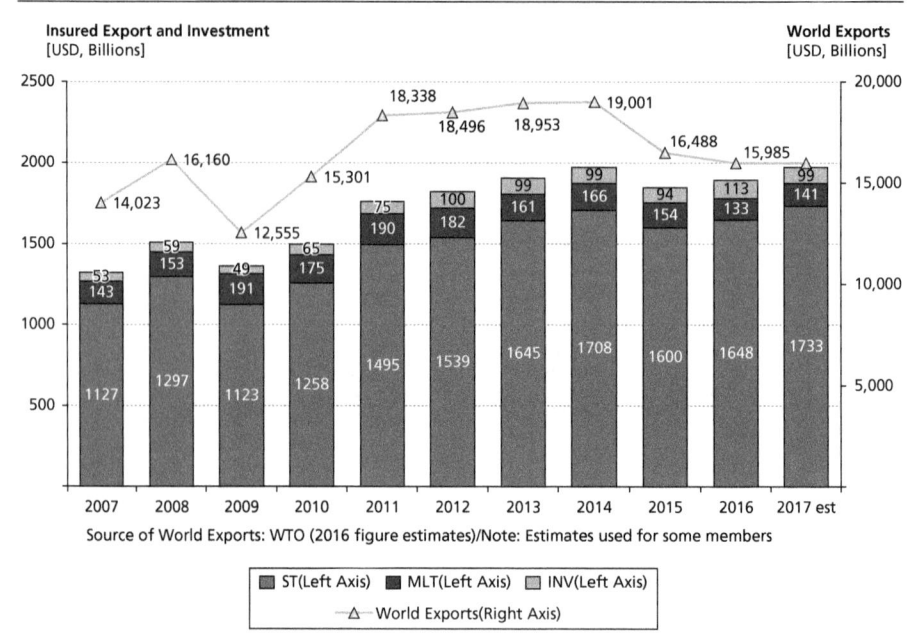

Figure 6.2 Insured exports and investments vs world exports
Adapted with permission from Berne Union.

investment insurance (INV), we will focus on investment insurance which covers political risk perils and to some extent, medium and long-term credit (which might be non-honouring or contract frustration, as mentioned).

6.05 As the Figure 6.2 illustrates, the smallest category is investment insurance and together these three categories of cover represent about 12 per cent of world cross-border trade.

C. Size and Growth

6.06 Numbers vary on the maximum capacity of the CPRI market, and on how many underwriters offer political risk insurance, but in general there are some sixty private market insurers offering political risk cover with a combined, theoretical maximum coverage capacity of around $3 billion per insured transaction. Note that these figures do not factor considerable additional capacity that can be offered by public agencies. The numbers are smaller for structured credit as some markets which offer 'pure' political risk cover do not provide structured credit cover (eg Sovereign, OPIC, MIGA), their maximum limits are also lower, and the maximum term of insurance cover they can offer is shorter. Nevertheless, Figure 6.3 indicates the dramatic growth in structured credit, also

Trends and Developments in the Credit and Political Risk Insurance Market in 2017

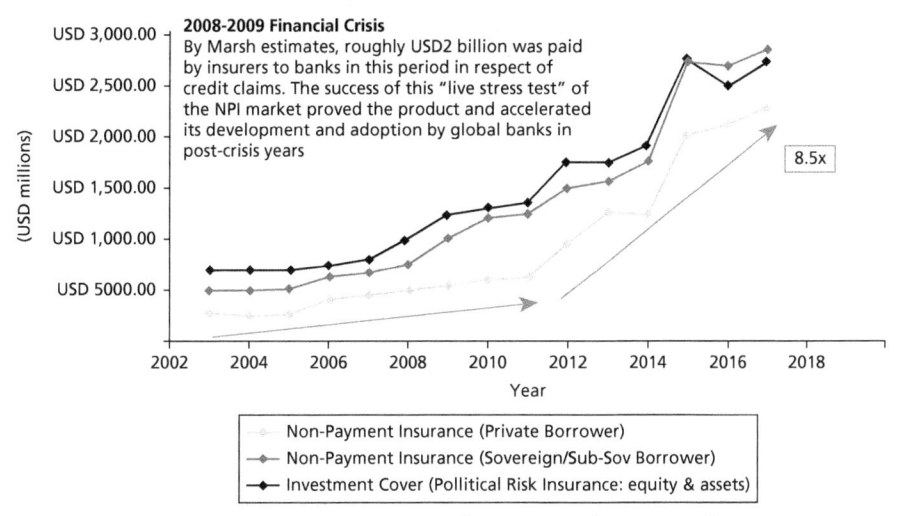

Figure 6.3 Non-payment insurance market—record capacity for any single risk
Reproduced with permission from Marsh USA.

known as non-payment insurance (by a private obligor) over the last period as well as political risk and non-payment (sovereign obligor). Figure 6.3 is based on Marsh's at least annual survey of CPRI market participants.

D. Trends and Developments in the Private Market

1. Private market trends and developments

In recent years the private CPRI market has been characterized by a dramatic increase in available capacity and tenors, as noted, and by increasing flexibility in the types of risk which insurers are able to consider, as described in the commentary on the structured credit market and demonstrated in Figure 6.1. **6.07**

The result has been a diversification of insurer portfolios and the mobilization of capital towards the needs of both commercial banks and multilateral institutions and their clients. This portfolio diversification involves insurers taking on an array of different sovereign and private commercial credit risks, and is best illustrated by the increase in capacity to insure medium and long-term credit risk on loans where the underlying proceeds are not designated for the financing of the sale of goods or services between two parties, sometimes known as 'non-trade'. It is also illustrated by the increase in capacity to insure credit risk on private, non-recourse project financings. These developments are important for private market participants that have mobilized capital to support economic activity in both developed and **6.08** developing markets, but the CPRI market continues to be anchored by its willingness and ability to support trade and investments in emerging and frontier market countries.

6.09 The continued dominance of emerging and frontier market countries is demonstrated in the 2017 claims and exposure figures collected by the Berne Union. The background on these trends in the private CPRI market is also provided in this chapter, followed by commentary on developments in 2017 relating to claims activity and to individual countries where insurers' risk appetites have changed.

2. Private CPRI market trends and developments

a. Non-trade and project finance

6.10 The providing of property and casualty insurance is the primary business of most insurance companies that participate in the private market for credit and political risk insurance. As premium growth in the property and casualty insurance market has flattened in recent years due to a surplus of underwriting capacity, the capital of many insurers has flowed into specialty products, like CPRI (as well as cyber and other specialty areas), where growth in new business and higher returns can still be found.

6.11 Credit and political risk insurers have traditionally focused on providing either named peril cover for the 'pure' political risks mentioned at the beginning of this chapter, or structured credit insurance covering loans used to finance the export and sale of commodities in emerging markets.

6.12 In recent years, two main factors have contributed to the decision being taken by many insurers to diversify their portfolios:

- In the 2017–2018 Marsh Market Survey, underwriters have reported that their traditional benign view of the risk involved in insuring loans that directly finance the export and sale of commodities (where lenders have security over the physical commodities being bought and sold) has been challenged by claims where the underlying commodities pledged to lenders either do not exist due to fraud or do not provide for adequate recoveries. This has led some underwriters to reconsider their traditional emphasis on insuring trade-related transactions and to consider supporting non-trade business where it is the credit quality of the underlying borrower, rather than security in the form of physical commodities, that is treated as a key risk mitigant in a transaction.
- Commercial banks are increasingly able to recognize structured credit insurance policies as providing capital relief under local law applications of the Basel II and III (and potentially under Basel IV) accords which provide guidance on the setting of banks' capital requirements.[5] Banks have increasingly called on

---

[5] Regulation (EU) 575/2013 of 26 June 2013 on prudential requirements for credits institutions and investment firms and amending Regulation (EU) 648/2012 [2013] OJ L176/1.

insurers not only for risk mitigation but as a way to more efficiently mobilize capital towards their key clients and industry verticals, and towards asset-types.

In trying to adapt their coverage offering, many insurers have expanded their risk appetite to insuring senior secured and unsecured loans where the underlying loan proceeds are not designated to finance an underlying trade transaction, but to finance the borrower's working capital. This type of risk is categorized by market participants as 'non-trade' for which a key underwriting criteria is that insurers be able to provide cover at a level where the insured lender commits to retaining approximately 50 per cent or more of their initial participation in the insured loan. The risk-sharing, or 'indemnity level', found in non-trade exists in stark contrast to the traditional trade finance described where insurers commonly agree to cover up to 90 per cent of their insured's credit risk on an underlying loan. These transactions provide insurers with diversity in the kind of credit risk they are taking (borrowers are often required to be investment-grade) and in the geographies where they have exposure (borrowers are usually in OECD countries). The amount of capacity available to cover this type of business increased significantly in 2017, with insurers' theoretical maximum coverage capacity for any one non-trade risk totalling US$1–1.5 billion.

6.13 The same factors which motivated insurers to consider non-trade business have also played an important role in insurers increasingly seeking to support private, non-recourse project financings for which per-risk market capacity now exceeds US$850 million. While infrastructure and energy projects in emerging and frontier market countries had previously been insured in the CPRI market, insurers only provided cover for named political risk perils where lenders and investors benefited from government guarantees. In response to the factors described, as well as the ability of some insurers to assess construction risk and the historically low default rates in project finance, some insurers have adapted to cover the risk of default by a project on its repayment obligations for any reason where lenders do not have recourse to the project's equity investors or to the government. This development has mobilized significant amounts of capital in the insurance industry to support both commercial banks and development finance agencies in the building of public and private infrastructure in both developed and developing countries.[6]

6.14 Non-payment insurance cover for project finance loans has generally been limited to developed countries, but is expanding into emerging markets. Given that the underlying transaction needs to be credit worthy, many emerging market infrastructure projects do not meet that criterion. In such cases lenders and investors

---

[6] Moody's Investors Service, *Default and Recovery Rates for Project Finance Bank Loans, 1983–2015* (2017); Jinjoo Lee, 'Insurers Increase Presence in Project Finance Deals' (*InfraAmericas*, 18 May 2016) <www.inframationnews.com> accessed 1 March 2018.

can rely on political risk cover for arbitration award default when remedies for non-payment are pursued under the key project documents. For example, if an emerging market state-owned utility fails to pay for the power off-take, the sponsors and lenders would generally have the ability to terminate the project and receive a termination payment from the government. If the government fails to pay the termination amount, then the project participants may take the government to arbitration under the project agreements. If they win an award and the government still fails to pay, they may then turn to the insurers for payment under the Breach of Contract (also known as Arbitral Award Default) insurance.

b. Structured credit versus traditional political risk

6.15 Over the last two decades, private CPRI insurers have succeeded beyond expectations by responding to opportunity, growing what is now a very robust market for 'pure' or non-credit political risk insurance (covering overseas contracts, or assets and operations, financed with debt or equity in emerging markets). The private market for this type of coverage has grown at a steady and moderate pace, in many ways matching the cover provided by public agencies in the case of the better risks. Taking advantage of their underwriting speed and flexibility, private insurers might prove a better choice over public agencies to insure, for example, a manufacturing operation in India or a call centre in the Philippines. Conversely, public agencies would remain dominant for more complex projects in higher-risk countries, such as a power project in Sub-Saharan Africa.

6.16 As already described, the same cohort of private CPRI insurers has also branched out into single situation structured credit insurance, which caters mainly to banks and is far surpassing the traditional 'pure' political risk market in scope. Alongside the insurance of sovereign credit default risk, single situation structured credit insurance is providing a major source of new growth. For some private insurers, this has created a dilemma of how to allocate scarce capital and other resources between new structured credit opportunities and traditional pure political risk ones.

Example
Investment insurance policies are often structured on a multi-country basis, covering a dozen or more scheduled countries where the insured has assets and operations, for a locked-in term and pricing for three or five years. Because the ability to offer this product is so common in the CPRI market, insurance pricing, similar to that in standard property insurance, has been soft, with an 'average risk' portfolio of a corporate client's country risk costing a premium equivalent of approximately sixty basis points per annum (calculated against the policy limit). If the insured portfolio includes a large limit in India, the same insurers may prefer to use their limited India capacity to cover a single situation structured credit risk opportunity with an Indian borrower, where they can earn close to double the return of a pure political risk, multi-country investment insurance policy, at 115 basis points per annum.

In this example, the ability to write single situation structured credit risk insurance (which covers borrower default for any reason including country risk) effectively highlights for insurers the opportunity cost of 'locking up' valuable capacity for twelve countries on a traditional investment insurance programme. This compares to the higher risk, but much higher return on capacity employed for just one country, in a single situation structured credit opportunity.

6.17 The dynamic described, which has operated for the last decade, may have restrained the growth of the private market for pure political risk insurance, but may have also kept pricing from dropping, as insurer supply was attracted elsewhere. In 2017, some markets have moved away from offering the traditional multi-country political risk programme in favour of single risk situations. This has especially been the case in countries such as Brazil or Turkey.

c. Claims activity in 2017

6.18 Claims in the PRI market are notable for being diverse in product type and country of origin. However, reported claims that have been paid, for both credit and political risks, have risen in the last eight years following the peak of the global financial crisis in 2010, and the peak of the commodities super-cycle in 2011.[7]

6.19 While insurer risk portfolios are increasingly balanced to include OECD countries, the bulk of their exposure is still in commodity-exporting countries in the emerging markets.[8] Anecdotally, private insurers have reported a lower number of claims in 2017 compared to 2015 and 2016, but with claims activity remaining steady in the market. Some notable claims witnessed by the market in 2017 include Latin America (political risk for infrastructure), Morocco (default by a state-owned enterprise), and Tanzania (Ministry of Finance non-honouring of guarantee).

6.20 In addition, in 2017 the market closely monitored the restructurings of sovereign obligations in Mozambique and Azerbaijan which are believed to have resulted in insurers avoiding sizeable claims. Berne Union data for investment insurers (see Figure 6.4 and Figure 6.5), which includes both public and private markets, outlines where claims have occurred over the last five years and the top ten largest countries for that period.

---

[7] Berne Union, 'The Bulletin on International Trade, Finance and Investment from the Export Credit and Political Risk Insurance Industry' (2017) 23–27 <https://www.berneunion.org/DataReports> accessed 20 June 2018; Lloyd's Paid Political Risk Claims, 1 January 1997–30 June 2016 (on file with authors).

[8] ibid.

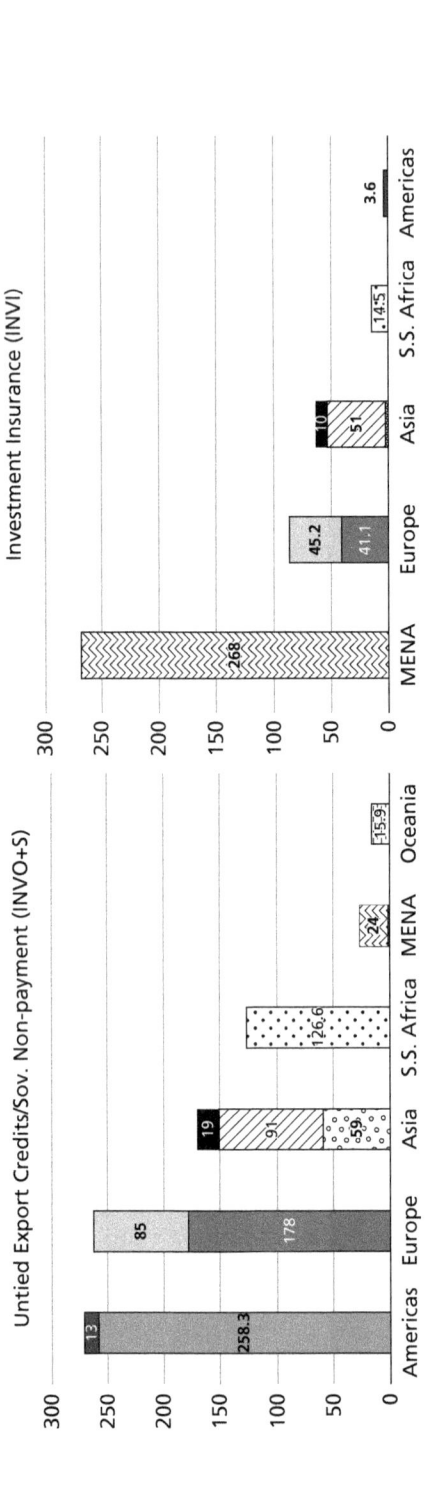

[USD millions]

Untied Export Credits/Sov. Non-payment (INVO+S)

- Americas: 13, 258.3
- Europe: 85, 178
- Asia: 19, 91, 59
- S.S. Africa: 126.6
- MENA: 24
- Oceania: 15.9

Investment Insurance (INVI)

- MENA: 268
- Europe: 45.2, 41.1
- Asia: 10, 51
- S.S. Africa: 14.5
- Americas: 3.6

Legend:
- Rest of Europe
- Russia & CIS
- S. Asia
- ASEAN
- E. Asia
- South and Central America
- N. America
- Other Middle East
- GCC
- N. Africa
- S.S. Africa
- Australia & Oceania

Figure 6.4 INV Claims in the last five years
Adapted with permission from Berne Union.

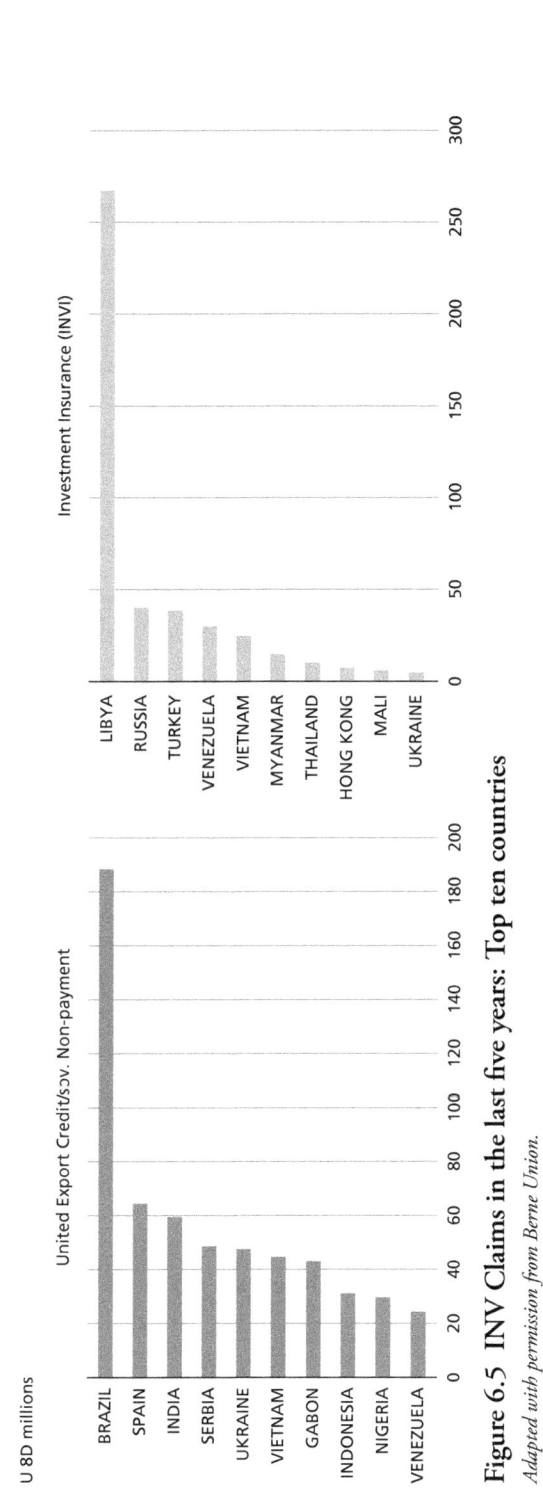

Figure 6.5 INV Claims in the last five years: Top ten countries

Adapted with permission from Berne Union.

For 2016, the latest individual year for which data is available, Berne Union members paid US$300 million in claims with the bulk as 'unspecified' as to peril. The top countries included India, Spain, Brazil, Indonesia, and Ukraine.

d. Country risk appetite in 2017

6.21 An insurer's appetite for taking on exposure in a given country is more tangibly shaped by individual country limits which are set by agreement with the insurer's actuaries, and by agreements with their reinsurers who agree to accept a portion of the insurer's losses. When demand for coverage in a country increases but an insurer has reached its maximum exposure level allowed under its agreed country limit, or where political or economic circumstances in that country have deteriorated, insurers will seek to reduce their exposure. Insurers are consistent in declaring their willingness and ability to underwrite 'good risks in bad countries'. In an effort to not scare off potential business, it is unusual for them to declare that they are closed for business in a country.

6.22 In 2017, one notable shift in insurer appetite was Argentina, where previously insurers had largely declined to write new business. With the election in 2015 of Mauricio Macri and his coalition party's victory in legislative elections held in October 2017, many underwriters have responded by taking on new risk in the country to support lending to and investment in Argentine businesses and infrastructure projects. However, by the time of publication, given Argentina's economic woes, this trend had reversed.

6.23 In 2018, as a result of high levels of existing exposure and/or recent events in these countries, private CPRI insurers have anecdotally reported a reluctance or inability to support new business in Ethiopia, Turkey, Kenya, and Tanzania. Other hot spots remaining include Brazil (where insurer appetite is restrained by the fallout of the massive and still ongoing corruption scandals), Russia (always a strong source of demand but which has been tempered by sanctions), and Turkey (possibly the second most insured country in the private CPRI market, after China). Berne Union data provides a view by region of where new coverage was issued in 2017, as shown in Figure 6.6.

6.24 Top countries for investment insurers for aggregate exposure include China, Russia, Brazil, Vietnam, and Kazakhstan, with the top exposure in China at US$20.7 billion. For new business in 2016, Kazakhstan topped the list at US$10.2 billion.

e. Sectors

6.25 While we don't have data on exposure by sector, the Berne Union surveyed its members as to expected demand as well as those sectors of concern for the medium- and long-term business. No data is publicly available for the Investment Insurance group of underwriters, but we expect that it mirrors Figure 6.7.

Figure 6.6 New commitments in INV 2017

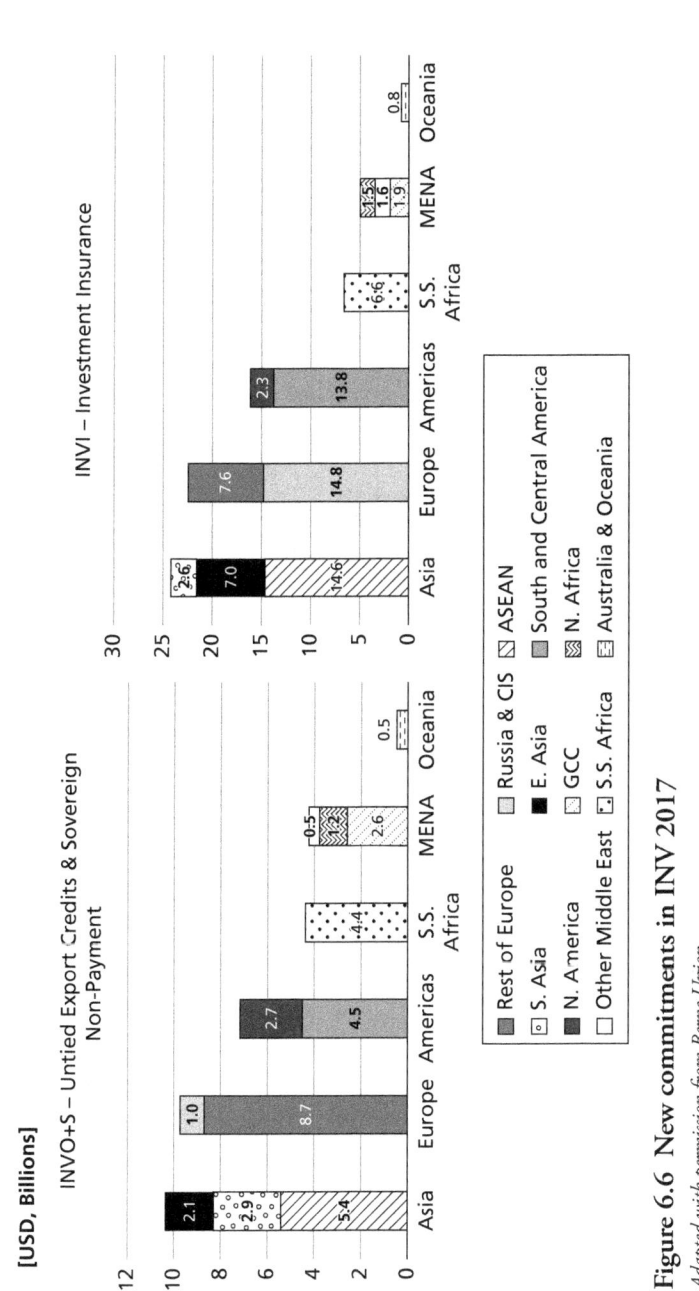

Adapted with permission from Berne Union.

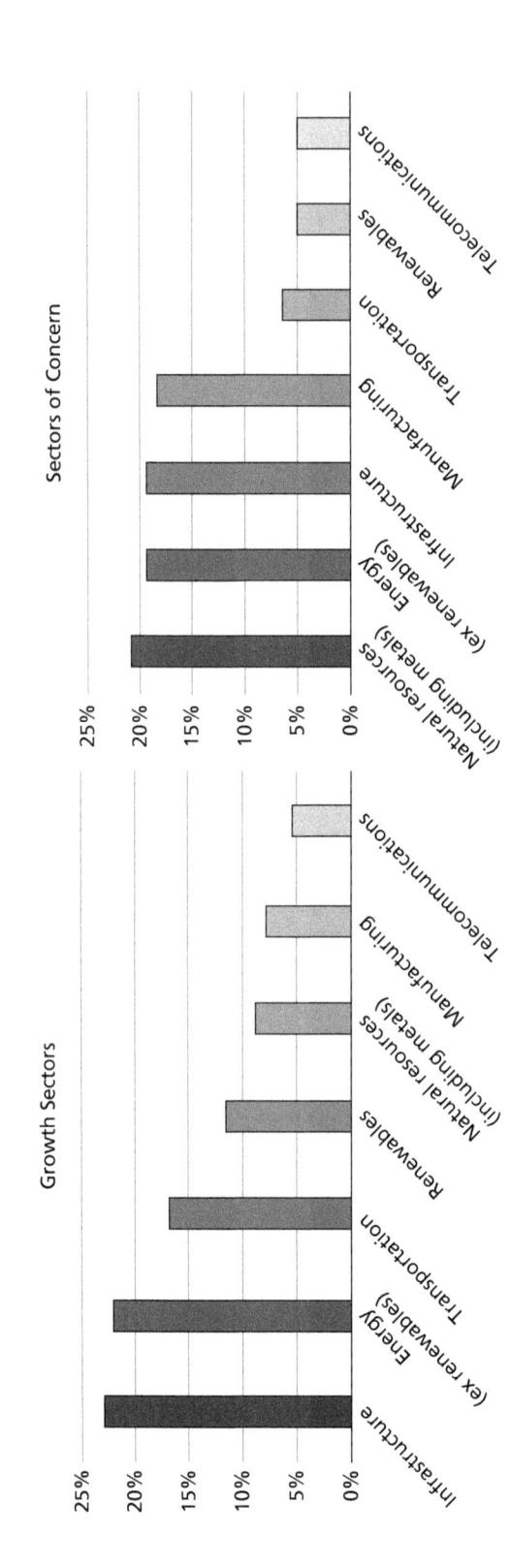

Figure 6.7 Member survey: Outlook for 2018 (MLT)

Adapted with permission from Berne Union.

E. Market Trends and Developments: Focus on Public Sector

1. OPIC

6.26 During 2017, OPIC continued its collaboration with the private sector through reinsurance and, under new leadership, its focus on projects that support US national security and foreign policy priorities. An example of this was December 2017's OPIC board approval of the Eurocape wind power project in the Ukraine. In February 2018, OPIC also issued political risk insurance for a US$250 million US capital markets financing, the proceeds of which are being used by Energoatom, Ukraine's state-energy nuclear energy utility, to construct and bring into operation a spent nuclear fuel storage facility.[9]

6.27 The insurance coverage for this project is a new application of a time-tested insurance product. The innovation is the application to a US capital markets financing, which resulted in a fifteen-notch upgrade to Ukraine's sovereign rating of Caa2 to Aa2. The coverage protects bondholders against default on an arbitral award by the borrower (Energoatom) and the sovereign guarantor, and denial of justice by the sovereign guarantor. This successful placement, twenty-year loan tenor, and investment-grade rating for an issuer from Ukraine, suggests that this form of coverage may be used for other sovereign related projects in emerging markets.

2. MIGA

6.28 MIGA concluded its financial year 2017 (end June 2017) with record-setting insurance issuance of US$4.8 billion in coverage. MIGA is proud of its innovations in coverage in response to its client requests.[10] Such coverage developments were used to support the Elazig Hospital in Turkey and the Tierra Mojada power project in Mexico. In Turkey, a twenty-year MIGA guarantee along with a liquidity facility by the European Bank for Reconstruction and Development, led to a Moody's rating of Baa2 (two notches above the sovereign) for the project bond that was issued to support the project. This was the first time an infrastructure project bond was used to finance a greenfield public-private partnership (PPP) for a hospital in Turkey.

6.29 In Mexico, MIGA issued more than US$900 million in coverage (realized with the help of private market reinsurance) for one of the first projects implemented under the new energy law. The policy contained an innovation in the breach of contract cover for potentially multiple arbitrations. MIGA's mandate is focused

---

[9] Moody's Investors Services, 'Rating Action: Moody's Assigns Aa2 Rating to Energoatom Tranaction Supported by OPIC Political Risk Insurance' (18 January 2018).
[10] MIGA, 'Annual Report' (2017) 13 <http://www.miga.org/sites/default/files/archive/Documents/Annual-Report-2017.pdf> accessed 20 June 2018.

on working in the poorest countries and addressing climate change.[11] MIGA is working ever more closely with the World Bank to maximize finance for development (the 'MFD' initiative) by catalysing private sector participation, so that World Bank infrastructure lending is the financing of last resort.[12] Given this, MIGA expects that about half of its projects will be in Africa, including power, and some of the road projects currently being planned in Kenya. It is also seeing increased demand in Latin America for PPP projects. As noted, Argentina is just returning to the PRI market, and MIGA provided substantial support in FY2017 by issuing US$1.1 billion in cover for expropriation of funds to Banco Santander.[13] The purpose of the cover was to enable Santander to reduce the risk of some of its assets, thereby reducing the group's risk weighted average on a consolidated basis and in turn freeing up capacity to extend more credit in Argentina, including for priority sectors and SME borrowers.

3. African Trade Insurance Agency (ATI)

6.30 In 2017, ATI continued to register record results and focus on creating innovative solutions to Africa's challenges. ATI's financial performance continued a six-year growth trend recording a 56 per cent increase in its bottom line.[14] This growth is buttressed by significant portfolio growth, where ATI issued US$2.4 billion coverage in 2017, and supported by an expanded mandate across Africa, where it can now underwrite deals in non-member countries. ATI's regional expansion remains tied to new member countries (Côte d'Ivoire, Ethiopia, South Sudan, and Zimbabwe), but now also includes, for the first time, deals underwritten in non-member countries, such as Angola, Gabon, and Nigeria. This expansion underpins ATI's strategy to provide more value to its member countries while becoming a linchpin to pivotal deals in the rest of Africa for its partners. An example of this strategic positioning is ATI's cover of a US$159 million loan from African Development Bank to support Ethiopian Airlines' fleet expansion. With regard to innovation, two partnerships that involve the European Investment Bank, KfW and Munich Re, have also helped ATI provide solutions to energy-sector challenges in Africa. The first initiative, the Regional Liquidity Support Facility (RLSF), provides US$72 million to cover the liquidity risks of independent power producers

---

[11] In this regard, MIGA has received some market criticism for insuring the Tierra Mojada project, being that Mexico is a middle income, investment grade-rated country and private insurers, which have long been decidedly open and receptive to insuring Mexican project political and credit risks, are not seen as needing MIGA involvement to 'crowd them in' to participating.

[12] MIGA, 'Annual Report' 1–2.

[13] MIGA, Project Brief, 'Santander Central Bank Mandatory Reserves Coverage' (2017) <https://www.miga.org/pages/projects/project.aspx?pid=3613> accessed 20 June 2018.

[14] ATI is a pan-African multilateral institution based in Nairobi that provides political and credit risk solutions to companies, investors, and lenders doing business in Africa. Its mission is to attract investments and facilitate trade in Africa, but especially in its member countries (currently thirteen). It has an A rating from Standard & Poor's.

specializing in small-scale renewable energy projects, while the second, a US$1.4 billion initiative—the African Energy Guarantee Facility (AEGF)—provides the first dedicated reinsurance for sustainable energy projects across Africa. ATI's support of priority sectors has reinvigorated partnerships with member governments as they strive to meet long-term financing needs for infrastructure development. This reengagement has helped ATI provide more value while also helping its partners source secure transactions in Africa.

4. Other Agencies

6.31 Other multilaterals, such as the Asian Development Bank (ADB), work with the private market to increase line size. Last year ADB utilized $750 million of private market credit reinsurance. While ADB did not issue any political risk coverage in 2017, it expects to do so for several transactions in 2018.

F. Conclusion

6.32 The political risk insurance market has been characterized by more focus on structured credit, increased cooperation between public and private markets, and steady claims activity. As globalization and environmental issues put social and economic stress on both emerging and developed market countries, investors in these countries are dealing with an uncertain risk environment, but they are finding more flexible and client-focused risk-sharing partners in the credit and political risk insurance market. While credit and political risk insurance, whether covering a foreign investment or a loan, is not a solution to the problem of a poorly-structured loan or investment, private and public insurers alike continue to commit more capital to support investors who are seeking long-term partnerships with insurers in the taking and sharing of credit and political risks.

APPENDIX

Political Risk and Credit Insurance Coverages[15]

Coverages For Investments or Physical Assets	Protects Owners of Tangible Assets and Foreign Direct Investments Against:	Compensation Based On:
Expropriation	Acts by the Host Gov't interfering with fundamental ownership rights of the insured's investment including but not limited to confiscation and nationalization.	• Net Investment Value or Net Book Value of the insured investments
Forced Abandonment	Abandonment of a foreign enterprise as a result of advice by the home government to evacuate key operations personnel from the host country or a relevant region because of Political Violence (see below).	• Net Investment Value or Net Book Value of the insured investments
Forced Divestiture	Requirement by Insured's own government to permanently divest of all or part of a shareholding in the foreign enterprise.	• Net Investment Value or Net Book Value of the insured investments
Non -Repossession, Deprivation	Refusal or failure of the Foreign Government to allow the Insured to exercise its right to repossess the Insured Equipment (if held as collateral for a lease or loan), in accordance with the terms and conditions of the Agreement, or to remove the Equipment or Commodity from the Foreign Country.	• Value of the insured goods
Political Violence	Physical damage to investments and assets located overseas caused by political violence (war, civil war, revolution, insurrection, strikes, riots, sabotage and terrorism).	• Lesser of repair or replacement cost of assets • Usually can't exceed the Expropriation limit
Arbitration Award Default	Risk of non-payment of an arbitration award obtained by a foreign investor against a host government or state-owned enterprise, in accordance with the terms & conditions of a project agreement such as a power purchase agreement.	• The lesser of the investment, or the amount of the unpaid award
Business Interruption	Consequential financial losses to a non-financial corporate Insured directly resulting from the Insured's business operations having been interrupted by political violence or expropriation.	• Ongoing operating expenses, extra expense and lost profit during the period of restoration • Usually sub-limited

[15] This appendix is a reproduction of Marsh, 'Menu of Political Risk Coverages' (2011).

Coverages For Investments or Physical Assets	Protects Owners of Tangible Assets and Foreign Direct Investments Against:	Compensation Based On:
Contingent Business Interruption	Consequential financial losses to a non-financial corporate Insured directly resulting from the Insured's business operations having been interrupted due to political violence damage to a third party's assets.	• Ongoing operating expenses, extra expense and lost profit during the period of restoration • Usually sub-limited
Inconvertibility / Non-Transfer	Delay or inability of a foreign enterprise to exchange local currency into hard currency or to repatriate funds to the insured parent corporation.	• Estimated profits or dividends to be remitted, parent company loans to be repaid, etc • Usually sub-limited
Contract Frustration Insurance	Losses resulting from a canceled or frustrated contract as result of political events in the host country, including non-payment due to political action or inaction (not limited to war, civil war, government act, law, order, decree or regulation; cancellation of import or export licenses, expropriation of the foreign buyer [or supplier], and currency inconvertibility/ non-transfer risk).	• Unpaid and contractually due invoices, plus accrued but uninvoiced expenses
Contract Repudiation Insurance / Non-Honoring of a Guarantee - Buyer	Contract losses resulting from cancellation of contract and credit losses following non-payment of sums due by a buyer on a trade contract; non-payment by any guarantor.	• Unpaid and contractually due invoices, plus accrued but uninvoiced expenses
Contract Repudiation Insurance / Non-Honoring of a Guarantee - Seller	Contract losses resulting from actions of a Seller including cancellation of contract and non-performance / non-delivery / non-refundment of Buyer's advances; includes non-payment by a guarantor if applicable.	• Accrued and unrecoverable expenses • Failure to refund advances following non-delivery
Trade Disruption Insurance	Financial consequences / losses for corporations following delays / interruptions in movements of goods [fills a gap in conventional business interruption, which requires political violence or expropriation loss to the Insured's own assets in the Host Country, as TDI has no such requirement].	• Lost profit/extra expense. • (very limited market)
Wrongful Calling of Guarantees	(A) The unfair drawing down by a government buyer of an on-demand, callable standby letter of credit posted by the Insured as a bid, advance payment, warranty or performance guarantee, or (B) a fair drawing (by a government or a private buyer) where the contract terms are unfulfilled due to occurrence of a political risk.	• Amount of L/C drawn and debited from the Insured's account

TRADE CREDIT INSURANCE

Coverage for Sales Receivables	Protects Sellers of Goods or Services and Their Lenders, Against:	Compensation Based on:
Lenders' Form	*Financial Loss resulting from default(s) on short term, open account trade receivables that have been factored or discounted by a Lender. Applies to approved buyers only, on Loss due to protracted default, insolvency or bankruptcy.*	• *The amount of the unpaid accounts receivable.*
Whole Turnover	• *Financial Loss to a corporate seller of goods or services resulting from default(s) on short term, open account trade receivables due to protracted default, insolvency or bankruptcy.* • *Coverage operates on a portfolio "whole-turnover" basis covering all of the Insured company's trade receivables.*	• *The amount of the unpaid accounts receivable.*
Excess of Loss	• *Financial Loss to a corporate seller of goods or services resulting from default(s) on short term, open account trade receivables due to protracted default, insolvency or bankruptcy.* • *Coverage operates on major buyers only where there are large exposures and excessive concentrations of risk, or on losses that lie above a predetermined threshold of loss held by the Insured for its own account - thus covering catastrophic losses only.*	• *The amount of the unpaid accounts receivable.*

B. DEVELOPMENTS IN TREATIES AND TREATY POLICY

7

INTERNATIONAL INVESTMENT AGREEMENTS, 2017

A Review of Trends and New Approaches

Jesse Coleman, Lise J Johnson, Lisa E Sachs, and Nathan Lobel

A. Introduction	7.01	D. Protecting Public Interest Objectives?	7.36
B. Covered Investors and Investments	7.09	E. Conclusion	7.59
C. Substantive Obligations: Focus on Fair and Equitable Treatment	7.20		

A. Introduction

In 2017, at least twenty-two new investment treaties were signed, down from the thirty-five, thirty-four, and thirty-seven treaties concluded in 2014, 2015, and 2016, respectively (see Table 7.1).[1] While the United Nations Conference on Trade and Development (UNCTAD) reports that 2017 saw the lowest number of concluded investment treaties since 1983, four of these treaties were multilateral agreements (although none included investor–state dispute settlement provisions), involving around eighty countries total in all concluded agreements. Thirteen of the new agreements were bilateral investment treaties (BITs) and nine were other agreements, including free trade agreements (FTAs) or multilateral agreements on investment, bringing the total number of treaties concluded and 7.01

---

[1] Investment treaties, or international investment agreements (IIAs), are defined herein as bilateral and multilateral instruments for the protection and/or promotion of foreign investment. A complete list of the IIAs concluded in 2017 is provided in Table 7.1 at the end of this chapter.

in force to 3,322 by the end of 2017.[2] At least sixteen treaties entered into force in 2017.[3]

7.02 A number of notable regional developments in treaty-making are covered in other chapters. In Chapter 16, Catharine Titi provides an overview of Europe's negotiations regarding the creation of an investment court system, which was successfully included in several 2017 agreements (although Belgium has requested an opinion on the legality of such a court under the laws of the European Union from the Court of Justice of the European Union[4]). The European Union will also have to further consider its future approach to investment protection and investor–state dispute settlement (ISDS) after the Court of Justice ruled in May 2017 that the European Union does not have exclusive competence to enter into agreements including portfolio investment and ISDS clauses in the context of the European Union (EU)–Singapore Comprehensive Free Trade Agreement.[5]

7.03 The outlook is similarly uncertain in the United States, where the Trump Administration has initiated renegotiation of the North American Free Trade Agreement (NAFTA)[6] with Mexico and Canada, and is more generally changing course on decades-long investment policies including, in particular, its stance on ISDS. Indeed, the only investment treaty concluded by the United States in the review period is the Trade and Investment Facilitation Agreement with Paraguay, a text without ISDS provisions. David Schneiderman covers related developments in Chapter 18. Many Latin American countries might also be moving away from ISDS, following the lead of famously ISDS-averse Brazil. In Chapter 17, Facundo Perez Aznar discusses MERCOSUR's new Protocol for Cooperation and the Facilitation of Investment that excludes ISDS and narrows substantive protections for investors.

---

[2] This figure represents the total number of treaties concluded and in force at the end of 2017. UNCTAD, 'Recent Developments in the International Investemnt Regime' <http://investmentpolicyhub.unctad.org/Upload/IIA%20Issues%20Note%20May%202018.pdf> accessed 4 June 2018. In addition, UNCTAD's Navigator indicates that the total number of treaties terminated or replaced by the end of 2017 is 243. UNCTAD's Navigator indicates that the total number of treaties concluded by 2017 year-end (including treaties signed, in force, and terminated, and not excluding treaties replaced by other treaties) is 3,616. See UNCTAD, *International Investment Agreements Navigator* <http://investmentpolicyhub.unctad.org/IIA/AdvancedSearchBITResults> accessed 4 June 2018.

[3] UNCTAD, *International Investment Agreements Navigator* (n 2).

[4] Kingdom of Belgium, 'Belgian Request for an Opinion from the European Union Court of Justice' <https://diplomatie.belgium.be/sites/default/files/downloads/ceta_summary.pdf> accessed 4 June 2018.

[5] European Union Court of Justice, 'Opinion 2/15 of the Court' (16 May, 2017) <http://curia.europa.eu/juris/document/document.jsf;jsessionid=9ea7d0f130d6ac64193d4a9542d581fa98233892177f.e34KaxiLc3eQc40LaxqMbN4Pax4Se0?text=&docid=190727&pageIndex=0&doclang=en&mode=req&dir=&occ=first&part=1&cid=650959> accessed 4 June 2018; European Union–Singapore Comprehensive Free Trade Agreement (EU–Singapore FTA).

[6] North American Free Trade Agreement (signed 17 December 1992, entered into force 1 January 1994) (NAFTA).

7.04 These conversations have spread to many international fora as well. In Chapter 3, Taylor St John highlights the multilateral negotiations and discussions related to the procedural and substantive standards of these treaties, as well as the rules of arbitration, facilitated by UNCTAD, the United Nations Commission on International Trade Law (UNCITRAL), the Organisation for Economic Co-operation and Development (OECD), and the International Centre for Settlement of Investment Disputes (ICSID). The World Trade Organization (WTO) also touched upon international investment policy in 2017; as Reji Joseph discusses in Chapter 5, several states have requested that the WTO host a discussion on global policy for investment facilitation.[7]

7.05 While many changes in investment treaty policy have taken place on the regional or international stage, a number of countries continue to take unilateral action to change their investment commitments. At least twenty-two terminations went into effect in 2017.[8] India formally terminated seventeen of its treaties, at the time of writing making effective about one third of its nearly fifty notices of intent to terminate issued in 2016,[9] and seeking renegotiations based on its revised model BIT (published in December 2015). In Europe, after the European Commission recommended that member states terminate intra-EU BITs and, in 2015, initiated infringement actions against five of the twenty-six European Union member states with intra-European Union treaties,[10] Romania and Poland took strides to exit such treaties. Romania, one of the five states targeted by the infringement action, terminated its BIT with Denmark,[11] and the Romanian parliament

---

[7] Sidhartha, 'China, Pak, Others Seek Talks on Investment at WTO' *The Times of India* (Buenos Aires, 11 December 2017) <https://timesofindia.indiatimes.com/business/international-business/china-pak-others-seek-talks-on-investment-at-wto-meet/articleshow/62025120.cms> accessed 4 June 2018.

[8] UNCTAD, 'Recent Developments in the International Investment Regime' (n 2) 2.

[9] Prabhash Ranjan and Pushkar Anand, 'More Than a BIT of Protectionism' *The Hindu* (14 December 2016) <www.thehindu.com/opinion/op-ed/More-than-a-BIT-of-protectionism/article16801222.ece> accessed 4 June 2018. It has also begun to negotiate new treaties based on its December 2015 model BIT, which limits investor protections, requires exhaustion of local remedies for five years before the initiation of ISDS proceedings, and precludes arbitral review of domestic judicial decisions. Jesse Coleman and Kanika Gupta, 'India's Revised Model BIT: Two Steps Forward One Step Back?' (Columbia Center on Sustainable Investment, 4 October 2017) <http://ccsi.columbia.edu/files/2017/10/Investment-Claims_-India%E2%80%99s-Revised-Model-BIT_-Two-Steps-Forward-One-Step-Back_.pdf> accessed 4 June 2018; 'India, Peru to Start FTA Negotiations This Week' *The Times of India* (7 August 2017) <https://timesofindia.indiatimes.com/business/india-business/india-peru-to-start-fta-negotiations-this-week/articleshow/59957621.cms> accessed 4 June 2018; Amiti Sen and Surabhi, 'India May Deviate from Model BIT to Meet Canada's Demands' *The Hindu Business Line* (New Delhi, 4 August 2017) <www.thehindubusinessline.com/economy/policy/india-may-deviate-from-model-bit-to-meet-canadas-demands/article9803014.ece> accessed 4 June 2018.

[10] European Commission Press Release, 'Commission Asks Member States to Terminate their Intra-EU Bilateral Investment Treaties' (18 June 2015) <http://europa.eu/rapid/press-release_IP-15-5198_en.htm> accessed 25 June 2018. The infringement proceeding initiated in 2015 targeted Austria, the Netherlands, Romania, Slovakia, and Sweden.

[11] UNCTAD, *International Investment Agreements Navigator* (n 2).

encouraged the president to terminate the twenty-two BITs with other European Union members,[12] while the Polish parliament considered a bill to terminate its BIT with Portugal.[13] Denmark also terminated its agreement with Estonia.[14] Other terminations included the Germany–Indonesia BIT, the Argentina–South Africa BIT, and the Ecuador–Peru BIT.[15]

7.06 The termination of the Ecuador–Peru BIT follows several other terminations by Ecuador in prior years, since the new constitution in 2008 prohibited the state from entering into treaties that yield sovereign jurisdiction to ISDS.[16] Like India, Ecuador terminated these agreements unilaterally, thereby triggering sunset clauses of five to twenty years.[17] Ecuador also issued notices of termination for its remaining fifteen treaties in May 2017 in the midst of a political transition.[18] However, the subsequent Ecuadorian government has also pledged to renegotiate these treaties, potentially foretelling the emergence of a new investment policy in the years to come.

7.07 Argentina and Colombia also developed new model BITs in 2017, and South Africa and the Dominican Republic continued work to develop new treaty models.

7.08 This background suggests an evolving landscape, with several states changing their approach to investment protection. Yet a number of states continued to sign agreements in 2017, some with innovations in treaty practice and others reflecting a degree of path dependency and a relatively consistent approach to investment protection. This chapter examines these agreements and specific developments in treaty drafting practice that took place over the course of 2017. It reviews publicly available investment treaties concluded and published in 2017, with some developments through May 2018 noted where relevant, in addition to one model BIT that was not publicly available at the time of writing but is on file with the authors.[19] Section B explores the modest but still isolated innovations in treaty definitions of 'investor'

---

[12] Volterra Fietta 'Romania Set to Terminate its Intra EU BITs' (*Volterra Fietta Client Alert*, 27 March 2017) <www.volterrafietta.com/romania-set-to-terminate-its-intra-eu-bits/> accessed 4 June 2018.

[13] Marcin Orecki, 'Let the Show Begin: Poland Has Commenced the Process of BITs' Termination' (*Kluwer Arbitration Blog*, 8 August 2017) <http://arbitrationblog.kluwerarbitration.com/2017/08/08/let-show-begin-poland-commenced-process-bits-termination/> accessed 4 June 2018.

[14] UNCTAD, *International Investment Agreements Navigator* (n 2).

[15] ibid.

[16] Christian Leathley and Daniela Paez, 'Ecuador's Legislative Branch Approves Termination of 12 Bilateral Investment Treaties' (Herbert Smith Freehills LLP, 5 May 2017) <www.lexology.com/library/detail.aspx?g=eefa16ea-93e5-44e2-b36f-1b64cdbd8bd4> accessed 4 June 2018.

[17] International Institute for Sustainable Development, 'Ecuador Denounces its Remaining 16 BITs and Publishes CAITISA Audit Report' Investment Treaty News (12 June 2017) <https://www.iisd.org/itn/2017/06/12/ecuador-denounces-its-remaining-16-bits-and-publishes-caitisa-audit-report/> accessed 4 June 2018.

[18] ibid.

[19] The chapter focuses on texts published in English, with more limited consideration also given to agreements published in Spanish.

and 'investment'. Section C illustrates the limited evolution and experimentation in treaties' core substantive obligations by focusing on developments in 2017 texts regarding the fair and equitable treatment (FET) obligation. Lastly, in Section D, we examine treaty drafting developments concerning three thematic areas: (1) sustainable development and the public interest; (2) climate change and environmental measures; and (3) human rights and investor obligations.

B. Covered Investors and Investments

The most elemental component of investment treaties, defining the scope and application of investment protections and access to investor–state dispute settlement, are the treaties' definitions of covered investors and investments. As treaty practice has evolved, two opposing dynamics are at play with respect to these definitions. On the one hand, recognizing that 'capital is fungible and investment of capital takes a multitude of forms in the world today', governments seeking to provide protections to 'foreign investment in all its forms' continue to include definitions of investment in their treaties that are 'broad and open-ended, with a list of specific types of covered investments that is indicative rather than definitive'.[20] Indeed, consistent with past practice, all of the publicly available 2017 treaties include the traditionally broad definition of 'investment', covering, in most cases, 'every asset that an investor owns or controls, directly or indirectly', including shares, stocks, intellectual property rights, licences, and loans, among other forms of tangible and intangible assets.[21] Despite the varied contribution of different forms of investment to economic development, treaties concluded in 2017 continue to define investment in the broadest way, for the purposes of affording protections.

7.09

On the other hand, some governments have taken steps to clarify criteria for investors and investments that are covered under their treaties.[22] As with many

7.10

---

[20] Barton Legum, 'Defining Investment and Investor: Who is Entitled to Claim?' (2006) 22(4) Arbitration International 521, 522–23.
[21] See eg Investment Agreement between the Government of the Hong Kong Special Administrative Region of the People's Republic of China and the Government of the Republic of Chile (signed 18 November 2016) (Chile–Hong Kong BIT); China–Hong Kong Comprehensive and Enhanced Partnership Agreement (signed 28 June 2017, entered into force 28 June 2017) (China–Hong Kong CEPA); Investment Promotion and Protection Agreement between the Government of the Federal Republic of Nigeria and the Government of the Republic of Singapore (signed 4 November 2016) (Nigeria–Singapore BIT); Agreement between Japan and the State of Israel for the Promotion and Protection of Investment (signed 1 February 2017, entered into force 5 October 2017) (Japan–Israel BIT); Agreement between the Republic of Rwanda and the United Arab Emirates on the Promotion and Reciprocal Protection of Investments (signed 1 November 2017) (Rwanda–UAE BIT); and the Pacific Agreement on Closer Economic Relations Plus (signed 14 June 2017) (PACER Plus), among others.
[22] For instance, it has become standard treaty practice to exclude from the definition of an 'investment' for the purposes of treaty coverage sovereign debt or claims to money arising from commercial contracts for the sale of goods (see eg Japan–Israel BIT (n 21); Bilateral Investment

other treaty protections, the evolution of the definitions of covered investors and investments has been incremental and innovation limited: most of the 2017 treaties remain in lock-step with one another and with older generation treaties. Nevertheless, the slight divergences in the 2017 treaties merit a closer look. The definitions of investors and investments in the 2017 treaties are as notable for their innovations as they are for their adherence to traditional treaty practice despite growing concerns about ISDS practices and outcomes.

7.11 Of particular concern to many respondent governments have been the increased practices of round-tripping, whereby a domestic investor gains treaty protections by routing an investment through a foreign subsidiary or other economic vessel,[23] and treaty-shopping, whereby a foreign investor either not covered by an investment treaty or covered by a weaker agreement uses a subsidiary or shareholder from a third country to gain stronger protections.[24] As noted by a tribunal, 'it is not uncommon in practice and—absent a particular limitation—not illegal to locate one's operation in a jurisdiction perceived to provide a beneficial regulatory and legal environment in terms, for example, of taxation or the substantive law of the jurisdiction, including the availability of a BIT'.[25] By this

---

Agreement for the Promotion and Protection of Investments Between the Government of the Republic of Colombia and the Government of the United Arab Emirates (signed 13 November 2017) (Colombia–UAE BIT); Rwanda–UAE BIT (n 21); and PACER Plus (n 21); see also UNCTAD 'Recent Developments in the International Investment Regime' (n 2)), as well orders or judgments entered in judicial or administrative actions (see eg China–Hong Kong CEPA (n 21); Agreement on Investment Among the Governments of the Hong Kong Special Administrative Region of the People's Republic of China and The Member States of The Association of Southeast Asian Nations (signed 12 November 2017) (Hong Kong–ASEAN FTA); Free Trade Agreement between Argentina and Chile (signed 2 November 2017) (Argentina–Chile FTA); and the Colombia model BIT).

[23] See *Tokios Tokelés v Ukraine* Case No ARB/02/18 (29 April 2004); *The Rompetrol Group NV v Romania*, ICSID Case No ARB/06/3, Decision on Respondent's Preliminary Objections on Jurisdiction and Admissibility (18 April 2008) <http://italaw.com/documents/RomPetrol.pdf/> accessed 4 June 2018; *Société Ouest Africaine des Bétons Industriels v Senegal* (1994) Decision on Jurisdiction of 1 August 1984, 2 ICSID Reports, 175, 182–83; *Autopista Concesionada de Venezuela v Venezuela* (2004) Decision on Jurisdiction of 27 September 2001, 6 ICSID Reports, 419, 442–43; *Wena Hotels Limited v Egypt* (2004) Decision on Jurisdiction of 29 June 1999, 6 ICSID Reports, 67, 81–84; *Champion Trading Company and Ameritrade International, Inc v Egypt* (2004) Decision on Jurisdiction of 21 October 2003, 19 ICSID Rev—FILJ, 275, 290.

[24] See *Saluka Investments BV v The Czech Republic*, under UNCITRAL Rules, Partial Award 17 March 2006; *Lauder v Czech Republic* (2001) Final award, Ad hoc—UNCITRAL Arbitration Rules <www.mfcr.cz/scripts/hpe/default.asp> accessed 4 June 2018; *Plama Consortium Limited v Bulgaria*, Decision on Jurisdiction of 8 February 2005, 20 ICSID Rev—FILJ (2005) 262; *Aguas del Tunari SA v Bolivia*, Decision on Jurisdiction of 21 October 2005, 20 ICSID Rev—FILJ (2005) 450; *ADC Affiliate Limited and ADC & ADMC Management Limited v Hungary*, Award of 2 October 2006 <https://www.italaw.com/documents/ADCvHungaryAward.pdf> accessed 4 June 2018.

[25] *Aguas del Tunari SA v Republic of Bolivia*, ICSID Case No ARB/02/3, Decision on Respondent's Objections to Jurisdiction (21 October 2005) para 330.

logic, 'a restructure solely for the purpose of taking advantage of a dispute settlement clause in an IIA is not illegal or abusive merely for that reason'.[26]

In order to limit the ease of treaty shopping, many more modern treaties require some combination of incorporation and substantial business activity in the home country and/or effective control of the investment in order for an investor to be covered under the treaty. These limitations can be found both in the definition of (covered) investors as well as in denial of benefits provisions, which each publicly available 2017 treaty contains. **7.12**

The Rwanda–Turkey agreement, for instance, defines an investor as a legal entity 'incorporated or constituted under the law in force of a Contracting Party and having [its] registered offices together with substantial business activities in the territory of that Contracting Party'.[27] The Argentina–Qatar BIT clarifies that 'a company formed under the legislation of such Contracting Party shall not be deemed an "investor" under this treaty where it does not conduct substantial business activities within the territory of such Contracting Party'.[28] Given the latitude afforded to tribunals in interpreting 'substantial business activity' in clauses like those discussed in this chapter,[29] the Colombia model BIT notably includes clear criteria for establishing the existence of substantial business activity, giving guidance to tribunals in their determination of such.[30] These definitions limit the ability of investors to set up or use shell companies to benefit from investor protections. **7.13**

One innovative provision of the Colombia model BIT further limits the ability of investors to treaty-shop by requiring not only substantial business activities in the **7.14**

---

[26] Vidushi Gupta, 'Exclusion From Within the Ambit of a Protected Investor, a Fair Price to Pay for the Act of Abusive Treaty Shopping?' (2014) 1 Transnational Dispute Management 9.
[27] Article 1(2)(b). See also Rwanda–UAE BIT (n 21).
[28] The Reciprocal Promotion and Protection of Investments between the Argentine Republic and the State of Qatar (signed 6 November 2016) (Argentina–Qatar BIT), art 1d.
[29] See *Masdar Solar & Wind Cooperatief v Spain*, ICSID Case No ARB/14/1, Award (16 May 2018) paras 252–56.
[30] Substantial business activity requires all of the following:

   a. The nature and scope of business conducted by the Enterprise, including the amount and type of clients and contracts, the amount of sales, turnover declared in tax returns, payment of taxes, years of establishment in the Contracting Party;
   b. The activities developed in the Home Party's Territory are similar to those developed by the entity operating in the Host Party's Territory, or are directly related to the active holding of shares in subsidiaries operating in the Host Party's Territory;
   c. The Enterprise's employee structure in the Home Party's Territory (number of employees, share of employees in respect to global operations of the Enterprise who work in the Home Party's Territory; permanent staff);
   d. The continuous physical presence of the Enterprise in the Home Party's Territory (ownership or rental of premises, costs related to the maintenance of physical location, phone, fax and mailing information offered to clients and third parties for contact with the Enterprise).

home country but also that the covered investor meet certain criteria to establish effective control of the covered investment in the host country:

> the holding of majority ownership or voting rights that allow for a decisive position in, or the right to select or exercise substantial influence over the selection of, the entity's managing bodies; the ability to effectively decide and implement the key decisions of the business activity of an enterprise; and participation in the day-to-day management of the entity.[31]

This type of provision presumably limits the treaty's protection to majority or controlling shareholders, precluding protection of minority or non-controlling investors and the parallel claims that protection of such investors can enable.

7.15 In addition to circumscribing the definition of covered investors, all of the publicly available 2017 treaties that include ISDS include a 'denial of benefits' provision, allowing the host state effectively to deny the benefits of the treaty protections to some or all 'shell companies owned by nationals of a third-country or the host State and companies owned by enemy aliens'.[32] The scope of this provision, however, varies among treaties. The scope of the provision in the Japan–Israel agreement is extremely limited, limiting the ability of a Contracting Party to deny benefits only in cases in which persons of a non-Contracting Party own more than 50 per cent of equity interest in the investor or have the power to legally direct its action, and only if the denying Party '(a) does not maintain diplomatic relations with the non-Contracting Party; or (b) adopts or maintains measures with respect to the non-Contracting Party ... that would prohibit transactions with the enterprise or that would be violated or circumvented if the benefits of this Agreement were accorded to the enterprise or to its investments ...'.[33] On the other hand, the Colombia model includes an extensive denial of benefits clause, which allows contracting states also to deny benefits to an investor of the other contracting party if 'an international court or a judicial or administrative authority of any State with which the Contracting Parties have diplomatic relations has proven that such investor has directly or indirectly' committed human rights violations, caused environmental damage, committed serious fraudulent actions against the tax laws, committed corruption, violated the host state's labour laws, or other enumerated violations.[34]

7.16 A recurring issue facing arbitral tribunals is whether a respondent state may invoke a denial of benefits clause after an arbitration has been commenced. Some tribunals have agreed with respondent states (and intervening non-disputing state

---

[31] Colombia model BIT, Definitions.
[32] Legum (n 20) 524.
[33] Japan-Israel BIT (n 21) art 21.
[34] Colombia model BIT, Denial of Benefits.

parties) that pre-dispute denial would be impractical and is not required.[35] In a number of other cases, tribunals have declared that denial of benefits provisions cannot be invoked 'retrospectively' after the ISDS claim has been launched,[36] although no treaty expressly supports that conclusion. Only a few treaties covered in this review period clarify the issue by stating explicitly that a party may deny the benefits of the agreement to an investor of the other party on specified grounds even after the institution of arbitral proceedings.[37]

7.17 The China–Hong Kong agreement includes a notably lengthy annex, seemingly to address the persistence of round-tripping and shell companies more generally. Annex 1 includes complex provisions on the requirements and criteria for an investor, particularly from Hong Kong, to benefit from the protections in the agreement. For instance, one footnote in Annex 1 states that '[a]ny overseas company, representative office, liaison office, "mail box company" and company specifically established for providing certain services to its parent company, which is registered in Hong Kong, is not a Hong Kong investor under this Annex'. The annex specifies that for an investor to be covered under the agreement, it must be '1.1. incorporated or established pursuant to the Companies Ordinance or other relevant laws of the Hong Kong Special Administrative Region, and have obtained a valid Business Registration Certificate; and 1.2. engage in substantive business operations in Hong Kong', with additional criteria relating to the years engaged in substantial business operations, having paid profits taxes, having substantial business premises, and employing Hong Kong residents.

7.18 A final consideration with respect to covered investors and investments is the nature of the investment in the host country, and the scope and nature of assets and interests in the host country afforded treaty protections. As noted, all of the publicly available 2017 treaties continue to afford protection to a broad range of tangible and intangible assets; however, some treaties add certain additional criteria for an investment to qualify as such under a treaty and to be afforded the respective protections. Several treaties and the Colombia model BIT, for instance, apply a partial *Salini* test,[38] defining an investment as one that includes

---

[35] See *Pac Rim Cayman LLC. v Republic of El Salvador*, ICSID Case No ARB/09/12, Decision on Jurisdictional Objections (1 June 2012) paras 4.83–4.90.

[36] See eg *Khan Resources Inc v Mongolia*, UNCITRAL, Decision on Jurisdiction (25 July 2012) paras 425–29; *Ampal-American Israel Corporation v Egypt*, ICSID Case No ARB/12/11, Decision on Jurisdiction (1 February 2016) paras 124–73.

[37] See eg China–Hong Kong CEPA (n 21), Hong Kong–ASEAN FTA (n 22), and Argentina–Chile FTA (n 22). Although in some cases, those grounds may be difficult to establish; for instance, the Colombia–UAE agreement denies benefits of the treaty 'if the main purpose behind the acquisition of the nationality of [the] Contracting Party was to obtain benefits under this Agreement that would not otherwise be available to such Investor' (art 25 (1)) arguably requiring a host country to prove 'main purpose'. The Rwanda–UAE BIT (n 21) also mirrors this language.

[38] Alex Grabowski, 'The Definition of Investment Under the ICSID Convention: A Defense of Salini' (2014) 15(1) Chicago Journal of International Law (2014) 287.

'the commitment of capital, the expectation of gain or profit, or the assumption of risk'.[39] A few treaties have taken the further step of explicitly requiring that an investment contributes 'to the economic development' of the host state, rounding out the requirements of the *Salini* test, though this remains rare.[40] Some treaties further require 'the objective of establishing a lasting interest' in the host country,[41] seem to protect only 'responsible' investors,[42] or require that an investment be 'made in accordance with applicable laws and regulations'.[43] (The latter two requirements are discussed later in this chapter.)

7.19 Surprisingly, little has been included in treaties to prevent the increasing incidence of shareholder claims for reflective loss, whereby a foreign shareholder, even if minority and non-controlling, is able to bring a claim for relief based on harm to the company in which they hold shares.[44] The Rwanda–Turkey agreement excludes portfolio shareholders from coverage;[45] Argentina's agreements with Chile and Qatar contain provisions similar to those found in agreements such as the NAFTA and the Trans-Pacific Partnership (TPP), which attempt to exclude claims by minority or non-controlling shareholders for reflective loss;[46] and the Colombia model BIT limits protected investors to majority or controlling shareholders.[47] However none of the other 2017 treaties reviewed take steps to limit this type of claim, despite the growing frequency with which states have critiqued multiple claims by non-controlling minority shareholders and the extensive work

---

[39] Nigeria–Singapore BIT (n 21). See also Rwanda–UAE BIT (n 21); Hong Kong–ASEAN FTA (n 22); PACER Plus (n 21); Protocol for Cooperation and Investment Facilitation Between the Members of MERCOSUR (signed 7 April 2017) (MERCOSUR Investment Protocol); and the Colombia model BIT.

[40] Argentina–Chile FTA (n 22); see also Turkey's treaties with Burundi, Mozambique, and Ukraine as referenced in UNCTAD, 'Recent Developments in the International Investment Regime' (n 2).

[41] MERCOSUR Investment Protocol (n 39). See also, Rwanda–Turkey BIT (' ... acquired for the purpose of establishing lasting economic relations ... ' art 1(1)); Rwanda–UAE BIT (n 21) (requiring 'certain duration'); Colombia model BIT (noting in its 'Definitions' article that the investment must reflect 'an intention to maintain a long-term presence in the Host Party').

[42] Colombia–UAE BIT (n 22).

[43] Japan–Israel BIT (n 21). See also eg Rwanda–UAE BIT (n 21). Some treaties further indicate that licenses, authorizations, permits, and similar rights are only deemed to be investments insofar as they are conferred pursuant to the host country's laws. See eg China–Hong Kong CEPA (n 21); Argentina–Chile FTA (n 22); and PACER Plus (n 21). Other treaties require that for intellectual property rights to be protected, they must be recognized as such under domestic law. See eg Hong Kong–ASEAN FTA (n 22) and Colombia model BIT.

[44] See *Saluka Investments BV v The Czech Republic*, under UNCITRAL Rules, Partial Award (17 March 2006); *Siemens AG v Argentine Republic*, ICSID Case No ARB/02/8, Decision on Jurisdiction (3 August 2004) paras 137–144.

[45] The treaty states that 'investments are not in the nature of acquisition of shares or voting power amounting to, or representing of, less than ten (10) per cent of a company through stock exchanges which shall not be covered by this Agreement' (art 1(e)).

[46] Argentina–Chile FTA (n 22) art 8.25, Argentina–Qatar BIT (n 28) art 5.4.

[47] Colombia model BIT, definition of 'covered investor'.

on this issue by the OECD,[48] as well as model language that has been used in other treaties that limit shareholders to bringing such claims only if the company itself provides a waiver of other litigation options, and if any damages awarded revert to the company.

C. Substantive Obligations: Focus on Fair and Equitable Treatment

7.20 While there are multilateral negotiations focused on procedural reform now taking place in UNCITRAL, there is no ongoing multilateral process focused on reforming or harmonizing substantive standards. And in this respect, while we have witnessed convergence among groups of states in connection with negotiation of mega-regionals such as the TPP, now the Comprehensive and Progressive Agreement for Trans-Pacific Partnership (CPTPP), and the Regional Comprehensive Economic Partnership (RCEP), we continue to see a range of approaches and experimentation. Nevertheless, such experimentation seems to be confined within a certain set of parameters regarding investment protection, with standard definitional approaches and core substantive obligations largely continuing to characterize investment treaties.

7.21 A key theme defining the 2017 treaties' approaches to questions of scope also applies to issues of substance: as with the limited evolution and experimentation in states' definitions of covered investors and investments, so too do the 2017 treaties' core substantive obligations, including decisions to exclude certain provisions, largely follow the path of previous agreements, with certain limited innovations. This section illustrates these patterns by focusing on the FET obligation, an arguable proxy for states' overall approaches to investment treaty policy.

7.22 Notably, all agreements covered by this chapter included the FET obligation, except the Protocol for the Cooperation and Facilitation of Investment within the MERCOSUR (MERCOSUR Investment Protocol). That agreement clearly expresses the treaty parties' desire to exclude the FET standard.[49] This does not mean that the state parties declined to reference any standards of treatment that may also form part of the FET obligation. Rather, it means that they clearly sought to distance themselves from the 'FET' concept and the myriad interpretations it has been given, and instead provide specific guarantees against denials of

---

[48] David Gaukrodger, 'Investment Treaties and Shareholder Claims: Analysis of Treaty Practice' (2014) OECD Working Papers on International Investment <http://www.oecd.org/daf/inv/investment-policy/WP-2014-3.pdf> accessed 4 June 2018.

[49] MERCOSUR Investment Protocol (n 39) art 4(3). ('Para mayor certeze, los estándares de "trato justo y equitativo", de "protección y seguridad plena" … no son cubiertos por el presente Protocolo'). See ch 17 in this volume by Facundo Pérez-Aznar.

justice and of due process.[50] This is similar to approaches taken by countries such as India and Brazil in their models.[51]

1. (How) does FET relate to the customary international law minimum standard of treatment?

7.23 Of the publicly available 2017 treaties with FET obligations, most link the FET obligation to the minimum standard of treatment under customary international law.[52] The nature and significance of the link between the FET obligation and the minimum standard of treatment, however, is not always clear. The agreement between Hong Kong and China, for instance, only references customary international law in the relevant article's title, labelling it 'Minimum Standard of Treatment'.[53] It does not otherwise specify the relationship between the concepts, namely whether the FET obligation is meant to be an element of, synonymous with, or additive to customary international law rules.[54] The Japan–Israel treaty raises similar questions: the treaty requires state parties to provide investors the 'customary international law standard of treatment including fair and equitable treatment'. This phrasing is akin to that used in the NAFTA's Article 1105 and the NAFTA parties' subsequent clarification of that article,[55] as well as approaches used in more modern agreements such as the TPP,[56] the post-TPP CPTPP,[57] and 2017's Pacific Agreement on Closer Economic Relations (PACER) Plus[58] and the Argentina–Chile[59] agreement.[60] Nevertheless, the Japan–Israel BIT lacks some

---

[50] ibid art 4.
[51] Jesse Coleman, Lise Johnson, Lisa Sachs, and Kanika Gupta, 'International Investment Agreements, 2015–2016: A Review of Trends and New Approaches' in Lisa Sachs and Lise Johnson (eds), *Yearbook on International Investment Law & Policy 2015–2016* (OUP 2018).
[52] This pattern is consistent with the observation that states appear to be increasingly tying the FET obligation to the minimum standard of treatment. See David Gaukrodger, 'Addressing the Balance of Interests in Investment Treaties: The Limitation of Fair and Equitable Treatment Provisions to the Minimum Standard of Treatment under Customary International Law' (2017) OECD Working Papers on International Investment 2017/03, 18–20 <http://dx.doi.org/10.1787/0a62034b-en> accessed 26 June 2018.
[53] China–Hong Kong CEPA (n 21) ch 1, art 4.
[54] ibid.
[55] On 31 July 2001, the Free Trade Commission (FTC), comprising the NAFTA Parties' cabinet-level representatives, issued an interpretation reaffirming that 'Article 1105(1) prescribes the customary international law minimum standard of treatment of aliens as the minimum standard of treatment to be afforded to investments of investors of another Party'. (NAFTA Free Trade Commission, Notes of Interpretation of Certain Chapter 11 Provisions, para B.1 (31 July 2001) (FTC Interpretation)). The FTC further stated that the FET obligation does 'not require treatment in addition to or beyond that which is required by the customary international law minimum standard of treatment of aliens'. (ibid para B.2).
[56] Trans-Pacific Partnership (signed 4 February 2016) (TPP), art 9.6(1).
[57] Comprehensive and Progressive Agreement for Trans-Pacific Partnership (signed 8 March 2018) (CPTPP), art 9.6(1).
[58] PACER Plus (n 21) art 9(1).
[59] Argentina–Chile FTA (n 22) art 8.7.
[60] The Hong Kong–ASEAN FTA (n 22) similarly links the FET obligation to customary international law, but does not state that customary international law *includes* fair and equitable

potentially significant clarifying features that those other agreements possess including, in particular, any clause expressly clarifying that the FET obligation is not intended to go beyond the customary international law minimum standard of treatment, or create any additional substantive rights.[61] Without such a clarification, it is arguable that the Japan–Israel BIT (1) represents a concession by these two states that they view customary international law as including an FET obligation, an otherwise disputed proposition,[62] and (2) may give rise to interpretations more favourable to investors than treaties more clearly limiting the FET obligation to obligations under customary international law.

The Colombia–United Arab Emirates (UAE) BIT represents a different approach: it states that '[e]ach Contracting Party shall accord to investments of investors of the other Contracting Party "fair and equitable treatment" and "full protection and security" in accordance with the law and regulations of the Host State, and the customary or international law standard of treatment and protection.'[63] In this agreement, one interpretation is that customary international law is treated not as a cap on the meaning of the FET obligation (as under, for instance, the NAFTA, TPP, PACER Plus, Hong Kong–Association of Southeast Asian Nations (ASEAN), and Argentina-Chile agreements' vision of that provision), but as one of several sources for understanding the FET obligation and what it requires. The treaty also arguably suggests that either a breach of domestic law or the 'international law standard of treatment and protection' can give rise to an FET violation.

7.24

Some agreements, following a model advanced by the European Union in its agreements, do not connect the FET obligation to the minimum standard of treatment but instead seek to identify its components. The treaty between the UAE and Rwanda is an example, opting not to reference customary international law and instead stating the obligation ('Each Contracting party shall accord fair and equitable treatment') and then elaborating on the types of conduct that will constitute a breach (discussed further in this chapter).[64] Colombia's model BIT is similar.[65]

7.25

---

treatment. The Hong Kong–ASEAN FTA states in art 5(1), 'Treatment of Investment': 'Each Party shall accord to covered investments fair and equitable treatment and full protection and security ... [T]he concepts of "fair and equitable treatment" and "full protection and security" do not require treatment in addition to or beyond that which is required under customary international law, and do not create additional substantive rights.'

[61] Japan–Israel BIT (n 21) art 4; cf TPP (n 56) art 9.6(2); CPTPP (n 57) art 9.6(2); PACER Plus (n 21) art 9(2); Hong Kong–ASEAN FTA (n 22) art 5(1)(c); Argentina–Chile FTA (n 22) art. 8.7(2).

[62] See Patrick Dumberry, 'Has the Fair and Equitable Treatment Standard Become a Rule of Customary International Law?' (2016) 8(1) Journal of International Dispute Settlement 155. See also n 53 (representing an approach in which the FET obligation is tethered to customary international law, but not described as being an element of it).

[63] Colombia–UAE BIT (n 22) art 5(1).

[64] Rwanda–UAE BIT (n 21) art 4.

[65] Colombia model BIT, Fair and Equitable Treatment.

2. What is the content of 'FET' and how is a breach established?

7.26 The treaties adopt (or allow) different approaches to deciphering the precise meaning of FET.

7.27 In the treaties explicitly linking the FET obligation to customary international law, such as the PACER Plus, Hong Kong–ASEAN, and Argentina–Chile texts, the treaties indicate expressly[66] or implicitly[67] that the tribunal must approach the question of the meaning of the FET obligation by determining whether there is a relevant customary international law rule arising from a 'general and consistent practice of States that they follow from a sense of legal obligation'.[68] Tribunals evaluating whether the FET standard has been breached would presumably then need to decide first whether a relevant rule of customary international law exists, and then whether that rule has been breached.

7.28 How to establish that a rule of customary international law exists is a complex topic, one under study in recent years by the International Law Commission, among others.[69] In addition to the question of how a rule of customary international law is established, another important question with implications for ISDS case outcomes is *who* has the burden of establishing such a rule in the context of a dispute. This has been a recurring issue in the context of the NAFTA, with the state parties unanimously and routinely arguing that the burden of establishing a rule of customary international law falls on the investor,[70] and tribunals offering competing views.[71]

7.29 A more recent development, which can be seen in the TPP/CTPPP[72] and in 2017's Argentina–Chile FTA,[73] is for state parties to attempt to preempt litigation

---

[66] PACER Plus (n 21) art 2, n 6; Argentina–Chile FTA (n 22) art 8.7, n 4.
[67] Hong Kong–ASEAN FTA (n 22) art 5(1).
[68] PACER Plus (n 21) art 2, n 6; Argentina–Chile FTA (n 22) art 8.7, n 4.
[69] For an overview, see International Law Commission, 'Analytical Guide to the Work of the International Law Commission: Identification of Customary International Law' <http://legal.un.org/ilc/guide/1_13.shtml> accessed 4 June 2018. For a review of the NAFTA parties' views on this, see Gaukrodger, 'Addressing the Balance of Interests' (n 52) 27–35.
[70] See eg *Apotex Holdings Inc and Apotex Inc v United States*, ICSID Case No ARB(AF)/12/1 (*Apotex II*), Counter-Memorial on Merits and Objections to Jurisdiction of Respondent United States of America (14 December 2012) para 354; *Windstream Energy LLC v Canada*, PCA Case No 2013-22 (*Windstream*), [Non-disputing State Party] Submission of the United States of America (12 January 2016) para 20; *Windstream*, Government of Canada Rejoinder Memorial (6 November 2015) para 199; Gaukrodger, 'Addressing the Balance of Interests' (n 52) 34.
[71] *Apotex II* (n 70) Award (25 August 2014) para 9.6 (noting that the claimants bear the burden of proving their case, and ultimately rejecting the claimants' contention regarding the existence of relevant rules of customary international law on certain administrative procedural matters); cf *Windstream* (n 70) Award, para 350 ('The Tribunal is ... unable to accept the Respondent's argument that the burden of proving the content of the rule falls exclusively on the Claimant. In the Tribunal's view, it is for each Party to support its position as to the content of the rule with appropriate legal authorities and evidence.').
[72] TPP (n 56) art 9.23(7).
[73] Argentina–Chile FTA (n 22) art 8.36(3).

of these issues by clarifying in the treaty text that the investor bears the burden of all elements of its claim including, presumably, the content of customary international law.

Several treaties have nevertheless provided tribunals guidance on related issues. For instance, the PACER Plus, Hong Kong–ASEAN, and Argentina–Chile texts indicate what their contracting states consider a customary international law-tethered FET obligation to mandate, saving tribunals some of the work of deciding whether a relevant rule exists. In an approach similar to that employed in the TPP/CTPPP,[74] the PACER Plus,[75] Hong Kong–ASEAN,[76] and Chile–Argentina[77] agreements state that the customary international law-tied FET obligation 'includes the obligation not to deny justice … in accordance with the principle of due process …'.[78] By using the word 'includes', the state parties to these three agreements leave open the possibility that the customary international law notion of FET includes other obligations regarding treatment of aliens, but do not list any elements other than the denial of justice in accordance with due process. Those elements will need to be determined in accordance with methods for determining the content of customary international law. 7.30

Some treaties that are more ambiguous than the PACER Plus, Hong Kong–ASEAN, and Chile–Argentina IIAs on the relationship between the FET obligation and the customary international law standard of treatment contain additional language providing guidance to tribunals regarding what FET means and/or does not mean. Common elements are protection against denials of justice[79] and guarantees of due process.[80] Several texts also state the FET obligation protects against 'manifestly 7.31

---

[74] TPP (n 56) art 9.6(2)(a).
[75] PACER Plus (n 21) art 9(2)(a).
[76] Hong Kong–ASEAN FTA (n 22) art 5(1)(a) ('"fair and equitable treatment" requires each Party not to deny justice in any legal or administrative proceedings in accordance with the principle of due process of law').
[77] Argentina–Chile FTA (n 22) art 8.7(2)(a) ('"Trato justo y equitativo" incluye la obligación de las Partes de no incurrir en una denegación de justicia en procedimientos penales, civiles o contencioso administrativos, de acuerdo con el principio del debido proceso incorporado en los principales sistemas legales del mundo').
[78] The wording varies slightly between some of these agreements, with potential substantive significance. For instance, the Hong Kong–ASEAN FTA (n 22) explains denial of justice by reference to due process 'in accordance with the principle of due process of law'. In contrast, the PACER Plus (n 21) refers to 'the principle of due process embodied in *the principal legal systems of the world*' (emphasis added).
[79] Colombia–UAE BIT (n 22) art 5(2)(a); Rwanda–UAE BIT (n 21) art 4(2)(a); China–Hong Kong CEPA (n 21) ch 1, art 4(2)(i).
[80] Colombia–UAE BIT (n 22) art 5(2)(b); Rwanda–UAE BIT (n 21) art 4(2)(b). Notably, in apparent contrast to the PACER Plus (n 21), Hong Kong–ASEAN, and Argentina–Chile (n 22) IIAs, which seem to link determinations of whether there has been a denial of justice with breach of due process, some of the list-based IIAs, such as Colombia–UAE (n 22), Rwanda–UAE (n 22), and the CETA, seem to treat issues of denial of justice and breach of due process as being separate elements of the FET obligation (cf China–Hong Kong CEPA (n 21) ch 1, art 4(2)(i)).

arbitrary' treatment, a concept that is similarly expressly reflected in texts concluded by the European Union, such as the Comprehensive Economic and Trade Agreement (CETA),[81] but that has given rise to controversial decisions in cases such as *Bilcon v Canada*.[82] The Colombia model BIT,[83] Colombia–UAE BIT,[84] and China–Hong Kong Comprehensive and Enhanced Partnership Agreement (CEPA),[85] for instance, each specify that the FET obligation protects against manifestly arbitrary conduct. In a slightly different approach, the Rwanda–UAE treaty does not include 'manifestly arbitrary' conduct among the list of measures that are said to constitute FET violations,[86] but adds a separate provision in the FET article stating, 'Neither Contracting Party shall hamper, by arbitrary or discriminatory measures, the development, management, use, expansion, sale and the liquidation of [covered] investments.'[87]

7.32 'Manifestly arbitrary' conduct has been cited by various tribunals as conduct amounting to a breach of FET;[88] thus, some of the 2017 treaties seem to reflect such arbitral decisions. In this context, it is interesting to note that those treaties following a list-based approach to defining the content of the FET obligation have not similarly seemed to accept and restate an understanding of the FET obligation as requiring 'transparency', 'proportionality', or an adherence to 'specific commitments',[89] elements some tribunals have identified as also being a part of the FET obligation.[90]

7.33 Finally, among the group of treaties reviewed in this chapter, the agreement between Israel and Japan follows a minority approach of declining to provide any further elaboration on the meaning of FET, other than, as noted, briefly connecting it to customary international law.

3. A note on other substantive standards

7.34 As with the FET obligation, a similar degree of limited experimentation can be seen in states' approaches to other substantive obligations such as the

---

[81] CETA, art 8.10(2)(c).
[82] *Bilcon of Delaware v Canada*, UNCITRAL, PCA Case No 3009-04, Award on Jurisdiction and Liability (17 March 2015) paras 442–43, 591.
[83] Colombia model BIT, Fair and Equitable Treatment, 2(c).
[84] Colombia–UAE BIT (n 22) art 5(2)(c).
[85] China–Hong Kong CEPA (n 21) ch 1, art 4(2)(i).
[86] Rwanda–UAE BIT (n 21) art 4(2).
[87] Rwanda–UAE BIT (n 21) art 4(5).
[88] See eg *Bilcon* (n 82) and cases cited therein.
[89] The investment chapter of the EU–Singapore FTA (n 5) had originally stated that a breach of the FET obligation would arise from 'a breach of the legitimate expectations of a covered investor arising from specific or unambiguous representations from a Party so as to induce the investment and which are reasonably relied upon by the covered investor'. (art 9.4(e)) (footnotes omitted). The text as released in 2018 no longer lists such breach of legitimate expectations as a standalone basis for an FET violation.
[90] It may be that elements of transparency are considered to be subsumed within notions of due process, or that a breach of a 'specific commitment', or conduct that is disproportionate, are considered to be examples of conduct that is 'manifestly arbitrary'.

expropriation obligation (with treaties, for instance, adopting different formulas to guide tribunals in determining whether an indirect expropriation has occurred,[91] or in assessing compensation for expropriations[92]); the most favoured nation (MFN) obligation (with treaties differing on whether procedural and/or substantive provisions can be imported[93]); and overarching provisions, such as a provision in the Hong Kong–ASEAN FTA 'recognizing that commitments by each newer ASEAN Member State may be made in accordance with its stage of development'.[94] These differences may be traced to diverse causes, including states' priorities domestically as well as in relation to their negotiating party(ies), negotiating capacities, power dynamics among negotiating parties, and experiences with investment treaties and dispute settlement to date.

Overall, it appears that, notwithstanding convergence obtained in some mega-regionals, and the relatively limited number of negotiations ongoing and treaties being concluded (as compared to patterns in the 1990s in particular), there are interesting variations in current approaches to investment protection, as agreements are typically more specific and precise than their predecessors of a decade or more ago. Nevertheless, it also appears that the diversity that exists within the substantive provisions of the treaties covered in this chapter still fits within a basic trajectory. In the context of the FET obligation, this means that, based on the sample of publicly available treaties reviewed for this chapter, the treaties concluded generally opt to link the obligation to customary international law and/or specify what the FET obligation means or does not mean. These approaches find precedent in 7.35

---

[91] cf eg the Colombia–UAE BIT (n 22) art 7 (requiring the tribunal to examine the 'scope', and 'economic impact' of the measure(s), and its/their 'level of interference on the reasonable and distinguishable expectations concerning the investment'), and not including a 'police powers' provision, with the Hong Kong–ASEAN FTA, annex 2 (requiring examination of, among other factors, the 'economic impact' and 'character' of the government action, and whether it 'breaches the government's prior binding written commitment to the investor . . .', and including a 'police powers' clarification).

[92] cf eg PACER Plus (n 21) art 13(2) (noting compensation shall be determined in accordance with the generally recognized principles of valuation and *equitable principles*) (emphasis added), with the Colombia–UAE BIT (n 22) (noting that '[w]here the fair market value cannot be ascertained, the compensation shall be determined *in equitable manner*'), and the Hong Kong–ASEAN FTA (n 22) art 10(2), 10(4), and n 10 (providing for different compensation depending on whether the expropriating party is an ASEAN member state (fair market value) or Hong Kong (real value), connecting compensation standards for expropriation 'relating to land' to domestic laws and regulations, and specifying that for certain ASEAN member states, payment of interest is also subject to non-discriminatory domestic laws, regulations and policies).

[93] See eg Hong Kong–ASEAN FTA (n 22) art 4(3) (preventing importation of obligations from other existing and some future treaties), and art 4(5) (clarifying that the most favoured nation (MFN) obligation does not permit importation of any dispute resolution proceedings found in other treaties); and Colombia–UAE BIT (n 22) (adding that '[f]or greater clarity', the MFN obligation does not encompass the treaty's sections on definitions or dispute settlement, an approach that prevents investors or investments otherwise not covered from seeking protection, and prevents those investors and investments that are covered from accessing more favourable dispute resolution mechanisms).

[94] Hong Kong–ASEAN FTA (n 22) art 18(d).

D. Protecting Public Interest Objectives?

7.36 As noted in past *Yearbook* chapters, global and national dialogue on reform of the investment treaty regime has included calls from a range of stakeholders for negotiating states to improve protection of policy space and measures adopted in pursuit of public interest objectives.[95] However, in addition to varying refinements and innovations in substantive host state obligations, other provisions included in 'new generation' treaties that purport to better protect policy space appear to vary in terms of their explicit reference to public interest objectives. Moreover, while it is too soon to assess their effectiveness in practice, some provisions may be limited by their conditionality, lack of specificity, or non-binding nature. This section explores treaty drafting developments in 2017 with respect to three thematic areas: (1) sustainable development and the public interest; (2) climate change and environmental measures; and (3) human rights and investor obligations.

1. Sustainable development and the public interest

7.37 Of the treaties reviewed in this chapter, several include explicit references to sustainable development in their preambles and/or in operative provisions. The Rwanda–UAE BIT, for example, contains a number of preambular references to sustainable development, though it does not refer to sustainable development in its operative text.[96] PACER Plus also refers to sustainable development in its preamble, underscoring the character of the agreement as a 'development tool' and reaffirming the parties' commitments to *inter alia* 'sustainable development agreements'.[97] References to sustainable development can also be found in the preamble of the MERCOSUR Investment Protocol, which recognizes the role of investment in the promotion of sustainable development, poverty reduction, and expansion of human capacity and development.[98] The Protocol's preamble also provides that investors and their investments should behave in a socially responsible manner, and contribute to the sustainable development of state parties.[99] Colombia's model BIT explicitly links investment promotion and protection with

---

[95] See eg Coleman, Johnson, Sachs, and Gupta (n 51); Lisa Sachs, Lise Johnson, and Jesse Coleman, *International Investment Agreements, 2014: A Review of Trends and New Approaches* (OUP 2016).
[96] Rwanda–UAE BIT (n 21) preamble.
[97] PACER Plus (n 21) preamble.
[98] MERCOSUR Investment Protocol (n 39) preamble.
[99] ibid.

sustainable development, with the model's preamble noting that the parties are '[s]eeking to promote and protect foreign investments that favour the prosperity and the sustainable development of both Parties'.[100]

Some of the texts reviewed in this chapter also include references to sustainable development within the operative portions of their respective texts. The stated objective of the MERCOSUR Investment Protocol is to promote cooperation amongst state parties in order to facilitate investment that enables the sustainable development of state parties.[101] The Protocol's corporate social responsibility (CSR) provision also provides that investors and their investments shall endeavour to achieve the highest possible level of contribution to sustainable development in the host state by adopting the voluntary standards outlined in that provision.[102] In conditioning access to dispute settlement, Colombia's model BIT provides that protection under the agreement to covered investors and investments 'stems from the Covered Investor's contribution to the sustainable development and welfare of their Host Party'.[103] The specific mechanism or means for assessing this contribution is not outlined in the treaty. BITs concluded by Turkey in 2017 also reportedly condition treaty protection on the basis of covered investors' or investments' contribution 'to the host State's economy or sustainable development'.[104] 7.38

While these examples expand the set of 'new generation' treaties that explicitly link investment promotion and protection to sustainable development within the treaty texts, they seem by comparison less powerful than the references to sustainable development found in recently concluded FTAs. The European Union–Armenia CEPA,[105] which does not contain substantive obligations regarding investment protection, contains an explicit commitment by state parties to principles of sustainable development,[106] along with a confirmation of the parties' 7.39

---

[100] Colombia model BIT, preamble.
[101] MERCOSUR Investment Protocol (n 39) art 1.
[102] ibid art 14.
[103] Colombia model BIT, Section DD (Dispute Settlement), art X(3) (Scope of Application of ISDS).
[104] UNCTAD, 'Recent Developments in the International Investment Regime' (n 2) 5, referring to Bilateral Investment Treaty Between Burundi and Turkey (signed 14 June 2017) (Burundi–Turkey BIT); Bilateral Investment Treaty between Mozambique and Turkey (signed 24 January 2017) (Mozambique–Turkey BIT); Bilateral Investment Treaty between Turkey and Ukraine (signed 9 October 2017) (Turkey–Ukraine BIT). These treaties were not publicly available at the time of writing; the authors were therefore unable to verify the manner in which protection is conditioned in the texts of these agreements.
[105] The Comprehensive & Enhanced Partnership Agreement between the European Union and Armenia (signed 24 November 2017) (EU–Armenia CEPA). The European Union–Armenia CEPA does not contain substantive obligations on investment (though it does contain, in art 203, a commitment to 'review the environment and legal framework for investment, no later than three years after the entry into force of' the agreement to consider opportunities for including provisions on investment). That it and similar trade and broader economic partnership agreements contain more advanced provisions concerning matters of public interest is noteworthy.
[106] ibid art 2 (General Principles).

'commitment to enhance the contribution of trade to the goal of sustainable development'.[107] The latter provision lists specific steps that the parties will take in this regard, including seeking greater policy coherence between labour and trade policies; striving to facilitate and promote trade and investment in environmental goods and services; striving to remove obstacles to trade or investment concerning goods and services of relevance for climate change mitigation and adaptation; promoting 'trade in goods that contribute to enhanced social conditions and environmentally sound practices'; and promoting CSR.[108] While these commitments remain broad in their scope and content, they appear more concrete and tailored towards achieving certain sustainable development objectives than those found in other recently concluded texts.[109] The extent to which these provisions may be enforced by state parties may, however, be limited by the application of Article 285, which provides that provisions regarding compliance in the dispute settlement chapter do not apply to Chapter 9 (Trade and Sustainable Development), including the provisions referred to previously in this chapter.[110]

7.40 In addition to explicit references to sustainable development, investment treaties concluded in 2017 include general provisions that seek to protect policy space and measures adopted in pursuit of public interest objectives, including promotion of sustainable development. Most treaties reviewed in this chapter contain a version of a right to regulate provision (whether implicit or explicit), along with non-lowering of standards provisions and general exceptions.[111] As the authors reported last year,[112] it is too soon to tell whether these provisions will have a tangible impact on protection of measures adopted by host states in pursuit of public interest objectives. Moreover, the strength of these provisions continues to vary across agreements.[113] Indeed, as discussed further in Chapter 9 and Chapter 19, early signs from the interpretation and application of existing exceptions indicate that they may narrow, rather than expand, states' defences.[114] It is, however,

---

[107] ibid art 276 (Trade and Investment Favouring Sustainable Development).

[108] ibid art 276 (a)–(e) (Trade and Investment Favouring Sustainable Development). See also art 284 (Working Together on Trade and Sustainable Development).

[109] Some recent BITs, including the Reciprocal Investment Promotion and Protection Agreement between the Government of the Kingdom of Morocco and the Government of the Federal Republic of Nigeria (signed 3 December 2016) (Morocco–Nigeria BIT), provide noteworthy exceptions to this general trend. The Morocco–Nigeria BIT contains several references to sustainable development in its preamble and art 1(3) links the definition of a covered investment to that investment's contribution to sustainable development.

[110] European Union–Armenia CEPA (n 105) art 285 (Dispute Settlement).

[111] UNCTAD also reports that several treaties not reviewed in this chapter (as they were not public at the time of writing) also contain non-lowering of standards provisions and general exceptions. See Table 1 in UNCTAD, 'Recent Developments in the International Investment Regime' (n 2) 4.

[112] Coleman, Johnson, Sachs, and Gupta (n 51).

[113] For example, the general exception included in the Colombia model BIT is explicitly self-judging, while the general exception included in the Japan–Israel BIT (n 21) (art 15) is not.

[114] See ch 9 by Jarrod Hepburn and ch 19 by Tania Voon, Andrew Mitchell, and James Munro.

difficult to draw this conclusion with certainty, given the discretion available to investor–state tribunals.

7.41 Lastly, two unique provisions that seek to protect public interest objectives should be highlighted. The first is a broad provision that seeks to address the potential impact of investments on the public interest: the China–Hong Kong CEPA provides that '[o]ne side reserves the right to establish or maintain any restrictive measures relating to investors and covered investments of the other side in the event that the implementation of this Agreement causes substantial impact on its sectors or public interests'.[115] The second is an exception included in PACER Plus, which explicitly provides that nothing in the agreement 'shall preclude the adoption by New Zealand of measures *it deems necessary* to accord more favourable treatment to Māori in respect of matters covered by this Agreement including in fulfilment of its obligations under the Treaty of Waitangi'.[116] This provision is self-judging and does not contain language requiring the measures adopted to otherwise comply with the provisions of PACER Plus, implying that it will provide stronger protection for the measures it seeks to cover than certain right to regulate or exception provisions found in other treaties. For avoidance of doubt, it also specifically states that the measures adopted by New Zealand may concern matters covered by PACER Plus, precluding confusion regarding whether specific trade and investment-related measures come within the scope of the provision, or whether only general measures regarding rights and obligations arising from the Treaty of Waitangi can be covered. However, although self-judging, and while the 'otherwise compliant with' language is absent from the provision, the use of 'necessary' means that the exception maintains a stricter nexus requirement.

2. Climate change and environmental measures

7.42 During the review period, one economic partnership agreement that refers to climate objectives was signed, and negotiations regarding a second were concluded. Although these agreements do not, for the moment, include provisions on investment protection, their inclusion of these explicit references to climate change is noteworthy, and they provide a valuable (though distinct) benchmark against which investment treaty developments can be compared. In November 2017, the European Union–Armenia CEPA was signed.[117] One month later, negotiations on the European Union–Japan Economic Partnership Agreement (EPA) were finalized, though the agreement has not yet been signed.[118] Both of these treaties explicitly refer to state parties' commitment to implement the objectives of the

---

[115] China–Hong Kong CEPA (n 21) art 22(6).
[116] PACER Plus (n 21) ch 11, art 6 (emphasis added).
[117] EU–Armenia CEPA (n 105).
[118] European Union-Japan Economic Partnership Agreement (EU–Japan EPA) <http://ec.europa.eu/trade/policy/in-focus/eu-japan-economic-partnership-agreement/> accessed 4 June 2018.

United Nations Framework Convention on Climate Change (UNFCCC)[119] and the Paris Agreement.[120] [121]

7.43 In addition to general obligations regarding multilateral environmental agreements (discussed further in this chapter), Article 275 of the European Union–Armenia CEPA provides:[122]

> The Parties reaffirm their commitment to implementing and reaching the objectives of the United Nations Framework Convention on Climate Change of 1992 (UNFCCC), the Kyoto Protocol thereto of 1998 and the Paris Agreement of 2015. They commit to work together to strengthen the multilateral, rules-based regime under the UNFCCC and to cooperate on the further development and implementation of the international climate-change framework under the UNFCCC and agreements and decisions related thereto.

7.44 This provision is complemented by a full chapter dedicated to Climate Action.[123] The chapter contains, among other things, commitments by state parties to: strengthen cooperation to address climate change;[124] promote measures at domestic, regional, and international levels address to climate change;[125] exchange information and expertise to achieve climate objectives;[126] and engage in a regular dialogue on matters covered by the Climate Action chapter.[127] The current draft of the European Union–Japan EPA does not contain a 'climate action' chapter; however, the language used to refer to the UNFCCC and Paris Agreement is marginally more decisive than that used in the European Union–Armenia CEPA.[128]

---

[119] United Nations Framework Convention on Climate Change (adopted 9 May 1992, entered into force 21 March 1994) 1771 UNTS 107 (UNFCCC).
[120] Paris Agreement (adopted 12 December 2015, opened for signature on 22 April 2016, entered into force on 4 November 2016).
[121] See eg EU–Armenia CEPA (n 105) art 275(4); European Union–Japan EPA (n 118) art 16.6(4). Note with respect to the European Union-Japan EPA that this is referred to on the European Commission's website as the text of the agreement as it stands (after legal revision), but which may undergo further modifications. See European Commission, 'EU–Japan Economic Partnership Agreement: Texts of the Agreement' <http://trade.ec.europa.eu/doclib/press/index.cfm?id=1684> accessed 4 June 2018. The 'Key Elements' of the treaty are listed here: European Commission, 'Key Elements of the EU-Japan Economic Partnership Agreement: Fact Sheet' (18 April 2018) <http://europa.eu/rapid/press-release_MEMO-18-3326_en.htm> accessed 4 June 2018.
[122] EU–Armenia CEPA (n 105) art 275(4).
[123] ibid ch 4 (Climate Action).
[124] ibid arts 51 and 54. Article 54 mentions specific objectives cooperation should to address.
[125] ibid art 52.
[126] ibid art 53.
[127] ibid art 55.
[128] European Union–Japan EPA (n 118), ch 16 (Trade and Sustainable Development), art 16.4(4) provides:

> The Parties recognize the importance of achieving the ultimate objective of the United Nations Framework Convention on Climate Change, done at New York on 9 May 1992 (hereinafter referred to as "UNFCCC"), in order to address the urgent threat of climate change, and the role of trade to that end. The Parties reaffirm their commitments to effectively implement the UNFCCC and the Paris Agreement, done at Paris on 12 December 2015 by the Conference of the Parties to the UNFCCC at its 21st session. The

Other texts reviewed for the purposes of this chapter do not include comparable references to climate change, the UNFCCC, or the Paris Agreement. Three additional features of texts concluded in 2017 are worth highlighting with respect to how they address—or do not address—state parties' environmental obligations and measures adopted in pursuit of those obligations. 7.45

First, in addition to the provisions explicitly dealing with climate change, the European Union–Armenia CEPA contains more general provisions regarding state parties' obligations arising from multilateral environmental agreements. These provisions: explicitly recognize the links between trade and environmental issues; stress the importance of multilateral environmental governance in addressing these impacts; reaffirm parties' commitments to implementing 'in their laws and practices the multilateral environmental agreements (MEAs) to which they are party'; commit the parties to regularly exchanging information about progress regarding ratification of these MEAs; and provide that nothing in the CEPA prevents state parties 'from adopting or maintaining measures to implement the MEAs to which they are party, provided that such measures are not applied in a manner that would constitute a means of arbitrary or unjustifiable discrimination between the Parties or a disguised restriction on trade'.[129] Similar general commitments to multilateral environmental obligations are also contained in the current draft text of the European Union–Japan EPA,[130] and in the concluded China–Georgia FTA.[131] 7.46

By contrast, most other treaties concluded in 2017 do not contain comparable commitments to multilateral environmental obligations. Although PACER Plus includes a preambular reference to state parties' commitments regarding multilateral (and sustainable development) agreements,[132] none of the other agreements reviewed in this chapter contain a similar express acknowledgment or affirmation of these obligations, either in the preamble or operative portion of the texts. 7.47

Second, some general exceptions contained in the treaties reviewed herein explicitly note that environmental measures come within the scope of the provision. For example, the Japan–Israel BIT's general exception explicitly covers 'environmental measures necessary to protect human, animal or plant life or health'.[133] The general exception in the China–Hong Kong CEPA covers environmental measures 7.48

Parties shall cooperate to promote the positive contribution of trade to the transition to low greenhouse gas emissions and climate-resilient development. The Parties commit to working together to take actions to address climate change towards achieving the ultimate objective of the UNFCCC and the purpose of the Paris Agreement.

[129] EU–Armenia CEPA (n 105) art 275.
[130] EU–Japan EPA (n 118) ch 16 (Trade and Sustainable Development), art 16.4.
[131] See eg Free Trade Agreement Between China and Georgia (signed 13 May 2017, entered into force 1 January 2018) (China–Georgia FTA), arts 9.1–9.3 in ch 9 (Environment and Trade).
[132] PACER Plus (n 21) preamble.
[133] Japan–Israel BIT (n 21) art 15(1)(a).

necessary to achieve other stated objectives in the exception, which mirror those commonly found in such provisions regarding compliance with laws, protection of life, and conservation of natural resources.[134] PACER Plus also explicitly provides that environmental measures necessary to achieve the other stated objectives in the provision are covered by the exception.[135] The Colombia–UAE BIT provides that measures *appropriate* 'to protect human, animal, or plant life, health, *or the environment*' are covered by the exception.[136] This provision therefore both includes environmental measures in the list of objectives covered by the exception, and contains a slightly more flexible nexus requirement than that usually found in general exceptions modelled on General Agreement on Tariffs and Trade (GATT) Article XX[137] or General Agreement on Trade in Services (GATS) Article XIV.[138] Colombia's model BIT, by contrast, includes the 'necessary' nexus, but the exception is self-judging.[139]

7.49 Lastly, as noted with respect to sustainable development, right to regulate and non-lowering of standards provisions are increasingly found in more recently negotiated treaties. Where they are included, they often refer to environmental measures or protection of the environment. However, the strength of their wording varies, and it is difficult to assess at this stage in the development of investment law whether they will be effective.

7.50 Looking ahead, it will be interesting to observe whether states' commitments to addressing climate change objectives will shape, in a more decisive and concrete manner, the provisions included in future trade and investment agreements. Growing interest in 'climate-friendly' approaches to trade and investment are spurring the development by non-state entities of new models that could promote more creative thinking on these issues. In late 2016, the Sierra Club outlined a model that, if adopted by negotiating states, would require the inclusion of more concrete and specific provisions capable of guarding the regulatory space needed to protect and implement climate policies.[140] In 2017, the Stockholm Chamber of Commerce launched the 'Stockholm Treaty Lab', a competition designed to promote development of innovative model investment treaties to encourage investment in climate change mitigation and adaptation.[141] It remains

---

[134] China–Hong Kong CEPA (n 21) art 22(1).
[135] PACER Plus (n 21) ch 11, art 1(6) (which applies to ch 9 on investment).
[136] Colombia–UAE BIT (n 22) art 11(b) (emphases added).
[137] General Agreements on Tariffs and Trade (1947 and 1994) 55 UNTS 194 and 1867 UNTS 190, art XX.
[138] General Agreement on Trade in Services (1994) 1869 UNTS 183, art XIV.
[139] Colombia model BIT, General Exceptions.
[140] Sierra Club, 'A New, Climate-Friendly Approach to Trade' < www.sierraclub.org/sites/www.sierraclub.org/files/uploads-wysiwig/climate-friendly-trade-model.pdf> accessed 4 June 2018.
[141] Stockholm Treaty Lab, 'The Prize'<http://stockholmtreatylab.org/the-prize/> accessed 4 June 2018.

3. Human rights and investor obligations

7.51 As reported in previous *Yearbook* chapters, explicit references to human rights within the texts of investment treaties are rare: most of the treaties concluded to date, and the vast majority of those in force, do not contain explicit references to human rights (as the obligations of states, the responsibility of investors to respect human rights, or to the human rights of investment-affected rights holders).[143] The texts concluded in 2017 continued this general trend. Where treaties concluded in 2017 included non-lowering of standards provisions, right to regulate provisions, and/or general exceptions, most of these provisions did not include explicit references to human rights. Additionally, when non-lowering of standards provisions were included in the treaties, those provisions covered environmental measures, but did not always cover labour law or enforcement.[144]

7.52 However, a small number of texts reviewed in this chapter provide an exception to the continued general trajectory of limited explicit reference to human rights. The MERCOSUR Investment Protocol refers explicitly to human rights in Article 14(2), where the Protocol provides that investors and their investments must commit their best efforts to comply with principles and voluntary standards concerning respect for the human rights of investment-affected rights holders.[145] The Argentina–Chile FTA's Investment Chapter includes a provision on CSR wherein the parties reaffirm their commitment to CSR standards approved by the parties, including those addressing human rights, and 'endeavour to encourage investors' to incorporate these standards into their policies and practices.[146] PACER Plus also reaffirms the importance of state parties encouraging investors to voluntarily

---

[142] While beyond the scope of the review period for this chapter, the European Union announced in early 2018 that it would conclude trade agreements only with states that ratified the Paris Agreement. See eg EA Crunden, 'EU Will Only Make Trade Deals with Nations that Ratify Paris Climate Agreement' *Think Progress* (6 February 2018) <https://thinkprogress.org/eu-paris-us-decd4aad9145/> accessed 4 June 2018.

[143] For discussion of past treaty drafting practice, see eg Coleman, Johnson, Sachs, and Gupta (n 51) 90–96. See also Johnson, Sachs, and Coleman (n 95) and Jesse Coleman, Kaitlin Cordes, and Lise Johnson, 'Human Rights Law and the Investment Treaty Regime' in Surya Deva (ed), *Research Handbook on Human Rights and Business* (Edward Elgar, *forthcoming*).

[144] cf China–Hong Kong CEPA (n 21) art 25 (which limits the non-lowering of standards to environmental measures, and there is no other non-lowering of standards provision that addresses labour measures) and PACER Plus (n 21) art 19(1) (which refers to non-enforcement of environmental, health, labour, safety, or other regulatory standards). The non-lowering of standards provision in the Investment Chapter of the Argentina–Chile FTA (n 22) (art 8.14) also refers explicitly to environmental and health objectives, but not to labour.

[145] MERCOSUR Investment Protocol (n 39) art 14(2).

[146] Argentina–Chile FTA (n 22) art 8.17. Other references to human rights may be included in the full FTA; this chapter reviewed explicit references to human rights in the Investment Chapter only.

incorporate into their policies internationally recognized CSR standards, guidelines, and principles.[147] All three of these provisions mirror the approach adopted by Brazil in the CSR provision of its Cooperation and Facilitation of Investment Agreements (CFIAs) with certain states.[148]

7.53 Colombia's model BIT includes several explicit references to human rights. The model's reaffirmation of state parties' right to regulate, which appear both in the preamble and the operative portion of the text, explicitly refers to human rights as one of the listed legitimate public welfare objectives.[149] Measures deemed by the adopting state necessary to protect human rights are also explicitly listed as being covered by the general exception included in the model.[150] The model further provides that state parties may: (1) condition or prevent a transfer of funds to enforce investor compliance with judicial, arbitral, or administrative decisions concerning *inter alia* human rights obligations;[151] and (2) deny the benefits of the treaty where an international court or judicial or administrative authority of any state with which the state parties have diplomatic relations has proven that the investor, directly or indirectly, *inter alia* 'committed serious human rights violations' or sponsored others to do so, 'caused serious environmental damage in the Territory of the Host Party', or 'caused grave violations of the Host Party's labour laws'.[152] These references to human rights in the context of conditioning transfers and denying treaty benefits are unique amongst recently reviewed texts.

7.54 Related to the promotion of sustainable and human rights-compliant trade and investment, at least two agreements are worth highlighting for their inclusion of specific provisions or chapters concerning gender. The Argentina–Chile FTA reportedly includes a full chapter on trade and gender.[153] Canada and Chile also signed an amendment to the existing Canada–Chile FTA[154] to incorporate a trade

---

[147] PACER Plus (n 21), ch 9 (Investment), art 5(2).
[148] See eg Agreement on Cooperation and Facilitation of Investments between the Federal Republic of Brazil and the Republic of Colombia (signed 9 October 2015), art 13 (hereafter Brazil–Colombia CFIA). Note that Brazil adopted a more decisive approach in its model and in certain other treaties. See eg Investment Cooperation and Facilitation Agreement between the Federative Republic of Brazil and the Republic of Malawi (signed 25 June 2015), art 9 (Brazil–Malawi CFIA).
[149] Colombia model BIT, preamble and Chapeau on Investment and Regulatory Measures.
[150] ibid, General Exception.
[151] ibid, Freedom of Transfers.
[152] ibid, Denial of Benefits.
[153] Ministerio de Relaciones Exteriores de Chile, 'Chile and Argentina sign a trade agreement: "There are many countries in our region that talk about integration, we are achieving integration"' (2 November 2017) <https://minrel.gob.cl/chile-and-argentina-sign-a-trade-agreement-there-are-many-countries-in/minrel/2017-11-03/152244.html> accessed 4 June 2018.
[154] Government of Canada, 'Canada Chile FTA' <http://international.gc.ca/trade-commerce/trade-agreements-accords-commerciaux/agr-acc/chile-chili/fta-ale/background-contexte.aspx?lang=eng> accessed 4 June 2018; Free Trade Agreement between the Government of Canada and the Government of the Republic of Chile (signed 5 December 1996, entered into force 5 July 1997) (Canada–Chile FTA).

and gender chapter into that agreement.[155] The chapter *inter alia*: reaffirms state parties' commitment to implementing obligations under the Convention on the Elimination of all Forms of Discrimination Against Women (CEDAW)[156] and other international agreements addressing gender equality and women's rights;[157] outlines areas of cooperation to promote women's participation in national and international economies;[158] and establishes a trade and gender committee to support implementation of the chapter.[159] Canada and Chile also updated the investment chapter of the FTA by, among other things, reaffirming state parties' right to regulate, including a CSR provision, and clarifying other existing treaty standards.[160]

While references to explicit human rights obligations and responsibilities remained rare in 2017,[161] treaties concluded during the review period do include several noteworthy provisions that seek to strengthen the connection between the responsibility of investors for their conduct and protection under the relevant treaty. First, several treaties seek to, in different ways, condition protection on compliance with host state laws, which could include human rights obligations. The Colombia–UAE BIT, for example, defines an 'investor' as a state party, state enterprise, or an enterprise or national of a state party that has made an investment 'in accordance with the law of the other Contracting Party'.[162] Similarly, the Rwanda–UAE BIT includes compliance with the laws and regulations of the host state as a characteristic of the definitions of 'investor' and 'investment' under the treaty.[163] PACER Plus emphasizes compliance with host state laws in a separate provision, with state parties explicitly acknowledging in the treaty 'that investors of a Party and their investments are subject to the laws, regulations and standards

7.55

---

[155] Government of Canada, 'Highlighting Gender in Trade' <http://international.gc.ca/gac-amc/publications/blueprint_2020-objectif_2020/highlighting_gender_trade-mettre_accent_sur_genre_commerce.aspx?lang=eng> accessed 4 June 2018.

[156] Convention on the Elimination of All Forms of Discrimination against Women (opened for signature 1 March 1980, entered into force 3 September 1981) 1249 UNTS 13 (CEDAW).

[157] Canada–Chile FTA (n 151) appendix II, ch N bis (Trade and Gender), art N bis-02 (International Agreements).

[158] ibid appendix II, ch N bis (Trade and Gender), art N bis-03 (Cooperation Activities).

[159] ibid appendix II, ch N bis (Trade and Gender), art N bis-04 (Trade and Gender Committee).

[160] UNCTAD 'Recent Developments in the International Investment Regime' (n 2) 7.

[161] A 2014 study of 2,107 investment treaties found that only 0.5 per cent of treaties included in the study contained references to human rights, with a majority of those references falling within the preambles of the texts studied. The sample included all treaties concluded by countries invited to participate in OECD-hosted investment dialogue (fifty-four countries, in addition to the European Commission) with other countries, provided that the text of the agreement was available in early 2014. The study indicates that the sample covered 'more than 70% of the global investment treaty population' at the time. See Kathryn Gordon, Joachim Pohl, and Marie Bouchard, 'Investment Treaty Law, Sustainable Development and Responsible Business Conduct: A Fact Finding Survey' OECD Working Papers on International Investment 2014/01, 10–18 http://dx.doi.org/10.1787/5jz0xvgx1zlt-en.

[162] Colombia–UAE BIT (n 22) art 2.1(b). See also the definition for 'enterprise' in art 2.1(c).

[163] Rwanda–UAE BIT (n 21) arts 1.1 and 1.2.

of the host state Party'.¹⁶⁴ As noted with respect to human rights, the Colombia model BIT includes two provisions (the first regarding free transfers and the second concerning denial of benefits) designed to encourage responsible investor conduct and compliance with host state laws.¹⁶⁵

7.56 Second, some treaties appear to condition protection on other defined characteristics that seek to promote responsible or sustainable investment. The Colombia–UAE BIT provides that an 'investor' refers to an enterprise or national of a state party 'that has made a *responsible* investment'.¹⁶⁶ The meaning of the term 'responsible', and the process for determining whether an investment is 'responsible', does not appear to be explicitly outlined in the text of the treaty; however, the phrasing suggests that whether or not an investment is 'responsible' seems to be a threshold question for determining whether the investor is covered by the treaty. As noted above, other treaties reportedly condition treaty coverage on the basis of investors' contribution to sustainable development.¹⁶⁷

7.57 Lastly, at least one treaty explicitly establishes a mechanism for obtaining covered investors' consent for the submission of counterclaims. The Colombia–UAE BIT provides that, in order for a covered investor to submit a claim to arbitration under the dispute resolution section of the BIT, the investor must submit its consent to 'the possibility of facing claims by the Respondent against them'.¹⁶⁸ While allowing the submission of counterclaims has, in recent cases, enabled states to raise environmental and human rights issues in the context of investor–state disputes,¹⁶⁹ submission of these claims is not without its challenges for host states and the public interest, particularly where the rights of investment-affected individuals and communities are affected by the dispute and/ or underlying investment.¹⁷⁰

7.58 What these developments regarding human rights and investor obligations more generally might mean for the interpretation and application of investment treaty standards remains unclear. As further explored in Chapters 10 and 24 of this *Yearbook*, investment tribunals have in many cases been reluctant to interpret and apply human rights law in investment disputes. Whether or how that position

---

¹⁶⁴ PACER Plus (n 21) ch 9 (Investment), art 5(1).
¹⁶⁵ Colombia model BIT, Freedom of Transfers and Denial of Benefits.
¹⁶⁶ Colombia–UAE BIT (n 22) art 2.1(b) (emphasis added).
¹⁶⁷ UNCTAD, 'Recent Developments in the International Investment Regime' (n 2) 5.
¹⁶⁸ Colombia–UAE BIT (n 22) art 13(3).
¹⁶⁹ See eg *Urbaser SA and Consorcio de Aguas Bilbao Bizkaia, Bilbao Biskaia Ur Partzuergoa v Argentine Republic*, ICSID Case No ARB/07/26; *Burlington Resources Inc v Republic of Ecuador*, ICSID Case No ARB/08/5 (formerly *Burlington Resources Inc and others v Republic of Ecuador and Empresa Estatal Petróleos del Ecuador (PetroEcuador)*).
¹⁷⁰ See eg Lise Johnson and Brooke Skardvedt Güven, 'The Settlement of Investment Disputes: A Discussion of Democratic Accountability and the Public Interest' *Investment Treaty News* (13 March 2017) <https://www.iisd.org/itn/2017/03/13/the-settlement-of-investment-disputes-a-discussion-of-democratic-accountability-and-the-public-interest-lise-johnson-and-brooke-skartvedt-guven/> accessed 4 June 2018.

would shift with the inclusion of more explicit references to human rights within the four corners of investment treaties, and with greater emphasis on the obligations of investors, has yet to be determined.

E. Conclusion

7.59 The political landscape that underpins the formulation of investment law and policy is changing: debates regarding the merits of investment treaties, and the impacts of international investment more generally, have attracted the attention of broader stakeholder groups, and the long-established public-facing positions of capital-importing and capital-exporting states appear, at least on the surface, to be shifting. Some of this shifting landscape can be seen in recent terminations and in the evolution of model treaties. The treaties reviewed in this chapter are, therefore, a narrow subset—including only countries who continue to pursue treaty making and who have concluded texts in 2017.

7.60 Of this small selection, however, it is perhaps notable that in the midst of the broader public policy discussions, and discontent, with certain substantive and procedural aspects of investment treaties and investor–state arbitration, many of the 2017 texts seem to be taking more time than one might expect to incorporate reforms. Although certain texts, some of which are highlighted herein, stand out for their attempts to integrate sustainability and protection of policy space into their revised provisions, most seem to reflect a degree of path dependency with respect to investment protection. Exploring why this might be the case, and the specific factors that may be influencing the slower pace of textual change (including, for example, path dependency and pressure groups, negotiating leverage, lack of awareness of challenges and best fit reforms) would require further inquiry. Identifying which factors, if any, may be at play could be instructive for those international organizations and others working to reform investment governance. Moreover, as the impacts of global challenges affecting international investment become more tangible, it will be interesting to observe whether negotiating states act with greater urgency to formulate investment laws at the global and national levels that effectively promote sustainable investment.

Table 7.1 2017 International Investment Agreements

S No	Full treaty name (when available)	Short name (* denotes agreement is publicly available as of May 2018)	Date signed	Date entered into force (status as of May 2018)
1.	Indonesia–Chile Comprehensive Economic Partnership Agreement	Chile–Indonesia CEPA	Signed 15 December 2017	Not in force
2.	The Comprehensive & Enhanced Partnership Agreement between the European Union and Armenia	EU–Armenia CEPA*	Signed 24 November 2017	Not in force
3.	Bilateral Investment Agreement for the Promotion and Protection of Investments Between the Government of the Republic of Colombia and the Government of the United Arab Emirates	Colombia–United Arab Emirates BIT*	Signed 13 November 2017	Not in force
4.	Agreement on Investment Among the Governments of the Hong Kong Special Administrative Region of the People's Republic of China and The Member States of The Association of Southeast Asian Nations	Hong Kong, China SAR–ASEAN (Association of South-East Asian Nations) Investment Agreement*	Signed 12 November 2017	Not in force
5.	Free Trade Agreement between Argentina and Chile	Argentina–Chile FTA	Signed 2 November 2017	Not in force
6.	Agreement between the Republic of Rwanda and the United Arab Emirates on the Promotion and Reciprocal Protection of Investments	Rwanda–United Arab Emirates BIT*	Signed 1 November 2017	Not in force
7.	Bilateral Investment Treaty between Turkey and Uzbekistan	Turkey–Uzbekistan BIT	Signed 25 October 2017	Not in force
8.	Bilateral Investment Treaty between the United Arab Emirates and the Maldives	United Arab Emirates–Maldives BIT	Signed 17 October 2017	Not in force
9.	Bilateral Investment Treaty between Turkey and Ukraine	Turkey–Ukraine BIT	Signed 9 October 2017	Not in force
10.	Mainland and Hong Kong Closer Economic Partnership Agreement	China–Hong Kong CEPA Investment Agreement*	Signed 28 June 2017	28 June 2017

Table 7.1: Continued

S No	Full treaty name (when available)	Short name (* denotes agreement is publicly available as of May 2018)	Date signed	Date entered into force (status as of May 2018)
11.	Bilateral Investment Treaty Between Burundi and Turkey	Burundi–Turkey BIT	Signed 14 June 2017	Not in force
12.	The Pacific Agreement on Closer Economic Relations Plus	PACER Plus*	Signed 14 June 2017	Not in force
13.	Free Trade Agreement Between China and Georgia	China–Georgia FTA*	Signed 13 May 2017	1 January 2018
14.	Agreement Between the Government of the Republic of Mauritius and the Government of the Republic of Cabo Verde for the Avoidance of Double Taxation and the Prevention of Fiscal Evasion with Respect to Taxes on Income	Cabo Verde–Mauritius BIT*	Signed 13 April 2017	Not in force
15.	Protocol for Cooperation and Investment Facilitation Between the Members of MERCOSUR	Intra-MERCOSUR Investment Facilitation Protocol*	Signed 7 April 2017	Not in force
16.	Bilateral Investment Treaty between Angola and the United Arab Emirates	Angola–United Arab Emirates BIT	Signed 5 April 2017	Not in force
17.	Bilateral Investment Treaty between Jordan and Saudi Arabia	Jordan–Saudi Arabia BIT*	Signed 27 March 2017	Not in force
18.	Bilateral Investment Treaty between the Islamic Republic of Iran and Luxembourg	Iran, Islamic Republic of–Luxembourg BIT	Signed 14 February 2017	Not in force
19.	Bilateral Investment Treaty Between the United Arab Emirates and Burundi	United Arab Emirates–Burundi BIT	Signed 6 February 2017	Not in force
20.	Agreement Between Japan and The State of Israel for The Liberalization, Promotion And Protection of Investment	Israel–Japan BIT*	Signed 1 February 2017	5 October 2017
21.	Bilateral Investment Treaty between Mozambique and Turkey	Mozambique–Turkey BIT	Signed 24 January 2017	Not in force
22.	Trade and Investment Framework Agreement Between Paraguay and the United States of America	Paraguay–United States of America TIFA	Signed 13 January 2017	Not in force

C. DEVELOPMENTS IN INVESTOR–STATE ARBITRATION

8

RECENT DEVELOPMENTS IN ISDS
Jurisdiction and Admissibility—Procedure and Conduct

Catharine Titi

A. Jurisdiction and Admissibility	8.01	C. Conclusions	8.29
B. Procedure and Conduct	8.20		

A. Jurisdiction and Admissibility

1. Existence of covered investment

In *Bear Creek v Peru*, the dispute revolved around a mining investment project close to Peru's border with Bolivia.[1] According to the Peruvian Constitution, foreigners can obtain rights to natural resources in border regions only after approval by the Peruvian authorities.[2] Jenny Karina Villavicencio, a Peruvian national and an employee of Bear Creek, had acquired the mining concession and, subsequently, Bear Creek exercised an option to acquire these rights with approval from the Peruvian authorities. Bear Creek conducted exploration work but the project was plagued by protests. In an effort to quell them, the Peruvian government revoked the rights effectively putting an end to the project. The respondent argued that the alleged investment was invalid under Peruvian law and that the tribunal had no jurisdiction.[3] The tribunal rejected the objection, noting that the Peruvian authorities had authorized the claimant to acquire mining rights. The claimant had acquired seven mining concessions and engaged in a considerable number of activities. The authorizations and other costs

8.01

---

[1] *Bear Creek Mining Corp v Peru*, ICSID Case No ARB/14/21, Award (30 November 2017).
[2] Peruvian Constitution, art 71.
[3] *Bear Creek* (n 1) paras 275ff.

incurred by the claimant meant that there was investment covered under the applicable investment treaty.[4] The respondent had also contended in the alternative that the claimant never acquired the rights to operate the mining project.[5] The tribunal determined that the claimant had an exclusive right to *seek* a right to mine and to pursue a mining project; this was sufficient to confirm the tribunal's jurisdiction.[6]

2. Nationality and foreign control

8.02 In *Kim v Uzbekistan*, the tribunal rejected Uzbekistan's jurisdictional objection that two of the claimants were not Kazakh nationals. The claimants had provided a copy of their passport, thus furnishing *prima facie* evidence that they fulfilled the nationality requirement.[7] The respondent had argued that according to the Kazakh Constitution and national laws it is not possible for a citizen to hold dual citizenship.[8] The tribunal noted that according to Kazakh law, it appeared that an individual may see his or her citizenship terminated but such termination would require a concrete act by the Kazakh Office of Internal Affairs.[9] The tribunal found no proof that the first of the two claimants did not have the Kazakh nationality.[10] With respect to the second claimant, his Kazakh nationality had in effect been terminated, but this happened after the crucial dates, that is after registration of the claim; such subsequent loss of his nationality was without significance for the tribunal's jurisdiction.[11]

8.03 In *Valores Mundiales v Venezuela*, the tribunal rejected the respondent's jurisdictional objection that the Spanish investors were owned and controlled by a Mexican company.[12] In particular, the respondent had argued that the claimants were 'paper companies', but the bilateral investment treaty (BIT) did not contain a denial-of-benefits clause. The tribunal reasoned that nationality depends on the national law of the state of nationality and, as the BIT did not add further criteria, the incorporation requirement was fulfilled, and the claimants were both investors under the BIT and nationals for the purposes of the Convention on the

---

[4] ibid paras 282–85.
[5] ibid paras 286ff.
[6] ibid paras 295–98.
[7] *Vladislav Kim and others v Uzbekistan*, ICSID Case No ARB/13/6, Decision on Jurisdiction (8 March 2017) para 182.
[8] ibid paras 195ff.
[9] ibid para 207.
[10] ibid paras 213–18.
[11] ibid paras 219–25.
[12] *Valores Mundiales, SL and Consorcio Andino SL v Venezuela*, ICSID Case No ARB/13/11, Award (25 July 2017) (unpublished). The award is discussed in Damien Charlotin, 'In Now-surfaced Valores Mundiales Award, Arbitrators Highlight why Venezuela's Denunciation of the ICSID Convention Did Not Prevent a Claimant from Later Filing for Arbitration' 10(23) *Investment Arbitration Reporter* (13 November 2017) 1.

Settlement of Investment Disputes between States and Nationals of Other States (ICSID Convention).[13]

In *Eskosol v Italy*, the tribunal discussed whether Eskosol's bankruptcy was sufficient to divest it of foreign control, although the company had been both solvent and under foreign control prior to the contested measures.[14] The tribunal reasoned that it would be inconsistent with the purpose of the ICSID Convention to render the investor 'ineligible to access its protections', because of its bankruptcy. That would have implied that a state could avoid scrutiny of its conduct, although it could be 'partially or wholly responsible for the financial straits that led to the bankruptcy', as was Eskosol's allegation in that case.[15] The tribunal concluded that Eskosol's bankruptcy did not deprive it of foreign control.[16]

8.04

3. Umbrella clause and most favoured nation treatment

In *WNC v Czech Republic*, the tribunal upheld the respondent's argument that the investor could not use the BIT's umbrella clause, since the allegedly breached share purchase agreement (SPA) was not signed by the investor but by its subsidiary.[17] The parties disagreed on whether an umbrella clause requires privity. The tribunal resolved that, even if umbrella clauses couched in general terms did not require privity, the BIT applicable *in casu* contained very precise language, requiring 'specific agreements' to be concluded between the host state and the foreign investor.[18] Consequently, the SPA was not a specific agreement and the umbrella clause was not applicable.[19] The tribunal elaborated further that the claimant's contention that umbrella clauses do not require privity does not find 'authoritative support' in investment case law; rather to the contrary, tribunals have consistently decided that they have no jurisdiction under umbrella clauses for contractual obligations undertaken by host states and the investors' locally incorporated subsidiaries.[20] Ultimately, the tribunal stated that, even if the treaty did not include a narrowly worded umbrella clause, it would still uphold the requirement of privity.[21] The tribunal also examined whether it had jurisdiction

8.05

---

[13] Charlotin (n 12) 18.
[14] *Eskosol SpA in liquidazione v Italy*, ICSID Case No ARB/15/50, Decision on Respondent's Application Under Rule 41(5) (20 March 2017) paras 100ff.
[15] ibid para 106.
[16] ibid para 108.
[17] *WNC Factoring Ltd (UK) v Czech Republic*, PCA Case No 2014-34, Award (22 February 2017) paras 312ff.
[18] *Contrast Supervision y Control SA v Costa Rica*, ICSID Case No ARB/12/4, Final Award (18 January 2017), where the same approach, ie textual analysis of the umbrella clause, led to the conclusion that the clause was broad enough to encompass contractual relationships between the state and the investor's subsidiary (paras 283ff).
[19] ibid paras 320ff.
[20] ibid para 334.
[21] ibid para 335.

under the umbrella clause on the basis of Czech law.[22] Eventually, it rejected this claim both because it considered that the investor had not proved the existence of the host state's implied duty of good faith in Czech law and because umbrella clauses do not cover general obligations under the law of the host state.[23]

8.06 In *WNC v Czech Republic*, the tribunal had further to determine whether the treaty's most favoured nation (MFN) clause allowed the claimant to rely on more favourable umbrella clauses. The tribunal observed that the BIT contained a particularly narrow arbitration clause granting it jurisdiction over some investment protections only, excluding the BIT's MFN clause.[24] Consequently, it rejected the investor's claims on the basis of the MFN standard.[25]

8.07 In *Teinver v Argentina*, the tribunal rejected the claimant's attempt to import an umbrella clause from the Argentina–US BIT into the Argentina–Spain BIT through the MFN standard. It reasoned that the 'critical words' '[i]n all matters governed by this Agreement' in the MFN provision related to 'the various rights or forms of protection contained in the individual provisions *of the Treaty*'.[26] The parties had selected not to draft an umbrella clause, and its incorporation into the Argentina–Spain BIT through the MFN treatment would result in creating new investment protections not provided for in the treaty.

8.08 In *Beijing Urban Construction v Yemen*, the tribunal was unconvinced by the claimant's efforts to enlarge jurisdiction by importing a wider range of investment protections through the BIT's MFN clause. It focused on the express territorial limits imposed by the BIT ('*treatment accorded to investors … in its territory*') and held that these words tether the MFN treatment to activities ' "in the territory" associated geographically with the investment'. This limitation did not allow the tribunal to expand the scope of the arbitration clause through the MFN standard.[27]

4. Scope of arbitration clause in Chinese BITs

8.09 In *Beijing Urban Construction v Yemen*, the applicable arbitration clause in the China–Yemen BIT gave investors access to arbitration to determine the amount of compensation due in case of expropriation.[28] The respondent argued in favour of a narrow interpretation that would limit the tribunal's jurisdiction to deciding on *quantum*.[29] As in *Tza Yap Shum v*

---

[22] ibid paras 342ff.
[23] ibid paras 342ff.
[24] ibid paras 349ff.
[25] ibid para 358.
[26] *Teinver SA, Transportes de Cercanías SA and Autobuses Urbanos del Sur SA v Argentina*, ICSID Case No ARB/09/1, Award (21 July 2017) para 884 (emphasis added).
[27] *Beijing Urban Construction Group Co Ltd v Yemen*, ICSID Case No ARB/14/30, Decision on Jurisdiction (31 May 2017) paras 112–21.
[28] ibid.
[29] ibid paras 48ff.

Peru,³⁰ the *Beijing Urban Construction* tribunal decided in favour of a broad interpretation of the BIT's arbitration clause allowing it to determine both liability and quantum, in light of the object and purpose of the BIT.³¹ In contrast, in *China Heilongjiang v Mongolia*, the tribunal decided in favour of a narrow interpretation of the arbitration clause in the China–Mongolia BIT, considering that interpretation only with respect to the amount of compensation—but not liability—gives *effet utile* to the provision; the tribunal subsequently declined jurisdiction.³²

5. Intra-EU BITs

In *WNC v Czech Republic*, the tribunal dismissed claims arising out of the UK–Czech Republic BIT.³³ Relying on earlier investment case law, it rejected the argument that the UK–Czech Republic BIT has been superseded by EU law when the Czech Republic joined the EU. In particular, it noted that 'tribunals have consistently held that EU law and BITs do not have the same subject matter on the basis that EU law does not offer equivalent procedural or substantive protections to foreign investors'.³⁴ It relied especially on the fact that EU law does not offer investors access to arbitration against their host state and it rejected the argument that EU member state courts have the same advantages as international arbitration.³⁵ The tribunal found no incompatibility between EU law and the BIT, considering that the BIT does not discriminate on nationality grounds against EU investors from third states and that the fact that 'the BIT affords certain rights not available to other EU investors does not make the BIT discriminatory'.³⁶ The tribunal added that, although there is no doctrine of binding precedent in international law, 'to the extent that they are based on sound legal reasoning, the decisions of tribunals in prior international law cases can provide useful insights to subsequent tribunals considering those issues'.³⁷ Notice that reference is made here not only to the case law of previous investment tribunals but tribunals applying international law more generally. Intra-EU investment treaty objections were also discussed at length and eventually dismissed in at least three other cases: *Blusun v Italy*,³⁸ *Eiser v Spain*,³⁹ and *PL Holdings v*

8.10

---

³⁰ *Sr Tza Yap Shum v Peru*, ICSID Case No ARB/07/6, Decision on Jurisdiction and Competence (19 June 2009) para 188.
³¹ *Beijing Urban Construction* (n 27) paras 78ff, see also para 87.
³² *China Heilongjiang International Economic & Technical Cooperative Corp., Beijing Shougang Mining Investment Company Ltd., and Qinhuangdaoshi Qinlong International Industrial Co Ltd. v Mongolia*, PCA Case No 2010-20, Award (30 June 2017) paras 423–54.
³³ *WNC Factoring Ltd* (n 17).
³⁴ ibid para 298.
³⁵ ibid paras 298 and 300.
³⁶ ibid para 309.
³⁷ ibid para 310.
³⁸ *Blusun SA, Jean-Pierre Lecorcier and Michael Stein v Italy*, ICSID Case No ARB/14/3, Award (27 December 2016). This award was not public until a few months later.
³⁹ *Eiser Infrastructure Limited and Energía Solar Luxembourg Sàrl v Spain*, ICSID Case No ARB/13/36 Award (4 May 2017).

Poland.⁴⁰ A related significant development needs to be stressed before closing this paragraph. On 6 March 2018, the Court of Justice of the European Union held an intra-EU BIT to be incompatible with the law of the European Union.⁴¹ The impact of this judgment is yet to be fully appreciated.⁴²

6. Counterclaims

8.11 In *Urbaser v Argentina*, in an apparent first,⁴³ a tribunal upheld jurisdiction over the respondent's counterclaim that the investors had violated their obligations with respect to the human right to water.⁴⁴ *In casu*, the claimants had argued that the asymmetric nature of BITs prevents host states from 'invoking any right based on such a treaty, including through the submission of a counterclaim'.⁴⁵ The tribunal rejected this argument, noting that the BIT's arbitration clause was neutral as to the identities of claimant and respondent making simple reference to disputes arising 'between the parties'.⁴⁶ This meant that, in contrast with other narrower arbitration clauses, the applicable provision indicated that 'either the investor or the host State can be a party submitting a dispute in connection with an investment to arbitration'.⁴⁷ The claimants had further argued that they had never consented to Argentina bringing a counterclaim and that the scope of their consent was limited to the damage caused to their investment.⁴⁸ The tribunal also rejected this claim. It remarked that the claimants' acceptance of the offer to arbitrate did not specifically exclude eventual counterclaims.⁴⁹ In addition, if the scope of the claimants' acceptance were narrower than Argentina's offer to arbitrate, there would be no valid arbitration agreement and the tribunal would lack jurisdiction.⁵⁰ The claimants had also argued that Argentina had not complied with the BIT's limited local remedies clause. The tribunal described this claim as 'absurd', *inter alia* because the claimants themselves had failed to comply with that requirement and had successfully argued that they could bypass it.⁵¹ Having upheld

---

⁴⁰ *PL Holdings Sàrl v Poland*, SCC Case No V 2014/163, Partial Award (28 June 2017).
⁴¹ Case C-284/16 *Slovak Republic v Achmea BV* (ECJ, 6 March 2018).
⁴² For further discussion on this see Chapter 16.
⁴³ Jarrod Hepburn, 'In a First, BIT tribunal Finds that it has Jurisdiction to Hear a Host State's Counterclaim Related to Investor's Alleged Violation of International Human Rights Obligations' 10(2) *Investment Arbitration Reporter* (23 January 2017).
⁴⁴ *Urbaser SA and Consorcio de Aguas Bilbao Bizkaia, Bilbao Biskaia Ur Partzuergoa v Argentina*, ICSID Case No ARB/07/26, Award (8 December 2016).
⁴⁵ ibid para 1143.
⁴⁶ ibid.
⁴⁷ ibid.
⁴⁸ ibid para 1145.
⁴⁹ ibid para 1146.
⁵⁰ ibid para 1147.
⁵¹ ibid para 1149.

jurisdiction over Argentina's counterclaim,[52] the tribunal eventually rejected it on its merits.[53]

7. Energy Charter Treaty claims against Russia

In 'second wave' Yukos arbitrations against Russia, two tribunals held that Russia is bound by the provisional application of the Energy Charter Treaty (ECT). Russia signed the ECT in 1994 and in 2009 it notified the ECT Depositary that it did not intend to ratify it.[54] In *Yukos Capital SARL v Russia*, a United Nations Commission on International Trade Law (UNCITRAL) tribunal held by majority that the ECT is provisionally applicable to Russia; it appears that arbitrator Brigitte Stern dissented.[55] In *Luxtona v Russia*, the tribunal dismissed Russia's objections relating to the provisional application of the ECT and denial of benefits.[56]

8.12

8. Denunciation of the ICSID Convention

In *Valores Mundiales v Venezuela*, the tribunal found that Venezuela's denunciation of the ICSID Convention did not prevent the claimant from accessing ICSID arbitration.[57] Pursuant to Articles 71 and 72 of the ICSID Convention, denunciation takes effect six months after written notice of denunciation and it does not affect rights or obligations 'arising out of consent to the jurisdiction of the Centre' before such denunciation. Venezuela gave notice of its denunciation on 24 January 2012. In *Valores Mundiales v Venezuela*, the respondent argued that there was no perfected consent; the claimant had sent the notice of dispute in

8.13

---

[52] ibid para 1155.

[53] ibid para 1221. See also Jarrod Hepburn, '2017 Developments in Investment Treaty Arbitration' in Lisa E Sachs, Lise Johnson, and Jesse Coleman (eds), *Yearbook on International Investment Law and Policy 2017* (OUP 2018).

[54] Sergey Ripinsky, 'Russia' in Chester Brown (ed), *Commentaries on Selected Model Investment Treaties* (OUP 2013) 596.

[55] *Yukos Capital Sarl v the Russian Federation*, UNCITRAL, Interim Award on Jurisdiction (18 January 2017) (unpublished). See Luke Eric Peterson, 'In Second-wave Yukos Arbitration, McLachlan and Rowley See Russia as Provisionally Bound by Energy Charter Treaty' 10(4) *Investment Arbitration Reporter* (20 February 2017).

[56] *Luxtona Limited v the Russian Federation*, UNCITRAL, Decision on Jurisdiction (22 March 2017) (unpublished). See Jarrod Hepburn, 'Interim Award in Luxtona v. Russia Arbitration Comes to Light, Offering New Reasoning on Provisional Application of Energy Charter Treaty and Russia's Attempted Denial of Benefits to this Yukos Shareholder' 11(1) *Investment Arbitration Reporter* (8 January 2018) 8–16. Proceedings on the merits are currently suspended, see Damien Charlotin and Luke Eric Peterson, 'Russia Set-aside Round-up: Swiss Court Rules that Russia Does Not Need to Post Security for Costs as it Seeks to Set Aside Crimea BIT Award; Set-Aside Applications Continue in First and Second Wave Yukos Cases' (2017) Investment Arbitration Reporter < https://www.iareporter.com/iar-search/?iarsearch=Russia+set-aside+round-up%3A+Swiss+court+rules+that+Russia+does+not+need+to+post+security+for+costs+as+it+seeks+to+set+aside+Crimea+BIT+award%3B+set-aside+applications+continue+in+first+and+second+wave+Yukos+cases&iar_dt=5&cdfrom=&cdto=> accessed 1 May 2018.

[57] *Valores Mundiales, SL and Consorcio Andino SL v Venezuela*, ICSID Case No ARB/13/11, Award (25 July 2017) (unpublished). See Charlotin (n 12) 14ff.

November 2011 and the BIT included a mandatory six-month waiting clause; by the time the waiting period had come to its term, Venezuela had denounced the ICSID Convention. The tribunal held that the BIT's waiting clause was only relevant—if at all—to the commencement of the arbitration proceedings but not to consent. It added that the notice of dispute expressly mentioned the claimants' consent to arbitration.[58] Another jurisdictional objection put forward by Venezuela concerned the allegation of expropriation through an Administrative Order enacted in January 2013, one year after Venezuela's denunciation of the ICSID Convention. The tribunal remarked that the claimants had already invoked the investment treaty's expropriation provisions in the notice of dispute and that it would make no sense to ask them to file a new claim every time Venezuela adopted a new measure relating to the dispute.[59]

8.14 In *Fábrica de Vidrios v Venezuela*, the parties were at loggerheads over the meaning of 'consent' in Article 72 of the ICSID Convention; the respondent argued that Article 72 requires perfected consent and the claimant that a party's own consent to the jurisdiction of ICSID suffices.[60] *In casu*, perfected consent only came into existence on 20 July 2012, when the investor registered its claim. After canvassing the issue at considerable length, the tribunal concluded that 'consent' in Article 72 of the ICSID Convention is perfected consent.[61] The tribunal observed that Articles 71 and 72 of the ICSID Convention are intended, *inter alia*, to facilitate an 'orderly exit' from the ICSID Convention in case of denunciation. If Article 72 of the ICSID Convention were to be interpreted to cover not only perfected but also *potential* agreements to arbitrate, a state that denounced the Convention could be respondent 'in an unlimited and unforeseeable number of future ICSID arbitrations for decades after its denunciation …. This would be antithetical to an orderly exit from the ICSID Convention.'[62]

8.15 The award in *Fábrica de Vidrios v Venezuela* breaks with other arbitral decisions on the effects of denunciation of the ICSID Convention, including the award in *Blue Bank v Venezuela*. In the latter case, the tribunal held, *inter alia*, that the relevant date for consent is the date when the claimant filed its request for arbitration, rather than the date when the claimant's request was registered by the ICSID secretariat;[63] and that effective interpretation of Article 71 of the ICSID Convention requires that the state's offer of arbitration last for six months following the notice

---

[58] Charlotin (n 12) 16.
[59] ibid 17.
[60] *Fábrica de Vidrios Los Andes, CA and Owens-Illinois de Venezuela, CA v Venezuela*, ICSID Case No ARB/12/21, Award (13 November 2017) para 272.
[61] ibid paras 273ff.
[62] ibid para 289.
[63] *Blue Bank International & Trust (Barbados) Ltd v Venezuela*, ICSID Case No ARB/12/20 (26 April 2017) paras 115–16.

of denunciation.⁶⁴ Having therefore found that consent had been perfected before Venezuela's denunciation of the ICSID Convention took effect, the majority of the tribunal considered that it was not necessary to discuss Article 72 of the ICSID Convention, since the latter addresses only 'the post-termination survival of certain of a State's rights or obligations'.⁶⁵

Similarly, in *Transban v Venezuela*, a tribunal majority found that nothing in Article 72 debarred investors from accessing arbitration before Venezuela's denunciation took effect, that is in the six months following denunciation.⁶⁶ *In casu*, the majority accepted a scanned copy of the notice of arbitration as consent 'in writing'. It remarked that emails did not exist at the time when the ICSID Convention came into being and cited the evolutionary interpretation of treaties by the International Court of Justice (ICJ). The majority concluded that it had temporal jurisdiction over the claim, with Santiago Torres Bernandez dissenting.⁶⁷ Nonetheless, a different tribunal majority eventually declined jurisdiction on unrelated grounds.⁶⁸ 8.16

9. Corruption and other illegality

In *Spentex v Uzbekistan*, the tribunal decided that multi-million dollar payments in consultancy fees made by the claimant's parent company prior to acquisition of the investment constituted corruption.⁶⁹ The finding led the tribunal to dismiss all claims, although the issue of whether this went to jurisdiction or admissibility divided the tribunal.⁷⁰ In *Bear Creek v Peru*, the tribunal rejected the respondent's argument of illegality and bad faith of the investment, since the treaty expressly provided for special formalities that may be imposed by the host state, but no express legality requirement had actually been imposed by Peru. Illegality was therefore not relevant to jurisdiction. However, the tribunal noted that illegality or lack of good faith may be relevant to the merits.⁷¹ 8.17

---

⁶⁴ ibid paras 118ff.
⁶⁵ ibid paras 108ff.
⁶⁶ *Transban Investments Corp v Venezuela*, ICSID Case No ARB/12/24 (unpublished). The award and separate opinions are discussed in Jarrod Hepburn, 'Tomka-chaired Tribunal Declines Jurisdiction over Transban Claim—but Majority Diverges from Fabrica Tribunal, and Sees No Problem with Investor Consent Given after Venezuela's ICSID Denunciation Notice' 10(24) *Investment Arbitration Reporter* (27 November 2017) 15–20.
⁶⁷ Hepburn, 'Tomka-chaired Tribunal Declines Jurisdiction over Transban Claim' (n 66) 15–20.
⁶⁸ ibid 18.
⁶⁹ *Spentex Netherlands, BV v Uzbekistan*, ICSID Case No ARB/13/26, Award (27 December 2016) (unpublished). The award is discussed in Vladislav Djanic, 'In Newly Unearthed Uzbekistan Ruling, Exorbitant Fees Promised to Consultants on Eve of Tender Process are Viewed by Tribunal as Evidence of Corruption, Leading to Dismissal of all Claims under Dutch BIT' 10(13) *Investment Arbitration Reporter* (26 June 2017) 3, 3ff.
⁷⁰ Djanic (n 69) 5ff.
⁷¹ *Bear Creek* (n 1) paras 299–324.

10. Abuse of right

8.18 In a rare finding, in *Orascom v Algeria*, the tribunal held that the investor's 'pursuit of its claims' constituted an abuse of right under the circumstances.[72] Investment tribunals have sometimes found an abuse of right when an investment was restructured to benefit from a treaty's dispute settlement clause in situations where a dispute was foreseeable.[73] A notable recent example in this vein is the award in *Philip Morris v Australia*.[74] However, in *Orascom v Algeria* the facts were different. The investor, who controlled different entities in a vertical chain of ownership, sought to impugn host state measures by instituting various claims at different levels of the chain for the same harm.[75] The tribunal reasoned that the host state had not accepted to be challenged 'multiple times by various entities under the same control that are part of the vertical chain in relation to the same investment, the same measures and the same harm'.[76] It held that such conduct does not serve the purpose of investment treaties; rather, it creates a risk of contradictory decisions and multiple recovery.[77] It concluded that such abuse of rights was (an additional) ground for the inadmissibility of the claims.[78] The award in *Orascom v Algeria* could have a significant impact, since it identified as abuse of right a situation that can regularly arise in investment arbitration. The award has already been invoked in anti-suit injunction proceedings in India in the context of the *Vodafone v India II* dispute,[79] where the High Court of Delhi temporarily enjoined the investor not to pursue the arbitration because that would constitute 'abuse of process of law'.[80]

11. Jurisdictional objections in the merits phase

8.19 In *PL Holdings v Poland*, a tribunal operating under the rules of the Stockholm Chamber of Commerce (SCC) considered jurisdictional objections in the merits phase, notwithstanding their belatedness. The respondent

---

[72] *Orascom TMT Investments Sàrl v Algeria*, ICSID Case No. ARB/12/35, Award (31 May 2017) paras 539ff.

[73] ibid para 540.

[74] *Philip Morris Asia Ltd v Australia*, UNCITRAL, PCA Case No 2012-12, Award on Jurisdiction and Admissibility (17 December 2015).

[75] *Orascom* (n 72) paras 542ff.

[76] ibid para 542.

[77] ibid para 543.

[78] ibid para 545.

[79] *Vodafone Group Plc and Vodafone Consolidated Holdings Limited v India*, UNCITRAL, 2017. For more on the case, see <http://investmentpolicyhub.unctad.org/ISDS/Details/819> accessed 24 March 2018.

[80] *Union of India v Vodafone Group Plc United Kingdom*, CS(OS) 383/2017, Judgment, High Court of Delhi (22 August 2017). The other dispute is *Vodafone International Holdings BV v India*, PCA Case No 2016-35. The temporary restraint has now been lifted, see Ridhi Kabra, 'Indian Supreme Court Allows Appointment of Tribunal President in Vodafone's Second Arbitration against India, but Restrains Arbitration Hearings until January' 10(26) *Investment Arbitration Reporter* (25 December 2017).

had argued *inter alia* that the purportedly applicable BIT had been superseded by EU law when Poland joined the EU. The tribunal remarked that the respondent's objection was untimely and that the tribunal might be justified in considering that it had been abandoned.[81] Nonetheless, the tribunal preferred to examine the objection, both because it related to its jurisdiction and because it concerned 'sovereign assertions made not only by Poland but also by the European Union'.[82] The objection was eventually dismissed on its merits.[83]

B. Procedure and Conduct

1. Arbitrator challenges

In *Pey Casado v Chile*, the Chairman of the ICSID Administrative Council rejected the claimant's request to disqualify two arbitrators, Franklin Berman and VV Veeder.[84] The challenge, which was rejected for untimeliness, had primarily relied on the discovery that Alan Boyle, a barrister at Essex Court Chambers in London, had represented Chile in a case against Bolivia before the ICJ. The claimant took issue with Berman and Veeder, also barristers at Essex Court Chambers, for their alleged failure to disclose this connection between a member of their chambers and the respondent state.[85] A new challenge to Veeder was made a few days later,[86] followed by a request to disqualify Berman from deciding on the challenge.[87] In a letter addressed to the Secretary-General of ICSID, Berman himself suggested that the challenge to Veeder should not be decided by himself and his unchallenged co-arbitrator but by the ICSID Administrative Council. He considered that, were he to decide on the challenge, any ruling he made would be open to an accusation of lack of objectivity and partiality, no less so because he himself had been challenged and because both the old and new challenges targeted 'the relationship between members of the same Barristers' Chambers'.[88] A new request

8.20

---

[81] *PL Holdings* (n 40) paras 298 and 306.
[82] ibid paras 298 and 307.
[83] ibid paras 310ff.
[84] *Victor Pey Casado and President Allende Foundation v Chile*, ICSID Case No ARB/98/2, Decision on the Proposal to Disqualify Sir Franklin Berman QC and Mr V. V. Veeder QC (21 February 2017).
[85] Jarrod Hepburn, 'The NeverEnding Story: Latest Developments in the Pey Casado v. Chile Case Include Arbitrator Challenge Ruling; Another Challenge; and a Slowed Rectification Process' 10(5) *Investment Arbitration Reporter* (6 March 2017) 8–9.
[86] *Victor Pey Casado and President Allende Foundation v Chile*, ICSID Case No ARB/98/ Claimants' Request for Disqualification of the Arbitrator Mr. V.V. Veeder (23 February 2017).
[87] ibid.
[88] The letter is available here <https://www.italaw.com/sites/default/files/case-documents/italaw8484_0.pdf> accessed 24 March 2018.

to disqualify Berman himself followed a few days later.[89] The Chairman of the ICSID Administrative Council eventually rejected both requests.[90]

8.21 In *Tethyan Copper v Pakistan*, the respondent challenged arbitrator Stanimir Alexandrov. In the case, the claimant's evaluation experts, the Brattle Group, advocated a variation of the discounted cash flow (DCF) method that had formed part of Peru's case in *Bear Creek v Peru*, where Alexandrov acted as counsel for Peru.[91] Pakistan indicated its preference for the challenge to be decided by a third party and for the co-arbitrators to comply with such decision, stressing the long duration of the proceeding and the 'convivial' ties that can grow among arbitrators.[92] In an unexpected twist, Alexandrov's challenge in *Tethyan Copper v Pakistan* led Spain to lodge a complaint in the *Eiser v Spain* case, currently at annulment. Through *Tethyan Copper v Pakistan*, Spain discovered that the arbitrator had been working with the Brattle Group, Eiser's evaluation experts.[93] While it was late for a request for disqualification in *Eiser v Spain*, Spain challenged Alexandrov in *SolEs Badajoz v Spain*, SolEs Badajoz having also engaged the Brattle Group as experts.[94] The co-arbitrators called to decide on the latter challenge declared themselves 'equally divided' within the meaning of Article 58 of the ICSID Convention and left the decision to ICSID.[95] Alexandrov eventually stepped down explaining that he was reluctant to continue to serve on a tribunal where one of his co-arbitrators doubts his impartiality.[96] The foregoing cases demonstrate a willingness to delegate to ICSID the decision on disqualification, allowing the unchallenged co-arbitrators to 'sidestep one of the more thankless tasks in investment treaty arbitration'.[97]

8.22 In *Iskandar Safa and Akram Safa v Hellenic Republic*, a dispute over a shipyard brought under the Greece–Lebanon BIT, a challenge to Brigitte Stern, appointed

---

[89] Available here <https://www.italaw.com/sites/default/files/case-documents/italaw8486_0.pdf> accessed 24 March 2018.

[90] *Victor Pey Casado and President Allende Foundation v Chile*, ICSID Case No ARB/98, Decision on the Proposals to Disqualify Mr V.V. Veeder and Sir Franklin Berman QC (13 April 2017).

[91] *Tethyan Copper Company Pty Limited v Pakistan*, ICSID Case No ARB/12/1. See Luke Eric Peterson, 'As Damages Phase Unfolds in Pakistan Mining Case, a Challenge is Lodged against Stanimir Alexandrov—Citing his client's Alleged Interest in a Rarely-used Valuation Method under Scrutiny' 10(15) *Investment Arbitration Reporter* (24 July 2017) 14–15.

[92] Peterson, 'As Damages Phase Unfolds in Pakistan Mining Case' (n 91) 14–15.

[93] Luke Eric Peterson, 'As Spain Seeks to Annul Energy Charter Treaty Award, Government Hires Outside Law Firm and Complains about Arbitrator's Relationship with Damages Experts' 10(22) *Investment Arbitration Reporter* (30 October 2017) 15–16.

[94] Luke Eric Peterson, 'Co-arbitrators Declare Themselves to be "Equally Divided" on Challenge to Third Tribunal Member, thus Putting ICSID in the Driver's Seat' 10(22) *Investment Arbitration Reporter* (7 August 2016) 15.

[95] ibid.

[96] Jarrod Hepburn, 'While Rejecting Merits of Pending Challenge, Alexandrov Resigns, Citing the Fact that One of his Two Co-arbitrators Has Seeming Doubts of his Impartiality; Joubin-Bret Also Steps Aside to Take Key UNCITRAL Post' 10(22) *Investment Arbitration Reporter* (30 October 2017) 14.

[97] Luke Eric Peterson, 'Sir Frank Berman Seeks to Recuse Himself from Deciding Challenge to Fellow Arbitrator and then Pey Casado Claimants Challenge Him Again' 10(6) *Investment Arbitration Reporter* (20 March 2017) 13.

by the respondent, failed.⁹⁸ According to the *Investment Arbitration Reporter*, Stern has faced the biggest number of arbitrator challenges but has never been disqualified; in *Murphy v Ecuador*, she 'and a colleague' both resigned.⁹⁹

2. Bifurcation

Contrasting decisions have been taken in relation to bifurcation of proceedings in two arbitrations under the Turkey–Libya BIT in relation to construction projects thwarted following political unrest in Libya.¹⁰⁰ In *Güriş v Libya*, the respondent sought to bifurcate the proceedings, denying the tribunal's jurisdiction on the argument *inter alia* that the dispute predates the BIT's entry into force. Libya raised an additional objection based on the existence of an investment. The tribunal held that deciding on the existence of an investment would require an investigation into the claimant's activities which would be closely related to the merits phase. In addition, the tribunal considered that determining the exact moment in time when the alleged facts took place would require a complicated inquiry and bifurcation would not be helpful. Consequently, it dismissed the request for bifurcation.¹⁰¹ By contrast, in *Nurol Construction v Libya*, the tribunal accepted bifurcation 'on questions of material and temporal jurisdiction' on the understanding that 'whether the claimant holds an investment in Libya, and when exactly the dispute arose in relation to the BIT's entry-into-force, *could* entirely dispose of the Nurol case, justifying bifurcation even despite some factual overlap with merits issues'.¹⁰² In *Lao Holdings and Sanum v Laos*, the tribunal accepted that it had the power to reconsider its earlier decision not to bifurcate, if circumstances so warranted.¹⁰³ While rejecting the request to bifurcate proceedings as between jurisdiction and liability, the tribunal agreed to separate the proceedings with respect to quantum.¹⁰⁴

8.23

---

⁹⁸ *Iskandar Safa and Akram Safa v Greece*, ICSID Case No ARB/16/20, registered 5 July 2016. The decision to reject the challenge to arbitrator Brigitte Stern is not at the time of writing public but it is reported on the ICSID website <https://icsid.worldbank.org/en/Pages/cases/casedetail.aspx?CaseNo=ARB/16/20> accessed 24 March 2018 and in Investment Arbitration Reporter, 'Challenge to Brigitte Stern is Rejected in Greece Arbitration; Effort Was Latest of at least 8 Attempts by Claimants to Dislodge her from Tribunals' 10(6) *Investment Arbitration Reporter* (20 May 2017).

⁹⁹ *Murphy Exploration & Production Company—International v Ecuador (II)*, PCA Case No 2012-16. See further *Investment Arbitration Reporter* (n 98).

¹⁰⁰ The cases are *Güriş İnşaat ve Mühendislik AŞ v Libya*, Procedural Order (29 June 2017) and *Nurol İnşaat ve Ticaret AŞ v Libya*. Very little is known about the two cases. They are discussed in Ridhi Kabra, Jarrod Hepburn, and Luke Eric Peterson, 'As Series of Turkey-Libya BIT Arbitrations Proceed, Tribunals are Taking Different Approaches to Libya's Contention that Treaty's Entry-into-force Rules Out Civil War-related Claims' 10(20) *Investment Arbitration Reporter* (2 October 2017) 27–30.

¹⁰¹ Kabra, Hepburn, and Peterson (n 100) 28–29.

¹⁰² ibid 29–30.

¹⁰³ *Lao Holdings NV and Sanum Investments Limited v Laos*, ICSID Case No ARB(AF)/16/2 and ICSID Case No ADHOC/17/1, Procedural Order No 2 (23 October 2017) para 41.

¹⁰⁴ ibid paras 46 and 52.

3. Privilege

8.24 In *Niko Resources v Bangladesh*, a contractual arbitration under the ICSID Convention, the tribunals[105] rejected the respondent's request that Niko produce the results of an internal investigation into its alleged corruption in Bangladesh.[106] The investigation, commissioned by Niko, was conducted by Deloitte in 2009. The question of privilege was governed by Canadian law, and the tribunals considered appointing an expert on Canadian privilege law to inspect the documents but eventually decided against it; the parties had argued in depth the relevant rules and principles of Canadian law and the issue could be decided without a need to inspect the documents in question.[107] The tribunals distinguished between solicitor–client privilege and litigation privilege in Canadian law.[108] While solicitor–client privilege aims to protect the confidential relationship between counsel and client, litigation privilege drives at the process of litigation; it aims to facilitate investigation and preparation of an adversarial process.[109] The tribunals found that the investigation had been conducted to prepare Niko's defence in legal proceedings relating to allegations of corruption in Bangladesh and the claimant's defence in the arbitration proceeding was closely linked to that investigation.[110] It was therefore covered by the litigation privilege in Canadian law and the claimant could assert it against the respondent's request for production of the documents.[111]

4. Power to reconsider pre-award decisions under the ICSID Convention

8.25 A procedural question that gained currency in recent disputes is whether a tribunal has the power to reconsider a pre-award decision under the ICSID Convention.[112] In *ConocoPhillips v Venezuela*, the issue had already been addressed twice, with two tribunal majorities expressing the view that pre-award decisions were *res iudicata*

---

[105] ICSID Case Nos ARB/10/11 and ARB/10/18 are heard by two identically composed tribunals.

[106] *Niko Resources (Bangladesh) Ltd v Bangladesh Petroleum Exploration and others*, ICSID Case Nos ARB/10/11 and ARB/10/18, Procedural Order No 22 (27 July 2017). See further Jarrod Hepburn, 'Niko v. Bangladesh: In a New Ruling, Arbitrators Reject Respondent's Bid to Obtain Documents from Internal Corruption Investigation; Deloitte Report is Deemed Privileged under Local Law' (2017) 10 Investment Arbitration Reporter 24, 24ff.

[107] *Niko Resources* (n 106) para 14.

[108] ibid paras 25ff.

[109] ibid para 25 and paras 64ff.

[110] ibid paras 88 and 98.

[111] ibid paras 88ff.

[112] For a detailed discussion, see Catharine Titi, '*Res Iudicata* and Interlocutory Decisions under the ICSID Convention: Antinomies over the Power of Tribunals to Review' (2018) 33 (2) ICSID Review—Foreign Investment Law Journal <https://academic.oup.com/icsidreview/advance-article-abstract/doi/10.1093/icsidreview/siy002/5023828?redirectedFrom=fulltext>.

and could not be revisited and two dissenting arbitrators (Georges Abi-Saab and Andreas Bucher) arguing in favour of the tribunal's power to reopen.[113] In an apparent volte-face, a newly constituted tribunal[114] addressed Venezuela's Third Application for Reconsideration and ultimately reviewed the 2013 Decision on Jurisdiction and the Merits (subject of the initial request for reconsideration) on its merits.[115] It did so, while using ambiguous language about its formal power to reopen the decision ('irrespective of whether the Tribunal would have, or does not have the power to reconsider the Application').[116] The tribunal examined Venezuela's application insomuch as it related to its purported failure to negotiate with the claimant on the basis of fair market value.[117] Eventually, after reviewing Venezuela's conduct during the negotiations, the tribunal dismissed the request.

8.26 The power of ICSID tribunals to reopen interlocutory decisions was also the subject of another proceeding. In *Burlington v Ecuador*, the respondent had requested a reconsideration of an earlier decision contending that the tribunal had erred as a matter of law and that it had been misled by the claimant and reached its decision on the basis of incomplete facts.[118] The tribunal decided that pre-award decisions are not *res iudicata*.[119] To reach this conclusion, it relied on the 'structure or architecture' of the ICSID Convention,[120] and notably 'the requirement for incorporation of earlier decisions into the award, the absence of remedies against these decisions, and the fact that the Contracting States' obligation to recognize and enforce only attaches to the award, not to earlier decisions'.[121] The respondent's motion for reconsideration was eventually dismissed on its merits.[122] The tribunal reasoned that the fact that decisions lack *res iudicata* effect does not necessarily mean that they must be reopened.[123] It argued that, irrespective of *res iudicata*, the rationale for this decision is 'obvious':

> a contrary view would defeat the purpose of efficient dispute settlement, entailing constant re-litigation of issues already resolved, with unavoidable adverse consequences in terms of increased costs and length of proceedings. In addition, the

---

[113] *ConocoPhillips Petrozuata BV, ConocoPhillips Hamaca BV and ConocoPhillips Gulf of Paria BV v Venezuela*, ICSID Case No ARB/07/30, Decision on Respondent's Request for Reconsideration (10 March 2014 and 9 February 2016).

[114] Eduardo Zuleta replaced Kenneth J Keith as President. Kenneth J Keith alongside L Yves Fortier were the arbitrators who formed the tribunal majorities that had rejected the tribunal's power to reopen its earlier decision.

[115] *ConocoPhillips Petrozuata BV, ConocoPhillips Hamaca BV and ConocoPhillips Gulf of Paria BV v Venezuela*, ICSID Case No ARB/07/30, Interim Decision (17 January 2017).

[116] ibid para 62.

[117] ibid paras 94ff.

[118] *Burlington Resources Inc v Ecuador*, ICSID Case No ARB/08/5, Decision on Reconsideration and Award (7 February 2017) paras 80ff.

[119] ibid paras 86ff.

[120] ibid para 86.

[121] ibid para 89.

[122] ibid paras 81ff.

[123] ibid para 90.

possibility of re-litigating issues would jeopardize legal certainty and ultimately undermine the confidence of the users in the system.[124]

8.27 Outside the ICSID framework, the question of reopening an *award* was raised in *Murphy Exploration v Ecuador II*, an arbitration conducted under the 1976 UNCITRAL Arbitration Rules. Unlike the ICSID Convention, the UNCITRAL Arbitration Rules do not provide for any 'pre-award' decisions.[125] The tribunal rejected the investor's motion to reconsider the respondent's liability, since it had already decided upon the issue in its Partial Final Award.[126] The tribunal reasoned that had it acquiesced to the investor's request, there would be 'an unnecessary and duplicative re-examination of the merits'.[127]

5. Power of ICSID tribunals to seek assistance from domestic courts

8.28 In *Niko Resources v Bangladesh*, the arbitrators addressed the power of ICSID tribunals to seek assistance from domestic courts.[128] The parties joined issue on whether an ICSID tribunal could turn to a municipal court to request support in the production of evidence.[129] The tribunals were mindful of the fact that the ICSID Convention did not confer an express power on tribunals to seek assistance from domestic courts and that the latter had no obligation to offer such assistance if sought.[130] Nonetheless, they held that if a request under Article 43(a) of the ICSID Convention were unavailing, and in light of Article 44 of the Convention, a tribunal could request assistance in the collection of evidence from a municipal court or it could authorize a party to do so directly.[131] Presently, the tribunals were unconvinced that there was a sufficient reason to exercise that power.[132] The decision points to the complex relationship between investment tribunals and local courts. It will be recalled that an earlier decision in *Niko Resources v Bangladesh* asserted the tribunals' exclusive jurisdiction over the matters validly brought before them and essentially issued anti-suit injunction orders against courts in Bangladesh.[133]

---

[124] ibid para 91.
[125] See UNCITRAL Arbitration Rules of 1976, art 32(1) and (2).
[126] *Murphy Exploration and Production Company International v Ecuador [II]*, PCA Case No 2012-16, Final Award (10 February 2017) para 32.
[127] ibid para 32.
[128] *Niko Resources* (n 106).
[129] ibid para 54.
[130] ibid para 69.
[131] ibid para 70.
[132] ibid para 71.
[133] *Niko Resources (Bangladesh) Ltd v Bangladesh Petroleum Exploration and others*, ICSID Case Nos ARB/10/11 and ARB/10/18, Decision Pertaining to the Exclusivity of the Tribunals' Jurisdiction (19 July 2016) para 20.

C. Conclusions

The review of arbitral decisions delivered in the last year for jurisdiction, admissibility, procedure, and conduct reveals both the breath and the variation of the issues that arise in investment arbitration. Some of them have remained on the agenda for some time. This is the case of contestations about the existence of a covered investment or about an investor's nationality, but also arbitrator challenges—with an apparent preference to defer to ICSID for a decision on disqualification. Other issues, such as application of the MFN standard to the treaty's arbitration clause, have featured less prominently in this recent case law. Tribunals continue to reach different solutions, such as in relation to the scope of the arbitration clause of old generation Chinese BITs or the effects of denunciation of the ICSID Convention. Last year's decisions also show that some issues increasingly find uniform solutions. The paradigmatic example is the consistent dismissal of objections in relation to intra-EU BITs. Finally, some decisions have a certain element of novelty about them, such as the treatment of counterclaims.

8.29

9

2017 DEVELOPMENTS IN INVESTMENT TREATY ARBITRATION

Jarrod Hepburn

A. Introduction	9.01	D. Remedies and Settlements	9.42
B. Merits	9.02	E. Annulment and Set-Aside	9.51
C. Provisional Measures	9.32		

A. Introduction

9.01 Investment treaty jurisprudence continued to develop at a rapid rate during 2017. This contribution highlights certain notable contributions made by tribunals during the year in the areas of merits, provisional measures, remedies and settlements, and annulments and challenges to awards.

B. Merits

9.02 Across the spectrum of investment treaty case law in 2017, tribunals addressed many interesting issues relating to the substance of treaty guarantees. This section categorizes those issues into six sections, as follows: (1) human rights, social and environmental issues; (2) domestic judicial conduct; (3) cases against Venezuela; (4) solar power incentives; (5) delays in domestic administrative/judicial action; and (6) proportionality.

1. 'Investment and …'—human rights, social, and environmental issues in investment treaty case law

9.03 The possible tensions between investor interests and social or environmental interests have long been at the heart of the investment treaty regime, stretching back to the earliest cases such as *Ethyl v Canada* or *Methanex v USA* relating to environmentally motivated bans on certain chemicals. In 2017, three high-profile cases demonstrated that these tensions remain on centre stage.

In January 2017, an award from December 2016 was made public in *Urbaser v Argentina*. The case was one of the numerous cases stemming from utility concessions cancelled in the wake of Argentina's financial crisis in the early 2000s. The two claimants were shareholders in an Argentine company that held a concession to operate water and sewage services in parts of Greater Buenos Aires province. The concession struggled during Argentina's crisis, and was renegotiated with provincial authorities in 2003–05, before being terminated by the government in 2006. In assessing the investors' claims that Argentina and its provincial authorities had breached investment treaty obligations, the tribunal emphasized the investors' own obligations in the sensitive and important industry of water services, and ultimately held that the state was justified in terminating the contract due to the claimants' own failings.[1]

9.04

Notably, amongst other findings, the tribunal held that investors' expectations might be relevant under the fair and equitable treatment (FET) standard, but that these expectations must be formed within a legal environment covering 'core interests of the host State'—in particular, here, public health and access to water. Thus, the tribunal said, 'the protection of this universal basic human right [namely, access to water] constitutes the framework within which Claimants should frame their expectations'.[2] Furthermore, the tribunal found that the customary international law defence of necessity was satisfied during the crisis period, with Argentina having no alternative but to restrict the tariffs that the concessionaire could charge to customers in order to ensure continuity of essential services during the crisis.[3] The *Urbaser* tribunal thus viewed Argentina's conduct more leniently than in a case brought by another foreign investor in the same Buenos Aires water concession, where a separate tribunal ruled by majority in 2011 that Argentina could *not* rely on the necessity defence because its own conduct had contributed to the onset of the financial crisis.[4] Although Argentina did breach FET in one respect—pressuring the claimants into contract renegotiations which, the tribunal said, were already doomed to fail due to political developments—the tribunal held that the concession was worthless by this stage, since the claimants had failed to make the investments necessary to sustain it. As a result, the investors received no damages despite Argentina's breach.[5]

9.05

As well as dismissing the investors' claims on the merits, the tribunal also entertained a counterclaim filed by Argentina alleging that the investors had breached

9.06

---

[1] *Urbaser SA v Argentina*, ICSID Case No ARB//07/26, Award (8 December 2016) para 950.
[2] ibid paras 622–24.
[3] ibid para 718.
[4] *Impregilo v Argentina*, (ICSID Case No ARB/07/17, Award (21 June 2011) para 359.
[5] *Urbaser* (n 1) paras 845–47.

obligations under the human right to water. In a potentially important finding, the tribunal held that it had jurisdiction over a claimed breach of human rights by the investors.[6] Perhaps unusually, the BIT permitted *either party*, not merely the investor, to commence arbitration, and the tribunal found that Argentina's counterclaim had a factual and legal connection to the investors' primary claim, allowing the tribunal to hear it. Moreover, the tribunal dismissed the claimants' suggestion that international law imposed obligations only on states (and that the claimants could therefore not be liable for any breach of international human rights obligations). Instead, the tribunal noted that contemporary international law granted rights to individuals and corporations (for instance, under investment treaties), and could therefore impose obligations on them as well. The tribunal cited a range of human rights materials, including the Universal Declaration on Human Rights, the International Covenant on Economic, Social and Cultural Rights, the Ruggie Guiding Principles on Business and Human Rights, and UN General Assembly resolutions, and concluded that investors did indeed have an international law obligation not to engage in activity aimed at destroying the enjoyment of human rights.[7]

9.07 Nevertheless, the tribunal saw no suggestion that the investors had violated this negative obligation, which was 'not a matter for concern in the instant case'.[8] Argentina, meanwhile, retained the positive obligation to fulfil human rights (including the right to water), and the investors could not have violated that positive obligation since it did not apply to them. Thus, the counterclaim was dismissed on the merits.

9.08 Overall, the *Urbaser* award appears to place more emphasis on investor conduct than in most earlier investment treaty decisions, and it may signify the early stages of a trend towards the imposition of international law obligations on investors.[9]

9.09 In a similar vein is the November 2017 award in *Bear Creek v Peru*, which highlighted the potential for conflict between indigenous communities and mining projects, and discussed the social duties imposed on foreign investors in these projects. The investor in the case complained that Peru had revoked its mining rights at the Santa Ana silver mine, near the country's border with Bolivia. Peruvian authorities had initially supported the project, but it had also faced significant opposition from local indigenous communities, enduring large and sometimes violent protests. After a prolonged period of unrest in 2011, under considerable pressure to act on the situation, the authorities convened a late-night meeting

---

[6] ibid paras 1155.
[7] ibid paras 1193–221.
[8] ibid para 1210.
[9] But see Martins Paparinskis, 'Investment Treaty Arbitration and the (New) Law of State Responsibility' (2013) 24 European Journal of International Law 617, 647 for some more cautious remarks on this trend.

with protesters, and the following morning a decree was adopted, revoking the claimant's rights.[10]

9.10 In assessing whether this revocation amounted to an expropriation, the ICSID tribunal drew on the concept of a 'social licence', citing the United Nations Declaration on the Rights of Indigenous Peoples. Amongst other things, this concept entailed a degree of consultation with and acceptance by local communities living near large-scale mining projects. The tribunal noted that Bear Creek had indeed run numerous workshops and information sessions, and offered employment to many residents in the area. However, the tribunal found that the investor could have done more to obtain the 'social licence' needed for its project to be successful. Despite this, the tribunal also noted that Peru had approved of the investor's outreach activities, and it ultimately held that Bear Creek was entitled to assume that it had done everything legally required (under Peruvian law) in terms of consultation. According to the tribunal, this meant that Peru could not justify revoking the rights as a response to the social unrest; instead, the revocation was an indirect expropriation. Given the rushed, late-night procedure and the evident lack of compensation, the expropriation was ruled unlawful.[11]

9.11 A notable aspect of the tribunal's decision was its view of the interaction between Peru's police powers claim and a general exceptions clause in the treaty. (This clause stated in part that 'nothing in this Agreement shall be construed to prevent a Party from adopting or enforcing measures necessary ... to protect human ... life or health.')[12] Peru had alleged that its revocation measures were not an expropriation but were instead an ordinary exercise of 'police powers'. However, the tribunal (perhaps unusually) treated the 'police powers' claim not as negating the existence of any expropriation, but as an exception to a finding of expropriation. Since the treaty already contained a general exceptions clause, the tribunal said, this excluded the possibility of any other implied exceptions such as a 'police powers' argument. As a result, the only exceptions that Peru could rely on were those defined in the general exceptions clause.[13] Although long familiar to trade lawyers, general exceptions clauses have only recently become a more regular feature of investment treaties, particularly where investment commitments form part of a larger free trade agreement (such as the US–Peru agreement underpinning the *Bear Creek* case). One longstanding concern in relation to such clauses is that, although intended to preserve states' regulatory flexibility and powers to pass laws to meet environmental, social, health, or other public purposes, the greater legal definition entailed by the clauses might instead serve to *narrow* the flexibility

---

[10] *Bear Creek Mining Corporation v Peru*, ICSID Case No ARB/14/21, Award (30 November 2017) paras 378–83.
[11] ibid paras 400–16, 442–49.
[12] US–Peru Trade Promotion Agreement, art 2201.
[13] *Bear Creek* (n 10) para 473.

available.¹⁴ This concern was potentially borne out by the *Bear Creek* decision, given the tribunal's decision that the general exceptions clause excluded the availability of other defences such as police powers.

9.12 Peru then sought to rely on the general exceptions clause itself, arguing that the clause covered the state's revocation of the mining rights since this was necessary to protect human life or health. The tribunal was sceptical of this claim, but in any case held that the exception would not protect against unlawful expropriations. In the tribunal's reasoning, the expropriation obligation did not *prevent* Peru from revoking the rights, as long as the revocation complied with the obligation—that is, as long as compensation was paid.¹⁵

9.13 Ultimately, the *Bear Creek* case appears to place some significant limits on the usefulness of general exceptions clauses, since (according to the tribunal's interpretation) they not only exclude all other exceptions, but also do not remove obligations to pay compensation for measures found to be expropriatory, despite the measures' legitimate social or environmental objectives. The case suggests that a better approach, from states' perspective, would be to focus arguments (and treaty drafting) not on general exceptions clauses but on clauses defining the primary obligations. Annex 812.1(c) of the US–Peru treaty, for instance, already provides in part that 'non discriminatory measures of a Party that are designed and applied to protect legitimate public welfare objectives, such as health, safety and the environment, do not constitute indirect expropriation'. Although this clause might not have been satisfied on the facts of *Bear Creek* (given Peru's lack of due process), its successful application would entail a finding of no expropriation, with no compensation thereby due.

9.14 In a dissenting opinion, Peru's nominee to the tribunal, Philippe Sands, placed much greater emphasis on foreign investors' own conduct in engaging in large-scale projects located in indigenous lands. While the majority had suggested that the investor had done as much as could be expected, arbitrator Sands drew more broadly on international law to find that Bear Creek should bear more responsibility for its failure to obtain a sufficient 'social licence' from the local Peruvian indigenous population. The dissenter challenged the traditional view that international law imposed obligations only on states, citing the findings of the *Urbaser v Argentina* tribunal that private parties had obligations not to engage in activity aimed at destroying human rights.¹⁶ Sands also cited ILO Convention 169 on Indigenous and Tribal Peoples, characterizing that instrument as an 'applicable

---

¹⁴ Jarrod Hepburn, 'Specific Exceptions in Investment Law Protecting Domestic Policy Space' in Thomas Cottier and Krista Nadakavukaren Schefer (eds), *Elgar Encyclopaedia of International Economic Law* (Edward Elgar 2017) 273.
¹⁵ *Bear Creek* (n 10) para 477.
¹⁶ *Bear Creek Mining Corporation v Peru*, ICSID Case No ARB/14/21, Partial Dissenting Opinion of Professor Philippe Sands QC (12 September 2017) para 10.

rule of international law' that must be applied in the case under the underlying treaty's applicable law clause.[17] These legal instruments suggested to the dissenter that Bear Creek should have done much more to engage with the community before it pursued its mining project. In his view, Bear Creek's failure to obtain a 'social licence' meant that it was equally responsible with Peru for the protests and subsequent revocation of rights. Sands commented: 'As an international investor the Claimant has legitimate interests and rights under international law; local communities of indigenous and tribal peoples also have rights under international law, and these are not lesser rights.'[18] The tangible consequence of Bear Creek's failings, Sands concluded, was that its compensation award (later discussed) should be halved, reflecting its equal responsibility with Peru for its loss.[19]

9.15 *Bear Creek* and the late 2016 award in *Urbaser* thus both represent early signs that tribunals may become more willing to look for obligations on investors under international law, alongside the rights that investors currently enjoy under investment treaties.

9.16 Meanwhile, obligations on investors in *domestic* law were central to the February 2017 decision on counterclaims in *Burlington v Ecuador*. The state's primary liability in the case had already been determined in 2012,[20] and a separate February 2017 decision on quantum (later discussed) awarded Burlington nearly $380 million in compensation.[21] In the parallel counterclaims decision, however, Burlington was ordered to pay back $41.7 million to Ecuador for its own breaches—not of the US–Ecuador BIT, but of Ecuadorian environmental law. The tribunal's ability to hear the counterclaim was made easier by the fact that Burlington agreed with Ecuador not to contest jurisdiction, thus skirting the challenges that other tribunals have faced in this regard.[22] As in the 2015 counterclaim in the related *Perenco v Ecuador* case, the three arbitrators—presumably appointed to the tribunal for their expertise in international law—proceeded to spend several hundred pages instead analysing and applying Ecuadorian law. The tribunal found a range of breaches relating to oil contamination at various sites, and certain breaches of maintenance obligations, leading to the $41.7 million award (plus interest).[23] Successful counterclaims against investors are rare in investment treaty arbitration, as the relevant issues are often brought before domestic courts instead. However,

---

[17] ibid para 7.
[18] ibid para 36.
[19] ibid para 39.
[20] *Burlington Resources Inc v Ecuador*, ICSID Case No ARB/08/5, Decision on Liability (14 December 2012).
[21] *Burlington Resources Inc v Ecuador*, ICSID Case No ARB/08/5, Decision on Reconsideration and Award (7 February 2017).
[22] See eg *Rusoro v Venezuela*, *Roussalis v Romania* or *Urbaser v Argentina*.
[23] *Burlington Resources Inc v Ecuador*, ICSID Case No ARB/08/5, Decision on Counterclaims (7 February 2017).

the treatment of foreign investors in domestic courts sometimes itself becomes the subject of an investment treaty claim, when investors allege that domestic courts have fallen below international minimum standards of justice.[24] The *Burlington* approach might therefore represent a more palatable alternative for both parties for resolution of counterclaims, as the claimant itself appeared to accept (in not contesting jurisdiction), despite the problems raised by arbitrators being called on to apply unfamiliar law.[25]

2. Domestic judicial conduct and investment treaties: *Eli Lilly v Canada*

9.17 In March 2017, a tribunal under the North American Free Trade Agreement (NAFTA)[26] issued its final award in *Eli Lilly v Canada*.[27] The case centred on claims by US pharmaceutical company Eli Lilly that the Canadian courts had judicially developed a new doctrine of patent law, resulting in the invalidation of two of the claimant's patents. According to Eli Lilly, the allegedly abrupt reversal of the prior law by the Canadian judiciary amounted to an expropriation of its intellectual property rights, and a breach of the minimum standard of treatment enshrined in NAFTA Article 1105.

9.18 One notable issue addressed in the case was whether denial of justice was the only rule of international law that could potentially be breached by domestic judicial conduct. The three NAFTA states all supported this contention (Canada in its pleadings, and the US and Mexico in non-disputing party submissions under NAFTA Article 1128), taking the view that a 'judicial expropriation' was therefore not legally cognizable (ie that an expropriation could only be committed by executive or legislative conduct, not judicial conduct).[28] However, the *Eli Lilly* tribunal doubted this, observing that all the standards of investment treaties applied to all state organs, including the judiciary. This suggested that judicial conduct could lead to an expropriation, for instance if 'a judicial decision crystallizes a taking alleged to be contrary to NAFTA Article 1110'.[29] The tribunal also noted that expropriations under NAFTA required due process of law, meaning that

---

[24] See eg the claimants' allegations of a denial of justice inflicted by the Ecuadorian court system in *Chevron Corporation v Ecuador*, UNCITRAL, Claimant's Supplemental Memorial on the Merits (20 March 2012).

[25] Jarrod Hepburn, *Domestic Law in International Investment Arbitration* (OUP 2017).

[26] North American Free Trade Agreement (signed 17 December 1992, entered into force 1 January 1994) (NAFTA).

[27] *Eli Lilly and Company v Canada*, ICSID Case No UNCT/14/2, Final Award (16 March 2017).

[28] *Eli Lilly and Company v Canada*, ICSID Case No UNCT/14/2, Counter-Memorial of Canada (27 January 2015) paras 230–45; *Eli Lilly and Company v Canada*, ICSID Case No UNCT/14/2, Submission of the United States of America (18 March 2016) paras 20–24; *Eli Lilly and Company v Canada*, ICSID Case No UNCT/14/2, Submission of Mexico Pursuant to NAFTA Article 1128 (18 March 2016) para 14.

[29] *Eli Lilly* (n 27) para 221.

domestic judicial conduct could be relevant to an expropriation claim, and not only to a denial of justice claim. Furthermore, the tribunal also commented that judicial conduct might breach the elements of 'manifest arbitrariness' and 'blatant unfairness' commonly agreed to form part of the minimum standard of treatment under Article 1105, alongside denial of justice.[30] The tribunal ultimately saw no need to make a finding on this, since it saw no breaches of NAFTA in any case, but the *Eli Lilly* award reiterates the wide scope of NAFTA (and other investment treaty) obligations.

Also of interest in the *Eli Lilly* award was its confirmation that the ordinary processes of legal development in common law countries such as Canada—potentially including reversal of legal doctrines established in lower courts by later, binding higher court judgments—did not necessarily amount to a breach of the legal stability envisioned by investment treaties. In the tribunal's view, 'evolution of the law through court decisions is natural, and departures from precedent are to be expected'[31]—at least, provided that the legal changes were not 'fundamental or dramatic'.[32] Even where judicially developed rules were unclear, this was also not a cause for concern; 'questions about the precise scope of application of legal rules abound in nearly all legal regimes'.[33] While perhaps not surprising, the dicta illustrate the gulf between the current understanding of the minimum standard of treatment and the strict rules set out in early cases such as *Tecmed v Mexico*, calling for states to act 'free from ambiguity',[34] or *CMS v Argentina*, requiring a 'stable legal and business environment'.[35]

9.19

3. Venezuela and the investment treaty regime

Venezuela's fortunes in investment treaty arbitration continued to slide in 2017, as the state was ordered to pay at least $800 million in compensation (before interest) across four awards. Two of these decisions, the November 2017 *Saint-Gobain* award on damages and the November 2017 *Longreef* final award, remain unpublished, although the *Longreef* tribunal reportedly ordered $43 million plus interest in compensation for Venezuela's unlawful expropriation and breaches of fair and equitable treatment in relation to an investment in the coffee sector.[36]

9.20

---

[30] ibid paras 222–25.
[31] ibid para 310.
[32] ibid para 387.
[33] ibid para 429.
[34] *Técnicas Medioambientales Tecmed SA v Mexico*, ICSID Case No ARB(AF)/00/2, Award (29 May 2003) para 154.
[35] *CMS Gas Transmission Company v Argentina*, ICSID Case No ARB/01/8, Award (12 May 2005) para 274.
[36] Investment Arbitration Reporter, 'Venezuela Sees Three Final Awards in a Little Over a Week, as Dutch Investor, Longreef Investments AVV, Nets 50+ Million Dollars in Latest BIT Ruling' *Investment Arbitration Reporter* (8 November 2017) <http://tinyurl.com/ydxcyrnr>.

9.21 The other two decisions, a July 2017 award in *Valores Mundiales v Venezuela* and an October 2017 award in *Koch v Venezuela*, both discuss merits, and merit discussion. First, the awards differed on the long-standing question of the relations between treaty-based 'fair and equitable treatment' provisions and the customary international law minimum standard of treatment. According to the *Koch* tribunal, a treaty granting FET 'in accordance with the rules and principles of international law' connected that standard to the customary minimum standard, rather than an (arguably) higher 'autonomous' standard of FET.[37] In *Valores Mundiales*, however, the tribunal drew no connection between FET and the minimum standard, finding that the two concepts were technically separate, despite similar wording ('fair and equitable treatment, in accordance with international law') in the relevant treaty. Nevertheless, the *Valores Mundiales* tribunal accepted that the minimum standard had evolved over time, and was now essentially the same as the treaty-based FET standard in any case.[38] (The two tribunals' positions contrast with another 2017 award, *Teinver v Argentina*, where the tribunal viewed the treaty-based and customary standards separately, and suggested that the 'autonomous' FET standard included protection of legitimate expectations, while the customary standard did not.)[39]

9.22 Second, the *Koch* tribunal found an expropriation but no FET breach, while the *Valores Mundiales* tribunal found a breach of FET but no expropriation. In the latter award, the tribunal held that certain interferences with the management of a company did not amount to an indirect expropriation, since there was no overall loss of control of the company by the claimant.[40] However, Venezuela had committed a breach of FET by imposing two confusing sets of measures on the claimant's operations, partly justified by a criminal investigation against an unrelated party and partly justified by state objectives of food security. The timeline for these interferences was left unspecified, and the 'lack of coherence and transparency' contributed to a treaty violation.[41] As well, while a formal expropriation process had been commenced, Venezuela took no further action on it for nearly ten years, leaving the claimants in a 'situation of uncertainty'.[42] Combined with a long-delayed local court decision (required to be issued within five days, but still not issued after six years), the tribunal was satisfied that Venezuela had breached FET.

---

[37] *Koch Minerals Sarl v Venezuela*, ICSID Case No ARB/11/19, Award (30 October 2017) para 8.42.
[38] *Valores Mundiales SL v Venezuela*, ICSID Case No ARB/13/11, Award (25 July 2017) paras 528–36.
[39] *Teinver SA v Argentina*, ICSID Case No ARB/09/1, Award (21 July 2017) paras 666–67.
[40] *Valores Mundiales* (n 38) para 479.
[41] ibid para 586.
[42] ibid para 582.

In *Koch*, meanwhile, the tribunal rejected claims that a series of measures—tax **9.23** increases, delays in issuing VAT refunds, orders to sell products below cost price—amounted to a FET violation. The measures were not arbitrary, discriminatory, or in bad faith at the time, the tribunal said, and the fact that the claimant's investment was later subjected to a formal expropriation could not colour the past events.[43] By contrast, the failure to pay compensation for the formal expropriation clearly rendered it in breach of the relevant treaty, the tribunal held. Notably, the *Koch* tribunal did not enter into debates over whether an expropriation that is unlawful merely due to a lack of compensation should be treated differently to an expropriation held unlawful on other grounds, as has been discussed in other cases against Venezuela in recent years (eg *Tidewater v Venezuela* or *ConocoPhillips v Venezuela*). The *Koch* tribunal did, however, acknowledge that a genuine effort to negotiate compensation may satisfy the compensation requirement, even if no amounts are actually agreed and paid.[44] As for the other conditions for lawful expropriation, the tribunal rejected the claimants' argument that their lack of advance warning (having first learned of the expropriation via a TV address from President Chavez) rendered the expropriation in breach of due process.[45] (By contrast, in *Bear Creek v Peru*, as discussed, a tribunal held that a lack of advance warning of an indirect expropriation, effected via revocation of mining rights, breached the due process condition.) Similarly, the *Koch* tribunal held that the public purpose condition was satisfied via the state's claimed objective of ensuring food security: 'the standard of review of a State's conduct to be undertaken by an international tribunal includes a significant measure of deference towards the State making the impugned measure'.[46]

The Venezuela cases also touched on two other less-commonly pleaded investment **9.24** treaty standards. In *Valores Mundiales*, the tribunal unusually found a breach of the 'free transfers' provision, when Venezuela declined (without reasons) to permit the investor to repatriate certain funds.[47] In *Koch*, as well as the FET clause, the tribunal also tied the less prominent 'full protection and security' clause to customary international law. For the tribunal, this limited the clause's remit to protection from physical interference, and doomed the claimant's arguments under that provision.[48] Continuing a more long-running debate, the *Koch* award contrasts again with *Teinver v Argentina*, where the tribunal held that full protection and security could extend to protection of 'intangible assets', not merely physical security.[49]

---

[43] *Koch* (n 37) para 8.62.
[44] ibid para 7.28.
[45] ibid para 7.23.
[46] ibid para 7.20.
[47] *Valores Mundiales* (n 38) para 639.
[48] *Koch* (n 37) para 8.46.
[49] *Teinver* (n 39) para 905.

4. Investment treaty regulation of solar power incentives

9.25 During 2017, three awards surfaced in the numerous cases relating to withdrawal of solar power incentives in Spain and Italy. In *Eiser v Spain*, a tribunal at ICSID awarded €128 million in compensation following changes in Spain's regulatory regime for solar power plants. The tribunal held that the Energy Charter Treaty's FET obligation did not grant a right to absolute regulatory stability for investors, but that it did protect against states instituting 'unprecedented' or 'totally different' regulatory regimes. In the tribunal's view, Spain's changes from 2012 onwards were so drastic—and, in addition, appeared to lack a meaningful substantive basis—that FET was found to have been breached.[50] The case contrasts with *Isolux v Spain*, a Stockholm Chamber of Commerce (SCC) award from 2016 that became public during 2017, which related to the same measures at issue in *Eiser*. In *Isolux*, the tribunal majority saw no treaty breaches, observing that the investor had made its investment in October 2012, after Spain had made certain earlier (and less drastic) changes to its solar power regulatory regime. (Those earlier changes were held not to breach Energy Charter Treaty commitments in the 2016 *Charanne v Spain* case.)[51] For the *Isolux* tribunal, the claimant could not have any expectations of legal stability when circumstances already suggested in October 2012 that further regulatory changes were likely. Furthermore, the claimant's damages submissions indicated to the tribunal that its returns had actually been higher than its own forecasts, despite the regulatory changes, suggesting that any claim of expropriation could not succeed.[52]

9.26 Meanwhile, Italy also survived a claim at ICSID in the *Blusun* case, where the late 2016 award was also made public in 2017. Like the *Eiser* tribunal, the *Blusun* tribunal considered that the FET obligation was not a guarantee of complete stability and preserved states' rights to change their laws. The relevant test for breach, in the tribunal's mind, was proportionality, ensuring that a new regime had sufficient regard for the interests of those committed under the previous regime.[53] The *Blusun* tribunal majority appeared to view Italy's measures in relation to solar power as being less drastic as in the *Eiser* case against Spain; the reduction in tariffs that Italy had imposed was substantial, but not crippling for the investors, and the tariffs remained higher than in other countries. A dissenting arbitrator, however, considered that Italy's reduction in the permitted size of solar plants was unexpected, and amounted to an expropriation.[54]

---

[50] *Eiser Infrastructure Ltd v Spain*, ICSID Case No ARB/13/36, Award (4 May 2017) 111–33.
[51] *Charanne BV v Spain*, SCC Case No 062/2012, Final Award (21 January 2016).
[52] *Isolux Infrastructure Netherlands BV v Spain*, SCC Case No V2013/153, Award (12 July 2016) 201–25.
[53] *Blusun SA v Italy*, ICSID Case No ARB/14/3, Award (27 December 2016) para 318.
[54] ibid para 409.

The various solar cases reviewed here all turn on different facts, with different measures at stake, and different times of investment generating different expectations regarding solar incentives. Nevertheless, they suggest a degree of flexibility in the FET standard, which does not necessarily prevent all change in legal regimes—as observed above in relation to *Eli Lilly v Canada*.

9.27

5. Domestic delays in administrative or judicial conduct

Delays in domestic administrative or judicial action featured in three cases during 2017. In *PL Holdings v Poland*, Polish banking authorities had postponed a reconsideration of a decision adversely affecting the claimant five times. Since the reconsideration decision was required to be issued before the claimant could pursue the matter in local courts, the tribunal held that Poland's 'prolonged and repeated failure to act on Claimant's petition for reconsideration effectively barred Claimant's fundamental right of access to court for redress'.[55] This finding then fed into a broader finding of expropriation. Similarly, in *Cervin & Rhone v Costa Rica*, a regulatory decision on tariff-setting in the gas industry was required to be issued within a certain eight-day period, but ultimately took more than two years. Since Costa Rican law provided that the decision would not have retroactive effect, the impact of the delayed decision was, in theory, even worse for the investor. In the tribunal's view, this administrative delay amounted to a breach of FET.[56] (However, the claimant was unable to prove any loss arising from this delay, partly because the regulatory decision eventually went against the claimant anyway. Thus, no damages were awarded.)[57] In the third case, *Valores Mundiales v Venezuela* (as discussed above), a preliminary local court decision on admissibility that should have taken at most five days failed to be issued within six years. This extensive judicial delay contributed to a finding of FET breach.[58]

9.28

6. Proportionality in investment treaty case law

The much-discussed concept of proportionality appeared in the merits reasoning of two awards in 2017. In *Ampal-American v Egypt*, a tribunal at ICSID held in February 2017 that Egypt had committed an unlawful expropriation in terminating a gas supply contract with the claimant for non-payment of an invoice. According to the tribunal, the termination was not only unlawful under its governing law (English law), but had also come during a period of political opposition to the gas pipeline that was central to the project, which transported gas from Egypt to Israel. This rendered the termination a 'disproportionate act',

9.29

---

[55] *PL Holdings Sarl v Poland*, SCC Case No V2014/163, Partial Award (28 June 2017) para 408.
[56] *Cervin Investissements SA v Costa Rica*, ICSID Case No ARB/13/2, Award (7 March 2017) para 663.
[57] ibid para 703.
[58] *Valores Mundiales* (n 38) paras 556–63.

contributing to the finding of unlawful expropriation.[59] Notably, the *Ampal-American* tribunal was chaired by Yves Fortier, who also chaired the *Occidental v Ecuador* tribunal which, in 2012, held that a contract termination deemed disproportionate to the underlying wrong amounted to an expropriation and breach of FET.[60] The *Ampal-American* decision is perhaps less significant, given that the termination in *Occidental* was permitted by the contract (but nevertheless held in breach of treaty), and given that the *Occidental* tribunal was at much greater pains to establish a role for proportionality in the assessment than the *Ampal-American* tribunal's brief references. Nevertheless, perhaps together with *Blusun* discussed above, the ruling seems to form part of a growing trend of cases supporting the relevance of proportionality, in some sense, to investment treaty arbitration.

9.30 The June 2017 ruling in *PL Holdings v Poland* also fits into this trend. There, the SCC tribunal reviewed Polish banking authorities' conduct in relation to the claimant, measuring it against a three-pronged test for proportionality: suitability for achieving a public purpose; necessary for achieving that purpose; and not 'excessive in that its advantages are outweighed by its disadvantages'. The tribunal found none of these prongs satisfied: the measures taken were in fact held to make it *more* difficult for the claimant bank to address the regulatory concerns expressed by the authorities. Rather than taking the draconian steps of imposing a deprivation of voting rights and, eventually, a forced sale, 'any number of lesser measures … could readily be imagined', the tribunal said.[61] The legal basis for the tribunal's proportionality assessment is not entirely clear in the award, although it clearly contributed in some form to the (sole) finding of expropriation. The parties argued over the legal source of any potential principle of proportionality to be applied in the case, but the tribunal concluded only that, '[r]egardless of the law specifically applicable to the principle of proportionality in this case, the principle is understood in largely similar terms across jurisdictions'.[62]

9.31 As noted above, proportionality also appeared in the 2016 award in *Blusun v Italy*, made public during 2017. The tribunal in that case held that proportionality was the relevant test for breach of FET, although it ultimately found that Italy's changes to its solar incentives scheme were not so drastic as to engender a breach.[63]

---

[59] *Ampal-American Israel Corp v Egypt*, ICSID Case No ARB/12/11, Decision on Liability and Heads of Loss (21 February 2017) para 346.
[60] *Occidental Petroleum Corporation v Ecuador*, ICSID Case No ARB/06/11, Award (5 October 2012).
[61] *PL Holdings* (n 55) para 375.
[62] ibid para 355.
[63] *Blusun* (n 53) para 318.

C. Provisional Measures

Alongside merits developments, 2017 also saw many developments in provisional measures. **9.32**

Three cases addressed the contested issue of tribunals ordering states to suspend domestic criminal proceedings against investment treaty claimants. In February 2017, an ICSID tribunal in *Italba v Uruguay* held that it did not have the power to make such an order. In the tribunal's view, a claimant at ICSID should have no expectation that their international case conferred a 'blanket immunity upon its principals and witnesses from a [domestic] criminal investigation'.[64] The tribunal saw no irreparable harm, in any case, in Uruguay pursuing its investigations against two of the claimant's witnesses in the arbitration.[65] **9.33**

The following month, however, another ICSID tribunal in *Nova Group v Romania* held that it did have power to issue provisional measures restraining states from pursuing domestic criminal proceedings, at least in exceptional circumstances.[66] The *Nova Group* tribunal also suggested that there was no strict rule that only criminal proceedings commenced *after* an arbitration had been launched could be restrained via provisional measures. Although such proceedings might more likely be viewed as a bad faith response to the claimant's move to commence arbitration, the tribunal considered that the timing of the criminal proceedings was merely an additional factor affecting the justifiability of a provisional measures order.[67] In the case at hand, however, the *Nova Group* tribunal saw no grounds to exercise that power, rejecting the claim that the criminal proceedings were discouraging witnesses from testifying in the ICSID arbitration.[68] **9.34**

Later, in July 2017, an UNCITRAL rules tribunal in *Pugachev v Russia* similarly upheld its power to restrain domestic criminal proceedings, even if 'the Tribunal's analysis must be cautious in order to prevent unjustified interferences in the sovereign judicial decisions of States'.[69] For the *Pugachev* tribunal, the timing of the criminal proceedings would affect the calculations; it was particularly reluctant to interfere with criminal proceedings that were already underway when the arbitration was launched, doubting the proportionality of doing so.[70] Notably, the tribunal contrasted its powers in relation to domestic proceedings within the host **9.35**

---

[64] *Italba Corporation v Uruguay*, ICSID Case No ARB/16/9, Decision on Claimant's Application for Provisional Measures and Temporary Relief (15 February 2017) para 118.
[65] ibid para 121.
[66] *Nova Group Investments BV v Romania*, ICSID Case No ARB/16/19, Decision on Claimant's Request for Provisional Measures (29 March 2017) para 248.
[67] ibid para 257.
[68] ibid para 365.
[69] *Sergei Pugachev v Russia*, UNCITRAL, Interim Award (7 July 2017) para 293.
[70] ibid para 275.

state, on the one hand, to proceedings playing out in third-party jurisdictions, on the other hand. While it had powers in relation to the former (even if subject to a high threshold), the tribunal doubted that it could grant the claimants' request to order alleged Russian state entities to desist from pursuing civil proceedings in third states that were not even parties to the relevant BIT underlying the case.[71]

9.36 The *Pugachev* and *Nova Group* cases also both addressed the separate, but related, question of restraining states from issuing extradition orders over investment treaty claimants or their affiliates. In *Nova Group*, the tribunal granted the claimant's request for an order preventing Romania from pursuing the extradition from the UK of the claimant's principal shareholder and manager. The tribunal held that the individual was a key witness in the case, who had exclusive knowledge of certain events, and could not meaningfully direct the case from a Romanian prison.[72] To assuage Romania's concerns that preventing his extradition would lead to his flight from the UK to a jurisdiction without extradition arrangements with Romania, the tribunal ordered the individual to surrender his passport to a neutral party. However, the tribunal dismissed concerns that the provisional measures ruling would disproportionately interfere with Romania's sovereignty. At pains to explain itself, the tribunal's order amounted to 139 pages, described by the tribunal itself in a subsequent ruling as 'the most detailed exposition to date of provisional measures issues arising in the context of domestic proceedings'.[73] Similarly, the *Pugachev* tribunal agreed that the extradition and incarceration of the claimant in Russia would threaten his ability to consult with his lawyers in France and present his case to the arbitrators. Since Russia could still extradite the claimant once the arbitration had concluded, the tribunal said, an order of provisional measures did not disproportionately interfere with Russian prerogatives.[74]

9.37 Two further provisional measures orders were issued during 2017 that addressed domestic civil proceedings in the host state. In July 2017, a sole arbitrator in the UNCITRAL rules case *Centerra v Kyrgyzstan* ordered Kyrgyzstan to suspend its pursuit of domestic proceedings which had already led to a disputed $98 million judgment against the investor for breaches of Kyrgyz environmental law. The state was ordered to give thirty days' notice to the investor and the tribunal if it intended to resume the domestic proceedings, to allow Centerra to seek appropriate relief. According to the arbitrator, this ruling was 'necessary to ensure that the

---

[71] ibid para 226. Ultimately, the tribunal held that the entities in question were *prima facie* not connected to the Russian state, making an order against Russia in relation to the entities' conduct even less justifiable: ibid para 227.
[72] *Nova Group* (n 66) para 301.
[73] *Nova Group Investments BV v Romania*, ICSID Case No ARB/16/19, Decision on Respondent's Request for Reconsideration of Procedural Order No 7 (18 April 2017) para 33.
[74] *Pugachev* (n 69) paras 319, 332.

Kyrgyz Court Claims will not proceed to final judgments or enforceable orders during the pendency of these arbitrations'.[75]

Meanwhile, in *Puma Energy Holdings v Benin*, a sole arbitrator at the SCC issued an emergency measures order preventing Benin from enforcing a disputed $15 million judgment against the claimant's Beninese subsidiary. The requirement of irreparable harm was found to be justified in the case on the grounds that enforcing the judgment would 'effectively and conclusively extinguish' the claimant's operations in Benin. While the arbitrator acknowledged that, '[b]rought to its extreme, almost all damage in any commercial context could be economically compensated', he held that compensation did not always reverse all the consequences of a loss, for instance where compensation could not be allocated to any appropriate alternative investment.[76] This wider view of 'irreparable harm' has seemingly been endorsed in earlier cases as well, such as *Evrobalt v Moldova*, where another sole arbitrator at the SCC considered that the total 'economic ruination' of a claimant could amount to irreparable harm despite appearing to be remediable via monetary compensation.[77] 9.38

The *Puma* case is also notable for apparently pushing the boundaries of the SCC emergency arbitration process, the contours of which are still being worked out in the investment treaty context, in at least two respects. First, previous SCC emergency orders (such as in the *Evrobalt* and *Kompozit v Moldova* cases) have been issued in investment treaty cases where the claimant had at least filed a notice of dispute with the respondent state, taking a step towards a full arbitration, before requesting an emergency order. In *Puma*, however, the claimant had not filed a notice of dispute, but grounded its emergency measures claim merely on Benin's consent to SCC arbitration in the Luxembourg–Benin BIT. The sole arbitrator accepted this, and indicated that Benin was bound to comply with the emergency order as part of its obligations under the treaty.[78] Second, twenty-eight days after the emergency order, the claimant filed a notice of arbitration with Benin under the BIT, purporting to formally commence arbitration. However, Benin contested this, observing that the BIT required a preliminary notice of dispute, followed by a six-month negotiation period before a formal notice of arbitration could be filed to commence proceedings. The state suggested that the claimant had only filed its notice of arbitration because, under the SCC Rules, an emergency order 9.39

---

[75] CenterraGold, 'Centerra Provides Update on International Arbitration' (19 July 2017) <s3.amazonaws.com/cg-raw/cg/news-releases/nr-20170719-1.pdf>.
[76] Jarrod Hepburn, 'ANALYSIS: Stockholm Arbitration Finds Emergency Measures Justified Against Benin Where Entire Investment Faces Extinguishment Due to Alleged Denial of Justice' *Investment Arbitration Reporter* (14 June 2017) <tinyurl.com/ybofz7tn>.
[77] *Evrobalt LLC v Moldova*, SCC Emergency Arbitration EA 2016/082, Award on Emergency Measures (30 May 2016) para 53.
[78] Hepburn, 'ANALYSIS: Stockholm Arbitration Finds Emergency Measures Justified Against Benin' (n 76).

ceases to be binding if 'arbitration is not commenced within 30 days'.[79] This raises the question of what suffices to 'commence' arbitration under the SCC Rules. Although typically an arbitration would not commence until a notice of arbitration is filed,[80] this position would mean that emergency orders in investment treaty cases would only ever remain binding for thirty days, since—because investment treaties very often contain negotiation periods of six months or more, like the Luxembourg–Benin BIT—formal arbitration could not be commenced within the required thirty-day period.[81] This limited lifespan may not matter if the mere issuance of the order essentially fulfils the claimant's strategic purposes. In other cases, though, unless a more expansive view of 'commencing' arbitration were taken, the usefulness of emergency arbitrator orders in investment treaty disputes might remain limited.

9.40 Two other provisional measures rulings issued in 2017 stemmed from efforts to restrain states from calling on performance guarantees posted by claimants in relation to construction projects. In both cases (*Rizzani de Eccher v Kuwait*[82] and *Guris v Libya*),[83] however, the claimants were unable to convince the tribunal that there was any risk of imminent harm, as there was no evidence that the respondent states were actually planning to call on the guarantees. Furthermore, the tribunals both saw no irreparable harm (such as insolvency) that the claimants would suffer even if the guarantees were called on. In *Rizzani de Eccher*, the tribunal also declined to order provisional measures requested by Kuwait, aimed at forcing the claimant to continue working on the disputed highway construction project during the arbitration's pendency. The tribunal saw no risk of irreparable harm to Kuwait if the project stalled.[84]

9.41 Lastly, on 3 December 2017 (a Sunday), an UNCITRAL rules tribunal at the Permanent Court of Arbitration (PCA) issued an *ex parte* emergency provisional measures order one day after the claimant's request, instructing Ukraine to protect the life, health, and physical safety of the claimant, a Russian/US dual national. The claimant alleged that he had been arrested the previous day and beaten in custody, and (at the time of the request) was in emergency care in a Kiev hospital.

---

[79] Jarrod Hepburn, 'Benin Seeks Revocation of Emergency Award, As Investor Follows up with Formal Claim' *Investment Arbitration Reporter* (11 July 2017) <tinyurl.com/y7z3wtkz>.

[80] See eg SCC Arbitration Rules, art 8; UNCITRAL Arbitration Rules, art 3(2).

[81] Unless, of course, the emergency order was obtained within the final thirty days of the BIT's negotiation period; or unless the claimant is able to plead a 'futility' exception, contending that the envisaged negotiations with the respondent would have anyway been futile, such that an ordinarily premature notice of arbitration is effective.

[82] *Rizzani de Eccher SpA v Kuwait*, ICSID Case No ARB/17/8, Decision on Provisional Measures (23 November 2017) para 130.

[83] See Jarrod Hepburn, 'Arbitrators in ICC BIT Case Reject Investor's Request for Interim Measures to Prevent Government from Calling on Project Guarantees' *Investment Arbitration Reporter* (9 May 2017) <tinyurl.com/ybyxty8t>.

[84] *Rizzani de Eccher* (n 82) para 148.

The tribunal agreed to issue a temporary protective measure, while ordering the parties to file full submissions on the provisional measures application several days later.[85] Shortly after the emergency order was issued, Ukraine's nominee to the tribunal indicated that he dissented from the order, apparently on the grounds that Ukraine had not been given due process in the extremely rapid proceedings.

D. Remedies and Settlements

9.42 Damages awards issued in 2017 continued to favour the discounted cash flow (DCF) approach to valuing investments. Its use was, however, rejected in *Bear Creek v Peru*, with the tribunal determining that the project was still at an early stage.[86] In that case, the tribunal (majority) held instead that it would award the amount invested by the claimant, an undisputed figure of $18.2 million.

9.43 Two tribunals discussed questions of country risk in damages. The issue has arisen in numerous cases against Venezuela in the past (for instance in *Gold Reserve v Venezuela* and *Tidewater v Venezuela*), and 2017 proved no exception on this front. In *Valores Mundiales v Venezuela*, the tribunal adopted the claimant's proposed country risk premium, much lower than the state's proposal, finding that the investment had actually grown even despite the apparently larger political risks of operating in Venezuela.[87] Meanwhile, in *Saint-Gobain v Venezuela*, the tribunal split on the question of whether to even include a country risk premium (intended to factor in the risks of doing business in the particular respondent state). While the *Saint-Gobain* majority held that country risk was merely an economic factor that any hypothetical purchaser would take into account when valuing an investment, the dissenting arbitrator considered that damages calculations must exclude the very risk that investment treaties are (in his view) designed to protect against—namely, sovereign interference. Otherwise, countries would benefit (via lower damages awards due to large country risk premiums being applied) from creating a climate of uncertainty and risk.[88]

9.44 Tribunals also addressed another long controversial question in 2017, whether compensation is determined differently for lawful and unlawful expropriations. The *Koch* tribunal referred to this 'unresolved debate',[89] but managed to side-step

---

[85] *Igor Boyko v Ukraine*, PCA Case No 2017-23, Procedural Order No 3 on Claimant's Application for Emergency Relief (3 December 2017).
[86] *Bear Creek* (n 10) para 604.
[87] *Valores Mundiales* (n 38) para 790.
[88] *Saint-Gobain Performance Plastics Europe v Venezuela*, ICSID Case No ARB/12/13, Decision on Liability and the Principles of Quantum (30 December 2016) para 723; *Saint-Gobain Performance Plastics Europe v Venezuela*, ICSID Case No ARB/12/13, Concurring and Dissenting Opinion of Judge Charles N Brower (21 December 2016).
[89] *Koch* (n 37) para 9.193.

the question, while the *Burlington* tribunal majority took the view that the appropriate valuation date for an unlawful expropriation was the date of award, rather than date of expropriation. Recalling her earlier dissent on this issue in *Quiborax v Bolivia*, arbitrator Brigitte Stern dissented again in *Burlington* on the point, maintaining that the date of expropriation remained the correct valuation date regardless of the lawfulness of the expropriation.[90] The *Burlington* tribunal also differed amongst itself on the use of *ex post* data in valuation (ie data and information from time periods coming after the expropriation date). The majority preferred the more reliable *ex post* data, reflecting actual events occurring since the expropriation, while arbitrator Stern again supported her *Quiborax* position of excluding reference to this data.[91]

9.45 Otherwise of note, the *PL Holdings v Poland* tribunal held that it would determine interest according to the rates set in domestic (Polish) law.[92] Tribunals rarely take this approach, contending instead that international law should solely govern the consequences of a breach of international law. However, other earlier tribunals (such as *CME v Czech Republic*)[93] have looked to domestic law, reasoning that international law did not set any specific rate to use, and that domestic law was part of the applicable law in the case.

9.46 Lastly, a (possibly) more general comment on damages calculations was offered by the *Koch v Venezuela* tribunal, which lamented the fact that the parties' damages experts in the case had offered wildly differing valuations of the investment. Given the discrepancy, the tribunal held that it had no confidence in either figure: 'It is as if two boxers in the ring knocked each other out simultaneously, with neither winning the contest.'[94] Instead, the tribunal relied on reports commissioned earlier by the state for negotiations with other shareholders in the same plant the expropriation of which was at issue in the case. Arbitrators are of course rarely trained in economics or financial modelling, and are not likely to have extensive experience in the valuation of businesses, leaving them highly reliant on expert views in the typical case. When these expert views are also unhelpful, as in *Koch*, tribunals will be left in difficult positions which may not satisfy either disputing party in the case.

9.47 Apart from damages awards by tribunals, various states opted to settle cases during 2017, either in advance of awards or even after awards had been issued. Argentina, for instance, settled another outstanding compensation award during 2017, after settling with a number of investor claimants the previous year. The state agreed to pay French investor Total $210 million, after the *Total* award, reportedly worth

---

[90] *Burlington* (n 21) para 337.
[91] ibid.
[92] *PL Holdings* (n 55) para 648.
[93] *CME Czech Republic BV v Czech Republic*, UNCITRAL, Final Award (14 March 2003) 158.
[94] *Koch* (n 37) para 9.206.

$300 million, withstood an annulment bid by Argentina in 2016.⁹⁵ Bolivia settled its case with Spanish investor Abertis in May 2017, following hearings in December 2015.⁹⁶ The parties agreed to settle for around $23 million, representing roughly a quarter of the amount claimed by Abertis in the case relating to a dispute over tariffs for airport services provided by the investor. Venezuela also settled cases with mining companies Gold Reserve and Crystallex, in billion-dollar deals.⁹⁷

Ukraine announced in February 2017 that US pharmaceutical company Gilead Sciences Inc agreed to withdraw its (potential) BIT claim against the country. The parties had been in dispute over the rights of competing companies to sell a generic version of Gilead's hepatitis C drug in Ukraine. It was not clear whether Gilead had in fact filed a formal notice of arbitration with the state (and under what instrument, if so), or whether the case remained only at the level of a preliminary notice of dispute. Nevertheless, Ukraine portrayed the settlement as comprising an agreement from Gilead to withdraw its case and lower the price of its drug, in return for the de-registration of the competing drug.⁹⁸ 9.48

A short-lived claim by Turkish construction company Görkem against Turkmenistan was settled in December 2017, when the claimant reached a separate settlement with its Turkmen contracting partner in a case relating to the construction of a shopping and trade centre. The claim was filed at ICSID in August 2016, but a tribunal was constituted only in October 2017, two months before the parties agreed to discontinue the case.⁹⁹ 9.49

In December 2017, Ecuador announced that it had settled its case with US oil investor Burlington Resources Inc for a reported $337 million.¹⁰⁰ As noted above, the tribunal at ICSID had awarded Burlington nearly $380 million in damages, 9.50

---

⁹⁵ Reuters, 'Argentina Gives France's Total Bonds in Settlement' (*Reuters*, 19 July 2017) <www.reuters.com/article/uk-argentina-total-bonds/argentina-gives-frances-total-bonds-in-settlement-idUKKBN1A320V>.
⁹⁶ Damien Charlotin and Luke Peterson, 'Bolivia: An Update on Three Investment Treaty Arbitrations (Glencore, Abertis, Quiborax)' *Investment Arbitration Reporter* (12 May 2017) <tinyurl.com/kyqc98j>.
⁹⁷ Katia Dmitrieva, Katia Porzecanski, and Bob van Voris, 'Crystallex, Venezuela Agree to Settle $1.2 Billion Mine Dispute' (*Bloomberg*, 25 November 2017) <www.bloomberg.com/news/articles/2017-11-24/crystallex-venezuela-agree-to-settle-1-2-billion-mine-dispute>; Reuters, 'Gold Reserve Gets $40 Million of $1.03 Billion Settlement Deal with Venezuela' (*Reuters*, 17 June 2017) <www.reuters.com/article/us-gold-reserve-arbitration-venezuela/gold-reserve-gets-40-million-of-1-03-billion-settlement-deal-with-venezuela-idUSKBN1972O7>.
⁹⁸ Luke Peterson and Zoe Williams, 'Pharma Corp Withdraws Investment Arbitration After Ukraine Government Agrees to Settlement of Dispute over Monopoly Rights to Market Anti-Viral Drug' *Investment Arbitration Reporter* (16 March 2017) <tinyurl.com/htdpaf2>.
⁹⁹ Investment Arbitration Reporter, 'Turkmenistan BIT Arbitration Comes to an End' *Investment Arbitration Reporter* (13 December 2017) <tinyurl.com/y7pomzpe>.
¹⁰⁰ Reuters, 'ConocoPhillips to Receive $337 in Accord with Ecuador' (*Reuters*, 5 December 2017) <www.reuters.com/article/us-conocophillips-ecuador/conocophillips-to-receive-337-million-in-accord-with-ecuador-idUSKBN1DY1KP>.

offset by a nearly $42 million award in favour of Ecuador under a successful counterclaim. The agreed settlement figure thus appears to represent the amount ordered by the tribunal, once the counterclaim set-off is factored in, suggesting that the settlement effectively amounts to Ecuador's agreement to comply in full with the original compensation award. The parties further agreed to discontinue Ecuador's request for annulment of the award, a decision on which was still pending at the time of settlement.

E. Annulment and Set-Aside

9.51 Investors and states alike sought to annul a range of investment treaty decisions during 2017. While ICSID's annulment process is perhaps the most prominent forum for such challenges, a significant number of awards not governed by the ICSID Convention were the subject of set-aside attempts in various domestic courts during 2017.

9.52 At ICSID, an annulment committee rejected Argentina's bid to annul the $400 million *Suez* award in May 2017. Argentina had pleaded the less common ground of a defect in tribunal constitution (under Article 52(1)(a) of the ICSID Convention), focusing on a directorship held by one arbitrator, Gabrielle Kaufmann-Kohler, at Swiss bank UBS, which owned shares in the claimants.[101] However, confirming the high bar required for annulment at ICSID, the ad hoc annulment committee considered that it would only annul the award on this basis if the decision not to disqualify Ms Kaufmann-Kohler was so unreasonable that no reasonable person could have made it. While the committee expressed some sympathy for criticisms of the arbitrator in failing to disclose the directorship to the parties, the disqualification decision was not 'plainly unreasonable'.[102] Other grounds for annulment raised by Argentina were also rejected, with the committee declining to second-guess the tribunal's reasoning on the use of an MFN clause to avoid an eighteen-month local litigation requirement in the treaty, and on the application of the customary defence of necessity.

9.53 Similarly, in October 2017, an ICSID annulment committee upheld a June 2015 jurisdictional decision in *Gambrinus v Venezuela*, which had dismissed the investor's claim. The committee again confirmed its limited mandate of review, and declined to re-open all the claimed errors in the tribunal's reasoning,

---

[101] The same facts had also underpinned several other unsuccessful challenges against Ms Kaufmann-Kohler in other cases.
[102] *Suez v Argentina*, ICSID Case No ARB/03/19, Decision on Argentina's Application for Annulment (5 May 2017) paras 201, 218.

particularly where (the committee held) some of the claims raised by the aggrieved investor had not been put to the original tribunal.[103]

9.54 Venezuela had already enjoyed annulment success that year, succeeding in its bid to annul the $1.4 billion *Exxon* damages award at ICSID in March 2017. The original tribunal had found the state in breach of the Netherlands–Venezuela BIT in 2014, and had awarded the massive sum partly due to its decision to disregard a clause in the underlying investment contract that limited compensation. Instead of abiding by the contractual limitation clause, the tribunal determined that it should apply international law compensation standards. However, the annulment committee recalled that the legal rights underpinning an investment were defined by domestic law, not international law, and that the market value of these rights would be affected by their scope as determined by domestic law. The committee held that, in calculating compensation, the tribunal should have factored in the contractual limitation clause, since the domestic law clause would have implications for the international law test of market value of the investment.[104] Furthermore, according to the committee, the tribunal had also wrongly applied customary international law standards on compensation when in fact the BIT standards should have applied for the lawful expropriation at issue in the case.[105] These failures to apply the proper law led the committee to find that the high bar for annulment had been overcome in this case. While the original tribunal's finding of liability was left untouched, the $1.4 billion damages component was set aside.

9.55 Outside ICSID, Venezuela had less success in set-aside efforts in 2017. In relation to another $1.4 billion award, the United States District Court for the District of Columbia declined to set aside the (later-settled) 2016 ICSID Additional Facility award in *Crystallex v Venezuela*. Like ICSID annulment committees, the DC court confirmed the high threshold needed for set-aside in that jurisdiction, holding that it would not review the merits of the underlying decision. Amongst other arguments, Venezuela had contended that confirming the award would be contrary to US public policy, which (Venezuela said) recognized states' rights to regulate the environmental impacts of industry. However, the DC court rejected this, doubting that Venezuela's expropriation of the investment was truly motivated by environmental concerns. In any case, the court viewed itself merely as holding Venezuela to the terms of its treaty, which did not violate any basic US notions of justice.[106] Meanwhile, Venezuela also lost its bid to set aside another

---

[103] *Gambrinus Corp v Venezuela*, ICSID Case No ARB/11/31, Decision on Annulment (3 October 2017).
[104] *Venezuela Holdings BV v Venezuela*, ICSID Case No ARB/07/27, Decision on Annulment (9 March 2017) para 184.
[105] ibid para 188.
[106] *Crystallex International Corporation v Venezuela*, Civil Action 16-0661, United States District Court for the District of Columbia (25 March 2017).

(later settled) ICSID Additional Facility award worth $700 million, in the *Gold Reserve* case before the Paris Court of Appeal in February 2017. Taking a slightly more substantive approach to review of the jurisdictional issues in that award, the Paris court held that it agreed with the tribunal's decision that there had been no abuse of process in the claimant's acquisition of its investment in Venezuela. As for the merits, the court held simply that the tribunal's decision fell within its mandate.[107]

9.56 In June 2017, the same DC court that ruled in *Crystallex v Venezuela* also dismissed a challenge to the 2016 decision in *Mesa Power v Canada*, which had rejected the investor's claim. The court noted that a mere disagreement with the tribunal's merits decision would not be enough for set-aside. In particular, the court observed that a dissenting arbitrator in the case had used the same interpretive tools as the majority, but had come to a different view, suggesting that there was no underlying flaw with the tribunal's reasoning methods but purely differences of appreciation.[108]

9.57 Two other notable set-aside claims—one successful, the other not—arose during 2017. In July, the Hague Court of Appeal upheld a lower court judgment dismissing Ecuador's challenge to several awards issued by a tribunal in the ongoing *Chevron v Ecuador* case. The appeal court was satisfied that the tribunal had properly accepted jurisdiction in the case, and held that its review powers did not extend to second-guessing the merits of the tribunal's decisions. Most notably, the Dutch court disagreed with Ecuador's argument that the tribunal's interim measures order—directing the state to prevent enforcement of the multi-billion-dollar 'Lago Agrio' judgment against Chevron—interfered with the state's sovereignty. According to the court, Ecuador had agreed to the application of the UNCITRAL rules when it consented to arbitration in the underlying BIT, and this entailed agreement to be subjected to any interim measures ordered by UNCITRAL rules tribunals. As well, by definition, the interim measures might be revoked later. Thus, the court found no conflict with public policy in upholding this element of the tribunal's decisions.[109]

9.58 Lastly, the Singapore High Court ruled in August 2017 in a complex case brought by South African investors against the Kingdom of Lesotho, relying on the Finance and Investment Protocol (FIP) of the Southern African Development Community (SADC). In April 2016, an UNCITRAL rules tribunal had held (by majority) that Lesotho breached the FIP when it participated in the process of shutting down the supposedly-permanent SADC Tribunal, which at the time was

---

[107] *Venezuela v Gold Reserve Inc*, RG 14/21103, Paris Court of Appeal (7 February 2017).
[108] *Mesa Power Group LLC v Canada*, Civil Action 16-1101, United States District Court for the District of Columbia (15 June 2017).
[109] *Ecuador v Chevron Corporation*, 200.193.418/01, Hague Court of Appeal (18 July 2017) para 12.2.

hearing a claim of expropriation against Lesotho, brought by the South African investors. No compensation was awarded, but Lesotho was ordered to establish a new ad hoc tribunal to hear the expropriation claim again.[110] Reviewing the *Swissbourgh v Lesotho* award, the Singapore court focused on the FIP tribunal's finding that the right to bring a claim to the SADC Tribunal was indeed an investment protected by the FIP. Analysing this jurisdictional finding *de novo* under Singaporean law, the court doubted that the right to bring a claim fit the FIP definition of investment—which, it noted, was narrower than most equivalent definitions in BITs. Firstly, the court considered that the claimed investment was not grounded in Lesotho's territory, nor governed by its domestic law, as (the court said) was required by the FIP (contrary to the tribunal, which had held that the investment did not need to meet these requirements). Secondly, the court saw an insufficient connection between the right to bring a claim and the 'bundle of rights' forming the actual investment in the case, namely, the claimants' mining rights in Lesotho. Thirdly, the court noted that the FIP required an investment to be 'admitted' into the host state; in the court's view, a right to bring a claim before an international tribunal was simply not capable of being 'admitted' in the manner envisaged by the FIP. Ultimately, the court held, the right to bring a claim was not itself an investment, but was a protection granted by the FIP in respect of the actual investment—the underlying mining project.[111] On a separate issue, the court also examined the FIP's (unusual) requirement of exhausting local remedies before pursuing a claim under that instrument. The tribunal had concluded that a particular remedy in the Lesotho legal system did not offer effective redress for the lost opportunity to claim before the SADC Tribunal, and therefore did not need to be pursued by the claimants. The Singapore court entered into a substantive review of this finding, ultimately disagreeing with the FIP tribunal. Noting the importance of permitting respondent states an opportunity to correct errors within their own systems before being subjected to international claims, the court held that the investors should have pursued this remedy, even if it was unclear whether it would be successful.[112] While the *Swissbourgh* case is atypical in many respects, the Singapore court challenge offers some useful discussion of the definition of investment and the exhaustion of local remedies rule, which has at times displayed complicated interactions with investment treaty jurisprudence.[113]

---

[110] Luke Peterson, 'INVESTIGATION: Lesotho is Held Liable for Investment Treaty Breach Arising Out of its Role in Hobbling a Regional Tribunal That Had Been Hearing Expropriation Case' *Investment Arbitration Reporter* (14 July 2016) <tinyurl.com/jx4a5zr>.
[111] *Lesotho v Swissbourgh Diamond Mines (Pty) Ltd* [2017] SGHC 195, 90–106.
[112] ibid 140–56.
[113] See eg Zachary Douglas, 'International Responsibility for Domestic Adjudication: Denial of Justice Deconstructed' (2014) 63 International & Comparative Law Quarterly 867.

D. INVESTMENT AND . . .

10

HUMAN RIGHTS IN INTERNATIONAL INVESTMENT LAW
Recent Trends in Arbitration and Treaty-Making Practice

Markus Krajewski

A. Introduction	10.01	D. Recent Developments in Human Rights Law-making	10.28
B. Neither Foes nor Friends? Investment Law and International Human Rights	10.03	E. Conclusion	10.38
C. Recent Developments in Investment Law	10.09		

A. Introduction

The relationship between international investment law and human rights has been a contentious topic of political and scholarly debates, at least since the 2003 Report of the United Nations High Commissioner for Human Rights on 'Human rights, trade and investment'.[1] In this report, the High Commissioner recommended that states should maintain sufficient policy space to promote and protect human rights and clarify investors' obligations vis-à-vis human rights when drafting investment agreements.[2] Many academic contributions evolve around similar issues and discuss whether investment treaties and arbitral practice restricts states in pursuing policies aimed at the full realization of human rights.[3] The focus of the

10.01

---

[1] United Nations Commission on Human Rights (Sub-Commission on the Promotion and Protection of Human Rights), 'Report of the High Commissioner for Human Rights on Economic, Social and Cultural Rights: Human rights, trade and investment' (2 July 2003) UN Doc E/CN.4/Sub.2/2003/9.
[2] ibid paras 58–59.
[3] Pierre-Marie Dupuy, Ernst-Ulrich Petersmann, and Francesco Francioni (eds), *Human Rights in International Investment Law and Arbitration* (OUP 2009); Marc Jacob, 'International Investment

debate has largely been on the impact of the interpretation and application of the terms of investment agreements on the states' ability to regulate and to maintain policy space, often dubbed as the 'right to regulate'.[4] In 2017, the debate gained momentum through new approaches in investment arbitration and treaties as well as in human rights practice and treaty-making. These developments relate predominantly to the second aspect of the High Commissioner's 2003 report, that is the clarification of investor obligations with regard to human rights.

10.02 This present contribution discusses these developments in the framework of the larger debates on investment law and human rights and seeks to assess whether they are theoretically convincing and practically relevant. The contribution begins with a brief summary of the main elements of the debate on investment law and human rights protection until today (section B). It will then move to developments within the field of international investment law assessing both recent jurisprudence (section C.1) as well as newly concluded treaties (section C.2). Subsequently, the contribution will discuss recent developments in the field of human rights practice relating to new developments in treaty drafting (section D.1) and approaches taken by human rights treaty bodies (section D.2). Finally, the contribution suggests preliminary results and conclusions (section E).

B. Neither Foes nor Friends? Investment Law and International Human Rights

10.03 International human rights are human rights enshrined in global and regional human rights treaties such as the International Covenants on Civil and Political Rights and on Economic, Social and Cultural Rights of 1966 or the European, American, and African Conventions on human rights, as well as human rights established as customary international law. With the exception of those human rights which constitute *jus cogens*, there is no formal hierarchy between international human rights law and international investment law. Hence, any potential conflicts[5] need to be resolved through the formal rules on treaty conflicts as enshrined in *inter alia* Article 30 of the Vienna Convention on the Law of Treaties or through the interpretation or redrafting of the relevant investment treaties.

Agreements and Human Rights' (2010) INEF Research Paper Series: Human Rights, Corporate Responsibility and Sustainable Development 03/2010 < http://www.humanrights-business.org/files/international_investment_agreements_and_human_rights.pdf> accessed 22 May 2018.

[4] David Gaukrodger, 'The Balance between Investor Protection and the Right to Regulate in Investment Treaties: A Scoping Paper' (2017) OECD Working Papers on International Investment No 2017/02; Aikaterini Titi, *The Right to Regulate in International Investment Law* (Hart Publishing 2014).

[5] On the notion of conflicts: Erich Vranes, 'The Definition of "Norm Conflict" in International Law and Legal Theory' (2006) (17)(2) European Journal of International Law 395.

However, since the rules on treaty conflicts only apply to treaties relating to the same subject matter,[6] conflicts need to be resolved by interpreting the clauses of the applicable treaty in light of the obligations of the other treaty.[7]

The relationship between human rights and international investment law manifests itself in different contexts and directions. Two general and broad approaches concerning substantive law exist from the perspective of investment protection: human rights can be used to support or enlarge claims of investors or they can be used to strengthen the state's defence of its actions which are taken to respect, protect, and fulfil human rights. Similarly, investment law can be viewed in two different ways from the perspective of human rights: the requirements of investment law, in particular as interpreted and applied through investment tribunals, can be seen as restrictions on the state's ability to respect, protect, and fulfil human rights or as reinforcement of individual rights of investors under international investment law. 10.04

The different perspectives on substantive law broadly correspond with different procedural settings in investor–state disputes.[8] First, human rights can be introduced by the investor to support or complement his or her claims. Second, human rights may be relied upon by the state to defend its actions or to raise counterclaims against the investor. Third, human rights can be the subject of an *amicus curiae* brief. Fourth, they can be addressed by the investment tribunal independent of the arguments of the parties or the *amici*. As a variation of the last possibility, human rights could also be raised by one arbitrator in a separate or dissenting opinion. 10.05

These diverse approaches and variations show that there is a potential for conflict but also for mutual reinforcement in the relationship between human rights and international investment law. Many authors claim that international investment agreements and arbitration practice restrict the ability of states to fulfil their human rights obligations and that investment agreements may therefore conflict with human rights, because the latter would require certain state measures which the former would inhibit.[9] This has been 10.06

---

[6] Vienna Convention on the Law of Treaties (adopted 23 May 1969, entered into force 27 January 1980) 1155 UNTS 331 (VCLT), art 30(1).
[7] Bruno Simma and Theodore Kill, 'Harmonizing Investment Protection and Human Rights: First Steps Towards a Methodology' in Christina Binder, Ursula Kriebaum, and August Reinisch (eds), *International Investment Law for the 21st Century: Essays in Honour of Christoph Schreuer* (OUP 2009) 694; Jacob, (n 3) 29–30.
[8] Clara Reiner and Christoph Schreuer, 'Human Rights and International Investment Arbitration' in Pierre-Marie Dupuy, Ernst-Ulrich Petersmann, and Francesco Francioni (eds), *Human Rights in International Investment Law and Arbitration* (OUP 2009) 82, 88–94. For an overview see Vivian Kube and Ernest-Ulrich Petersmann, 'Human Rights Law in International Investment Arbitration' (2016) 11(1) Asian Journal of WTO & International Health Law & Policy 65.
[9] Moshe Hirsch, 'Interactions Between Investment and Non-Investment Obligations' in Peter Muchlinski et al (eds), *The Oxford Handbook of International Investment Law* (OUP 2008) 179; Bruno Simma, 'Foreign Investment Arbitration: A Place for Human Rights?' (2011) 60 International &

disputed by other authors who have claimed that investment arbitration practice hardly displays any real conflicts between the protection of human rights and the obligations of investment agreements, because human rights treaties do not require specific measures that would be inconsistent with investment agreements.[10]

10.07 Furthermore, other commentators have underlined the similarities of the principles of investment protection and human rights, and have argued that they serve the same functions. In the view of these authors, both legal regimes reinforce each other.[11] However, it should be noted that the potential for reinforcement only concerns human rights of the investor, which would normally be restricted to an individual right to property or basic principles of due process. Contrary to this, the conflictive relationship between human rights and investment law encompasses a broader range of human rights and rights holders, because the respective conflicts usually affect a large number of people, evident from the cases concerning the investment disputes surrounding water supply and services by foreign investors.[12]

10.08 As pointed out, while the different approaches to human rights and investment law have so far been the subject of many public and academic debates, their practical relevance has been relatively limited. International investment tribunals have occasionally referred to human rights but have not engaged in substantive analysis or based their decisions on human rights arguments.[13] Recent developments in investment arbitration practice and treaty-making, as well as in the field of human rights law, suggest that this may change and that the practical relevance of the relationship between human rights and investment could be growing.

Comparative Law Quarterly 573, 578; Cristina Bodea and Fangjin Ye, 'Investor Rights versus Human Rights: Do Bilateral Investment Treaties Tilt the Scale?' (2018) British Journal of Political Science 1–23. doi:10.1017/S0007123418000042.

[10] James D Fry, 'International Human Rights Law in Investment Arbitration: Evidence of International Law's Unity' (2006) 18 Duke Journal of Comparative & International Law 77.

[11] Francesco Francioni, 'Access to Justice, Denial of Justice and International Investment Law' in Pierre-Marie Dupuy, Ernst-Ulrich Petersmann, and Francesco Francioni (eds), *Human Rights in International Investment Law and Arbitration* (OUP 2009) 63–81; Pierre-Marie Dupuy and Jorge E Viñuales, 'Human Rights and Investment Disciplines: Integration in Progress' in Marc Bungenberg, Jörn Griebel, Stephan Hobe, and August Reinisch (eds), *International Investment Law* (Hart Publishing 2015) 1739–67.

[12] Pierre Thielbörger, *The Right(s) to Water: The Multi-Level Governance of a Unique Human Right* (Springer 2014) 152.

[13] Silvia Steininger, 'What's Human Rights Got To Do With It? An Empirical Analysis of Human Rights References in Investment Arbitration' (2018) 31(1) Leiden Journal of International Law 33; see also Kube and Petersmann (n 8) 72–94.

C. Recent Developments in Investment Law

1. Investor–state dispute settlement cases

a. Urbaser v Argentina

Although investment tribunals have mentioned human rights law in their awards in the past, the deliberation of the ICSID tribunal in the matter of *Urbaser v Argentina* of 8 December 2016 on potential human rights obligations of international investors has been the most innovative and thought-provoking approach so far.[14] The case was part of the saga of investment disputes following the Argentinian financial and economic crisis between 1998 and 2001.[15] It concerned a concession for water and sewage services in the Province of Greater Buenos Aires granted to a company established *inter alia* by Urbaser. During the Argentinian crisis, the concession ran into a deadlock after Argentina depreciated the value of the Peso and failed to revaluate the tariffs of the concession. The Province of Greater Buenos Aires then chose to terminate the concession.[16] Unlike in previous cases in which Argentina—although reluctantly—referred to its obligations under human rights law, especially the right to water, to defend its measures,[17] in *Urbaser* Argentina filed a counterclaim based on the investor's alleged failure to provide the necessary investment into the water concession. According to Argentina this constituted a violation of the investor's 'commitments and its obligations under international law based on the human right to water'.[18] 10.09

After determining that the claim fell within its jurisdiction, the tribunal held that international human rights were part of the applicable law in the dispute because the relevant bilateral investment treaty (BIT) between Spain and Argentina 10.10

---

[14] *Urbaser SA and Consorcio de Aguas Bilbao Bizkaia, Bilbao Biskaia Ur Partuergoa v The Argentine Republic*, ICSID Case No ARB/07/26, Award (8 December 2016). For an analysis see Jarrod Hepburn, 'In a First, BIT Tribunal Finds that it Has Jurisdiction to Hear a Host State's Counterclaim Related to Investor's Alleged Violation of International Human Rights Obligations' *Investment Arbitration Reporter* (12 January 2017) <https://www.iareporter.com/articles/in-a-first-bit-tribunal-finds-that-it-has-jurisdiction-to-hear-a-host-states-counterclaim-related-to-investors-alleged-violation-of-international-human-rights-obligations/> accessed 22 May 2018; Caroline Richard and Elliot Luke, 'Human Rights in International Investment Law: Where to After Urbaser?' (Freshfields Bruckhaus Deringer, 22 December 2017) <http://humanrights.freshfields.com/post/102enaj/human-rights-in-international-investment-law-where-to-after-urbaser> accessed 22 May 2018; and Monica Feria-Tinta, 'Like Oil and Water? Human Rights in Investment Arbitration in the Wake of Philip Morris v. Uruguay' (2017) 34 Journal of International Arbitration 601, 625–28.

[15] Kevin Crow and Lina Lorenzoni Escobar, 'International Corporate Obligations, Human Rights, and the Urbaser Standard: Breaking New Ground?' (2018) 35 Boston University International Law Journal 87, 92.

[16] *Urbaser v Argentina* (n 14) para 34.

[17] See for example: *Suez et al v The Argentine Republic*, ICSID Case No ARB/03/19, Decision on Liability (30 July 2010) para 252; *SAUR International SA v The Argentine Republic*, ICSID Case No ARB/04/4, Decision on Jurisdiction and Liability (6 June 2012) para 328.

[18] *Urbaser v Argentina* (n 14) para 37.

included a reference to 'general principles of international law'.[19] Subsequently and to the surprise of many observers in the field of international investment law, the tribunal was of the opinion that private parties could have obligations for compliance in relation to human rights.[20] The tribunal began its reasoning by stating that the existence of human rights obligations of investors could not be categorically dismissed based on the fact that they are not subjects of international law.[21] Indeed, the tribunal rightly observes that BITs confer rights on investors which means that they can generally be also bearers of obligations.[22] While it is true that the existence of BITs indicates that corporations can be partial subjects of public international law, this does not establish which obligations they have.

10.11 The tribunal based its finding on the growing importance of corporate social responsibility (CSR) standards as well as on specific provisions of human rights instruments.[23] Its first argument concerned the Universal Declaration of Human Rights (UDHR), in particular Article 30 UDHR, which provides that provisions in the Declaration may not be interpreted as allowing a state, group, or person to destroy the rights and freedoms enshrined in the UDHR. According to the tribunal, this provision indicates that private entities can also be bound by human rights in general.[24] The tribunal then recalled various articles of the International Covenant on Civil and Political Rights (ICCPR). Some of these refer to specific rights which confer the human right to water. However, the tribunal also pointed to Article 5 ICCPR, which is comparable to Article 30 UDHR.[25] Ultimately, the tribunal concluded that these provisions show that the right of an individual is complemented by an obligation by public and private entities 'not to engage in an activity which is aimed at destroying those rights'.[26] Hence, the human rights obligation of private entities was construed by the tribunal as an obligation to abstain from an activity.

10.12 The tribunal then turned to the specific question of whether the claimant in the case of *Urbaser* was bound by an international law obligation to provide the people living in the area of the concession with drinking water and sanitation services. The tribunal pointed out that the contractual obligation of Urbaser to provide water based on the Concession would not include an international legal obligation of the investor.[27] The tribunal also noted that none of the provisions of the BIT contain such a specific human rights obligation.[28] The tribunal further

---

[19] ibid para 1192.
[20] ibid para 1193.
[21] ibid para 1194.
[22] ibid.
[23] ibid paras 1195–99.
[24] ibid para 1196.
[25] ibid paras 1197–99.
[26] ibid para 1199.
[27] ibid para 1206.
[28] ibid para 1207.

recalled the doctrine of human rights law according to which the obligation to ensure the population's access to water is based on the host state's laws and not an independent obligation of the investor.[29] The tribunal underlined the state's obligations in is context:

> The human right to water entails an obligation of compliance on the part of the State, but it does not contain an obligation for performance on part of any company providing the contractually required service. Such obligation would have to be distinct from the State's responsibility to serve its population with drinking water and sewage services.[30]

The tribunal therefore dismissed the counterclaim. However, it noted that its conclusions might have been different 'in case an obligation to abstain, like a prohibition to commit acts violating human rights would be at stake', because such an obligation would be of 'immediate application, not only upon States, but equally to individuals and other private parties.'[31]

10.13 The determination of the tribunal and its legal reasoning have already led to a number of academic reflections. Some have questioned the doctrinal support for the broad claims concerning the idea of human rights obligations of corporations,[32] while others have argued that the practical impact of the approach taken by the tribunal may be minimal because the standards set by the tribunal for an investor's duty to actually perform certain services or activities to discharge human rights obligations will usually not be met.[33] Nevertheless, it has also been pointed out that the tribunal's approach may lead the way to future cases in which investors could be held liable for violations of human rights.[34]

10.14 Regardless of its imminent practical impact, the tribunal's approach raises important conceptual questions. The tribunal acknowledged that CSR standards alone cannot provide a legal basis for human rights obligations of private companies. However, its interpretation of Article 30 UDHR and Article 5 ICCPR is not based on the conventional understanding of human rights. Both provisions can be used as context when interpreting specific clauses of the human rights

---

[29] ibid para 1209.
[30] ibid para 1208.
[31] ibid para 1210.
[32] Edward Guntrip, 'Urbaser v Argentina: The Origins of a Host State Human Rights Counterclaim in ICSID Arbitration?' (*EJIL: Talk!*, 10 February 2017) <https://www.ejiltalk.org/urbaser-v-argentina-the-origins-of-a-host-state-human-rights-counterclaim-in-icsid-arbitration/> accessed 22 May 2018.
[33] Crow and Escobar (n 15) 116–17.
[34] Naomi Briercliffe, 'Holding Investors to Account for Human Rights Violations through Counterclaims in Investment Treaty Arbitration' (Allen & Overy, 30 January 2017) <http://www.allenovery.com/publications/en-gb/Pages/Holding-investors-to-account-for-human-rights-violations-through-counterclaims-in-investment-treaty-arbitration.aspx> accessed 22 May 2018.

instruments, but they do not address the question of potential duty-bearers under the relevant international instruments.[35]

10.15 The tribunal's determination provides no reference to existing standards of interpretation (textual, contextual, or object and purpose of human rights treaties) nor suggests any case law which might lead into the direction of human rights obligations for private entities. The tribunal could, for example, have asked if the existence of international standards and domestic laws on corporate responsibility leads to customary investor obligations. While the tribunal recalled these standards, it only concludes that 'it can no longer be admitted that companies operating internationally are immune from becoming subjects of international law'.[36] However, the tribunal also stated that these standards are not 'on their own, sufficient to oblige corporations to put their policies in line with human rights law.'[37] Yet, the tribunal does not base this conclusion on any specific doctrinal arguments.

10.16 Furthermore, the tribunal could have analysed if the interpretation of the applicable BIT could be developed into human rights obligations of investors. However, by not engaging with these approaches, the tribunal does not connect its reasoning with the wider debate. It is hence difficult to situate the approach adopted by the tribunal in the broader context of current thinking on corporate obligations in human rights law.[38] Consequently, the search for doctrinal support of the tribunal's approach continues.

b. Separate opinion of Philippe Sands in Bear Creek v Peru

10.17 So far it does not seem that other tribunals have taken up the *Urbaser* approach. However, Professor Philippe Sands, QC referred to it in his separate opinion to the award of the tribunal in the case of *Bear Creek v Peru* of 30 November 2017.[39] The case concerned a Canadian mining company that sought to invest in a Peruvian silver mine. The tribunal unanimously decided that Peru's revocation of a decree which was necessary to operate the mine amounted to an indirect expropriation on the basis of the Free Trade Agreement between Canada and the Republic of Peru. The tribunal therefore awarded Bear Creek compensation for its sunk costs.

---

[35] Guntrip (n 32).
[36] *Urbaser v Argentina* (n 14) para 1195.
[37] ibid.
[38] On this debate see: Andrew Clapham, *Human Rights Obligations of Non-State Actors* (OUP 2006) and Adam McBeth, *International Economic Actors and Human Rights* (Routledge 2010).
[39] *Bear Creek Mining Corporation v Republic of Perú*, ICSID Case No ARB/14/21, Partial Dissenting Opinion of Philippe Sands (30 November 2017) paras 1–41. For an analysis see also Jarrod Hepburn, 'Tribunal Rejects DCF Approach in Bear Creek Case; Dissenter Sees ILO Convention on Indigenous and Tribal Peoples as Imposing Obligations in Context of Miner's ICSID Claim' *Investment Arbitration Reporter* (4 December 2017) <https://www.iareporter.com/articles/tribunal-rejects-dcf-approach-in-bear-creek-case-dissenter-sees-ilo-convention-on-indigenous-and-tribal-peoples-as-imposing-obligations-in-context-of-miners-icsid-claim/> accessed 22 May 2018.

However, Philippe Sands was of the opinion that certain activities of the investor, especially its role in causing or contributing to social unrest in the area of the project, should have been taken into account when calculating the amount of compensation. In his reasoning, Professor Sands referred to International Labour Organization (ILO) Convention No 169 concerning Indigenous and Tribal Peoples in Independent Countries which is generally accepted as part of human rights law.[40] Sands conceded that the obligation to implement ILO Convention 169 falls on states and not on private parties. Yet, he also stated that 'the fact that the Convention may not impose obligations directly on a private foreign investor as such does not, however, mean that it is without significance or legal effects for them'.[41] This statement was associated with a specific reference to the *Urbaser* tribunal. Sands went on to argue that ILO Convention 169 was applicable in the case at hand and that the tribunal could take it into consideration when assessing the behaviour of the investor.[42] Adhering to those rules would in turn have also reduced its own damage.[43] As the investor had not obtained a 'social licence' to operate by consulting and cooperating with the indigenous peoples affected by the project, it contributed to the failure of the project according to Sands.[44] **10.18**

Although it incorporates some of the reasoning of the *Urbaser* tribunal, the separate opinion of Philippe Sands does not seem to share its main conclusion, that is that private parties could have direct obligations based on human rights law. Instead, Sands seems to argue that violation of human rights by investors can be taken into account when determining the level of compensation if adhering to human rights requirements would have minimized potential damages which the investors suffered. This approach seems less burdensome on investors, but may prove more powerful than the *Urbaser* approach because its practical effects may be significant. First, the approach taken by Philippe Sands does not require the responding state to actually file a counterclaim. Instead it would be sufficient for the state to allege that the investor did not adhere to the requirements of international human rights law. Second, taking human rights violations of an investor into account when determining the amount of the damages could have a potentially larger effect on investors than theoretical speculations about the nature of their human rights obligations. **10.19**

However, it should also be noted that the assessment of the conduct of an investor would be better suited in the merits part of an award and less so as part of the calculation of the damages. Yet, in the absence of enforceable **10.20**

---

[40] *Bear Creek v Peru*, Partial Dissenting Opinion of Philippe Sands (n 39) para 7.
[41] ibid para 10.
[42] ibid para 11.
[43] ibid.
[44] ibid para 38.

obligations of the investor enshrined in the investment agreement, the damages stage may be the only opportunity to assess the conduct of the investor in this regard.

c. Conclusion

10.21 Despite its limited scope the arbitral practice positively engaging with human rights obligations of investors so far indicates the benefits and dangers of this approach. One of the benefits of investment tribunals applying human rights obligations of investors is that the application takes place in the context of a specific case and considers the particular circumstances of that case. The development of 'human rights case law' in investment arbitration could therefore contribute to the establishment of clearer rules and expectations for investors. Even though investment law is not based on a formal system of precedent, tribunals often rely on the reasoning of others. For example, Professor Sands referred to the *Urbaser* case in his separate opinion. The conclusion reached by Professor Sands in the *Bear Creek* case is also an example of a concretization of human rights obligations through specific cases as it was based on the facts of the case and the actual behaviour of the investor. It is clear that Professor Sands was of the opinion that this behaviour of the investor did not meet the requirements of ILO Convention 169.

10.22 However, it has to be conceded that the development of investment arbitration human rights case law through a piecemeal approach may lead to further fragmentation and bears the danger of being disconnected with the human rights discourse. It is not surprising that the decision in *Urbaser*—though welcomed by some based on its general approach—was received with some scepticism by human rights scholars.[45] It seems that establishing a convincing legal basis for human rights obligations of private entities remains as necessary and important as ever.

2. Human rights obligations for investors in investment treaties

10.23 The most obvious and straightforward legal basis for investor obligations concerning human rights would be the establishment of such obligations in international investment agreements. This could be done through the binding incorporation of international standards such as the OECD Guidelines for Multinational Enterprises,[46] or through direct investor obligations. While this idea had been suggested in the literature,[47] by international organizations such

---

[45] Guntrip (n 32).
[46] See eg Eva van der Zee, 'Incorporating the OECD Guidelines in International Investment Agreements: Turning a Soft Law Obligation into Hard Law?' (2013) 40 Legal Issues of Economic Integration 33.
[47] Barnali Choudhury, 'Spinning Straw into Gold: Incorporating the Business and Human Rights Agenda into International Investment Agreements' (2017) 38 University of Pennsylvania Journal of International Law 425, 469–70.

as the United Nations Conference on Trade and Development (UNCTAD),[48] and by civil society actors for a long time, it was not until December 2016 that the idea was actually finally realized.[49] Until then, even the most progressive investment treaties only contained hortatory language encouraging investors to adhere to principles of corporate social responsibility.[50] Specific references to human rights obligations of investors in investment treaties remained vague and without binding force.

The new BIT between Morocco–Nigeria of 2016 departs from previous practice.[51] Its Article 18(2) states: 'Investors and investments shall uphold human rights in the host state.' Upon entry into force, the Morocco–Nigeria BIT would be the first international investment agreement that establishes binding obligations on investors to uphold human rights. This would make it one of the most innovative agreements of recent times.[52] In this event the legal basis for human rights obligations of investors of the respective parties to the treaty investing in the other country would be crystal clear. However, while the legal basis would be clear, its exact contents would remain vague as the BIT only refers to human rights in broad terms and does not specify concrete obligations. 10.24

The approach taken by Morocco and Nigeria in their BIT does not stand alone. It seems to be part of a general trend in African investment treaty practice and law-making. For example, Article 14(2) of the ECOWAS Supplementary Act on Investment of 2009 holds: 10.25

> Investors shall uphold human rights in the workplace and the community in which they are located. Investors shall not undertake or cause to be undertaken, acts that breach such human rights. Investors shall not manage or operate the investments in a manner that circumvents human rights obligations, labour standards as well as regional environmental and social obligations, to which the host State and/or home State are Parties.[53]

---

[48] UNCTAD, 'Investment Policy Framework for Sustainable Development' (2015) <http://unctad.org/en/PublicationsLibrary/diaepcb2015d5_summary_en.pdf> accessed 22 May 2018, 110.

[49] For a review of agreements until 2014 see Lise Johnson, Lisa E Sachs, and Jesse Coleman, 'International Investment Agreements, 2014: A Review of Trends and New Approaches' in Lisa E Sachs and Lise Johnson (eds), *Yearbook on International Investment Law and Policy 2015–2016* (OUP 2018) 58.

[50] Peter Muchlinski, 'The Impact of a Business and Human rights Treaty on Investment Law and Arbitration' in Surya Deva and David Bilchitz (eds), *Building a Treaty on Business and Human Rights: Context and Contours* (CUP 2017) 351–52.

[51] The treaty was signed on 3 December 2016 but is not yet in force. Its text is available at <http://investmentpolicyhub.unctad.org/Download/TreatyFile/5409> accessed 22 May 2018.

[52] Tarcisio Gazzini, 'The 2016 Morocco–Nigeria BIT: An Important Contribution to the Reform of Investment Treaties' (September 2017) 3(8) <https://www.iisd.org/sites/default/files/publications/iisd-itn-september-2017-english.pdf> accessed 22 May 2018.

[53] ECOWAS, 'Supplementary Act A/SA.3/12/08 Adopting Community Rules on Investment and the Modalities for their Implementation with ECOWAS of 19 December 2008' <http://investmentpolicyhub.unctad.org/Download/TreatyFile/3266> accessed 22 May 2018.

In a similar, but slightly less strict language, Article 24 of the African Union's Draft Pan-African Investment Code of 2016[54] requires that 'the following principles should govern compliance by investors with business ethics and human rights: (a) support and respect the protection of internationally recognized human rights; (b) ensure that they are not complicit in human rights abuses; ….' It can therefore be argued that establishing human rights obligations for investors is part of a new African approach to investment treaty-making.[55]

10.26 The benefit of the explicit establishment of binding human rights obligations in international agreements appears clear: it provides for an unambiguous legal basis to apply human rights obligations to private investors. However, it should also be noted that both Article 18 of the Morocco–Nigeria BIT as well as the legal documents upon which this provision may be based remain vague in terms of their contents. This is especially problematic as the exact elements of human rights obligations of private entities are unclear. This is why a mere reference to the adherence of investors to human rights may not be sufficient.

10.27 Non-binding standards such as the OECD Guidelines or the United Nations Guiding Principles on Business and Human Rights (UNGPs) provide for greater clarification and contain more details. For example, both the UNGPs and the OECD Guidelines specify the elements of human rights due diligence which a company is expected to undertake. The UNGPs clarify that due diligence is based on human rights expertise and consultations with stakeholders.[56] Furthermore, the OECD Guidelines are also applied in concrete cases deliberated at National Contact Points which lead to a concretization of these Guidelines. However, so far these standards do not impose any legally binding obligations on corporations. If, however, investment treaties incorporated these standards and made them binding, this approach would likely be more effective than the inclusion of a more general obligation for investors to uphold human rights.

D. Recent Developments in Human Rights Law-making

10.28 International investment law is not the only field of law that has displayed innovative developments concerning investment protection and human rights in the recent past. Human rights law has also seen some new approaches.

---

[54] African Union Commission, 'Economic Affairs Department, Draft Pan- African Investment Code' (December 2016) <https://au.int/sites/default/files/documents/32844-doc-draft_pan-african_investment_code_december_2016_en.pdf> accessed 22 May 2018.

[55] Makane Moïse Mbengue and Stefanie Schacherer, 'The "Africanization" of International Investment Law: The Pan-African Investment Code and the Reform of the International Investment Regime' (2017) 18 The Journal of World Investment & Trade 414, 434–36.

[56] United Nations Office of the High Commissioner, 'UN Guiding Principles on Business and Human Rights' (2011), Principle 18.

1. Treaty on business and human rights

The most interesting development in the past years has been the re-emergence of the idea of creating binding obligations for business entities through an international human rights law instrument.[57] The United Nations Human Rights Council established an open-ended intergovernmental working group (IGWG) on transnational corporations and other business enterprises with respect to human rights by resolution 26/9 in 2014 and entrusted it with the mandate 'to elaborate an international legally binding instrument to regulate, in international human rights law, the activities of transnational corporations and other business enterprises'. The IGWG held two informative sessions in 2015 and 2016.[58] In its third session, the IGWG commenced formal negotiations on a treaty on business and human rights even though a number of developed countries and the EU are still opposing this approach. Hence, it is currently still unclear if the debates will lead to a treaty at the end.

10.29

The negotiations have not yet produced draft texts. However, the Chairmanship of the IGWG published a paper which outlines the possible elements of a treaty on business and human rights (the Elements Paper).[59] While the Elements Paper is not meant to be a formal negotiating document, but rather a collection of possible elements for discussion, it can be used as an indicator of what could be part of the treaty. Given the early stage of negotiations, it is difficult to predict whether these elements will inform any treaty that emerges on the basis of current discussions, or if a treaty will emerge at all.

10.30

Nevertheless, it is useful to note that the Elements Paper outlines potential obligations of transnational corporations and other business enterprises (TNCs and OBEs). For example, it is suggested that TNCs and OBEs shall comply with all applicable laws and respect internationally recognized human rights, wherever they operate, and throughout their supply chains. Furthermore, the Elements Paper proposes that TNCs and OBEs shall prevent human rights impacts of their activities and provide redress. In addition, TNCs and OBEs shall design, adopt, and implement internal policies consistent with internationally recognized

10.31

---

[57] David Bilchitz, 'The Necessity for a Business and Human Rights Treaty' (2016) 1 Business and Human Rights Journal 203; Surya Deva and David Bilchitz (eds), *Building a Treaty on Business and Human Rights: Context and Contours* (CUP 2017).

[58] See Carlos Lopez, 'Struggling to Take Off?: The Second Session of Intergovernmental Negotiations on a Treaty on Business and Human Rights' (2017) 2 Business and Human Rights Journal 365.

[59] 'Open-ended intergovernmental working group on transnational corporations and other business enterprises with respect human rights, Elements for a Draft Legally Binding Instrument on transnational corporations and other business enterprises with respect to human rights, Chairmanship of the OEIGWG established by HRC Res. A/HRC/RES/26/9, 29 September 2017', <http://www.ohchr.org/Documents/HRBodies/HRCouncil/WGTransCorp/Session3/LegallyBindingInstrumentTNCs_OBEs.pdf> accessed 22 May 2018.

human rights standards and establish effective follow-up and review mechanisms, to verify compliance throughout their operations. Finally, the Elements Paper refers to an obligation of TNCs and OBEs to refrain from activities that would undermine the rule of law as well as governmental and other efforts to promote and ensure respect for human rights and shall use their influence in order to help promote and ensure respect for human rights. If adopted and implemented these proposals would establish significant and far-reaching binding human rights obligations for private corporations in the field of human rights.

10.32 In addition to direct obligations for private entities, the Elements Paper also suggests including provisions in a treaty on business and human rights which would establish a primacy of human rights obligations over trade and investment agreements.[60] This rather vague proposal needs to be complemented and concretized by suggestions for state obligations to include clauses in investment treaties which clarify their relationship to the obligations of the investment treaty or which provide for specific investor obligations. In addition, states could be required to raise human rights arguments in investor–state dispute settlement proceedings.[61] Most importantly, states should be required to carry out human rights impact assessments before, during, and after the negotiations of an investment treaty.[62]

10.33 In light of the early stage of the negotiating process it is difficult to predict if, when, and with which results the negotiations may conclude. In any case, it is unclear how a potential treaty on business and human rights would affect an existing BIT or the decision of an investment arbitration tribunal. If both parties of a BIT would also be parties to a potential business and human rights treaty, the latter might constitute context in the meaning of Article 31(3)(c) of the Vienna Convention on the Law of Treaties and could therefore become relevant when interpreting an investment agreement.[63] However, if a BIT does not contain any references to investor obligations, the terms of the investment agreements cannot be interpreted in such a way that they would establish human rights obligations of investors. Furthermore, the impact of a treaty on business and human rights on an investment treaty with only one party also being a party to the business and human rights treaty may be even less clear. Addressing these challenges seems

---

[60] For an analysis of the idea of establishing a hierarchy, see Markus Krajewski, 'Framing the Broader Context of Business and Human Rights: The Impact of Trade Agreements on Human Rights' in Surya Deva (ed), *Research Handbook on Business and Human Rights* (forthcoming).
[61] Muchlinski (n 50) 374.
[62] For detailed proposals, see Markus Krajewski, 'Model Clauses for a UN Treaty on Transnational Corporations, Other Businesses and Human Rights' (CIDSE 2017) < https://www.cidse.org/publications/business-and-human-rights/business-and-human-rights-frameworks/ensuring-the-primacy-of-human-rights-in-trade-and-investment-policies.html> accessed 22 May 2018.
[63] Muchlinski (n 50) 367.

possible but would require careful drafting of the treaty on business and human rights.[64]

2. General Comment No 24 of the Social, Economic and Cultural Rights Committee

10.34 Another relevant event in the area of investment and human rights in 2017 was the adoption of General Comment No 24 by the Committee on Social, Economic and Cultural Rights in August 2017.[65] This comment summarizes the Committee's past practice and current understanding of the connection between business and human rights, in particular concerning the rights enshrined in the International Covenant on Social, Economic and Cultural Rights (ICSECR) of 1966. General Comments are considered to be non-binding, but they constitute semi-official authoritative interpretations of the respective human rights treaty as they are adopted by consensus and usually based on the practice of the corresponding treaty body.[66]

10.35 In its General Comment No 24 the Committee stated that '[s]tates parties should identify any potential conflict between their obligations under the Covenant and under trade or investment treaties, and refrain from entering into such treaties where such conflicts are found to exist, as required under the principle of the binding character of treaties.'[67] Furthermore, the General Comment suggested that the conclusion of investment agreements should be preceded by human rights impact assessments that take into account both the positive and negative human rights impacts of trade and investment treaties.[68] Finally, states 'are encouraged to insert, in future treaties, a provision explicitly referring to their human rights obligations, and to ensure that mechanisms for the settlement of investor-State disputes take human rights into account in the interpretation of investment treaties or of investment chapters in trade agreements.'[69]

10.36 The last passage is of particular relevance as it clearly establishes a human rights duty to ensure that investment agreements do not conflict with human rights. However, the Committee does not go as far as to say that states are obliged to insert human rights provisions in international investment agreements in order to discharge their duties under the ICESCR. Nevertheless, the Committee makes

---

[64] See also: Krajewski, 'Model Clauses for a UN Treaty on Transnational Corporations, Other Businesses and Human Rights' (n 62).
[65] United Nations Committee on Economic, Social and Cultural Rights, 'General Comment No. 24 (2017) on State obligations under the International Covenant on Economic, Social and Cultural Rights in the context of business activities' (10 August 2017) E/C.12/GC/24.
[66] Jane Connors and Markus Schmidt, 'United Nations' in Daniel Moeckli, Sangeeta Shah, and Sandesh Sivakumaran (eds), *International Human Rights Law* (2nd edn, OUP 2014) 379–80.
[67] General Comment No 24 (n 65) para 13.
[68] ibid.
[69] ibid.

it clear that reforming investment agreements by including specific references to human rights would ensure that human rights are better protected in the context of investment agreements.

10.37 Unlike a potential provision in a treaty on business and human rights, General Comment No 24 does not establish binding legal obligations for investors in investment treaties and investment arbitration. Yet, while the treaty process is still subject to significant political contestations, the General Comment No 24 already establishes a useful reference point for investment policymakers and treaty-drafters. General Comment No 24 therefore also indicates that including state obligations for investment policies in a treaty on business and human rights could be based on an authoritative interpretation of existing human rights.

E. Conclusion

10.38 The recent developments in investment arbitration practice and treaty-making as well as in the fields of human rights described in this contribution, indicate that some investment tribunals, human rights bodies, and states are willing and prepared to move beyond the mere recognition of the impact of international investment law on human rights law and vice versa. However, it is yet too early to determine whether the instances observed will lead to a general trend and which practical, legal, and political consequences will follow from this general trend. Approaches of investment tribunals towards human rights are clearly not yet based on consistent practice. It is also questionable to what extent states seem willing to include references to human rights in investment agreements as an appropriate means to mitigate potential conflicts between the two fields of law.

10.39 In any case, general and broad clauses without any specifications as to exactly how states and investors should behave may not be sufficient. Incorporating investor obligations in investment treaties or establishing human rights obligations of private companies in a treaty on business and human rights will only have an impact if it is clear to investors and states what they should do and what they should avoid. In order to reach such clarity, it might be useful to refer to concrete cases decided by human rights courts and committees, investment tribunals, or other dispute settlement institutions.

10.40 In the *Urbaser* and *Bear Creek* cases, the concrete activities of an investor were assessed in light of the particular circumstances of the case. Even though in both cases the tribunals did not reach a decision against the investor vis-à-vis its concrete behaviour, it became clear which activities of the investors were seen as problematic and which not. Subsequent decisions of investment tribunals could build on this and establish a case law on investor expectations and duties concerning human rights. However, the difficulty of such an approach is that it depends on the language of the applicable treaty and the willingness and ability of the arbitrators to take human rights arguments into account and accept that the arbitration tribunal has jurisdiction to hear claims about human rights violations of companies. This underlines why reforms of investment treaties remain necessary to ensure consistency and to provide the tribunals with a clear legal basis for the development of a future case law on human rights and investment. Such reforms would include changes of the substantive rules as well as the procedural settings of the dispute settlement mechanism including the qualification of the arbitrators.

11

DEVELOPMENTS IN INTERNATIONAL INVESTMENT LAW IN RELATION TO INTELLECTUAL PROPERTY IN 2017

Carlos M Correa

A. Introduction	11.01	C. Arbitral Award: *Eli Lilly v Canada*	11.11
B. Intellectual Property Rights as Investment	11.02	D. Final Remarks	11.25

A. Introduction

11.01 This chapter reviews the developments in international investment law that took place in 2017 in relation to intellectual property rights. It examines, firstly, the extent to which such rights have been deemed a protected investment under bilateral investment treaties (BITs) and other international investment agreements (IIAs) signed during that year.[1] Secondly, it reviews a final arbitral decision that addressed issues relating to intellectual property rights (specifically patents) in the context of the North American Free Trade Agreement (NAFTA).[2]

---

[1] Fourteen BITs and other IIAs were signed in 2017 according to the database of the United Nations Conference on Trade and Development (UNCTAD) <http://investmentpolicyhub.unctad.org/IIA/AdvancedSearchBITResults> accessed 18 May 2018. The analysis in this chapter covers seven of those instruments for which an English or Spanish text is available.

[2] *Eli Lilly and Company v The Government of Canada*, ICSID Case No UNCT/14/2, UNCITRAL, Final Award (16 March 2017). Issues relating to trademarks as protected investments were also raised in *Bridgestone Licensing Services, Inc and Bridgestone Americas, Inc v Republic of Panama*, ICSID Case No ARB/16/34, Decision on Expedited Objections (13 December 2017), where the tribunal accepted jurisdiction over the case.

B. Intellectual Property Rights as Investment

As discussed elsewhere,[3] BITs and other IIAs such as the investment chapters contained in free trade agreements (FTAs), generally contain an all-encompassing definition of covered 'investment' based on the concept of 'assets'. All assets of an enterprise, such as movable and immovable property, equity in companies, claims to money, contractual rights, concessions, licences, and similar rights have been normally included in BITs and other IIAs as protected investments.

11.02

References to intellectual property rights as one of the 'assets' that constitute an investment are pervasive in BITs and other IIAs;[4] however, the specificity regarding the extent of covered rights varies among the treaties. In many cases, a general reference to 'intellectual property rights' is made with or without any qualifications,[5] while in others a list of the covered intellectual property rights is included.[6]

11.03

The references to intellectual property rights as covered assets are generally problematic, particularly as it is unclear whether the mere acquisition and maintenance of such rights in a host state would give rise to a protected investment, or whether other conditions should be met, such as the actual use of such rights by an enterprise established in the host state in relation to goods or services produced there.

11.04

---

[3] See eg Organisation for Economic Co-operation and Development, 'International Investment Law: Understanding Concepts and Tracking Innovations' (OECD 2008) 49 <https://www.oecd.org/investment/internationalinvestmentagreements/40471468.pdf> accessed 18 May 2018; UNCTAD, 'Scope and Definition: UNCTAD Series on Issues in International Investment Agreements II' (2011) <http://unctad.org/en/Docs/diaeia20102_en.pdf> accessed 18 May 2018.

[4] See eg Carlos Correa and Jorge Vinuales, 'Intellectual Property Rights as Protected Investments: How Open Are the Gates?' (2016) 19(1) Journal of International Economic Law 91.

[5] Such as references to rights 'recognized in a party', 'established in accordance with the Agreement on Trade Related Aspects of Intellectual Property Rights' (TRIPS Agreement) or 'related to an investment'. This latter qualification (found in art 1.2(d) of the Rwanda–United Arab Emirates BIT (signed 1 November 2017 but not yet in force) <http://investmentpolicyhub.unctad.org/Download/TreatyFile/5665> accessed 20 May 2018) suggests that intellectual property rights are not an investment *per se*.

[6] For instance, the BIT between the United States and El Salvador (signed 10 March 1999 but not yet in force) <http://investmentpolicyhub.unctad.org/Download/TreatyFile/1139> accessed on 12 May 2018 specifies that 'investment' includes:

- copyrights and related rights,
- patents,
- rights in plant varieties,
- industrial designs,
- rights in semiconductor layout designs,
- trade secrets, including know-how and confidential business information,
- trade and service marks, and
- trade names.

11.05 There is some precedent in arbitral decisions dealing with situations where no manufacturing capacity was established, and in which the existence of a protected investment was dismissed. In *Grand River Enterprises, Inc v United States*, for instance, the tribunal declined to consider that an 'investment' had been made in the United States on the grounds that claimants did not manufacture cigarettes at Grand River's plant but in Canada for export to the United States.[7] The extent to which similar arguments could be made in cases where intellectual property rights are acquired but not exploited (through the production of goods or services) would need to be clarified under most BITs and other IIAs.

11.06 The final decision in *Bridgestone v Panama* will be particularly relevant in this regard. The tribunal's December 2017 decision establishing jurisdiction held problematically that 'a registered trademark will constitute a qualifying investment provided that it is exploited by its owner by activities that, together with the trademark itself, have the normal characteristics of an investment'.[8] This means that the registration of a trademark and its use (eg for licensing or exports) could be deemed a protected investment 'despite the absence of any other form of investment commonly associated with investment, e.g. shares or real property. Thereby, the tribunal has opened an additional possibility to litigate IP disputes in an ISDS context.'[9]

11.07 The model BIT adopted by India has directly addressed this issue as the concept of 'investment' requires the presence in India of an 'enterprise' that meets certain requirements (Article 1.6).[10] In the case of Brazil, although the definition of 'investment' is broader, the model BIT provides that 'Investors and their investment shall strive to achieve the highest possible level of contribution to the sustainable development of the Host State and the local community' (Article 14.1).[11]

11.08 Despite the uncertainty created by an assets-based approach in relation to intellectual property rights, the BITs and other IIAs signed in 2017 have not introduced more clarity in this regard. Under most of them, for an investment to be protectable, it should entail the commitment of capital or other resources, the expectation of gains or profits, or the assumption of risk.[12] It is uncertain whether

---

[7] *Grand River Enterprises Six Nations Ltd v United States*, NAFTA/UNCITRAL, Award (12 January 2011) paras 85–89.
[8] *Bridgestone Licensing Services, Inc and Bridgestone* Americas, *Inc v Republic of Panama*, ICSID Case No ARB/16/34, Decision on Expedited Objections (13 December 2017) para 177.
[9] Simon Klopschinski, 'Investment Disputes, Trademarks and licenses, and ICSID Tribunals—"Bridgestone v. Panama"' (23 March 2018) <http://ipkitten.blogspot.com/2018/03/investment-disputes-trademarks-and.html> accessed on 2 June 2018.
[10] See the India Model Bilateral Investment Treaty (December 2015) <http://investmentpolicyhub.unctad.org/Download/TreatyFile/3560> accessed on 18 May 2018).
[11] See 'Cooperation And Facilitation Investment Agreement Between The Federative Republic Of Brazil And . . .' <http://investmentpolicyhub.unctad.org/Download/TreatyFile/4786> accessed 8 June 2018.
[12] Bilateral Investment Treaty between Colombia and the United Arab Emirates (signed 13 November 2017 but not yet in force) <http://investmentpolicyhub.unctad.org/Download/

this vague qualification would be enough to counter intellectual property owners' claims in case, for instance, of a prohibition on the use of trademarks,[13] or the invalidation of the rights (as in the case against Canada reviewed in section C), particularly where the right owner does not produce goods or services in the country where the rights were acquired. In particular, if the 'expectations of gains' were considered as a sufficient and independent qualifier of investment, in those situations the owner of intellectual property rights might claim a breach of the state's obligations as an indirect expropriation and/or a breach of legitimate expectations protected under the fair and equitable treatment standard.[14]

Notably, the reference to qualifications of a protected investment—the commitment of capital or other resources, the expectation of gains or profits or the assumption of risk—is not mentioned in the Israel–Japan BIT signed in 2017.[15] However, this treaty contains a specific clause on intellectual property (Article 18). This clause recognizes, on the one hand, the Contracting Parties' rights and obligations under the TRIPS Agreement, and provides for consultations as well as an obligation to remove, depending on the results of such consultation and in accordance with the Contracting Party's laws and regulations, 'the factors which are recognized in the consultation as having adverse effects to the investments of

11.09

TreatyFile/5668> accessed 20 May 2018; Agreement on Investment between the Governments of the Hong Kong Special Administrative Region of the People's Republic of China and the Member States of the Association of South East Asian Nations (ASEAN) (signed 12 November 2017 but not yet in force) <http://investmentpolicyhub.unctad.org/Download/TreatyFile/5656> accessed 20 May 2018; Free Trade Agreement between Argentina and Chile (signed 2 November 2017 but not yet in force); Agreement between the Republic of Rwanda and the United Arab Emirates on the Promotion and Reciprocal Protection of Investments <http://investmentpolicyhub.unctad.org/Download/TreatyFile/5665> accessed 20 May 2018; Investment Agreement of the Mainland and Hong Kong Closer Economic Partnership Agreement (signed and entered into force on 28 June 2017) <http://investmentpolicyhub.unctad.org/Download/TreatyFile/5580> accessed 20 May 2018; Pacific Agreement on Closer Economic Relations Plus (signed 14 June 2017) <http://investmentpolicyhub.unctad.org/Download/TreatyFile/5586> accessed 20 May 2018; and Intra-MERCOSUR Cooperation and Facilitation Investment Protocol (signed 7 April 2017) <http://investmentpolicyhub.unctad.org/IIA/treaty/3772> accessed 20 May 2018.

[13] This was one of the issues at stake in *Philip Morris Asia Limited v The Commonwealth of Australia*, PCA Case No 2012-12, UNCITRAL, Award on Jurisdiction and Admissibility (17 December 2015) where the complaint was dismissed. The same issue was raised in *Philip Morris Brands Sàrl, Philip Morris Products SA and Abal Hermanos SA v Oriental Republic of Uruguay*, ICSID Case No ARB/10/7, Award (8 July 2016) para 271: where the tribunal concluded that 'under Uruguayan law or international conventions to which Uruguay is a party the trademark holder does not enjoy an absolute right of use, free of regulation, but only an exclusive right to exclude third parties from the market so that only the trademark holder has the possibility to use the trademark in commerce, subject to the State's regulatory power'.

[14] The breach of legitimate expectations has become one of the major factors considered in applying the fair and equitable treatment standard in the arbitral jurisprudence on investment law. See eg Michele Potestà, 'Legitimate Expectations in Investment Treaty Law: Understanding the Roots and the Limits of a Controversial Concept' (2013) 28 ICSID Review 88.

[15] Agreement between Japan and the State of Israel for the Liberalization, Promotion and Protection of Investment (signed 1 February 2017, entered into force 5 October 2017) <http://investmentpolicyhub.unctad.org/Download/TreatyFile/5575> accessed 18 May 2018.

investors of the other Contracting Party'.[16] On the other, it allows the Contracting Parties not to extend to an investor of the other Contracting Party the 'treatment accorded to investors of a non-Contracting Party by virtue of any existing or future bilateral or multilateral agreements in respect of protection of intellectual property rights, to which the former Contracting Party is a party, provided that the former Contracting Party complies with the TRIPS Agreement'.[17]

11.10 The commented provision introduces, thus, a limitation to the principle of most favoured nation as provided for in Article 3 of the BIT.[18] There is no record available of the negotiation that would help to understand the concerns behind this provision, which could protect both Israel and Japan from TRIPS-plus obligations (such as data exclusivity for biological products) that either of them may agree upon in negotiations with non-contracting parties. Israel has signed a number of FTAs (with EU, EFTA, the United States, and Canada),[19] that were negotiated at a time when TRIPS-plus provisions were not a common feature in such agreements. Japan, on the contrary, has entered into agreements that provide for such TRIPS-plus protections,[20] and has been active in the negotiation and later revision of the Trans-Pacific Partnership (TPP).[21] Although Israel has introduced in its legislation some TRIPS-plus elements (such as the extension of the patent term and data exclusivity for medical preparations comprising a new chemical entity),[22] it will not be obliged to confer on Japanese firms any additional protection Israel may eventually agree on in future BITs or IIAs. On the other hand, Israel's firms would not benefit from TRIPS-plus protections provided for in other agreements entered into by Japan.

C. Arbitral Award: *Eli Lilly v Canada*

11.11 The final award in *Eli Lilly v Canada* was a major development in 2017 relating to intellectual property in investment case law. Eli Lilly, a major US pharmaceutical company, filed an investment complaint against Canada as a result of a

---

[16] ibid art 18(1).
[17] ibid art 18(3).
[18] ibid art 3.
[19] See Federation of Israeli Chambers of Commerce, 'Israel's Trade Agreements' (26 June 2015) <https://www.chamber.org.il/38991/39012/israels-trade-agreements/> accessed 18 May 2018; and Export.gov, 'Israel—Trade Agreements' <https://www.export.gov/article?id=Israel-Trade-Agreements> accessed 18 May 2018.
[20] See Export.gov, 'Japan—Trade Agreements' <https://www.export.gov/article?id=Japan-Trade-Agreements> accessed 18 May 2018.
[21] Now renamed as the 'Comprehensive and Progressive Agreement for Trans-Pacific Partnership' (CPTPP).
[22] See Luzzato & Luzzato, 'The Drug Industry and Intellectual Property in Israel' <https://www.luzzatto.co.il/en/learn/thought-pieces/155-the-drug-industry-and-intellectual-property-in-israel> accessed 7 June 2018.

2010 Federal Canadian court decision that confirmed the invalidity of two patents that Eli Lilly had obtained there. The claimant relied, *inter alia,* on NAFTA Chapter 17 on intellectual property rights, the TRIPS Agreement, and the laws of the United States and Mexico, to argue that the way the court had applied the patentability requirement of 'utility' was in breach of Canada's obligations under the NAFTA Chapter 11 on investment.

1. The revoked patents: an example of 'evergreening'

11.12 Eli Lilly's complaint was based on the revocation of two patents: No 2,041,113 (1998) relating to olanzapine, a product to treat schizophrenia, and No 2,209,735 (2002) that covered atomoxetine, which is used to treat attention deficit/hyperactivity disorder. These two patents provide a telling example of what has been termed 'evergreening' in the field of patent law, a quite common strategy in the pharmaceutical industry. In order to extend the patent protection on a medicine beyond the term of a basic patent (on an active ingredient), companies usually apply for patents on variants (such as salts, polymorphs, formulations, isomers, etc) that may be routinely developed (without any inventive activity) or on new medical uses of existing medicines. The objective of obtaining these 'secondary' patents is to delay the entry of generic versions of the medicines concerned.[23]

11.13 In the case of olanzapine, Eli Lilly originally obtained patent CA 1,075,687 (1980) based on what is known as a broad 'Markush claim', that is a claim that covers a multitude of compounds through a generic description of the relevant chemical formula. Eli Lilly's patent covered in this case several million compounds that were claimed to be 'useful in the treatment of mild anxiety states and certain kinds of psychotic conditions such as schizophrenia'. Despite the broad coverage of the patent, olanzapine was identified as one of the 'most preferred compounds'.

11.14 Since Eli Lilly only started to commercialize olanzapine (under the commercial name 'Zyprexia') in 1996 and the patent was about to expire, it filed and obtained patent No 2,041,113 (filed in 1991, granted in 1998) covering olanzapine *per se,* as a selection from the genus of compounds of the previous patent, as well as the use of olanzapine for the treatment of schizophrenia. Eli Lilly claimed it had discovered that olanzapine had a 'marked superiority in the treatment of schizophrenia' compared with other compounds of the larger group it had previously patented.[24] However, according to the Canadian statement of defence, '[E]vidence at trial revealed that Claimant had claimed the second monopoly on the basis of studies which failed to establish any particular treatment advantage of olanzapine over the already-patented class to which it belonged.'[25] Significantly,

---

[23] See eg Sandeep K Rathod, 'Ever-greening: A Status Check in Selected Countries' (2010) 7 Journal of Generic Medicine 227.
[24] See *Eli Lilly v Canada* (n 2) Government Statement of Defence (30 June 2014) para 3.
[25] ibid.

Eli Lilly filed at least twenty-nine other Canadian patent applications relating to olanzapine, claiming to have found at least sixteen new medical uses for the compound, ranging from sexual dysfunction to autism.[26]

11.15 The second revoked patent, filed in 1996 and granted in 2002 (CA 2,209,735) covered a method of treatment of attention-deficit hyperactivity disorder. Eli Lilly had initially obtained a patent on atomoxetine (CA 1,051,034, filed in1979) (commercial name 'Strattera') for the treatment of depression. In filing the later revoked patent, Eli Lilly asserted that it had identified a new medical use for that product. Between 1992 and 2004 the company filed additional patent applications for ten other pathologies, including treatment of psoriasis, stuttering, incontinence, and hot flashes.[27]

11.16 Given the nature of the invalidated patents it was reasonable for Eli Lilly to expect invalidity challenges by the generic pharmaceutical industry and the possibility of revocation. In fact, the rate of invalidation of granted patents is high, even in the United States, Eli Lilly's home country. It has been noted, for instance, that 80 per cent of the more than 5,000 patent challenges brought to the Patent Trial and Appeals Board (PTAB) of the US Patent and Trademark Office since September 2012 ended up with the invalidation of patent claims.[28]

2. Patents as a protected investment

11.17 The broad definition of 'investment' typically contained in BITs and other IIAs was the starting point of Eli Lilly's complaint. NAFTA incorporated an all-encompassing concept of 'investment'. Although it does not explicitly refer to intellectual property rights, according to Article 1139(g), 'investment' includes 'real estate or other property, tangible or *intangible*, acquired in the expectation or used for the purpose of economic benefit or other business purposes'.[29] The absence of a specific reference in Article 1139 to patents perhaps explains why the claimant attempted to broadly characterize its investment as 'exclusive property rights' and 'intangible property'.[30]

11.18 In cases where BITs and other IIAs do not specifically refer to intellectual property rights, whether there is or is not a protected investment will depend on the characterization made by the domestic law of the particular asset. While a patent and other intellectual property rights would fall under the category of 'intangible' property, an outstanding question is whether the asset should

---

[26] ibid para 67.
[27] ibid para 55.
[28] David Kline, 'Has the Government Made it Too Easy to Invalidate Patents?' (24 April 2017) <http://michelsonip.com/government-made-easy-invalidate-patents/> accessed 24 May 2018.
[29] Emphasis added.
[30] See *Eli Lilly v Canada* (n 2) Claimant's Memorial (29 September 2014) para 163.

meet other requirements before being deemed as an 'investment'. As noted by a commentator,

> At a minimum, a determination that an intellectual property rights owner is also an investor cannot plausibly be based solely on acquiring rights, particularly since member states of the WTO have no choice but to accord such rights, and to do so on the terms set by the TRIPS Agreement. Moreover, all intellectual property rights are to some extent contingent rights only ... whether a granting agency has appropriately granted (or denied) such rights are always subject to question before national courts. To transform such contingent rights into property-like assets gives graver import than contemplated by States to the role of intellectual property treaties.[31]

Notably, in *Eli Lilly v Canada* the respondent did not introduce a defence around the concept of investment as applied to patents granted in its territory. It seemed to admit that they could be characterized as a protected investment under NAFTA, independently of whether the patents had been effectively exploited or not in Canada through the production of olanzapine and atomoxetine. Instead, Canada argued that the examination of the patent office was only an 'initial' review and that the validity of a patent was finally determined by the courts. It stated in this respect:

11.19

> At the heart of Claimant's allegations is a fundamental mischaracterization of the nature of the patent grant in Canada. It suggests that this initial grant conferred upon it an irrevocable property right ... This is incorrect. Under Canadian law, an initial patent grant is always made subject to invalidation by the Federal Court, the ultimate arbiter of patent validity and the authoritative interpreter of Patent Act requirements ...[32]

Canada argued that a property right never existed,[33] and did not enter into the discussion of whether the patents as such constituted a protected investment under NAFTA. As a result, the main grounds for the defence required a judgment by the arbitral tribunal regarding its competence to review a judicial decision and the patent policy applied in Canada. This legal strategy exposed Canada to significant risks given the latitude that investment tribunals enjoy in interpreting states' obligations regarding investors, as illustrated by the tribunal's judgment relating to its own competence to review judicial decisions.

11.20

3. NAFTA safeguards

According to NAFTA Article 1110.7, the provision mandating compensation in cases of direct or indirect nationalization or expropriation 'does not apply to the

11.21

---

[31] Ruth L Okediji, 'Is Intellectual Property "Investment"? Eli Lilly v. Canada and The International Intellectual Property System' (2014) 35(4) University of Pennsylvania Journal of International Law 1121, 1126.
[32] *Eli Lilly v Canada* (n 2) Statement of Defence (30 June 2014) para 43.
[33] ibid para 111.

issuance of compulsory licenses granted in relation to intellectual property rights, or to the revocation, limitation or creation of intellectual property rights, to the extent that such issuance, revocation, limitation or creation is consistent with Chapter Seventeen (Intellectual Property)'.[34] This means that an investor's compensation cannot be claimed in cases of invalidation of a patent, the very basis of Eli Lilly's complaint, unless there is violation of any of the NAFTA obligations concerning the protection of intellectual property rights set forth in Chapter 17.

11.22   The safeguard against considering revocation as an expropriation is a logical corollary of the nature of the rights conferred by a patent grant. The examination made by a patent office, as noted in Canada's Statement of Defence, does not create an irrevocable right since its decision may be reviewed and, hence, ultimately confirmed or dismissed by a court.[35] Although other rights (such as exploration permits and public services concessions) may also be revoked, this is generally the case when fraud or other wrongdoing is found in concluding or executing a contract (including failure to comply with its terms). Patents, however, may be revoked even when the applicable procedures have been legally complied with, on the basis of a re-examination of the extent to which the patentability standards have been met.

11.23   According to NAFTA's Article 1709.8, a party may revoke a patent when '(a) grounds exist that would have justified a refusal to grant the patent; or (b) the grant of a compulsory license has not remedied the lack of exploitation of the patent'.[36] Utility is one of the grounds on which a patent application may be refused, and NAFTA Chapter 17 does not contain a definition limiting NAFTA parties' right to determine how that requirement can be interpreted and applied.[37] Although Article 1110.7 was invoked by Canada,[38] and was relevant for deciding the case, the tribunal did not make any reference to that article in its final award.

---

[34] NAFTA Secretariat, 'North American Free Trade Agreement—Chapter 11: Investment' <https://www.nafta-sec-alena.org/Home/Texts-of-the-Agreement/North-American-Free-Trade-Agreement?mvid=1&secid=539c50ef-51c1-489b-808b-9e20c9872d25#A1110?> accessed 25 May 2018.

[35] See *Eli Lilly v Canada* (n 2) Government Statement of Defence (30 June 2014) para 43.

[36] NAFTA Secretariat, 'North American Free Trade Agreement - Chapter 17: Intellectual Property' <https://www.nafta-sec-alena.org/Home/Texts-of-the-Agreement/North-American-Free-Trade-Agreement?mvid=1&secid=b6e715c1-ec07-4c96-b18e-d762b2ebe511> accessed 25 May 2018.

[37] NAFTA art 1709 provides that 'each Party shall make patents available for any inventions, whether products or processes, in all fields of technology, provided that such inventions are new, result from an inventive step and are capable of industrial application. For purposes of this Article, a Party may deem the terms "inventive step" and "capable of industrial application" to be synonymous with the terms "non-obvious" and "useful", respectively'.

[38] Canada also argued that the consideration of Canada's compliance with NAFTA Chapter 17— or with other international obligations outside of Chapter 11—was beyond the mandate of the tribunal and that allegations of a breach of NAFTA Chapter 17 had to be brought on a state-to-state basis before a tribunal constituted pursuant to NAFTA Chapter 20 (*Eli Lilly v Canada* (n 2) Statement of Defence (30 June 2014) para 83–84).

It did not elaborate, in fact, on the possible inconsistency between Canada's court decision and NAFTA Chapter 17.[39] The tribunal rather examined whether there was a 'legitimate justification' for Canada's definition of 'utility'; it concluded that such was the case: '[i]n exchange for the monopoly granted, the patentee must disclose to the public the basis of its prediction of utility and what makes it sound. Whether or not this is the preferred approach, it is plainly not an irrational one.'[40]

That conclusion was reached by the tribunal on the basis of a detailed examination of the three elements[41] of the 'promise utility' doctrine as applied by the Canadian courts, which was carried out with the purpose of determining whether '[i]n the mid-2000s, after the patents for Zyprexa and Strattera had been examined and granted, but prior to their invalidation by the courts, Canada's patent utility law underwent a dramatic transformation'.[42] The focus of the tribunal was not the analysis of the utility standard as such nor of its compatibility with NAFTA or TRIPS, but rather whether that standard had substantially changed as claimed by Eli Lilly. The tribunal found that, although there were some incremental and evolutionary changes, actually foreseeable in a common law system,[43] the claimant had been unable to show a dramatic transformation of the utility doctrine. It also concluded that the challenged Canadian court's decision was 'neither arbitrary nor discriminatory, nor can it be said that the judicial measures taken were expropriatory within the meaning of Article 1110'.[44] **11.24**

D. Final Remarks

The review of the BITs and other IIAs signed during 2017 shows that the treatment of intellectual property has followed the same patterns found in most earlier agreements. This is despite the concerns raised by the use of these agreements to challenge measures that affect the scope or validity of intellectual property rights. **11.25**

---

[39] The tribunal did not dismiss either 'the possibility that domestic patent laws that are consistent with NAFTA or the World Trade Organization's Agreement on Trade Related Aspects of Intellectual Property Rights (TRIPS) could nevertheless be impugned for disappointing expectations of profit under bilateral investment agreements' Brook K Baker and Katrina Geddes, 'The Incredible Shrinking Victory: Eli Lilly v. Canada, Success, Judicial Reversal, and Continuing Threats from Pharmaceutical ISDS' (2017) Northeastern University School of Law Research Paper No 296–2017 <https://papers.ssrn.com/sol3/papers.cfm?abstract_id=3012538> accessed 26 May 2018.
[40] *Eli Lilly v Canada* (n 2) Final Award (16 March 2017) para 428.
[41] These elements are: (1) the identification of a 'promise' in the patent disclosure, against which utility is measured; (2) a prohibition against use of post-filing evidence; and (3) the requirement that pre-filing evidence to support a sound prediction of utility must be included in the patent.
[42] *Eli Lilly v Canada* (n 2) Final Award (16 March 2017) para 308.
[43] ibid para 386.
[44] ibid para 418.

11.26 In the *Eli Lilly v Canada* case, the claimant challenged the generally accepted principle that the courts of the country that grants a patent enjoy exclusive jurisdiction to address issues of invalidation. But by considering itself competent to review a Canadian court's decision, the tribunal has raised more general concerns regarding the role of arbitral tribunals in reviewing judicial decisions. Although it recognized that 'a NAFTA Chapter Eleven tribunal is not an appellate tier in respect of the decisions of the national Judiciary',[45] the tribunal 'rejected the important protection for state sovereignty provided in the principle that a state is only responsible internationally for decisions of its courts applying that state's own laws, where a *denial of justice* has occurred'.[46]

11.27 In *Eli Lilly v Canada*, the tribunal ultimately dismissed the case on the argument that Eli Lilly had failed to establish that the change to Canadian patent regulation was dramatic or radical, rather than on articulating a legal standard for 'expropriation' under NAFTA. Indeed, even if an expropriation were not established, it might still be possible for an investor to argue that there has been a violation under the fair and equitable standard if the change was too fundamental or dramatic and frustrated investor's expectations. This reasoning suggests that in agreeing to an investment treaty, a government may be deemed to take on 'an affirmative obligation to constrain the evolution of national legal standards, or to limit the public policy that fuels such evolution to the equilibrium that existed at the time the treaty was signed'.[47]

11.28 If the tribunal's approach—based on a vast investigation to determine whether the utility standard in Canada had just incrementally evolved or undertaken a 'dramatic' change—were adopted in other cases, investment tribunals would be given the discretion to judge under imprecise criteria when a legal change has been merely 'evolutionary' or otherwise 'dramatic', thereby threatening the states' right to dynamically adapt their policies in response to changing economic, social and environmental circumstances. As the United States argued in *Glamis Gold, Ltd v United States*, 'if States were prohibited from regulating in any manner that frustrated expectations—or had to compensate for any diminution in profit—they would lose the power to regulate'.[48]

11.29 The tribunal's approach in *Eli Lilly v Canada* may be regarded as an opportunity by rights holders to challenge the revocation of patents, trademarks, or other intellectual property rights, as well as compulsory licences and other legitimate

---

[45] ibid para 224.
[46] Robert Howse, 'Eli Lilly v Canada: A Pyrrhic Victory Against Big Pharma' (*International Economic Law and Policy Blog*, March 26 2017) <http://worldtradelaw.typepad.com/ielpblog/2017/03/eli-lilly-v-canada-a-pyrrhic-victory-against-big-pharma-.html> accessed 27 May 2018.
[47] Okediji (n 31) 1122.
[48] *Glamis Gold, Ltd v United States of America*, Ad hoc—UNCITRAL Arbitration Rules, Award (8 June 2009) para 576.

measures adopted to mitigate the exclusionary effects of intellectual property rights. Significantly, while that case was pending, Novartis (a Swiss pharmaceutical firm) filed a formal notice of dispute under the Switzerland–Colombia BIT challenging Colombia's declaration of public interest in relation to imatinib (a drug for leukaemia) as a basis to grant a compulsory licence.[49] Another investment claim (for a $800 million compensation) was notified by the US pharmaceutical company Gilead against Ukraine, arguing a breach of test data protection,[50] on the argument that the drug regulatory authority had illegitimately registered a generic equivalent to its hepatitis C medicine, sofosbuvir.[51]

While the definition of 'investment' under the innovative model BITs developed by Brazil and India may provide a defence against investor–state litigation involving intellectual property rights,[52] governments engaged in the reform of current BITs and other IIAs or in the negotiation of new ones should be conscious of the far-reaching implications of including such rights as a protected 'asset', particularly when, in the absence of qualifications regarding the concept of investment, the mere registration may be used as a basis for multi-million dollar investor-to-state complaints. 11.30

---

[49] Brook K Baker, 'Eli Lilly's ISDS Patent Claim against Canada Defeated' (6 April 2017) <http://www.madhyam.org.in/eli-lillys-isds-patent-claim-against-canada-defeated/> accessed 28 May 2018.

[50] This is a *sui generis* protection granted—in some countries on the basis of an exclusive right to use—in relation to test data on the efficacy and safety of pharmaceutical and agrochemical products. See eg Owais Shaikh, *Access to Medicine Versus Test Data Exclusivity: Safeguarding Flexibilities Under International Law* (Springer 2016).

[51] The product of the generic competitor of Gilead was de-registered by the Ukraine's authorities pursuant to an agreement under which Gilead withdrew the claim. See Luke Eric Peterson and Zoe Williams, 'Pharma Corp Withdraws Investment Arbitration after Ukraine Agrees to Settlement of Dispute over Monopoly Rights to Market Anti-viral Drug' *Investment Arbitration Reporter* (16 March 2016) <http://isds.bilaterals.org/?gilead-pharma-corp-withdraws> accessed 28 May 2018.

[52] Some BITs provide that intellectual property rights should be determined in accordance with domestic law. For instance, the BIT between Hong Kong and ASEAN (n 12) stipulates that the intellectual property rights protected are those 'which are recognised pursuant to the laws and regulations of a host Party' (art 1(e)(3)). While the nature and scope of the rights may be ultimately determined by domestic laws, a clarification of this kind would not exclude the characterization of such rights as protected assets if an unqualified asset-based approach is followed.

12

INVESTOR–STATE ARBITRATION IN THE EXTRACTIVE INDUSTRIES

Zoe Phillips Williams

A. Introduction	12.01	C. Concluded Cases	12.21
B. New Cases	12.07	D. Conclusion	12.38

A. Introduction

12.01 This chapter focuses on select investment arbitration claims—either initiated or concluded in 2017—which relate to extractive industries. It is not a complete overview of all arbitral proceedings initiated or concluded in this year, but rather seeks to highlight cases which have broader policy relevance due to the policy measures and interests involved.

12.02 Investors in the extractive industries initiate the most claims against host states of any sector; approximately 25 per cent of all investment disputes relate to oil, gas, or mining investments.[1] Given the highly politicized nature of the extractive industry, this is unsurprising. Large extractive projects often have a negative impact on the environment and communities in the vicinity of operations. Moreover, given the long time-horizon of most oil and mining projects, deals that were signed with foreign investors by one government may be understood by subsequent administrations as disadvantageous. Unequal bargaining power at the time of entry often leads to contracts which favour investor over state interests, but as market or political conditions change, states are incentivized to alter the regulatory framework governing extractive sector activity, or renegotiate or terminate

---

[1] Zoe Phillips Williams, 'What, Where, When and Why? Patterns in Investment Arbitration' in Kavaljit Singh and Burghard Ilge (eds), *Rethinking Bilateral Investment Treaties: Critical Issues and Policy Choices* (Both Ends 2016) 29–40.

contracts.² This dynamic was clearly at work during the mid-2000s in particular, when investors in the extractive industry were subject to expropriation, contractual changes, and the application of windfall taxes in resource-dependent states in Latin America and Asia, attributed at least in part to the boom in commodities prices.³

12.03 However, both during the commodities boom and in more recent periods of lower prices, investment claims have been provoked by a much wider range of measures than attempts by the host state government to capture resource rents alone. Both in developed and developing host states, disputes have arisen relating to environmental and livelihood concerns, particularly in communities which either have traditionally been dependent on artisanal mining, or in which key economic sectors such as agriculture, fishing, and tourism, are seen to be incompatible with large-scale resource development. Thus, some of these investor–state disputes are the result of community–company conflicts in which the state has recognized the concerns of affected communities as legitimate and worth defending, even in the face of the costs posed by arbitration.

12.04 With one exception, the new cases that will be discussed fall into this latter category—the majority relate to measures taken by the state in response to the (potential) negative environmental or social externalities of extractive industry projects. As will be discussed in greater detail, these cases highlight some of the areas of concern for critics of the investment protection regime—namely, the impact of investment arbitration on domestic groups which may be negatively affected by an investment but do not have recourse to arbitration to address their concerns. More broadly, these disputes suggest the potential for conflict between the obligations placed on host states by international investment law and the interests and demands of citizens and civil society in democratic states.⁴ Ultimately, this has the potential to limit, or at least put a price on, state responsiveness to democratic pressures.

12.05 While these types of disputes are often framed by claimants as the result of 'politically motivated' decision-making by host states, states' duties to communities affected by extractive projects are also enshrined in domestic regulation relating to environmental and social impact assessments of these projects. Moreover, international standards such as ILO 169 and the UN-led efforts on business and human rights suggest an emerging international consensus on the duties that various actors—both states and investors—have towards communities affected by investment projects. Thus, investment arbitration related to extractive industry

---

² Christopher Hajzler, 'Expropriation of Foreign Direct Investments: Sectoral Patterns from 1993–2006' (2012) 1 Review of World Economics 148.
³ ibid.
⁴ Jonathan Bonnitcha, Lauge Poulsen, and Michael Waibel, *The Political Economy of the Investment Treaty Regime* (OUP 2017).

projects highlights the tensions between states' legal obligations to investors and other actors. A number of the cases discussed, particularly *Bear Creek v Peru*, clearly exemplify this dynamic.

12.06 The following section will give a brief overview of investment claims brought by extractive industry investors in 2017. The third section will discuss two cases in which an award was rendered in 2017. The final section will discuss the broader policy trends and implications of these cases and conclude.[5]

B. New Cases

1. Acacia Mining and AngloGold Ashanti v Tanzania

12.07 Tanzania was served with two requests for arbitration by mining companies in 2017, following the passage of controversial legislation which significantly altered the regulatory framework governing the country's mining sector. Unlike the other cases discussed in this and the following section, these disputes more closely resemble those between mining, oil, and gas investors and several Latin American governments in the mid-2000s and appear to be motivated by changing views on what role the extractive sector should play in the country's development—particularly that the country was not benefitting from large-scale foreign investment in the extractive industry.

12.08 Tanzanian president John Magufuli was elected in 2015, pledging to reduce corruption[6] and industrialize the natural resource-dependent country.[7] A series of measures aimed at the mining industry have been central to Tanzania's new approach to development. The first of these was a ban on exports of copper, gold, and silver ore in the spring of 2017, which was justified by the government as part of a push to ensure that value-added activities are carried out in the country. In July 2017, the Tanzanian National Assembly passed legislation which directly affects foreign investors in the extractive industry. Specifically, the Natural Wealth and Resources Contracts (Review and Renegotiation of Unconscionable Terms) Act 2017 empowers the National Assembly to review and renegotiate all existing contracts with investors in the extractive industry that are seen to restrict the state's full exercise of sovereignty over its natural resources.[8] The legislation also

---

[5] Cases not discussed here include several for which the state measure at issue was not clearly related to the industry of the investor, eg bankruptcy proceedings and state responses to the alleged failure of an investor to uphold contractual obligations.
[6] Dan Paget, 'Tanzania: Shrinking Space and Opposition Protest' (2017) 28(13) Journal of Democracy 153.
[7] Thabit Jacob, 'Competing Energy Narratives in Tanzania' (2017) 116(34) African Affairs 341.
[8] Natural Wealth and Resources Contracts (Review and Renegotiation of Unconscionable Terms) Act 2017.

requires that the government acquire at least a 16 per cent stake in extractives projects and allows for an increase in royalty rates.[9] A second act—the Natural Wealth and Resources (Permanent Sovereignty) Act, 2017—takes specific aim at investment arbitration, requiring that all '[d]isputes arising from extraction, exploitation or acquisition and use of natural wealth and resources shall be adjudicated by bodies or other organs established in the United Republic and accordance with laws of Tanzania.'[10]

Following the passage of this legislation, Acacia Mining, a UK-registered company in which Barrick Gold holds a majority stake, initiated contract-based arbitration at the London Court of International Arbitration. Acacia has been embroiled in a longer-running dispute with the government over alleged tax evasion and the aforementioned export ban. Indeed, it had been subject to investigation by two government committees which concluded it had been underreporting its exports and owed the government $190 billion in taxes. While there are reasons to doubt the findings of the committees, it is highly plausible that the company has been underpaying taxes to the Tanzanian government through base erosion and profit shifting; indeed, the company did not pay any income tax in the country from 2010 to 2015.[11] Moreover, Acacia's CEO publicly stated that the company had struck very advantageous tax deals with the government, which incentivize investment, but can subsequently 'come back to bite us'.[12]

12.09

However, despite these earlier disputes, Acacia did not turn to arbitration until July 2017, following the passage of the aforementioned legislation, claiming that it was necessary to do so at this juncture to protect the company. Shortly thereafter, South African mining giant AngloGold Ashanti initiated contract-based arbitration under UNCITRAL rules against Tanzania. In October 2017, Barrick Gold reached a settlement with the government, agreeing to a $3 million payment to the government as 'good will' gesture to the government, in addition to a partnership going forward in which the government is assured a greater proportion of the economic benefits of the mining activity. However, despite this agreement, the arbitration proceeding is ongoing.[13]

12.10

---

[9] United Nations Conference on Trade and Development (UNCTAD), 'Investment Policy Monitor Issue 18' <http://unctad.org/en/PublicationsLibrary/webdiaepcb2017d9_en.pdf> accessed 21 February 2017.

[10] Natural Wealth and Resources (Permanent Sovereignty) Act, 2017, 7.

[11] Alexandra Readhead, 'Inflated Expectations about Mineral Export Misinvoicing are Having Real Consequences in Tanzania' (2017)<https://www.alexandrareadhead.com/blog/2017/6/26/inflated-expectations-about-mineral-export-misinvoicing-are-having-real-consequences-in-tanzania> accessed 10 May 2018.

[12] Jon Yeomans, 'Acacia Mining Shares Surge as Barrick Strikes Deal with Tanzania' *The Telegraph* (19 October 2017) <https://www.telegraph.co.uk/business/2017/10/19/acacia-mining-shares-surge-barrick-strikes-deal-tanzania/> accessed 10 May 2018.

[13] Acacia Mining, 'Acacia Annual Report 2017' <http://www.acaciamining.com/~/media/Files/A/Acacia/reports/2018/2017-acacia-annual-report-accounts.pdf> accessed 14 April 2018.

12.11 These disputes are the result of a broader shift towards a more state-led model of development in the country, as well as concerns about tax evasion in the sector. Whatever the underlying reason, these disputes stand out in 2017 for so closely resembling the type described in the literature on the obsolescing bargain. They also recall the disputes between investors and Latin American states in the mid-2000s, when governments were incentivized to capture higher than average resource rents during the commodities boom. At the time of writing, investors are warning over similar proposed changes to the Democratic Republic of Congo's mining code and Zambia has also charged foreign investors in the mining sector with tax evasion. Thus, these disputes in Tanzania may be the beginning of a new wave of cases in sub-Saharan Africa.

2. Kingsgate v Thailand

12.12 Thailand was served with a notice of dispute by Australian company Kingsgate Consolidated under the Thailand–Australia free trade agreement (FTA) in November 2017. The dispute relates to the Chatree gold mine, operated by Kingsgate's local subsidiary. Kingsgate has been operating the mine since 2001, and the mine had an expected lifetime of twenty-seven years.[14] This is an example of an investor–state dispute which has arisen because of a broader dispute between industry actors and local communities.

12.13 This is the second dispute between Thailand and foreign-owned mining companies in recent years (although this appears to be the first to proceed to formal arbitration[15]), both of which relate to opposition from local communities to extractive activity. As has been reported by a Thai non-governmental organization (NGO), Fortify Rights, local communities have opposed gold mining due to what they perceive to be the negative environmental and human health effects of the industry. The NGO reports that active opposition has been ongoing for several years, and until recently, met with significant repression from government security forces.[16]

12.14 In December 2016, the military issued an order under Section 44 of the interim constitution, suspending all mining operations in the country. The government reportedly justified the measure on the grounds that it would allow

---

[14] Jarrod Hepburn, 'Australian Investment Makes Good on BIT arbitration threat against Thailand and also Takes its Political Risk Insurer to Court' *Investment Arbitration Reporter* (2017) <https://www.iareporter.com/articles/australian-investor-makes-good-on-bit-arbitration-threat-against-thailand-and-takes-its-political-risk-insurer-to-court/> accessed 22 February 2018.
[15] ibid.
[16] Sutharee Wannasiri and Kingsley Abbott, 'Struggle against Mining Violations Leaves Activists Exposed' (*Fortify Rights*, 2016) <http://www.fortifyrights.org/commentary-20160505.html> accessed 22 February 2018.

government agencies to address the environmental and health concerns of affected communities.

12.15 In response, Kingsgate turned to arbitration under the FTA, with proceedings underway in November 2017. The company has also initiated domestic legal proceedings against its own political risk insurer, Zurich Insurance Australia. While the policy reportedly covered expropriatory acts under the Thailand–Australia FTA, the company was denied compensation by the insurer.

12.16 The dispute between Kingsgate and Thailand is similar to a number of disputes between governments and mining companies, in which states took measures to which investors objected at the behest of local community groups and NGOs. The declaration of a moratorium on mining by the executive in particular is reminiscent of elements of *Pacific Rim Cayman v El Salvador*.

3. Rockhopper v Italy

12.17 UK oil company Rockhopper Exploration Plc initiated ICSID arbitration proceedings against Italy in March 2017, under the Energy Charter Treaty (ECT). Like *Kingsgate v Thailand* discussed, this is another example of a dispute in which government measures taken in response to the concerns of citizens are challenged by the investor.

12.18 The dispute relates to legislation, passed by the Italian parliament in 2016, banning offshore oil drilling within twelve miles of Italy's coastline. Similar legislation had previously been introduced in 2010, justified on precautionary grounds following BP's oil spill in the Gulf of Mexico that year. This original legislation was later repealed by the Prime Minister Mario Monti's administration, in the wake of the financial crisis.[17]

12.19 Prior to the ban, Rockhopper had been engaged in exploration activity under the Ombrina Mare concession, and the company claims it was denied a production permit due to the new legislation. The company's claim includes compensation for lost profits.[18]

12.20 Italy has been hit with several claims from investors in its energy sector, most of which are related to the country's renewables sector. In response, Italy withdrew from the ECT in 2015. However, protections afforded to existing investments

---

[17] Christopher Coats, 'Italy Looks for Relief with First New Energy Plan in 25 Years' (*Forbes* 2012) <https://www.forbes.com/sites/christophercoats/2012/11/12/italy-looks-for-relief-with-first-new-energy-plan-in-25-years/#23f8569063fa> accessed 10 May 2018.
[18] IAReporter, 'Italy's Ban on Oil and Gas Development near its Coastline Leads to Investment Treaty Arbitration Claim' *Investment Arbitration Reporter* (2017) <https://www.iareporter.com/articles/italys-ban-on-oil-and-gas-development-near-its-coastline-leads-to-investment-treaty-arbitration-claim/> accessed 22 February 2018.

C. Concluded Cases

1. Bear Creek v Peru

12.21 In 2017, an arbitral tribunal rendered its final award in the dispute between Bear Creek Mining Corporation and Peru, finding the latter liable for breaches of the Canada–Peru FTA. This case is notable for the significant involvement of third parties, including in the events leading up to the dispute, the proceeding itself, as well as the implications of the tribunal's decision for mining-affected communities.

12.22 Canadian mining company Bear Creek was granted rights to acquire, own and operate the Santa Ana silver mine in Puno in 2007.[19] The concession is within 50 kilometres of the Peru–Bolivia border, and was thus, according to Peruvian law, ineligible for foreign ownership unless the project was deemed a public necessity. While a Peruvian Bear Creek employee initially acquired the rights, the company was granted authorization to hold the rights to the concession via Supreme Decree 083 in 2007 and was allowed to begin exploration activities in 2008.

12.23 In its eventual submissions to the arbitral tribunal, Peru argued that the project was met with local opposition from the outset, citing physical altercations and mine site invasions as proof that Aymara groups living in the area rejected the proposed mine. Nevertheless, the Ministry of Mines approved the company's Community Participation Plan in 2011. At the same time, local communities continued to communicate their opposition to the project to both national and local government authorities, with concerns focusing on the impact that the mine might have on subsistence farming and drinking water.[20] Community protests against the mine continued throughout the spring of 2011.

12.24 In the summer 2011, in response to the widespread protests, newly elected President Ollanta Humala issued Supreme Decree 32, revoking Decree 83 which had allowed the claimants to hold the legal title to the mine, and Supreme Decree 33, suspending the issuance of all mining permits for the Puno region. Over the next several months, Peru additionally adopted a law requiring consultation with local indigenous groups prior to the implementation of projects which could affect them.

---

[19] *Bear Creek Mining Corporation v Republic of Peru*, ICSID Case No ARB/14/21, Final Award (2017) para 149.
[20] ibid.

12.25 Bear Creek first attempted to overturn Decree 32 through domestic legal proceedings, and when a judgment favourable to the company was appealed by the government, Bear Creek initiated arbitration proceedings in August 2014. The company claimed that Peru had breached the Canada–Peru FTA by unlawfully expropriating its investment.

12.26 Peru based its defence on the alleged illegality of the claimant's initial investment due to prohibitions on foreign ownership, as well as the sustained opposition to the project, claiming that Bear Creek had not obtained the necessary social licence to operate from local communities.

12.27 The arbitral tribunal allowed a joint *amicus* submission from local civil society organization Derechos Humanos y Medio Ambiente Puno (DHUMA) and Peruvian lawyer Carlos Lopez. These parties had initially been approached to act as witnesses for the respondent but preferred to independently submit an *amicus* brief. Their submission details Bear Creek's lack of sufficient engagement with the local communities, and in particular, those communities which were deemed to be only indirectly affected by the project. The *amicus* submission asserted that the company demonstrated a lack of understanding of the ways in which the project could jeopardize their rights to their land and water. Moreover, attempts to conduct community outreach were insufficient—for example, the brief discusses technical presentations to local communities conducted in Spanish, in buildings which could not accommodate all interested community members. Consequently, the company was never able to obtain a social licence to operate.[21]

12.28 The majority of the tribunal agreed that Bear Creek could have done more to address the concerns of all communities likely to be affected by the mine's operations. However, it noted that Peru had been aware of community opposition to the project from early 2011, and nevertheless endorsed Bear Creek's community outreach activities in the months preceding the issuing of Decree 32. Thus, the tribunal argued that Peru could not retroactively claim that Bear Creek's conduct was in contravention of ILO Convention 169, nor that it was the cause of the social unrest in the region. The tribunal concluded that Decree 32 could not therefore be justified on the grounds that it was issued in response to the community protests, with the intention of 'safeguarding social and environmental conditions'.[22] Ultimately, the tribunal found that Peru had indirectly expropriated the claimant's investment in violation of the FTA and awarded damages of over $18 million plus interest.

12.29 The majority's findings were met with a partial dissent from Peru's arbitral nominee Philippe Sands. Sands agreed with the majority that Peru had unlawfully

---

[21] ibid.
[22] ibid paras 412–14.

expropriated the claimant's investment, as other means were available to the government to respond to the communities' opposition to the project and related unrest. However, he departed from the majority in their decision on costs, finding that the claimant's actions contributed to the failure of the project. Specifically, he argued that although ILO Convention 169 only imposes duties on signatory states to consult with indigenous populations prior to the implementation of projects which could affect them, investors are also required to act in ways which do not contravene domestic or international law. Moreover, he concluded that the claimant evinced a clear lack of understanding of ILO Convention 169 and its duties to consult with local communities and was thus unprepared to undertake an investment on indigenous lands. On these grounds, he found contributory fault on the part of the claimant and determined that the damages award to Bear Creek should be reduced by half, and the costs of the tribunal should be split between the parties.[23]

12.30 In the face of these objections, the majority restated its conclusion that as the affected indigenous groups were not a party to the dispute, it could only assess measures taken by Peru. While the local communities had perhaps not given consent to the project, Peru's continual approval of the project up until the issuing of Decree 32 demonstrated that in the eyes of the state, the claimant had fulfilled all obligations with respect to third parties.

12.31 The tribunal's decision in this case demonstrates the tensions between domestic policymaking and investment protection. As the dissenting arbitrator notes, both investors and indigenous groups have rights under international law. However, their access to dispute resolution mechanisms differs greatly. While Bear Creek was able to enforce its rights under the Canada–Peru FTA by means of investment arbitration, the Aymara communities who feared the impact of the mine had no means to ensure that they were adequately consulted as required by ILO Convention 169. Moreover, if Peru's actions were taken in an attempt to comply with its obligations toward its indigenous communities under ILO 169, it has been successfully challenged by an investor for doing so.

12.32 Finally, this case highlights the tension between policy flexibility and commitments to individual investors. As was noted by the tribunal, Peru issued approvals for the claimant's various activities until it enacted Decree 32, implying that, until that point, it judged that Bear Creek was complying with duties under Peruvian law. However, it is notable that this decree was issued by the newly elected Humala government. By 2011, there were 102 active socio-environmental conflicts in Peru, almost all of which were related to the activities of mining companies.[24]

---

[23] ibid.
[24] Defensoria del Pueblo (2011). Reporte de conflictos sociales No 149. Defensoria del Pueblo <http://www.defensoria.gob.pe/conflictos-sociales> accessed 26 March 2018.

Humala had run on a platform that was more critical towards foreign mining than his predecessor Alan Garcia, and his election was an indication of the political preferences of Peruvians. Decree 32 and the subsequent indigenous people's consultation law were arguably reflections of the shifting preferences of Peruvian citizens toward the industry.[25] Therefore, this case illustrates the ways in which investment treaties and arbitration may put a price on a state's responsiveness to domestic policy preferences.

2. Burlington Resources v Ecuador

In 2017, an ICSID tribunal hearing the claim brought by Burlington Resources Inc against Ecuador rendered its final award. In addition to ruling on Ecuador's request to reconsider some elements of the award and on costs, the tribunal considered Ecuador's counterclaim, which alleged that Burlington had breached domestic environmental law.[26] **12.33**

In its decision on liability, the tribunal situates the dispute between the parties in the context of rising oil prices in the early 2000s. In 2001, Burlington acquired minority interests in several oil blocks, operating them jointly with Perenco Ecuador Ltd, and entering into a production sharing contract (PSC) with the state. In 2005, following an increase in the price of oil, Ecuador attempted to renegotiate the PSC. Following the failure of this attempt, Congress enacted Law 42, implementing a windfall tax of 50 per cent, which was subsequently increased to 99 per cent. Burlington initiated arbitration proceedings in 2008, claiming that the windfall tax amounted to an indirect expropriation. Subsequently, Ecuador seized Burlington's assets in an attempt to collect on this outstanding tax. Burlington and its partners later abandoned the contested oil blocks.[27] **12.34**

In 2017, the tribunal ruled that Ecuador was liable for $379.8 million for breaches of the Ecuador–US BIT, on the grounds that it had unlawfully expropriated the claimant's investments in the contested oil blocks.[28] **12.35**

During the arbitration proceedings, Ecuador submitted a counterclaim against Burlington (and against Burlington's concession partner Perenco Ecuador Ltd in a separate arbitration) for environmental damages incurred when the investor abandoned the oil site. Under Ecuadoran law, operators of oil blocks are liable for environmental harm to the areas in which they operate. In response, the **12.36**

---

[25] Indeed Alan Garcia had been particularly welcoming of foreign investment and mining and his time in office had been dominated by widespread social conflict related to the industry.

[26] Jarrod Hepburn, 'Analysis: Successful Counterclaim in Burlington v. Ecuador Breaks Ground' *Investment Arbitration Reporter* (2017) <https://www.iareporter.com/articles/analysis-successful-counterclaim-in-burlington-v-ecuador-breaks-new-ground/> accessed 22 February 2018.

[27] *Burlington Resources v Republic of Ecuador*, ICSID Case No 08/5, Decision on Liability (2012).

[28] *Burlington Resources v. Republic of Ecuador*, ICSID Case No 08/5, Decision on Counterclaims (2017).

members of the tribunal carried out a site visit to determine the existence of environmental damage, finding evidence of soil and groundwater contamination attributable to the claimant's activities. It thus ordered Burlington to pay damages of $41.7 million.

12.37 While the amount awarded to Ecuador falls far short of the $2.8 billion sought by the state, this decision confirms that states can successfully make counterclaims against investors in the context of treaty arbitration on environmental grounds. This is particularly relevant for Ecuador, as the state plans to submit claims for environmental damage to the tribunal in the long-running arbitration with Chevron.[29]

D. Conclusion

12.38 This chapter has provided an overview of some key cases of investment arbitration either initiated or concluded in 2017 involving extractive industry investors. It has focused on cases which have a clear relevance for non-disputing parties—not a difficult feat, as disputes between states and oil and mining companies often touch on environmental and social issues, as well as broader development strategies, and thus frequently involve the interests of affected communities and citizens more generally.

12.39 These cases can be roughly divided into two broad categories—those which relate directly to efforts to combat the negative environmental and social externalities of extractive projects and those which relate to the state's reassessment of the role of the extractive industry in its approach to economic development. *Acacia and AngloGold Ashanti v Tanzania* are clear examples of the latter. Over the last year, Tanzania has taken steps which attempt to ensure that foreign investment in the extractive industry does more to contribute to the country's development, including pursuing companies which have allegedly committed tax evasion and increasing state participation in mining projects. As discussed, these policy developments have been accompanied by similar moves in a number of other southern African countries and can be seen as part of a potentially regional trend. Although the public response from investors apart from Acacia and AngloGold has been limited to threats of arbitration,[30] these claims illustrate the ways in which investment treaties and arbitration may limit the models of development that states are able to pursue.

---

[29] Hepburn, 'Analysis: Successful Counterclaim in Burlington v. Ecuador Breaks Ground' (n 26).
[30] Harry Sanderson, 'Randgold Says Prepared to Take Legal Action against DRC Mining Code' *Financial Times* (2018)<https://www.ft.com/content/4f8d6010-0a82-11e8-8eb7-42f857ea9f09> accessed 27 March 2018.

12.40 The second type of case is exemplified by the remaining disputes discussed in this chapter. In these, the disputes are related to measures taken by states to allegedly mitigate the (potential) negative externalities of extractive industry activity on the environment and local communities. While the cases discussed here are arguably all related to the interests of non-disputing parties, they can also be framed as investor challenges to the application of domestic policies and international standards which seek to regulate extractive industry activity, quite apart from the immediate political considerations facing host-state actors.

12.41 In the case of *Rockhopper v Italy*, the state has responded to the preferences of regional governments and communities which feared the negative impact of underwater drilling off the Italian coast. While the legislation at issue was enacted in 2016, similar legislation had been passed in 2010 shortly after a massive oil spill in the Gulf of Mexico. There are important parallels between this case and both *Lone Pine Resources v Canada* and *Vatenfall v Germany II*, such as the potential for environmental degradation resulting from extractive activity influenced state policy measures subsequently challenged by the investor.

12.42 In both *Kingsgate v Thailand* and *Bear Creek v Peru*, the state has responded to citizens' concerns regarding extractive projects. While the implications of the Kingsgate dispute remain to be seen, *Bear Creek v Peru* clearly encapsulates the tension between state commitments to protect the public interest, and commitments made to investors. In this way, both cases recall the state–local community dynamics underlying *Pacific Rim v El Salvador* and *Bilcon v Canada* among others.

12.43 All of these cases highlight the inability of investment arbitration to truly resolve these disputes, as the system is unable to bring all disputing parties and relevant interests to the table—particularly as it would be a mistake to assume that state and community interests are always aligned. What then, is the solution? One approach could be to ensure host state commitment to consultation with local communities, particularly processes which give affected communities the right to veto a project that, if allowed to go forward, would only become the target of sustained opposition. However, as the outcome of *Bilcon v Canada* suggests, decisions to deny permits to investors based on community consultations can also create liability under an investment treaty. Thus, the current design of the investment protection regime commits states to uphold agreements made with investors, even when these conflict with the domestic public interest. Until the system is reformed to allow states greater flexibility to respond to the interests of citizens and communities, investor–state disputes in the extractive industries are likely to remain a common occurrence.

13

FARMLAND IN INTERNATIONAL INVESTMENT LAW AND DISPUTE SETTLEMENT
Developments in 2017

Lorenzo Cotula and Thierry Berger

A. Introduction	13.01	C. Developments in Investment Disputes	13.12
B. Policy Developments	13.05	D. Future Outlook	13.17

A. Introduction

13.01 In 2017, farmland was at the centre of significant developments in international investment law and dispute settlement. This short chapter reviews those developments, covering both policy shifts and investment disputes.[1] The chapter does not discuss evolutions concerning the agriculture sector upstream and downstream of the production stage, such as the manufacturing and commercialization of agricultural inputs,[2] or investments in aggregation, processing, and distribution.[3] It is also worth noting that land issues can be at stake in disputes concerning sectors other than agriculture, such as the extractive industries,[4] or the leisure

---

[1] The chapter covers developments that occurred in 2017 up to March 2018. For a more comprehensive discussion of the place of farmland in international investment law, including both historical and contemporary analysis, see Lorenzo Cotula, '"Land grabbing" and International Investment Law: Toward a Global Reconfiguration of Property?' in Andrea K Bjorklund (ed), *Yearbook on International Investment Law & Policy 2014–2015* (OUP 2016) 177–214; and Lorenzo Cotula, 'Land, property and sovereignty in international law' (2017) 25 Cardozo Journal Of International & Comparative Law 219, 286.

[2] See eg *Koch Minerals Sàrl and Koch Nitrogen International Sàrl v Bolivarian Republic of Venezuela*, ICSID Case No ARB/11/19, Award (30 October 2017), relating to a fertiliser plant.

[3] See eg *Valores Mundiales, SL and Consorcio Andino SL v Bolivarian Republic of Venezuela*, ICSID Case No ARB/13/11, Award (25 July 2017), relating to the production and sale of corn and wheat.

[4] See Chapter 12.

industry,⁵ but these are outside the scope of this chapter.

13.02 Farmland has formed the object of international dispute settlement since the early twentieth century, for example where agrarian reforms or land occupations in Latin America affected land owned by foreign nationals.⁶ In the 1930s, Mexico's agrarian reform triggered celebrated diplomatic correspondence between the US and Mexican governments, whereby US Secretary of State Cordell Hull argued that international law required states to pay prompt, adequate, and effective compensation where foreign investment is expropriated.⁷ This standard of compensation has come to be known as the 'Hull formula', and is widely used in contemporary investment treaties.⁸ In more recent times, the first ever investor–state arbitration brought under an investment treaty related to the destruction of a shrimp farm in an armed conflict situation.⁹

13.03 Farmland has also long featured, explicitly or implicitly, in investment policy at both international and national levels. Broad asset-based definitions of investment contained in international investment treaties would usually cover farmland-related investments. Several asset types typically mentioned in investment treaties are particularly relevant—including immovable property, company shares, and natural resource concessions. Immovable property would cover proprietary interests in farmland and agribusiness installations. Natural resource concessions would cover farmland concessions or leases, and some investment treaties explicitly refer to 'concessions to search for, *cultivate*, extract or exploit natural resources'.¹⁰ Company shares would typically encompass shares in farmland-holding companies. Several investment treaties deal with farmland issues more explicitly, particularly when setting exceptions to pre-establishment obligations.¹¹

---

⁵ See eg the cases *Ansung Housing Co Ltd v People's Republic of China*, ICSID Case No ARB/14/25, Award (9 March 2017) concerning a dispute arising from the acquisition of land use rights for the development of a golf resort; and *Lao Holdings NV v Lao People's Democratic Republic*, ICSID Case No ARB(AF)/12/6, Decision on the Claimant's Second Material Breach Application (15 December 2017), relating to a casino investment.

⁶ See eg *United States of America on Behalf of Marguerite de Joly de Sabla v The Republic of Panama*, U.S.–Panama Arbitration Commission, Award (29 June 1933).

⁷ Department of State, 'Mexico-United States: Expropriation by Mexico of agrarian properties owned by American citizens' (1938) 32 American Journal of International Law 181.

⁸ August Reinisch, 'Legality of Expropriations' in August Reinisch (ed), *Standards of Investment Protection* (OUP 2008) 196.

⁹ *Asian Agricultural Products Ltd v Sri Lanka*, ICSID Case No ARB/87/3, Award (27 June 1990).

¹⁰ See eg Agreement between the Government of the United Kingdom of Great Britain and Northern Ireland and the Federal Democratic Republic of Ethiopia for the Promotion and Protection of Investments (signed 19 November 2009) art 1(a)(v), emphasis added. Other UK treaties use similar formulations. So do some treaties concluded by Malaysia—eg the Convenio entre el Gobierno de Malasia y el Gobierno de la República de Chile sobre la Promoción y Protección de las Inversiones (signed 11 November 1992) art 1(a)(v).

¹¹ For example Agreement between the Government of Canada and the Government of the Republic of Côte d'Ivoire for the Promotion and Protection of Investments (signed 30 November 2014). See Annex I, Illustrative Schedule of Côte d'Ivoire (section 5), which refers to national law measures that exclude non-nationals from rural land ownership.

At the national level, the terms of access to land for prospective investors have featured in many investment laws.[12]

13.04 In contemporary economic relations, the agriculture sector accounts for a small share of investment disputes—for example, less than 3 per cent of the case load of the International Centre for Settlement of Investment Disputes (ICSID) to date.[13] However, agrarian reform cases have continued to feature in recent disputes,[14] including some cases with reverberations in the review period. And while there is a long history of foreign-controlled agribusiness plantations in low and middle-income countries, a new surge in deal making from at least 2005, and at an accelerated pace from 2007–2008, injected new momentum into debates about the place of farmland in international investment law.[15] Although the pace of this transnational deal making has since slowed,[16] in the review period investor–state arbitration was threatened or actually resorted to in connection with recent agribusiness plantation deals. The review period also witnessed policy evolutions in relation to agrarian reform, national land and investment legislation, and international investment treaty-making. The next two sections discuss developments in investment policy and dispute settlement, respectively, while the conclusion identifies trends worth monitoring in the future.

---

[12] For example Lao People's Democratic Republic, Law on Investment Promotion (2016), arts 4, 8(3), 15–16, 41–50, 67(9)–(11), and 92(3) (referring generally to land, rather than specifically to farmland).

[13] Calculated by the authors based on data from <https://icsid.worldbank.org/en/Pages/cases/searchcases.aspx> accessed 27 February 2018. Figures from UNCTAD's Investment Dispute Settlement Navigator are similar: the agriculture sector accounts for just over 2 per cent of known treaty-based investor–state arbitrations to date (calculated by the authors based on UNCTAD data from <http://investmentpolicyhub.unctad.org/ISDS> accessed 6 April 2018).

[14] See eg *Bernardus Henricus Funnekotter and Others v Republic of Zimbabwe*, ICSID Case No ARB/05/6, Award (22 April 2009); *Bernard Von Pezold and Others v Republic of Zimbabwe*, ICSID Case No ARB/10/15, Award (28 July 2015); *Border Timbers Limited, Border Timbers International (Private) Limited and Hangani Development Co (Private) Ltd v Republic of Zimbabwe*, ICSID Case No ARB/10/25, Award (28 July 2015); and *Vestey Group Ltd v Bolivarian Republic of Venezuela*, ICSID Case No ARB/06/4, Award (15 April 2016). See also Luke E Peterson and Ross Garland, *Bilateral Investment Treaties and Land Reform in Southern Africa* (2010) Rights & Democracy.

[15] See eg Carin Smaller and Howard Mann, 'A Thirst for Distant Lands: Foreign Investment in Agricultural Land and Water' (2009) International Institute for Sustainable Development; Lorenzo Cotula, *Land Rights and Investment Treaties: Exploring the Interface* (2015) International Institute for Environment and Development; and Kaitlin Y Cordes, Lise Johnson and Sam Szoke-Burke, *Land Deal Dilemmas: Grievances, Human Rights, and Investor Protections* (2016) Columbia Center on Sustainable Investment.

[16] Lorenzo Cotula and Thierry Berger, *Trends in Global Land Use Investment: Implications for Legal Empowerment* (2017) International Institute for Environment and Development.

B. Policy Developments

13.05 In relation to land issues, the investment treaties (and chapters in wider trade and investment treaties) that were concluded in the review period do not significantly depart from established treaty practice.[17] In treaties containing pre-establishment provisions, land continued to form the object of recurring exceptions to national treatment. For example, all the states parties to the Pacific Agreement on Closer Economic Relations Plus (PACER Plus), which was signed on 14 June 2017, inscribed land-related exceptions in their respective schedules of commitments. This includes restrictions on the proposed acquisition by a foreign investor of an interest in agricultural land or an agribusiness the value of which exceeds specified thresholds;[18] maximum durations for land leases;[19] conditioning land-related transactions to prior approval by the relevant authorities;[20] and more fundamental restrictions on land ownership by foreign investors.[21]

13.06 Also in substantial continuity with some earlier treaty practice, at least one treaty concluded in 2017 featured land-related exceptions in the main body of the treaty. In its expropriation clause, the Hong Kong–ASEAN Investment Agreement includes a caveat in relation to land that purports to grant a significant role to national law. The clause reads as follows:

> any measure of expropriation relating to land shall be as defined in the existing laws and regulations of the expropriating Party on the date of entry into force of this Agreement, and shall be, for the purposes of and upon payment of compensation, in accordance with the aforesaid laws and regulations. Such compensation shall be subject to any subsequent amendments to the aforesaid laws and regulations relating to the amount of compensation where such amendments follow the general trends in the market value of the land.[22]

---

[17] Unless otherwise stated, treaty provisions refer to land in general terms, which is broader than farmland.

[18] Pacific Agreement on Closer Economic Relations Plus (PACER Plus) (signed 14 June 2017), Annex 9-A Schedule of Commitments on Investment, Schedule of Australia.

[19] ibid, Schedules of Cook Islands, Federated States of Micronesia, Kiribati, Palau, Samoa and Tuvalu.

[20] ibid, Schedules of Cook Islands, Kiribati, Nauru, New Zealand, Tuvalu.

[21] ibid, Schedules of Cook Islands, Federated States of Micronesia, Kiribati, Nauru, Niue, Palau, Samoa, Solomon Islands, Tonga, Tuvalu, Vanuatu. See also the Mainland and Hong Kong Closer Economic Partnership Arrangement (signed 28 June 2017), Investment Agreement, art 5 and Table 2 Item 3—Land: 'The Mainland reserves the right to adopt or maintain any measures with respect to restricting Hong Kong investors and their investments in the use of or contracting for the operation of agricultural lands'.

[22] Agreement on Investment among the Governments of Hong Kong Special Administrative Region of the People's Republic of China and the Member States of the Association of Southeast Asian Nations (ASEAN) (signed 12 November 2017), cl 10.4. Earlier treaties concluded by Singapore, including in the context of ASEAN, included similar provisions; see eg Agreement on Investment under the Framework Agreement on Comprehensive Economic Cooperation between the Association of Southeast Asian Nations and the Republic of India (signed 12 November 2014), art 8.8.

13.07 At the national level, some investment codes that were adopted or that entered into force in 2017 contain explicit provisions on investors' access to land. Myanmar's Investment Law of 2016, which came into force with full effect in April 2017,[23] includes a chapter on 'Right to Use Land' to regulate the establishment, duration and renewal of land leases.[24] Egypt's Investment Law of 2017 specifically covers agriculture, and contains several provisions on land access for commercial investors.[25] Meanwhile, a number of high-income country governments took or announced measures to restrict the acquisition of farmland by foreign investors. For instance, Australia announced that foreign investors would normally need to show that Australian entities were given the opportunity to bid for the land which they seek to acquire;[26] in France, the President announced measures to restrict the large-scale acquisition of farmland by foreign investors;[27] and New Zealand clarified the requirements to screen farmland acquisitions by foreign investors.[28]

13.08 In recent years, investment issues have featured prominently in some national land law reform processes, including as part of continued efforts to support the implementation of the Voluntary Guidelines on the Responsible Governance of Tenure of Land, Fisheries and Forests in the Context of National Food Security. These guidelines are an international soft-law instrument which the United Nations Committee on World Food Security endorsed in 2012, and which addresses farmland investment issues.[29] In recent years, several policy and legislative revisions have partly built on the Voluntary Guidelines, leading to cross-referencing in some national policy and legislative instruments.[30] In the review period, the Voluntary Guidelines continued to be resorted to in ongoing land law reforms, including in the form of multi-stakeholder dialogue to sustain reform initiatives.[31]

---

[23] Maximilian Clasmeier, *Myanmar's New Investment Law and its Confidence in International Arbitration* (*Kluwer Arbitration Blog*, 2017) <http://arbitrationblog.kluwerarbitration.com/2017/01/25/myanmars-new-investment-law-and-its-confidence-in-international-arbitration/> accessed 27 February 2018.

[24] Myanmar Investment Law No 40/2016 of 18 October 2016, art 50.

[25] Egypt Investment Law No 72 of 31 May 2017, arts 1 and 26.

[26] UNCTAD, *Investment Policy Monitor 2018*, Issue 19, UNCTAD/DIAE/PCB/2018/1.

[27] Rory Mulholland, 'Emmanuel Macron Promises to Stop Foreign Investors Buying up French Farms after China Land Grab' *The Telegraph* (Paris, 22 February 2018).

[28] Ministerial Directive Letter on Land Information in New Zealand, 'Legislation, Ministers & Delegated Powers' (28 November 2017) <https://www.linz.govt.nz/sites/default/files/media/doc/oio_directive-letter_20171128.pdf> accessed 27 February 2018.

[29] Committee on World Food Security, *Voluntary Guidelines on the Responsible Governance of Tenure of Land, Fisheries and Forests in the Context of National Food Security* (Food and Agriculture Organization of the United Nations, 2012), s 12.

[30] For example, the National Land Policy of Sierra Leone (1 August 2015) explicitly acknowledges the influence of the Voluntary Guidelines in the policy reform (s 1.3); and in Scotland the Land Reform (Scotland) Act 2016 refers twice to the Voluntary Guidelines, as an international instrument that the Scottish government 'must have regard to the desirability of ... promoting respect for' when developing national instruments envisaged by the Act (ss 1 and 44).

[31] In Liberia, eg, a multi-stakeholder dialogue supported by the Food and Agriculture Organization of the United Nations was reported to have resulted in the development of recommendations and renewed calls for the adoption of the draft Land Rights Bill. See Food and Agriculture Organization

13.09 Finally, national level policy developments arose in connection with agrarian reform in southern Africa—particularly Zimbabwe and South Africa. These developments followed political change at the highest level of government. At the time of writing, the nature, implications, and outcomes of these policy shifts were still unclear. Over the years, Zimbabwe's controversial 'fast-track' agrarian reform programme was at the centre of several investor–state arbitrations and other international dispute settlement proceedings.[32] In 2017, the swearing in of a new president was followed by announcements of a policy shift. In his inauguration speech, the new President Emmerson Mnangagwa stated that 'complex issues of land tenure will have to be addressed both urgently and definitely'.[33] This remark was followed up through the issuance of new 'Investment Guidelines and Opportunities in Zimbabwe',[34] which identified agriculture as one priority area for investment.[35] While the government did not seek to reverse land redistribution,[36] it promised to compensate the commercial farmers who lost their land through the agrarian reform, and to honour obligations under applicable investment treaties, as part of a wider renewed emphasis on markets and private investment.[37] In this context, the government was considering the establishment of an ad hoc tribunal based on international best practice to determine the value of compensation and modalities of payment.[38] Meanwhile, expropriated commercial farmers were reported to be claiming compensation, with quoted amounts varying between $9 billion and $30 billion, and with a small minority of farmers reportedly considering recourse to international arbitration.[39]

13.10 In early 2018, South Africa also experienced the swearing in of a new president. Incoming President Cyril Ramaphosa announced in his first state of the nation

---

of the United Nations, *Governance of Tenure Newsletter* (10 December 2017) <http://www.fao.org/tenure/newsletters/detail-events/en/c/1073549/> accessed 27 February 2018.

[32] See the arbitrations cited n 14, and the case *Mike Campbell (Pvt) Ltd. & Others v The Republic of Zimbabwe*, Southern African Development Community (SADC) Tribunal, SADC (T) Case No 2/2007, Judgment (28 November 2008).

[33] President Mnangagwa's inauguration speech in full, *Chronicle* (25 November 2017) <http://www.chronicle.co.zw/president-mnangagwas-inauguration-speech-in-full/> accessed 27 February 2018.

[34] Government of Zimbabwe, *Investment Guidelines and Opportunities in Zimbabwe* (2018) <http://www.cfuzim.org/~cfuzimb/images/investguides.pdf> accessed 8 March 2018.

[35] ibid paras 9.9 and 9.10.

[36] 'Zimbabwe Won't Return Land to White Farmers: Mnangagwa' *News 24* (Harare, 11 February 2018) <https://www.news24.com/Africa/Zimbabwe/zimbabwe-wont-return-land-to-white-farmers-mnangagwa-20180210-2> accessed 27 February 2018.

[37] *Investment Guidelines and Opportunities in Zimbabwe* (n 34) paras 1.4-1.6, 1.8(b) and 1.9(a).

[38] ibid para. 1.9(a). The guidelines do not elaborate on the nature of relevant 'international best practice'.

[39] 'Ex-Zim Farmers Demand $9 Billion Compensation' *Business Daily* (25 January 2018) <http://www.businessdaily.co.zw/index-id-National-zk-39797.html> accessed 27 February 2018.

address that South Africa would accelerate its land redistribution programme to 'redress a grave historical injustice', and to increase the number of agricultural producers and the amount of cultivable land.[40] The political transition was accompanied by lively debates about the place of expropriation and compensation in an agrarian reform programme that had traditionally been based on 'willing seller, willing buyer' principles—an approach that was perceived as slow in delivering change. In this context, the parliament debated whether to amend the constitution in order to allow expropriation without compensation.[41] The need for such an amendment was disputed by some, who argued that the constitution already allows the state to expropriate without compensation under certain circumstances.[42]

13.11 By way of background, it is worth recalling that South Africa concluded a number of bilateral investment treaties (BITs) from the 1990s. While the South African Constitution requires specified social and historical circumstances to be considered when determining the amount of compensation,[43] the expropriation clauses found in South Africa's investment treaties typically refer to market value alone.[44] A model investment treaty developed by the Southern African Development Community (SADC) does require consideration of social and historical factors,[45] but this approach is yet to be reflected into actual investment treaties concluded by South Africa. However, the Protection of Investment Act of 2015 provides that payment of compensation in case of expropriation shall be according to the terms set in the Constitution.[46] South Africa is reported to have lost at least one investor–state arbitration in connection with its agrarian

---

[40] 'In full, Read Cyril's Ramaphosa's First State of the Nation Address' *Times Live* (16 February 2018) <https://www.timeslive.co.za/politics/2018-02-16-in-full--read-cyril-ramaphosas-first-state-of-the-nation-address/> accessed 27 February 2018.

[41] Samuel Osborne, 'South Africa Votes to Seize Land from White Farmers without Compensation' *The Independent* (1 March 2018) <http://www.independent.co.uk/news/world/africa/south-africa-white-farms-land-seizure-anc-race-relations-a8234461.html> accessed 1 March 2018.

[42] Ruth Hall, 'Land Expropriation without Compensation: What Does it Mean?' *News 24* (4 March 2018) <https://m.news24.com/Columnists/GuestColumn/land-expropriation-without-compensation-what-does-it-mean-20180304-5> accessed 8 March 2018. Article 25(3) of the Constitution of the Republic of South Africa of 1996 provides that '[T]he amount of the compensation [in case of expropriation] … must be just and equitable'; Ruth Hall argued that this provision would allow for compensation to be set at nil, provided this is 'just and equitable' in the circumstances.

[43] These circumstances include the market value of the property, but also the current use of the property, the history of its acquisition and use, and the purpose of the expropriation; Constitution of the Republic of South Africa of 1996, art 25(3).

[44] For example Agreement between the Government of the People's Republic of China and the Government of the Republic of South Africa concerning the Reciprocal Promotion and Protection of Investments (signed 30 December 1997), art 4.

[45] SADC Model Investment Treaty (2012), art 6.2, options 1 and 2.

[46] Protection of Investment Act No 22 of 15 December 2015, s 10.

reform programme, though the relevant award is not publicly available.⁴⁷ The government has since terminated several (but not all) investment treaties.⁴⁸ However, the treaties terminated continue to cover existing investments for periods specified in the relevant 'survival' clause.⁴⁹ Depending on future evolutions, the potential policy shifts might thus give rise to further treaty-based disputes.

C. Developments in Investment Disputes

In 2017, several investor–state arbitrations were initiated that presented connections to farmland. One such arbitration stemmed from the cancellation of a sugarcane project in Tanzania. The claim was brought under the BIT between Sweden and Tanzania, and it was registered with ICSID on 11 September 2017.⁵⁰ The dispute concerns an agreement the investor signed with the Tanzanian government to develop some 20,000 hectares of land for a sugarcane plantation and an ethanol processing facility.⁵¹ At the time of writing, there was little publicly available information about the legal arguments and the relevant facts at stake in the arbitration. However, the case attracted public commentary by virtue of its being the first—and thus far the only—publicly known investor–state arbitration that originated from the post-2005 wave of agribusiness plantation deals in low and middle-income countries.⁵²

13.12

---

⁴⁷ Luke E Peterson, 'Swiss Investor Prevailed in 2003 in Confidential BIT Arbitration over South Africa Land Dispute' *Investment Arbitration Reporter* (22 October 2008) <http://www.iareporter.com/articles/20091001_2> accessed 27 February 2018.

⁴⁸ Including treaties with Austria, Belgium–Luxembourg Economic Union, Denmark, France, Germany, Netherlands, Spain, Switzerland, and the United Kingdom.

⁴⁹ For example, the investment treaty with Belgium and Luxembourg, terminated in October 2012, continues to apply for ten years after termination. Accord entre l'Union Economique Belgo-Luxembourgeoise et la République d'Afrique du Sud Concernant l'Encouragement et la Protection Réciproques des Investissements (signed 14 August 1998).

⁵⁰ Agreement between the Government of the United Republic of Tanzania and the Government of the Kingdom of Sweden on the Promotion and Reciprocal Protection of Investments (signed 1 September 1999). The arbitration is *EcoDevelopment in Europe AB & others v United Republic of Tanzania*, ICSID Case No ARB/17/33.

⁵¹ EcoEnergy Group, *White Paper on the Bagamoyo EcoEnergy Project in Tanzania*, <http://www.ecoenergy.co.tz/fileadmin/user_upload/Ecoenergy_whitepaper.pdf> accessed 8 March 2018.

⁵² Jesse Coleman and Kaitlin Y Cordes, 'Not So Sweet: Tanzania Confronts Arbitration over Large-Scale Sugarcane and Ethanol Project' (*CCSI Blog*, 21 September 2017) <http://ccsi.columbia.edu/2017/09/21/not-so-sweet-tanzania-confronts-arbitration-over-large-scale-sugarcane-and-ethanol-project/> accessed 27 February 2018; Nathalie Bernasconi-Osterwalder and Carin Smaller, 'Farmland Investments Are Finding Their Way to International Arbitration' (*IISD Blog*,

13.13 In addition, there were media reports of an Indian investor threatening to bring arbitration proceedings against the government of Ethiopia in connection with another post-2005 agribusiness plantation deal.[53] However, the BIT between Ethiopia and India did not appear to be in force,[54] and Ethiopia's investment code does not seem to offer consent to arbitration.[55] Unless the corporate structure underlying the investment allows the investor to invoke other BITs, or unless the relevant contractual arrangements include an arbitration clause,[56] it is not clear how the investor could give effect to the threat of arbitration.

13.14 In the review period, arbitration notices were also served in connection with older agribusiness plantations. According to reports, investors served a notice to the government of Tanzania under the Italy–Tanzania BIT, arguing that an agricultural estate they acquired in 1997 was unduly expropriated to make way for a manufacturing plant.[57] Further, commercial farmers in Zimbabwe were reported to have served a notice of arbitration over the country's agrarian reform programme. At the time of writing, little information about this case was publicly available, but would-be claimants were reported to have relied on the SADC Finance and Investment Protocol.[58] A further arbitration claim was reported to have been initiated against Hungary in connection with the alleged expropriation of a British-linked potato and dairy farming operation.[59]

---

20 September 2017) <http://www.iisd.org/blog/farmland-investments-are-finding-their-way-international-arbitration> accessed 27 February 2018.

[53] Birhanu Fikade, 'Karuturi Contemplates Legal Recourse for Loss in Ethiopia' *The Reporter* (30 September 2017) <http://www.thereporterethiopia.com/business/karuturi-contemplates-legal-recourse-loss-ethiopia> accessed 27 February 2018.

[54] According to UNCTAD's IIA Navigator <http://investmentpolicyhub.unctad.org/IIA/CountryBits/67#iiaInnerMenu> (accessed 27 February 2018). Agreement between the Republic of India and the Federal Democratic Republic of Ethiopia for the Reciprocal Promotion and Protection of Investments (signed 5 July 2007).

[55] Investment Proclamation No 769/2012 of 17 September 2012 <http://investmentpolicyhub.unctad.org/InvestmentLaws/laws/180> accessed 27 February 2018.

[56] OpenLandContracts.org, an online repository of publicly available investment contracts for land, agriculture, and forestry projects, includes a copy of a contract between the Indian investor and Ethiopia (<http://www.openlandcontracts.org/contract/ocds-591adf-3081785170/view#/> accessed 27 February 2018). If this is the applicable contract, it does not include an arbitration clause.

[57] Zoe Williams, 'Tanzania Put on Notice of Potential $30 Million BIT Arbitration by Italian Agricultural Investor' *Investment Arbitration Reporter* (29 August 2017) <https://www.iareporter.com/articles/tanzania-put-on-notice-of-potential-30-million-bit-arbitration-by-uk-agricultural-investor/> accessed 27 February 2018.

[58] IAReporter, 'Dispossessed Landowners in Zimbabwe Reportedly Attempt to Use the SADC Finance and Investment Protocol' *Investment Arbitration Reporter* (21 August 2017) <https://www.iareporter.com/articles/dispossessed-landowners-in-zimbabwe-reportedly-attempt-to-use-sadc-finance-and-investment-protocol/> accessed 27 February 2018. SADC Protocol on Finance and Investment (signed 18 August 2006).

[59] Zoe Williams, 'UK Investor's Lost Hungarian Farm Lease Leads to BIT Arbitration' *Investment Arbitration Reporter* (3 August 2017) <https://www.iareporter.com/articles/uk-investors-lost-hungarian-farm-lease-leads-to-bit-arbitration/> accessed 27 February 2018.

13.15 Also worth noting are developments concerning ongoing arbitrations. Hearings were reported to have been held for a farmland-related arbitration brought by a US investor against Moldova.[60] In a separate development concerning two of Zimbabwe's agrarian reform cases,[61] an ICSID Annulment Committee lifted the stay on enforcement of the arbitral award.[62] The Committee was not swayed by Zimbabwe's argument that lifting the stay would cause 'catastrophic' consequences for its public finances.[63] The Committee subsequently dismissed Zimbabwe's request for a new stay.[64] The deadline for Zimbabwe to honour the award was reported to have since expired, which effectively put the state in a position of non-compliance.[65] At the time of writing, the annulment proceedings were ongoing.

13.16 By way of background, in one of Zimbabwe's agrarian reform cases, investors challenged Zimbabwe's 'fast-track' land reform programme on the grounds that their land was expropriated without compensation and that they suffered from land invasions, violence, and racial discrimination.[66] The arbitral tribunal held that the state had breached several provisions of the BIT between Germany and Zimbabwe.[67] Local groups supported by a non-governmental organization filed a petition to seek permission from the arbitral tribunal to make an *amicus curiae*

---

[60] Damien Charlotin, 'US Investor Says it Resorted to Third-party Funding due to State's Non-payment of Advances; at Hearings Parties Spar over an Investor's Need to Use Local Courts before Turning to BIT Arbitration' *Investment Arbitration Reporter* (18 January 2108) <https://www.iareporter.com/articles/us-investor-says-it-resorted-to-funding-due-to-states-non-payment-of-advances-at-hearings-parties-spar-over-an-investors-need-to-use-local-courts-before-turning-to-bit-arbitration/> accessed 27 February 2018.

[61] *Bernard Von Pezold and Others v Republic of Zimbabwe*, ICSID Case No ARB/10/15; *Border Timbers Limited, Border Timbers International (Private) Ltd and Hangani Development Co (Private) Limited v Republic of Zimbabwe*, ICSID Case No ARB/10/25.

[62] Damien Charlotin, 'In Previously Confidential Ruling, Stay of Enforcement Was Lifted in Zimbabwe Case, and ICSID Panel Gave the State Another Shot at Effecting Restitution of Seized Properties—but no Payment for Restitution was Forthcoming' *Investment Arbitration Reporter* (27 August 2017) <https://www.iareporter.com/articles/28229/> accessed 27 February 2018. See *Bernard Von Pezold and Others v Republic of Zimbabwe*, ICSID Case No ARB/10/15, Decision on Stay of Enforcement of the Award (24 April 2017); *Border Timbers Limited, Border Timbers International (Private) Ltd and Hangani Development Co (Private) Limited v Republic of Zimbabwe*, ICSID Case No ARB/10/25, Decision on Stay of Enforcement of the Award (24 April 2017).

[63] *Border Timbers Ltd* (n 62) paras 49–50, 83–87.

[64] Charlotin, 'In Previously Confidential Ruling, Stay of Enforcement Was Lifted' (n 62); and *Bernard Von Pezold and Others v Republic of Zimbabwe*, ICSID Case No ARB/10/15 and *Border Timbers Ltd, Border Timbers International (Private) Limited and Hangani Development Co (Private) Limited v Republic of Zimbabwe*, ICSID Case No ARB/10/25, Joint Decision on the Applicant's Urgent Application for Provisional Measures Regarding the Temporary Stay of Execution and the Escrow Agreement (22 August 2017).

[65] Andrew Mizner, 'Multi-million Dollar Payment Hangs over Zimbabwe' *African Law and Business* (14 September 2017), <https://www.africanlawbusiness.com/news/7593-multi-million-dollar-payment-hangs-over-zimbabwe> accessed 27 February 2018.

[66] *Von Pezold* (n 14) paras 103–59. The two agrarian reform cases were jointly heard by the same arbitral tribunal. However, the award in *Border Timbers Ltd, Border Timbers International (Private) Limited and Hangani Development Co (Private) Ltd v Republic of Zimbabwe*, ICSID Case No ARB/10/25 has not yet been published.

[67] *Von Pezold* (n 14) paras 445–48, 645, 652–57, 918–20, 1016–17.

submission. However, the tribunal did not give permission partly because it found that there were legitimate doubts as to the independence or neutrality of the petitioners.[68]

D. Future Outlook

13.17 The review period points to developments that are worth following in the future. From a policy perspective, the legal and institutional implications of the shifting approaches to agrarian reform in Southern Africa, and ultimately their practical outcomes, were as yet unclear at the time of writing and deserve continued tracking. Depending on how events will unfold, these developments could result in new departures in public policy at the interface between land governance and investment protection, and possibly in new farmland-related investor–state arbitrations.

13.18 Continued tracking of new and ongoing farmland-related arbitrations could shed light on how international investment law addresses complex investment disputes, including (depending on the factual circumstances of the case) in situations where the investor–state dispute is embedded in wider relations also involving other actors such as local farmers. The large number of failed investments in the recent wave of agribusiness plantation deals in low and middle-income countries, and the fact that a substantial majority of these deals were covered by at least one applicable investment treaty,[69] mean that the deals may well result in additional investor–state arbitrations.

13.19 Finally, it will be interesting to see whether the measures taken or announced by some high-income country governments to restrict the acquisition of farmland by foreign investors will develop into a consolidated trend, and what reverberations, if any, this may have in the wider investment policy landscape. It is worth noting that businesses originating from some of those countries have been active in large-scale farmland acquisitions abroad.[70]

---

[68] *Von Pezold & Others v Zimbabwe*, ICSID Case No ARB/10/25, and *Border Timbers Ltd, Border Timbers International (Private) Limited and Hangani Development Co (Private) Ltd v Republic of Zimbabwe*, ICSID Case No ARB/10/25, Procedural Order No 2 (2012) paras 25–27, 51, 55–56.

[69] As of 2015, 64 per cent of publicly reported land deals concluded since the year 2000 were found to be covered by at least one applicable treaty; see Lorenzo Cotula and Thierry Berger, *Land Deals and Investment Treaties: Visualising the Interface* (2015) International Institute for Environment and Development.

[70] See eg Land Matrix, an online public database of land deals <http://www.landmatrix.org> accessed 27 February 2018.

E. REGION REPORTS

14

INTERNATIONAL INVESTMENT LAW AND POLICY
2017 Developments in Africa

Mouhamadou Madana Kane

A. Introduction	14.01	C. Investment Treaty Policy: The Positives, the Negatives, and the *Rendez-Vous Manques*	14.16
B. Investment Treaty Practice: Overview of Trends and Lessons Learned	14.04	D. Conclusion	14.33

A. Introduction

Africa is blessed with tremendous natural resources, which strategically position the continent to attract foreign direct investment (FDI) funds required to finance the sustainable development programmes of African nations. Despite recent declines in FDI flows to Africa,[1] due mainly to the fall in commodity prices, FDI inflows to the continent have generally increased since 2005[2] owing to the various structural reforms adopted by African countries to improve governance, and enhance the investment climate and business environment, thus giving private investors confidence and incentives to explore the African market. However, despite solid achievements, Africa remains vulnerable to external shocks and meeting the

14.01

---

[1] According to the UNCTAD World Investment Report (WIR), FDI inflows to Africa have continued to decrease during 2012–2016. See Annex Table 1 of the 2017 WIR <http://unctad.org/en/PublicationsLibrary/wir2017_en.pdf > accessed 28 May 2018.

[2] According to UNCTAD 2011 WIR, FDI inflows to Africa were at only $38 million in 2005 and continued to increase significantly in the following years. The only periods of decline were in 2009 and 2010 due obviously to the world financial crisis. From 2011, FDI flows to Africa again picked up from $55 million in 2010 to $66 million in 2011 and $77 million in 2012. See Annex Table 1 of the 2011 WIR. <http://unctad.org/en/PublicationsLibrary/wir2011_en.pdf> accessed 28 May 2018.

14.01 investment needs of African countries remains a huge challenge, especially in the context where large infrastructure deficits continue to hamper Africa's economic and developmental growth.³

14.02 In this context of increased need for private capital, many African countries have signed international investment agreements (IIAs), particularly bilateral investment treaties (BITs),⁴ with the aim to promote FDI flows.⁵ However, the uncertainties raised by these treaties, in terms of their economic benefits and impact on the policy space of host countries, have resulted in debates regarding their relevance and the emergence of a new international investment law agenda at the global level. Since the international investment law landscape is changing, it is necessary to monitor trends and developments in Africa, with the view to identifying gaps and assessing the contribution of the continent to the development of international investment law. This chapter tries to achieve that objective by shedding light on the 2017 investment treaty policy and practice of African countries.

14.03 The chapter is organized in two further sections. Section B provides an overview of trends and lessons learned from the investment treaty practice in Africa, whereas section C zooms in on the positive and negative developments in investment treaty policy.

B. Investment Treaty Practice: Overview of Trends and Lessons Learned

14.04 For Africa, the year 2017 was particularly rich with lessons from many perspectives. A number of important developments regarding the investment treaty practice of African countries deserve to be highlighted.

1. International investment agreements: negotiation, signature and ratification

a. BITs

14.05 One key lesson learnt is the important reduction of the number of BITs signed by African countries in 2017. Indeed, only three new BITs were signed in 2017 against

---

³ As reported by the New Partnership for Africa's Development (NEPAD) Agency, $93 billion is needed annually to meet Africa's infrastructure needs and close the gap by 2040, as targeted under the Programme for Infrastructure Development in Africa (PIDA), is a continental initiative launched in 2010 to tackle infrastructure gaps in Africa by 2040. Further details about the PIDA are available at <http://www.nepad.org/programme/programme-infrastructure-development-africa-pida> accessed 28 May 2018.

⁴ At the end of 2017, African countries were party to 973 BITs. Our search in the UNCTAD International Investment Agreement Database is accessible at <http://investmentpolicyhub.unctad.org/IIA> accessed 18 February 2018.

⁵ The objective to promote FDI is consistently set out in the preamble of African investment treaties.

fifteen in 2016.⁶ The slow-down in the African BIT practice, which is consistent with the global trend, is relevant to note given the increased criticism of BITs, both in terms of their economic impact and effect on the policy space of host countries. Also important to note is the fact that no new BIT was signed between African countries in 2017. This indicates that intra-African bilateral investment cooperation is also slowing down compared to 2016 where six intra-African BITs were concluded,⁷ with Mauritius⁸ and the Kingdom of Morocco⁹ leading the way. Another notable highlight in 2017 is the continuous interest of the Republic of Turkey in signing BITs with African countries. Indeed, pursuing a trend initiated back in 2004–2005 with North African countries,¹⁰ and since 2010, with sub-Saharan African countries,¹¹ Turkey has been the primary external partner of African countries in 2017, having been party to two of the three BITs signed in that year.¹²

In terms of ratification trends, the rate of ratification of African BITs continues to be low. At the end of 2017, African countries were party to 973 BITs, out of which only 366 are in force, which represents nearly one-third of the total BITs signed.¹³ Only two BITs entered into force during 2017, which represents a significant decrease compared to 2016 where nine BITs were ratified.¹⁴   **14.06**

---

⁶ See UNCTAD International Investment Agreement Navigator <http://investmentpolicyhub.unctad.org/IIA> accessed 14 March 2018.

⁷ Six intra-African BITs were signed in 2016, see UNCTAD International Investment Agreement Database <http://investmentpolicyhub.unctad.org/IIA> accessed 14 March 2018.

⁸ Mauritius signed three BITs in 2016, all of which were with African states, see UNCTAD International Investment Agreement Database <http://investmentpolicyhub.unctad.org/IIA> accessed 14 March 2018. A trend has been noticed with Mauritius recently adopting strategic measures to foster the presence of Mauritian companies in other African destinations. It is in this context that the country had recently launched an Rs.500 million Mauritius–Africa Fund aiming to encourage Mauritian companies to invest in Africa, in addition to signing joint development agreements with other African countries for the establishment and management of special economic zones, including with Senegal, Madagascar, and Ghana, see Mauritius Investment Authority <http://www.investmauritius.com/media/422818/BOI-Corporate-Brochure-Apr-2017-ENG.pdf> accessed 29 May 2018.

⁹ Morocco is one of the most active African signatory states, having signed in 2016 four BITs: three with African countries and one with a non-African country, see UNCTAD International Investment Agreement Database <http://investmentpolicyhub.unctad.org/IIA> accessed 14 March 2018. The Kingdom has an African strategy, which has recently been reinforced by the decision to reintegrate the country in the African Union, and the country's pending request to become a member state of the Economic Commission of West African States (ECOWAS).

¹⁰ BITs with Morocco (2004), Tunisia (2004), and Egypt (2005).

¹¹ BITs with Senegal (2010), Nigeria (2011), Cameroon (2012), Gabon (2012), Mauritius (2013), Gambia (2013), Guinea (2013), Djibouti (2013), Benin (2013), Kenya (2014), and Sudan (2014).

¹² These are the Mozambique–Turkey BIT (signed 24 January 2017) and the Burundi–Turkey BIT (signed 14 June 2017), see UNCTAD International Investment Agreement Database <http://investmentpolicyhub.unctad.org/IIA> accessed 18 February 2018.

¹³ See UNCTAD International Investment Agreement Database <http://investmentpolicyhub.unctad.org/IIA> accessed 18 February 2018.

¹⁴ The Kenya–Korean Republic BIT and Kenya–Japan BIT entered into force respectively on 3 May 2017 and 14 September 2017, see UNCTAD International Investment Agreement Database <http://investmentpolicyhub.unctad.org/IIA> accessed 14 March 2018.

b. Trade agreements with investment chapters

14.07 Acknowledging the crucial link between investment and trade, African countries and Regional Economic Communities (RECs) have pursued efforts to mainstream investment, by incorporating investment chapters or provisions in larger trade or economic partnership agreements. In this context, the Tripartite Free Trade Agreement (TFTA), signed between the Common Market for Eastern and Southern Africa (COMESA), the East African Community (EAC), and the Southern African Development Community (SADC) contemplates the negotiation of additional protocols on trade-related matters including cross-border investment.[15, 16] It may also be recalled that an investment chapter is expected to be included in the Continental Free Trade Agreement (CFTA) and negotiated after the conclusion of the first phase of CFTA negotiations.[17] Given that the CFTA Agreement was recently signed during the African Union summit in March 2018 in Kigali,[18] it is therefore expected that negotiations of the CFTA investment chapter will kick off soon.

14.08 The TFTA and the CFTA are examples confirming the trend of mainstreaming investment issues in trade instruments. This trend also exist at the bilateral level with the Economic Partnership Agreements (EPA) between the European Union and African RECs. For example, the European Union and SADC member states concluded in 2016 an EPA providing that 'the EU and the Participating SADC EPA States agree to cooperate on investment … and may in [the] future consider negotiating an agreement on investment in economic sectors other than services'.[19]

2. Investor–state disputes

14.09 African countries' share in the world total investment disputes is not negligible.[20] Focusing on ICSID caseload, data shows that, as of 31 May 2017, African

---

[15] The Agreement Establishing a Tripartite Free Trade Area among the Common Market for Eastern and Southern Africa, the East African Community and the Southern African Development Community (TFTA), which was officially launched in 2015, established a free trade area between the twenty-six member states of the three RECs (COMESA, EAC, and SADC). At the time of writing this chapter, twenty-two member states signed the TFTA Agreement. Fourteen ratifications are required for the Agreement to enter into force.

[16] Article 45 of the TFTA ('Phase II Negotiations') provides for the negotiation of additional protocols within twenty-four months from the entry into force of TFTA.

[17] For a useful link to African Continental Free Trade Area (CFTA) negotiation milestones (including the outcome of human right impact assessment conducted), legal texts and policy documents, check <https://www.tralac.org/resources/our-resources/6730-continental-free-trade-area-cfta.html> accessed 9 May 2018.

[18] Tralac, 'African Continental Free Trade Area (AfCFTA) Legal Texts and Policy Documents' <https://www.tralac.org/resources/our-resources/6730-continental-free-trade-area-cfta.html> accessed 9 May 2018.

[19] The Agreement is available at <http://trade.ec.europa.eu/doclib/docs/2015/october/tradoc_153915.pdf> accessed 14 March 2018.

[20] UNCTAD Investment Dispute Settlement Navigator lists 855 investment disputes, out which 97 involved an African country <http://investmentpolicyhub.unctad.org/ISDS> accessed 18 February 2018.

countries participated in 22 per cent of the total ICSID cases thus far registered under the ICSID Convention and the ICSID Additional Facility Rules.[21] Indeed, out of the 613 cases registered,[22] 135 involved an African state,[23] resulting in the continent ranking third after South America (23 per cent) and Eastern Europe and Central Asia (25 per cent).[24] Specifically regarding investment treaty disputes,[25] UNCTAD data indicates that seventy-two treaty-based disputes are known to have been initiated worldwide in 2017,[26] out of which eleven involved African countries as respondents,[27] which represents roughly 15 per cent African participation as a respondent state. One important factor to note is that, out of the 2017 cases, only one is an intra-African investment dispute.[28] The limited number of intra-African disputes in 2017 is actually consistent with the global picture. For example, intra-African disputes share only 21 per cent of the total ICSID African cases.[29] Furthermore, out of the ninety-seven treaty-based African cases listed by UNCTAD, only seven are between an African country and an African investor,[30] which is also consistent with the fact that intra-African investment treaties represent less than 20 per cent of the total investment treaties signed by African countries.[31]

14.10 In terms of the legal basis of the claims, it is worth noting that all the eleven investment treaty cases reported in 2017, which are all pending, were submitted pursuant to a BIT,[32] similar to most of the other African investment treaty cases initiated before.[33] Finally, important to note is the fact that most of the majority of the 2017 African disputes are in the services (with six cases reported in this

---

[21] ICSID, 'ICSID Caseload 2017–Special focus on Africa' 7. <https://icsid.worldbank.org/en/Documents/resources/ICSID%20Web%20Stats%20Africa%20(English)%20June%202017.pdf> accessed 18 February 2018.
[22] These cases include not only IIA-based disputes but also disputes under investment laws and investment contracts.
[23] Out of the 135 cases, African States were claimant in only two, namely: *Gabon v Société Serete SA*, ICSID Case No ARB/76/1 (2017) and *Republic of Equatorial Guinea v CMS Energy Corporation and Others*, Case No CONC(AF)/12/12 (2017). See ICSID, 'ICSID Caseload 2017–Special focus on Africa' (n 21) 32–39.
[24] ICSID, 'ICSID Caseload 2017—Special focus on Africa' (n 21) 7.
[25] Refers to disputes based on an international investment agreement.
[26] See UNCTAD Investment Dispute Settlement Navigator (n 6).
[27] ibid.
[28] 'Intra-African dispute' refers to a dispute between an African state and an African investor. The subject case is *LTME Mauritius Limited and Madamobil Holdings Mauritius Limited v Republic of Madagascar*, ICSID Case No ARB/17/28 (2017) <http://investmentpolicyhub.unctad.org/ISDS/Details/840> accessed 9 May 2018.
[29] ICSID, 'ICSID Caseload 2017–Special focus on Africa' (n 21) 13.
[30] See UNCTAD Investment Dispute Settlement Navigator (n 6).
[31] Out of the 975 international investment agreements reported, 190 are intra-African, see UNCTAD International Investment Agreement Database <http://investmentpolicyhub.unctad.org/IIA> accessed 9 May 2018.
[32] See UNCTAD Investment Dispute Settlement Navigator (n 6).
[33] Out of ninety-seven cases listed in UNCTAD Dispute Settlement Navigator, ninety-two are based on a BIT <http://investmentpolicyhub.unctad.org/ISDS> accessed 9 May 2018.

sector), followed by the primary sector (three cases), and the manufacturing sector (two cases).[34] This finding is in line with the global picture since, out the ninety-seven African cases reported by UNCTAD, fifty-five revolve around the tertiary (services) industries, and the remaining respectively in the primary and the secondary sectors.

14.11   It may be noted, in the aftermath of the Arab Spring revolution, that Libya and Egypt have each faced a new claim in 2017. The claim against Libya was brought by a Turkish investor based on the 2009 Libya–Turkey BIT,[35, 36] in addition to the four cases initiated in 2016 based on the same treaty.[37] As far as Egypt is concerned, the country faced a claim by a Dutch investor pursuant to the Egypt–Netherlands BIT,[38, 39] thereby reinforcing the country's top ranking among African countries as a respondent in investor–state arbitration.[40]

14.12   Last but not least, it is relevant to note that two new claims have been initiated by African investors in 2017 respectively against India[41] and Madagascar[42] based on the India–Mauritius BIT,[43] and the Madagascar–Mauritius

---

[34] See UNCTAD Investment Dispute Settlement Navigator (n 6).

[35] Agreement between the Republic of Turkey and the Great Socialist People's Libyan Arab Jamahiriya on the Reciprocal Promotion and Protection of Investments (signed 25 November 2009).

[36] The subject case is *Ustay Yapi Taahhut ve Ticaret AS v Libya* (ICC) (2017) <http://investmentpolicyhub.unctad.org/ISDS/Details/818> accessed 29 May 2018.

[37] The four cases are Cengiz İnşaat Sanayi ve Ticaret A.S v. Libya (ICC)(2016) <http://investmentpolicyhub.unctad.org/ISDS/Details/776> accessed 29 May 2018; *Etrak İnşaat Taahut ve Ticaret Anonim Sirketi v Libya* (ICC) (2016) <http://investmentpolicyhub.unctad.org/ISDS/Details/774> accessed 29 May 2018; *Güriş İnşaat ve Mühendislik AŞ v Libya* (ICC) (2016) <http://investmentpolicyhub.unctad.org/ISDS/Details/778> accessed 29 May 2018; and *Nurol İnşaat ve Ticaret AŞ v Libya* (ICC) (2016) <http://investmentpolicyhub.unctad.org/ISDS/Details/777> accessed 29 May 2018. The country also faced a sixth case (ad hoc arbitration under UNCITRAL Rules) based on the Agreement on Promotion, Protection and Guarantee of Investments amongst the Member States of the Organization of the Islamic Conference (entered into force February 1988) (OIC Investment Agreement), namely *DS Construction FZCO v Libya* (2016) <http://investmentpolicyhub.unctad.org/ISDS/Details/775> accessed 29 May 2018. All the six cases were pending at the time of writing this chapter. It will be interesting to observe the outcome as lessons may be learnt for fragile countries or countries in transition.

[38] Agreement on Encouragement and Reciprocal Protection of Investments between the Arab Republic of Egypt and the Kingdom of the Netherlands (Egypt–Netherlands BIT) (signed 17 January 1996).

[39] The subject case is *Future Pipe International BV v Arab Republic of Egypt*, ICSID Case No ARB/17/31 <http://investmentpolicyhub.unctad.org/ISDS/Details/844> accessed 29 May 2018.

[40] So far, Egypt is respondent in thirty-one cases, see UNCTAD Investment Dispute Settlement Navigator (n 6).

[41] *Carissa Investments LLC v India* (UNCITRAL) (2017) <http://investmentpolicyhub.unctad.org/ISDS/Details/862> accessed 9 May 2018.

[42] *LTME Mauritius Limited and Madamobil Holdings Mauritius Limited v Republic of Madagascar*, ICSID Case No ARB/17/28 <http://investmentpolicyhub.unctad.org/ISDS/Details/840> accessed 9 May 2018.

[43] Agreement between the Government of the Republic of Mauritius and the Government of the Republic of India for the Promotion and Protection of Investments (India–Mauritius BIT) (signed 4 September 1998).

BIT.[44] Adding the two cases to the previous ones, African investors have been involved as claimants in sixteen investment treaty cases in total, including nine against non-African countries and seven against African countries.[45]

c. Investment promotion and protection: beyond investment treaties

Besides BITs, many African nations are exploring alternative approaches to investment promotion and regulation, including through national investment policies, domestic investment laws, trade treaties, and economic partnership agreements. Following the South African experience,[46] countries such as Namibia and Kenya have elaborated a national approach to investment promotion and protection, with a strong emphasis on investment facilitation measures. The following statement of the representative of Namibia at the UNCTAD 2017 High Level IIA Conference,[47] confirms this trend: 14.13

> "Weighing the size of the country's economy against the ongoing reforms regarding the IIA regime, the Namibian Government submitted that perhaps a single investment policy should rather be considered against investment treaties as a possible option for Namibia to improve its attractiveness to draw investors. *It remains our current opinion that entering into treaty negotiations is not obviously likely to be more effective than more targeted measures*".[48]

While Namibia's regulatory preference is towards refraining from negotiating BITs, the approach of the government of Kenya has been to develop a *Kenya Investment Policy*[49] to serve as a 'single, comprehensive and harmonized policy to guide attraction, facilitation, retention, monitoring and evaluation of investments'.[50] It is in this context that the Kenyan representative at the UNCTAD IIA Conference submitted that: 14.14

> The Kenya Investment Policy which provided for provisions that safeguard the country's right to regulate, ensuring responsible investment, while providing protection to investor, *are in consonance with the proposals contained in the UNCTAD's Road*

---

[44] *Accord de Promotion et de la Protection Réciproque des Investissements entre le Gouvernement de la République de Maurice Et Le Gouvernement de la République de Madagascar* (Madagascar–Mauritius BIT) (signed 6 April 2004).

[45] See UNCTAD Investment Dispute Settlement Navigator (n 6).

[46] It may be recalled that in 2015, South Africa decided to terminate most of its BITs and adopted a Protection of Investment Act.

[47] The conference took place during 9 to 11 October 2017. For further information, see <http://investmentpolicyhub.unctad.org/Pages/unctad-annual-high-level-iia-conference-phase-2-of-iia-reform> accessed 28 February 2018.

[48] Statement by HE Sabine Böhlke-Möller, Permanent Representative of Namibia<http://investmentpolicyhub.unctad.org/Upload/Documents/Namibia-%20SABINE%20B%C3%B6HLKE-M%C3%B6LLER-%20No%20session.pdf> accessed 28 February 2018 (emphasis added).

[49] *Kenya Investment Policy, Investment Growth for Sustainable Development* (June 2017) <https://www.tralac.org/news/article/11795-draft-kenya-investment-policy-investment-growth-for-sustainable-development.html> accessed 28 February 2018.

[50] ibid 6.

Map for IIA Reform and its Guiding Principles for Investment Policy for Sustainable Development and investment facilitation.[51]

14.15 Investment facilitation is indeed gaining momentum in Africa. The Abuja Statement on 'Deepening Africa's Integration in the Global Economy through Trade and Investment Facilitation for Development',[52] which was adopted in November 2017 as the outcome document of the High Level Trade and Investment Facilitation Forum for Development[53] testifies to this. From a domestic perspective, many African countries have adopted new investment laws aiming to facilitate investments. In 2017, Egypt and Mauritius respectively introduced a new Investment Law[54] and a new Business Facilitation Act[55] that provide incentives to foreign and domestic investors and streamline administrative processes. In 2016, Algeria and Tunisia also enacted new investment laws with various investment facilitation measures, including *inter alia*, tax incentives.[56] Kenya also enacted a law on Special Economic Zones, which offers a number of investment incentives.[57]

C. Investment Treaty Policy: The Positives, the Negatives, and the *Rendez-Vous Manqués*

14.16 The main highlights of 2017 are presented in this section, focusing respectively on the positives, the negatives, and the *rendez-vous manqués*.

1. The positives

a. Investment treaty reform: increased awareness, ownership and policy space

14.17 A significant development in the African international investment law and policy landscape has been the increased awareness of African countries about the potential negative impact of BITs on state regulatory power, and the need to undertake review and reform of the old generation of treaties. Many African countries

---

[51] Statement by HE Sabine Böhlke-Möller (n 48) (emphasis added).
[52] The Statement can be accessed at <https://docs.wto.org/dol2fe/Pages/FE_Search/FE_S_S009-DP.aspx?language=E&CatalogueIdList=239992,239877,239866,239841,239807,239717,239704,239247,239189,238858&CurrentCatalogueIdIndex=0&FullTextHash=&HasEnglishRecord=True&HasFrenchRecord=True&HasSpanishRecord=False> accessed 28 February 2018.
[53] The Forum was organized by the Federal Republic of Nigeria, the Economic Community for West African States (ECOWAS) in partnership with the WTO Friends of Investment Facilitation for Development (FIFD) from 2 to 3 November 2017, in Abuja, Nigeria.
[54] The text of the new law is available at <http://www.gafi.gov.eg/English/StartaBusiness/Laws-and-Regulations/PublishingImages/Pages/BusinessLaws/Investment%20Law%20english%20ban.pdf> accessed 28 February 2018.
[55] The text of the new law is available at<http://mauritiusassembly.govmu.org/English/bills/Documents/intro/2017/bill0517.pdf> accessed 28 February 2018.
[56] See UNCTAD Investment Policy Monitor, Issue 16 (November 2016) 5 < http://unctad.org/en/PublicationsLibrary/webdiaepcb2016d2_en.pdf > accessed 28 February 2018.
[57] ibid 3.

expressed this concern during the 2017 UNCTAD IIA conference.[58] The awareness has translated into concrete actions in certain countries. In this respect, it is possible to classify African countries into three groups: countries at 'awareness stage', 'reforming stage', and 'implementation stage'. African countries in the first group have just initiated their thinking about reviewing and reforming their BITs, and include, for example, The Gambia and Mauritania. The representative of the Gambian delegation at the conference noted interestingly that:

> Gambia has not undertaken any review of these [investment] treaties … and will request UNCTAD to assist the Government of the Gambia in closing the gaps to enhance competitiveness of the investment environment. This would include the review of BITs and the overlapping roles and functions of different institutions relating to investment promotion with the view to having an intergovernmental committee on investment.[59]

14.18 The Mauritanian representative issued a similar statement as follows:

> We have decided that it was important for us to reflect on the model of treaty we want for our country. It is in this context that Mauritania has approached the African Legal Support Facility, a subsidiary of the African Development Bank, to study the matter.[60]

14.19 In reality, most African countries are in the 'awareness' group because the debate about reforming the international investment regime has picked up in the continent only very recently, thanks partly to the capacity building initiatives of UNCTAD and other organizations including the African Legal Support Facility (ALSF).

14.20 The second group of countries, the 'reforming' group, include for example Egypt, Botswana, Burkina Faso, Madagascar, and Senegal. Contrary to the countries in the first group, the 'reforming' countries have gone one step beyond awareness by setting up frameworks or undertaking preliminary diagnosis of the issues that require attention. Burkina Faso[61] and Senegal[62] have set up inter-ministerial task forces or meetings for this purpose. Madagascar has completed the review of its BIT stock, and the Council of Ministers has approved the outcome report, which provides direction for revising the country's existing BIT stock and

---

[58] See the various statements of Representatives of Nigeria, Gambia, Botswana, Mauritania, Kenya, Madagascar, Burkina Faso <http://investmentpolicyhub.unctad.org/Pages/2017-edition-of-unctad-s-high-level-annual-iia-conference-phase-2-of-iia-reform> accessed 28 February 2018.

[59] See excerpt from the statement of Mr Lamin Dampha, Gambian Deputy Permanent Secretary, Ministry of Trade, Industry, Regional Integration and Employment Gambian at the UNCTAD IIA Conference <http://investmentpolicyhub.unctad.org/Upload/Documents/The%20Gambia_BoS%203_Kick-off%20Speaker.pdf> accessed 28 February 2018.

[60] See excerpt from the statement of Mr Moctar Kane, Director of Private Investment and International Cooperation at the Ministry of Economy and Finance, Mauritania, at the UNCTAD IIA Conference <http://investmentpolicyhub.unctad.org/Upload/Documents/IIA%20Conference_Moctar%20Kane%20(Mauritania)_plenary%20statement.pdf> accessed 28 February 2018.

[61] See Hamed El Kady's tweet dated 15 February 2018 <https://twitter.com/ElKady_Hamed/status/964143033901035521> accessed 28 February 2018.

[62] Confidential information on file with the author.

negotiating new treaties.⁶³ It has been announced that the next step will be to develop a national negotiation strategy aiming to result in the adoption of a model BIT for Madagascar, and build the capacity of BIT negotiators.⁶⁴ As far as Egypt and Botswana are concerned, the process is in a more advanced stage. Botswana previously adopted a model BIT and is currently envisaging its revision, as well as reforming the existing BIT stock.⁶⁵ Egypt also adopted a BIT model in 2007, the revision of which has apparently been initiated and completed.⁶⁶

14.21 The third group of countries have finalized the reform of their BITs and are already living it. Few countries fall into this category. Nigeria approved a model BIT in 2016,⁶⁷ which apparently is now serving as basis of new BITs, including the well-received Nigeria–Morocco BIT.⁶⁸ Nigeria also reviewed its BIT stock, and given the finding pointing out the poor quality of these BITs vis-à-vis desired policy outcomes,⁶⁹ it would not be surprising if the country reconsiders ratifying most of its treaties yet to enter into force. Another outcome of the review is the plan of the government of Nigeria to amend the relevant provisions of the Nigerian Investment Promotion Commission Act 'to ensure that the safeguards inserted in [the] model BIT are replicated in the National Law'.⁷⁰

---

⁶³ See statement of Mr Ratozomanana, Director General in Charge of the Development of the Private Sector, representing Madagascar at the UNCTAD IIA Conference <http://investmentpolicyhub.unctad.org/Upload/Documents/IIA%20Conference_Madagascar_RATOZOMANANA_plenary%20statement.pdf> accessed 28 February 2018.
⁶⁴ ibid.
⁶⁵ See statement of Her Excellency Dr Athaliah L Molokomme Ambassador and Permanent Representative of Botswana to the United Nations Office in Geneva <http://investmentpolicyhub.unctad.org/Upload/Documents/STATEMENT%20BY%20DR%20MOLOKOMME%20AT%20IIA%20MEETING%20OCTOBER%202017.pdf> accessed 28 February 2018. Para 4 of the statement indicates that Botswana amended its model BIT in 2010. Para 6 informs that the country 'imposed in 2013 a moratorium on the negotiation and conclusion of BITs', and the subsequent paras informs of the country's action plan with regards to future IIA reform and amendment of the BIT model.
⁶⁶ See Arabic statement of Mr Hayam El-Banna, Head of International Cooperation Department at the Egyptian General Authority for Investment (GAFI), representing Egypt at the UNCTAD IIA Conference <http://investmentpolicyhub.unctad.org/Upload/Documents/IIA%20Conference_Egypt%20statement_El-Banna.pdf> accessed 28 February 2018.
⁶⁷ See statement of Ms Patience Okala, Deputy Director/Legal Adviser at the Nigerian Investment Promotion Commission at the UNCTAD IIA Conference <http://investmentpolicyhub.unctad.org/Upload/Documents/Nigeria-%20Ms.%20Patience%20Okala-%20Closing%20Plenary.pdf> accessed 28 February 2018.
⁶⁸ Reciprocal Investment Promotion and Protection Agreement between the Government of the Kingdom of Morocco and the Government of the Federal Republic of Nigeria (Morocco–Nigeria BIT) (signed 3 December 2016). The Morocco–Nigeria BIT includes novel provisions such as, among others, investor obligations. It also clarifies precisely the notion of 'investment', as well as the obligations of the host state, and provides for the right of the state to regulate admitted investments.
⁶⁹ Source: statement of Ms Yewande Sadiku, Executive Secretary, Nigerian Investment Promotion Commission at the UNCTAD IIA Conference < http://investmentpolicyhub.unctad.org/Upload/Documents/Nigeria-%20Ms.%20Yewande%20Sadiku-%20Opening%20plenary.pdf > accessed 28 February 2018. . In accordance with the statement, the review of Nigerian BIT stock revealed that few BITs signed passed the test of checking whether they were compliant with twenty desired parameters.
⁷⁰ Source: excerpts of the statement of Ms Patience Okala, Deputy Director/Legal Adviser at the Nigerian Investment Promotion Commission (n 67).

14.22 At the regional level, investment regulation has become a core pillar of the work of RECs, most of which have adopted legal instruments aiming to promote integration and regulation of regional investment. Back in 2006, the East African Community (EAC) adopted a non-legally binding Model Investment Code to guide the investment policy practice of EAC member countries.[71] In the same year, member states of the Southern African Development Community (SADC) adopted a Protocol on Finance and Investment (SADC-FIP), which entered into force in 2010, as well as a model BIT in 2012.[72] In 2007, member states of the Common Market for Eastern and Southern Africa (COMESA) adopted an Investment Agreement for the COMESA Common Investment Area (COMESA Investment Agreement), which is yet to enter into force. In 2008, countries forming the Economic Commission for West African States (ECOWAS) enacted a Supplementary Act regarding Community Rules on Investment and the Modalities for their Implementation, which came into force in 2009.[73]

14.23 Similar to the efforts made by African countries to reform their BITs, some of the RECs have, in recent years taken steps to modernize their regional investment instruments. It may be recalled that a review of the SADC-FIP was undertaken in 2016, resulting in the adoption of an Agreement amending Annex-1 (Co-Operation on Investment) of the protocol.[74] The Agreement addressed the criticism by SADC Member States that some provisions of the original text could have 'unintended consequences for SADC Member States ... and ... fail to adequately balance investor protection and development policy space of host states',[75] with the inclusion in the amended Annex-1 of several innovations including,[76] *inter alia*:

- The limitation of the benefit of investment protection to investors from SADC countries only;[77]

---

[71] Note that the Model Investment Code was revised in late 2015.
[72] SADC Protocol on Finance and Investment (entered into force 16 April 2010). Note that the 2012 Model BIT has been revised in 2017 and adopted at technical level.
[73] Supplementary Act A/SA.3/12/08 Adopting Community Rules on Investment and the Modalities for their Implementation with ECOWAS (entered into force 19 January 2009). ECOWAS also initiated the project of developing a Common Investment Code in 2008, but the author has no information as regards the current negotiation status of this instrument.
[74] The Agreement Amending Annex-1 (Co-Operation on Investment) of the Protocol on Finance and Investment was adopted at the 36th SADC Summit held in Swaziland from 30 to 31 August in 2016. The text of the Agreement can be accessed at < http://investmentpolicyhub.unctad.org/Download/TreatyFile/5527>.
[75] Quote from the Preamble of the Agreement Amending Annex-1 of the SADC Protocol on Finance and Investment as signed and ratified by SADC Member States.
[76] For a comparison with the old definition, see the original Annex-1, which is accessible at <http://www.sadc.int/files/4213/5332/6872/Protocol_on_Finance__Investment2006.pdf>.
[77] Refer to the definition of 'Investment', which has been amended to refer to 'an enterprise within the territory of one State Party established, acquired or expanded by an investor of the other State Party . .. '.

- The removal of the fair and equitable and most favoured nation provisions and the inclusion of national treatment standard;[78]
- The replacement of 'prompt, adequate and effective compensation' in case of expropriation with 'fair and adequate compensation' using the fair market value valuation method;[79]
- The preservation of the right of the host state to adopt regulatory measures pursuing sustainable development and policy objectives;[80] and
- The recourse to domestic courts and tribunals for the settlement of investor–state disputes.[81]

14.24 COMESA member states are also expected to adopt a revised COMESA Investment Agreement soon. Indeed, following the review of the Agreement also initiated in 2016 with the objective to 'incorporate modern trends in the international investment arena',[82] a revised version of the Agreement was submitted, in late 2017, to the COMESA Committee on Legal Affairs.[83]

b. Regionalization of investment arbitration

14.25 A noteworthy development in the field of arbitration in Africa has been the inclusion in the 2017 revision of the Organization for the Harmonization of Business Laws in Africa (OHADA)[84] Uniform Act on Arbitration and the revised Arbitral Rules of the OHADA Common Court of Justice and Arbitration (CCJA)[85] of provisions allowing for investment arbitration, including investor–state

---

[78] Old art 6 of the Annex-1 (Investors of the Third State) contained two sub-clauses respectively granting fair and equitable treatment and most favoured nation treatment. In the amended Annex-1, such references have been removed and a national treatment provision included in the same article.

[79] The provision on compensation against expropriation is set out in art 5 of both the new and old Annex-1.

[80] The provision of art 12 (Right to Regulate) has been expanded in the amended Annxe-1 to refer specifically to 'principles of sustainable development', 'balance of the rights and obligations of investors and investment and Host States', and the 'non-discriminatory' character of measures adopted by the host state to comply with other international obligations.

[81] The previous reference to 'international arbitration' in art 28 (Settlement of Investment Disputes) of the original Annex-1 has been removed in the amended Annex-1 which now focuses only on state-to-state dispute.

[82] See statement in the COMESA website <http://www.comesa.int/revised-comesa-common-investment-agreement-tabled-before-legal-affairs-committee/> accessed 28 February 2018.

[83] ibid.

[84] OHADA is a French acronym that stands for 'Organization pour l'Harmonization du Droit des Affaires en Afrique'. OHADA is a supranational organization established by a treaty ratified by its seventeen member states from West and Central Africa (the list of state parties can be found at <http://www.ohada.org/index.php/en/ohada-in-a-nutshell/ohada-space> accessed 28 February 2018). The Uniform Acts issued by OHADA are directly applicable and mandatory in the territory of the states parties. They take precedence over the national laws of Member States. In that sense, they rank as treaties.

[85] The OHADA Common Court of Justice and Arbitration (CCJA) has a unique feature as it combines a dual function of a community court of justice and arbitral institution.

arbitration.[86] Article 3 of the new Uniform Act on Arbitration adds a provision stipulating that 'arbitration may be based on an arbitration agreement or an *investment instrument, such as an investment code or a bilateral or multilateral investment treaty*'.[87] Pursuant to this provision, arbitral tribunals can, unlike before, be established under the CCJA to hear investment disputes in general and investment treaty disputes in particular, provided that the tribunal should be seated in an OHADA state party.[88] In addition, the CCJA Revised Arbitral Rules incorporate a clause clearly aiming to establish the CCJA as a centre of choice for the settlement of both intra-African and extra-African investment disputes. Indeed, a new paragraph 2 has been added to Article 2.1 now giving the CCJA the power to 'administer arbitration procedures based on an investment instrument, notably an investment code, or a bilateral or multilateral investment treaty'.[89]

14.26 The revision of the OHADA Uniform Act on Arbitration and the CCJA Arbitration Rules, allowing an African supranational institution the possibility to hear investment disputes, is a welcome development and represents an important paradigm shift for Africa.

c. From theory to practice: the G20 Compact with Africa initiative and investment treaties

14.27 In the context of increased criticism regarding the economic impact of international investment treaties, one of the main gaps found in these agreements is the absence of investment facilitation provisions.[90] The objective of facilitating investments is generally included as a vague statement in the preamble of most investment treaties signed by African countries, without specific provisions committing capital-exporting countries to transfer technology or making concrete investments that would improve the enabling environment of the host country.

14.28 The G20's Compact with Africa initiative,[91] adopted in 2017 as part of the G20 Africa Partnership,[92] may contribute to bridging this gap. The stated objective of the initiative is to strengthen frameworks in African countries to support

---

[86] The new texts can be accessed at <http://www.ohada.org/index.php/en/news/latest-news/2294-online-publication-of-the-new-ohada-laws-on-arbitration-and-mediation> accessed 28 February 2018. The new Uniform Acts and the CCJA Revised Rules will enter into force on 15 March 2018.
[87] Author's translation of the French text (emphasis added).
[88] Article 1 of the Uniform Arbitration Act contains a territorial condition which requires arbitral tribunals to be seated in a state party.
[89] Author's translation of the French text (emphasis added).
[90] For a recent analysis, see Makane Moise Mbengue, 'Facilitating Investment for Sustainable Development: it Matters for Africa' (2018) *Columbia FDI Perspectives No* 222 <http://ccsi.columbia.edu/files/2016/10/No-222-Mbengue-FINAL.pdf> accessed 31 May 2018.
[91] More details available at <https://www.compactwithafrica.org> accessed 31 May 2018.
[92] A copy of the Partnership document can be accessed at <http://www.g20.utoronto.ca/2017/2017-g20-annex-partnership-africa.html> accessed 31 May 2018.

'sustainable private investments', by providing those countries the support needed to undertake investment policy reforms that are necessary to attract private capital.[93] Such reforms would be targeted at, *inter alia*, 'improv[ing] the business framework by implementing reliable regulation and institutions, *improving investor protection and dispute resolution mechanisms* ...'[94] at the domestic level.

14.29 Since the launch of the initiative, it appears that eleven African countries are working on investment compacts.[95] Looking at the concrete measures being envisaged under some of the draft compacts, it may be noted that these offer practical investment facilitation solutions which African developing countries opting to continue signing BITs can explore as part of modernizing their model BITs or enhancing their investment treaty policy frameworks. For example, a potential pillar under the proposed investment compact with Senegal is to enhance investor protection and dispute resolution mechanisms by 'systematiz[ing] and professionaliz[ing] the amicable settlement of disputes, operationaliz[ing] the commercial court, establish[ing] an electronic register of guarantees, operationaliz[ing] the electronic Company and Moveable Credit Registry etc'.[96] Ideally, African countries should be able to negotiate the inclusion of provisions of this nature, targeted at achieving specific outcomes, in their investment treaties.

2. The negatives and the *rendez-vous manqués*

a. Fragmented international investment law regime

14.30 The fragmentation of the international investment law regime does not spare the African continent. As we have seen, this fragmentation is the result of African countries signing BITs, regional investment treaties, plurilateral treaties,[97] trade treaties with investment chapters, and economic partnership agreements with investment provisions. African countries are signatories of double taxation treaties and are party to other multilateral investment regulations and frameworks. In addition to that, a large body of soft investment laws relevant to African countries is emerging, including the Joint African, Caribbean and Pacific Group of States (ACP)—UNCTAD Guiding Principles for Investment Policymaking that were approved by the ACP Committee of Ambassadors in May 2017.[98] It also

---

[93] It has been reported that Côte d'Ivoire, Ethiopia, Ghana, Morocco, Rwanda, Senegal, and Tunisia have already expressed interest to sign investment compacts.
[94] See the document at <http://www.g20.utoronto.ca/2017/2017-g20-annex-partnership-africa.html> accessed 31 May 2018 (emphasis added).
[95] Information extracted from the G20 Compact with Africa website <https://www.compactwithafrica.org/content/compactwithafrica/home/compact-countries.html> accessed 9 May 2018.
[96] The Senegal Policy Matrix is available at <https://www.compactwithafrica.org/content/compactwithafrica/home/compact-countries/senegal.html> accessed 9 May 2018.
[97] See eg the OIC Investment Agreement (n 37).
[98] See UNCTAD Investment Policy Monitor, Issue 18 (December 2017) 11 < http://unctad.org/en/PublicationsLibrary/webdiaepcb2017d9_en.pdf > accessed 28 February 2018.

appears that the development of EU–Africa Investment Principles is also being considered.[99]

In this context of continuous fragmentation of the regime, both within and outside Africa, some policy coherence will be needed to ensure that African countries do not fall into the trap of subscribing to conflicting obligations and commitments. In this respect, it is unfortunate to note the *rendez-vous manqué* of the Pan-African Investment Code. When, back in 2008, the African Ministers of Trade and Integration recommended the African Union Commission (AUC) to develop a comprehensive investment code, the idea was to consolidate the international investment law regime in Africa, taking stock of the vast network of BITs, other international investment agreements and RECs investment instruments, taking into account African countries' sustainable development aspirations. Unfortunately, during the last round of negotiation of the text of the Code in 2016, it was decided that the Code would be 'a guiding instrument to Member States as well as investors and their investments in the territory of Member States as defined by this Code',[100] therefore limiting the chances for achieving the consolidation objectives.[101] However, the Code can reach back to its original ambition if, as contemplated in Article 3.1, African Union member states decide that the code 'become[s] a binding instrument and to replace the intra-African bilateral investment treaties (BITs) or investment chapters in intra-African trade agreements … '.[102] This would indeed be a positive development given the Code's sustainable development dimensions and its consideration of African specificities.[103] Until such time, it is hoped that the Code will influence the content of future African BITs and other instruments being negotiated at the regional and continental levels.

14.31

b. Weak African participation in ongoing multilateral initiatives

African countries have not been significantly engaged in recent multilateral discussions relating to the reform of the international investment regime. While such discussions have reached their peak, it is unfortunate to note that the African voice has so far not been heard much. African countries have almost been absent from the debate about establishing a multilateral investment court, and only few have contributed to the ongoing work of the United Nations Commission on

14.32

---

[99] ibid 10.
[100] Article 2.1 of the last December 2016 Draft Pan-African Investment Code.
[101] For an analysis of the Pan-African Investment Code, see Mouhamadou Madana Kane, 'The Pan-African Investment Code: A Good First Step, but More is Needed' (2018) *Columbia FDI Perspectives No 217* <http://ccsi.columbia.edu/files/2016/10/No-217-Kane-FINAL.pdf> accessed 9 May 2018.
[102] The Pan-African Investment Code 2018 <https://au.int/web/en/newsevents/20170323/2017-AU-ECA-Conference-of-Ministers-Senegal-March-23-28> accessed 28 February 2018.
[103] See eg Pan-African Investment Code, art 38, which provides that 'Member States may adopt policies on cultural and linguistic diversity in promotion of investments'.

International Trade Law (UNCITRAL) regarding the reform of the investor–state dispute settlement (ISDS) system. Despite the importance of the latter initiative, only few countries have so far submitted comments to UNCITRAL, including Algeria, Côte d'Ivoire, Mauritania, Mauritius, and Tunisia.[104] The fact that African countries are missing the opportunity to submit comments poses the risk that they end up being subject to outside-made rules that do not suit their policy interests.

D. Conclusion

14.33 As these developments have shown, the investment law practice of African countries has been very rich during 2017. There have been many positive initiatives making Africa a new hub for innovative approaches in the area of investment treaty policy, the most notable ones being the increased consciousness about the pros and cons of investment treaties, and particularly the focus on investment facilitation and investment treaty reform both at country and regional levels. The trend for increased regional cooperation and integration on investment matters also constitutes a step in the right direction, as well as other initiatives such as the upgrading of the OHADA arbitration system to cater for investment arbitration.

14.34 In terms of perspectives, it should be hoped that the body of investment rules in Africa are consolidated for greater coherence and effectiveness. In this respect, the upcoming negotiations of the CFTA investment chapter offer a formidable opportunity to achieve this objective, especially if the Pan-African Investment Code inspires its future content. Finally, Africa has a lot to offer and to contribute to current discussions about ISDS reforms. As a priority action, the international community should explore innovative ways to engage African nations and involve the wider African public on these crucial matters.

---

[104] See UNCITRAL Compilation of Comments documents <http://www.uncitral.org/uncitral/en/commission/working_groups/3Investor_State.html> accessed 28 February 2018.

15

EXPANDING ISDS, ACTIVE NATIONAL COURTS, AND CONCLUDING MEGA-REGIONAL TREATIES

2017 Developments in International Investment Law in Asia

*Diane A Desierto**

A. Introduction	15.01	C. Active National Courts on Investor–State Arbitration	15.13
B. Contested Gateway Issues over Jurisdiction and Admissibility	15.03	D. Conclusion	15.19

A. Introduction

Developments in international investment law in Asia for the year 2017 attest to Asia's continuing rapid rise as a new centre of gravity for global economic activities.[1] Unlike North America and Europe, Asia in 2017 saw more Asian companies seeking recourse through investor–state arbitration;[2] more Asian states sued under

15.01

---

* I can be reached at ddesiert@nd.edu. My thanks to Atty Lenie Rocha of the Desierto & Desierto Law Firm (PH) for research assistance.

[1] See International Monetary Fund, 'Asia's Dynamic Economies Continue to Lead Global Growth' (9 May 2017) <https://www.imf.org/en/News/Articles/2017/05/08/NA050917-Asia-Dynamic-Economies-Continue-to-Lead-Global-Growth> accessed 14 June 2018; World Bank, *Global Economic Prospects: East Asia and the Pacific* (January 2018) <http://pubdocs.worldbank.org/en/115561512062597137/Global-Economic-Prospects-Jan-2018-East-Asia-and-Pacific-analysis.pdf> accessed 14 June 2018; OECD, *Economic Outlook for Southeast Asia, India, and China 2018* (OECD Publishing 2018) <http://dx.doi.org/10.1787/9789264286184-en> accessed 14 June 2018.

[2] Based on publicly available records at ITALAW.com, as of 2017, there were seven known notice of claims and/or notice of arbitrations initiated by Asian companies or against Asian states for investor–state arbitration proceedings: *Ras-al Khaimah Investment Authority v India*, UNCITRAL (PCA), Minutes of the Meeting of the Indian Inter-Ministerial Group on the Notice of Arbitration (5 January 2017); *Strategic Infrasol Foodstuff LLC UAE et al v India*, UNCITRAL, Second Notice of

investor–state arbitration;[3] more Asian national courts issuing decisions relating to pending investor–state arbitrations;[4] and more Asian states reaching agreements in principle to conclude mega-regional economic treaties, such as the ASEAN-led and China-promoted[5] sixteen-member Regional Comprehensive Economic Partnership (RCEP) and the Japan-led eleven-member renamed Comprehensive and Progressive Agreement for Trans-Pacific Partnership (CPTPP).[6] 2017 also

---

Intention to Submit to Arbitration and Notice of Arbitration (20 May 2016); *Kingsgate Consolidated v Thailand*, Notice of Dispute (7 April 2017); *Surfeit Harvesting Investment Holding v Republic of China (Taiwan)*, UNCITRAL, Notice of Arbitration (9 June 2017); *Hela Schwartz GmbH v People's Republic of China*, Notice of Arbitration (29 June 2017); and *Boonsom Boonyanit v Malaysia*, Notice of Dispute (1 August 2017). Decisions were issued in several cases where claimants were Asian companies, such as *Standard Chartered Bank (Hong Kong) v Tanzania*, ICSID Case No ARB/10/20, Decision on Applicant's Request for a Continued Stay on Enforcement of the Award (2017); *Beijing Urban Construction Group Co Ltd v Republic of Yemen*, ICSID Case No ARB/14/30, Decision on Jurisdiction (2017).

[3] Based on publicly available records at ITALAW.com, in 2017, there were ten known investor–state arbitral awards or decisions issued in investor–state arbitrations involving Asian states as respondents or Asian claimants: *Baggerwerken Decloedt En Zoon NV v Republic of the Philippines*, ICSID Case No ARB/11/27, Award (2017) (award not public but details are narrated in Marvyn N Benaning, 'PHL to Pay P800 Million for Laguna Lake Project Scrapped by Aquino Administration' *BusinessMirror* (7 February 2017) <https://businessmirror.com.ph/phl-to-pay-p800-million-for-laguna-lake-project-scrapped-by-aquino-administration/> accessed 14 June 2018); *Ansung Housing Co Ltd. v People's Republic of China*, ICSID Case No ARB/14/25, Award (2017); *Tethyan Copper Co Pty Ltd v Islamic Republic of Pakistan*, ICSID Case No ARB/12/1, Decision on Liability (2017) (decision not public but details are narrated in Barrick Press Release, 'ICSID Issues Decision in Favor of Antofagasta plc and Barrick in Reko Diq Arbitration Proceedings' (21 March 2017) <https://www.italaw.com/sites/default/files/case-documents/italaw8560.pdf> accessed 14 June 2018); *Lao Holdings NV v Lao People's Democratic Republic*, ICSID Case No ARB(AF)/16/2, Decision on Bifurcation (2017); *Lao Holdings NV v Lao People's Democratic Republic*, ICSID Case No ARB(AF)/16/2, Decision on Document Production (2017); *China Heilongjiang International Economic Cooperative Corporation et al v Mongolia*, PCA, Award (2017) (award not public but details are narrated in Luke Eric Peterson, 'Mongolia Prevails in Long-running Chinese BIT Arbitration, as Arbitrators Distinguish their Reading of Constricted Jurisdiction Clause from More Generous Readings in Prior Cases' *Investment Arbitration Reporter* (7 July 2017) <https://www.iareporter.com/articles/mongolia-prevails-in-long-running-chinese-bit-arbitration-as-arbitrators-distinguish-their-reading-of-constricted-jurisdiction-clause-from-more-generous-readings-in-prior-cases/> accessed 14 June 2018); *Philip Morris Asia Ltd v The Commonwealth of Australia*, PCA Case No 2012-12, Final Award Regarding Costs (2017); *Laos Holdings NV v Lao People's Democratic Republic*, ICSID Case No ARB(AF)/16/2, Decision on the Merits of Claimants' Second Material Breach Application (2017); *Lighthouse Corp Pty Ltd v Timor-Leste*, ICSID Case No ARB/15/2, Award (2017).

[4] See eg *Union of India v Vodafone Group Plc*, CS(OS) 383/2017, Judgment of the High Court of Delhi Restraining Claimant from Proceeding with its Arbitration Claim (22 August 2017) <https://www.italaw.com/sites/default/files/case-documents/italaw9452.pdf> accessed 14 June 2018; *Union of India v Vodafone Group Plc*, CS(OS) 383/2017, Order of the Delhi High Court re Second Arbitration Proceeding (26 October 2017) <https://www.italaw.com/sites/default/files/case-documents/italaw9370.pdf> accessed 14 June 2018; *Union of India v Vodafone Group Plc*, (SLP (C) No 33885/2017), India Supreme Court Order (14 December 2017) <https://www.italaw.com/sites/default/files/case-documents/italaw9451.pdf> accessed 14 June 2018.

[5] Giovanni Di Lieto, 'RCEP the Grand Blueprint of Xi Jinping's World Trade Game' *Asia Times* (28 September 2017) <http://www.atimes.com/rcep-grand-blueprint-xi-jinpings-world-trade-game/> accessed 14 June 2018.

[6] Trans-Pacific Partnership Ministerial Statement (10 November 2017) <https://www.mfat.govt.nz/assets/FTAs-in-negotiations/TPP/2017.11.10-Ministerial-Statement-FINAL.pdf> accessed 14 June 2018; Trans-Pacific Partnership List of Suspended Provisions (10 November 2017) <https://

witnessed the first decisions issued under the landmark Bangladesh Accord,[7] which, with oversight from the International Labour Organization (ILO), Bangladesh, and home states of multinational corporations involved in the Rana Plaza tragedy, enabled labour unions to sue foreign companies for redress in arbitration proceedings. Asia's year-end major economic summits for 2017, namely, the Asia-Pacific Economic Cooperation (APEC),[8] the East Asia Summit (EAS),[9] and the Association of Southeast Asian Nations (ASEAN) Heads of State Summit[10]—all articulated strong concern over the felt human impacts of unmanaged globalization on domestic populations, particularly on widening inequality, transnational environmental threats, climate change, and regional disasters, the continuing lack of protections for Asian migrant labourers, and ongoing threats of community displacement. Collectively, China's US$4 trillion to US $8 trillion One Belt One Road (OBOR) infrastructure programme and its leadership of the Asian Infrastructure Investment Bank (AIIB),[11] Japan's Quality Infrastructure programme and sovereign lending under the Japan International Cooperation Agency (JICA),[12] Korea's increased presence in regional infrastructure projects,[13]

---

www.mfat.govt.nz/assets/FTAs-in-negotiations/TPP/ANNEX-II_LIst-of-suspended-Provisions.pdf> accessed 14 June 2018; Comprehensive and Progressive Agreement for Trans-Pacific Partnership Outline (10 November 2017) <https://www.mfat.govt.nz/assets/FTAs-in-negotiations/TPP/Annex-I_Outline-of-Agreement.pdf> accessed 14 June 2018; Joint Leaders' Statement on the Regional Comprehensive Economic Partnership (14 November 2017) <http://dfat.gov.au/trade/agreements/rcep/news/Pages/joint-leaders-statement-on-the-rcep-negotiations-14-november-2017-manila-philippines.aspx> accessed 14 June 2018.

[7] Permanent Court of Arbitration Press Release, 'Bangladesh Accord Arbitrations: Arbitrations under the Accord on Fire and Building Safety in Bangladesh between IndustriALL Global Union and UNI Global Union (as Claimants) and two Global Fashion Brands (as Respondents), Decision on Admissibility of Claims and Confidentiality' (16 October 2017) <https://pcacases.com/web/sendAttach/2238> accessed 14 June 2018.

[8] APEC 2017 Leaders' Declaration, Da Nang (Viet Nam, 11 November 2017) <https://www.apec.org/Meeting-Papers/Leaders-Declarations/2017/2017_aelm> accessed 14 June 2018.

[9] Chairman's Statement of the 12th East Asia Summit (Manila, Philippines, 14 November 2017) <http://asean.org/chairmans-statement-of-the-12th-east-asia-summit/> accessed 14 June 2018.

[10] Chairman's Statement of the 31st ASEAN Summit (Manila, Philippines, 13 November 2017) <http://asean.org/storage/2017/11/final-chairman%E2%80%99s-statement-of-31st-asean-summit.pdf> accessed 14 June 2018.

[11] See David Dollar, 'The AIIB and the "One Belt One Road"' *Brookings* (Summer 2015) <https://www.brookings.edu/opinions/the-aiib-and-the-one-belt-one-road/> accessed 14 June 2018; Wade Shepard, 'The Real Role of the AIIB in China's New Silk Road' *Forbes* (15 July 2017) <https://www.forbes.com/sites/wadeshepard/2017/07/15/the-real-role-of-the-aiib-in-chinas-new-silk-road/#1b5e3b3d7472> accessed 14 June 2018.

[12] See Wade Shepard, 'Japan Ups its Game against China's Belt and Road' *Forbes* (1 December 2016) <https://www.forbes.com/sites/wadeshepard/2016/12/01/japan-ups-its-infrastructure-game-against-chinas-belt-and-road/#3be0d0513223> accessed 14 June 2018.

[13] See Jung Min-hee, 'Korean Gov't to Focus More on Quality of Overseas Construction Projects' *Business Korea* (25 July 2017) <http://www.businesskorea.co.kr/english/news/national/18763-focusing-quality-korean-gov%E2%80%99t-focus-more-quality-overseas-construction-projects> accessed 14 June 2018.

as well as ASEAN's expanding external partnerships throughout the world,[14] have all spurred Asia to a fast march of massive infrastructure development throughout and across individual Asian jurisdictions, spanning a vast spectrum of regional maritime, territorial, and information connectivity projects.[15]

15.02 The result is Asia's deepening influence over the trajectory of international investment law through both treaties and jurisprudence. The following subsections highlight four recurring themes from investor–state jurisprudence and investment treaty developments in Asia: (1) contested gateway issues over jurisdiction and admissibility; (2) unsuccessful public policy or regulatory defences; (3) active national courts on investor–state arbitration; and (4) new models of mega-regional or regional investment treaties and Asian arbitral rules reforms.

B. Contested Gateway Issues over Jurisdiction and Admissibility

15.03 In 2017, some Asian states were relatively successful in mustering jurisdictional objections against investor claims. Timor-Leste prevailed in raising jurisdictional objections in *Lighthouse Corporation Pty Ltd and Lighthouse Corporation LTD IBC v Democratic Republic of Timor Leste*,[16] a claim brought invoking a set of contractual arrangements for the supply and fuel of generators, the Timor-Leste Foreign Investment Law, and the ICSID Convention. In this case, the *Lighthouse* tribunal[17] first emphasized that under the legal maxim *iura novit curia,* it was not bound by the arguments or sources invoked by the parties, and thus 'the Tribunal is required to apply the law of its own motion, provided always that it gives the Parties an opportunity to comment if it intends to base its decision on a legal theory that was not addressed and that the Parties could not reasonably anticipate.'[18] The *Lighthouse* tribunal also declared that 'it is not bound by previous decisions. At the same time, it is of the opinion that it should pay due consideration to earlier decisions of international tribunals....subject to compelling grounds, it should be respectful of the reasoning and solutions established in a series of consistent cases.'[19] The *Lighthouse* tribunal rejected that Timor-Leste consented to arbitration through any of its contracts, finding that, on the evidence:

---

[14] See Philippines Mission to ASEAN, 'ASEAN's External Partners Pledge Support for ASEAN Connectivity' (5 October 2017) <http://www.jakartapm.dfa.gov.ph/sample-sites/pr/268-asean-s-external-partners-pledge-support-for-asean-connectivity> accessed 14 June 2018.
[15] See Asian Development Bank, *Meeting Asia's Infrastructure Needs* No FLS168388-2, 2017.
[16] *Lighthouse* (n 4).
[17] Composed of Professor Gabrielle Kaufmann-Kohler (President), Mr. Stephen Jagusch QC (Arbitrator), Professor Campbell McLachlan QC (Arbitrator).
[18] *Lighthouse* (n 4) para 109.
[19] ibid para 111.

it has not been demonstrated to the Tribunal's satisfaction that the Parties agreed to refer their disputes to ICSID arbitration ... not only is reference to the document containing the ICSID dispute settlement clause ambiguous as to its intent, but it also has not been sufficiently established that the Respondent knew the document existed or that it was supplied to the Respondent, or that it was discussed with the Respondent.[20]

More significantly, the *Lighthouse* tribunal found that Timor-Leste's Foreign Investment Law did not confer automatic consent to arbitration, by holistically examining Timor-Leste's constitutional, statutory, and administrative regime governing foreign investment: **15.04**

[F]irst, it is clear that the Respondent intended to exercise administrative control on incoming foreign investments. This is evident from the Timorese Constitution, the Foreign Investment Law (FIL) ... and from other legislation enacted at that time. Indeed, shortly after the enactment of the FIL, Timor-Leste issued implementing regulation ... which details the procedures and practical measures under the FIL, particularly the application process, and issuance as well as revocation of foreign investment certificates. As foreign investment certificates are strictly regulated, it seems counterintuitive to suggest that an investor who does not comply with clear administrative requirements may nevertheless benefit from the FIL. The various provisions of the FIL, constituted with the existence of a Decree setting out the detailed rules, requirements and procedures for the application, assessment, approval or denial, and revocation of foreign investor's certificates in Timor Leste suggest that the requirement of these certificates is not to be disregarded.[21]

Strongly finding that 'the Claimants have failed to make out their case ... [and] raised additional arguments and filed new evidence before the Hearing which added complexity',[22] the *Lighthouse* tribunal held the claimants liable for the entirety of the ICSID arbitration costs and direct costs of the proceedings (US$ 546,868.51), and for respondent's share of those costs (US$ 273,434.26) and respondent's legal representation (US$1.3 million).

The People's Republic of China similarly prevailed in its jurisdictional objections in *Ansung Housing Co Ltd v People's Republic of China*,[23] where the tribunal dismissed all claims and awarded China its share of the direct costs of the proceedings (US$69,760.55), 75 per cent of its legal fees and expenses (US$ 4853.25 plus EUR 67,443.10 plus CNY 1,387,500), plus interest at LIBOR three-month rate plus 2 per cent compounded quarterly.[24] This case is the second investment arbitration claim brought against China, brought by a South Korean investor over investment in a golf course and condominium **15.05**

---

[20] ibid para 255.
[21] ibid para 321.
[22] ibid para 344.
[23] *Ansung* (n 4).
[24] Tribunal composed of Prof Lucy Reed (President), Dr Michael Pryles (Arbitrator), and Prof Albert Jan Van Den Berg (Arbitrator). *Ansung* (n 4) (Decision) (1) and (2).

development project in Sheyang-Xian, China. China lodged an objection that the claim is 'manifestly without legal merit' under ICSID Arbitration Rule 41(5) and (6), because the claimant had instituted the arbitration 'more than three years after it first acquired knowledge that it had incurred loss or damage, rendering the claim time-barred under Article 9(7) of the China-Korea BIT'.[25] Article 9(7) of the China–Korea bilateral investment treaty (BIT) states that '[a]n investor may not make a claim pursuant to paragraph 3 of this Article if more than three years have elapsed from the date on which the investor first acquired, or should have first acquired, knowledge that the investor had incurred loss or damage'.[26]

15.06 The *Ansung* tribunal upheld the time limitation under Article 9(7) of the China–Korea BIT, finding that the claimant had 'repeatedly pleaded facts setting the date at which it first acquired the knowledge that it had incurred loss or damage to be *before* October 2011'.[27] Ansung belatedly filed its Request for Arbitration on 7 October 2011, beyond the three-year period under Article 9(7) of the China–Korea BIT.[28] The *Ansung* tribunal also rejected the claimant's argument to disregard the three-year limitation period in Article 9(7) of the China–Korea BIT on the basis of a most favoured nation (MFN) clause in Article 3(3) of the same China–Korea BIT: 'a plain reading of this Article does not extend MFN treatment for a State's consent to arbitrate with investors and, in particular, not to the temporal limitation period for investor-State arbitration in Article 9(7) of the China-Korea BIT'.[29]

15.07 In *China Heilongjiang International Economic and Technical Cooperative Corp, Beijing Shougang Mining Investment Company Ltd, and Qinhuangdaoshi Qinlong International Industrial Co Ltd v. Mongolia*,[30] Mongolia also succeeded in its jurisdictional objection based on Article 8(3) of the Mongolia–China BIT:

> If a dispute involving the amount of compensation for expropriation cannot be settled within six months after resort to negotiations as specified in paragraph 1 of this Article, it may be submitted at the request of either party to an ad hoc arbitral tribunal. The provisions of this paragraph shall not apply if the investor concerned has

---

[25] *Ansung* (n 4) paras 28, 56.
[26] ibid para 74.
[27] ibid para 107.
[28] ibid para 122.
[29] ibid para 138.
[30] *China Heilongjiang International Economic and Technical Cooperative Corp, Beijing Shougang Mining Investment Company Ltd, and Qinhuangdaoshi Qinlong International Industrial Co Ltd v Mongolia*, PCA Case No 2010-20, Award (2017) (China Heilongjiang) (full text made available at the Investment Arbitration Reporter service, <https://www.iareporter.com/articles/in-depth-a-first-look-inside-the-now-surfaced-award-in-the-case-of-china-heilongjiang-v-mongolia-award-claimants-pursuing-set-aside/>) accessed 14 June 2018 (requires subscription), based on the claimants' filing of a petition to set aside in United States Federal Court which attached the said arbitral award.

resorted to the procedure specified in the paragraph 2 of this Article [i.e. recourse to domestic courts].[31]

15.08 While the *China Heilongjiang* tribunal[32] found that it had jurisdiction *ratione personae* over the dispute since the claimants were all qualified investors within the meaning of the Mongolia–China BIT,[33] the tribunal ultimately declined jurisdiction *ratione materiae* in the dispute because the claimants brought claims alleging expropriation, and not necessarily on a dispute on the amount of compensation for expropriation:[34]

> The Tribunal is of the view that the purpose of the words *"involving the amount of compensation for expropriation"* is to qualify a category of disputes which may fall within the jurisdiction of an ad hoc arbitral tribunal. The purpose of this phrase is thus to restrict the jurisdiction of an ad hoc arbitral tribunal to encompass only disputes which involve the amount of compensation for expropriation. While the ordinary meaning of the term "the amount of compensation for expropriation" does not seem to cause a difficulty, the same is not the case as far as the term "involving" is concerned. Does the term "involving" restrict the scope of that phrase only to disputes about the amount of compensation for expropriation and nothing else? Or does it cover all disputes which may arise in relation to expropriation, provided that the amount of compensation for expropriation is an element of such disputes? The Tribunal agrees with the view of the Court of Appeal of the Republic of Singapore in *Sanum v. Laos,* which had to interpret an identical provision in the China-Laos BIT, that the word 'involve' is certainly capable of supporting either of the Broad or Narrow Interpretations and to cavil over the possible definitions of the world "involve" will not help us interpret Article 8(3) ... Rather, the words in Article 8(3) can only be accurately, and more meaningfully, understood by considering the context of this provision ... In the view of the Tribunal the term "involving" is a neutral one. It does not by itself enlarge nor restrict the category of disputes falling within the Tribunal's jurisdiction; nothing turns on it. The critical terms are rather the terms *"the amount of compensation for expropriation"*.
>
> ... Arbitration before an ad hoc arbitral tribunal would be available in cases where an expropriation has been formally proclaimed and what is disputed is the amount to be paid by the State to the investor for its expropriated investment ... The Tribunal is thus not of the view that an investor will be left without a meaningful opportunity to make use of the Treaty's provisions for arbitration before an ad hoc arbitral tribunal ... the Contracting States of the Treaty have carefully worded the text of Article 8, paragraph 3, as relating "to a dispute involving the amount of compensation for expropriation". Only this narrow issue falls within the jurisdiction of an arbitral tribunal while all disputes, including those involving the amount of compensation for expropriation, can be submitted to the competent court of the Contracting State

---

[31] Agreement between the Government of the People's Republic of China and the Government of the Mongolian People's Republic Concerning the Encouragement and Reciprocal Protection of Investments, 1991, at art 8(3), full text available at <http://investmentpolicyhub.unctad.org/Download/TreatyFile/760> accessed 14 June 2018.

[32] Composed of Judge Peter Tomka (President), Dr Yas Banifatemi (Arbitrator), and Mr Mark Clodfelter (Arbitrator).

[33] *China Heilongjiang* (n 31) paras 404–22.

[34] ibid para 452.

accepting the investment. This is what the two States, Mongolia and China, agreed on in 1991 when they signed the Treaty. This arrangement should not be surprising as both States then had similar political and economic systems and did not have any reason to question the judicial system of the other Treaty Party and consequently to favour international arbitration for the settlement of investment disputes.[35]

15.09 The *Lighthouse*, *Ansung*, and *China Heilongjiang* arbitrations all give evidence that limitations to arbitration devised by Asian states in their treaties and legal regimes—whether through carefully worded domestic foreign investment law and administrative rules such as those of Timor-Leste, prescriptive periods or time limitations to initiating claims as found in the China–Korea BIT, or the specific language adopted in the jurisdictional clause in the Mongolia–China BIT—are proving successful. They illustrate practical legal options that other host states can emulate to control their consent to investor–state arbitration.

15.10 Finally, recalling Australia's successful jurisdictional objection against an Asian claimant in *Philip Morris Asia Ltd v The Commonwealth of Australia*,[36] the tribunal issued an interestingly detailed (albeit redacted to the public) Final Award Regarding Costs[37] in July 2017. The *Philip Morris* tribunal first held that the conduct of the parties or their counsel in the context of the proceedings should not affect the allocation of costs.[38] Because the claimant had prevailed on two of the jurisdictional objections, the tribunal acknowledged that the claimant would not bear the entirety of costs, and exercised its discretion to only have the claimant bear a (redacted) percentage of the costs.[39] Examining Australia's unique representation issues in great detail, the tribunal held that the costs claimed by Australia for its legal representation were reasonable.[40]

1. Unsuccessful public policy or regulatory defences

15.11 Asian states were less successful in marshalling public policy or regulatory defences on the merits in 2017. The Philippines lost its first investor–state arbitration in *Baggerwerken Decloedt En Zoon NV v the Philippines*,[41] reportedly found

---

[35] ibid paras 439, 446, 448, 449, 450, and 451.
[36] *Philip Morris Asia Ltd v The Commonwealth of Australia*, PCA Case No 2012-12, Award on Jurisdiction and Admissibility (2015).
[37] *Philip Morris Asia Ltd v The Commonwealth of Australia*, PCA Case No 2012-12, Final Award Regarding Costs (2017).
[38] ibid para 37.
[39] ibid paras 68–70.
[40] ibid paras 94–104.
[41] *Baggerwerken Decloedt En Zoon NV v Republic of the Philippines*, ICSID Case No ARB/11/27, Award (2017) (award not public, details at 'On the wires: Philippines Liable for BIT Breach; Investor that Won Emergency Orders vs. Ukraine Does Not Fare as Well in Final Result; Iranians Pursue Bahrain over Bank Closure' *Investment Arbitration Reporter* (12 February 2017) <https://www.iareporter.com/articles/on-the-wires-philippines-liable-for-bit-breach-investor-that-won-emergency-orders-vs-ukraine-does-not-fare-as-well-in-final-result-iranians-pursue-bahrain-over-bank-closure/> accessed 14 June 2018.

liable under the Belgium–Luxembourg Economic Union–Philippines BIT to the total claimed amount of almost US$16 million for the Philippine government's cancellation of a lake dredging project, based on the unsubstantiated corruption allegations of the Philippines' Aquino administration against the claimants.[42] Then Philippines President Aquino had ordered the cancellation of this project for allegedly being 'overpriced and technically deficient',[43] preferring that the Philippines spend the project contract amount on the conditional cash transfer programme for the poor. Pakistan also lost on the merits for its governmental denial of a mining lease for the Reko Diq project in 2011, leading to a successful claim of investors in *Tethyan Copper Company Pty Ltd v Islamic Republic of Pakistan*.[44] Prior to the cancellation of the project, Pakistan was reported to have ordered the reassessment of the project 'to protect the country's national interests … [and] avoid selling valuable national interests at throwaway prices'.[45]

15.12 A settlement reached in *Lao Holdings NV v Government of the Lao People's Democratic Republic* was deemed to have been breached in a 15 December 2017 Decision on the Merits of the Claimants' Second Material Breach Application.[46] Claimants had alleged expropriation without compensation of their investment in gambling projects and other contracts (expansion of airport, development of special economic zone), through governmental measures such as an 80 per cent tax on casino revenues, alleged oppressive and unfair audits, among others, leading to an investment loss estimated at between US$690 million to US$1 billion.[47] A settlement was reached between the parties in June 2014. The claimants alleged the government of Laos breached this settlement, entitling them to revive the treaty arbitration (designated as the First Material Breach Application). This First Material Breach Application was dismissed on the merits by the arbitral tribunal[48] in June 2015. In the Second Material Breach Application, the claimants alleged that the government of Laos had seized and unilaterally operated the casinos,

---

[42] ibid. See also Benaning (n 4).
[43] Associated Press, 'Aquino Stops More "Overpriced, Technically Deficient" Foreign-funded Work' *Philippine Daily Inquirer* (18 June 2011) <http://globalnation.inquirer.net/4506/aquino-stops-more-'overpriced-technically-deficient'-foreign-funded-work accessed 14 June 2018>.
[44] *Tethyan Copper Company Pty Ltd v Islamic Republic of Pakistan*, ICSID Case No ARB/12/1, Award (2017) (award not public, details at <https://www.italaw.com/sites/default/files/case-documents/italaw8560.pdf> accessed 14 June 2018; see also 'World Bank Tribunal Rules against Pakistan in Reko Diq Project Case' *Dawn.com* (21 March 2017) <https://www.dawn.com/news/1321955> accessed 14 June 2018.
[45] Farhan Bokhari, 'Pakistan Threatens to Cancel Exploration Deal' *The Financial Times* (14 January 2010) <https://www.ft.com/content/1df0dad6-0145-11df-8c54-00144feabdc0> accessed 14 June 2018.
[46] *Lao Holdings NV v The Government of the Lao People's Democratic Republic*, ICSID Case No ARB(AF)/12/6, Decision on the Merits of the Claimants' Second Material Breach Application (2017).
[47] ibid para 5
[48] Composed of Hon Ian Binnie CC, QC (President), Prof Bernard Hanotiau (Arbitrator), and Prof Birgitte Stern (Arbitrator).

terminating the project development agreement with the claimants, reducing the value of the gaming assets of the claimants, imposing discriminatory taxes, while the government of Laos alleged, *inter alia*, that the claimants committed multiple acts of fraud and bribery.[49] The tribunal held that it would allow the Second Material Breach Application, reviving the treaty arbitration on the basis of alleged governmental breaches of the 2014 settlement (on the imposition of a 28 per cent ad valorem tax on gross gaming revenues instead of a flat tax, and on the government's revival of current criminal investigations against claimants where the settlement promised relief from such investigations).[50] On these grounds, the tribunal ordered the revival of the treaty-based claims against Laos.

C. Active National Courts on Investor–State Arbitration

15.13   2017 also witnessed remarkable developments from Asian national courts with respect to investor–state arbitration. On 14 August 2017, the Singapore High Court issued its first judgment[51] setting aside the investor–state arbitration award in *Swissbourgh Diamond Mines (Pty) Ltd, Josias Van Zyl, The Josias Van Zyl Family Trust and Others v The Kingdom of Lesotho*.[52] The Singapore High Court declared that the investment arbitration award 'dealt with an issue not contemplated by and not falling within the terms of the submission to arbitration and thereby fell foul of Art 34(2)(a)(iii) of the Model Law … because jurisdiction has been wrongly assumed … [the Court] therefore set aside the Award in entirety'.[53] Speaking for the Singapore High Court, Judge Kannan Ramesh stated:

> As I observed earlier, investment treaties are fine-tuned to balance the interests of host States and investors, and it would be ultimately counteractive to a treaty's object and purpose to extend its protections to situations clearly beyond its contemplation. While the defendants are understandably disappointed with the turn their investment has taken, that cannot be cured by doing violence to a dispute resolution provision in the treaty. The defendants' difficulties in establishing jurisdiction stem from the fact that their true investment—the Mining Leases—was made before Annex 1's entry into force …[54]

---

[49] *Lao Holdings* (n 47) paras 91–98.
[50] ibid paras 227–233.
[51] *Kingdom of Lesotho v Swissbourgh Diamond Mines (Pty) Ltd, Josias Van Zyl, The Josias Van Zyl Family Trust and Others*, High Court of the Republic of Singapore, Judgment of 14 August 2017.
[52] *Swissbourgh Diamond Mines (Pty) Ltd, Josias Van Zyl, The Josias Van Zyl Family Trust and Others v The Kingdom of Lesotho*, PCA Case No 2013-29, Partial Award on Jurisdiction and Merits (2016) (not public, details narrated in Luke Eric Peterson, 'Investigation: Lesotho is Held Liable for Investment Treaty Breach Arising Out of its Role in Hobbling a Regional Tribunal that Had Been Hearing Expropriation Case' *Investment Arbitration Reporter* (14 July 2016) <https://www.iareporter.com/articles/investigation-lesotho-is-held-liable-for-investment-treaty-breach-arising-out-of-its-role-in-hobbling-a-regional-tribunal-that-had-been-hearing-expropriation-case/> accessed 14 June 2018.
[53] *Lesotho v Swissbourgh Diamond Mines* (n 52) para 341.
[54] ibid para 342.

15.14 The Singapore High Court sought further submissions from the parties on whether the court has jurisdiction to remit the costs of the arbitration to the PCA tribunal or to make an order of the costs of arbitration itself; and the quantum of such costs assuming the court has jurisdiction.

15.15 Indian national courts have been similarly active with respect to the *Vodafone v India* arbitration. Vodafone brought a notice of arbitration in 2014 against India, alleging the latter's violations of the India–Netherlands BIT.[55] India challenged jurisdiction in that arbitration. In 2017, Vodafone instituted a second arbitration against India under the India–UK BIT, assailing similar governmental measures changing the tax regime. On 22 August 2017, the High Court of Delhi issued a judgment restraining Vodafone from proceeding with its arbitration claim under the India–UK BIT, declaring that it was of the

> prima facie opinion that as the claimants in the two arbitral proceedings form part of the same corporate group being run, governed, and managed by the same set of shareholders, they cannot file two independent arbitral proceedings as that amounts to abuse of process of law ... there is a risk of parallel proceedings and inconsistent decisions by two separate arbitral tribunals in the present case ... it would be inequitable, unfair, and unjust to permit the defendants to prosecute the foreign arbitration.[56]

This judgment has been elevated and is pending before the Indian Supreme Court.[57] The Delhi High Court judgment ultimately operates as a novel 'anti-investment arbitration injunction', the international legality of which has not yet been determined by the pending *Vodafone v India* tribunals.

1. New models of mega-regional or regional investment treaties and Asian arbitral rules reform

15.16 Finally, 2017 also witnessed more developments in mega-regional economic agreements, such as the agreement in principle over the renamed Comprehensive and Progressive Agreement for Trans-Pacific Partnership (CPTPP), with eleven states parties (Australia, Brunei Darussalam, Canada, Chile, Japan, Malaysia, Mexico, New Zealand, Peru, Singapore, Viet Nam), minus the United States which had withdrawn from the original Trans-Pacific Partnership Agreement under the Trump Administration.[58] The CPTPP suspended many of the original provisions

---

[55] Details furnished in Luke Eric Peterson, 'As Vodafone Sues India—and Nokia Threatens the Same—Company Could Seek Interim Arbitral Order Blocking India from Pursuing Billions in Taxes' *Investment Arbitration Reporter* (13 May 2014) <https://www.iareporter.com/articles/as-vodafone-sues-india-and-nokia-threatens-the-same-company-could-seek-interim-arbitral-order-blocking-india-from-pursuing-billions-in-taxes/> accessed 14 June 2018.

[56] *Union of India v Vodafone Group Plc United Kingdom and Another*, Judgment of 22 August 2017, 9.

[57] *Union of India v Vodafone Group Plc United Kingdom and Another*, Order of 14 December 2017.

[58] See Trans-Pacific Ministerial Statement of 11 November 2017 <http://dfat.gov.au/trade/agreements/tpp/news/Pages/trans-pacific-partnership-ministerial-statement.aspx>

of the investment chapter in TPP, ensuring a much narrower scope to investor–state dispute settlement.[59] The sixteen-member Regional Comprehensive Economic Partnership (RCEP), led by China, contains a draft investment chapter that also provides for investor–state dispute settlement,[60] which the RCEP ministers declared in 2017 would 'create an enabling investment environment in the region covering four pillars of investments—protection, liberalization, promotion, and facilitation'.[61] The Association of Southeast Asian Nations (ASEAN) concluded a new regional investment treaty with the Hong Kong Special Administrative Region on 11 December 2017.[62] China concluded an investment agreement with Hong Kong in 2017.[63] Japan concluded a new BIT with Israel on 1 February 2017.[64]

15.17 Finally, Asian arbitral institutions published revised or annotated versions of their arbitral rules.[65] As an alternative to ICSID rules, the Singapore International Arbitration Centre (SIAC) issued its first edition of the SIAC Investment Arbitration Rules on 1 January 2017, packaged as a set of rules that

> … have been developed with a view towards the issues unique to international investment arbitration. These Rules may be agreed and applied in any type of arbitration, the application of which shall not be subject to objective criteria, such as the existence of a qualifying "investor" or "investment" or the presence of a State, State-controlled entity or intergovernmental organisation, without prejudice to any requirements set out in the underlying contract, treaty, statute or other instrument. Where the parties to a dispute have previously consented, or a party has previously

---

accessed 14 June 2018; Mireya Solis, 'Trump Withdrawing from the Trans-Pacific Partnership' *Brookings* (24 March 2017) <https://www.brookings.edu/blog/unpacked/2017/03/24/trump-withdrawing-from-the-trans-pacific-partnership/> accessed 14 June 2018.

[59] See New Zealand Ministry statement at <https://www.mfat.govt.nz/en/trade/free-trade-agreements/free-trade-agreements-concluded-but-not-in-force/cptpp/tpp-and-cptpp-the-differences-explained/> accessed 14 June 2018, declaring that '[s]uspensions in the Investment Chapter will mean that claims are no longer permitted in relation to investment contracts and approvals (called "investment agreements" and "investment authorisations" in the TPP). This means that under CPTPP private companies who enter into an investment contract with the Government will not be able to use ISDS clauses if there is a dispute about that contract'.

[60] Unconfirmed leaked documents from the RCEP negotiations are detailed here <https://www.keionline.org/23305/> accessed 14 June 2018.

[61] RCEP Ministerial Statement, November 2017 <http://asean.org/storage/2017/11/RCEP-Summit_Leaders-Joint-Statement-FINAL1.pdf> accessed 14 June 2018 para (k).

[62] See full text of Agreement on Investment among the Governments of the Hong Kong Special Administrative Region of the People's Republic of China and the Member States of the Association of Southeast Asian Nations (signed 12 November 2017).

[63] See full text of Investment Agreement of the Mainland and Hong Kong Closer Economic Partnership Agreement (entered into force 28 June 2017).

[64] See Agreement between Japan and the State of Israel for the Liberalization, Promotion and Protection of Investment (entered into force 5 October 2017).

[65] See Hong Kong International Arbitration Centre Press Release, 'Guide to the HKIAC Arbitration Rules Released' (4 May 2017) <http://www.hkiac.org/news/guide-hkiac-arbitration-rules-released> accessed 14 June 2018; Shenzhen Court of International Arbitration 2016 Arbitration Rules <http://www.sccietac.org/web/doc/view_rules/861.html> accessed 14 June 2018.

offered to consent, to arbitration in accordance with rules of arbitration other than the SIAC Investment Arbitration Rules, whether in a contract, treaty, statute or other instrument, the dispute may be referred instead to arbitration in accordance with the SIAC Investment Arbitration Rules if the parties have subsequently consented to refer such dispute to arbitration in accordance with the SIAC Investment Arbitration Rules.[66]

Subsequently, the China International Economic and Trade Arbitration Commission (CIETAC) issued its International Investment Arbitration Rules, which came into force on 1 October 2017.[67] There are no publicly reported cases thus far filed under the SIAC or CIETAC Investment Arbitration Rules. 15.18

D. Conclusion

2017 has been a significant year for Asia in international investment law. While arbitral awards such as *Lighthouse v Timor-Leste, Ansung v People's Republic of China, China Heilongjiang et al v Mongolia* have shown Asian states' deft and successful use of jurisdictional objections and narrow jurisdictional clauses in investment treaties, Asian states also failed in advancing substantive public policy or regulatory defences brought under older investment treaty models. The mixed results arguably fuel Asian states' continued experimentation to date with new investment treaty design, through mega-regional, regional, and new BITs, as well as by prescribing alternative investment rules to ICSID. 15.19

---

[66] See full text of SIAC Investment Arbitration Rules 2017 <http://www.siac.org.sg/images/stories/articles/rules/IA/SIAC%20Investment%20Arbitration%20Rules%20-%20Final.pdf> accessed 14 June 2018.
[67] See full text of CIETAC Investment Arbitration Rules 2017 <http://www.cietac.org/index.php?m=Page&a=index&id=390&l=en> accessed 14 June 2018.

16

DEVELOPMENTS IN INTERNATIONAL INVESTMENT LAW AND POLICY IN THE EUROPEAN UNION

Catharine Titi

A. Introduction	16.01	D. International Investment Court and Multilateral Reform of ISDS	16.08
B. State-of-Play of EU Negotiations and Investment Agreements	16.02	E. Compatibility with EU Law: Investment Court and Intra-EU BITs	16.12
C. Division of Competences between the EU and its Member States	16.04	F. Conclusions	16.18

A. Introduction

16.01 Since the entry into force of the Treaty of Lisbon, the EU has been fine-tuning its international investment policy. Recent developments reveal just how vibrant and fast-paced the field is. This chapter reviews 2017 developments in international investment law and policy in the EU. It commences with the state-of-play of EU negotiations. Then it turns to the apportionment of competences between the EU and its member states. In a following step, it examines the EU's efforts to establish a multilateral investment court system. Finally, the chapter canvasses developments in relation to the compatibility of the investment court, arbitration clauses and intra-EU BITs with EU law.

B. State-of-Play of EU Negotiations and Investment Agreements

16.02 In 2017, the EU continued to negotiate international investment agreements (IIAs) and a number of these agreements are now a step closer to coming into being. In December 2017, the EU and Japan finalized negotiations on an Economic Partnership Agreement, although negotiations on investment protection standards and dispute settlement are still afoot.[1] The EU has put its investment court system on the table as well as its work towards the establishment of a multilateral investment court.[2] While closer to conclusion, the EU–Singapore free trade agreement (EUSFTA) is subject to ongoing deliberations in relation to that treaty's investment protection provisions.[3] It appears that the European Commission is holding discussions with Singapore in order to align the 'investment protection provisions in the draft agreement' with the EU's new approach.[4] This statement should be understood to refer among others to the introduction of an investment court system. At the time of writing, legal scrubbing for the EU–Vietnam free trade agreement (FTA) is almost complete. The next step will be for the agreement to be translated into all official EU languages and into Vietnamese.[5] According to the European Commission, the FTA could enter into force by the end of 2018.[6] The EU–Canada Comprehensive Economic and Trade Agreement (CETA), which was signed in October 2016, obtained the consent of the European Parliament on 15 February 2017,[7] and was ratified by Canada on 16 May 2017.[8] On 21 September 2017, part of CETA came into provisional application; however, the investment chapter and CETA's investment court system remain outside the scope of the agreement's provisional application.[9] CETA will

---

[1] European Commission, Press Release, 'EU and Japan finalise Economic Partnership Agreement' (8 December 2017) <http://trade.ec.europa.eu/doclib/press/index.cfm?id=1767> accessed 30 April 2018.

[2] See <http://trade.ec.europa.eu/doclib/docs/2006/december/tradoc_118238.pdf> accessed 30 April 2018.

[3] European Parliament, Legislative Train Schedule, 'EU-Singapore free trade agreement' (EUSFTA) (updated 20 December 2017)<http://www.europarl.europa.eu/legislative-train/theme-a-balanced-and-progressive-trade-policy-to-harness-globalisation/file-eu-singapore-fta> accessed 2 May 2018. The EUSFTA will be canvassed later in light of Opinion 2/15 of the Court of Justice of the European Union.

[4] See <http://trade.ec.europa.eu/doclib/docs/2006/december/tradoc_118238.pdf> accessed 2 May 2018.

[5] European Commission, 'Overview of FTA and Other Trade Negotiations' (updated January 2018) <http://trade.ec.europa.eu/doclib/docs/2006/december/tradoc_118238.pdf> accessed 30 April 2018. At the time of going to publication, the EUSFTA's investment chapter has become the EU–Singapore Investment Protection Agreement, in apparent reaction to Opinion 2/15 (see below (paras 16.05–16.07)) and investment arbitration has been replaced by a permanent investment court.

[6] European Commission, 'Overview of FTA and Other Trade Negotiations' (updated January 2018) <http://trade.ec.europa.eu/doclib/docs/2006/december/tradoc_118238.pdf> accessed 30 April 2018.

[7] European Commission, Fact Sheet, 'CETA—a Trade Deal that Sets a New Standard for Global Trade' (15 February 2017) <http://europa.eu/rapid/press-release_MEMO-17-271_en.htm> accessed 30 April 2018.

[8] European Commission, Press release, 'EU-Canada Trade Agreement Enters into Force' (20 September 2017) <http://europa.eu/rapid/press-release_IP-17-3121_en.htm> accessed 2 May 2018.

[9] ibid.

come into force 'fully and definitively' upon ratification by all EU member states.[10] According to the European Parliament, as of October 2017, seven member states had ratified CETA or were 'at a very advanced stage of doing so'.[11] Despite these steps forward, the path to CETA's ratification does not have the all-clear yet: the Court of Justice of the European Union (CJEU) is currently seized of a request for an Opinion on the compatibility of CETA's investor–state dispute settlement (ISDS) mechanism with EU law.[12] The Opinion of the CJEU, while issued in the CETA context, will doubtless be of relevance to all EU investment agreements.

16.03 The EU is further negotiating or looking into negotiating *inter alia* with the Association of South East Asian Nations (ASEAN) and MERCOSUR, and individually with Australia, China, India, Indonesia, Mexico, Myanmar, and New Zealand.[13] At the same time, the future of the EU–US Transatlantic Trade and Investment Partnership (TTIP) has become uncertain under the Trump administration. Despite a joint EU–US report dated 17 January 2017,[14] TTIP negotiations are on hold and no formal commitment has taken place with the new US administration.[15]

C. Division of Competences between the EU and its Member States

16.04 In 2017, the impassioned debate on the apportionment of competences between the EU and its member states for the conclusion of EU investment agreements[16] seemed to find its resolution. The controversy turned on whether EU investment agreements fall within the exclusive competence of the EU and should therefore

---

[10] ibid.
[11] The member states in question are Croatia, the Czech Republic, Denmark, Latvia, Malta, Portugal, and Spain. See European Parliament, 'At a Glance—CETA Ratification Process: Latest Developments' (October 2017) <http://www.europarl.europa.eu/RegData/etudes/ATAG/2017/608726/EPRS_ATA(2017)608726_EN.pdf> accessed 2 May 2018. It is interesting to note that in July 2017, the French Constitutional Council (*Conseil constitutionnel*) held that CETA is compatible with the French Constitution, see Decision No 2017-749 DC, Comprehensive Economic and Trade Agreement between Canada, on the one hand, and the European Union and its Member States, on the other, 31 July 2017.
[12] This topic is discussed in section E.
[13] European Commission, 'Overview of FTA and Other Trade Negotiations' (updated January 2018) <http://trade.ec.europa.eu/doclib/docs/2006/december/tradoc_118238.pdf> accessed 30 April 2018.
[14] European Commission and Executive Office of the President of the United States, 'US-EU Joint Report on TTIP Progress to Date' (17 January 2017) <http://trade.ec.europa.eu/doclib/docs/2017/january/tradoc_155242.pdf> accessed 30 April 2018.
[15] European Commission, 'Transatlantic Trade & Investment Partnership Advisory Group, Meeting Report (9 March 2017) <http://trade.ec.europa.eu/doclib/docs/2017/april/tradoc_155484.pdf> accessed 30 April 2018, 2.
[16] The term 'EU investment agreements' is agnostic about whether these are pure or mixed EU agreements. It is used in contradiction with EU member state bilateral investment treaties.

be concluded as pure EU agreements without member state participation; or whether they belong to a shared competence and must be concluded jointly by the EU and the member states ('mixed' agreements). Since the very beginning, the European Commission contended that the competence was exclusive, while some member states argued that the competence was mixed.[17]

In 2016, the Commission proposed CETA as a mixed agreement. According to EU Trade Commissioner Cecilia Malmström, this was not because the Commission considered that the agreement fell under shared competence but rather due to the political situation in the Council and the need for a swift signature.[18] The case was different with EUSFTA; once that agreement was initialled,[19] the European Commission sought an Opinion from the CJEU under Article 218(11) of the Treaty on the Functioning of the European Union (TFEU) in relation to the apportioning of competences between the EU and its member states.[20] The Commission argued that the EU had exclusive competence to sign and conclude the EU–Singapore FTA.[21] On 21 December 2016, Advocate General Sharpston issued her Opinion. The Advocate General considered that EUSFTA could only be concluded as a mixed agreement, that is jointly by the EU and the member states.[22] Her Opinion was largely confirmed when the CJEU rendered Opinion 2/15 on 16 May 2017.

16.05

---

[17] For a scholarly discussion on the topic, see Steffen Hindelang and Niklas Maydell, 'The EU's Common Investment Policy—Connecting the Dots' in Marc Bungenberg et al (eds), *European Yearbook of International Economic Law 2011: Special Issue: International Investment Law and EU Law* (Springer 2011); Marc Bungenberg, 'The Division of Competences Between the EU and Its Member States in the Area of Investment Politics' in Marc Bungenberg et al (eds), *European Yearbook of International Economic Law 2011: Special Issue: International Investment Law and EU Law* (Springer 2011); August Reinisch, 'The Division of Powers Between the EU and Its Member States "After Lisbon"', in Marc Bungenberg et al (eds), *European Yearbook of International Economic Law 2011: Special Issue: International Investment Law and EU Law* (Springer 2011); Marc Bungenberg, 'Going Global? The EU Common Commercial Policy After Lisbon' in Christoph Herrmann and Jörg Philipp Terchechte (eds), *European Yearbook of International Economic Law 2010* (Springer 2010); August Reinisch, 'The EU on the Investment Path—Quo Vadis Europe' (2013) Santa Clara Journal of International Law 2012 136 *et seq*; Marc Bungenberg and Catharine Titi, 'The Evolution of EU Investment Law and the Future of EU-China Investment Relations' in Wenhua Shan and Jinyuan Su (eds), *China and International Investment Law: Twenty Years of ICSID Membership* (Brill,2014) 300 *et seq*; Catharine Titi, 'Investment Law and the European Union: Towards a New Generation of International Investment Agreements' (2015) 26(3) European Journal of International Law 643.
[18] European Commission, Press Release, 'European Commission Proposes Signature and Conclusion of EU-Canada Trade Deal' (5 July 2016) <http://europa.eu/rapid/press-release_IP-16-2371_en.htm> accessed 2 May 2018.
[19] CJEU, Opinion 2/15 of the Court, 16 May 2017, ECLI:EU:C:2017:376, para 9.
[20] Court of Justice of the European Union, Press Release No 147/16, 'Advocate General Sharpston considers that the Singapore Free Trade Agreement can only be concluded by the European Union and the Member States acting jointly' (21 December 2016) <https://curia.europa.eu/jcms/upload/docs/application/pdf/2016-12/cp160147en.pdf> accessed 30 April 2018.
[21] CJEU, Opinion 2/15 of the Court (n 19) paras 12 *et seq*.
[22] CJEU, Opinion of Advocate General Sharpston, Opinion procedure 2/15, 21 December 2016, ECLI:EU:C:2016:992.

16.06 According to Opinion 2/15, the EU–Singapore FTA belongs for the most part to the exclusive competence of the EU; however, some of its provisions fall within the shared competence of the EU and the member states, that is (a) the provisions on investment protection insomuch as they relate to forms of non-direct investment, such as portfolio investment;[23] (b) the provisions on investor–state dispute settlement; and the provisions of Chapters 1 (Objectives and General Definitions), 14 (Transparency), 15 (Dispute Settlement between the Parties), 16 (Mediation Mechanism), and 17 (Institutional, General and Final Provisions) insomuch as they relate to EUSFTA's investment chapter (Chapter 9) and to issues of shared competence.[24] In essence then, Opinion 2/15 defined the EU's competence over investment protection as 'partly exclusive and partly shared'.[25] The Opinion also addressed the power of the EU to replace EU member state agreements by EUSFTA. Article 9.10 of the agreement provides that upon its entry into force, bilateral investment treaties (BITs) concluded between EU member states and Singapore shall cease to exist and will be replaced with and superseded by EUSFTA. Similar provisions exist in the other negotiated EU investment agreements. In contrast to the Opinion of the Advocate General,[26] the CJEU stressed that member states are 'prohibited from adopting acts producing legal effects in areas which fall within an exclusive competence of the European Union'.[27] As a corollary, the member states could not exercise further powers in the field of the EU's exclusive competence, that is to the extent that the commitments concern foreign *direct* investment.[28]

16.07 The European Commission 'welcomed' Opinion 2/15 for the 'legal clarity and stability on competences and responsibilities' that it provides for the future of EU investment agreements.[29] It is uncertain at this stage whether the Opinion may encourage the Commission to negotiate separately FTAs and standalone IIAs, so as to conclude FTAs on the basis of its traditional exclusive competence and investment treaties on the basis of the newly defined mixed competence.

---

[23] Readers will recall that art 207 of the TFEU provides that the EU's exclusive competence covers 'foreign direct investment' but is silent about other types of investment, such as portfolio investment. Indeed part of the disagreement between the EU and the member states stemmed from this 'omission' in art 207 of the TFEU.

[24] CJEU, Opinion 2/15 of the Court (n 19) para 305.

[25] European Commission, 'Recommendation for a Council decision authorising the opening of negotiations for a Convention establishing a multilateral court for the settlement of investment disputes' COM (2017) 493 final, 13 September 2017, 4.

[26] CJEU, Opinion of Advocate General Sharpston (n 22) paras 371 *et seq*.

[27] CJEU, Opinion 2/15 of the Court (n 19) para 250.

[28] CJEU, Opinion 2/15 of the Court (n 19) paras 251–52.

[29] European Commission, Factsheet, 'The Opinion of the European Court of Justice on the EU-Singapore Trade Agreement and the Division of Competences in Trade Policy' (September 2017) <http://trade.ec.europa.eu/doclib/docs/2017/september/tradoc_156035.pdf> accessed 30 April 2018), p. 2.

This certainly appeared likely at some stage,[30] although in September 2017 the Commission declared that it did not intend to do so.[31]

D. International Investment Court and Multilateral Reform of ISDS

In the last couple of years, the EU has intensified its efforts to accelerate multilateral reform of ISDS. The fulcrum of these efforts is the establishment of a multilateral investment court. Before addressing the more recent developments, a brief timeline of the project for the creation of the court may be useful. The European Commission first unveiled its proposal for an international investment court in September 2015.[32] Its draft text was broadly endorsed by the EU and served as the blueprint for the official negotiating document that was tabled for discussions with the United States in November 2015.[33] In December 2015, when negotiations on the EU–Vietnam FTA were concluded, the Commission announced that the treaty contained an investment court system with an appellate body.[34] In February 2016, the new—post-legal scrubbing—text of CETA was released. The new text includes an international investment court instead of the traditional investor–state dispute settlement mechanism. While providing for a bilateral EU–Canada investment court, CETA has the particularity that it commits both the EU and Canada to pursue negotiations on a *multilateral* investment court.[35]

16.08

---

[30] Hans Von Der Burchard, 'Juncker Proposes Fast-tracking EU Trade Deals' *Politico* (31 August 2017, updated 4 September 2017) <http://www.politico.eu/article/juncker-proposes-fast-tracking-eu-trade-deals/> accessed 30 April 2018. See further European Commission, 'Proposed New Architecture for Splitting EU FTAs and EU Investment Agreements' <http://g8fip1kplyr33r3krz5b97d1.wpengine.netdna-cdn.com/wp-content/uploads/2017/08/COM-proposal-splitting-trade-deals.pdf> accessed 30 April 2018.

[31] European Commission, Factsheet, 'The Opinion of the European Court of Justice on the EU-Singapore Trade Agreement and the Division of Competences in Trade Policy' (September 2017) <http://trade.ec.europa.eu/doclib/docs/2017/september/tradoc_156035.pdf> accessed 30 April 2018, 3. At the time of going to publication, the EU appears to have started to separate investment chapters from the rest of the FTA, see above n 5 on the EU–Singapore Investment Protection Agreement.

[32] European Commission draft TTIP text on investment (16 September 2015) <http://europa.eu/rapid/press-release_MEMO-15-5652_en.htm> accessed 30 April 2018). For an overview of this early draft, see Catharine Titi, 'The European Commission's Approach to the Transatlantic Trade and Investment Partnership (TTIP): Investment Standards and International Investment Court' (2015) 6 Transnational Dispute Management 1.

[33] The proposal is available at http://trade.ec.europa.eu/doclib/docs/2015/november/tradoc_153955.pdf. For a discussion see Catharine Titi, 'The European Union's Proposal for an International Investment Court: Significance, Innovations and Challenges Ahead' (2017) Transnational Dispute Management 1.

[34] European Commission, News, 'EU and Vietnam Finalise Landmark Trade Deal' (2 December 2015) <http://trade.ec.europa.eu/doclib/press/index.cfm?id=1409> accessed 30 April 2018).

[35] CETA art 8.29 ('The Parties shall pursue with other trading partners the establishment of a multilateral investment tribunal and appellate mechanism for the resolution of investment disputes').

The ambition to create a multilateral investment court was repeated in the EU–Canada Joint Interpretative Instrument accompanying CETA.[36] The intention is that 'once a minimum critical mass of participants is established', the multilateral court will replace bilateral court systems established by individual treaties such as CETA and that it will be open to accession by third states.[37] In December 2016, the Commission and Canada co-hosted an inter-governmental expert meeting in order to facilitate the establishment of a multilateral investment court with competence over disputes under existing and future investment agreements.[38] The EU further plans to allow transition to the multilateral investment court not only for EU investment agreements but also for EU member state BITs authorized under Regulation No EU 1219/2012.[39]

16.09 On 21 December 2016, the European Commission launched a public consultation on its proposal for multilateral reform of investment dispute resolution,[40] building on its earlier Inception Impact Assessment.[41] The consultation sought to collect stakeholders' views on the EU's approach to investment dispute settlement and options for multilateral reform, including the creation of a standing multilateral investment court. The consultation further broached the possible establishment of a multilateral appellate mechanism.[42] The consultation was completed on 15 March 2017. It revealed 'overall broad support for a multilateral reform of investment dispute settlement', although the European Commission acknowledged that some questions remain unresolved, especially in relation to 'technical aspects'.[43] The summary report of the public consultation was annexed

---

[36] Joint Interpretative Instrument on the Comprehensive Economic and Trade Agreement (CETA) between Canada and the European Union and its Member States, 27 October 2016 <http://data.consilium.europa.eu/doc/document/ST-13541-2016-INIT/en/pdf> accessed 30 April 2018, 6.

[37] ibid. See also Statement 36 (Statement by the Commission and the Council on investment protection and the Investment Court System (ICS) of the Statements and Declarations to be entered on the occasion of the adoption by the Council of the decision authorising the signature of CETA, 27 October 2016 <http://data.consilium.europa.eu/doc/document/ST-13463-2016-REV-1/en/pdf> accessed 30 April 2018.

[38] European Commission, Press Release, European 'Commission and Canadian Government Co-host Discussions on a Multilateral Investment Court' (13 December 2016) <http://europa.eu/rapid/press-release_IP-16-4349_en.htm> accessed 2 May 2018.

[39] European Commission, Inception Impact Assessment, 'Establishment of a Multilateral Investment Court for Investment Dispute Resolution' (1 August 2016) 3.

[40] European Commission, 'Questionnaire on Options for a Multilateral Reform of Investment Dispute Resolution' <http://trade.ec.europa.eu/consultations/index.cfm?consul_id=233> accessed 2 May 2018.

[41] ibid. See also European Commission, Consultation Strategy, 'Impact Assessment on the Establishment of a Multilateral Investment Court for Investment Dispute Resolution' (1 August 2016) <http://trade.ec.europa.eu/doclib/docs/2016/october/tradoc_154997.pdf> accessed 2 May 2018.

[42] European Commission, 'Questionnaire on options for a multilateral reform of investment dispute resolution' (n 40).

[43] European Commission, 'Recommendation for a Council decision authorising the opening of negotiations for a Convention establishing a multilateral court for the settlement of investment disputes' (n 25) 5.

Developments in the European Union

to the Commission's Impact Assessment Report.[44] On 13 September 2017, the Commission issued a Recommendation for a Council decision authorizing the opening of negotiations for a Convention establishing a multilateral court for the settlement of investment disputes.[45]

The EU's proposal for the establishment of a multilateral investment court or discussion with the EU may have encouraged some institutions to wish to play host to such negotiations or at least assume a role in the reform efforts. On 14 July 2017, at its fiftieth session, the United Nations Commission on International Trade Law (UNCITRAL) entrusted its Working Group III with a mandate to study the possible reform of investor–state dispute settlement.[46] Working Group III should accordingly (a) identify and examine concerns regarding the current system of investment dispute settlement; (b) consider whether reform is desirable in light of the identified concerns; and (c) if it finds that reform is desirable 'develop any relevant solutions' to be recommended to UNCITRAL.[47] It was agreed that the Working Group should exercise broad discretion in discharging its mandate while ensuring that deliberations are 'government-led with high-level input from all governments'[48] and that 'any solutions devised would be designed taking into account the ongoing work of relevant international organizations and with a view to allowing each State the choice of whether and to what extent it wished to adopt the relevant solution(s)'.[49] This is in line with UNCITRAL's working methods, which generally avoid bringing pressure to bear on states to adopt proposed solutions.   16.10

For the time being, UNCITRAL has taken over the discussions on the creation of a multilateral investment court, insomuch as the EU is currently 'channeling its multilateral ambitions into the UNCITRAL forum'.[50] The EU is not a formal member of UNCITRAL although many EU member states are.[51] In a document   16.11

---

[44] European Commission Staff Working Document, 'Impact Assessment on Multilateral reform of investment dispute resolution, annexed to the Recommendation for a Council decision authorising the opening of negotiations for a Convention establishing a multilateral court for the settlement of investment disputes' SWD (2017) 302 final, 13 September 2017.

[45] European Commission, 'Recommendation for a Council decision authorising the opening of negotiations for a Convention establishing a multilateral court for the settlement of investment disputes' (n 25).

[46] United Nations, Report of the United Nations Commission on International Trade Law, Fiftieth session (3–21 July 2017) A/72/17, para 264.

[47] ibid.

[48] United Nations, Report of the United Nations Commission on International Trade Law, Thirty-fourth session (27 November–1 December 2017), Annotated provisional agenda (15 September 2017) para 10.

[49] United Nations, Report of the United Nations Commission on International Trade Law, Fiftieth session (n 46) para 264.

[50] Luke Eric Peterson, 'UNCITRAL Meetings on ISDS Reform Get Off to Bumpy Start, as Delegations Can't Come to Consensus on who Should Chair Sensitive Process—Entailing a Rare Vote' 10(25) *Investment Arbitration Reporter* (11 December 2017) 3.

[51] See Origin, Mandate and Composition of UNCITRAL <http://www.uncitral.org/uncitral/en/about/origin.html> accessed 2 May 2018.

dated 20 November 2017, the Commission rendered public its comments prepared for the first meeting of UNCITRAL Working Group III.[52] It was reported that the participation of the EU in the UNCITRAL process has rendered anxious some states sceptical about radical reforms to the ISDS mechanism.[53] In March 2018, the Council officially adopted and made public its negotiating mandate to the Commission to negotiate a convention establishing a multilateral court.[54]

E. Compatibility with EU Law: Investment Court and Intra-EU BITs

16.12 While the EU has been actively pursuing the creation of a multilateral investment court, on 6 September 2017, Belgium submitted a request for an Opinion to the CJEU concerning the compatibility of the investment court system with EU law.[55] This request is pertinent in light of earlier opinions rendered by the CJEU, including Opinion 1/09 on the European and Community Patents Court[56] and Opinion 2/13 on the EU's accession to the European Convention on Human Rights (ECHR).[57] Broadly speaking, the provisions on the investment court system have been drafted in a way so as to circumvent objections expressed vis-à-vis other court systems in the CJEU's Opinions.[58] It should also be recalled that

---

[52] EU, 'The Identification and Consideration of Concerns as Regards Investor to State Dispute Settlement' (20 November 2017) <http://trade.ec.europa.eu/doclib/docs/2017/november/tradoc_156402.pdf> accessed 2 May 2018.

[53] Peterson (n 50) 3.

[54] Council of the European Union, 'Negotiating Directives for a Convention Establishing A Multilateral Court for the Settlement of Investment Disputes' (20 March 2018) <http://data.consilium.europa.eu/doc/document/ST-12981-2017-ADD-1-DCL-1/en/pdf> accessed 2 May 2018. The Commission had already engaged in 'exploratory talks' even before the negotiating directives were issued. The negotiating directives are also noteworthy in that they refine some clauses of the EU's investment court system. For instance, according to para 11, judges should be appointed for 'fixed, long and non-renewable' terms, in contrast with CETA's court, where members of the first instance tribunal are appointed for a five-year term, renewable once.

[55] This is Opinion 1/17. There is some uncertainty as to the exact date the request for Opinion 1/17 was lodged. According to the CJEU, the application was registered on 7 September 2017, according to the Belgian Ministry of Foreign Affairs, Foreign Trade and Development Cooperation, the request was submitted on 6 September 2017. See respectively <http://curia.europa.eu/juris/liste.jsf?language=en&td=ALL&num=C-1/17> (accessed 30 April 2018) and Belgian Ministry of Foreign Affairs, Foreign Trade and Development Cooperation, Minister Reynders submits request for opinion on CETA, 6 September 2017, <https://diplomatie.belgium.be/en/newsroom/news/2017/minister_reynders_submits_request_opinion_ceta> accessed 30 April 2018.

[56] CJEU, Opinion 1/09, European and Community Patents Court [2011] ECR I-1137.

[57] CJEU, Opinion 2/13, Accession of the European Union to the European Convention for the Protection of Human Rights and Fundamental Freedoms, 18 December 2014. For a discussion, see Stephan Schill, Editorial: Opinion 2/13—'The End for Dispute Settlement in EU Trade and Investment Agreements?' (2015) 16 Journal of World Investment and Trade 379.

[58] Catharine Titi, 'The European Union's Proposal for an International Investment Court: Significance, Innovations and Challenges Ahead' (2017) 1 Transnational Dispute Management, 29.

the EU is already party, together with the member states, to the Energy Charter Treaty (ECT), which gives access to international dispute settlement.

16.13 Belgium's request for an Opinion follows an internal agreement between the federal government and the governments of the federated entities that was reached on 27 October 2016 on the signing of CETA.[59] The internal agreement included 'a national unilateral declaration regarding the Belgian conditions for signing CETA, for which the undertaking was made to request an opinion from the [CJEU] regarding the compatibility of certain aspects of CETA with the European Treaties, in particular with [regard] to Opinion 2/15'.[60] A working group made up of representatives of the federal government and the governments of the federated entities had been preparing Belgium's request for an Opinion since December 2016.[61]

16.14 The Belgian request for an Opinion focuses on the compatibility of the EU's investment court system with: (a) the exclusive competence of the CJEU to interpret EU law; (b) the general principle of equality and the 'practical effect' requirement of EU law; (c) the right of access to courts; and (d) the right to an independent and impartial judiciary.[62] The questions submitted to the CJEU extend beyond the 'traditional' concern about the compatibility of the proposed dispute settlement mechanism with the jurisdictional autonomy of the CJEU. In fact, the first three questions recall arguments raised by the European Commission in its various submissions in arbitral proceedings conducted on the basis of intra-EU investment treaties and in the context of infringement proceedings it initiated against EU member states seeking the termination of intra-EU BITs.[63] With respect to the fourth question, Belgium has concretely requested the opinion of the CJEU in relation to the conditions regarding the remuneration of the members of the tribunal and the appellate tribunal; their appointment and other terms of appointment (the 'release' of the members); the guidelines of the International Bar Association (IBA) on Conflicts of

---

[59] Belgian Ministry of Foreign Affairs, Foreign Trade and Development Cooperation, CETA—Belgian Request for an Opinion from the European Court of Justice <https://diplomatie.belgium.be/sites/default/files/downloads/ceta_summary.pdf> accessed 2 May 2018.
[60] ibid.
[61] Belgian Ministry of Foreign Affairs, Foreign Trade and Development Cooperation, Minister Reynders submits request for opinion on CETA <https://diplomatie.belgium.be/en/newsroom/news/2017/minister_reynders_submits_request_opinion_ceta> accessed 30 April 2018.
[62] Belgian Ministry of Foreign Affairs, Foreign Trade and Development Cooperation, CETA—Belgian Request for an Opinion from the European Court of Justice <https://diplomatie.belgium.be/sites/default/files/downloads/ceta_summary.pdf> accessed 30 April 2018.
[63] Damien Charlotin, 'EU's Highest Court is Asked Once More to Weigh in on International Investment Law Questions—This Time by Belgium in Relation to CETA's "Investment Court System"' 10(19) *Investment Arbitration Reporter* (18 September 2017) 22. See also European Commission, Press Release, 'Commission Asks Member States to Terminate their intra-EU Bilateral Investment Treaties' (18 June 2015) <http://europa.eu/rapid/press-release_IP-15-5198_en.htm; and http://europa.eu/rapid/press-release_MEMO-16-3125_en.htm> accessed 30 April 2018.

Interest in International Arbitration and the introduction of a code of conduct for members of the tribunal and the appellate tribunal; and the 'external professional activities' of members of the tribunal and the appellate tribunal related to investment disputes.[64] In its request for an Opinion, Belgium further notes that the state does not take any position regarding the questions submitted to the CJEU and that it 'is also conscious of the fact that the ICS is the first step towards the creation of a multilateral Investment Court which, in the long run, shall become the responsible legal institution to resolve conflicts between investors and states'.[65]

16.15 Belgium's request for an Opinion joined another case concerning investment law issues that until recently had been pending before the CJEU. The case related to a request for a preliminary ruling on the question of compatibility of an intra-EU BIT's arbitration clause with EU law and was submitted by Germany's Federal Court of Justice (*Bundesgerichtshof*) in the context of the *Achmea* (formerly Eureko) *v Slovakia* case.[66] Advocate General Wathelet issued his Opinion in relation to the *Achmea* case on 19 September 2017.[67] According to the Advocate General, the arbitration clause in the Netherlands–Slovakia BIT constitutes no discrimination on grounds of nationality prohibited by EU law;[68] arbitral tribunals established under the investment treaty can submit requests for preliminary rulings and are therefore not incompatible with that mechanism;[69] the BIT's protections are broader than protections under EU law and the EU treaties, and they are different from them; however, that does not make them incompatible with EU law;[70] finally, the BIT's dispute settlement clause is compatible both with the allocation of powers fixed by the EU treaties and with the autonomy of the EU legal order.[71] If the investment-law friendly interpretation of the Advocate General were a precursor of things to come, this might have meant that intra-EU BITs need not be terminated. However, the Advocate General's Opinion is not binding on the CJEU.

---

[64] Belgian Ministry of Foreign Affairs, Foreign Trade and Development Cooperation, Minister Reynders submits request for opinion on CETA <https://diplomatie.belgium.be/en/newsroom/news/2017/minister_reynders_submits_request_opinion_ceta> accessed 30 April 2018.

[65] Belgian Ministry of Foreign Affairs, Foreign Trade and Development Cooperation, CETA—Belgian Request for an Opinion from the European Court of Justice <https://diplomatie.belgium.be/sites/default/files/downloads/ceta_summary.pdf> accessed 30 April 2018.

[66] The decision of German Federal Court of Justice of 3 March 2016 is available here (in German) <http://juris.bundesgerichtshof.de/cgi-bin/rechtsprechung/document.py?Gericht=bgh&Art=en&client=12&nr=74612&pos=0&anz=1&Blank=1.pdf> accessed 2 May 2018.

[67] CJEU, Case C-284/16 *Slovak Republic v Achmea BV*, Opinion of Advocate General Wathelet, 19 September 2017, ECLI:EU:C:2017:699.

[68] ibid para 65.

[69] ibid paras 126 *et seq*.

[70] ibid paras 183–228.

[71] ibid paras 229–72.

16.16 The judgment of the CJEU was issued on 8 March 2018,[72] and its conclusions are diametrically opposed to Advocate General Wathelet's. The CJEU did not discuss the issue of discrimination but focused on the autonomy of the EU legal order. It held that an arbitral tribunal constituted under the BIT 'may be called on to interpret or indeed to apply' provisions of EU law, such as notably provisions relating to the freedom of establishment and the freedom of movement of capital.[73] The fact that an arbitral tribunal does not qualify as a court or tribunal of a member state means it cannot request a preliminary ruling.[74] (The preliminary ruling procedure would allow for debated questions of EU law to be submitted to the CJEU.) An arbitral award is only subject to review by courts of member states depending on the tribunal's own choice of seat and the extent to which national law allows such review.[75] In the present case, it was the choice of Germany as the seat of the arbitration that enabled Slovakia to seek review of the award.[76] In short, the CJEU concluded that the Netherlands–Slovakia BIT includes a dispute settlement mechanism which 'could prevent … disputes from being resolved in a manner that ensures the full effectiveness of EU law, even though they might concern the interpretation or application of that law'.[77] The BIT's dispute settlement clause has 'an adverse effect on the autonomy of EU law' and similar provisions are incompatible with EU law.[78]

16.17 While the CJEU's judgment lands a blow on intra-EU BITs, it is yet early to draw general conclusions. The court's position is expressed in the particular context of the *Achmea* case. New questions already abound, including questions with respect to its implications for pending intra-EU disputes, including under the ECT,[79] disputes brought under the Convention on the Settlement of Investment Disputes between States and Nationals of Other States (ICSID Convention), and non-ICSID disputes with a seat outside the EU. Finally, it should also be noted that the CJEU emphasized that its analysis regarding the compatibility of a dispute settlement clause with the autonomy of the EU legal order took place in the context of an investment treaty concluded by a member state and *not* by the EU.[80] In other words, no conclusions should be drawn from the judgment about

---

[72] Case C-284/16 *Slovak Republic v Achmea BV*, Judgment (Grand Chamber), 8 March 2018, ECLI:EU:C:2018:158.
[73] ibid para 42.
[74] ibid para 49.
[75] ibid paras 51–53. The applicable arbitration clause provided for an ad hoc tribunal that 'shall determine its own procedure applying [the UNCITRAL Arbitration Rules]' art 8(5) of the Netherlands–Slovakia BIT.
[76] ibid para 52.
[77] ibid para 56.
[78] ibid paras 59–60.
[79] At the time of writing, and following the CJEU judgment, Spain is seeking to reopen two closed ECT proceedings. See Luke Eric Peterson, 'Spain Immediately Seeks to Test Whether ECJ Judgment Reaches to Energy Charter Treaty Cases; However Request to Reopen Two Closed Proceedings Also Raises Specter of Arbitrator Challenge' *Investment Arbitration Reporter* (9 March 2018).
[80] *Slovak Republic v Achmea BV* (n 72) para 58.

the compatibility of dispute settlement clauses in EU investment agreements with EU law.

F. Conclusions

16.18 This review of recent developments in the EU reveals that negotiations are ongoing and several agreements are a step closer to being approved or ratified. CETA is already in provisional application, although not its investment chapter. Now that the controverted issue of the division of competences between the EU and the member states has been settled by the CJEU, the topic that has moved centre stage and is likely to continue to dominate the agenda is the establishment of a permanent multilateral investment court. Nonetheless, as of the beginning of 2018, discussions on this project have moved to UNCITRAL and the latter's preoccupation is *multilateral reform of investment law* rather than the establishment of a multilateral court. Finally, some questions are currently pending before the CJEU and their resolution is eagerly awaited, while the recent CJEU judgment in the *Achmea* case will doubtless generate a lot of debate and fuel scholarly discussions. A lot is in flux and developments will surely be important in the years to come, even if their direction remains eminently uncertain.

17

RECENT TRENDS IN INVESTMENT LAW AND POLICY IN LATIN AMERICA

*Facundo Pérez-Aznar**

A. Introduction	17.01	C. Trends at the Regional Level and their Implications for Multilateral Forums	17.22
B. Trends in the Conclusion of Bilateral Agreements and in the Enactment of Legislation Related to Foreign Investments	17.07	D. Conclusion	17.36

A. Introduction

The purpose of this chapter is to provide a brief overview of new issues, approaches, or trends in the Latin American region relating to investment law and policy during 2017 and the first part of 2018.[1] The relationship of Latin America with investment arbitration is one of complexity, diversity, and nuance.[2] As this chapter will show, these characteristics can be seen in the experiences of the region during the period under analysis. **17.01**

During 2017 Latin American states have continued their engagement with international investment law. For instance, over the course of 2017, at least five **17.02**

---

* The author is grateful to Ariel Martins Mogo, Hugo Romero Martínez, Henrique Choer Moraes, Rodrigo Polanco Lazo, Lukas Montoya, Rodrigo Castillo de la Cerda, and other persons who preferred to remain anonymous for exchanges during the preparation of this work.

[1] For an analysis of some approaches to foreign investment in the region during the period 2013–2016, see Katia Fach Gómez and Catharine Titi, 'International Investment Law and ISDS: Mapping Contemporary Latin America' (2016) 17 Journal of World Investment & Trade 515. For an analysis of recent trends in the international investment regime in different developing countries (including Brazil and Chile from Latin America) see Fabio Morosini and Michelle Ratton Sanchez Badin (eds), *Reconceptualizing International Investment Law from the Global South* (CUP 2017).

[2] Catharine Titi, 'Investment Arbitration in Latin America: The Uncertain Veracity of Preconceived Ideas' (2014) 30 Arbitration International 357, 358.

international investment agreements (IIAs) were negotiated and signed by countries in the region.[3] There have also been an important number of IIAs being renegotiated, including IIAs concluded by Argentina and Chile. In addition, the year under analysis has been a productive one in terms of legislative work at the local level, both for the approval of IIAs (as it was the case in Brazil and Mexico) and for their termination (as was the case in Ecuador).

17.03 The political changes in Latin America (in particular the new administrations in Argentina, Brazil, and Ecuador with a more 'pro-market' view of the economy) during the last couple of years (coupled with the political changes in the United States with the Trump administration) have had an impact on the investment policy landscape in the region. The attempts to disengage from the existing investment regime in the region appear to have decreased. The outcome of the negotiations on the creation of a regional dispute settlement centre under the aegis of the Union of South American Nations (UNASUR) is unclear since six countries suspended membership to that organization. The states parties of the MERCOSUR (Argentina, Brazil, Paraguay, and Uruguay) signed the Protocol on Investment Cooperation and Facilitation (MERCOSUR Protocol) in April 2017. More recently, in January 2018, the updated version of the now so-called Progressive Agreement for Trans-Pacific Partnership (CPTPP), without the United States, was signed between eleven states, including Chile, Mexico, and Peru from Latin America. In addition, since August 2017, Canada, Mexico, and the United States have been renegotiating the North American Free Trade Agreement (NAFTA).[4]

17.04 Latin American countries have been very active in the rethinking of investment standards and investor–state dispute settlement (ISDS) mechanisms at the multilateral level. There appears to be a consensus among Latin American states that there are areas in which reform of the existing investment regime and ISDS mechanisms would be beneficial, although 2017 evidenced a variety of opinions on the specific areas requiring reform, the extent of reform needed, and how to proceed with that reform. There appears to be a division among those countries that support ISDS and see the solutions in bilateralism (eg Chile and Mexico), and those that consider that multilateralism should be the preferred tool for reform (eg Argentina and Ecuador). In a third view Brazil argues that the ISDS mechanism is flawed per se and for that reason it is focusing on state to state dispute settlement (SSDS) and investment facilitation.

17.05 Although it is not the purpose of this chapter to analyse the arbitral claims against Latin American countries, it is important to highlight that, in 2017, there were

---

[3] See United Nations Conference on Trade and Development (UNCTAD), *International Investment Agreements Navigator* <http://investmentpolicyhub.unctad.org/IIA> accessed 14 February 2018.

[4] North American Free Trade Agreement (signed 17 December 1992, entered into force 1 January 1994) (NAFTA).

an important number of arbitral decisions involving Latin American countries discussing important issues related to the investment regime.[5] According to the UNCTAD's database, from a total of sixty-seven cases with decisions in the different stages of the proceedings rendered during 2017, nineteen cases involved Latin American countries.[6] There were also an important number of new cases against countries from the region. From the fifty-three cases registered in 2017 under the ICSID Convention and the ICSID Additional Facility Rules, ten cases were against Latin American countries.[7] According to the UNCTAD database (which includes not only ICSID cases) twelve out of sixty-five investment cases involving IIAs initiated during 2017 were against Latin American countries.[8] The subject of the dispute in these cases is varied, covering different economic sectors such as transportation, telecommunications, hydrocarbons, services, and finance. The respondent states in these cases are Venezuela, Mexico, Peru, Argentina, Chile, Nicaragua, Panama, Uruguay, and Colombia, this last country being one of the 'newcomers' in the long list of respondent states.

In the following pages, we will first focus on the trends in the conclusion of bilateral agreements and the enactment of legislation related to foreign investments in Latin America, then we will turn to the trends at the regional level and its implications for multilateral forums, and finally we will elaborate some general conclusions from these findings. 17.06

B. Trends in the Conclusion of Bilateral Agreements and in the Enactment of Legislation Related to Foreign Investments

There were important developments in the region concerning the conclusion of bilateral agreements and the enactment of legislation related to foreign investments, which shows the engagement of Latin America with investment agreements but also distinctive approaches in the search of balanced solutions for the negotiation of IIAs. 17.07

The new administration that took office in Argentina in December 2015 made clear that the attraction of foreign investments was a key factor in its economic policy and returned to the IIA arena with the negotiation of new agreements, 17.08

---

[5] For a discussion of some of the arbitral decisions involving the region rendered during 2017 see Chapters 8 and 9.
[6] UNCTAD, *Investment Dispute Settlement Navigator* <http://investmentpolicyhub.unctad.org/ISDS> accessed 14 February 2018.
[7] International Centre for Settlement of Investment Disputes (ICSID), 'The ICSID Caseloads–Statistics' (Issue 2018-1) <https://icsid.worldbank.org/en/Documents/resources/ICSID%20Web%20Stats%202018-1(English).pdf> accessed 14 February 2018.
[8] UNCTAD, *Investment Dispute Settlement Navigator* (n 5).

which (with the exception of the MERCOSUR Protocol discussed) maintain traditional substantive provisions and ISDS. However, as discussed further in this chapter, Argentina's approach appears to be cautious in terms of drafting; and the country seeks to use its experience in previous investment disputes in order to improve the investment regime.

17.09 Roughly fifteen years after concluding its last bilateral investment treaty (BIT), Argentina has begun again to negotiate new BITs and, most recently, renegotiate some of its fifty-eight old investment treaties (eg with Mexico and Canada). In 2016, it concluded a BIT with Qatar and started negotiations with Japan.[9] In 2017 it signed two new IIAs: a free trade agreement (FTA) with Chile and the MERCOSUR Protocol on investments. The main characteristics of Argentina's negotiations are that it does not use a model BIT and the first draft generally comes from the negotiating counterparty. These three agreements with Qatar, Chile, and MERCOSUR show that Argentina focuses on introducing more advanced provisions vis-à-vis some particular issues (eg definition of investments, security exceptions, obligations for investors, more detailed procedural rules) rather than on any revolutionary change, and that it negotiates more on a case-by-case basis. In 2016 Argentina also concluded a trade and investment framework agreement (TIFA) with the United States, establishing an institutional framework between the parties to promote and cooperate on investment and trade through a bi-national Council on Trade and Investment.[10]

17.10 Argentina signed the FTA with Chile in November 2017.[11] Unlike Chile, this is the first time Argentina concludes an FTA with an investment chapter. With this treaty Argentina departs considerably from the Qatar BIT, which was a more traditional BIT. The investment chapter in the FTA with Chile includes provisions not common in Argentine BITs, such as non-conforming measures (Article 8.11) and denial of benefits (Article 8.15). A comparison among different IIAs of the Contracting Parties shows that the chapter is based on the Pacific Alliance Additional Protocol on Investments between Colombia, Mexico, and Peru signed in 2014, which in turn is based on the US–Chile FTA and NAFTA. The main innovations that appear in the Argentina–Chile FTA (and not in the Pacific Alliance Protocol) include a negative list of what does not constitute an investment (Article 8.1.1), an article on the right to regulate (Article 8.4), a definition

---

[9] Facundo Pérez-Aznar, 'The Recent Argentina–Qatar BIT and the Challenges of Investment Negotiations' *Investment Treaty News* (12 June 2017) <https://www.iisd.org/itn/2017/06/12/recent-argentina-qatar-bit-challenges-investment-negotiations-facundo-perez-aznar/> accessed 14 February 2018.

[10] The text of the agreement is available at UNCTAD, *Investment Policy Hub* <http://investmentpolicyhub.unctad.org/Download/TreatyFile/5099> accessed 14 February 2018.

[11] The text of the agreement is available at UNCTAD, *Investment Policy Hub* <http://investmentpolicyhub.unctad.org/IIA/CountryOtherIias/8#iiaInnerMenu> accessed 14 February 2018.

of 'like circumstances' (Articles 8.5.3 and 8.6.3), express language indicating that the most favoured nation clause does not apply to jurisdiction and substantive obligations (Article 8.6.4), the obligation for investors to comply with the legislation of the host state (Article 8.16), general exceptions inspired by GATT Article XX (Article 8.19), and the right to regulate on intellectual property matters (Article 8.20). Concerning dispute settlement, the agreement also includes innovative provisions, such as the possibility to resort to mediation (Article 8.23), the duty to disclose the existence of third-party funders (Article 8.27), the duty of the tribunal to decide on objections related to its competence or its jurisdiction as a preliminary manner (Article 8.33), and the challenge of arbitrators when there are justifiable doubts as to their impartiality or independence (Article 8.41).[12]

17.11 During 2017 Brazil continued with its policy of negotiating agreements on cooperation and facilitation of investments (ACFIs). The Brazilian model investment agreement departs from the traditional design of BITs, particularly due to the exclusion of key standards such as fair and equitable treatment and indirect expropriation, the focus on cooperation, and on the facilitation of investments and by eliminating the possibility of ISDS.[13] From 2015, Brazil has signed agreements based on its model ACFI with Angola, Chile, Colombia, India, Malawi, Mexico, Mozambique, Peru (as a chapter in the Economic and Trade Expansion Agreement signed in 2016), and within the MERCOSUR with the Intra-MERCOSUR Protocol on investments signed in 2017.

17.12 The next step for Brazil is to put ACFIs into operation. It is auspicious that the approval processes in the Brazilian Congress advanced rapidly during 2017. The Agreement between Brazil and Peru signed in 2016 was the first investment agreement approved in the last sixty years.[14] The Brazilian Congress has also approved the ACFIs with Angola, Chile, Malawi, Mexico, and Mozambique. The Brazil–Angola ACFI became the first ACFI to enter into force, after its ratification in 2017.[15] This shows a departure from the 1990s when the Brazilian Congress refused to approve the traditional BITs Brazil had signed at that time, and reflects a

---

[12] Article 8.41 provides that when an arbitrator has been challenged by a disputing party, the other disputing party may accept the challenge. If the other disputing party does not agree to the challenge or the challenged arbitrator does not resign, the challenging party may, at its election, request the president of the ICSID Administrative Council or the Secretary of the Permanent Court of Arbitration (PCA) to adopt a decision on the challenge.

[13] For a detailed analysis of Brazilian ACFIs, see generally Michelle Ratton Sanchez Badin and Fabio Morosini, 'Navigating between Resistance and Conformity with the International Investment Regime: The Brazilian Agreements on Cooperation and Facilitation of Investments (ACFIs)' in Morosini and Ratton Sanchez Badin *Reconceptualizing International Investment Law* (n 1) 188–210.

[14] Carlos M Cozendey and Abrão M Árabe Neto, 'Um balanço até aqui dos acordos de investimentos' (29 May 2017) <http://www.itamaraty.gov.br/pt-BR/discursos-artigos-e-entrevistas-categoria/outras-autoridades-artigos/16357-um-balanco-ate-aqui-dos-acordos-de-investimentos-valor-economico-29-05-2017> accessed 14 February 2018.

[15] Decreto Nº 9.167, Diário Oficial da União (13 October 2017) 1 <http://www.planalto.gov.br/ccivil_03/_ato2015-2018/2017/decreto/D9167.htm.> accessed 14 February 2018.

political will to make ACFIs effective. In 2017, the Brazilian Chamber of Foreign Trade (CAMEX) approved the regulation governing the functioning of the ombudsman for direct investments provided for in the different ACFIs.[16]

17.13 The Brazilian model has prevailed in Brazil's negotiation with other Latin American countries. However, no Latin American country so far has adopted the Brazilian model as its own. This can be explained in part by Brazil's economic and political weight and in the fact that the country has not offered ISDS as an alternative. However, there can be other policy reasons. It is reported that during negotiations of IIAs within the region, one country's requests to use SSDS instead of ISDS were quickly rejected by their negotiating counterparties.

17.14 There have been important changes in Ecuador's investment policy during 2017. The Ecuadorian President Rafael Correa had formalized, on 16 May 2017, Ecuador's withdrawal from BITs concluded with sixteen countries: Argentina, Bolivia, Canada, Chile, China, France, Germany, Italy, the Netherlands, Peru, Spain, Sweden, Switzerland, the United Kingdom, the United States, and Venezuela. Ecuador had previously denounced its other BITs between 2008 and 2010.[17] The denunciations followed the recommendations of CAITISA, an audit commission composed of government officials, academics, lawyers, and civil society groups that examined Ecuador's BITs between 2013 and 2015.[18]

17.15 However, the new Ecuadorian government that took office some days later announced that it may renegotiate and renew these BITs (and even readopt the ICSID Convention) because it believes the absence of foreign investor protections could deter potential new FDI.[19] In October 2017 the Ecuadorian hydrocarbons minister considered that the departure of Ecuador from ICSID was a 'problem' that investors would have to consider and that Ecuador was willing to consider other solutions, including allowing the submission of complaints before the local courts of the investors' home states.[20]

---

[16] Secretaria Executiva da Câmara de Comércio Exterior, Resolution 12 (16 February 2017) <http://camex.gov.br/ombudsman-de-investimentos-diretos-oid?id=1792.> accessed 14 February 2018.

[17] 'Ecuador Denounces its Remaining 16 BITs and Publishes CAITISA Audit Report' *Investment Treaty News* (12 June 2017) <https://www.iisd.org/itn/2017/06/12/ecuador-denounces-its-remaining-16-bits-and-publishes-caitisa-audit-report/> accessed 14 February 2018.

[18] Comisión para la Auditoría Integral Ciudadana de los Tratados de Protección Recíproca de Inversiones y del Sistema de Arbitraje Internacional en Materia de Inversionesiones en Ecuador, *Informe Ejecutivo* (May 2017) <http://caitisa.org/index.php/home/enlaces-de-interes> accessed 14 February 2018.

[19] César Coronel Ortega, 'Ecuador and ISDS—A Rough Journey and a Possible New Beginning' (21 December 2017) <http://oxia.ouplaw.com/page/Ecuador-and-ISDS> accessed 14 February 2018.

[20] 'Carlos Pérez García (Ministro de Hidrocarburos de Ecuador): no pertenecer al Ciadi afecta a potenciales inversores de Ecuador' *El Universo* (6 October 2017) <https://www.eluniverso.com/noticias/2017/10/06/nota/6417607/no-pertenecer-ciadi-afecta-potenciales-inversores-ecuador-detalla> accessed 14 February 2018.

17.16 In January 2018, the President of Ecuador declared the attraction and promotion of investment was a state policy, created the Strategic Committee on Promotion and Attraction of Investment and assigned the Ministry of Foreign Affairs the role of formulating and renegotiating future IIAs.[21] The government has stated that it already has a draft of a model BIT.[22] Recently an Ecuadorian delegate expressed that her country 'is prepared to give good investors the tools to invest in [Ecuador] through the investment contracts' and that 'the new BITs would be drafted to ensure the investor will have obligations too'.[23]

17.17 Chile has continued with its policy of negotiating investment agreements as part of FTAs influenced by treaties previously negotiated with developed countries.[24] During 2017, Chile, as noted, signed the FTA with Argentina and updated the FTAs with China and Canada, including those FTAs' investment chapters. In the case of the Chile–Canada FTA, the updated version includes language clarifying the Contracting Parties' understanding of already existing obligations in the treaty, provisions that seek to re-affirm a states' right to regulate, a new article on corporate social responsibility, improvements to the ISDS mechanism (including with respect to preliminary objections, awarding of costs, ethical considerations, third-party funding, and transparency), encouragement of alternatives to arbitration (such as mediation and consultation), and a clause enjoining the Parties to adopt a permanent multilateral tribunal.[25] In the investment chapter in its FTAs, Chile still follows the US–Chile FTA, which in turn follows the NAFTA model.[26] During 2016, Chile has signed a BIT with Hong Kong[27] and an FTA with Uruguay.[28] The latter treaty does not include an investment chapter (investment relations are covered by the 2010 Chile–Uruguay BIT) but it includes different provisions that refer expressly to 'investments', in particular those dealing with labour, environment, and health matters.

---

[21] Decreto Ejecutivo No 252, Registro Oficial (11 January 2018) <https://minka.presidencia.gob.ec/portal/usuarios_externos.jsf> accessed 14 February 2018.

[22] 'Los 10 temas económicos que marcarán al Ecuador en el 2018' *El Comercio* (2 January 2018), <http://www.elcomercio.com/actualidad/temas-economicos-ecuador-economia-2018.html> accessed 14 February 2018.

[23] UNCTAD, *Investment Policy Hub*, Statement by the Ecuatorian delegate <http://investmentpolicyhub.unctad.org/Upload/Documents/Blanca%20Gomez%20de%20la%20Torre%20(Ecuador)_plenary.pdf> accessed 14 February 2018.

[24] For an analysis of Chile's investment policy and agreements see Rodrigo Polanco Lazo, 'The Chilean Experience in South-South Investment and Trade Agreements' in Morosini and Ratton Sanchez Badin, *Reconceptualizing International Investment Law* (n 1) 47–94.

[25] UNCTAD, *Investment Policy Hub*, Statement by the Chilean delegate <http://investmentpolicyhub.unctad.org/Upload/Documents/Jorge%20Vidal_Chile_IIA%20Conference_plenary%20statement.pdf. > accessed 14 February 2018.

[26] ibid.

[27] The text of the agreement is available at UNCTAD, *Investment Policy Hub* < http://investmentpolicyhub.unctad.org/Download/TreatyFile/5413> accessed 14 February 2018.

[28] The text of the agreement is available at UNCTAD, *Investment Policy Hub* <http://investmentpolicyhub.unctad.org/Download/TreatyFile/5408> accessed 14 February 2018.

17.18 In the case of Mexico, during 2017, the Mexican government ratified BITs with the United Arab Emirates, Turkey, and Haiti, and the ACFI with Brazil.[29] In December 2017 the president promulgated the BIT with Turkey[30] and in January 2018 the one with the United Arab Emirates.[31] Also in an important shift in its investment policy, Mexico signed the ICSID Convention in January 2018, which now has to be approved by the Mexican Senate for its ratification.[32]

17.19 There were also other important developments in Latin America on the adoption of internal legislation related to international investment policy. In 2016, Argentina had enacted Law 27,328 on public-private partnership (PPP) contracts.[33] The Law allows for PPP contracts between the national government and private parties to agree to international arbitration on issues related to infrastructure projects, but requires the executive power to approve and report to the National Congress on any international arbitration clauses that may be so agreed upon. During 2017, Regulatory Decree 118/2017, amended by Decree 936/2017, was adopted providing that international arbitration is limited to situations where the PPP contractors have foreign shareholders with the minimum percentage that is established in the bidding documents of each project.[34] In addition, in September 2017, the Argentine Senate approved the draft Law on International Commercial Arbitration, which incorporates contents of the UNCITRAL Model Law.[35] The Argentine minister of justice explained that the law 'constitutes a fundamental tool to attract foreign investment'.[36]

---

[29] The approval decrees of the treaties are available at DOF: 17/11/2017, DOF: 22/12/2017 in <http://dof.gob.mx/> accessed 14 February 2018.

[30] Acuerdo entre el Gobierno de los Estados Unidos Mexicanos y el Gobierno de la República de Turquía para la Promoción y Protección Recíproca de las Inversiones, DOF: 15/12/2017 <http://dof.gob.mx/nota_detalle.php?codigo=5507960&fecha=15/12/2017> accessed 14 February 2018.

[31] Acuerdo entre el Gobierno de los Estados Unidos Mexicanos y el Gobierno de los Emiratos Árabes Unidos para la Promoción y Protección Recíproca de Inversiones, DOF: 24/01/2018, <http://www.dof.gob.mx/nota_detalle.php?codigo=5504958&fecha=17/11/2017> accessed 14 February 2018.

[32] Secretaría de Economía de México, 'México firma el Convenio sobre Arreglo de Diferencias Relativas a Inversiones entre Estados Nacionales y de Otros Estados' (11 January 2018) <https://www.gob.mx/se/prensa/mexico-firma-el-convenio-sobre-arreglo-de-diferencias-relativas-a-inversiones-entre-estados-nacionales-y-de-otros-estados> accessed 14 February 2018.

[33] Law 27, 328, BO: 30/11/2016 <http://servicios.infoleg.gob.ar/infolegInternet/anexos/265000-269999/268322/norma.htm> accessed 14 February 2018.

[34] Regulatory Decree 118/2017, BO: 20/02/2017 <http://servicios.infoleg.gob.ar/infolegInternet/anexos/270000-274999/271968/texact.htm> accessed 14 February 2018.

[35] The text of the draft law and the current status can be found at <http://www.senado.gov.ar/parlamentario/parlamentaria/verExp/parla/PE-228.16-PL> accessed 14 February 2018.

[36] Ministerio de Justicia y Derechos Humanos de Argentina, 'El Senado dio media sanción a la normativa de arbitraje comercial internacional' (11 September 2017) <https://www.justicia2020.gob.ar/senado-dio-media-sancion-la-normativa-arbitraje-comercial-internacional/> accessed 14 February 2018; 'Media sanción en el Senado para la ley de arbitraje' *El Cronista* (8 September 2017) <https://www.cronista.com/economiapolitica/Media-sancion-en-el-Senado-para-la-ley-de-arbitraje-20170908-0061.html> accessed 14 February 2018.

17.20 In Venezuela the National Constituent Assembly enacted the Constitutional Law on Productive Foreign Investments in December 2017.[37] The law provides that foreign investments will be subject to the jurisdiction of the courts of Venezuela, but it also states that Venezuela may make use of other dispute resolution mechanisms created within the framework of integration schemes 'provided that internal judicial remedies have been exhausted' (Article 6). The chapter on 'Duties and rights of foreign investors and investment conditions for investments' includes, *inter alia*, provisions on legal security, national treatment, remission of profits or dividends, responsible business conduct, and other obligations for foreign investors (Articles 25–36). The final provision provides that 'any investment framework agreement or international commercial agreement on investments' subscribed or renegotiated by Venezuela, shall be based on the provisions established in the law.

17.21 Coming back to the conclusion of IIAs, other countries from the region that have concluded BITs in recent years are Uruguay and Paraguay, in addition to their participation in the MERCOSUR Protocol, and the countries from Central America. Uruguay signed a BIT with Japan in 2015 that entered into force in April 2017, which includes different provisions preserving the right to regulate, *inter alia*, on health matters.[38] At the same time, after about seventeen years without signing any BIT (and in a pattern similar to that of Argentina), Paraguay signed a BIT with Qatar in February 2018.[39] In 2017, Paraguay concluded a TIFA with the United States. Concerning Central America, Costa Rica, El Salvador, Honduras, Nicaragua, and Panama signed with South Korea the South Korea–Central America FTA in February 2018, which includes an investment chapter with an ISDS mechanism.[40] In 2015, Guatemala had signed a BIT with Turkey and Honduras had signed an FTA with Peru.

C. Trends at the Regional Level and their Implications for Multilateral Forums

17.22 The political changes in Latin America in the last two years have had an impact not only on the conclusion of bilateral agreements and the enactment of

---

[37] Gaceta Oficial de la República Bolivariana de Venezuela, 439.406–412 (29 December 2017) the text is also available in the UNCTAD, *Investment Policy Hub* <http://investmentpolicyhub.unctad.org/InvestmentLaws> accessed 14 February 2018.

[38] The text of the agreement is available at UNCTAD, *Investment Policy Hub* <http://investmentpolicyhub.unctad.org/Download/TreatyFile/3284> accessed 14 February 2018.

[39] 'Paraguay y Qatar firman acuerdos económicos' *La Nación* (12 February 2018) <https://www.lanacion.com.py/negocios_edicion_impresa/2018/02/12/paraguay-y-qatar-firman-acuerdos-economicos/ > accessed 14 February 2018.

[40] Yoon Ja-young, 'Korea Signs FTA with Central America' *The Korea Times* (21 February 2018) <http://www.koreatimes.co.kr/www/common/vpage-pt.asp?categorycode=367&newsidx=244537> accessed 22 February 2018.

legislation related to foreign investments, but also on the investment policies in the region and the position of Latin American countries in multilateral forums.

17.23   The incorporation of Argentina in the Pacific Alliance (comprising Chile, Colombia, Mexico, and Peru) was one of the foreign policy promises wielded during the electoral campaign by President Mauricio Macri and the first step was taken in June 2016, when the Alliance granted Argentina the status of 'observer'. This perhaps can explain in part a more conciliatory position of Argentina towards IIAs and ISDS in line with the Pacific Alliance contracting states. The Pacific Alliance is an integration initiative that focuses more on commercial rather than political integration, unlike the original idea under the MERCOSUR. The preference of Argentina and other countries for the first option could have long-term implications in terms of models of integration for Latin America.

17.24   In the case of Brazil, the changes of government in August 2016 appears not to have impacted its policy of concluding ACFIs, although the new government has made clear that the Pacific Alliance is also a priority for Brazil, which is one of the reasons it has concluded ACFIs with all of the Pacific Alliance members.[41] Brazil was also one of the countries that suspended its membership in UNASUR, something unthinkable a couple of years ago. Bolivia and Venezuela appear to have kept their critical positions towards the existing investment regime, while the new Ecuadorian administration appears, as discussed, to have a more friendly position towards IIAs and ISDS.

17.25   In April 2017, the states parties of the MERCOSUR signed the Intra-MERCOSUR Protocol on Investments. The Protocol draws significantly on the Brazilian model ACFI. The emergence of that agreement has implications at the level of investment policy, as it represents a step towards the regionalization of the Brazilian model, although it also introduces provisions not found in previous ACFIs.[42] An important aspect of the agreement is that the MERCOSUR members, by signing the Protocol, have decided to discipline the relations amongst themselves based on this model.[43] In addition, the Protocol borrows the existing MERCOSUR dispute settlement mechanisms (Article 24), which include a permanent appeal

---

[41] Ministério da Indústria, Comércio Exterior e Serviços, 'Senado aprova Acordo de Cooperação e Facilitação de Investimentos entre Brasil e México' (20 April de 2017) <http://www.mdic.gov.br/noticias/2452-senado-aprova-acordo-de-cooperacao-e-facilitacao-de-investimentos-entre-brasil-e-mexico> accessed 14 February 2018.

[42] Facundo Perez Aznar and Henrique Choer Moraes, 'The MERCOSUR Protocol on Investment Cooperation and Facilitation: Regionalizing an Innovative Approach to Investment Agreements' *EJIL: Talk!* (12 September 2017) <https://www.ejiltalk.org/the-mercosur-protocol-on-investment-cooperation-and-facilitation-regionalizing-an-innovative-approach-to-investment-agreements/> accessed 14 February 2018.

[43] ibid.

jurisdiction.⁴⁴ In doing so, it marks a difference from prior ACFIs and a step in the institutionalization of investment dispute settlement.

Another important development with effects in Latin America is that, since August 2017, Canada, Mexico, and the United States have been renegotiating the NAFTA. During renegotiations Mexico was a staunch defender of the ISDS mechanism in Chapter 11.⁴⁵ The United States pushed for the elimination of ISDS or at least for an amendment that would allow a country to 'opt-out' of ISDS. However, rather than accept an ISDS opt-out right, Mexico and Canada responded that they would prefer to simply remove ISDS altogether.⁴⁶ Mexico has even proposed having a permanent dispute resolution body to resolve investor–state disputes under the NAFTA similar to that in the Comprehensive Economic and Trade Agreement (CETA) between the European Union and Canada in an attempt to break the impasse in the renegotiations.⁴⁷ Mexico also considered passing an investment protection law including ISDS mechanisms similar to the ones appearing in the NAFTA to reassure foreign investors in its energy sector.⁴⁸

17.26

A further development also involving other regions but with effects directly in Chile, Mexico, and Peru is the conclusion of CPTPP in January 2018.⁴⁹ The CPTPP is modelled on the Trans-Pacific Partnership (TPP), which was signed in February 2016, but never entered into force following the withdrawal of the United States. The CPTPP incorporates the entire TPP into the new treaty (Article 1), but it suspends the application of certain provisions of the previous text (Article 2). In relation to the TPP's investment chapter, in the new agreement investor–state arbitration will not be permitted for alleged breaches of investment agreements or investment authorizations and the possibility of claiming a breach of the minimum standard of treatment by investors in the financial services sector

17.27

---

⁴⁴ ibid.
⁴⁵ 'Canada, Mexico Reject Proposal to Rework Nafta Corporate Arbitration System William Mauldin' *Wall Street Journal* (29 January 2018) <https://www.exportaz.org/2018/02/01/wsj-canada-mexico-reject-proposal-rework-nafta-corporate-arbitration-system/> accessed 14 February 2018.
⁴⁶ 'NAFTA in Play: The State of Play Following the Sixth Round of Negotiations' *Baker Mckenzie* (1 February 2018) <https://www.bakermckenzie.com/en/insight/publications/2018/02/the-state-of-play-following-the-sixth/> accessed 14 February 2018.
⁴⁷ Cosmo Sanderson, 'Mexico Proposes Permanent Dispute Resolution Body for NAFTA' *Global Arbitration Review* (30 November 2017) <https://globalarbitrationreview.com/article/1151247/mexico-proposes-permanent-dispute-resolution-body-for-nafta?utm_source=Law%20Business%20Research&utm_medium=email&utm_campaign=8944140_GAR%20Headlines%2030%2F11%2F2017&dm_i=1KSF,5BPCC,JIQNZ9,KK4AS,1> accessed 14 February 2018.
⁴⁸ 'Mexico Offers to Match Oil Groups Nafta wish' *Argus* (27 September 2017), <http://www.argusmedia.com/news/article/?id=1542543#.Wc-1J1atuEo.twitter> accessed 14 February 2018.
⁴⁹ The text of the CPTPP is available at <https://www.mfat.govt.nz/assets/CPTPP/Comprehensive-and-Progressive-Agreement-for-Trans-Pacific-Partnership-CPTPP-English.pdf> accessed 14 March 2018.

is excluded (Annex).⁵⁰ Australia and New Zealand excluded the application of the ISDS clause in the context of their reciprocal relationship, but no other country (including Latin American ones) has resorted to this option.

17.28 The last development at the regional level took place at UNASUR. Since 2008 the creation of the proposed Centre for the Settlement of Investment Disputes (*Centro de solución de controversias en materia de inversiones*) has been negotiated under the auspices of UNASUR.⁵¹ It was reported that there were at least four meetings of negotiators during 2017 in Buenos Aires and Quito and that the text of the document was almost finished.⁵² However, the political changes in the region, the different points of view among the member states with regards to the functioning of the organization, and key issues related to ISDS in particular, coupled with the need for consensus required inside the organization in order to adopt a final document, have prevented faster progress. Decisions by Argentina, Brazil, Chile, Colombia, Peru, and Paraguay in April 2018 to suspend membership in UNASUR,⁵³ creates uncertainty about the future of this organization and the outcome of that initiative.

17.29 Moving to the multilateral level, there were interesting discussions at the 'UNCTAD Annual International Investment Agreements Conference: Phase 2 of IIA Reform' held in Geneva in October 2017 with an active participation from Latin American countries.⁵⁴ The discussions among participants appear to show a consensus among states that there are areas in which reform of the existing international investment regime would be beneficial, although there were a variety of opinions on the specific areas requiring reform, the extent of reform needed, and how to proceed to that reform.

17.30 In terms of investment policy, in general terms Argentina was of the view that in order to guarantee the well functioning of the system and ultimately its survival, states should negotiate treaties with balanced and coherent provisions, including not only procedural but also substantive provisions.⁵⁵ Argentina considered that in order to achieve this all states should engage in multilateral negotiations rather than in bilateral solutions. Ecuador underlined the need for

---

⁵⁰ ibid.
⁵¹ See Fach Gómez and Titi, 'International Investment Law and ISDS: Mapping Contemporary Latin America' (n 1) 518–22.
⁵² Diario Oficial El Peruano, No 14204 (9 September 2017) 47–48 <http://elperuano.pe> accessed 14 February 2018.
⁵³ Santiago Dapelo, 'La Argentina y otros cinco países abandonan la Unasur' *La Nación* (21 April 2018) <https://www.lanacion.com.ar/2127623-la-argentina-y-otros-cinco-paises-abandonan-la-unasur> accessed 30 April 2018.
⁵⁴ For documents related to the conference including the statements of many delegations see <http://investmentpolicyhub.unctad.org/EventsCalendar/Details/546> accessed 14 February 2018.
⁵⁵ UNCTAD, *Investment Policy Hub*, Statement by the Argentine delegate (October 2017) <http://investmentpolicyhub.unctad.org/Upload/Documents/IIA%20Conference_ARGENTINA'S%20%20FINAL%20SPEECH%20PLENARY_Ariel%20Martins.pdf> accessed 14 February 2018.

reform expressing that the country was sympathetic with the efforts to implement an appeal system.[56] Colombia expressed that the investment regime needed flexible provisions to allow itself to progress and evolve, and it shared the idea of a 'lighter approach to multilateralism'.[57] The position of Chile reflected a preference for bilateralism underlining its experience in negotiating investment chapters in FTAs.[58] Brazil noted the challenges of discussing contentious issues at the multilateral level, such as protection rules and dispute settlement clauses, and believed that investment facilitation could be a pragmatic way to advance in the multilateral arena.[59]

The differences in the views of Latin American countries with regard to dispute settlement mechanisms were more clearly revealed in the meeting of the UNCITRAL working group on ISDS reform held in Vienna in November and December of 2017.[60]   17.31

On one side, Chile and Mexico joined the position of the United States, Japan, and Russia and very often moderated the extent of certain problems and stressed that bilateral tools and drafting techniques already exist that can be used to address any perceived problems, as an alternative to multilateralism.[61] Chile and Mexico argued that many of the criticisms were based on perceptions rather than on actual data and, regarding the duration of proceedings, wondered whether ISDS was slower than other dispute settlement methods at the national and international level. They further expressed their preferences for ad hoc arbitration instead of any permanent mechanism.[62] In a similar line, Costa   17.32

---

[56] UNCTAD, *Investment Policy Hub*, Statement by the Ecuatorian delegate (October 2017) <http://investmentpolicyhub.unctad.org/Pages/unctad-annual-high-level-iia-conference-phase-2-of-iia-reform> accessed 14 February 2018.

[57] UNCTAD, *Investment Policy Hub*, Statement by the Colombian delegate (October 2017) <http://investmentpolicyhub.unctad.org/Upload/Documents/Colombia%20-%20Nicolas%20Palau%20van%20Hissenhoven_final%20plenary.pdf> accessed 14 February 2018.

[58] UNCTAD, *Investment Policy Hub*, Statement by the Chilean delegate (October 2017) <http://investmentpolicyhub.unctad.org/Upload/Documents/Jorge%20Vidal_Chile_IIA%20Conference_plenary%20statement.pdf> accessed 14 February 2018.

[59] UNCTAD, *Investment Policy Hub*, Statement by the Brazilian delegate (October 2017) <http://investmentpolicyhub.unctad.org/Upload/Documents/Brazil-%20Mr.%20Abrão%20Neto-%20Plenary%20Session.pdf. > accessed 14 February 2018.

[60] For documents related to the meeting including the recordings of the discussions see <http://www.uncitral.org/uncitral/en/commission/working_groups/3Investor_State.html> accessed 14 February 2018.

[61] Luke E Peterson 'Analysis: What did Governments Agree (and Disagree) on at Recent UNCITRAL Meetings on Investor-State Dispute Settlement Reform?' *Investment Arbitration Reporter* (4 January 2018) <https://www.iareporter.com/articles/analysis-what-did-governments-agree-and-disagree-on-at-recent-uncitral-meetings-on-investor-state-dispute-settlement-reform/> accessed 14 February 2018.

[62] See Statement by Mexico, Working Group III (Dispute Settlement), 34th session, Recordings 28/11/2017 14:00:00—28/11/2017 17:00:00 and Statement by Chile Working Group III (Dispute Settlement), 34th session, Recordings 29/11/2017 09:30:00—29/11/2017 12:30:00.

Rica stated that ISDS was an important tool in its policy of attracting foreign investments.[63]

17.33 Meanwhile, Argentina, and Ecuador (and perhaps to a lesser degree Colombia and Honduras) together with the European Union and Canada, cast doubt on the efficacy of following only bilateral solutions, and saw a need for a more systemic, multilateral set of solutions.[64] Argentina pointed out that it is common for states to receive negative responses to their requests to renegotiate BITs, an issue making bilateral approaches to reform inadequate. Argentina opined that an appeal authority could guarantee the necessary coherence and consistency.[65] Argentina also stated that the discussion on dispute settlement is a very important one, but that it was necessary to also discuss substantive issues.[66]

17.34 Representing a third approach, Brazil stressed that its experience in the design of ACFIs could contribute to finding solutions to the problems raised. Brazil stated that among the reasons why it decided not to have ISDS in its agreements was the fact that it may be considered discriminatory against national investors who do not have the chance to resort to international arbitration.[67] That argument is debatable since ACFIs still create a special regime for foreign investors not available for nationals. From Brazil's perspective, ISDS was intrinsically 'flawed', so no reforms would be enough to redeem the system.[68] The general position held by Brazil during the discussions was that many of the criticisms raised towards the ISDS regime such as in terms of costs, time, transparency, and dispute prevention, were covered under the Brazilian ACFIs.[69]

17.35 Finally, it is important to highlight the increasing participation of Latin American countries in the discussions at the Organisation for Economic Co-operation and Development (OECD) Investment Committee[70] and its Freedom of Investment Roundtable, where since 2011 governments have been evaluating key aspects of investment treaties at regular bi-annual meetings.[71] The OECD has played an

---

[63] Statement by Costa Rica, Working Group III (Dispute Settlement), 34th session, Recordings 29/11/2017 14:00:00—29/11/2017 17:00:00.

[64] See Peterson (n 61). See also Statement by Argentina, Working Group III (Dispute Settlement), 34th session, Recordings 29/11/2017 09:30:00—29/11/2017 12:30:00.

[65] See statement by Argentina, Working Group III (Dispute Settlement), 34th session, Recordings 30/11/2017 14:00:00—30/11/2017 17:00:00.

[66] ibid.

[67] See Statement by Mexico, Working Group III (Dispute Settlement), 34th session, Recordings 28/11/2017 14:00:00—28/11/2017 17:00:00.

[68] ibid.

[69] See eg Statement by Brazil, Working Group III (Dispute Settlement), 34th session, Recordings 29/11/2017 14:00:00—29/11/2017 17:00:00.

[70] The list of Latin American countries participating in the OECD Investment Committee includes Mexico and Chile as OECD member countries, and Argentina, Brazil, Colombia, Costa Rica, and Peru as associates.

[71] The list of Latin American countries participating in the OECD Freedom of Investment Roundtable includes Argentina, Brazil, Chile, Colombia, Costa Rica, Mexico, Paraguay, and Peru.

important role in defining the investment policy at the global level in the last years and the participation of Latin American countries in the discussions have allowed the organization to have a more complete view regarding the different positions within the region in order to find balanced approaches.

D. Conclusion

17.36 Latin American countries continue to see IIAs as a tool to promote foreign investments, although they follow different approaches in the conclusion of such agreements depending on the different models of development that each country follows. Quite often they try to find innovative solutions to identified problems based in their own experiences. Attempts to disengage from the existing investment regime in the region appear to have decreased. However, there appears to be a consensus among Latin American states that there are areas in which reform of the existing investment regime and ISDS mechanisms would be beneficial. The main challenge is that there is a variety of opinions on the specific areas requiring reform, the extent of reform needed, and how to proceed with that reform.

17.37 The Intra-MERCOSUR Protocol on Investments has important implications at the level of investment policy, as it represents a step towards the regionalization of the Brazilian ACFI model and the institutionalization of investment dispute settlement through the existing MERCOSUR dispute settlement mechanisms. However, it is questionable whether ACFIs could become a model for the entire region since that model has not been followed in the negotiation of IIAs when Brazil is not involved. The negotiations of the creation of a regional dispute settlement centre under the aegis of UNASUR is another very important development that requires closer scrutiny by states and academics since it has been the laboratory of many interesting ideas, notwithstanding the new developments concerning that organization.

17.38 At the multilateral level Latin American countries appear to share a rhetoric that more equilibrium is needed in IIAs and agree that some changes in the current investment regime would be desirable although they have different views as to whether bilateral or multilateral reform processes are appropriate, as well as what outcomes should be pursued. In order to enrich the discussion it would be desirable for additional Latin American countries to become engaged in the relevant discussions at UNCITRAL and other forums. In this respect it has to be recalled that many of the current proposals for reform are based on the experiences of Latin American countries. It is also necessary to broaden the discussion concerning transparency, since the negotiations of IIAs and investment disputes involving Latin American governments remain to a great extent confidential, hampering public debate on this important issue for the economic development that the region is continuously seeking.

17.39 The practice of foreign investment regulation involving Latin American countries has profoundly influenced the way we understand international investment law today.[72] Latin America has long been a 'laboratory' for the development of international law and, more specifically, for taking an independent approach to law on the treatment of aliens and their property.[73] In recent years the region has been experimenting with novel approaches to the ongoing international investment law process and Latin America may play a decisive role in the worldwide design of the future investment dispute settlement system.[74] There is still, however, work to be done in order to fully take advantage of the experience and ideas from the region in defining the investment policy at the global level.

---

[72] Jorge E Viñuales, 'Concluding Observations: The Laws and the Judge of Foreign Investment' in Attila Tanzi et al (eds), *International Investment Law in Latin-America: Problems and Prospects* (Brill 2016) 823–33, 824.

[73] Attila Tanzi, Alessandra Asteriti, Rodrigo Polanco Lazo, and Paolo Turrini, 'Introduction' in Attila Tanzi et al (eds), *International Investment Law in Latin-America: Problems and Prospects* (Brill 2016) 1–20, 3.

[74] Fach Gómez and Titi, 'International Investment Law and ISDS: Mapping Contemporary Latin America' (n 1) 534.

18

NORTH AMERICA INVESTMENT LAW AND POLICY

2017

*David Schneiderman**

A. Introduction	18.01	C. Investment Treaty Policy	18.11
B. Jurisprudence	18.02	D. NAFTA Renegotiation	18.21

A. Introduction

It has been a consequential year for North America investment law and policy. This chapter addresses developments in three distinct sections. It turns, first, to a discussion of the *Eli Lilly v Canada* dispute. Second, new investment treaty policy adopted by the three North American Free Trade Agreement (NAFTA)[1] partners is addressed. Lastly, NAFTA renegotiations are taken up. The latter turned out to be the most important set of North American developments since 1994, the year NAFTA entered into force.

B. Jurisprudence

Only a single investment arbitration dispute warrants discussion, namely, the dispute between the Indiana-based pharmaceutical Eli Lilly and the government of Canada.[2] Eli Lilly sought to protect two drugs from generic competition. Having

---

* I am grateful to Ladan Mehranvar, Armand de Mestral, and to Hugo Perezcano Díaz for guidance, two anonymous reviewers for comments, and the Social Science and Humanities Research Council for support. The chapter was substantially completed in March 2018 and reports on events to the end of 2017.

[1] North American Free Trade Agreement (signed 17 December 1992, entered into force 1 January 1994) (NAFTA).

[2] *Eli Lilly and Company v The Government of Canada*, ICSID Case No UNCT/14/2, Award (16 March 2017) paras 232, 235. *TransCanada Corporation and TransCanada PipeLines Limited v United*

secured these patents—in the case of one drug, for a seventeen-year period—renewals were denied by the regulatory authority, Health Canada, and subsequently in Canadian courts. Eli Lilly's patents, Canadian authorities concluded, were invalid for 'lack of utility'. Eli Lilly claimed that Canada's patent rules amounted to a radical and discriminatory departure from Canada's traditional utility test, upsetting the company's expectations concerning renewal of its patents.[3] This institutional behaviour offended the minimum standard of treatment under international law (MST) and amounted to an unlawful expropriation under NAFTA resulting in Cdn $500 million in damages.[4]

18.03   The tribunal unanimously rejected every one of the investor's claims (not all of which will be discussed here).[5] The tribunal's reasoning turned on the question of whether the Canadian policy change was a radical and dramatic change. This question—described as 'the fundamental question'[6]—is the common thread that unites the tribunals' discussion of the standard of treatment due to Eli Lilly. Before turning to that unifying thread, it is worth mentioning the tribunal's views about liability for judicial measures under NAFTA.

1. Judicial misconduct

18.04   Each of the patent decisions were affirmed by the Federal Court of Canada (Trial and Appellate levels) while leave to appeal to the Supreme Court of Canada was denied. Given these facts, Canada argued that only a denial of justice warranted a tribunal finding a treaty breach. Both the United States and Mexico (under Article 1128) agreed with Canada's submission. The United States argued, more specifically, that there was no ground for liability in cases where the domestic legal

---

States of America, ICSID Case No ARB/16/21, was a high profile dispute concerning refusal to approve, for environmental reasons, construction of a pipeline from Alberta to refineries in the United States. The dispute was discontinued, by order of the Secretary-General of ICSID on 24 March 2017, as a consequence of the Trump administration's change in policy approving construction. See: Luke Eric Peterson, 'TransCanada Says It Has Permit For Keystone Pipeline, and ICSID Case Is Swiftly Discontinued' *Investment Arbitration Reporter* (24 March 2017) <https://www.iareporter.com/articles/transcanada-says-it-has-permit-for-keystone-pipeline-and-icsid-case-is-swiftly-discontinued/> accessed 29 May 2018.

[3] According to *Eli Lilly*, the traditional utility test enabled the introduction of commercial success and post-filing testing. This was replaced by a heightened promise of utility doctrine that, *inter alia*, ignored post-filing evidence of commercial use. *Eli Lilly* (n 1) para 232.

[4] The claimant also alleged that Canada was in violation of obligations arising under Chapter 17 of NAFTA, which the tribunal concluded it had no jurisdiction to consider in light of the NAFTA Free Trade Commission Note of 31 July 2001.

See NAFTA Free Trade Commission, 'Notes of Interpretation of Certain Chapter 11 Provisions' (31 July 2001) <http://www.international.gc.ca/trade-agreements-accords-commerciaux/topics-domaines/disp-diff/NAFTA-Interpr.aspx?lang=eng> accessed 24 February 2018: '3. A determination that there has been a breach of another provision of the NAFTA, or of a separate international agreement, does not establish that there has been a breach of Article 1105(1)'.

[5] Composed of Albert van den Berg (President), Daniel Bethlehem, and Gary Born.

[6] *Eli Lilly* (n 1) para 307 (the claimant 'must succeed on this issue to prevail in this arbitration').

system 'conforms to a "reasonable standard of civilized justice" and is fairly administered'. Otherwise tribunals 'would become supranational appellate courts'.[7] The tribunal responded by declining to address this specific point for reasons of judicial economy. It, nevertheless, reasoned that, as the judicial branches are organs of the state, judicial acts 'may engage questions of expropriation'. Judicial takings, if not recognized in US law, are possible under NAFTA.[8] The tribunal admitted, at the same time, that it cannot serve as an 'appellate tier' in respect of national judicial decisions.[9]

The tribunal also adopted the standard of 'egregious and shocking' behaviour detailed in *Glamis Gold*—behaviour that includes 'manifest arbitrariness, blatant unfairness, a complete lack of due process, evident discrimination, or a manifest lack of reasons'—violations of which give rise to a breach of MST.[10] The tribunal, in other words, preferred to distinguish between breaches of the international minimum standard and denials of justice. It was 'unwilling to shut the door to the possibility that judicial conduct', other than that characterized as a denial of justice, can give rise to a NAFTA MST claim.[11] As no special deference is due to judicial behaviour in MST claims, it is hard to imagine what meaningful role denial of justice will play in future NAFTA disputes where judicial behaviour is at issue.

18.05

2. Legitimate expectations

Two further doctrinal elements are worth noting. First, the tribunal addressed the circumstances that constitute a 'dramatic change' in the legal regime so as to upset legitimate expectations. Eli Lilly's expert argued that, previously, applicants for a patent could satisfy the promise of utility merely by showing a 'scintilla of utility'. A second strand emerged out of the case law that demanded an 'elevated standard' of review.[12] This amounted, it was claimed, to a change of the legal regime so dramatic as to give rise to state liability. The claimant's argument was underscored by a comparative review of the law of the other two NAFTA parties to the dispute, in addition to other jurisdictions, which revealed a 'global consensus' that rendered Canada an outlier.[13]

18.06

---

[7] ibid paras 204, 208.
[8] US law has served as an important source for takings analysis in investment law ever since *Pope & Talbot Inc v Canada*, Ad hoc—UNCITRAL Arbitration Rules, Interim Award (26 June 2000) para 99 nn 71–72. On the domestic constitutional law origins of US investment treaty policy, see Kenneth J Vandevelde, *The First Bilateral Investment Treaties: U.S. Postwar Friendship, Commerce, and Navigation Treaties* (OUP 2017) ch 8.
[9] *Eli Lilly* (n 1) para 207, 221.
[10] *Glamis Gold Ltd v United States*, Ad hoc—UNCITRAL Arbitration Rules, Award (8 June 2009) para 616.
[11] *Eli Lilly* (n 1) paras 222–23.
[12] *Eli Lilly* (n 1) para 237 (expert evidence of Professor Norman Siebrasse).
[13] ibid para 260.

18.07 The tribunal was unmoved. It would be 'difficult' for the claimant to succeed, they observed, in circumstances where judicial decisions that gave rise to these changes 'were handed down over a period of more than six years'. After all, 'evolution of the law through court decisions is natural, and departures from precedent are to be expected', the tribunal declared.[14] Nor did a comparative outlook shed light on the purported dramatic departure within a single jurisdiction.[15]

18.08 This is a significant pronouncement in so far as tribunals, in earlier disputes, have insisted that fair and equitable treatment (FET) does not amount to 'freezing' a state's regulatory capacity.[16] Instead, there remains room for legal change. The problem is that tribunals have not been all that clear about what constitutes legitimate legal change and what does not. Moshe Hirsch maintains that legitimate expectations doctrine under FET allows for more regulatory flexibility than many will admit. He insists that there must be something more—exceptional factors, is how he describes them—beyond mere regulatory changes that diminish investment value.[17] In *Eli Lilly*, the tribunal described circumstances in which a change in the law does not give rise to liability. Where change is 'incremental and evolutionary' and where evolving 'doctrine has a reasonably solid foundation in prior authority', there will be no treaty violation.[18] Having failed to establish a dramatic change, the tribunal, rather than ending the inquiry, continued to address Eli Lilly's allegations.

3. Arbitrariness

18.09 A second element worth noting concerns what amounts to arbitrary conduct. The investor claimed that, having changed the standard for patent protection, precipitating unpredictability and incoherence in the pursuit of no legitimate purpose, Canada acted arbitrarily and so violated MST.[19] The tribunal reasoned that Canada had a 'legitimate public policy justification' for its patent doctrine. The standard of review to be applied in such cases is suggested by the following passage:[20]

> The Tribunal need not opine on whether the promise doctrine is the only, or the best, means of achieving these objectives. The relevant point is that, in the Tribunal's view, the promise doctrine is rationally connected to these legitimate policy goals.

---

[14] ibid paras 309–10.
[15] ibid para 377.
[16] See eg *BG Group Public Limited Company v Argentina*, Ad Hoc—UNCITRAL Arbitration Rules, Final Award (24 December 2007) para 298.
[17] Moshe Hirsch, 'Between Fair and Equitable Treatment and Stabilization Clause: Stable Legal Environment and Regulatory Change in International Law' (2011) 12 Journal of World Investment & Trade 783, 799.
[18] *Eli Lilly* (n 1) para 386.
[19] ibid para 430.
[20] ibid para 423.

The tribunal appears to have set a low bar by which to test state action for arbitrariness. 'Some level of unpredictability is present in the application of all law', the tribunal admitted.[21] So long as there is a 'rational connection'—in constitutional law, this is understood to be a low threshold for review of state action—the respondent will be absolved of liability. A rational policy approach, the tribunal concludes, is 'not an indication of arbitrariness in law'.[22]

C. Investment Treaty Policy

1. Gender

Canadian investment treaty policy underwent 'recalibration' in amendments to the Chile–Canada Free Trade Agreement signed in 5 June 2017 and not yet in force. Of particular note is a novel chapter on 'Trade and Gender', which is independent of the Agreement's investment chapter. The Gender chapter acknowledges the importance of 'incorporating a gender perspective into the promotion of inclusive economic growth', invoking Goal 5 of the UN Sustainable Development Goals (on 'Gender Equality') and affirms a commitment to implementing the Convention on the Elimination of all Forms of Discrimination Against Women. These commitments and affirmations, however, will not be the subject of dispute resolution.[23]

The investment chapter's new article on 'Corporate Social Responsibility' (CSR), however, could give rise to a dispute regarding gender discrimination in the case of monopolies and state enterprises should an investor incur 'loss or damage'.[24] The relevant article reaffirms the parties' commitment to encouraging enterprises to incorporate standards and guidelines having to do with such things as labour, environment, and 'gender equality'. By insisting on gender neutrality in their investment policy, the parties might be understood to be signalling that formal equality as between the sexes is to be expected. In which case, where state monopolies or enterprises provide a greater advantage to women over men by preferring, for instance, their hiring or promotion, this could give rise to an investment

---

[21] ibid para 421.
[22] ibid para 426.
[23] Government of Canada, 'Canada-Chile Free Trade Agreement, Appendix II: Chapter N bis–Trade and Gender, Art. N bis-06' <http://international.gc.ca/trade-commerce/trade-agreements-accords-commerciaux/agr-acc/chile-chili/fta-ale/2017_Amend_Modif-App2-Chap-N.aspx?lang=eng> accessed 23 February 2018.
[24] Government of Canada, 'Canada-Chile Free Trade Agreement, Appendix I: Chapter G-Investment, Article G-14 *bis*' <http://international.gc.ca/trade-commerce/trade-agreements-accords-commerciaux/agr-acc/chile-chili/fta-ale/2017_Amend_Modif-App1-Chap-G.aspx?lang=eng> accessed 23 February 2018.

dispute if it results in loss or damage for those not so preferred. If read together with the 'Trade and Gender' chapter, however, such affirmative and differential treatment would be justifiable in the interests of advancing the economic situation of women.

18.13 One additional change to the Chile–Canada Free Trade Agreement investment chapter is worth mentioning. A new footnote 2 has been added to the article on national treatment: 'For greater certainty, whether treatment is accorded in "like circumstances" under Article G-02 (National Treatment) or Article G-03 (Most-Favoured-Nation Treatment) depends on the totality of the circumstances, including whether the relevant treatment distinguishes between investors or investments on the basis of legitimate public policy objectives.'[25] The reference to 'legitimate policy objectives' appears to link up with Article G-01: 'Scope and Coverage', which identifies 'legitimate policy objectives' such as 'the protection of health, safety, the environment or public morals, social or consumer protection or the promotion and protection of cultural diversity'. This additional footnote seems to accord well with the reasoning of the *Eli Lilly* tribunal,[26] which addressed legitimate public policy objectives in the context of its discussion of arbitrariness. The only additional footnote to the relevant MST provision is as follows: 'Article G-05 (Minimum Standard of Treatment) shall be interpreted in accordance with Annex G-05 (Customary International Law).' The Annex defines customary international law as arising from 'a general and consistent practice of States that they follow from a sense of legal obligation'.[27]

2. Investment court

18.14 Canada in 2017 continued to wage a campaign to promote an investment court, a proposal originating out of the European Commission during the negotiation of the Transatlantic Trade and Investment Partnership (TTIP) with the United States. A version of the model was incorporated into EU–Canada Comprehensive Economic and Trade Agreement (CETA) not long after the election of the federal Liberal government. CETA entered into provisional force in October 2017. The investment chapter will require, however, the consent of each European state. Only seven out of twenty-eight member states have, or nearly have, ratified CETA. The Belgian state of Wallonia requested an opinion of the European Court of Justice in 2017 on the compatibility of CETA, including its investment

---

[25] The footnote appears to incorporate the discussion of national treatment in *SD Myers Inc v Canada*, Ad hoc—UNCITRAL Rules, First Partial Award and Separate Opinion (13 November 2000) para 246 (referring to 'legitimate public policy measures that are pursued in a reasonable manner' as being justifiable).

[26] These amendments to the Chile–Canada FTA were signed 5 June 2017, several months after the release of the *Eli Lilly* (n 1) award on 16 March 2017.

[27] Government of Canada, 'Canada–Chile Free Trade Agreement' (n 23).

chapter, with EU law.[28] Much work on ratification remains to be done, therefore, before CETA's investment chapter comes into force.[29]

The investment court model was offered as a response to European critics of investor–state dispute settlement (ISDS) having, among other features, a tribunal of first instance and another to hear appeals. Americans have remained cool to the proposal. Canadians, without any public consultation, embraced it, marketing the abrupt policy change as advancing a 'progressive' trade and investment agenda. The new model of dispute settlement looks little like a 'court', however. It appears to be more similar to World Trade Organization (WTO) dispute settlement mechanisms than to Canadian or EU judicial systems.[30] The model does offer prospects of greater consistency and fewer arbitral conflicts when compared to the status quo.[31] Because the model does not address substantive investor protections—too controversial a subject says UNCITRAL[32]—it may contribute only marginally to improving investor–state arbitral outcomes.[33]

18.15

Mexico's stance on the investment court model remains ambivalent. During the course of negotiations for a free trade agreement with the European Union—the seventh round of negotiations were concluded in December 2017—Mexico indicated a willingness to join onto the EU project even as it expressed scepticism about the proposal.[34] Nevertheless, Mexico is doubling down on ISDS. In January

18.16

---

[28] See: Laurens Ankersmit, 'Investment Court System In CETA To Be Judged By The ECJ' (*European Law Blog*, 31 October 2016) < https://europeanlawblog.eu/2016/10/31/investment-court-system-in-ceta-to-be-judged-by-the-ecj/> accessed 8 May 2018 and David Schneiderman, 'A Day of Reckoning with Democracy for Investors' (*CIGI Online*, 27 October 2016) <https://www.cigionline.org/articles/day-reckoning-democracy-investors> accessed 23 February 2018.

[29] European Parliament, 'CETA Ratification process: Latest Developments' (October 2017) <http://www.europarl.europa.eu/RegData/etudes/ATAG/2017/608726/EPRS_ATA(2017)608726_EN.pdf> accessed 23 February 2018.

[30] See eg Laura Puccio and Roderick Harte, 'From Arbitration to Investment Court System (ICS): The Evolution of CETA Rules' (*European Parliamentary Research Service*, June 2017) http://www.europarl.europa.eu/RegData/etudes/IDAN/2017/607251/EPRS IDA(2017)607251_EN.pdf accessed 23 February 2018, 15: 'The proposals for both tribunals (First Instance and Appeal) are ... very similar to the WTO AB,' the authors write, while the selection of so-called 'judges ... is quite different'. Also see: August Reinisch, 'The European Union and Investor-State Dispute Settlement: From Investor-State Arbitration to a Permanent Investment Court' in Armand de Mestral (ed), *Second Thoughts: Investor-State Arbitration Between Developed Democracies* (Centre for International Governance and Innovation, 2017) 355.

[31] See Gus Van Harten, 'The European Union's Emerging Approach to ISDS: A Review of the Canada-Europe CETA, Europe-Singapore FTA, and European-Vietnam FTA' (2016) 1 University of Bologna Law Review 138 <https://bolognalawreview.unibo.it/article/view/6318/6095> accessed 9 May 2018.

[32] Secretariat of United Nations Commission on International Trade Law, 'Possible Future Work in the Field of Dispute Settlement: Reforms of Investor-State Dispute Settlement (ISDS)' (20 April 2017) A/CN.9/917, 4/16.

[33] Céline Lévesque, 'The European Commission Proposal for an Investment Court System: Out with the Old, In with the New?' in Armand de Mestral (ed), *Second Thoughts: Investor-State Arbitration Between Developed Democracies* (CIGI Press 2017) 75.

[34] See 'Report On The 7th Round Of Negotiations between the EU and Mexico for Modernising the Trade Part of the EU-Mexico Global Agreement' (12–22 December 2017) <http://trade.

2018, fearing NAFTA's demise in the face of intransigent demands by the US, Mexico finally signed onto the ICSID Convention.[35]

3. TPP

18.17 Both Canada and Mexico remained committed to finalizing the Transpacific Partnership Agreement (TPP), an accord originally having twelve signatory states, including the United States. On the first day of the Trump presidency, however, the United States withdrew from the pact. Such deals, negotiated by earlier administrations, Trump declared were 'ridiculous', even as the United States had determined the content of a number of such treaties.[36]

18.18 Canada took the opportunity, during the course of the US presidential campaign in 2016, to conduct hearings about TPP under the auspices of the House of Commons Standing Committee on International Trade. This appeared to be mostly a delaying tactic until the smoke cleared after the US presidential election. The Committee released its report in April 2017 and it contained very few surprises. Among the recommendations regarding ISDS, the Committee suggested that future FTAs include 'open and transparent' mechanisms for dispute settlement and 'reaffirm the ability of government to regulate in the public interest'.[37]

18.19 Despite US withdrawal, the remaining eleven treaty partners decided to proceed with a revised, but substantially similar, agreement in October 2017. Dropped from the text were twenty-two provisions that US negotiators had extracted at the negotiating table.[38] This might be viewed as an enticement for a subsequent

---

ec.europa.eu/doclib/docs/2018/january/tradoc_156557.pdf> and Iana Dreyer, 'EU and Mexico Fail to Conclude Political Agreement on Trade Deal' (*Euractiv*, 21 December 2017) <https://www.euractiv.com/section/economy-jobs/news/eu-and-mexico-fail-to-conclude-political-agreement-on-trade-deal/> both accessed 22 February 2018. The final text of the EU–Mexico agreement includes an 'Investment Court'. See European Commission, 'Fact Sheet: Key Features of the EU-Mexico Trade Agreement' (21 April 2018) <http://europa.eu/rapid/press-release_MEMO-18-1447_en.htm> accessed 9 May 2018.

[35] Stephanie Nolan, 'Amid NAFTA Uncertainty, Mexican Exporters Shift Thoughts South and East' *The Globe and Mail* (16 February 2018) <https://www.theglobeandmail.com/report-on-business/international-business/amid-nafta-uncertainty-mexican-exporters-shift-thoughts-south-and-east/article38011475/> accessed 29 May 2018.

[36] Peter Baker, 'Trump Abandons Trans-Pacific Partnership, Obama's Signature Trade Deal' *The New York Times* (24 January 2017) <https://www.nytimes.com/2017/01/23/us/politics/tpp-trump-trade-nafta.html> accessed 29 May 2018. On the enhanced bargaining power of the US in the context of NAFTA negotiations see Maxwell A Cameron and Brian W Tomlin, *The Making of NAFTA: How the Deal Was Done* (Cornell University Press 2000).

[37] House of Commons Canada, 'Report of the Standing Committee on International Trade, "The Trans-Pacific Partnership Agreement: Benefits and Challenges for Canadians"' (April 2017) <http://www.ourcommons.ca/DocumentViewer/en/42-1/CIIT/report-6 accessed 23 February 2018> 58.

[38] 'Comprehensive And Progressive Agreement For Trans-Pacific Partnership: Preamble' <https://www.mfat.govt.nz/assets/CPTPP/Comprehensive-and-Progressive-Agreement-for-Trans-Pacific-Partnership-CPTPP-English.pdf> accessed 23 February 2018.

US administration to re-join the agreement. Excised from the scope of ISDS are investment agreements (contracts between investors and host states in natural resource, public utilities, and public infrastructure sectors) and investment authorizations (licences and other approvals granted to investors by host states). In addition, actions taken in the financial services sector will not amount to a breach of MST. These excisions do not appear to substantially weaken the agreement's investment chapter.

Some drama subsequently ensued in the final stages of negotiation, on the sidelines of the APEC Summit in November. Canada's Prime Minister Trudeau was a no-show at what was designated as a signing ceremony. Canada maintained that no final agreement had been concluded, insisting on further adjustments including renaming the pact the Comprehensive and Progressive Agreement for Trans-Pacific Partnership (CPTPP).[39] This is a mouthful, intended to signal that this agreement was as 'progressive' as CETA. If it seemed that Canada was all-in with the EU's investment law and policy project, the investment court model noticeably was absent from the agreement. Japan, which took a lead in re-launching TPP, appears to have been the resistant to the EU proposal, with both Japan and the EU preferring to omit an investment chapter from their trade agreement announced in December 2017. The new prime minister of New Zealand also expressed scepticism of ISDS upon her election in May 2017, resulting in a side agreement removing ISDS in disputes between Australia and New Zealand.[40] The disorder around finalizing the CPTPP, however, pales in comparison to the drama associated with the renegotiation of NAFTA, to which this chapter turns next.

18.20

D. NAFTA Renegotiation

1. US ISDS proposal

Candidate Trump characterized NAFTA as a disaster for the United States. Renegotiation, if not cancellation, of NAFTA loomed on the horizon. As Trump never specifically addressed NAFTA's investment chapter on the campaign trail, it was unclear what the US position would be entering into renegotiations. If past Republican (and even Democratic) policy is any guide, Trump would have been

18.21

---

[39] Marie Danielle Smith, ' "We Don't Know What Canada Wants": Japanese Chorus of Confusion Grows over Trudeau's TPP Position' *National Post*, (21 December 2017) (the deal was 'renamed per a request from Canada') <http://nationalpost.com/news/politics/we-dont-know-what-canada-wants-japanese-chorus-of-confusion-grows-over-trudeaus-tpp-position> accessed 6 March 2018.

[40] New Zealand Foreign Affairs and Trade, 'CPTPP Overview' <https://www.mfat.govt.nz/en/trade/free-trade-agreements/free-trade-agreements-concluded-but-not-in-force/cptpp/cptpp-overview/> accessed 27 February 2018.

expected to insist upon including rights that are touted as mirroring those found in the US Constitution.[41]

18.22 This appeared to be the case on the eve of renegotiations.[42] In July 2017, United States Trade Representative (USTR) Robert Lighthizer indicated that the United States would be seeking to strengthen NAFTA's investment chapter by securing 'important rights consistent with U.S. legal principles and practice, while ensuring that NAFTA country investors in the United States are not accorded greater substantive rights than domestic investors'.[43] These USTR objectives were expanded upon in November 2017. In updated negotiating objectives, USTR indicated it would seek to include procedures that more efficiently resolved disputes, ensured open and accessible dispute settlement, and enabled the submission of amicus briefs.[44] It was also an objective to '[p]rovide meaningful procedures for resolving investment disputes, while ensuring the protection of U.S. sovereignty and the maintenance of strong U.S. domestic industries'.[45] However, in October 2017 the United States had placed before its counterparts a vague proposal that ISDS only be available when state parties 'opt in' to NAFTA's investment chapter. In testimony before a Canadian House of Commons Committee, Deputy Minister Steve Verheul of Global Affairs Canada revealed that '[a]t the table, the U.S. promptly said they would opt out.'[46]

18.23 The rationale for this policy change appears to have been addressed in USTR Lighthizer's closing statement at the conclusion of the fourth round of NAFTA renegotiations. Ambassador Lighthizer declared that 'it is unreasonable to expect that the United States will continue to encourage and guarantee U.S. companies to invest in Mexico and Canada primarily for export to the United States'.[47] If

---

[41] See David Schneiderman, 'Writing the Rules of the Global Economy: How America Defines the Contours of International Investment Law' (2018) 6 *London Review of International Law* 255. For a historical background, see Vandevelde (n 8).

[42] Negotiations commenced on 16 August 2017 in Washington DC, with the second round in Mexico City (1–5 September 2017), the third round in Ottawa (23–27 September 2017), fourth in Washington DC (11–15 October 2017), and then a fifth round in Mexico City (17–21 November 2017).

[43] Office of The United States Trade Representative (USTR), 'Summary of Objectives for the NAFTA Renegotiation' (17 July 2017) <https://ustr.gov/sites/default/files/files/Press/Releases/NAFTAObjectives.pdf> accessed 23 February 2018, 9,

[44] These negotiating objectives are drawn from the Bipartisan Congressional Trade Priorities and Accountability Act of 2015, H.R. 2146 (114th), s102(b)(4)(H).

[45] USTR 'Summary of Objectives for the NAFTA Renegotiation' (November 2017) <https://ustr.gov/sites/default/files/files/Press/Releases/Nov%20Objectives%20Update.pdf> accessed 23 February 2018, 8–9.

[46] Canada House of Commons Standing Committee on International Trade, 'Evidence: Meeting No 92, 42nd Parliament, 1st Session' (4 December 2017) <https://www.ourcommons.ca/DocumentViewer/en/42-1/CIIT/meeting-92/evidence> accessed 23 February 2018.

[47] USTR, 'Closing Statement of USTR Robert Lighthizer at the Fourth Round of NAFTA Renegotiations' (October 2017) <https://ustr.gov/about-us/policy-offices/press-office/press-releases/2017/october/closing-statement-ustr-robert> accessed 23 February 2018.

US investment policy previously encouraged the movement of capital across borders, it was now about discouraging investment abroad by not providing what Lighthizer described as a form of 'political risk insurance paid for by the United States government'. This was 'absurd', he declared. This was an argument, also advanced by critics, that ISDS privatizes profit but socializes risk. Firms should be expected to calculate their own risks according to market disciplines and without a 'thumb on the scale', Lighthizer announced. An ISDS opt-in would have the advantage, he acknowledged, of getting the US labour movement to buy in to a revised NAFTA.[48]

If the Trump administration appeared intent on killing ISDS in NAFTA, the Bipartisan Congressional Trade Priorities and Accountability Act of 2015 may prove to be a speed bump. The Act directs the president to 'further strengthen the system of international trade and investment disciplines and procedures, including dispute settlement'. He is also directed to secure for American investors abroad 'important rights comparable to those that would be available under United States legal principles and practice'.[49] Congress is expected to be consulted about such things and can impede approval of any replacement treaty.[50] This seems unlikely, however, so long as Republicans control both the House and the Senate. There also is some debate about whether the president can unilaterally terminate NAFTA without Congressional approval.[51] Peak business organizations are opposed to giving up on ISDS but failed, in 2017, to influence negotiations. If negotiations are not complete by mid-2018, progress likely will be stalled as federal elections are due to occur in Mexico in July 2018 and then the US mid-term election in November 2018.[52]

18.24

2. Two amigos respond

Canada has been promoting investment treaties modelled upon NAFTA's investment chapter since 1994. Canada has expressed a preference for keeping dispute settlement in NAFTA but adjusting it so that it is in line with CETA's investment

18.25

---

[48] Jenny Leonard, 'Lighthizer: NAFTA 2.0 Could Shift "Paradigm," Win Over Labor And Business' 35(42) Inside US Trade (20 October 2017) <https://insidetrade.com/inside-us-trade/lighthizer-nafta-20-could-shift-paradigm-win-over-labor-and-business> accessed 29 May 2018.

[49] Bipartisan Congressional Trade Priorities and Accountability Act of 2015, H.R. 2146 (114th), s 102(b)(4) <https://www.govtrack.us/congress/bills/114/hr2146/text> accessed 24 February 2018.

[50] The details are outlined in Christopher Sands, 'Table Stakes: Congress Will Be Sitting across from Canada at the NAFTA 2.0 Negotiations' (*C.D. Howe E-Brief*, 13 July 2017) <https://www.cdhowe.org/sites/default/files/attachments/research_papers/mixed/EBrief%20261.pdf> accessed 24 February 2018.

[51] Compare Joel P Trachtman, 'Power to Terminate U.S. Trade Agreements: The Presidential Dormant Commerce Clause Versus an Historical Gloss Half Empty' (15 October 2017) <https://ssrn.com/abstract=3015981> accessed 8 May 2018 and Curtis A Bradley and Jack L Goldsmith, 'Presidential Control over International Law (2018) 131 Harvard Law Review 1201, 1223–26.

[52] Similar talks are planned in 2018 regarding the US–Korea FTA.

court model. Both Mexico and the United States, as mentioned, expressed resistance to adopting the EU model.[53] It is doubtful that removal of ISDS would be a deal breaker for Canada in NAFTA renegotiations.

18.26 Mexico also has come to accept ISDS as a common feature of investment treaty blueprints, even vigorously defending it against detractors at a recent UNCITRAL working group meeting on ISDS.[54] It is also, negotiators believe, a way of gaining the confidence of foreign investors to invest in Mexico. Mexico has signed over thirty BITs and has, with Canada, resisted the US proposal to remove ISDS from a revised NAFTA. Yet it does not appear to be a deal breaker for Mexico either. No mention of it was made by a group of Mexican senators associated with the ruling PRI party, for instance, who outlined six 'red lines' that they would not cross in NAFTA renegotiations.[55] According to Canadian Deputy Minister Verheul: 'Both Canada and Mexico have said that if this were to be the case, if the U.S. is going to opt out, Canada would opt out as well, and Mexico said they also would opt out. If the U.S. proposal were to be adopted—at this point, we are still opposing it—there would be no ISDS between NAFTA members.'[56] He does not mention, however, that ISDS would continue to be available as between Canada and Mexico under the CPTPP.

3. Gender and indigenous chapters

18.27 Among the proposals the Canadian delegation placed on the table were new chapters on 'Trade and Gender' and 'Trade and Indigenous Peoples'. The implications for NAFTA's investment chapter are not obvious. The 'Trade and Gender' chapter is modelled upon the Chile–Canada agreement finalized in 2017 and the implications for investment treaty law might be as ambiguous. The Indigenous chapter, however, has not been made public. Reports indicate that the proposal include sections on education, health, and economic development. There is, in addition, a reference to the United Nations Declaration on the Rights of Indigenous Peoples (UNDRIP). The reaction of NAFTA parties to the Canadian proposals

---

[53] Canada House of Commons Standing Committee on International Trade, 'Evidence: Meeting No 92' (n 46).

[54] Luke Eric Peterson, 'Analysis: What Did Governments Agree (And Disagree) On At Recent UNCITRAL Meetings On Investor-State Dispute Settlement Reform?' *Investment Arbitration Reporter* (4 June 2018) < https://www.iareporter.com/articles/analysis-what-did-governments-agree-and-disagree-on-at-recent-uncitral-meetings-on-investor-state-dispute-settlement-reform/> accessed 29 May 2018.

[55] Robbie Whelan, 'Mexican Senators Lay Out Six "Red Lines" For NAFTA Renegotiation; Group Of Senators From Ruling PRI Party To Reject A Modified Deal If Any Of The Six Lines Are Crossed' *Wall Street Journal* (5 October 2017) <https://www.wsj.com/articles/mexican-senators-lay-out-six-red-lines-for-nafta-renegotiation-1507243496> accessed 29 May 2018.

[56] Canada House of Commons Standing Committee on International Trade, 'Evidence: Meeting No.92' (n 46).

was mixed. Mexico was 'optimistic and complimentary about the text', it is reported,[57] even as its negotiating team did not invite any Mexican indigenous participation in the talks. There is no expectation that the United States will agree to such binding commitments.

Investment law mostly has been indifferent to the fact that many disputes implicate the rights of indigenous peoples. According to the UN Special Rapporteur, an 'alarming number of cases ... have resulted in serious violations of indigenous peoples' land, self-governance and cultural rights'.[58] Yet only a handful of disputes have acknowledged this fact or invited indigenous peoples to have any kind of presence in investment arbitration.[59] Conflict in this field, however, is endemic given how '[c]ommunal holdings of land are not conducive to good mainstream business practices'.[60] It was for this reason—because indigenous land holdings were chronically 'underused'—that the Mexican government amended the Constitution in 1992, in the lead up to NAFTA, so as to permit individual land holding and the commodification of communal Indian lands. This helped precipitate the Zapatista uprising in Chiapas on 1 January 1994, on the eve of NAFTA's coming into force.[61] Canada did seek to foreclose some disputes by excluding, as 'Future Measures' under NAFTA, measures taken to confer 'rights or preferences provided to aboriginal peoples' that ran afoul of some, but not all, provisions in Chapter 11.[62]

18.28

It is this linkage between land and foreign investment that prompted the Hupacasath First Nation to seek to enjoin the government of Canada entering into a BIT with the People's Republic of China without first consulting the Hupacasath. The investment treaty would have impacted negatively on their pending Aboriginal rights claim against the government of Canada, they argued. According to their reading of Canada's constitutional law, entering into this international treaty

18.29

---

[57] Jorge Barrera, 'Canada Proposes "Groundbreaking" NAFTA Chapter on Indigenous Rights' (*CBC News*, 1 December 2017) <http://www.cbc.ca/news/indigenous/nafta-indigenous-chapter-1.4429145> accessed 23 February 2018.

[58] United Nations Human Rights Council, 'Report of the Special Rapporteur on the Rights of Indigenous Peoples' (11 August 2016) UN Doc. A/HRC/33/42.

[59] For example *Glamis Gold* (n 10). See generally Judith Levine, 'The Interaction of International Investment Arbitration and Indigenous Peoples' in Fraeya Baetens (ed), *Investment Law Within International Law: Integrationist Perspectives* (CUP 2013) 106–28.

[60] Sharon Venne, 'Aboriginal Peoples and NAFTA: Colonization Continues to Run Amok' (1994) 5(3 & 4) Constitutional Forum 78. See also Ovide Mercredi, 'The MAI and First Nations' in Andrew Jackson and Matthew Sanger (eds), *Dismantling Democracy: The Multilateral Agreement and its Impact* (Lorimer 1998) 69.

[61] Jorge A Vargas, 'NAFTA, The Chiapas Rebellion, and the Emergence of Mexican Ethnic Law' (1994) 25 California Western International Law Journal 1, 75.

[62] Referring to national treatment (art 1101), most favoured nation (art 1102), performance requirements (art 1106), and senior management and boards of directors (art 1107) in NAFTA, Annex II, 'Reservations for Future Measures' <http://www.international.gc.ca/trade-commerce/trade-agreements-accords-commerciaux/agr-acc/nafta-alena/fta-ale/24_a2.aspx?lang=eng> accessed 25 February 2018.

required prior consultation. The Hupacasath application was denied both in the first instance and on appeal.[63] Both levels of court admitted, however, that the duty to consult could be triggered in the appropriate circumstances.[64] It is noteworthy that Article 19 of UNDRIP dictates a lower threshold for triggering consultation, leading to consent, 'before adopting and implementing legislative or administrative measures that *may affect*' indigenous peoples.[65] Even investors have an interest in securing the consent and participation of indigenous peoples, in advance of undertaking resource exploitation on their lands, instead of relying only upon state approval. Success of such projects is far less likely without it.[66]

18.30 The tension between investment law and indigenous rights cannot be willed away by disparaging it as 'political correctness'.[67] As the pressures of economic development continue to encroach on traditional lands, the investment law community needs to reconcile itself to this fact and devise measures and mechanisms that address the likelihood of ongoing conflict.

---

[63] *Hupacasath First Nation v Canada*, 2013 FC 900 (TD) para 59 (describing the claim as 'speculative, remote and non-appreciable') and *Hupacasath First Nation v Canada*, 2015 FCA 4 (CA) paras 77–78 (the claimants rely upon 'assumptions, conjectures and guesswork'). For a more detailed account see David Schneiderman, 'Investor Rights and the Judicial Denial of the Neoliberal Constitutionalism' in Simon Archer, Daniel Drache, and Peer Zumbansen (eds), *The Daunting Enterprise Of Law: Essays In Honour Of Harry W. Arthurs* (McGill-Queen's University Press 2017) 169–85. The worry was that Canada, in order to avoid violating its treaty obligations, would take steps injurious to the First Nation's interests.

[64] *Hupacasath First Nation* (2013) (n 63) para 68.

[65] United Nations Declaration on the Rights of Indigenous Peoples, UN Doc A/RES/61/295 (emphasis added) and see discussion in Risa Schwartz, 'Moving Toward a Trade and Indigenous Peoples' Chapter in a Modernized NAFTA' CIGI Paper No 144 (27 September 2017) <https://www.cigionline.org/publications/moving-toward-trade-and-indigenous-peoples-chapter-modernized-nafta> accessed 23 February 2018.

[66] 'Establishing conditions of transparency and trust are a vital pre-requisite for the success of a project, which involves a corporation arriving from a faraway place to pursue an investment in the lands of indigenous and tribal peoples' observes Arbitrator Phillipe Sands in his partial dissenting opinion in *Bear Creek Mining Corporation v Republic of Peru*, ICSID Case No ARB/14/2, Award (30 November 2017) para 7.

[67] FH Buckley, 'Trump and Canada May Chill a NAFTA Deal: Trudeau's Politically Correct Demands Only Heighten Antagonism With the President' *Wall Street Journal* (22 February 2018) <https://www.wsj.com/articles/trump-and-canada-may-chill-a-nafta-deal-1519341951> accessed 29 May 2018.

Part II

GENERAL ARTICLES

19

IMPORTING WTO GENERAL EXCEPTIONS INTO INTERNATIONAL INVESTMENT AGREEMENTS

Proportionality, Myths, and Risks

*Andrew D Mitchell, James Munro, and Tania Voon**

A. Introduction	19.01	C. Impact of General Exceptions on the Interpretation of Investment Protections	19.60
B. Comparing Policy Space under Investment Protections and WTO General Exceptions	19.10	D. General Exceptions and Clarifications in Modern Investment Treaty Practice	19.81
		E. Conclusion	19.111

A. Introduction

Many states, non-governmental organizations (NGOs), and international organizations have become increasingly concerned about the impact of international investment law on host states' capacity to regulate in the public interest. These concerns arise in part from the increasing use of investor–state dispute settlement (ISDS),[1] against both developed and developing

---

* This research was supported by the Australian Research Council pursuant to the Future Fellowship scheme (project number FT130100416). For helpful comments on earlier drafts the authors thank Elizabeth Sheargold, the two anonymous referees, and the participants at the Asia FDI Forum III (11–12 May 2017, Chinese University of Hong Kong). Andrew is a member of the Australian Government's Expert Advisory Group for Plain Packaging of Tobacco Products (an honorary position). He and Tania also conduct independent research in collaboration with the McCabe Centre for Law and Cancer and have advised governments on public health matters in international economic law. The views expressed are the authors' own and are not necessarily shared by any employer or other entity.

[1] UNCTAD, 'Investor-State Dispute Settlement: Review of Developments in 2016' (IIA Issues Note No 1, May 2017) UNCTAD/DIAE/PCB/2017/8, fig 1.

countries,[2] with all the attendant resource implications regardless of the outcome.[3] The perceived non-transparency and illegitimacy of many aspects of the ISDS framework aggravate these developments.[4] In particular, concerns have arisen from investment treaty tribunals' sometimes expansive interpretations of investment obligations[5] and arguably excessive awards against host states.[6]

19.02 Relevant stakeholders have responded in various ways to these difficulties, with many of the implemented or proposed reforms focusing on ISDS. For example, the United Nations Commission on International Trade Law (UNCITRAL) created a new set of transparency rules for treaty-based ISDS, which entered into force on 1 April 2014,[7] and then a related treaty on transparency (the so-called Mauritius Convention), which entered into force on 18 October 2017,[8] with currently three states parties (Canada, Mauritius, and Switzerland) and nineteen signatories (including Australia, the United States, and the United Kingdom). The European Commission has proposed a new investment court,[9] which is now incorporated in its preferential trade agreements (PTAs) with Canada (CETA)[10] and Viet Nam,[11] and which UNCITRAL has now agreed to consider in connection with ISDS reforms.[12] The United Nations Conference on Trade and Development (UNCTAD)[13] and the Organisation for Economic Co-operation

---

[2] ibid 2.

[3] See eg *Philip Morris Brands Sàrl v Uruguay*, ICSID Case No ARB/10/7, Award (8 July 2016) paras 583, 590(2); cf *Philip Morris Asia Limited v Australia* PCA Case No 2012–12 (UNCITRAL), Final Award Regarding Costs (8 March 2017) paras 103, 105, 107; see also Jarrod Hepburn, 'Final Award is Released in Philip Morris v. Australia case, but Crucial Costs Information is Redacted from Public View' *Investment Arbitration Reporter* (9 July 2017).

[4] See eg Gus Van Harten et al, *Public Statement on the International Investment Regime* (Osgoode Hall Law School, York University, 31 August 2010) <http://www.osgoode.yorku.ca/public-statement-international-investment-regime-31-august-2010/> accessed 7 November 2017; Tania Voon, Andrew D Mitchell, and James Munro, 'Legal Responses to Corporate Manoeuvring in International Investment Arbitration' (2014) 5(1) Journal of International Dispute Settlement 41.

[5] See eg *William Ralph Clayton and Others v Canada*, PCA Case No 2009–04 (UNCITRAL), Dissenting Opinion (17 March 2015) para 49; cf *Windstream Energy LLC v Canada*, PCA Case No 2013–22 (UNCITRAL), Award (27 September 2016) paras 7, 515(b).

[6] See eg UNCTAD, 'Investor-State Dispute Settlement: Review of Developments in 2014' (IIA Issues Note No 2, May 2015) UNCTAD/WEB/DIAE/PCB/2015/2, 5.

[7] UNCITRAL Rules on Transparency in Treaty-based Investor-State Arbitration (2013).

[8] United Nations Convention on Transparency in Treaty-based Investor-State Arbitration (entered into force 18 October 2017).

[9] European Commission, 'Concept Paper: Investment in TTIP and beyond—the path for reform' (May 2015) 4.

[10] Comprehensive Economic and Trade Agreement between Canada and the European Union (signed 30 October 2016, not yet in force but provisionally applied in part) ch 8 arts 8.27–8.30 (CETA).

[11] Free Trade Agreement between the European Union and Vietnam (not yet signed or in force) ch II s 3 arts 12–15.

[12] See eg Nikos Lavranos, *The First Steps towards a Multilateral Investment Court (MIC)* <http://www.ciarb.org/news/ciarb-news/news-detail/news/2017/07/13/the-first-steps-towards-a-multilateral-investment-court-(mic)> accessed 7 November 2017.

[13] See eg UNCTAD, 'Investment Policy Framework for Sustainable Development' (2015) UNCTAD/DIAE/PCB/2015/5.

and Development (OECD)[14] also continue to promote ISDS reform as part of their broader investment policy frameworks.

States have also responded to concerns with international investment law through apparent changes in treaty practice not limited to ISDS reforms. As we have discussed elsewhere, some states have terminated international investment agreements unilaterally or by consent.[15] More generally, the number of international investment agreements (IIAs, including bilateral investment treaties (BITs) and PTAs with investment chapters) being signed each year since the early 2000s has fallen, following a peak in the 1990s.[16] Further, states have been modifying substantive IIA provisions in an apparent attempt to preserve policy space. Importantly for this chapter, states increasingly combine multiple approaches to treaty drafting to safeguard their ability to regulate while still affording investors protections under IIAs. 19.03

This chapter examines the increasingly common approach of including in IIAs 'general exceptions' modelled on, or incorporated from, the law of the World Trade Organization (WTO). Although traditional IIAs include no such exceptions, a 2017 study found them in 45 per cent of a sample of 113 IIAs concluded between 2010 and 2015.[17] We investigate the utility of this approach, in terms of its effectiveness in increasing host states' policy space,[18] as well as the risks and uncertainty it creates with respect to that goal. We do so not through empirical data-driven methods but through doctrinal analysis of WTO law, investment law, and treaty law, as well as investigation of case studies of particular kinds of modern IIAs. 19.04

The use of WTO-style exceptions in IIAs deserves closer examination because IIA negotiators and treaty drafters do not typically provide guidance as to their 19.05

---

[14] See eg OECD, 'Policy Framework for Investment' (2015).
[15] See Tania Voon and Andrew D Mitchell, 'Ending International Investment Agreements: Russia's Withdrawal from Participation in the Energy Charter Treaty' (2018) 111 AJIL Unbound; Tania Voon and Andrew D Mitchell, 'Denunciation, Termination and Survival: The Interplay of Treaty Law and International Investment Law' (2016) 31(2) ICSID Review 413; Tania Voon, Andrew D Mitchell, and James Munro, 'Parting Ways: The Impact of Mutual Termination of Investment Treaties on Investor Rights' (2014) ICSID Review 451.
[16] See eg UNCTAD, 'Recent Trends in IIAs and ISDS' (IIA Issue Note No 1, February 2015) UNCTAD/WEB/DIAE/PCB/2015/1, 2.
[17] Amelia Keene, 'The Incorporation and Interpretation of WTO-Style Environmental Exceptions in International Investment Agreements' (2017) 18 Journal of World Investment & Trade 62, 65, 69.
[18] For confirmation of this purpose of including general exceptions, see eg Department of Foreign Affairs and Trade, Australia, *Fact Sheet: Investor–State Dispute Settlement (ISDS)* <http://dfat.gov.au/trade/agreements/kafta/fact-sheets/Documents/kafta-fact-sheet-investor-state-dispute-settlement-isds.pdf> accessed 7 November 2017; Andrew Newcombe, 'General Exceptions in International Investment Agreements' in Marie-Claire Cordonnier Segger, Markus W Gehring, and Andrew Newcombe (eds), *Sustainable Development in World Investment Law* (Wolters Kluwer 2011) 354, n 10 (referring to the official commentary on the 2003 Canadian Model Foreign Investment Protection Agreement).

intended operation; nor have investment treaty tribunals developed much guidance as to their interpretation or application. Moreover, only limited literature exists on the use of such exceptions in IIAs. Generally promoting their use,[19] Kurtz develops a 'taxonomy' of approaches to including WTO-style general exceptions in IIAs, focusing on the structure and content exceptions themselves (rather than their interaction with the rest of the IIA)[20] and the relevance of WTO jurisprudence to investment treaty arbitration.[21] Wu also identifies WTO-style general exceptions in IIAs as 'one mechanism through which the trade regime has influenced the substantive provisions of the investment regime'.[22] Focusing on the impact of general exceptions on tobacco control measures challenged under IIAs, Chaisse concludes that they are unlikely to add much to existing flexibilities inherent in investment obligations, such as the 'customary international law doctrine of police powers' in the context of expropriation.[23] Addressing environmental measures, Keene generally favours the use of general exceptions in IIAs,[24] but she suggests that they may be rendered inutile, for example in the face of an annex clarifying the expropriation obligation.[25] Other commentators have warned of the potential for general exceptions to be counterproductive in IIAs, for example by limiting the police powers doctrine or justifications for discrimination and thus restricting policy space.[26] Building on this existing work, this chapter draws particularly on IIAs concluded in the past few years to reveal the specific implications of varied approaches to WTO-style general exceptions. These variations significantly influence the impact of exceptions on investment obligations and thus host states' policy space.

---

[19] Jürgen Kurtz, *The WTO and International Investment Law: Converging Systems* (CUP 2016) 168–71, 228.

[20] ibid 193–202 (but see 184–85, 193–94). See also Suzanne Spears, 'The Quest for Policy Space in a New Generation of International Investment Agreements' (2010) 13(4) Journal of International Economic Law 1037, 1060–62.

[21] Kurtz (n 19) 218–28.

[22] Mark Wu, 'The Scope and Limits of Trade's Influence in Shaping the Evolving International Investment Regime' in Zachary Douglas, Joost Pauwelyn, and Jorge E Viñuales (eds), *The Foundations of International Investment Law: Bringing Theory into Practice* (OUP 2014) 169, 199.

[23] Julien Chaisse, 'Exploring the Confines of International Investment and Domestic Health Protections—Is a General Exceptions Clause a Forced Perspective?' (2013) 39 American Journal of Law & Medicine 332, 354 (see also 359). See also Barton Legum and Ioana Petculescu, 'GATT Article XX and International Investment Law' in Robert Echandi and Pierre Sauvé (eds), *Prospects in International Investment Law and Policy* (CUP 2014) 344.

[24] Keene (n 17) 89, 91.

[25] ibid 77, 86.

[26] See eg Newcombe (n 18) 367–68; Armand de Mestral and Lukas Vanhonnaeker, 'Exception Clauses in Mega-Regionals (International Investment Protection and Trade Agreements)' in Thilo Rensmann (ed), *Mega-Regional Trade Agreements* (Springer 2017) 75, 114–15; Céline Lévesque, 'The Inclusion of GATT Article XX Exceptions in IIAs: A Potentially Risky Policy' in Robert Echandi and Pierre Sauvé (eds), *Prospects in International Investment Law and Policy* (CUP 2014) 363, 364, 366–67. See also Nicholas DiMascio and Joost Pauwelyn, 'Nondiscrimination in Trade and Investment Treaties: Worlds Apart or Two Sides of the Same Coin?' (2008) 102 American Journal of International Law 48, 82–83, cf Spears (n 20) 1063.

The chapter begins in section B by setting out the key differences in policy space **19.06**
reflected in three core investment obligations (regarding expropriation, fair and
equitable treatment, and non-discrimination)[27] compared to the WTO general
exceptions in Article XX of the General Agreement on Tariffs and Trade 1994
(GATT)[28] and Article XIV of the General Agreement on Trade in Services
(GATS).[29] These WTO exceptions are limited to specific lists of recognized legitimate policy objectives, some of which are subject to a 'necessity' test in terms of
the connection to the challenged measure, whereas policy space embedded in investment obligations is not usually limited to any particular objectives or subject
to an explicit nexus requirement. The stringent interpretation of the overarching
requirements of the opening paragraph or *chapeau* ('hat') of the WTO general
exceptions may also render them less flexible than the core investment standards.
However, our analysis identifies how WTO jurisprudence grants leeway to WTO
members in justifying their measures under the general exceptions, such that those
exceptions cannot be assumed to be less deferential than flexibilities within substantive investment obligations. In particular, the WTO Appellate Body explicitly
recognizes the right of WTO members to choose their own 'level of protection'
with respect to a given objective, whereas investment tribunals sometimes instead
engage in a strict proportionality analysis, comparing the benefits of a challenged
host state measure with its adverse impact on the relevant foreign investor or investment. A WTO member may therefore have a greater expectation of policy
space under WTO general exceptions than does a host state whose measure is
challenged under investment obligations.

Section C contains an in-depth investigation of how the inclusion of WTO-style **19.07**
general exceptions in IIAs may affect the interpretation of these three obligations
and thus the policy space within them. The customary rules of interpretation of

---

[27] We focus on the nature and extent of policy space in the two regimes. We do not address the differing structural character of policy space being embedded in a substantive provision rather than a general exception, such as differences in how the burden of proof might be allocated or the characterization of an exception as an affirmative defence or a carve-out from the scope of substantive provisions. Nor do we address the historical, institutional, and epistemic factors that may have led to the differing approaches to policy space reflected in the WTO regime vis-à-vis the international investment regime. For such discussions, see eg Caroline Henckels, 'Scope Limitation or Affirmative Defence? The Purpose and Role of Investment Treaty Exception Clauses' in Lorand Bartels and Federica Paddeu (eds), *Exceptions in International Law* (OUP, forthcoming); Jorge E Viñuales, 'Seven Ways of Escaping a Rule: Of Exceptions and Their Avatars in International Law' in Bartels and Paddeu (ibid); Joost Pauwelyn, 'Defenses and the Burden of Proof in International Law' in Bartels and Paddeu (ibid); Markus Wagner, 'Regulatory Space in International Trade Law and International Investment Law' (2014) 36 University of Pennsylvania Journal of International Law 1, 15–34, 71–85.

[28] GATT Doc LT/UR/A-1/A/1/GATT/2, signed 30 October 1947, as incorporated in Marrakesh Agreement Establishing the World Trade Organization (entered into force 1 January 1995) Annex 1A (General Agreement on Tariffs and Trade 1994) (GATT).

[29] Marrakesh Agreement Establishing the World Trade Organization (entered into force 1 January 1995) Annex 1B (General Agreement on Trade in Services) (GATS).

treaties including IIAs, particularly as set out in the Vienna Convention on the Law of Treaties (VCLT),[30] mean that the inclusion of general exceptions provides relevant context for interpreting investment provisions such as those concerning expropriation, FET, and non-discrimination. Depending on how they are incorporated, such exceptions may therefore narrow the scope for tribunals to consider a host state's legitimate policy objectives at earlier stages of analysis, namely in assessing conduct against an investment obligation. The potential for investment treaty tribunals to rely on WTO case law regarding general exceptions may further diminish the available policy space in the IIA if tribunals follow WTO tribunals' explanation of the necessity test and approach to balancing without recognizing the significant deference accorded to WTO members in choosing their level of protection.

19.08 Section D catalogues the ways in which WTO-style general exceptions are being integrated into IIAs, in order to evaluate the consequences of overlaying investment protections with such exceptions. Some modern IIAs apply general exceptions to the entire investment chapter, with the risk that the policy space within investment disciplines may be unintentionally diminished in the interpretative process. This overlap between the flexibilities under international trade law and international investment law may be particularly problematic for IIAs that do not also clarify the scope of investment obligations. Other modern IIAs reduce this risk of overlap by applying general exceptions to a limited number of investment obligations, excluding core obligations regarding expropriation and fair and equitable treatment, often pairing the latter obligations with clarifications to ensure regulatory autonomy for host states. However, some of these IIAs fail to clarify the relevance of regulatory purpose in identifying 'like circumstances' or otherwise applying non-discrimination obligations in the investment context. This omission again creates the interpretative risk that applying general exceptions to non-discrimination obligations will unintentionally reduce the acknowledgement of legitimate regulatory objectives in assessing non-discrimination under international investment law. The stringent treatment of discrimination under the *chapeau* to the general exceptions may exacerbate this outcome. Several other recent IIAs (particularly under US influence) rely almost entirely on clarifications to positive investment obligations instead of WTO-style general exceptions to account for non-economic policy objectives. This approach fails to benefit from the additional layer of protection for policy space offered by general exceptions, potentially exposing host states to a proportionality requirement under core investment obligations.

19.09 In sum, we urge treaty drafters and negotiators to act cautiously in introducing general exceptions from the WTO context into IIAs. The impact on the

---

[30] Vienna Convention on the Law of Treaties (entered into force 27 January 1980) (VCLT).

interpretation of investment obligations is not always foreseeable, and the expected interaction between different treaty provisions as well as the underlying WTO/investment treaty case law must be considered in detail. The concept of proportionality, which sounds favourable to host state sovereignty, may conceal a more utilitarian approach to regulatory balancing in international investment law than the so-called balancing in the WTO context, which in fact prioritizes WTO members' chosen level of protection with respect to legitimate regulatory objectives. Treaties that combine selective use of general exceptions with effective clarifications of the core investment disciplines regarding expropriation, fair and equitable treatment, and non-discrimination may be best placed to implement the treaty parties' intentions regarding their scope of regulatory autonomy.

B. Comparing Policy Space under Investment Protections and WTO General Exceptions

1. Proportionality requirements in substantive investment obligations

19.10 In this section, we show how investment treaty tribunals have used concepts of proportionality in analysing various investment obligations, including provisions on indirect expropriation, fair and equitable treatment, and non-discrimination. Such concepts may be understood as providing a legitimate means for considering the interests of both the host state and the claimant investor, recognizing that regulatory objectives may entail some interference with foreign investments.[31] However, if too stringently applied, proportionality may also intrude too much on host states' regulatory autonomy, replacing difficult domestic policy determinations with the tribunal's own values.[32] An understanding of the use of proportionality in the investment context provides a basis for comparing the arguably greater policy space available through WTO general exceptions as interpreted by the WTO Appellate Body.

a. Expropriation

19.11 Most IIAs provide that expropriations are lawful only where four cumulative conditions are met: (i) due process of law; (ii) a public purpose; (iii) non-discrimination; and (iv) payment of compensation.[33] However, before

---

[31] See eg Benedict Kingsbury and Stephan W Schill, 'Public Law Concepts to Balance Investors' Rights with State Regulatory Actions in the Public Interest—The Concept of Proportionality' in Stephan W Schill (ed), *International Investment Law and Comparative Public Law* (OUP 2010) 75, 102–04; Caroline Henckels, *Proportionality and Deference in Investor–State Arbitration* (CUP 2015) 122.

[32] Kurtz (n 19) 202.

[33] See eg North American Free Trade Agreement (entered into force 1 January 1994) art 1110.1 (NAFTA).

assessing compliance with those conditions, and hence the lawfulness of an expropriation, the claimant must establish that expropriation has occurred.[34] The unambiguous seizure of property or transfer of title involves *direct* expropriation. The distinction between compensable *indirect* expropriation and non-compensable regulation by the host state is less clear. The tribunal in *SD Myers v Canada* did 'not rule out [the] possibility' that '[r]egulatory conduct by public authorities' could be found expropriatory.[35] However, tribunals are faced with the difficult determination of 'when, how and at what point an otherwise valid regulation becomes, in fact and effect, an unlawful expropriation'.[36]

19.12 Some tribunals have recognized a doctrine of police powers,[37] according to which the legitimate and *bona fide* exercise of powers generally accepted as 'falling within the police or regulatory power of states'[38] does not amount to expropriation, allowing host states flexibility to regulate in the public interest. Unlike WTO general exceptions, this doctrine does not restrict *a priori* the legitimate policy objectives of a host state.[39] For instance, in the context of police powers, the tribunal in *Tecmed v Mexico* acknowledged 'the due deference owing to the state when defining the issues that affect its public policy or the interests of society as a whole, as well as the actions that will be implemented to protect such values'.[40]

19.13 However, as the tribunal in *Pope & Talbot v Canada* noted with respect to police powers, 'a blanket exception for regulatory measures would create a gaping loophole in international protections against expropriation'.[41] According to the tribunal in *Firemans Fund v Mexico*, factors such as whether the challenged

---

[34] *Chemtura Corporation v Canada*, Ad hoc (UNCITRAL), Award (2 August 2010) para 242.
[35] *SD Myers Inc v Canada*, Ad hoc (UNCITRAL), First Partial Award (13 November 2000) para 281.
[36] See *Saluka Investments BV v Czech Republic*, PCA (UNCITRAL), Partial Award (17 March 2006) para 264.
[37] See eg *Técnicas Medioambientales Tecmed v Mexico* ICSID Case No ARB(AF)/00/2, Award (29 May 2003) paras 115, 119 (Tecmed); *Saluka* (n 36) paras 258, 262; *Fireman's Fund Insurance Company v Mexico*, ICSID Case No ARB(AF)/02/01, Award (14 July 2006) para 176(j); *Suez v Argentina*, ICSID Case No ARB/03/17, Decision on Liability (30 July 2010) paras 128, 147; *Chemtura* (n 34) para 266; *Philip Morris v Uruguay* (n 3) paras 287, 295, 301, 307. See also Heikki Marjosola and Alain Pellet, 'Police Powers or the State's Right to Regulate' in Meg N Kinnear et al (eds), *Building International Investment Law: The First 50 Years of ICSID* (Kluwer Law International 2015) 447, 449, 460.
[38] *Saluka* (n 36) para 263.
[39] See eg *LG&E Energy Corp (United States) v Argentina*, ICSID Case No ARB 02/1, Decision on Liability (3 October 2006) para 195 (. Cf *Philip Morris v Uruguay* (n 3) paras 291, 295; Chaisse (n 23) 354; DiMascio and Pauwelyn (n 26) 76, 83.
[40] *Tecmed* (n 37) para 122.
[41] *Pope & Talbot Inc v Canada*, Ad hoc (UNCITRAL), Interim Award (26 June 2000) para 99. See also *ADC Affiliate Limited v Hungary*, ICSID Case No ARB/03/16, Award (2 October 2006) para 423.

measure is non-discriminatory, proportionate and *bona fide*, and contributes to a public purpose, are intended to close the perceived 'gaping loophole' described in *Pope & Talbot v Canada*.[42] Proportionality, in particular, has become a tool for distinguishing non-compensable regulation from compensable expropriation,[43] whether as a qualification to the police powers doctrine or even in the absence of explicit recognition of such a doctrine. Thus, following a review of relevant case law, Marjosola and Pellet concluded:

> The proportionality test, although unavoidably subjective, allows a distinction between deprivations of property which are compensable (those which amount to a disproportionate deprivation of property) and those which are not (since they are proportional to the aim of general interest pursued).[44]

19.14 Several scholars have opined on the nature of proportionality in international investment law, identifying a series of increasingly intrusive steps or forms of proportionality.[45] Unfortunately, as Henckels and Alvarez have observed, investment treaty tribunals rarely articulate their approach to proportionality with the same sophistication and nuance.[46] Nevertheless, tribunals can often be understood as imposing only the most intrusive form of proportionality:[47] 'proportionality *stricto sensu*'.[48] This manifestation of proportionality assesses whether the burden or harm resulting from the regulatory action in question is excessive or disproportionate to the regulatory objective pursued. Commentators have criticized the application of this form of proportionality in the context of investment treaty arbitration on the basis of its subjectivity and variability.[49]

---

[42] *Fireman's* (n 37) n 162.
[43] cf Thomas Cottier et al, 'The Principle of Proportionality in International Law: Foundations and Variations' (2017) 18 Journal of World Investment & Trade 628, 656, 659.
[44] Marjosola and Pellet (n 37) 458. See also Erlend M Leonhardsen, 'Looking for Legitimacy: Exploring Proportionality Analysis in Investment Treaty Arbitration' (2011) 3(1) Journal of International Dispute Settlement 95, 120–25.
[45] See eg Kingsbury and Schill (n 31) 85–88; Caroline Henckels, 'Indirect Expropriation and the Right to Regulate: Revisiting Proportionality Analysis and the Standard of Review in Investor–State arbitration' (2012) 15(1) Journal of International Economic Law 223, 226–28; Federico Ortino, 'Investment Treaties, Sustainable Development and Reasonableness Review: A Case Against Strict Proportionality Balancing' (2017) 30 Leiden Journal of International Law 71, 72–73, 87–88. See also Cottier et al (n 43), 629–30, 655–56.
[46] Henckels, 'Indirect Expropriation' (n 45) 233, 234; Henckels, *Proportionality and Deference* (n 31) 124; José E Alvarez, 'The Use (and Misuse) of European Human Rights Law in Investor–State Dispute Settlement' in Franco Ferrari (ed), *The Impact of EU Law on International Commercial Arbitration* (Juris 2017) 519, SSRN version 75.
[47] Henckels, 'Indirect Expropriation' (n 45) 233, 236; Ortino (n 45) 73.
[48] Henckels, 'Indirect Expropriation' (n 45) 228.
[49] See eg Henckels, 'Indirect Expropriation' (n 45) 250; Henckels, *Proportionality and Deference* (n 31) 193, 106–07, cf 123; Kurtz (n 19) 202; Ortino (n 45) 74, 90–91. cf Andreas Kulick, *Global Public Interest in International Investment Law* (CUP 2014) 171–73; Kingsbury and Schill (n 31) 102–04.

19.15 The tribunal in *Tecmed v Mexico* first arguably articulated proportionality *stricto sensu* in connection with expropriation as follows:

> the Arbitral Tribunal will consider, in order to determine if they are to be characterized as expropriatory, whether such actions or measures are proportional to the public interest presumably protected thereby and to the protection legally granted to investments, taking into account that the significance of such impact has a key role upon deciding the proportionality ... There must be a reasonable relationship of proportionality between the charge or weight imposed to the foreign investor and the aim sought to be realized by any expropriatory measure.[50]

In this dispute, the tribunal found an unlawful expropriation because Mexico's objective and the surrounding circumstances were not, in the tribunal's view, sufficiently 'serious' to justify the harm caused to the investor.[51] The tribunal in *Azurix v Argentina* subsequently found relevant to the question of proportionality in the context of indirect expropriation whether the person concerned bears 'an individual and excessive burden'.[52] Thus, if regulatory action imposes an excessive or disproportionate burden on the claimant investor or its interests or investments, the host state will not be able to rely on the police powers doctrine or the legitimacy of the objective to show that no expropriation occurred.

19.16 Other tribunals have adopted an arguably looser test of proportionality in the context of expropriation, for example emphasizing the need to take account of the gravity and urgency of the surrounding circumstances.[53] In 2016, the tribunal in *Philip Morris v Uruguay* reaffirmed the notion of proportionality in the context of the police powers doctrine and expropriation:

> As indicated by earlier investment treaty decisions, in order for a State's action in exercise of regulatory powers not to constitute indirect expropriation, the action has to comply with certain conditions. Among those most commonly mentioned are that the action must be taken *bona fide* for the purpose of protecting the public welfare, must be non-discriminatory and proportionate.[54]

Yet, even though the tribunal in this dispute unanimously found no expropriation, it did so on the basis that '[t]hey were *proportionate* to the objective they meant to achieve',[55] noting the 'limited adverse impact'[56] of the challenged measures on the investor's business and distinguishing them from 'banning the production and sale

---

[50] *Tecmed* (n 37) para 122. See also *LG&E* (n 39) para 195; *Deutsche Bank AB v Sri Lanka*, ICSID Case No ARB/09/02, Award (31 October 2012) para 522.
[51] *Tecmed* (n 37) paras 147, 151.
[52] *Azurix v Argentina*, ICSID Case No ARB/01/12, Award (23 June 2006) paras 311–12 (quoting European Court of Human Rights, *In the case of James and Others*, sentence of 21 February 1986 paras 50, 63).
[53] *Total SA v Argentina*, ICSID Case No ARB/04/1, Decision on Liability (27 December 2010) para 197.
[54] *Philip Morris v Uruguay* (n 3) para 305 (italics in original; underlining added).
[55] ibid para 306 (emphasis added).
[56] ibid.

of tobacco altogether'.⁵⁷ The corollary is that, if the extent of harm had been greater or the measures or their objectives less important in the tribunal's opinion, the tribunal could have found them 'disproportionate' and therefore expropriatory, even if Uruguay had no reasonably available alternative means of achieving an equivalent contribution to its policy goals. Thus, unlike in the context of WTO general exceptions, the proportionality requirement sometimes imposed in assessing expropriation in international investment law (whether strictly or loosely construed) may preclude the acceptance of the host state's chosen 'level of protection'.

Nevertheless, as in most issues, investment treaty tribunals have not been consistent in their application of proportionality in relation to indirect expropriation. Different tribunals adopt different approaches. At the opposite end to the police powers doctrine, some tribunals have applied a 'sole effect' doctrine,⁵⁸ pursuant to which the regulatory purpose is all but irrelevant and instead the impact of the measure itself determines the existence of expropriation.⁵⁹ The existence of a general exceptions provision may have less of an impact on the interpretation and application of an expropriation obligation where a tribunal applies the sole effects doctrine than where it applies some form of proportionality analysis, whether pursuant to the police powers doctrine or otherwise.

19.17

b. Fair and equitable treatment

In IIAs that explicitly link guarantees of 'fair and equitable treatment' (FET) to the minimum standard of treatment of aliens imposed under customary international law (CIL),⁶⁰ tribunals generally recognize that only sufficiently serious conduct will breach such guarantees, such as conduct that is:

19.18

> arbitrary, grossly unfair, unjust or idiosyncratic, is discriminatory and exposes the claimant to sectional or racial prejudice, or involves a lack of due process leading to an outcome which offends judicial propriety—as might be the case with a manifest failure of natural justice in judicial proceedings or a complete lack of transparency and candour in an administrative process.⁶¹

---

⁵⁷ ibid n 405.
⁵⁸ For discussion of the relationship between police powers, sole effect, proportionality, and related analytical tools, see Catharine Titi, 'Police Powers Doctrine and International Investment Law' in Andrea Gattini, Attila Tanzi, and Filippo Fontanelli (eds), *General Principles of Law and International Investment Arbitration* (Brill, 2018) 323.
⁵⁹ See eg *Compañía de Aguas del Aconquija SA and Vivendi Universal SA v Argentina* ICSID Case No ARB/97/3, , Award (20 August 2007) para 7.5.20.
⁶⁰ See also NAFTA Free Trade Commission, Notes of Interpretation of Certain Chapter 11 Provisions (31 July 2001) para 2.
⁶¹ *Waste Management, Inc v Mexico*, ICSID Case No ARB(AF)/00/3, Award (30 April 2004) para 98. See also eg *Loewen v United States*, ICSID Case No ARB(AF)/98/3, Award (26 June 2003) para 132; *International Thunderbird Gaming Corporation v Mexico*, Ad hoc (UNCITRAL), Award (26 January 2006) para 194; *Merrill & Ring Forestry LP v Canada*, UNCITRAL, Award (31 March 2010) para 236; *Mobil Investments Canada Inc v Canada*, ICSID Case No ARB(AF)/07/4, Decision on Liability (22 May 2012) para 152(2); *TECO Guatemala Holdings LLC v Guatemala*, ICSID Case No ARB/10/17, Award (19 December 2013) para 492.

19.19 In IIAs that do not explicitly link the FET obligation to CIL, some commentators and tribunals have interpreted FET as an autonomous standard,[62] which may suggest that a lower threshold or broader array of conduct will establish a violation.[63] However, the distinction between the CIL standard and an autonomous standard is unclear. Some tribunals have suggested that the CIL standard is capable of evolution, although the burden would be on the claimant to demonstrate particular activities today that might be considered to breach the high FET standard although they may not have done so previously.[64]

19.20 Tribunals have characterized the FET obligation as incorporating policy space in different ways. Some have suggested that the high threshold for violation allows policy space to pursue public welfare objectives.[65] Others have suggested that 'a State's reasonable right to regulate'[66] in the context of FET allows for public welfare measures.[67] The tribunal in *Philip Morris v Uruguay* articulated the contentious[68] position that 'national regulatory agencies' enjoy a 'margin of appreciation ... when dealing with public policy determinations'.[69]

19.21 The relationship between these different approaches and their connection to the police powers doctrine discussed in the context of expropriation is unclear. The tribunal in *EDF v Romania* referred to the 'legitimate and non-discriminatory exercise by the State of its police power in the public interest' in connection with the FET obligation,[70] whereas the tribunal in *Suez v Argentina* suggested that the

---

[62] See eg Christoph Schreuer, 'Fair and Equitable Treatment in Arbitral Practice' (2005) 6(3) Journal of World Investment & Trade 357, 360, 364; cf Santiago Montt, *State Liability in Investment Treaty Arbitration* (Hart Publishing 2009) 303, 306.

[63] See eg *Pope & Talbot v Canada*, UNCITRAL, Award on the Merits of Phase 2 (10 April 2001) para 118; *Saluka* (n 36) paras 292–93; Hussein Haeri, 'A Tale of Two Standards: "Fair and Equitable Treatment" and the Minimum Standard in International Law' (2011) 27(1) Arbitration International 27, 36–37. See also *Enron v Argentina*, ICSID Case No ARB/01/3, Award (22 May 2007) para 258; but see *Enron v Argentina*, ICSID Case No ARB/01/3, Decision on Annulment (30 July 2010) paras 406–07.

[64] See eg *Glamis Gold Ltd v United States*, Ad hoc (UNCITRAL), Award (14 May 2009) paras 601, 613, 614, 616.

[65] See eg *Frontier Petroleum v Czech Republic*, Ad hoc (UNCITRAL), Award (12 November 2010) [527]; *Thunderbird* (n 61) para 127.

[66] *Suez* (n 37) para 148.

[67] See eg *SD Myers* (n 35) para 263; *Saluka* (n 36) para 305; *Merrill* (n 61) para 224; *TECO* (n 61) paras 490, 493; *Philip Morris v Uruguay* (n 3) paras 409–10.

[68] See Alvarez (n 46) 65–66, 70–74; see generally Julian Arato, 'The Margin of Appreciation in International Investment Law' (2014) 54(3) Virginia Journal of International Law 545.

[69] *Philip Morris v Uruguay* (n 3) para 388 (see also para 398); see also *Electrabel v Hungary*, (Decision on Jurisdiction, Applicable Law and Liability) ICSID Case No ARB/07/19, Award (30 November 2012) paras 6.92, 8.35; but see *Philip Morris Brands Sàrl v Uruguay*, ICSID Case No ARB/10/7, Concurring and Dissenting Opinion (8 July 2016) paras 87, 138, 181, 186, 191; *Pezold v Zimbabwe*, ICSID Case No ARB/10/15, Award (28 July 2015) paras 465–66. cf *Chemtura* (n 34) para 123 (referring to but apparently not applying a margin of appreciation, in the context of expropriation).

[70] *EDF (Services) Ltd v Romania*, ICSID Case No ARB/05/13, Award (8 October 2009) paras 299, 301 (see also para 292).

doctrine of police powers has no place as an independent defence in the context of FET on the basis that it would be superfluous, since such considerations are already taken into account in the FET analysis as part of the state's right to regulate.[71] In *Electrabel v Hungary*, in the context of FET, the tribunal emphasized that its task was not 'to sit retrospectively in judgment upon Hungary's discretionary exercise of sovereign power, not made irrationally and not exercised in bad faith'.[72]

19.22 The relevance and significance of an investor's 'legitimate expectations' in the context of the FET obligation is also contested. However, the prevailing view appears to be that such considerations may be relevant to FET only where the respondent state has made a 'specific assurance or commitment to the investor so as to induce its expectations'[73] or has created 'reasonable and justifiable expectations'[74] '*in order to induce* investment'.[75] Thus, according to the tribunal in *Philip Morris v Uruguay*:

> It is common ground in the decisions of more recent investment tribunals that the requirements of legitimate expectations and legal stability as manifestations of the FET standard do not affect the State's rights to exercise its sovereign authority to legislate and to adapt its legal system to changing circumstances.[76]

Moreover, '[p]articularly in an industry like tobacco, ... there must be a reasonable expectation of regulation'.[77]

19.23 Despite recognition in the context of the FET obligation of the right to regulate, the legitimacy of non-discriminatory public welfare measures, and the limited relevance of an investor's expectations, some investment treaty tribunals have applied a proportionality test[78] akin to that discussed in respect of expropriation. One tribunal goes so far as to suggest that 'numerous investment treaty tribunals have found that the principle of proportionality is part and parcel of the overarching duty to accord fair and equitable treatment to investors'.[79]

---

[71] *Suez* (n 37) para 148.
[72] *Electrabel v Hungary*, ICSID Case No ARB/07/19, Decision on Jurisdiction, Applicable Law and Liability (30 November 2012) para 8.35 (also quoted in *Philip Morris v Uruguay* (n 3) para 399).
[73] *Glamis Gold* (n 64) para 620 (see also paras 767, 799–800, 807). See also *EDF v Romania* (n 70) para 219; Henckels, *Proportionality and Deference* (n 31) 72.
[74] *Thunderbird* (n 61) para 147.
[75] *Glamis Gold* (n 64) para 621 (original emphasis) (see also paras 627, 802).
[76] *Philip Morris v Uruguay* (n 3) para 422.
[77] ibid para 269 (see also para 430).
[78] See eg *MTD Equity Sdn Bhd v Chile*, ICSID Case No ARB/01/7, Award (25 May 2004) [109]; *Total* (n 53) para 162. See also Stephan W Schill, 'Fair and Equitable Treatment, The Rule of Law, and Comparative Public Law' in Stephan W Schill (ed), *International Investment Law and Comparative Public Law* (OUP 2010) 151, 169–70; Henckels, *Proportionality and Deference* (n 31) 70.
[79] *Occidental Petroleum Corporation v Ecuador*, ICSID Case No ARB/06/11, Award (5 October 2012) n 7 (see also para 404). See also Anne Marie Martin, 'Proportionality: An Addition to the International Centre for the Settlement of Investment Disputes' Fair and Equitable Treatment Standard' (2014) 37(3 E Supp) Boston College International & Comparative Law Review 58; Carmen Martinez Lopez and Lucy Martinez, 'Proportionality in Investment Treaty Arbitration

In the context of FET, requiring proportionality entails assessing whether the challenged measure excessively or disproportionately burdens the claimant investor or their investment, in view of the objectives and benefits of the measure, or 'a weighing of the Claimant's legitimate and reasonable expectations on the one hand and the Respondent's legitimate regulatory interests on the other'.[80]

19.24 For instance, in *EDF v Romania*, the tribunal considered in the context of FET that 'in addition to a legitimate aim in the public interest there must be "a reasonable relationship of proportionality between the means employed and the aim sought to be realized"', and that 'proportionality would be lacking if the person involved "bears an individual and excessive burden"'.[81] More recently, in *Philip Morris v Uruguay*, the majority of the tribunal concluded that the so-called 'single presentation requirement' did not breach FET because it 'was an attempt to address a real public health concern, ... *was not disproportionate to that concern* and that it was adopted in good faith'.[82] The tribunal found unanimously that the requirement of 80 per cent graphic health warnings on the front and back of tobacco packages did not breach FET because it was 'not an arbitrary, grossly unfair, unjust discriminatory or a *disproportionate* measure, in particular given its relatively minor impact on Abal's business'.[83]

19.25 The notion of proportionality in the context of FET means that a tribunal may find a breach of FET where it considers that the burden on the claimant investor outweighs the benefits of the challenged measure, even where no alternative is reasonably available to the respondent to achieve those benefits in a less burdensome manner. That result is similar to that in the expropriation context but different from that in the WTO context. However, as with expropriation, the precise impact of a general exceptions clause on the fair and equitable treatment obligation depends on the tribunal's particular approach, which may or may not include elements of proportionality. The proportionality aspects of a tribunal's reasoning concern us in particular as regards the unintended impact of general exceptions discussed further below. In contrast, for example, a tribunal emphasizing an investor's legitimate expectations might be more rather than less likely to consider a policy purpose where that purpose is explicitly mentioned in general exceptions, which would tend to accord with the states parties' reasons for including such exceptions.

---

and Beyond: An "Irresistible Attraction"?' (2015) 2 BCDR International Arbitration Review 261, 274–84.

[80] *Saluka* (n 36) para 306.
[81] *EDF v Romania* (n 70) para 293 (quoting *Azurix* (n 52)).
[82] *Philip Morris v Uruguay* (n 3) para 409 (emphasis added).
[83] ibid para 420 (emphasis added) (see also para 410).

c. Non-discrimination

19.26 Some IIAs contain provisions that prohibit discrimination based on nationality. Such provisions are necessarily comparative, requiring an assessment of whether the investor in question is treated less favourably than domestic investors (national treatment)[84] or investors of third states (most favoured nation (MFN) treatment).[85] Thus, a comparator must be identified to assess discrimination. Some more recent IIAs use textual additions such as 'like circumstances' as a basis for identifying a comparator (eg a domestic investor in like circumstances to the claimant foreign investor),[86] but many older IIAs provide no guidance in this regard.[87] On one view, the inclusion or omission of such words is not legally significant:[88] the investors must be in like circumstances to be comparable anyway.

19.27 In the process of identifying an appropriate comparator for non-discrimination, some tribunals have facilitated policy space for regulatory action in the public interest.[89] In particular, for example, tribunals have regarded domestic investors as not in like circumstances to the foreign investor claimant, or otherwise not comparable to the claimant, where those investors are distinguishable from the claimant on a legitimate factual or policy basis.[90] For instance, the tribunal in *Pope & Talbot v Canada* stated:

> Differences in treatment will presumptively violate Article 1102(2) [National Treatment], unless they have a reasonable nexus to rational government policies that (1) do not distinguish, on their face or de facto, between foreign-owned and domestic companies, and (2) do not otherwise unduly undermine the investment liberalizing objectives of [the *North American Free Trade Agreement* (NAFTA)].[91]

19.28 The tribunal in *Bilcon v Canada* more recently affirmed this approach to the national treatment obligation:

---

[84] See eg Agreement between Germany and the Philippines for the Promotion and Reciprocal Protection of Investments (entered into force 1 February 2000) art 3.1.

[85] See eg Agreement between Hong Kong and Australia for the Promotion and Protection of Investments (entered into force 15 October 1993) art 3.1.

[86] See eg NAFTA (n 33) art 1102.

[87] See eg Agreement between the Swiss Confederation and the Oriental Republic of Uruguay on the Reciprocal Promotion and Protection of Investments (entered into force 22 April 1991) art 3.2. See also Andrew Newcombe and Lluís Paradell, *Law and Practice of Investment Treaties* (Kluwer Law International 2009) 158–59.

[88] See eg Newcombe and Paradell (n 87) 160.

[89] For extensive discussion see generally Andrew D Mitchell, David Heaton. and Caroline Henckels, *Non-Discrimination and the Role of Regulatory Purpose in International Trade and Investment Law* (Edward Elgar 2016).

[90] See *Windstream v Canada*, UNCITRAL, Award (27 September 2016) para 414; *SD Myers* (n 35) para 246; *Marvin Feldman v Mexico*, ICSID Case No ARB(AF)/99/1, Award (16 December 2002) para 170, cf para 182; *GAMI v Mexico*, UNCITRAL, Award (15 November 2004) para 114. See also Jorge A Huerta-Goldman, 'Cross-cutting Observations on National Treatment' in Jorge A Huerta-Goldman, Antoine Romanetti, and Franz X Stirnimann (eds), *WTO Litigation, Investment Arbitration, and Commercial Arbitration* (Kluwer Law International 2013) 263, 269.

[91] *Pope & Talbot* (n 63) para 78.

The approach taken in *Pope & Talbot*, would seem to provide legally appropriate latitude for host states, even in the absence of an equivalent of Article XX of the GATT, to pursue reasonable and non-discriminatory domestic policy objectives through appropriate measures even when there is an incidental and reasonably unavoidable burden on foreign enterprises.[92]

The tribunal's reliance on the absence of an equivalent to GATT Article XX highlights that this interpretation of national treatment is an alternative method of ensuring adequate policy space, and also that the inclusion of a general exception could have an impact on the interpretation of national treatment. The WTO Appellate Body has adopted a similar approach in relation to non-discrimination in Article 2.1 of the Agreement on Technical Barriers to Trade (TBT Agreement).[93] Relying in part on the absence of a GATT Article XX equivalent in the TBT Agreement, the Appellate Body has held that a technical regulation that imposes a detrimental impact on imported products does not accord less favourable treatment contrary to Article 2.1 if the detrimental impact 'stems exclusively from a legitimate regulatory distinction rather than reflecting discrimination against the group of imported products'.[94] According to the Appellate Body, that qualification does not apply to the national treatment obligation in GATT Article III because of the presence of GATT Article XX.[95] The Appellate Body has explained this interpretative difference with reference to the objectives of the two agreements:

> the balance that the preamble of the *TBT Agreement* strikes between, on the one hand, the pursuit of trade liberalization and, on the other hand, Members' right to regulate, is not, in principle, different from the balance that exists between the national treatment obligation of Article III and the general exceptions provided under Article XX of the GATT 1994.[96]

19.29 In the investment context, tribunals do not typically elaborate upon the contours of the policy space inherent in the non-discrimination obligation. Specifically,

---

[92] *Bilcon v Canada* PCA Case No 2009–04 (UNCITRAL), Award on Jurisdiction and Liability (17 March 2015) para 723. See also *SD Myers* (n 35) paras 245–46.

[93] Marrakesh Agreement Establishing the World Trade Organization (entered into force 1 January 1995) Annex 1A ('Agreement on Technical Barriers to Trade') (TBT Agreement).

[94] WTO, *United States: Measures Affecting the Production and Sale of Clove Cigarettes—Report of the Appellate Body* (4 April 2012) WT/DS406/AB/R para 182 (*US—Clove Cigarettes*). See also eg WTO, *United States: Measures Concerning the Importation, Marketing and Sale of Tuna and Tuna Products—Report of the Appellate Body* (16 May 2012) WT/DS381/AB/R para 215 (*US—Tuna II (Mexico)*); WTO, *United States: Certain Country of Origin Labelling (COOL) Requirements—Reports of the Appellate Body* (29 June 2012) WT/DS384/AB/R and WT/DS386/AB/R para 271 (*US—COOL*).

[95] WTO, *European Communities: Measures Prohibiting the Importation and Marketing of Seal Products—Reports of the Appellate Body* (22 May 2014) WT/DS400/AB/R and WT/DS401/AB/R para 5.105 (*EC—Seal Products*); WTO, *United States: Certain Country of Origin Labelling (COOL) Requirements—Recourse to Article 21.5 of the DSU by Canada and Mexico—Reports of the Appellate Body* (8 May 2015) WT/DS384/AB/RW and WT/DS386/AB/RW para 5.358 (*US—COOL (Article 21.5—Canada and Mexico)*).

[96] *US—Clove Cigarettes* (n 94) para 109.

whether the standard requires merely a rational or plausible connection between regulatory action and its public welfare objective,[97] or that such action be no greater than necessary for that objective or proportionate to that objective,[98] remains unsettled. Although some investment treaty tribunals have relied on WTO case law on necessity and the general exceptions in GATT Article XX in relation to the latter formulation,[99] their understanding of necessity and proportionality may tend to restrict policy space more than the WTO Appellate Body does in practice under the general exceptions.

2. Hidden policy space in GATT Article XX and GATS Article XIV

19.30 WTO respondents in only three disputes have successfully invoked a general exception in practice (one of which invocations is under appeal and two of which occurred only at the stage of compliance proceedings),[100] with others typically failing to fulfil the *chapeau* requirements due to discriminatory aspects of their challenged measures.[101] These results may lead to the assumption (or myth) that the WTO general exceptions are interpreted too restrictively to offer significant policy space to WTO members in defending their measures found otherwise to violate GATT or GATS obligations. However, as we explain below, the Appellate Body's broad interpretation of the scope of subparagraphs of GATT Article XX and GATS Article XIV renders them more easily applicable to a range of regulatory measures. The Appellate Body's application of the necessity test is also less onerous than might first appear, because of the Appellate Body's repeated recognition of WTO members' right to determine their own level of protection with

---

[97] See eg *Pope & Talbot* (n 63) para 78; *Feldman* (n 90) para 170; *GAMI* (n 90) para 114.
[98] See eg *In the Matter of Cross-Border Trucking Services* NAFTA Ch 20 Panel, USA-MEX-98-2008-01, Final Report of the Panel (6 February 2001) paras 259, 262, 270; *SD Myers* (n 35) para 252.
[99] See eg *Trucking Services* (n 98) paras 262, 270.
[100] See WTO, *European Communities: Measures Affecting Asbestos and Products Containing Asbestos—Report of the Appellate Body* (12 March 2001) WT/DS135/AB/R para 175 (*EC—Asbestos*); WTO, *United States: Import Prohibition of Certain Shrimp and Shrimp Products—Recourse to Article 21.5 of the DSU by Malaysia—Report of the Appellate Body* (22 October 2001) WT/DS58/AB/RW para 152 (*US—Shrimp (Article 21.5—Malaysia)*). See also WTO, *United States: Measures Concerning the Importation, Marketing and Sale of Tuna and Tuna Products—Recourse to Article 21.5 of the DSU by the United States—Report of the Panel* (26 October 2017) WT/DS381/RW/USA; WTO, *United States: Measures Concerning the Importation, Marketing and Sale of Tuna and Tuna Products—Second Recourse to Article 21.5 of the DSU by Mexico—Report of the Panel* (26 October 2017) WT/DS381/RW2 (both appealed by Mexico on 1 December 2017, including with respect to the Article XX finding).
[101] See eg WTO, *Brazil: Measures Affecting Imports of Retreaded Tyres—Report of the Appellate Body* (3 December 2007) WT/DS332/AB/R para 233 (*Brazil—Retreaded Tyres*); WTO, *United States: Measures Affecting the Cross-Border Supply of Gambling and Betting Services—Report of the Appellate Body* (7 April 2005) WT/DS285/AB/R paras 369–72 (*US—Gambling*); *EC—Seal Products* (n 95) paras 5.338–5.339. See also the summary and discussion in Lorand Bartels, 'The Chapeau of the General Exceptions in the WTO GATT and GATS Agreements: A Reconstruction' (2015) 109 American Journal of International Law 95, 96.

respect to a particular objective. In addition, the Appellate Body has more recently taken greater account of the reality that a challenged measure may have multiple policy objectives. In turn, its reasoning indicates that a member may succeed in justifying discrimination in the application of a measure under the *chapeau* on the basis of a legitimate objective that is not the main objective on which the measure is defended under the general exceptions and that is not necessarily included in the list of exceptions. These various aspects of the Appellate Body's approach mean that the WTO general exceptions are in some ways less restrictive than ordinarily assumed and potentially less restrictive than the policy space recognized within substantive investment obligations.

a. The two-step test established by the WTO Appellate Body

19.31 The WTO Appellate Body has interpreted and applied Article XX of GATT and Article XIV of GATS according to a two-step legal test to be applied in a specific order.[102] First, the impugned measure must be 'provisionally justified'[103] under one of the subparagraphs of GATT Article XX or GATS Article XIV. These subparagraphs set out a closed list of legitimate policy objectives that may justify an otherwise WTO-inconsistent measure under these general exceptions. The objectives on which respondents have most often relied are:[104]

(a) necessary to protect public morals;[105]
(b) necessary to protect human, animal or plant life or health; ...
(d) necessary to secure compliance with laws or regulations which are not inconsistent with the provisions of this Agreement ...

19.32 GATT Article XX includes an additional common subparagraph that is not available under GATS Article XIV:

(g) relating to the conservation of exhaustible natural resources if such measures are made effective in conjunction with restrictions on domestic production or consumption ...

19.33 The Appellate Body has stated that the first step of the test requires, with respect to a given paragraph of GATT Article XX or GATS Article XIV, 'that the challenged measure address the particular interest specified in that paragraph and that there be a sufficient nexus between the measure and the interest protected'.[106]

---

[102] WTO, *United States: Import Prohibition of Certain Shrimp and Shrimp Products—Report of the Appellate Body* (12 October 1998) WT/DS58/AB/R para 119 (*US—Shrimp*).
[103] ibid para 125.
[104] GATT art XX (also reflected in GATS art XIV).
[105] Article XIV(a) of GATS includes, in addition to 'public morals', measures necessary to 'maintain public order'. GATS n 5 states that the 'public order exception may be invoked only where a genuine and sufficiently serious threat is posed to one of the fundamental interests of society'.
[106] *US—Gambling* (n 101) para 292, quoted in *EC—Seal Products* (n 95) para 5.169. See also *US—Shrimp* (n 102) para 133.

If a respondent shows that the challenged measure is provisionally justified under one of the subparagraphs of GATT Article XX (or GATS Article XIV), it must in the second step of the legal test show that the measure complies with the *chapeau*, which reads (in the GATT): **19.34**

> Subject to the requirement that such measures are not applied in a manner which would constitute a means of *arbitrary or unjustifiable discrimination* between countries where the same conditions[107] prevail, or a *disguised restriction on international trade*, nothing in this Agreement shall be construed to prevent the adoption or enforcement by any Member of measures: ... [108]

According to the Appellate Body, the function of the *chapeau* is 'to prevent the abuse or misuse of a Member's right to invoke the exceptions contained in the subparagraphs'.[109]

We now address the two steps in more detail, elaborating on the relevant WTO jurisprudence (particularly in reports of the Appellate Body) to show the significant policy space of WTO members under the general exceptions in WTO law. **19.35**

b. Step one: provisional justification and the member's chosen level of protection

In the first step of the Appellate Body's test, the provisional justification of the challenged measure includes two main elements.[110] **19.36**

First, the respondent must demonstrate that the challenged measure is broadly 'designed'[111] to address, has a 'relationship'[112] with, or is 'not incapable of protecting'[113] one of the interests in the subparagraphs of GATT Article XX (or GATS Article XIV). As noted, GATT Article XX and GATS Article XIV contain exhaustive lists of legitimate objectives that may be justified under the general exceptions,[114] even though they do not necessarily encompass every possible legitimate regulatory objective of a WTO Member.[115] For example, the objective **19.37**

---

[107] GATS art XIV uses the term 'like conditions' rather than 'the same conditions'.
[108] GATT art XX (emphasis added).
[109] *EC—Seal Products* (n 95) para 5.297. See also WTO, *United States: Standards for Reformulated and Conventional Gasoline—Report of the Appellate Body* (29 April 1996) WT/DS2/AB/R, 22 (*US—Gasoline*).
[110] See n 106 and corresponding text.
[111] See eg *US—Gambling* (n 101) para 298; WTO, *Colombia: Measures Relating to the Importation of Textiles, Apparel and Footwear—Report of the Appellate Body* (7 June 2016) WT/DS461/AB/R paras 5.67–5.68 (*Colombia—Textiles*).
[112] ibid paras 5.68–5.69.
[113] ibid para 5.103.
[114] cf TBT Agreement, art 2.2, which contains a list of 'legitimate objectives' commencing with the words '*inter alia*'. See also eg WTO, *European Communities: Trade Description of Sardines—Report of the Appellate Body* (26 September 2002) WT/DS231/AB/R para 286; WTO, *United States: Measures Concerning the Importation, Marketing and Sale of Tuna and Tuna Products (Mexico)—Panel Report* (15 September 2011) WT/DS381/R para 7.437.
[115] See eg Frieder Roessler, 'Diverging Domestic Policies and Multilateral Trade Integration' in Jagdish Bhagwati and Robert E Hudec (eds), *Fair Trade and Harmonization: Prerequisites for Free Trade?* (MIT Press 1996) 21, 30.

of wealth redistribution (eg by way of a tax on luxury goods) is not obviously included in the general exceptions.[116] Similarly, human rights are covered only indirectly through the references to public morals in GATT Article XX(a) (and GATS Article XIV(a)), human life or health in GATT Article XX(b) (and GATS Article XIV(b)), and prison labour in GATT Article XX(e).[117] Unanswered questions also arise as to whether measures designed to protect extraterritorial interests such as animals or humans beyond the territory of the regulating member may be justified under every paragraph of GATT Article XX and GATS Article XIV.[118]

19.38 Nevertheless, WTO tribunals' expansive reading of some of the subparagraphs lends flexibility to the lists of objectives. Thus, for example, the Appellate Body has adopted an 'evolutionary'[119] interpretation of 'exhaustible natural resources' in Article XX(g), extending to living resources including endangered species such as certain species of turtle.[120] A WTO Panel has also read this term as including 'clean air'.[121] WTO Panels have also read 'public morals' broadly as 'standards of right and wrong conduct maintained by or on behalf of a community or nation',[122] acknowledging that such standards may differ between WTO members. US restrictions on online gambling,[123] Chinese monitoring of the content of audiovisual products,[124] European animal welfare measures,[125] and Colombian tariff measures to combat money laundering[126] have all been found to have a relationship with public morals. More generally, while the objective of the challenged

---

[116] ibid.
[117] See eg Lorand Bartels, 'Article XX of GATT and the Problem of Extraterritorial Jurisdiction: The Case of Trade Measures for the Protection of Human Rights' (2002) 36(2) Journal of World Trade 353, 354–56.
[118] See eg *US—Shrimp* (n 102) para 133; *EC—Seal Products* (n 95) para 5.173. See generally Lorand Bartels, 'Article XX' (n 117).
[119] *US—Shrimp* (n 102) para 130.
[120] ibid para 132.
[121] WTO, *United States: Standards for Reformulated and Conventional Gasoline—Panel Report* (29 January 1996) WT/DS2/R para 6.37 (this issue not appealed: *US—Gasoline* (n 109) 11–12).
[122] *US—Gambling* (n 101) para 296 (quoting WTO, *United States: Measures Affecting the Cross-Border Supply of Gambling and Betting Services—Panel Report* (10 November 2004) WT/DS285/R para 6.465 (*US—Gambling*, Panel Report)). See also Steve Charnovitz, 'The Moral Exception in Trade Policy' (1998) 38 Vanderbilt Journal of International Law 689; Oisin Suttle, 'What Sorts of Things are Public Morals? A Liberal Cosmopolitan Approach to Article XX GATT' (2017) 80(4) Modern Law Review 569.
[123] *US—Gambling* (n 101) para 296 (referring to *US—Gambling*, Panel Report (n 122) para 6.467).
[124] WTO, *China: Measures Affecting Trading Rights and Distribution Services for Certain Publications and Audiovisual Entertainment Products—Panel Report* (12 August 2009) WT/DS363/R paras 7.759, 7.763, 7.766 (*China—Publications and Audiovisual Products*, Panel Report). See also WTO, *China: Measures Affecting Trading Rights and Distribution Services for Certain Publications and Audiovisual Entertainment Products—Report of the Appellate Body* (21 December 2009) WT/DS363/AB/R para 243 (*China—Publications and Audiovisual Products*).
[125] *EC—Seal Products* (n 95) para 5.138 (referring to WTO, *European Communities: Measures Prohibiting the Importation and Marketing of Seal Products—Panel Reports* (25 November 2013) WT/DS400/R and WT/DS401/R para 7.409 (*EC—Seal Products*, Panel Reports)).
[126] *Colombia—Textiles* (n 111) paras 5.85, 5.89.

measure is discerned through 'the texts of statutes, legislative history, and other evidence regarding [its] structure and operation',[127] the threshold in connecting a challenged measure to its purported objective is relatively low here.[128]

Second, the respondent must establish the nexus between the measure and the objective specified in the relevant subparagraph of GATT Article XX or GATS Article XIV: most often, 'necessary to' or 'relating to'.[129] Establishing the requisite nexus is more onerous than the initial demonstration of whether a measure is designed to address a relevant objective. Under GATT Article XX(g), the respondent must demonstrate that the challenged measure 'relat[es] to' the conservation of natural resources. The words 'relating to' in Article XX(g) require only that the measure be 'primarily aimed at' the conservation of the relevant exhaustible natural resource;[130] the measure and the objective must be in 'a close and genuine relationship of ends and means'.[131] The words 'necessary to' give rise to a different (and more exacting)[132] legal standard.[133] For subparagraphs such as (a), (b), and (d), which begin with the words 'necessary to', the respondent must demonstrate that the challenged measure is 'necessary' with respect to the relevant objective (eg necessary to protect public morals, to protect human life or health, or to secure compliance with WTO-consistent laws), pursuant to the 'necessity' test established in WTO case law.

19.39

The Appellate Body in *China—Publications and Audiovisual Products*, citing jurisprudence on both GATT Article XX and GATS Article XIV, explained the necessity test as follows:[134] (i) '[t]he process begins with an assessment of the "relative

19.40

---

[127] *US—Tuna II (Mexico)* (n 94) para 314 (quoted in *EC—Seal Products* (n 95) para 5.144).

[128] *Colombia—Textiles* (n 111) para 5.70. But see eg WTO, *Indonesia: Importation of Horticultural Products, Animals and Animal Products—Panel Report* (22 December 2016) WT/DS477/R and WT/DS478/R para 7.632 (*Indonesia—Import Licensing Regimes*, Panel Report). The Appellate Body subsequently ruled the Panel's finding of justification under GATT art XX moot and of no legal effect: WTO, *Indonesia: Importation of Horticultural Products, Animals and Animal Products—Reports of the Appellate Body* (9 November 2017) WT/DS477/AB/R and WT/DS478/AB/R paras 5.103, 6.8(a) (*Indonesia—Import Licensing Regimes*).

[129] GATT art XX(j) applies to measures 'essential to the acquisition or distribution of products in general or local short supply'. The Appellate Body has held that the process of weighing and balancing and comparison with alternatives pursuant to the necessity test also applies to art XX(j): WTO, *India: Certain Measures Relating to Solar Cells and Solar Modules—Report of the Appellate Body* (16 September 2016) WT/DS456/AB/R para 5.63 (*India—Solar Cells*).

[130] *US—Gasoline* (n 109) 18–19 (quoted in WTO, *China: Measures Related to the Exportation of Various Raw Materials—Reports of the Appellate Body* (30 January 2012) WT/DS394/AB/R, WT/DS395/AB/R and WT/DS398/AB/R paras 357–58) (*China—Raw Materials*).

[131] *US—Shrimp* (n 102) para 136 (quoted in *China—Raw Materials* (n 130) para 355).

[132] See eg Donald M McRae, 'GATT Article XX and the WTO Appellate Body' in Marco Bronckers and Reinhard Quick (eds), *New Directions in International Economic Law* (Kluwer 2000) 219, 226.

[133] *US—Gasoline* (n 109) 16–18; WTO, *China: Measures Related to the Exportation of Rare Earths, Tungsten and Molybdenum—Reports of the Appellate Body* (7 August 2014) WT/DS431/AB/R, WT/DS432/AB/R and WT/DS433/AB/R para 5.87.

[134] *China—Publications and Audiovisual Products* (n 124) paras 239–42.

importance" of the interests or values furthered by the challenged measure';¹³⁵ (ii) '[h]aving ascertained the importance of the particular interests at stake, a panel should then turn to the other factors that are to be "weighed and balanced"', generally including 'the contribution of the measure to the realization of the ends pursued by it' and 'the restrictive impact of the measure on international commerce';¹³⁶ and (iii) a 'comparison between the challenged measure and possible alternatives should then be undertaken'.¹³⁷

19.41 Some commentators have suggested that identifying the 'relative importance' of the relevant objective and 'weighing and balancing' this importance against other factors entails a proportionality test akin to that arising in international investment law in relation to expropriation or FET.¹³⁸ However, the analysis undertaken in WTO case law does not conform to such a framework. In the following paragraphs, we explain why Regan's assessment in 2007 that WTO Panels and the Appellate Body do *not* engage in 'cost–benefit balancing'¹³⁹ under the general exceptions in GATT and GATS (comparing the 'benefits from the measure in the achievement of [its] goal against the cost of the measure in reduced trade')¹⁴⁰ is borne out by WTO jurisprudence in the subsequent decade. By focusing on WTO members' right to determine the level of protection they require with respect to a particular objective, the Appellate Body's interpretation of WTO general exceptions may be understood as more deferential to members' policy space than the proportionality tests sometimes applied in international investment law.

19.42 The WTO Appellate Body has repeatedly cited the 'relative importance of the interests or values further by the challenged measure' as a factor to consider in assessing necessity under the general exceptions.¹⁴¹ However, the Appellate Body

---

¹³⁵ *US—Gambling* (n 101) para 306 (quoted in *Brazil—Retreaded Tyres* (n 101) para 143). See also *EC—Asbestos* (n 100) para 172.
¹³⁶ *US—Gambling* (n 101) para 306. On the extent of contribution, see eg WTO, *Argentina: Measures Relating to Trade in Goods and Services—Report of the Appellate Body* (14 April 2016) WT/DS453/AB/R para 6.234 (*Argentina—Financial Services*). On trade-restrictiveness, see generally Tania Voon, 'Exploring the Meaning of Trade-Restrictiveness in the WTO' (2015) 14(3) World Trade Review 451.
¹³⁷ *US—Gambling* (n 101) para 307.
¹³⁸ See eg Lopez and Martinez (n 79) 271; see eg Kevin Crow, 'A Taxonomy of Proportionality in International Courts', iCourts Working Paper Series No 107 (November 2017) section IIb.
¹³⁹ Donald H Regan, 'The Meaning of "Necessary" in GATT Article XX and GATS Article XIV: the Myth of Cost–Benefit Balancing' (2007) 6 World Trade Review 347, 347. See also Axel Desmedt, 'Proportionality in WTO Law' (2001) 4(3) Journal of International Economic Law 441, 476; Kurtz (n 19) 201.
¹⁴⁰ Regan (n 139) 347.
¹⁴¹ *China—Publications and Audiovisual Products* (n 124) para 240. See also WTO, *Korea: Measures Affecting Imports of Fresh, Chilled and Frozen Beef—Reports of the Appellate Body* (11 December 2000) WT/DS161/AB/R and WT/DS169/AB/R para 162 (*Korea—Various Measures on Beef*); *US—Gambling* (n 101) para 306; *Brazil—Retreaded Tyres* (n 101) para 143; *EC—Seal Products* (n 95) para 5.214. This factor appears not to apply in the corresponding analysis under art 2.2 of the TBT Agreement: *US—COOL (Article 21.5—Canada and Mexico)* (n 95) para 5.277.

has not explained how to measure that importance. Moreover, the precise role of the objective's importance in the analysis is unclear. Usually, the Appellate Body refers to the importance of the relevant objective as a factor to be weighed and balanced alongside the measure's trade-restrictiveness and contribution to the objective.[142] Sometimes, the Appellate Body has suggested instead that the measure's contribution and trade-restrictiveness are to be weighed and balanced, 'in the light of' the importance of the objective.[143] The Appellate Body has also suggested that the comparison between the measure at issue and proposed alternatives should be undertaken 'in the light of' the importance of the objective pursued[144] (and also, in step 2, that discrimination under the *chapeau* is to be assessed 'in the light of the objectives listed in the paragraphs of Article XX').[145] But we have found no clear instance in which the importance of the objective, as determined by a WTO tribunal, has had any material impact on the 'necessity' analysis in WTO dispute settlement under GATT Article XX/GATS Article XIV.[146]

The Appellate Body stated in *Korea—Various Measures on Beef* that '[t]he more vital or important those common interests or values are, the easier it would be to accept as "necessary" a measure designed as an enforcement instrument'.[147] The Appellate Body did not explicitly ascertain the importance of the objective in that dispute, instead focusing on the availability of reasonable alternatives to achieve Korea's 'desired level of enforcement'[148] in concluding that Korea had failed to establish its defence under Article XX.[149] That dispute involved GATT Article XX(d), which contains an inclusive list of relevant laws or regulations, referring to measures: 19.43

> necessary to secure compliance with laws or regulations which are not inconsistent with the provisions of this Agreement, *including* those relating to customs enforcement, the enforcement of monopolies ... , the protection of patents, trade marks and copyrights, and the prevention of deceptive practices.[150]

---

[142] See eg *China—Publications and Audiovisual Products* (n 124) para 241; *US—Gambling* (n 101) para 306 (referring to the relative importance of the objective and 'the other factors that are to be "weighed and balanced"').

[143] *Brazil—Retreaded Tyres* (n 101) paras 156, 179, 182. On the significance of this qualification for deference to WTO Members, see Andrew D Mitchell and Caroline Henckels, 'Variations on a Theme: Comparing the Concept of "Necessity" in International Investment Law and WTO Law' (2013) 14 Chicago Journal of International Law 93, 129–30.

[144] *US—Gambling* (n 101) para 307; *Brazil—Retreaded Tyres* (n 101) para 178 (see also para 156) (both quoted in *China—Publications and Audiovisual Products* (n 124) paras 240–41). See also *US—COOL (Article 21.5—Canada and Mexico)* (n 95) para 5.269.

[145] *Brazil—Retreaded Tyres* (n 101) paras 225, 227.

[146] That is not to say that Panels and the WTO Appellate Body make no value judgments pursuant to this provision or other WTO provisions.

[147] *Korea—Various Measures on Beef* (n 141) para 162 (quoted in *EC—Asbestos* (n 100) para 172). See also *Colombia—Textiles* (n 111) para 5.71.

[148] *Korea—Various Measures on Beef* (n 141) para 180.

[149] ibid paras 181, 182, 185.

[150] GATT art XX(d) (emphasis added).

That provision leaves open the possibility for other relevant laws or regulations that are not inconsistent with WTO law to be covered by the exception, and hence other interests and objectives to be indirectly protected. In contrast, several other paragraphs of GATT Article XX and GATS Article XIV enshrine the legitimacy of particular objectives (eg public morals, human life, or health). The assessment of the relative importance of the objective may make more sense in the context of GATT Article XX(d) than in the context of some of these other paragraphs. Yet the Appellate Body has continued to incorporate in its necessity test both the measure of the relative importance of the objective and the language from *Korea—Various Measures on Beef* about how vital or important particular interests are.

19.44 For example, the Appellate Body stated in *EC—Asbestos*, with respect to a European Union ban on asbestos:

> the objective pursued by the measure is the preservation of human life and health through the elimination, or reduction, of the well-known, and life-threatening, health risks posed by asbestos fibres. The value pursued is both *vital and important in the highest degree*.[151]

19.45 A WTO Panel later used a similar description in characterizing online gambling restrictions arising from US concerns regarding matters such as money laundering, organized crime, fraud, and underage gambling.[152] Another WTO Panel applied the description 'vital and important in the highest degree' to a Brazilian ban on imports of retreaded tyres due to 'risks of dengue fever and malaria' and thus 'the objective of protecting human life and health against such diseases'.[153] Next, in examining challenged Chinese restrictions on the importation of certain publications and audiovisual products, a Panel determined that 'the protection of public morals ranks among the most important values or interests pursued by Members as a matter of public policy'.[154] Most recently, a Panel concluded that, 'in Colombia, the objective of combating money laundering reflects societal interests that can be described as vital and important in the highest degree'.[155]

19.46 These examples demonstrate that, despite the reference to 'weighing and balancing' and the notion of making an assessment in the light of the importance of the

---

[151] *EC—Asbestos* (n 100) para 172 (emphasis added).
[152] *US—Gambling* (n 101) para 301 (quoting *US—Gambling*, Panel Report (n 122) para 6.492, quoting *EC—Asbestos* (n 100) para 172).
[153] *Brazil—Retreaded Tyres* (n 101) para 179 (quoting WTO, *Brazil: Measures Affecting Imports of Retreaded Tyres*—Panel Report (12 June 2007) WT/DS332/R para 7.210 (*Brazil—Retreaded Tyres*, Panel Report)).
[154] *China—Publications and Audiovisual Products* (n 124) para 243 (quoting *China—Publications and Audiovisual Products,* Panel Report (n 124) para 7.817).
[155] *Colombia—Textiles* (n 111) para 5.105 (referring to WTO, *Colombia: Measures Relating to the Importation of Textiles, Apparel and Footwear*—Panel Report (27 November 2015) WT/DS461/R para 7.408; this finding not appealed).

relevant objective, WTO tribunals are not inclined to rank different policy objectives in order of importance as determined by them (or even by the respondent member). Rather, WTO tribunals typically assess the importance of the objective at stake as extremely high. The importance of the values in question may therefore be understood not as a variable factor but as always weighing in favour of justifying the measure under the general exceptions rather than disqualifying it. This more limited approach may acknowledge that WTO panels and the Appellate Body have specific (often trade-focused) expertise and reduced democratic legitimacy as compared to WTO member governments in determining regulatory policy objectives. In the context of the TBT Agreement, the United States, for example, has contended that 'panels are not in a position to judge and rank the importance of various objectives'.[156] Regan has also suggested that 'such judgments of importance by the Appellate Body' would involve 'a serious intrusion on the Members' regulatory autonomy',[157] 'at odds with the whole spirit of the WTO agreements, which leave the evaluation of domestic benefits to domestic regulators'.[158]

19.47 In our view, the defining feature of the necessity test in WTO law is not the holistic weighing and balancing (which some scholars view as a form of proportionality analysis)[159] or the relative importance of the objective pursued but, rather, substantial deference to the respondent's chosen 'level of protection' in achieving that objective.[160] WTO Panels and the Appellate Body have repeatedly emphasized WTO Members' autonomy in choosing their own level of protection, which is not open to review: 'a "reasonably available" alternative measure must be a measure that would preserve for the responding Member its *right to achieve its desired level of protection* with respect to the objective pursued'[161] under the relevant subparagraph of GATT Article XX or GATS Article XIV. In assessing necessity, the pre-eminence of the chosen level of protection markedly constrains the weighing and balancing exercise and the consideration of the relative importance of the values at stake. Ordinarily, therefore, a measure will fail the necessity test

---

[156] *US—COOL* (n 94) para 185 (summarizing United States submissions).
[157] Regan (n 139) 349.
[158] ibid 350 (see also 366–69). See also Prabhash Ranjan, 'Using the Public Law Concept of Proportionality to Balance Investment Protection with Regulation in International Investment Law: A Critical Appraisal' (2014) 3(3) Cambridge Journal of International and Comparative Law 853, 877.
[159] See (n 138).
[160] See also Cottier et al (n 43) 654; Ortino (n 45) 88–89.
[161] *US—Gambling* (n 101) para 308 (emphasis added; quoted in *Brazil—Retreaded Tyres* (n 101) para 156; *Colombia—Textiles* (n 111) para 5.115). See also *Korea—Various Measures on Beef* (n 141) paras 176, 178; *China—Publications and Audiovisual Products* (n 124) para 318; *India—Solar Cells* (n 129) para 5.59, n 214; *EC—Seal Products* (n 95) para 5.200. See also, in the context of different WTO agreements, WTO, *Australia: Measures Affecting Importation of Salmon—Report of the Appellate Body* (20 October 1998) WT/DS18/AB/R para 199; *US—COOL (Article 21.5—Canada and Mexico)* (n 95) para 5.266, n 761.

not through the weighing and balancing process but only where the complainant identifies a reasonably available alternative that is less trade-restrictive than the challenged measure while making an equivalent contribution to the objective.[162] Whether or not this comparison is described as being undertaken in the light of the importance of that objective[163] (which may affect the level of evidence required in justifying the challenged measure over alternatives), the result will be that the member's chosen level of protection is preserved.

19.48 However, the Appellate Body has not characterized the comparison between the measure at issue and a reasonably available alternative as determinative. Rather, it has described this comparison as a 'conceptual tool'[164] and part of a 'holistic' analysis of all relevant factors.[165] A comparison with alternatives may also not be required as part of the necessity test in certain circumstances, including[166] 'when the measure is not trade restrictive at all, or when a trade-restrictive measure makes *no* contribution to the achievement of the relevant legitimate objective'.[167] In both of these examples, the member's chosen level of protection nevertheless remains intact. If the challenged measure does not contribute to the member's objective, finding it unnecessary and therefore WTO-inconsistent will not affect the member's level of protection with respect to that objective. If the challenged measure is not trade restrictive at all, it will likely be found necessary under the general exceptions, again not disturbing the member's chosen level of protection.

19.49 The principle that WTO members may choose their level of protection is thus central to the necessity test for the purposes of GATT Article XX and GATS Article XIV. Based on this principle, a challenged measure cannot fail the necessity test solely on the basis that the harm it causes outweighs the public benefit that it seeks to achieve (ie that the measure is disproportionate to its objectives). In contrast, in the context of expropriation, FET, or non-discrimination, investment tribunals have sometimes determined that a host state's measure is disproportionate when comparing the state's objective with the adverse impact on the relevant investor or investment. That conclusion may mean that the measure violates international investment law even if the host state had no other reasonably available means to

---

[162] See eg *China—Publications and Audiovisual Products* (n 124) para 335. See also *US—COOL (Article 21.5—Canada and Mexico)* (n 95) para 5.266; Regan (n 139) 348–49, 351–52. cf Peter Van den Bossche, 'Looking for Proportionality in WTO Law' (2008) 35(3) Legal Issues of Economic Integration 283, 294; Mitchell and Henckels (n 143) 135; Filippo Fontanelli, 'Necessity Killed the GATT: Art XX GATT and the Misleading Rhetoric about "Weighing and Balancing"' (2012) 5 European Journal of Legal Studies 39, 55, 68.

[163] See n 144.

[164] *US—Tuna II (Mexico)* (n 94) para 320 (quoted in *US—COOL* (n 94) para 376, n 749).

[165] *Brazil—Retreaded Tyres* (n 101) para 182. See also *Argentina—Financial Services* (n 136) para 6.221; *Colombia—Textiles* (n 111) para 5.75.

[166] *US—COOL (Article 21.5—Canada and Mexico)* (n 95) para 5.231.

[167] *US—COOL* (n 94) para 376, n 748 (quoting *US—Tuna II (Mexico)* (n 94) para 322, n 647) (original emphasis) (in the context of TBT art 2.2).

make an equivalent contribution to the objective. International investment law contains no clear recognition of host states' right to determine their own level of protection with respect to a given objective, even though the potential range of legitimate objectives may be broader than those in the WTO general exceptions.

b. Step two: the *chapeau*—increasing recognition of multiple policy objectives?

19.50 If a WTO panel determines that a challenged measure is provisionally justified under one of the subparagraphs of GATT Article XX or GATS Article XIV, the panel turns to assess the measure's conformity with the *chapeau* of the relevant provision. To justify the measure under the general exceptions, the respondent must show that the measure was 'not applied in a manner which would constitute a means of arbitrary or unjustifiable discrimination between countries where the same conditions prevail, or a disguised restriction on international trade'.[168] As foreshadowed, several challenged measures have been found provisionally justified under a subparagraph of a general exception yet failed at the *chapeau* stage due to particular discriminatory elements.[169]

19.51 Another factor that has created difficulty for some WTO respondents in justifying their challenged measures under the general exceptions is that, as measures may have multiple objectives, discrimination in applying a particular measure may not necessarily be justified by the objective claimed under the relevant subparagraph of the general exceptions. Although the Appellate Body has recognized that measures may have multiple policy objectives,[170] its reasoning on the *chapeau* still requires some relationship between the discrimination and the claimed objective. This requirement is compounded by the exhaustive nature of the list of objectives in the general exceptions, as noted earlier, which may further limit the Appellate Body's willingness to recognize the legitimacy of unlisted objectives in justifying discrimination under the *chapeau*.

19.52 For example, in *Brazil—Retreaded Tyres*, Brazil exempted from its ban on the importation of retreaded tyres products imported from countries within the regional trade agreement MERCOSUR.[171] The Panel considered the discrimination effected by this exemption justified under GATT Article XX(b) because a MERCOSUR tribunal had ordered it.[172] However, the Appellate Body found the MERCOSUR exemption arbitrary or unjustifiable, contrary to the *chapeau*, because it was not rationally connected to the public health objective of the ban as claimed under Article XX(b) and undermined that objective.[173]

---

[168] GATT art XX; cf GATS art XIV.
[169] See (n 101).
[170] *US—Clove Cigarettes* (n 94) para 115. See also *US—Tuna II (Mexico)* (n 94) paras 325, 331.
[171] *Brazil—Retreaded Tyres*, Panel Report (n 153) para 7.235.
[172] ibid paras 7.272–7.274, 7.280–7.281, 7.289.
[173] *Brazil—Retreaded Tyres* (n 101) para 228. See also *US—Shrimp* (n 102) para 165.

19.53 Thus, if a measure is applied in a manner that discriminates against or between imported products (or otherwise restricts trade) on grounds that 'bear no rational connection to the objective falling within the purview of a paragraph of Article XX'[174] (specifically, the paragraph under which the measure has been provisionally justified), the measure cannot be justified under the general exceptions because it does not satisfy the *chapeau*. In practical terms, the Appellate Body's test in *Brazil—Retreaded Tyres* demands a strict alignment between the measure (and its application) and the policy objective under which it has been justified. This approach appears to discount the possibility of a measure with multiple legitimate policy objectives,[175] some of which may fall under different paragraphs of Article XX or outside Article XX altogether.

19.54 However, the more recent dispute involving *EC—Seal Products* suggests that the Appellate Body has softened the requisite degree of alignment or converted it from a legal requirement to just one of the factors to consider in assessing the available evidence. In that case, the Appellate Body stated in the context of the GATT Article XX *chapeau*:

> One of the most important factors* in the assessment of arbitrary or unjustifiable discrimination' in the context of the *chapeau* is ... whether the discrimination can be reconciled with, or is rationally related to, the policy objective with respect to which the measure has been provisionally justified under one of the subparagraphs of Article XX.[176]

19.55 Moreover, the Appellate Body emphasized that 'the relationship of the discrimination to the objective of a measure is one of the most important factors, but *not the sole test*, that is relevant to the assessment of arbitrary or unjustifiable discrimination'[177] under the *chapeau*. Rather, 'depending on the nature of the measure at issue and the circumstances of the case at hand, there could be additional factors that may also be relevant to that overall assessment'.[178] This slight change in language (subsequently repeated)[179] may increase the scope for a respondent to argue in a given dispute that discrimination explained by a different legitimate objective (such as an objective that is not listed in Article XX and perhaps not even listed elsewhere in the WTO agreements) is not arbitrary or unjustifiable and therefore meets the *chapeau* requirements.

---

[174] *Brazil—Retreaded Tyres* (n 101) para 227.
[175] Thus, the Appellate Body referred to discrimination 'explained by a rationale that bears no relationship to the objective of a measure provisionally justified under one of the paragraphs of Article XX, or goes against *that* objective': *Brazil—Retreaded Tyres* (n 101) para 232 (emphasis added).
[176] *EC—Seal Products* (n 95) para 5.306 (emphasis added).
[177] ibid para 5.321 (emphasis added).
[178] ibid para 5.321.
[179] See eg WTO, *United States: Measures Concerning the Importation, Marketing and Sale of Tuna and Tuna Products—Recourse to Article 21.5 of the DSU by Mexico—Report of the Appellate Body* (20 November 2015) WT/DS381/AB/RW para 7.316.

In *EC—Seal Products* itself, the Appellate Body found the EU seal regime not justified under Article XX(a) because it was applied in a manner constituting arbitrary or unjustifiable discrimination within the meaning of the *chapeau*. The EU exempted from its ban on the importation of seal products the products from indigenous community (IC) hunts. The Appellate Body found the discrimination effected by the exemption inconsistent with the *chapeau* because: **19.56**

> The European Union has failed to demonstrate … how the discrimination resulting from the manner in which the EU Seal Regime treats IC hunts as compared to 'commercial' hunts can be reconciled with, or is related to, the policy objective of addressing EU public moral concerns regarding seal welfare.[180]

On its face, this reasoning may seem to require the strict alignment the Appellate Body suggested in *Brazil—Retreaded Tyres*. But further examination reveals flexibility in acknowledging that the EU seal regime has more than one objective and that these different objectives may be capable of reconciliation. The Appellate Body found, based on the Panel findings, that 'the principal objective of the EU Seal Regime is to address EU public moral concerns regarding seal welfare, while accommodating IC and other interests so as to mitigate the impact of the measure on those interests'.[181] In other words, although the main objective of the regime was to protect public morals as contended under Article XX(a), the Appellate Body recognized that the regime also pursued other legitimate objectives or interests not framed as falling within Article XX(a).[182] Without refuting the legitimacy of IC interests, the Appellate Body stated: **19.57**

> the European Union has not established … why the need to protect the economic and social interests of the Inuit and other indigenous peoples necessarily implies that the European Union *cannot do anything further* to ensure that the welfare of seals is addressed in the context of IC hunts, given that 'IC hunts can cause the very pain and suffering for seals that the EU public is concerned about.'[183]

This more flexible reasoning of the Appellate Body[184] allowed the EU to bring its seal regime into conformity with WTO law by modifying the IC exemption to 'explicitly ad[d] animal welfare considerations as a condition for the use of the exception'.[185] Thus, although it has been modified to comply with the Appellate **19.58**

---

[180] *EC—Seal Products* (n 95) para 5.320.
[181] ibid para 5.167.
[182] See generally Robert Howse and Joanna Langille, 'Permitting Pluralism: The *Seal Products* Dispute and Why the WTO Should Accept Trade Restrictions Justified by Noninstrumental Moral Values' (2012) 37 Yale Journal of International Law 367.
[183] *EC—Seal Products* (n 95) para 5.320 (emphasis added) (quoting *EC—Seal Products*, Panel Reports (n 125) para 7.275).
[184] cf the analysis of this case in Bartels, 'The Chapeau' (n 101) 117–21; Emily Lydgate, 'Is it Rational and Consistent? The WTO's Surprising Role in Shaping Domestic Public Policy' (2017) 20 Journal of International Economic Law 571, 573–74.
[185] WTO, 'EC—Seal Products: Status Report by European Union—Addendum' (2015) WTO Docs WT/DS400/16/Add.7, WT/DS401/17/Add.7, 2.

Body's findings regarding the *chapeau*, the EU seal regime still discriminates between commercial and IC hunts on the basis of IC interests rather than on the public moral grounds concerning animal welfare that constitute the primary objective of the regime and on which it is justified under GATT Article XX(a).

19.59 This approach to the *chapeau* has the potential to enhance WTO members' regulatory autonomy in justifying measures under the GATT/GATS general exceptions, provided that any discrimination in the measure's application has a rational and legitimate policy basis. This reasoning also has the potential to overcome some of the stringency of the exhaustive nature of the list of legitimate policy objectives in the general exceptions, since neither the EU nor the Appellate Body appeared to attempt to establish that indigenous interests fell within one of the GATT Article XX subparagraphs (even though they might have done so, for example under Article XX(a) or XX(b)). However, whether the Appellate Body's approach in *EC—Seal Products* reflects a shift towards a more nuanced understanding of the relationship between the *chapeau* of Article XX and its subparagraphs or simply arose from the complicated circumstances of that dispute (particularly the involvement of indigenous community interests) is unclear. A more recent Panel report, *Indonesia—Import Licensing Regimes*, adopted a more traditional *Brazil—Retreaded Tyres* approach.[186] The Appellate Body in this dispute against Indonesia declined to rule on GATT Article XX and declared the Panel's findings of justification under Article XX 'moot and of no legal effect'.[187] Nevertheless, unfortunately (in our view), the Appellate Body in its brief reasoning on Article XX also seemed to adopt an approach closer to that in *Brazil—Retreaded Tyres* than to the more flexible approach we have understood as arising from *EC—Seal Products*.[188]

C. Impact of General Exceptions on the Interpretation of Investment Protections

19.60 Given our suggestion in section B that WTO general exceptions may offer more policy space than is generally assumed, the impact of including such exceptions in IIAs might be expected to increase regulatory autonomy for host states. General exceptions may have such an impact, for example when compared to older style IIAs that include no exceptions or clarifications. However, modern IIAs take various approaches to exceptions and clarifications, as elaborated in section D below. The impact of including general exceptions therefore varies considerably depending on the specific context, wording, and other drafting changes to

---

[186] *Indonesia—Import Licensing Regimes*, Panel Report (n 128) paras 7.818, 7.822, 7.833 (circulated 22 December 2016, appealed 17 February 2017).
[187] *Indonesia—Import Licensing Regimes* (n 128) para 5.103 (modifying the Panel Report).
[188] ibid paras 5.98–5.99.

traditional investment disciplines. In this section, we show how including general exceptions may have unintended consequences for policy space in the investment context because of the impact of customary rules of treaty interpretation and tribunals' approaches to such rules as well as the influence of WTO jurisprudence.

1. Interpreting general exceptions in IIAs pursuant to customary rules of interpretation

19.61 As treaties, IIAs are interpreted pursuant to the 'customary rules of interpretation of public international law',[189] which are generally accepted as being partially codified[190] in the VCLT, including Articles 31 and 32. The general rule of interpretation set out in Article 31 provides, most relevantly in Article 31(1):

> A treaty shall be interpreted in good faith in accordance with the ordinary meaning to be given to the terms of the treaty in their context and in the light of its object and purpose.

19.62 As recognized by the WTO Appellate Body in more recent years, this core rule requires a holistic interpretation rather than a mechanistic and sequential approach to ordinary meaning, context, and object, and purpose.[191] In our view, this provision does not specify a strict hierarchy prioritizing the text over the other relevant elements of interpretation.

19.63 In examining the 'ordinary meaning' of WTO general exceptions in the context of IIAs, the treaty interpreter must take into account the specific interaction adopted by the treaty drafters. As discussed further in section D, the use of general exceptions in IIAs is not uniform and varies as between IIAs and as regards the precise method of incorporating or reproducing the exceptions. For example, an exception might refer to a restriction on 'investment' or a restriction on 'international trade or investment' rather than a restriction on 'trade'. Such variations may affect the substantive outcome where an exception is invoked to justify conduct or measures that would otherwise breach investment obligations. Where the general exceptions are incorporated by reference, the impact may differ depending on

---

[189] Marrakesh Agreement Establishing the World Trade Organization (entered into force 1 January 1995) annex 2 ('Understanding on Rules and Procedures Governing the Settlement of Disputes') art 3.2 (DSU).

[190] In the WTO context, see eg WTO, *United States: Countervailing Duties on Certain Corrosion-Resistant Carbon Steel Flat Products from Germany—Report of the Appellate Body* (28 November 2002) WT/DS213/AB/R para 61; WTO, *Chile: Price Band System and Safeguard Measures Relating to Certain Agricultural Products—Report of the Appellate Body* (23 September 2002) WT/DS207/AB/R para 271; *US—Gasoline* (n 109) 23. On non-codified principles see Joseph Klingler, Yuri Parkhomenko and Constantinos Salonidis (eds), *Canons of Construction and Other Interpretive Principles in Public International Law* (Wolters Kluwer, forthcoming).

[191] See eg Federico Ortino, 'Treaty Interpretation and the WTO Appellate Body Report in *US—Gambling: A Critique*' (2006) 9(1) Journal of International Economic Law 117; Isabelle Van Damme, 'Treaty Interpretation by the WTO Appellate Body' (2010) 21(3) European Journal of International Law 605.

whether the incorporation is specified as *mutatis mutandis* (ie making necessary alterations as applicable, which could mean making relevant alterations in the context of the particular IIA or in the investment context more generally).

19.64 Simon Lester asks a more fundamental question in relation to the structure of the WTO general exceptions. In the WTO context, the core notion of 'nothing' in the GATT/GATS being 'construed to prevent' the measures specified in GATT Article XX and GATS Article XIV means that such measures do not violate WTO rules. In the investment context, could an investor contend that the exception simply confirms that the host state is free to regulate as it sees fit, without meaning that the host state can avoid paying compensation for a violation of an investment obligation? Lester rightly suggests that such an argument must fail as the exception would otherwise 'have no meaning'.[192] As Lester points out, in the WTO context the same argument could also be made on the basis that WTO members may regulate as they wish but may nevertheless face retaliation in the form of 'suspension of concessions' by a successful complainant member.[193] That suggestion brings to mind the old debate as to whether a WTO member is under an obligation as a matter of international law to comply with WTO rules (today the prevailing view,[194] as espoused by the late Professor John H Jackson),[195] or whether WTO members may instead choose to accept retaliation rather than bringing measures subject to adverse rulings into conformity with WTO law.[196] Similar principles and considerations apply in confirming the international law implications of international investment law and, hence, the inappropriateness of undermining general exceptions by reference to host state discretion to face the consequences of an adverse ruling.

19.65 The 'context' for the purposes of VCLT Article 31(1) is elaborated in Article 31(2) as including the 'text, including its preamble and annexes'. The existence of general exceptions in an IIA may therefore form part of the relevant context for interpreting investment obligations to which those exceptions apply, as discussed further in section C.2 below.

---

[192] Simon Lester, 'Improving Investment Treaties through General Exceptions Provisions: The Australian Example' IISD Investment Treaty News (2014). But see Lévesque (n 26) 368.
[193] DSU (n 189) art 22.
[194] See eg Yuval Shany, *Assessing the Effectiveness of International Courts* (OUP 2014) 210.
[195] See eg John H Jackson, 'The WTO Dispute Settlement Understanding—Misunderstandings on the Nature of Legal Obligation' (1997) 91(1) American Journal of International Law 60, 63. See also John H Jackson, *The World Trading System: Law and Policy of International Economic Relations* (2nd edn, MIT Press 2000) 126. See also Marco Bronckers and Freya Baetens, 'Reconsidering Financial Remedies in WTO Dispute Settlement' (2013) 16(2) Journal of International Economic Law 281, n 46.
[196] See eg Judith Bello, 'The WTO Dispute Settlement Understanding: Less is More' (1996) 90 American Journal of International Law 416, 418. See also Alan Sykes, 'The Dispute Settlement Mechanism: Ensuring Compliance?' in Martin Daunton, Amrita Narlikar and Robert M Stern (eds), *The Oxford Handbook on the World Trade Organization* (OUP 2012) 560, 563–66.

Article 31(3) of the VCLT also refers to additional material to be taken into account in interpreting a treaty, including: 19.66

(b) any subsequent practice in the application of the treaty which establishes the agreement of the parties regarding its interpretation;
(c) any relevant rules of international law applicable in the relations between the parties.

The WTO Appellate Body has held that WTO Panel and Appellate Body Reports, even if adopted, do not constitute 'subsequent practice' within the meaning of VCLT Article 31(3)(b).[197] This reasoning is supported by WTO provisions indicating that the WTO Ministerial Conference and General Council 'have the exclusive authority to adopt interpretations' of the WTO Agreements.[198] More generally, given that WTO Panel and Appellate Body Reports are adopted quasi-automatically pursuant to the negative consensus rule,[199] and that WTO members frequently express their objections to the reasoning or conclusions of reports upon their adoption in Dispute Settlement Body meetings, it could hardly be said that such reports 'establi[sh] the agreement'[200] of the disputing parties or the WTO members regarding interpretation of WTO provisions. Similarly, and particularly given the formally bilateral[201] and private nature of ISDS, investment treaty awards are unlikely to reflect the agreement of any particular treaty parties or disputing parties regarding the interpretation of a provision of an IIA.

Article 31(3)(c) is one of the most contentious provisions of the VCLT in the   19.67
context of WTO dispute settlement. In that context, does the reference in Article 31(3)(c) to 'relevant rules of international law applicable in the relations between the parties' mean the disputing parties or the entire WTO Membership? The VCLT defines 'party' as 'a State which has consented to be bound by the treaty and for which the treaty is in force',[202] which does not necessarily resolve the question, since both the disputing parties and all WTO members have consented to be bound by the WTO agreements. The WTO Appellate Body has not explicitly resolved the question either,[203] arguably adopting a strangely narrow approach to

---

[197] WTO, *Japan: Taxes on Alcoholic Beverages—Report of the Appellate Body* (4 October 1996) WT/DS8/AB/R, WT/DS10/AB/R and WT/DS11/AB/R, 14. See also WTO, *United States: Final Anti-Dumping Measures on Stainless Steel from Mexico—Report of the Appellate Body* (30 April 2008) WT/DS344/AB/R para 158.
[198] Marrakesh Agreement Establishing the World Trade Organization (entered into force 1 January 1995) art IX:2 (WTO Agreement). See also DSU (n 189) arts 3.2, 19.2.
[199] DSU (n 189) arts 16.4, 17.14.
[200] VCLT (n 30) art 31(3)(b).
[201] cf Stephan W Schill, *The Multilateralization of International Investment Law* (CUP 2009).
[202] VCLT (n 30) art 2.1(g).
[203] See eg WTO, *Peru: Additional Duty on Imports of Certain Agricultural Products—Report of the Appellate Body* (20 July 2015) WT/DS457/AB/R para 5.105 (*Peru—Agricultural Products*). cf WTO, *European Communities: Measures Affecting the Approval and Marketing of Biotech Products—Panel Reports* (29 September 2006) WT/DS291/R, WT/DS292/R and WT/DS293/R para 7.68 (not appealed) (*EC—Approval and Marketing of Biotech Products*, Panel Report).

the word 'relevant'[204] in order to avoid doing so while still restricting the role of Article 31(3)(c). WTO Panels and the Appellate Body have tended to emphasize the role of WTO dispute settlement in 'providing security and predictability to the multilateral trading system',[205] and the importance of the 'common intention of the parties to the treaty, and not just the intentions of some of the parties',[206] hence leaning towards consistent interpretations that apply to all WTO members and therefore an interpretation of 'parties' as all WTO members. Effectively, given the unusual WTO membership (including, eg, Chinese Taipei as a separate WTO member), this reading leaves no room for non-WTO treaties to affect interpretation pursuant to Article 31(3)(c), which provides an avenue primarily for customary international law[207] and perhaps general principles of law.[208] Non-WTO treaties (even to which the disputing parties are not necessarily party) may nevertheless influence interpretation of WTO law, for example as a 'factual reference'[209] or as evidence regarding the 'ordinary meaning' of terms pursuant to Article 31(1) of the VCLT.[210]

19.68 In the context of ISDS or state–state dispute settlement under IIAs, a similar question arises regarding VCLT Article 31(3)(c). Does the term 'parties' in Article 31(3)(c) refer to the disputing parties or the treaty parties? In this context, the definition of 'party' in the VCLT is more useful. Since a party according to that definition is both a 'State' and a party to the 'treaty' in question,[211] it cannot apply to an investor claimant. Therefore, Article 31(3)(c) provides for the interpretation of IIA provisions (including general exceptions) taking account of relevant rules

---

[204] See eg WTO, *European Communities: Measures Affecting Trade in Large Civil Aircraft—Report of the Appellate Body* (18 May 2011) WT/DS316/AB/R para 846; *Peru—Agricultural Products* (n 203) para 5.101.

[205] DSU art 3.2. See *EC—Approval and Marketing of Biotech Products*, Panel Report (n 203) para 7.70 (not appealed).

[206] *Peru—Agricultural Products* (n 203) para 5.95 (but see para 5.105 as noted).

[207] See Statute of the International Court of Justice (entered into force 24 October 1945) art 38(1)(b) and discussion below (ICJ Statute).

[208] See ICJ Statute art 38(1)(c) and discussion below; *US—Shrimp* (n 102) para 158. cf *EC—Approval and Marketing of Biotech Products*, Panel Report (n 203) para 7.67. See also Andrew D Mitchell, *Legal Principles in WTO Disputes* (CUP 2008); Stephan W Schill, 'General Principles of Law and International Investment Law' in Tarcisio Gazzini and Eric De Brabandere (eds), *International Investment Law: The Sources of Rights and Obligations* (Martinus Nijhoff Publishers 2012) 133.

[209] *US—Shrimp (Article 21.5—Malaysia)* (n 100) para 130. See also Joost Pauwelyn, *Conflict of Norms in Public International Law: How WTO Law Relates to Other Rules of International Law* (CUP 2003) 269; Gabrielle Marceau, 'WTO Dispute Settlement and Human Rights' (2002) 13(4) European Journal of International Law 753, 791.

[210] See eg *US—Shrimp* (n 102) para 171; WTO, *European Communities: Conditions for the Granting of Tariff Preferences to Developing Countries—Report of the Appellate Body* (7 April 2004) WT/DS246/AB/R para 163 (*EC—Tariff Preferences*). cf UN, International Law Commission, 'Fragmentation of International Law: Difficulties Arising from the Diversification and Expansion of International Law—Report of the Study Group—Finalized by Martti Koskenniemi' (2006) UN Doc A/CN.4/L.682 para 15.

[211] VCLT art 2.1(g).

of international law applicable between the IIA parties. What are those rules? Article 38(1) of the Statute of the International Court of Justice (ICJ Statute) is understood as an informal listing of the sources of international law, including treaties,[212] customary international law,[213] the 'general principles of law recognized by civilized nations',[214] and, as a 'subsidiary means for the determination of rules of law'[215] (or as evidence of the content of international law), 'judicial decisions and teachings of the most highly qualified publicists of the various nations'.[216] In the investment treaty context, while recognizing the status of arbitral tribunals' decisions as subsidiary sources, Schill maintains that '[a]rbitral precedent' is becoming 'the principal reference point to determine the content' of the law.[217]

As discussed below, at least where the states parties to an IIA are also WTO members, an investment treaty tribunal might properly use WTO jurisprudence as an interpretative tool pursuant to Article 31(3)(c) of the VCLT and Article 38(1)(d) of the ICJ Statute in providing evidence of the meaning of general exceptions imported from WTO law into IIAs. A tribunal might also use WTO case law in interpreting WTO-style general exceptions in IIAs in connection with the 'object and purpose' of the treaty within the meaning of VCLT Article 31(1) or as a 'supplementary means of interpretation' pursuant to VCLT Article 32, which provides:

19.69

> Recourse may be had to supplementary means of interpretation, including the preparatory work of the treaty and the circumstances of its conclusion, in order to confirm the meaning resulting from the application of article 31, or to determine the meaning when the interpretation according to article 31:
> (a) leaves the meaning ambiguous or obscure; or
> (b) leads to a result which is manifestly absurd or unreasonable.

Article 32 is often referred to in the context of ambiguity or absurdity, but its reference to confirming the meaning resulting from the application of VCLT Article 31 significantly widens its potential scope and use. WTO provisions and WTO case law do not strictly form part of the 'preparatory work' of an IIA or the 'circumstances of its conclusion', but again, since Article 32 refers to these as merely examples of 'supplementary means of interpretation' (by virtue of the

19.70

---

[212] ICJ Statute art 38(1)(a).
[213] ibid art 38(1)(b).
[214] ibid art 38(1)(c).
[215] ibid art 38(1)(d).
[216] ibid art 38(1)(d). But see Jorge E Viñuales, 'Sources of International Investment Law: Conceptual Foundations of Unruly Practices' in Jean d'Aspremont and Samantha Besson (eds), *The Oxford Handbook on the Sources of International Law* (OUP 2017) 1069, 1073 regarding the limitations of this provision with respect to 'foreign investment regulation'.
[217] Stephan W Schill, 'Sources of International Investment Law: Multilateralization, Arbitral Precedent, Comparativism, Soft Law' in Jean d'Aspremont and Samantha Besson (eds), *The Oxford Handbook on the Sources of International Law* (OUP 2017) 1095, 1104.

word 'including'), they might still be relevant to interpretation of general exceptions in IIAs in some circumstances.

2. Relevance of general exceptions in interpreting obligations

19.71 As noted in section B.1.c, both the WTO Appellate Body and certain investment tribunals have relied on the absence of general exceptions in given agreements to justify particular interpretations of non-discrimination obligations. Most notably, the Appellate Body has pointed to the absence of general exceptions in the TBT Agreement in concluding that a detrimental impact on imports does not breach TBT Article 2.1 where that impact 'stems exclusively from a legitimate regulatory distinction'.[218] In contrast, the presence of general exceptions means that such a qualification does not apply to the determination of less favourable treatment under the GATT.[219] Similarly, some investment tribunals have justified a broader approach to like circumstances (including reference to regulatory purpose) by the absence of general exceptions in the relevant IIA.[220]

19.72 The relevance of the *omission* of general exceptions to the interpretation of an investment obligation is questionable, in the light of the customary rules of interpretation of treaties just discussed. In the WTO context, the Appellate Body was comparing the TBT Agreement and the GATT, both of which form part of a single treaty (both being annexed to the Marrakesh Agreement Establishing the World Trade Organization).[221] In the investment context, tribunals might properly refer to the absence of a general exception for investment obligations where such an exception appears elsewhere in the treaty, such as under NAFTA as discussed further below.

19.73 However, where no WTO-style general exceptions appear in an IIA at all, a tribunal can take note of their omission by reference only to other IIAs or the WTO agreements. Such reference to third-party treaties would not normally form part of the relevant ordinary meaning, context, or object and purpose of the IIA being interpreted.[222]

19.74 However, the *inclusion* of general exceptions in an IIA is more relevant to interpreting substantive obligations in that IIA, most obviously as part of the context of those obligations. General exceptions may be contextually relevant in interpreting the obligations to which they apply, as well as other obligations in the same treaty to which they do not apply (in that sense their omission may be

---

[218] See n 94.
[219] See n 95.
[220] See n 92.
[221] WTO Agreement (n 198).
[222] See generally Andrew D Mitchell and James Munro, 'Someone Else's Deal: Interpreting International Investment Agreements in the Light of Third-Party Agreements' (2017) 28(3) European Journal of International Law 669.

noted).²²³ Treaty drafters must therefore consider their inclusion in relation to not only their content and independent impact but also their effect on the interpretation of other IIA provisions. The inclusion of general exceptions to enhance the regulatory autonomy of host states may unintentionally diminish the flexibility and recognition of regulatory purpose in substantive investment obligations to which those exceptions apply, as discussed further in section D below.

As an example, in the award released in late 2017 in *Bear Creek Mining v Peru*, the tribunal suggested that the existence of WTO-style general exceptions in the PTA between Canada and Peru,²²⁴ as well as detailed provisions on expropriation, meant that 'no other exceptions from general international law or otherwise can be considered applicable in this case'.²²⁵ In that case, a Canadian company, Beer Creek Mining Corporation, claimed, *inter alia*, that Peru had expropriated its investment by revoking a decree of public necessity, which was a legal prerequisite for certain of its mining operations in Peru.²²⁶ Peru responded that its actions entailed an exercise of its police powers,²²⁷ as supported by the PTA's 'carve-out for measures that are necessary to protect human life or health'.²²⁸ Yet the tribunal found the exceptions in Article 2201.1 of the PTA to have precisely the opposite effect: 'There is, thus, no need to enter into the discussion between the Parties regarding the jurisprudence concerning any police power exception for measures addressed to investments'.²²⁹ This ruling provides significant contemporary evidence highlighting the risk we have identified, namely that including WTO-style general exceptions may undermine the parties' intention of enhancing policy space by restricting existing exceptions or regulatory flexibilities in arbitral tribunals' interpretation of investment protections.

19.75

3. Relevance of WTO jurisprudence in interpreting IIAs

WTO case law on the interpretation and application of the general exceptions in GATT Article XX and GATS Article XIV is arguably relevant to the interpretation of such exceptions within IIAs. Where an IIA incorporates the WTO provisions by reference, WTO case law could conceivably be relevant in determining the 'ordinary meaning' of terms within the WTO general exceptions, pursuant to VCLT Article 31(1). WTO case law might also be regarded as relevant to

19.76

---

²²³ cf *Joseph Charles Lemire v Ukraine*, ICSID Case No ARB/06/18, Award (28 March 2011) paras 45–47.
²²⁴ Canada–Peru Free Trade Agreement (entered into force 1 August 2009) art 2201.
²²⁵ *Bear Creek Mining Corporation v Peru*, ICSID Case No ARB/14/21, Award (30 November 2017) para 473.
²²⁶ ibid paras 122, 149, 202, 341.
²²⁷ Ibid para 469.
²²⁸ ibid para 462.
²²⁹ ibid para 474. For further discussion of this dispute, see Joshua Paine, 'Bear Creek Mining Corporation v Republic of Peru: Judging the Social License of Foreign Investments and Applying New Style Investment Treaties' (2018) *ICSID Review* (forthcoming).

interpretation of general exceptions in IIAs either as a *subsidiary* means of identifying the relevant rules of international law applicable between the IIA parties pursuant to Article 31(3)(c) of the VCLT and Article 38(1)(d) of the ICJ Statute, or as a *supplementary* means of interpretation pursuant to VCLT Article 32. In practice, tribunals may not specify the legal basis on which they are referring to WTO case law (or WTO provisions) in terms of the VCLT,[230] and may not restrict their use of such materials to the circumstances and limits of the VCLT. The use of investment treaty tribunals of WTO case law in interpreting WTO-style general exceptions as applied to investment obligations, whether in accordance with or outside the scope of the VCLT, creates certain interpretative risks.

19.77 In the context of the WTO necessity test under GATT Article XX, Regan characterized the 'myth of cost-benefit balancing' as:

> dangerous because as long as the Appellate Body continues to state a standard cost–benefit balancing test in part of each opinion on 'necessity', and as long as trade lawyers continue to believe that such balancing is the applicable test, there is always the possibility that the Appellate Body will be taken in by its own misdescription of what it has been doing and will start actually trying to balance the domestic benefits of a measure against the cost in reduced trade.[231]

19.78 This risk is increased in the context of international investment law, where investment treaty tribunals—a step removed from the WTO—might simply transpose the Appellate Body's description of what the necessity test or the *chapeau* require without recognising or applying the nuances of that test in the same way as the Appellate Body does in practice. Investment tribunals might, for example, contrary to the realities of the WTO jurisprudence: fail to adopt a broad, evolutionary interpretation of the exhaustive list of objectives in the general exceptions; prohibit discrimination in the context of the *chapeau* where justified by a different legitimate objective from the respondent's claimed objective within that list; or undertake an independent process of ranking the importance of different policy objectives in place of the respondent state.

19.79 This scenario provides a particular example of the difficulties that may arise when an investment treaty tribunal relies on WTO case law concerning general exceptions. Such difficulties are inherent in the reliance of investment treaty tribunals on WTO law, unless the tribunal includes an arbitrator with deep experience of international trade law. Kurtz, for example, criticizes specific investment treaty tribunals for their reading of WTO law in the context of national treatment.[232]

---

[230] See eg *Continental Casualty Co v Argentina*, ICSID Case No ARB/03/9, Award (5 September 2008) para 192.
[231] Regan (n 139) 350.
[232] Kurtz (n 19) 97–108.

In one area, reference to WTO jurisprudence might assist in ensuring proper **19.80** interpretation of general exceptions in IIAs. Several investment treaty tribunals have suggested that exceptions should be interpreted narrowly.[233] In contrast, the WTO Appellate Body has made clear that no such interpretative rule applies,[234] and moreover that characterizing a provision as an exception does not detract from its importance in general or in comparison with other treaty provisions.[235] Greater reflection by investment treaty tribunals about WTO reasoning in this regard (without formal reliance on such reasoning as part of the interpretative process) might allow for a more accurate understanding of the customary rules of interpretation of treaties, which apply equally to obligations and exceptions, however framed.

D. General Exceptions and Clarifications in Modern Investment Treaty Practice

States have in recent years incorporated policy space in their IIAs in various ways. **19.81** Some have somewhat bluntly grafted WTO-style exceptions onto IIAs through the direct incorporation of Article XX of GATT or Article XIV of GATS, or the reproduction of the texts of those WTO agreements. Others have been more selective, applying WTO-style exceptions only to particular investment obligations, or qualifying investment obligations to ensure their interoperability with exceptions. A final alternative is to eschew such exceptions and instead include more extensive clarifications and qualifications in investment disciplines themselves to enhance policy space. We discuss each of these approaches in turn, after introducing the use of general exceptions in IIAs. Our analysis shows significant variation in the impact of general exceptions in IIAs, depending on the investment obligations covered by such exceptions and express clarifications within such obligations. General exceptions applied to all investment obligations may unintentionally reduce policy space, while a failure to rely on such exceptions at all may place too much reliance on textual clarifications to positive investment obligations.

---

[233] See eg *Noble Ventures Inc v Romania* ICSID Case No ARB/01/11, Award (12 October 2005) para 55; *Enron* (n 63) para 331; *Sempra Energy International v Argentina*, ICSID Case No ARB/02/16, Award (15 May 2007) para 373. cf *Aguas del Tunari SA v Bolivia*, ICSID Case No ARB/02/3, Decision on Respondent's Objections to Jurisdiction (21 October 2005) para 91.

[234] See WTO, *European Communities: Measures Concerning Meat and Meat Products (Hormones)—Report of the Appellate Body* (16 January 1998) WT/DS26/AB/R; WT/DS48/AB/R para 104 (*EC—Hormones*).

[235] See *EC—Tariff Preferences* (n 210) para 98. Although the Appellate Body in one instance relied on the concept of *in dubio mitius*, it has sensibly not done so again: *EC—Hormones* (n 234) para 165, n 154; cf *China—Publications and Audiovisual Products* (n 124) para 411.

1. Canada's 2004 model IIA: early use of WTO-style general exceptions

19.82 Although we have identified a recent trend towards reflecting WTO-style general exceptions in modern IIAs, they have been included in PTAs for much longer, albeit typically not applying to investment obligations. For example, NAFTA incorporated GATT Article XX (by reference) to certain provisions excluding services and investment[236] and included GATT Article XX(d) wording in relation to other provisions including services provisions.[237]

a. Article 10: general exceptions

19.83 Canada included a WTO-style exception for investment obligations in its (now-superseded)[238] 2004 model text. In particular, Article 10.1 provided:[239]

> 1. Subject to the requirement that such measures are not applied in a manner that would constitute arbitrary or unjustifiable discrimination between investments or between investors, or a disguised restriction on international trade or investment, nothing in this Agreement shall be construed to prevent a Party from adopting or enforcing measures necessary:
>
> (a) to protect human, animal or plant life or health;
> (b) to ensure compliance with laws and regulations that are not inconsistent with the provisions of this Agreement; or
> (c) for the conservation of living or non-living exhaustible natural resources.

This example provides a useful starting point for examining WTO-style exceptions in IIAs. It is reflected in a number of Canadian IIAs[240] and reveals several features.

19.84 First, it reproduces the text of Article XX of GATT and Article XIV of GATS with a number of modifications. In particular, its *chapeau* replaces references to 'discrimination between *countries where the same conditions prevail*'[241] with the phrase 'discrimination between *investments or between investors*'. Its *chapeau* also replaces 'disguised restriction on *trade in services*' (GATS) and 'disguised restriction on *international trade*' (GATT) with 'disguised restriction *on international trade or*

---

[236] NAFTA (n 33) art 2101.1.
[237] ibid art 2101.2.
[238] See also *Canadian Model Foreign Investment Promotion and Protection Agreement* (5 May 2014) art 18 ('General Exceptions').
[239] *Canadian Model Foreign Investment Promotion and Protection Agreement* (2004): <https://www.italaw.com/documents/Canadian2004-FIPA-model-en.pdf> accessed 7 November 2017. Other parts of art 10 provide additional agreement-wide exceptions relating to prudential measures, national security, and other matters. We confine our discussion to art 10.1, which most closely resembles GATT art XX/GATS art XIV.
[240] See eg Agreement between Canada and Ecuador for the Promotion and Reciprocal Protection of Investments, (entered into force 6 June 1997) art XVII:3; Agreement between Canada and the Slovak Republic for the Promotion and Protection of Investments (entered into force 14 March 2012) art IX:1; Agreement between Canada and the Republic of Peru for the Promotion and Protection of Investments (entered into force 20 June 2007) art 10.1.
[241] GATT art XX (emphasis added); GATS art XIV refers to 'like' conditions.

investment'. These modifications reflect the different focus of IIAs, namely, the promotion and protection of foreign investments and investors, as opposed to the liberalization of international trade in goods and services. However, precluding arbitrary or unjustifiable discrimination simply as between 'investors or between investments' without reference to their surrounding *conditions* arguably makes it harder for a host state to satisfy the Article 10.1 *chapeau* compared to the WTO equivalents.[242] Although the qualification of 'arbitrary or unjustifiable' discrimination remains, a complainant investor could invoke a broader array of comparators to evince such discrimination. It would nevertheless remain for the tribunal to determine whether the proposed investments or investors were comparable, which could entail an examination of their conditions.

A second noteworthy feature of the Canadian introduction of WTO general exceptions into its model IIA is its inclusion of only three policy objectives in the subparagraphs of Article 10.1, omitting other values that the WTO exceptions recognize as legitimate such as 'public morals', 'national treasures', and shortages in the supply of essential products. Further, Article 10.1(c) subjects measures pursuing all three objectives to a '*necessary*' requirement, whereas GATT Article XX(g) applies a less onerous nexus requirement of '*relating to*' with respect to measures for the conservation of *exhaustible natural resources*. Both these changes appear to increase the burden on the host state in defending its measure under the exception. In contrast, Article 10.1(c) omits the qualification from GATT Article XX(g) that such measures be 'made effective in conjunction with restrictions on domestic production or consumption', removing that requirement from the host state's responsibility. However, this difference may have little practical effect, given that protected investments would be operating within the host state's territory and therefore a comparison with domestic production or consumption may be inapt. **19.85**

2. General exceptions without clarifications to investment obligations

The 2016 signed Agreement between Japan and the Islamic Republic of Iran on Reciprocal Promotion and Protection of Investment also reproduces the text of GATT Article XX and GATS Article XIV, albeit with fewer modifications. As with the *chapeau* of the 2004 Canada model text—and unlike the WTO equivalents—its *chapeau* links the applicable discrimination or disguised restrictions to 'investors of the other Contracting Party and their investments in the Territory' without further qualification.[243] While its list of protected policy objectives more faithfully reproduces the WTO equivalents verbatim and additionally includes 'public morals' and 'national treasures', it omits an equivalent to Article XX(g) of GATT regarding the conservation of exhaustible natural resources. **19.86**

---

[242] Lester (n 192).
[243] Agreement between Japan and Iran on Reciprocal Promotion and Protection of Investment (not yet in force) art 13.

19.87 Significantly, while including a WTO-style general exception applicable to the whole agreement, this IIA omits any clarifications in the investment obligations. For instance, the agreement does not clarify the extent to which legitimate public welfare measures might constitute indirect expropriations. Nor does it clarify the scope of FET, apart from the traditional and rather conservative clarification that the requirement of FET does 'not require treatment in addition to or beyond that which is required by the customary international law minimum standard of treatment of aliens'.[244] Further, although the non-discrimination provision refers to investments or investors 'in like circumstances',[245] it does not specify whether legitimate regulatory distinctions can inform this requirement of likeness.

a. General exceptions

19.88 The Agreement between Rwanda and Turkey concerning the Reciprocal Promotion and Protection of Investments signed in 2016 also includes a broad general exceptions provision modelled on the WTO equivalents, but with significantly modified text.[246] Article 5 provides:

> 1. Nothing in this Agreement shall be construed to prevent a Contracting Party from adopting, maintaining, or enforcing any non-discriminatory legal measures:
>   (a) designed and applied for the protection of human, animal or plant life or health, or the environment;
>   (b) related to the conservation of living or non-living exhaustible natural resources.

19.89 As with the Canadian model IIA, Article 5 includes only two of the subparagraphs of the WTO general exceptions. Moreover, the substance of the *chapeau* of the WTO general exceptions is reduced to the term 'non-discriminatory legal measures'. Article 5 contains no further guidance on relevant comparators in identifying discrimination or whether all discrimination is captured, rather than only arbitrary, unjustifiable, or disguised discrimination. These changes could hinder a respondent's reliance on the Article 5.1 exceptions in comparison to WTO general exceptions.

19.90 Conversely, Article 5.1(a) replaces the word 'necessary' in the WTO general exceptions with the arguably broader words 'designed and applied', implying that a measure might fall within this paragraph even if it is not the least restrictive means of achieving the listed objective. The provision also appears to incorporate elements of the WTO Appellate Body's jurisprudence that broaden the scope of the exceptions, in favour of the respondent, by adding the words 'or the environment' to Article 5.1(a)[247] and 'living or non-living' to Article 5.1(b).[248]

---

[244] ibid art 5.
[245] ibid art 4.1.
[246] Agreement between Rwanda and Turkey concerning the Reciprocal Promotion and Protection of Investments (not yet in force) art 5.
[247] See *US—Shrimp* (n 102) para 128.
[248] See *Brazil—Retreaded Tyres* (n 101) para 151.

19.91 As with the IIA between Japan and Iran, the IIA between Turkey and Rwanda does not explain how its general exceptions provision relates to the policy space otherwise embedded in its substantive investment disciplines. For instance, the IIA between Turkey and Rwanda does not explain the relevance of regulatory purpose to the concept of likeness or clarify the scope of FET or the extent to which legitimate public welfare measures may be found to constitute indirect expropriations. Whether these general exceptions are intended to displace or supplement a host state's right to regulate under customary international law is also unspecified.

19.92 These two IIAs signed in 2016 thus provide examples of treaties incorporating WTO-style general exceptions without further clarification, creating a risk that an investment treaty tribunal might interpret the absence of clarifications to substantive investment obligations as indicating that the pre-existing policy space in those obligations is narrower or no longer required. For example, a tribunal might interpret the omission of reference to regulatory purpose in identifying investments in like circumstances in the light of the existence of general exceptions elsewhere in the treaty, such that the requirement of like circumstances does *not* entail a consideration of regulatory purpose. A reduction in the number or type of regulatory objectives mentioned in the general exceptions in an IIA as compared to the WTO provisions may also limit the scope of protection offered to a host state under such exceptions.

3. General exceptions to selected investment obligations or with clarifications

19.93 Unlike the stark approach of these IIAs signed in 2016 between Japan and Iran and between Rwanda and Turkey, some other IIAs incorporate WTO-style general exceptions only in relation to certain investment obligations and/or alongside clarifications on the scope or meaning of investment obligations. Although this more subtle approach mitigates the risk of a tribunal interpreting the general exceptions as removing policy space within investment obligations, some of these IIAs do not fully address this risk in connection with all relevant obligations.

19.94 Article 28.3.1 of CETA explicitly incorporates GATT Article XX with respect to 'Sections B (Establishment of investment) and C (Non-discriminatory treatment) of Chapter Eight (Investment)'. Sections B and C of CETA's investment chapter include investment obligations that are comparable to WTO obligations, including market access, performance requirements, national treatment, and MFN treatment. As Article 28.3.1 incorporates GATT Article XX as is, rather than *mutatis mutandis*, the reference in the *chapeau* of GATT Article XX to a 'disguised restriction on international trade' applies in the context of Sections B and C of CETA's investment chapter, potentially rendering that part of the *chapeau* inutile where any alleged discrimination does not affect international trade. As with the IIA between Turkey and Rwanda mentioned, Article 28.3.1 adds language taken from WTO jurisprudence ensuring that the GATT Article XX(b) exception extends to protection of the environment and the GATT Article XX(g) exception extends to non-living resources.

19.95 Article 28.3.2 of CETA applies an exception akin to GATS Article XIV to certain services obligations as well as Sections B and C of the Investment Chapter. The *chapeau* of this provision refers to 'trade in services', and its subparagraphs are limited to 'public morals', 'human health', and securing compliance with not-otherwise-inconsistent laws and regulations. As Article 28.3.2 is a non-identical textual reproduction of GATT Article XIV, a tribunal might be inclined to place less weight on WTO jurisprudence in construing Article 28.3.2 as compared to Article 28.3.1. Further, although CETA requires state–state dispute settlement panels to 'take into account relevant interpretations in reports of Panels and the Appellate Body adopted by the WTO Dispute Settlement Body',[249] no such rule applies explicitly to ISDS.

19.96 WTO-style general exceptions do not apply to Section D of CETA's investment chapter, which includes obligations traditionally characterized as flowing from customary international law, such as FET and expropriation. Instead, Article 8.9.1 clarifies that 'the Parties reaffirm their right to regulate within their territories to achieve legitimate policy objectives, such as the protection of public health, safety, the environment or public morals, social or consumer protection or the promotion and protection of cultural diversity'. CETA also enshrines a closed list of conduct that is capable of violating FET,[250] providing latitude to the host state in otherwise regulating, as well as an annex on expropriation clarifying that:

> except in the rare circumstance when the impact of a measure or series of measures is so severe in light of its purpose that it appears manifestly excessive, non-discriminatory measures of a Party that are designed and applied to protect legitimate public welfare objectives, such as health, safety and the environment, do not constitute indirect expropriations.[251]

19.97 The Australia–New Zealand Investment Protocol (ANZIP) signed in 2010 takes a similar approach to CETA.[252] Article 19 contains general exceptions similar to GATT Article XX and GATS Article XIV, but limited in application to national treatment, MFN treatment, performance requirements, and senior management and board of directors. Core investment disciplines such as expropriation and FET are not subject to these general exceptions, avoiding the question of how general exceptions affect the policy space already embedded or reflected in those disciplines. ANZIP also contains a clarification on expropriation corresponding

---

[249] CETA (n 10) art 29.17.
[250] ibid art 8.10.2.
[251] ibid annex 8-A para 3.
[252] Protocol on Investment to the Australia New Zealand Closer Economic Relations Trade Agreement (entered into force 3 January 2013) (ANZIP).

Importing WTO General Exceptions into IIAs

to that in CETA as noted.[253] ANZIP does not contain significant clarifications on the scope of FET,[254] although the treaty excludes ISDS altogether, which itself diminishes the risk of an adverse tribunal decision.

Neither CETA nor ANZIP includes textual clarifications concerning the meaning of 'like circumstances' in the context of the obligation of non-discrimination. As discussed in section C, a tribunal might therefore interpret the presence of general exceptions applicable to non-discrimination obligations as reducing the relevance of regulatory purpose in applying those obligations, just as the WTO Appellate Body has done in relation to GATT Article III in contrast to TBT Article 2.1.[255] Previous investment treaty awards might otherwise suggest that regulatory purpose is relevant in identifying like circumstances and therefore in precluding a breach of the non-discrimination obligation, without the need to rely subsequently on a general exception. **19.98**

A similar difficulty arises under the 2014 *Korea–Australia Free Trade Agreement* (KAFTA), which applies a WTO-style general exception to the whole investment chapter, although limited to the policy objectives concerning 'health', 'national treasures', 'exhaustible natural resources', and not-otherwise-inconsistent laws and regulations.[256] KAFTA includes textual clarifications aimed at ensuring that FET and expropriation do not impugn the ability to regulate,[257] without clarifying the meaning of 'like circumstances'. Two older agreements—the New Zealand–China Free Trade Agreement (NZCFTA)[258] and the ASEAN Comprehensive Investment Agreement[259]—also contain general exceptions applicable to all investment obligations[260] as well as a clarificatory annex on expropriation that explicitly requires indirect expropriation to be 'disproportionate to the public purpose'[261] (perhaps drawing on investment treaty awards discussed in section B.1.a). The agreements contain relatively minor clarifications regarding FET.[262] Neither of these agreements, however, clarifies the meaning of like circumstances. **19.99**

In contrast, the IIA between Nigeria and Singapore signed in 2016 includes a general exceptions provision applicable to the entire agreement, but subject to the following footnote: **19.100**

---

[253] ibid art 14, n 7.
[254] See ibid arts 12.3, 12.4.
[255] See section B.1.c.
[256] Free Trade Agreement between the Republic of Korea and Australia (entered into force 12 December 2014) art 22.1.3 (KAFTA).
[257] ibid annex 11-A, annex 11-B.
[258] Free Trade Agreement between New Zealand and the People's Republic of China (entered into force 1 October 2008) (NZCFTA).
[259] ASEAN Comprehensive Investment Agreement (entered into force 24 February 2012) (ASEAN CIA).
[260] NZCFTA (n 258) art 200; ASEAN CIA (n 259) art 17.
[261] NZCFTA (n 258) annex 13, para 3(b); ASEAN CIA (n 259) annex 2, para 3(c).
[262] NZCFTA (n 258) art 143; ASEAN CIA (n 259) art 11.

For greater certainty, the application of the general exceptions to these provisions shall not be interpreted so as to diminish the ability of governments to take measures where investors are not in like circumstances due to the existence of legitimate regulatory objectives.[263]

This agreement also contains clarifications enhancing policy space in connection with expropriation[264] and, to a lesser extent, FET.[265]

19.101 Some IIAs more comprehensively address policy space through both general exceptions and clarifications to investment obligations. The IIA signed between the Slovak Republic and Iran in 2016 includes a WTO-style general exceptions provision that applies to the agreement as a whole, although limited to objectives concerning 'health', 'national treasures', 'exhaustible natural resources', and to ensure compliance with laws and regulations.[266] This agreement overlays these general exceptions with textual clarifications that preserve the pre-existing policy space in expropriation,[267] fair and equitable treatment,[268] and non-discrimination provisions:

> A measure of the Contracting Party that treats investors of the other Contracting Party or their investments less favorably than:
>
> a) its own investors or their investments is not inconsistent with paragraph 1 of this Article; or
> b) investors of another State or their investments is not inconsistent with paragraph 2 of this Article;
>
> if it is adopted and applied by the Contracting Party in pursuit of a legitimate public purpose that is not based on the nationality of the investor or of nationality of the owner of an investment, either explicitly or factually, including the protection of health, safety, the environment, and internationally and domestically recognized labor rights, or the elimination of bribery and corruption, and it bears a reasonable connection to the stated purpose.[269]

19.102 The IIA signed in 2016 between Hong Kong and Chile takes a similar approach, including a general exceptions provision applicable to the whole agreement,[270] an annex clarifying indirect expropriation in connection with public welfare objectives,[271] and further policy specifications concerning fair and equitable treatment[272]

---

[263] Investment Promotion and Protection Agreement between Nigeria and Singapore (not yet in force) art 28, n 6.
[264] ibid annex I.
[265] ibid art 3.
[266] Agreement between the Slovak Republic and the Islamic Republic of Iran for the Promotion and Reciprocal Protection of Investments (not yet in force) art 11.
[267] ibid art 6.5.
[268] ibid art 4.2.
[269] ibid art 4.4.
[270] Investment Agreement between the Hong Kong Special Administrative Region of the People's Republic of China and the Republic of Chile (not yet in force) art 18.
[271] ibid annex I, para 3(b).
[272] ibid art 6.

and like circumstances.[273] Amendments to the Singapore–Australia Free Trade Agreement (SAFTA)[274] that were signed in 2016 and entered into force in 2017[275] also include WTO-style general exceptions[276] together with textual clarifications that preserve policy within investment obligations.[277] This more comprehensive approach provides maximum policy space to host states through both general exceptions and investment obligations, offsetting the possibility that the inclusion of general exceptions could unintentionally disrupt the existing interpretation of investment disciplines.

4. Clarifications to investment obligations without general exceptions

19.103 Another emerging approach eschews broad and general exceptions in favour of clarifications to investment obligations that to some extent appear designed to codify policy space already embedded in international investment law or to address overly expansive investment treaty interpretations of investment obligations.

19.104 The most prominent example of this approach is found in the investment chapter of the Trans-Pacific Partnership (TPP) as signed in 2016 by twelve countries,[278] but from which the United States has now withdrawn, precluding entry into force in that form. (Most of the TPP provisions are nevertheless now incorporated in the Comprehensive and Progressive Agreement on Trans-Pacific Partnership.) Although the TPP contains general exceptions in a separate chapter,[279] they do not apply to the investment chapter. The TPP investment chapter does contain some exceptions that adopt wording from the WTO general exceptions, but they apply only to certain investment obligations concerning performance requirements.[280] Instead, the TPP contains fairly extensive clarifications to the investment obligations concerning expropriation,[281] fair and equitable treatment,[282] and non-discrimination:

> For greater certainty, whether treatment is accorded in 'like circumstances' under Article 9.4 (National Treatment) or Article 9.5 (Most-Favoured-Nation Treatment) depends on the totality of the circumstances, including whether the relevant

---

[273] ibid art 4 n 4.
[274] Singapore–Australia Free Trade Agreement (entered into force 28 July 2003), as amended from 24 February 2006, 13 February 2007, 11 October 2007 and 2 September 2011 and 1 December 2017 (SAFTA).
[275] The amendments were signed on 13 October 2016 and entered into force on 1 December 2017.
[276] SAFTA (n 274) ch 8 art 19.
[277] ibid ch 8 art 6, art 13, n 8, annex 8-A.
[278] Trans-Pacific Partnership, text released following legal review 26 January 2016 (not in force) ch 9 (TPP).
[279] ibid ch 29, art 29.1.
[280] ibid arts 9.10.3(d), 9.10.3(h).
[281] ibid art 9.8, annex 9-B, annex 9-C.
[282] ibid art 9.6, annex 9-A.

treatment distinguishes between investors or investments on the basis of legitimate public welfare objectives.[283]

19.105 The TPP also imposes positive obligations on parties to uphold certain standards with respect to labour[284] and the environment.[285] An additional provision recognizes environmental, health and other regulatory objectives in the context of investment, but it is not an exception because it protects only measures that are 'otherwise consistent with' the investment chapter:

> Nothing in this Chapter shall be construed to prevent a Party from adopting, maintaining or enforcing *any measure otherwise consistent with this Chapter* that it considers appropriate to ensure that investment activity in its territory is undertaken in a manner sensitive to environmental, health or other regulatory objectives.[286]

19.106 This approach of the TPP may be understood to some extent as the US approach, given the similarity identified through empirical studies between the TPP text as signed and US FTAs.[287] The Korea–United States Free Trade Agreement (KORUS), for example, contains a similar provision regarding investment and environment,[288] no general exceptions, clarifications to fair and equitable treatment[289] and expropriation,[290] and dedicated chapters on labour[291] and the environment.[292] (However, unlike the TPP, KORUS does not clarify 'like circumstances' or otherwise indicate the relevance of regulatory purpose to non-discrimination.) The US approach also finds its way into non-US treaties. The IIA signed in 2016 between Nigeria and Morocco[293] similarly excludes general exceptions in favour of clarifications on fair and equitable treatment,[294] expropriation,[295] and non-discrimination,[296] alongside positive obligations concerning labour and human

---

[283] ibid arts 9.4–9.5, n 4.
[284] ibid ch 19. See eg Joo-Cheong Tham and KD Ewing, 'Labour Clauses in the TPP and TTIP: A Comparison without a Difference?' (2016) 17 Melbourne Journal of International Law 369.
[285] TPP (n 278) ch 20. See eg Joshua P Meltzer, 'The Trans-Pacific Partnership Agreement, the Environment and Climate Change' in Tania Voon (ed), *Trade Liberalisation and International Cooperation: A Legal Analysis of the Trans-Pacific Partnership Agreement* (Edward Elgar 2013) 207.
[286] TPP (n 278) art 9.16 (emphasis added).
[287] See eg Tomer Broude, Yoram Z Haftel and Alexander Thompson, 'The Trans-Pacific Partnership and Regulatory Space: A Comparison of Treaty Texts' (2017) 20 Journal of International Economic Law 391; Todd Allee and Andrew Lugg, 'Who Wrote the Rules for the Trans-Pacific Partnership?' (2016) Research and Politics DOI: 10.1177/2053168016658919; Wolfgang Alschner and Dmitriy Skougarevskiy, 'The New Gold Standard? Empirically Situating the Trans-Pacific Partnership in the Investment Treaty Universe' (2016) 17 Journal of World Investment and Trade 339.
[288] Free Trade Agreement between the United States of America and the Republic of Korea (entered into force 15 March 2012) art 11.10.
[289] ibid art 11.5, annex 11-A.
[290] ibid art 11.6, annexes 11-A, 11B.
[291] ibid ch 19.
[292] ibid ch 20.
[293] Reciprocal Promotion and Protection Agreement between Morocco and Nigeria (not yet in force).
[294] ibid art 7.
[295] ibid art 8.
[296] ibid art 6.3.

rights.[297] Additional provisions provide recognition and a targeted exception for 'environmental and social concerns'.[298]

19.107 As noted in section D.3, IIAs including general exceptions applicable to all investment obligations together with extensive clarification to core investment obligations (such as the 2017 amendments to SAFTA) maximize policy space for host states through both exceptions and obligations, potentially curtailing overly expansive interpretations of such obligations by investment treaty tribunals. In contrast, the TPP/US approach arguably more closely reflects the current state of international investment law, perpetuating its uncertainties. The absence of a layer of general exceptions may create more scope for investment treaty tribunals to impose a proportionality test, as identified in section B.1. As we have explained, in our view such a test is more intrusive than the interpretation of WTO general exceptions by the WTO Appellate Body, which grants significant deference to WTO members in choosing their appropriate level of protection with respect to a given legitimate policy objective.

19.108 The TPP approach may provide additional comfort to host states through its footnote in relation to non-discrimination, when compared to IIAs such as CETA and ANZIP that contain both general exceptions and clarifications with respect to certain investment obligations, while omitting clarifications regarding the meaning of like circumstances or the relevance of regulatory purpose to the non-discrimination obligation. In relation to fair and equitable treatment and expropriation, the TPP approach is similar to that in CETA and ANZIP, since they use clarifications rather than general exceptions with respect to those investment obligations.

19.109 The IIA signed in 2016 between Argentina and Qatar[299] adopts an approach somewhere between CETA and the TPP. Like the TPP, this agreement contains no WTO-style general exceptions applicable to investment obligations. However, unlike the TPP, it contains relatively minimal clarifications regarding fair and equitable treatment[300] and expropriation,[301] and no explicit likeness requirement in its non-discrimination obligation.[302] Like CETA, this agreement contains a dedicated provision enshrining the host state's 'right to regulate':

> None of the provisions of this Agreement shall affect the inherent right of the Contracting Parties to regulate within their territories through measures necessary to achieve legitimate policy objectives, such as the protection of public health, safety, the environment, public morals, social and consumer protection.[303]

---

[297] ibid art 15.
[298] ibid art 13.4.
[299] The Reciprocal Promotion and Protection of Investments between Argentina and Qatar (not yet in force).
[300] ibid art 3.4.
[301] ibid art 5.2(b).
[302] ibid art 4.
[303] ibid art 10.

19.110 This provision appears closer to an exception than the corresponding provision in CETA, which, as noted, simply 'reaffirms' the parties' right to regulate, leaving uncertain the result of any conflict between such reaffirmation and a positive investment obligation. Yet the Argentina–Qatar provision still seems less clear than GATT Article XX/GATS Article XIV in its intention to provide an exception to what would otherwise be a violation of the agreement. A tribunal might conclude that, notwithstanding its finding of violation, the host state's right to regulate remains intact.

E. Conclusion

19.111 In this chapter, we have highlighted underlying nuances of international investment law and WTO law that depart somewhat from common understandings of these two regimes. In relation to investment, we have pointed out that the use of the concept of proportionality in the form of a cost–benefit analysis or proportionality *stricto sensu* in relation to the investment disciplines concerning expropriation, FET, and non-discrimination significantly restricts host states' ability to determine and prioritize their own policy objectives and implementation.

19.112 Conversely, in the WTO sphere, we have explained how the WTO general exceptions in GATT Article XX and GATS Article XIV provide greater flexibility to WTO members than may be suggested by the low rate at which WTO respondent members have successfully invoked those provisions. The failure to establish that a challenged measure is justified by one of the general exceptions is typically due to discriminatory application of the measure contrary to the *chapeau* of the general exceptions, which WTO panels and the Appellate Body construe strictly.

19.113 Yet, absent discrimination, and notwithstanding frequent references to balancing different factors including the importance of the objective pursued, WTO Members have significant leeway to choose their own level of protection in pursuing particular objectives. Unless a complainant can point to a WTO-consistent alternative measure that is reasonably available to the respondent, less trade-restrictive than the challenged measure, and makes an equivalent contribution to the objective such that the respondent's chosen level of protection is maintained, the respondent's defence under the general exceptions is likely to succeed. The Appellate Body has also begun to demonstrate greater acceptance of the reality of multiple regulatory purposes in interpreting the *chapeau*.

19.114 Despite this hidden flexibility in the WTO general exceptions, applying them to investment obligations in IIAs will not necessarily increase host states' regulatory autonomy, as the treaty drafters apparently intend. The impact of the general exceptions on the intrusiveness of the IIA on host state regulation depends on the investment obligations to which it applies and the extent of any clarifications in the same IIA regarding those obligations. The impact of general exceptions also depends on the extent to which investment treaty tribunals rely on WTO jurisprudence, and more generally the way in which such tribunals engage in treaty interpretation, particularly in connection with the customary rules of interpretation as reflected in VCLT Articles 31 and 32. The VCLT rules provide scope for reference to general exceptions, for example as context in interpreting investment obligations within the same treaty. This approach may decrease the acknowledgement of regulatory purpose within investment protections such as expropriation, FET, and non-discrimination, in view of the existence of general exceptions. Tribunals may also be inclined to refer to the existence of general exceptions in WTO law or other IIAs in interpreting investment obligations, perhaps improperly reading into the omission of general exceptions from the treaty before them as evidence of the intention of the treaty parties not to take account of such non-economic policy goals. Reliance on WTO case law, which might also fall indirectly within the proper approach to treaty interpretation under the VCLT, could exacerbate this problem, if investment treaty tribunals pay more attention to what the WTO Appellate Body says it is doing than to what the Appellate Body does in applying the exceptions.

19.115 States have adopted various approaches in including WTO-style general exceptions in the context of investment provisions in recent years, perhaps in progressive acknowledgement of the interpretive difficulties discussed here. IIAs that rely solely on general exceptions (applicable to all investment obligations) to protect policy space may no longer benefit from the evolution of investment disciplines with in-built regulatory protections. IIAs that restrict general exceptions to particular investment obligations and pair them with clarifications to those obligations may leave gaps in protection for host states, for example where clarifications apply to expropriation and FET provisions but not non-discrimination. Nevertheless, IIAs that rely solely on clarifications in a more traditional approach to investment protection may miss out on the additional benefits provided by the WTO Appellate Body's true understanding of the general exceptions, which offers greater flexibility than the proportionality analysis sometimes favoured by investment treaty tribunals. In our view, careful use of general exceptions is best combined with modern clarifications to investment obligations in order to ensure that treaty parties achieve what they intend in importing general exceptions from the WTO into investment treaties.

20

THE FET STANDARD UNDER CETA
A Missed Opportunity to Restore the Balance between Private and Public Interests in the EU Investment Treaty Landscape?

Antonin Sobek

A. Introduction	20.01	E. Conclusion	20.69
B. The FET Standard and the Right to Regulate in Europe: From the Need to Safeguard States' Regulatory Freedom towards CETA	20.09	Appendix I: Examples of FET Clauses in BITs of EU Member States	
		Appendix II: The CETA Article on the FET Obligation	
C. The FET Standard under CETA: A Missed Opportunity to Restore the Balance between Private and Public Interests?	20.17	Appendix III: The CETA Article on the Applicable Law and Interpretation	
		Appendix IV: Extracts from the CETA Preamble	
D. A Call for a Further Reconsideration of the Scope and Place of the FET Standard in the European Investment Treaty Practice	20.54	Appendix V: The CETA Article on the Right to Regulate	

A. Introduction

20.01 Recent EU negotiations on ambitious trade agreements, including Comprehensive Economic and Trade Agreement (CETA)[1] and Transatlantic Trade and Investment

---

[1] Comprehensive Economic and Trade Agreement (CETA) between Canada, of the one part, and the European Union and its Member States, of the other part [2016] 10973/16 <http://data.consilium.europa.eu/doc/document/ST-10973-2016-INIT/en/pdf> accessed 2 May 2018.

Partnership (TTIP),[2] have been accompanied by an unprecedented backlash from the civil society regarding investment provisions contained therein.[3] This public opposition has been a strong call upon the EU representatives to further rethink the European investment treaty landscape, often associated with a legitimacy crisis for its failure to strike the right balance between private and public interests.[4] In order to remedy the current crisis, the EU has pushed for state-of-the-art changes in its investment treaty practice while negotiating ambitious international investment and trade agreements including CETA and TTIP.

20.02 Despite the similarity of their fair and equitable treatment (FET) clauses, this chapter deals with CETA rather than TTIP. Unlike the latter, improbable to be concluded in the near future,[5] CETA has been already approved by the European Parliament and Canada respectively on 15 February 2017 and on 17 May 2017.[6] Even though CETA has yet to be ratified by the EU national parliaments in order to take full effect, it has been provisionally applied as from 21 September 2017.[7]

20.03 The reasons for focusing the analysis on the FET obligation is not surprising. Historically, the FET obligation has been the most invoked protective standard by foreign investors.[8] Due to their vagueness, FET clauses have been subject to expansive interpretation by arbitral tribunals, and the FET obligation has gradually become the main ground for states' liability in investment claims.[9] FET is

---

[2] Transatlantic Trade and Investment Partnership between the EU and the US (TTIP) European Commission's draft text on investment <http://trade.ec.europa.eu/doclib/docs/2015/september/tradoc_153807.pdf > accessed 2 May 2018.

[3] Burghard Ilge, 'An Account of the EU's Engagement with Bilateral Investment Treaties' in Kavaljit Singh and Burghard Ilge (eds), *Rethinking Bilateral Investment Treaties: Critical Issues and Policy Choices* (Both Ends, Madhyam, SOMO 2016) 160.

[4] See eg M Waibel, A Kaushal, L Chung, and C Balchin, *The Backlash against Investment Arbitration: Perspectives and Reality* (Kluwer Law International 2010) 38; Suzanne A Spears, 'The Quest for Policy Space in a New Generation of International Investment Agreements' (2010) 13(4) Journal of International Economic Law 1037; Jan Kleinheisterkamp, 'Investment Treaty Law and the Fear for Sovereignty: Transnational Challenges and Solutions' (2015) 78(5) Modern Law Review 793, 794; Christian Tietje and Kevin Crow, 'The Reform of Investment Protection Rules in CETA, TTIP and Other Recent EU-FTAs: Convincing?' (2016) <https://ssrn.com/abstract=2884380> accessed 2 May 2018.

[5] European Commission, 'Transatlantic Trade and Investment Partnership (TTIP): Process' <http://ec.europa.eu/trade/policy/in-focus/ttip/about-ttip/process/> accessed 2 May 2018.

[6] European Commission, 'Countries and Regions: Canada' <http://ec.europa.eu/trade/policy/countries-and-regions/countries/canada/> accessed 10 November 2017.

[7] 'EU, Canada Agree Start of Free Trade Agreement' (EURACTIV.com, 10 July 2017) <https://www.euractiv.com/section/global-europe/news/eu-canada-agree-start-of-free-trade-agreement/> accessed 2 May 2018.

[8] Wenjuan Zhang, 'Will Greater Specificity with Respect to Fair and Equitable Treatment Obligation Lead to Greater Predictability in Investment Treaty Cases?' (2015) 12(1) Transnational Dispute Management 2.

[9] David Gaukrodger, 'The Limitation of Fair and Equitable Treatment Provisions to the Minimum Standard of Treatment under Customary International Law' OECD Working Papers on International Investment (OECD Publishing 2017) 1; Eric de Brabandere, 'States' Reassertion of Control over International Investment Law: (Re)Defining "Fair and Equitable Treatment" and

therefore at the very heart of the debate over the states' right to regulate within the EU investment treaty landscape.

20.04 Up to now, many scholars and non-governmental organizations have paid some attention to the novel formulation of the FET standard under CETA. Most often, scholarly work is nevertheless limited to comparing the new FET standard with existing FET clauses without assessing the implications of the new wording for the states' right to regulate.[10] The available literature is marked by a general overconfidence vis-à-vis the new formulation, generally seen as an improvement.[11] Only few scholars have expressed some sparse doubts about the merit of the new FET wording.[12] This chapter contributes to the debate by assessing the impact of the new FET formulation on the contracting states' right to regulate, by relativizing the general overconfidence on this point, and by proposing further refinements.

20.05 Throughout the chapter, the following research question will guide the analysis: *Will the FET standard under CETA allow the contracting states to better safeguard their legitimate regulatory freedom, and therefore restore the balance between private and public interests within the EU investment treaty landscape?*

20.06 This question deserves some clarification. First, it is based on the premise that under the current EU investment treaty landscape, which has been delimited by intra- and extra-EU BITs, is imbalanced and favours investors' protection (private interest) over states' regulatory space (public interest). While this view may not be shared by everyone, it reflects growing concerns of the public,[13] scholars,[14]

Indirect Expropriation' in Andreas Kulick (ed), *Reassertion of Control over the Investment Treaty Regime* (CUP 2017) 288.

[10] See eg Ursula Kriebaum, 'FET and Expropriation in the (Invisible) EU Model BIT' (2014) 15(3–4) The Journal of World Investment & Trade 454; Hanna Wilhelmer, 'The "Right to Regulate" in CETA's Investment Chapter—Fair and Equitable Treatment, Expropriation and Interpretative Powers' (2014) Seminar Paper <https://eur-int-comp-law.univie.ac.at/fileadmin/user_upload/i_deicl/VR/VR_Personal/Reinisch/Internetpublikationen/wilhelmer.pdf> accessed 2 May 2018; de Brabandere (n 9).

[11] Wilhelmer (n 10); Thomas Giegerich, 'Opening Statement' (Panel Discussion—TTIP: Prosperous future or endless dispute in Transatlantic Relations, 2015) <http://jean-monnet-saar.eu/?p=838> accessed 5 August 2017; Caroline Henckels, 'Protecting Regulatory Autonomy through Greater Precision in Investment Treaties: The TPP, CETA, and TTIP' (2016) 19 Journal of International Economic Law 27; Fabien Gélinas and Flavien Jadeau, 'CETA's Definition of Fair and Equitable Treatment Standard: Toward a Guided and Constrained Interpretation' (2016) 1 Transnational Dispute Management; de Brabandere (n 9).

[12] Zhang (n 8); Tietje and Crow (n 4).

[13] 'Protests in Germany against Transatlantic TTIP and Ceta Trade Deals' (*BBC News*, 17 September 2016). <http://www.bbc.com/news/world-europe-37396796> accessed 2 May 2018.

[14] See eg Gus Van Harten, *Investment Treaty Arbitration and Public Law* (OUP 2007); Muthucumaraswamy Sornarajah, 'A Coming Crisis: Expansionary Trends in Investment Treaty Arbitration' in Karl P Suavant and Michael Chiswick-Patterson (eds), *Appeals Mechanism in International Investment Disputes* (OUP 2008) 39; Waibel et al (n 4); Jonathan Bonnitcha, *Substantive Protection under Investment Treaties: A Legal and Economic Analysis* (CUP 2014); de Brabandere (n 9).

international organizations,[15] national governments,[16] and even arbitral tribunals.[17] Second, the expression '(legitimate) regulatory freedom' is used interchangeably with the 'right to regulate (in the public interest)' and refers to the ability of the contracting states to adopt regulation in the public interest without exposing themselves to the risk of having to compensate covered investors for breaches of obligations under CETA. Finally, this chapter does not attempt to answer what exactly the balance between the competing interests should be.[18] Rather, it departs from the idea that the aforementioned imbalance contributes in great part to the legitimacy crisis of international investment arbitration, and as such has to be remedied. In other words, when seeking to answer the question 'whether the new FET formulation can restore the balance between the competing interests', this chapter seeks to determine whether changes brought by the new FET clause are substantial enough to help moderate the legitimacy crisis of the EU investment regime.

In terms of methodology, the analysis will be based upon the existing corpus of arbitral awards, statistical data, principles of interpretation, the wording of relevant CETA provisions, and the available scholarly work. It is acknowledged that the findings in this chapter are approximate constructs. In practice, much will depend on how the CETA permanent tribunal (tribunal)[19] will interpret and enforce the new FET standard. 20.07

---

[15] See eg UNCTAD, Investment Policy Framework for Sustainable Development (2012) <http://unctad.org/en/PublicationsLibrary/diaepcb2012d5_en.pdf> accessed 28 June 2017; Greenpeace, 'Investor Protection in CETA: Gold Standard or Missed Opportunity' (International Centre for Trade Union Rights, October 2016) http://www.greenpeace.org/eu-unit/Global/eu-unit/reports-briefings/2016/ICS%20CETA%20Report%20WEB.pdf accessed 17 June 2017.

[16] See eg Australian Government Department of Foreign Affairs and Trade, 'Gillard Government Trade Policy Statement: Trading our way to more jobs and prosperity' (April 2011) <http://blogs.usyd.edu.au/japaneselaw/2011_Gillard%20Govt%20Trade%20Policy%20Statement.pdf> accessed 15 June 2017; Republic of South Africa, 'Bilateral Investment Treaty Policy Framework Review: Government Position Paper' (June 2009) <http://pmg-assets.s3-website-eu-west-1.amazonaws.com/docs/090626trade-bi-lateralpolicy.pdf> accessed 19 July 2017.

[17] Examples of tribunals that underlined the need for states to preserve their regulatory space: *Ulysseas, Inc v The Republic of Ecuador*, UNCITRAL Final Award (12 June 2012) paras 245–49; *Mobil Investments Canada Inc and Murphy Oil Corporation v Canada*, ICSID Case No ARB(AF)/07/4, Decision on Liability and on Principles of Quantum (redacted) (22 May 2012) para 153; *Plama Consortium Limited v Republic of Bulgaria*, ICSID Case No ARB/03/24, Award (27 August, 2008) paras 177, 219; *Parkerings-Compagniet AS v Republic of Lithuania*, ICSID Case No ARB/05/8, Award (11 September 2007) paras 327–38.

[18] This question has been discussed by many scholars. See eg Barnali Choudhury, 'Recapturing Public Power: Is Investment Arbitration's Engagement of the Public Interest Contributing to the Democratic Deficit?' (2008) 41 Vanderbilt Journal of Transnational Law 775; Stephan W Schill and Benedict Kingsbury, 'Public Law Concepts to Balance Investors' Rights with State Regulatory Actions in the Public Interest—the Concept of Proportionality' in Stephan W Schill (ed), *International Investment Law and Comparative Public Law* (OUP 2010) 75; Julie A Maupin, 'Public and Private in International Investment Law: An Integrated Systems Approach' (2014) 54(2) Virginia Journal of International Law 367; Bonnitcha (n 14).

[19] Tribunal established under art 8.27 CETA.

20.08 The chapter will start by briefly putting the topic in its context (section B). The second and core part will assess the impact of the new FET obligation on the states' right to regulate while challenging widespread assumptions about 'state-regulation friendly' nature of the FET clause,[20] and supposed reassertion of control by states over international investment law[21] (section C). Finally, some proposals will be made for a further reconsideration of the FET standard to prevent investors' overprotection, and to better safeguard the states' right to regulate (section D).

B. The FET Standard and the Right to Regulate in Europe: From the Need to Safeguard States' Regulatory Freedom towards CETA

20.09 This section briefly sets up the background to the topic and serves as a basis for the analysis in section C.

1. An expansive interpretation of the FET standard as a starting point for the debate on regulatory freedom

20.10 Before the entry into force of the Treaty of Lisbon[22] in 2009, the EU member states were responsible for their investment policies, and concluded around 1400 intra and extra-EU bilateral investment treaties (BITs).[23] This treaty practice is marked by a laconic drafting of FET clauses,[24] which can be divided into three traditional categories.[25] Most often, the European BITs, including the 2010 Austria–Kazakhstan BIT,[26] refer to 'fair and equitable treatment' without any further clarification. The second type of European BITs, which are much less common, links the FET standard to the 'principles of international law' such as in the 2007 France–China BIT.[27] Finally, the third type, also of minor importance

---

[20] Wilhelmer (n 10) 44–45.
[21] de Brabandere (n 9).
[22] Treaty of Lisbon amending the Treaty on European Union and the Treaty Establishing the European Community [2007] OJ C 306/01.
[23] Roland Klager, 'The Impact of the TTIP on Europe's Investment Arbitration Architecture' (2014) 2 Law Journal of the German – American Lawyers Association 68.
[24] Gélinas and Jadeau (n 11) 6–7.
[25] See Appendix I.
[26] Agreement for the Promotion and Reciprocal Protection of Investment between the Government of the Republic of Austria and the Government of the Republic of Kazakhstan (signed 12 January 2010, entered into force 21 December 2012) (Austria–Kazakhstan BIT) art 3.
[27] Accord entre le gouvernement de la République française et le gouvernement de la république populaire de Chine sur l'encouragement et la protection réciproques des investissements (signed 26 November 2007, entered into force 20 August 2010) (France–China BIT) art 3.

in the European investment treaty practice, ties the FET standard to customary international law such as in the Canada–Latvia BIT.[28]

20.11 The open-ended wording of FET was meant to ensure enough protection for capital-exporting countries from Western Europe as opposed to capital-importing countries from Eastern Europe.[29] Given that Europeans used to predominantly act as claimants in investment disputes, the 'catch-all' nature of the FET clauses was often in the interest of the EU member states.[30] However, this trend has gradually reversed as the EU member states have now become one of the main targets of ICSID cases as indicated by publicly available data from the International Centre for Settlement of Investment Disputes (ICSID).[31] In total, foreign investors brought seventy-eight ICSID claims, based at least in part on the FET standard, against the EU countries. That is around 20 per cent of all FET claims under ICSID.[32] Out of seventy-eight claims, nine are still pending, five were settled, and eighteen were successful, which amounts to approximately 28 per cent of all decided FET claims brought against the EU countries, and to around 20 per cent of all successful FET claims under ICSID.[33]

20.12 Gradually, the FET clauses of uncertain boundaries, together with the overly broad interpretation by arbitral tribunals, have become an important part of the debate over the EU member states' right to regulate.[34] Growing literature has started to either question or criticize investors' overprotection through open-ended FET clauses at the expense of legitimate state regulation.[35]

---

[28] Agreement between the Government of Canada and the Government of the Republic of Latvia for the Promotion and Protection of Investments (signed 5 May 2009, entered into force 24 November 2011) (Canada–Latvia BIT) art 3.

[29] Jeswald W Salacuse, *The Law of Investment Treaties* (2nd edn, OUP 2015) 104; Burghard Ilge, 'An Account of the EU's Engagement with Bilateral Investment Treaties' in Kavaljit Singh and Burghard Ilge (eds), *Rethinking Bilateral Investment Treaties: Critical issues and Policy Choices* (Both Ends, Madhyam and SOMO 2016) 157.

[30] ibid.

[31] ibid.

[32] Figures based on UNCTAD data, see Investment Policy Hub, 'Breaches of IIA Provisions Alleged and Found' <http://investmentpolicyhub.unctad.org/ISDS/FilterByBreaches> accessed 9 January 2018.

[33] ibid.

[34] Gaukrodger (n 9) 58; de Brabandere (n 9) 293.

[35] See eg UNCTAD, 'Interpretation of IIAs: What States Can Do' (IIA Issues Note No 3 2011) 8; Moshe Hirsch, 'Between Fair and Equitable Treatment and Stabilization Clause: Stable Legal Environment and Regulatory Change in International Investment Law (2011) 12 The Journal of World Investment & Trade 783; Bonnitcha (n 14) 21; Gus van Harten, 'Pro-Investor or Pro-State Bias in Investment Treaty Arbitration? Forthcoming Study Gives Cause for Concern' (*Investment Treaty News*, 13 April 2012) https://www.iisd.org/itn/2012/04/13/pro-investor-or-pro-state-bias-in-investment-treaty-arbitration-forthcoming-study-gives-cause-for-concern/ accessed 19 July 2017; Pia Eberhardt and Cecilia Olivet, 'Profiting from Injustice: How Law Firms, Arbitrations and Financiers are Fuelling an Investment Arbitration Boom' (Corporate Europe Observatory and the Transnational Institute 2012) 7; UNCTAD, Investment Policy Framework for Sustainable Development (n 15) 12.

2. A process of redefinition of the European investment landscape

20.13 The Treaty of Lisbon accorded to the Union an exclusive competence in the field of foreign direct investment (FDI)[36] including the negotiation of international investment agreements.[37] In this respect, one caveat should be kept in mind. In its recent Opinion 2/15, the European Court of Justice (ECJ) highlighted that when an international agreement relates to non-FDI investments, or to an investor–state dispute settlement (ISDS) mechanism, it falls within a shared competence between the EU and the member states.[38] In such a scenario, the agreement cannot be approved by the EU alone.[39] This has cast doubts on how the Union shall exercise its new exclusive competence in practice.[40]

20.14 Not surprisingly, the Lisbon Treaty has been a starting point for the process of redefinition of the European investment treaty landscape through which the EU gradually replaces intra- and extra-EU BITs by EU agreements, and engages in negotiating new comprehensive free trade agreements (FTAs) and international investment agreements (IIAs).[41] From the beginning, the European Commission made it clear that raising concerns about the right of states to regulate would need to be addressed in the new EU investment practice.[42] In 2015, under public

---

[36] Consolidated Version of the Treaty of the Functioning of the European Union [2012] OJ C326/47, arts 3(1)(e) and 207.

[37] See eg Marc Bungenberg, Joern Griebel, and Steffen Hindelang (eds), *International Investment Law and EU Law* (Springer 2011) 12; Catherine Titi, 'International Investment Law and the European Union: Towards a New Generation of International Investment Agreements (2015) 26(3) European Journal of International Law 639, 641–42.

[38] Opinion C-2/15 (2015/C 363/22) Request for an opinion submitted by the European Commission pursuant to Article 218(11) TFEU [2017] para 244.

[39] ibid para 245.

[40] To elaborate on this topic, see eg Bungenberg et al (n 37) 12; Daniel Thym, 'Mixity after Opinion 2/15: Judicial Confusion over Shared Competences' (*Verfassungsblog*, 31 May 2017) <https://verfassungsblog.de/mixity-after-opinion-215-judicial-confusion-over-shared-competences/> accessed 29 July 2017; Laurens Ankersmit, 'Opinion 2/15 and the Future of Mixity and ISDS' (*European Law Blog*, 18 May 2017) <http://europeanlawblog.eu/2017/05/18/opinion-215-and-the-future-of-mixity-and-isds/> accessed 29 July 2017. In light of this opinion and in order to avoid that future agreements be jeopardized by additional national ratification procedures, some authors recommend that portfolio investments and ISDS mechanisms be covered in separate agreements (see eg Guillaume Van der Loo, 'The Court's Opinion on the EU-Singapore FTA: Throwing off the Shackles of Mixity' (Centre for European Policy Studies, Policy Insights No 2017/17, May 2017) 10.

[41] See eg August Reinisch, 'The EU on the Investment Path—Quo Vadis Europe? The Future of EU BITs and other Investment Agreements' (2014) 12(1) Santa Clara Journal of International Law 111, 119; Euromines, 'A Quick Guide to EU/International Investment Agreements' (Euromines, 2016) <http://www.euromines.org/files/publications/a-quick-guide-to-eu-international-investment-agreements.pdf> accessed 27 June 2017, 4; to elaborate on the division of competences between the EU and the EU member states in the field of investment policies, see Bungenberg et al (n 37).

[42] European Commission, 'Towards a comprehensive European International Investment Policy' Communication from the Commission to the Council, the European Parliament, the European Economic and Social Committee and the Committee of the Regions (Brussels, 7 July 2010) COM (2010) 343 final, 8.

pressure, the European Parliament issued a resolution to the attention of the Commission with recommendations on the TTIP negotiations.[43] The Parliament recommended, *inter alia*, the incorporation into the TTIP of a more precise legal language with respect to the FET standard in order to avoid expansive protection by arbitral tribunals, and therefore protect the EU member states' regulatory freedom.[44] These policy choices also accompanied the CETA negotiations[45] and reflect the need to redefine the EU investment landscape while addressing concerns of the public. Strong public opposition to the TTIP and CETA investment provisions reflects a crisis of legitimacy for the investment regime,[46] and calls for a rebalancing of competing interests in favour of states' regulatory freedom.

3. The importance of CETA for the EU investment practice of tomorrow

The importance of CETA cannot be overstated in the process of redefinition of the European investment landscape. Indeed, it is one of the first important manifestations of the Union's new direction in the field of foreign direct investment,[47] which indicates how the face of the EU investment practice of tomorrow may look like.[48] Its investment provisions are likely to influence the wording of other agreements such as those currently negotiated with India, China, or Tunisia.[49] As implied from the statements of the European Commission, the CETA provisions aim at regaining the public support through, *inter alia*, the attempts to narrow the scope of the FET standard, and to guarantee the states' right to regulate.[50] 20.15

In the following section, it will be analysed whether the newly drafted FET standard, read in conjunction with the provisions on the right to regulate, can live up to their drafters' expectations to reverse the pro-corporate bias in favour of states' regulatory freedom, and therefore to restore the balance between private and public interests. 20.16

---

[43] European Parliament, 'European Parliament resolution of 8 July 2015 containing the European Parliament's recommendations to the European Commission on the negotiations for the Transatlantic Trade and Investment Partnership (Strasbourg, 8 July 2015) 2014/2228(INI).

[44] ibid 15.

[45] See eg European Commission, 'Investment Provisions in the EU–Canada Free Trade Agreement (CETA)' (European Commission, February 2016) <http://trade.ec.europa.eu/doclib/docs/2013/november/tradoc_151918.pdf> accessed 8 July 2017, 2.

[46] Kleinheisterkamp (n 4) 801.

[47] The EU also completed negotiations on the EU–Singapore FTA and the EU–Vietnam FTA, which both have yet to come into force (see European Commission, 'Overview of FTA and other Trade Negotiations' (March 2018) <http://trade.ec.europa.eu/doclib/docs/2006/december/tradoc_118238.pdf> accessed 28 February 2018).

[48] Gélinas and Jadeau (n 11) 1–2.

[49] European Commission, 'Overview of FTA and other Trade Negotiations' (n 47).

[50] For example European Commission, 'Investment provisions in the EU–Canada free trade agreement (CETA)' (n 45) 1–2; European Commission, 'Press Release: European Commission Proposes Signature and Conclusion of EU-Canada Trade Deal' (Strasbourg, 5 July 2016) <http://europa.eu/rapid/press-release_IP-16-2371_en.htm> accessed 12 July 2017

C. The FET Standard under CETA: A Missed Opportunity to Restore the Balance between Private and Public Interests?

20.17 Through the assessment of the FET standard and the provisions on the right to regulate, the following part of this chapter will attempt to relativize widespread assumptions about their contribution to the rebalancing of the antagonist interests.

1. The new approach to FET as a mere codification of past arbitral awards

20.18 The drafters of CETA have rethought the wording of the FET standard, which appears to be in striking contrast with previous European investment treaty practice.[51] Rather than opting for a vague and unqualified definition, or linking the open-ended FET standard to the 'principles of international law', or 'customary international law', Article 8.10 CETA provides a more specific definition listing elements that may violate FET.[52] This use of greater precision is usually equated with greater safeguards for states' regulatory freedom.[53] However, this may not be the case for several reasons.

20.19 First, it is often argued that the text narrows the scope of the FET standard as it provides for an 'exhaustive' list of elements.[54] Based on the maxim *expressio unius est exclusio alterius*, one could indeed argue that the list is intended to be exhaustive.[55] However, this is not necessarily the proper reading of the provision, which could also point to the non-exhaustive nature of the list.[56] Indeed, the disjunction 'or', mentioned at the end of the penultimate element of the list, as opposed to the use of 'or' after each element in TTIP, could suggest an indicative rather than exhaustive nature of the enumeration.[57] Since this key issue has not been clarified by the detailed Joint Interpretative Instrument of the Council of the European Union,[58] there is enough room for the tribunal to interpret the list as merely indicative. In such a scenario, *a fortiori*, the scope of the FET standard would not be limited.

---

[51] Zhang (n 8) 5.
[52] CETA (n 1) art 8.10; see Appendix II.
[53] See eg Zhang (n 8) 9; Tietje and Crow (n 4) 22.
[54] See eg Zhang (n 8) 5; Laura Puccio, 'CETA: Investment and the Right to Regulate' (European Parliament, February 2017) <http://www.europarl.europa.eu/RegData/etudes/ATAG/2017/599265/EPRS_ATA(2017)599265_EN.pdf> accessed 16 July 2017, 2.
[55] Gélinas and Jadeau (n 11) 7.
[56] ibid; Henckels (n 11) 36.
[57] Henckels (n 11) 36.
[58] Council of the European Union, Joint Interpretative Instrument on the Comprehensive Economic and Trade Agreement (CETA) between Canada and the European Union and its Member States (Brussels, 27 October 2016) 13541/16.

20.20 Even in the hypothesis that the list is to be considered exhaustive by the tribunal, it would be hasty to conclude that the 'clause has much more limited scope' as compared to the traditional FET clauses in EU BITs.[59] Looking at the analytical work by Catherine Yannaca-Small,[60] Christoph Schreuer,[61] or Patrick Dumberry,[62] it is possible to distil from arbitral awards several elements falling under the vague wording of 'fair and equitable treatment'. In the absence of clear definition of the FET standard, tribunals have most often considered that FET was composed of due process and transparency, denial of justice, and prohibition of arbitrariness, discrimination, and abusive treatment. These elements are listed in the wording of Article 8.10 CETA, which seems to merely codify the content of the vague FET clauses, as understood by many arbitral tribunals.[63]

20.21 Some authors suggest that the scope of the new FET clause is restrained by the fact that it does not list controversial elements such as 'good faith' and the requirement of 'stable and predictable legal and business environment'.[64] With respect to the former, however, it appears that the tribunals consider the good faith principle as a simple combination of legitimate expectations, transparency and lack of arbitrariness.[65] For instance, the *Tecmed* tribunal stated that good faith is a general principle under international law which includes basic expectations, transparency, and non-arbitrariness.[66] The same approach was followed, *inter alia*, by the *Glamis* tribunal.[67] Therefore, it does not seem necessary to list an additional element of good faith since its sub-elements are already arguably included in Article 8.10 CETA. In any case, tribunals often acknowledge that 'the principle of good faith is not an essential element of the standard of fair and equitable treatment and therefore violation of the standard would not require the existence of bad faith'.[68] With respect to the stable and predictable environment, it will be shown in the following section that the consecration of legitimate expectations in CETA can, in practice, amount to this requirement.

20.22 Interestingly and ironically, instead of being restricted, the scope of the new FET clause could actually be expanded as compared to some previous arbitral awards

---

[59] Giegerich (n 11).
[60] Catherine Yannaca-Small, 'Fair and Equitable Treatment Standard in International Investment Law' OECD Working Papers on International Investment 2004/03 (OECD Publishing 2004).
[61] Christopher Schreuer, 'Fair and Equitable Treatment in Arbitral Practice' (2005) 6(3) The Journal of World Investment & Trade 357.
[62] Patrick Dumberry, *The Fair and Equitable Treatment Standard: A Guide to NAFTA Case Law on Article 1105* (Kluwer Law International 2013).
[63] ibid; Yannaca-Small (n 60); Schreuer (n 61).
[64] See eg Zhang (n 8) 9; de Brabandere (n 9) 300.
[65] Yannaca-Small (n 60) 38.
[66] *Técnicas Medioambientales Tecmed, SA v The United Mexican States*, ICSID Case No ARB (AF)/00/2, Award (29 May 2003) para 154.
[67] *Glamis Gold, Ltd v The United States of America*, UNCITRAL, Award (8 June 2009) para 605.
[68] See eg *Enron Corporation and Ponderosa Assets, LP v Argentine Republic*, ICSID Case No ARB/01/3, Award (22 May 2007) para 263.

dealing with vague FET clauses. Indeed, some tribunals rejected the requirements of transparency and/or legitimate expectations as falling within the scope of the FET standard.[69] By codifying these two elements in CETA, the drafters have opted, to the detriment of regulatory freedom, for an expansive rather than restrained approach to FET.

20.23 It is also often suggested that the threshold for potential breaches of the newly formulated FET standard is higher and therefore guarantees more regulatory freedom for the contracting parties.[70] Indeed, it is often emphasized that the qualifiers under the new wording point to a particularly high threshold,[71] and that only grave breaches of due process or 'manifest arbitrariness' may amount to FET violations.[72] While the assumptions about the high threshold may be correct, it does not necessarily mean that the threshold should be different as compared to the threshold applied by tribunals to traditional open-ended FET clauses. Through analysing different NAFTA cases, where the FET standard is linked to customary international law, and some non-NAFTA awards, where the standard is either connected to international law or constitutes an autonomous standard, one may notice a general trend favouring a high threshold with respect to FET violations.

20.24 Regarding the requirement of 'manifest' arbitrariness under CETA, both NAFTA and some non-NAFTA tribunals have already specified that in order to breach the FET standard, be it equated with or additional to customary international law, arbitrariness has to be 'manifest'.[73] Even if not all tribunals mention 'manifest' as a qualifier, it is questionable whether it actually refers to a degree of severity, or more likely, to the ease to perceive/recognize/identify the arbitrariness pursuant to the dictionary or ordinary meaning.[74] The latter interpretation would be in line with tribunals' understanding of 'manifest' in *Mondev*[75] and *Enron*.[76]

20.25 With regard to the requirement of 'fundamental breach of due process' under CETA, while the same wording is not employed in past arbitral awards, NAFTA and non-NAFTA tribunals have generally adhered to the view that due process breaches under the FET standard should be subject to a high threshold. For instance, in the 2003 *Loewen* award, breaches of due process were equated with 'manifest injustice'.[77] Other tribunals referred to a 'lack of due process leading to

---

[69] Gélinas and Jadeau (n 11) 11.
[70] Tietje and Crow (n 4) 21.
[71] Wilhelmer (n 10) 22.
[72] ibid.
[73] *Enron* (n 68) para 281; *Glamis* (n 67) para 22.
[74] Kriebaum (n 10) 474.
[75] *Mondev International Ltd v United States of America*, ICSID Case No ARB(AF)/99/2, Award (11 October 2002) para 128.
[76] *Enron* (n 68) para 281.
[77] *Loewen Group, Inc and Raymond L Loewen v United States of America*, ICSID Case No ARB(AF)/98/3, Award (26 June 2003) para 132.

an outcome which offends a sense of judicial propriety'[78] or to a 'complete lack of due process'.[79] The use of different terminology does not appear to reflect significant, if any, differences in the applicable threshold.[80]

It appears from the following that the new FET standard under CETA merely codifies the scope and threshold of traditional open-ended FET clauses as commonly interpreted by different arbitral tribunals. While such a codification may provide greater certainty with respect to the normative content of the FET standard, which will also be subject to doubts in the following sections, it does not actually help restrict a broad interpretation of the FET standard in order to effectively safeguard states' regulatory freedom.

20.26

2. The consecration of legitimate expectations as a new Pandora's box

Traditionally, the most controversial element of the FET standard, which has been raising the main concerns regarding an expansive interpretation in favour of investors' overprotection, corresponds to the notion of legitimate expectations.[81] Its roots in investment law can be traced back to the now (in)famous *Tecmed* award,[82] in which the tribunal held that '(t)he foreign investor expects the host State to act in a consistent manner, free from ambiguity and totally transparently in its relations with foreign investor, so that it may know beforehand any and all rules and regulations that will govern its investments ....'[83] Through investors' expectations, the tribunal ended up with the controversial requirement of a stable legal and business environment.[84]

20.27

However, not all tribunals have accepted the view that investors' legitimate expectations form a part of the FET standard under customary international law or otherwise. For instance, in the 2009 *Cargill* award, the tribunal held that '[n]o evidence, has been placed before the Tribunal that there is such a requirement in the NAFTA or in customary international law, at least where such expectations do not arise from a contract or quasi-contractual basis'.[85] Moreover, scholarly work casts doubt on whether legitimate expectations should be regarded as an

20.28

---

[78] *Waste Management, Inc v United Mexican States ('Number 2')*, ICSID Case No ARB(AF)/00/3, Award (30 April 2004) para 98.
[79] *Glamis* (n 67) para 22.
[80] See the following section on interpretation for more details.
[81] Abdulladir Jailani, 'Indonesia's Perspective on Review of International Investment Agreements' in Kavaljit Singh and Burghard Ilge (eds), *Rethinking Bilateral Investment Treaties: Critical Issues and Policy Choices* (Both Ends, Madhyam and SOMO 2016) 113, 124.
[82] Michele Potestà, 'Legitimate Expectations in Investment Treaty Law: Understanding the Roots and the Limits of a Controversial Concept' (2013) 28(1) ICSID Review—Foreign Investment Law Journal 88, 101–02.
[83] *Tecmed* (n 66) para 154.
[84] UNCTAD, Investment Policy Framework for Sustainable Development (n 15) 64–65.
[85] *Cargill, Incorporated v United Mexican States*, ICSID Case No ARB(AF)/05/02, Award (redacted version) (18 September 2009) para 290.

element included in the FET standard, at least when linked to customary international law.[86] For instance, Dr Martins Paparinskis noted that 'it is not obvious that it [the principle of legitimate expectations] can be taken into account in interpreting the treaty rules on fair and equitable treatment or the customary standard ... or even operating as a separate obligation.'[87] By explicitly providing for legitimate expectations in Article 8.10(4), CETA drafters have therefore opted for an enlarged scope of the FET standard, which in practice may negatively affect states' regulatory freedom. The fact that under the said article, the tribunal has broad discretion whether to take investor's legitimate expectations into account,[88] further blurs the circumstances under which the FET standard may actually interfere with the states' right to regulate.

20.29 It has been argued that the formulation of legitimate expectations in CETA 'introduces significant constraints upon arbitral discretion' since only specific representations made [by governments] to induce a covered investment could be taken into account when applying the FET obligation.[89] However, the vague formulation of the provision could in practice accord to the tribunal a significant leeway when considering FET claims.[90] First, the notion of 'specific representation' lacks clarity,[91] and is prone to a broad interpretation so as to transform paragraph 4 of Article 8.10 CETA into a 'catch-all' provision. Since CETA does not limit the notion in scope, its interpretation by the tribunal could amount to the feared requirement of 'stable and predictable business and legal environment', as it used to be in the past,[92] whenever the tribunal considers that a government made and frustrated a 'specific representation' that an investor relied upon.

---

[86] Roland Kläger, *Fair and Equitable Treatment' in International Investment Law* (CUP 2011) 164; Martin Paparinskis, *The International Minimum Standard and Fair and Equitable Treatment* (OUP 2013) 256; Artemis Malliaropoulou, 'Legitimate Expectations in the TTIP Proposal, in CETA, in EU Law and in International Investment Law: A Paradigm of Heraclitean Hidden Harmony?' (EFILA Blog) <https://efilablog.org/2016/11/24/legitimate-expectations-in-the-ttip-proposal-in-ceta-in-eu-law-and-in-international-investment-law-a-paradigm-of-heraclitean-hidden-harmony/> accessed 10 July 2017; de Brabandere (n 9) 301; Enrique B Barrera, 'The Case for Removing the Fair and Equitable Treatment Standard from NAFTA' (2017) CIGI Paper No 128 <https://www.cigionline.org/sites/default/files/documents/Paper per cent20no.128web_2.pdf> accessed 25 July / 2017, 2.
[87] Paparinskis (n 86) 256.
[88] Indicated by the use of the word 'may'.
[89] Henckels (n 11) 38.
[90] Gélinas and Jadeau (n 11) 13.
[91] Malliaropoulou (n 86); Ilge, 'An Account of the EU's Engagement with Bilateral Investment Treaties' (n 3) 165.
[92] See eg Gus van Harten, Matthew C Porterfield, and Kevin P Gallagher, 'Investment Provisions in Trade and Investment Treaties: The Need for Reform' (*GEGI Exchange* Issue 005, September 2015) 3; Pia Eberhardt, Blair Redlin, and Cecile Toubeau, 'Trading Away Democracy: How CETA's Investor Protection Rules Threaten the Public Good in Canada and the EU' (November 2014) https://corporateeurope.org/sites/default/files/trading-away-democracy.pdf accessed 18 June 2017, 13.

Interestingly, Bernasconi and Mann from the International Institute for Sustainable Development (IISD) compared the wording of 'specific representation' in the provision on legitimate expectations with the wording of 'any specific written representation' in the initial proposal by the EU on the umbrella clause.[93] Their analysis suggests that the CETA drafters intended to cover more than representations in writing. In line with past awards, it could mean that governments may be bound by statements of individual officials who deal with covered investors, or by ambiguous commitments as inferred by tribunals from laws and regulations.[94] For instance, in the *Southern Pacific Properties* award, Egypt was bound by the acts, even if illegal, of Egyptian officials as they had created legitimate expectations for the covered investor.[95] Moreover, in the 2007 *Enron* award, Argentina was bound by commitments inferred from general gas regulation despite the fact that no specific rights had been conferred upon claimant.[96]

20.30

Besides that, the wording of the provision is silent on circumstances in which government's departure from legitimate expectations, once established, could be permissible. Some authors suggest that only a 'manifestly arbitrary' departure could be impermissible.[97] However, this conclusion does not necessarily flow from the wording of the FET standard. Nothing in Article 8.10 CETA specifies that the methodology with respect to legitimate expectations should follow the threshold of manifest arbitrariness. Since legitimate expectations are disconnected from the list of the FET elements, and represents a useful concept to assess FET violations as compared to a standalone FET element, they may actually lower the standard for breaching the listed FET elements, and erase the limits of the FET obligation.[98] Even in the hypothesis that the tribunal is to apply the threshold of manifest arbitrariness, it is open-ended what conduct the tribunal will consider as 'manifestly arbitrary'[99] (see section C.3 on the tribunal's interpretative power). In any case, the discretion provided for by paragraph 4 of Article 8.10 CETA can have the effect of creating serious obstacles to the states' right to regulate.[100]

20.31

Finally, it is sometimes argued that the scope of the concept of legitimate expectations is limited by virtue of Article 8.9(2) CETA, which clarifies that 'the mere fact that a Party regulates, including through a modification to its laws, in

20.32

---

[93] Nathalie Bernasconi-Osterwalder and Howard Mann, 'A Response to the European Commission's December 2013 Document "Investment Provisions in the EU-Canada Free Trade Agreement (CETA)"' (The International Institute for Sustainable Development, February 2014) 7.
[94] Kriebaum (n 10) 478; Greenpeace (n 15) 8.
[95] *Southern Pacific Properties (Middle East) Ltd v Arab Republic of Egypt*, ICSID Case No ARB/84/3, Award (20 May 1992) para 82.
[96] *Enron* (n 68) para 264.
[97] Henckels (n 11) 38.
[98] Barrera (n 86) 8.
[99] Henckels (n 11) 38.
[100] Singh and Ilge (eds), *Rethinking Bilateral Investment Treaties: Critical Issues and Policy Choices* (n 91) 165.

a manner which negatively affects an investment or interferes with an investor's expectations, including its expectations of profits, does not amount to a breach of an obligation under this Section'.[101] However, it is by no means clear whether and to what extent this provision would be interpreted by the tribunal as neutralizing the applicability of the concept of legitimate expectations enshrined in Article 8.10(4) CETA. First, Article 8.9(2) CETA does not mention 'legitimate' expectations. The article could therefore be interpreted as merely dealing with expectations that do not fall within the definition under Article 8.10(4) CETA. Second, Article 8.9(2) CETA specifies that 'the mere fact that a Party regulates' should not amount to the interference with investors' expectations. This formulation does not *a priori* cover situations where legitimate expectations are based on 'specific representations' and satisfy the threshold of Article 8.10(4) CETA. This would be in line with the existing body of arbitral awards where a state's regulatory action in the public interest is not prevented by investors' expectations unless they are based on 'specific representations'[102] or in breach of the FET standard.[103]

20.33 Yet again, these ambiguities may operate in favour of an extensive interpretation of the FET standard and to the detriment of states' regulatory freedom. In light of this, the concept of legitimate expectations may in practice amount to a Pandora's box capable of further extending state liability for legitimate state regulation.

3. The tribunal's interpretative power and an important room for discretion

20.34 The very heart of the debate on the interplay between the FET standard and states' regulatory freedom relates to the interpretative power of the tribunal and its margin of discretion when interpreting the Agreement. In its communication on CETA investment provisions, the European Commission stated that 'CETA introduces a precise and specific standard of treatment of investors and investment. Unlike other agreements, the standard of "fair and equitable treatment" in CETA … defines precisely the standard of treatment, without unwelcome discretion to the Members of the Tribunal.'[104] Moreover, scholars appear to be reassured and claim that the reforms 'have clarified within the limits of what can be clarified',[105] that '[i]t is reasonable to assume that drafting states' obligations with greater precision will constrain the scope of investment arbitrators' interpretative

---

[101] Puccio (n 54) 2.
[102] *EDF (Services) Ltd v Romania*, ICSID Case No ARB/05/13, Award (8 October 2009) para 217.
[103] *Saluka Investments BV v The Czech Republic*, UNCITRAL, Partial Award (17 March 2006) para 307.
[104] European Commission, Investment Provisions in the EU–Canada Free Trade Agreement (CETA) (n 45) 2.
[105] Tietje and Crow (n 4) 24.

discretion',¹⁰⁶ or that greater specificity will amount to a 'strictly circumscribed interpretation of FET'.¹⁰⁷

Contrary to these statements, the wording of the FET provision is all but precise, **20.35** and still leaves much discretion for the tribunal when balancing the states' obligation to provide fair and equitable treatment with the states' right to regulate. First, broad categories listed in Article 8.10(2) CETA have no fixed normative content and can cover a wide range of possible arguments about state misconduct.¹⁰⁸ It will be up to the tribunal to substantiate, interpret and apply them in practice.¹⁰⁹ For instance, Article 8.10(2)(b) CETA lists 'fundamental breach of due process, including a fundamental breach of transparency, in judicial and administrative proceedings'. The word 'including' indicates an open-ended range of elements that can constitute due process breaches. Moreover, broad concepts such as 'arbitrariness' or 'abusive treatment' are not subject to any clear definition.

A wide potential for the tribunal's discretion is also noticeable in terms of evaluative language,¹¹⁰ such as 'manifest' arbitrariness, 'fundamental' breach of due **20.36** process, 'fundamental' breach of transparency, 'rare' circumstances, or discrimination on 'manifestly wrongful' grounds. For instance, the use of the expression 'fundamental breach of due process' creates a potential for vast interpretative discretion. As rightly pointed out by Professor Ursula Kriebaum, it is unclear whether the expression refers to serious breaches of due process, or to fundamental rules/principles of due process.¹¹¹ Furthermore, when different tribunals have referred to the concept of 'manifest' arbitrariness, they have failed to explain how, if at all, it differs from the concept of arbitrariness.¹¹² The *Thunderbird* tribunal, for instance, limited itself to holding that Mexican proceedings were not 'arbitrary or unfair, let alone so manifestly arbitrary or unfair'.¹¹³ It is also noteworthy that past arbitral awards suggest that concepts with strong evaluative language such as 'manifest arbitrariness' do not shield states from liability for legitimate regulation.¹¹⁴ For instance, in the recent *Windstream* award, the tribunal implicitly accepted respondent's contention that its conduct had to be 'manifestly arbitrary' in order to breach the FET standard.¹¹⁵ The tribunal nevertheless concluded that

---

¹⁰⁶ Henckels (n 11) 27.
¹⁰⁷ Gélinas and Jadeau (n 11) 13.
¹⁰⁸ UNCTAD, Investment Policy Framework for Sustainable Development (n 15) 43.
¹⁰⁹ de Brabandere (n 9) 302.
¹¹⁰ Henckels (n 11) 30.
¹¹¹ Kriebaum (n 10) 474.
¹¹² See eg *International Thunderbird Gaming Corporation v The United Mexican States*, UNCITRAL, Arbitral Award (26 January 2006) para 197; *Glamis* (n 67) para 616; *Gemplus SA, SLP SA, Gemplus Industrial SA de CV v The United Mexican States*, ICSID Case No ARB(AF)/04/3, Award (16 June 2010) paras 7–72.
¹¹³ *Thunderbird* (n 112) para 197.
¹¹⁴ See eg ibid; *Gemplus* (n 112); *Windstream Energy LLC v Government of Canada*, PCA Case No 2013-22, Award (27 September 2016).
¹¹⁵ *Windstream* (n 114) paras 312, 358.

the government's conduct, presumably motivated by environmental purposes,[116] breached the FET standard.[117] Similarly, the *Bilcoin* tribunal agreed that the conduct must constitute a breach 'of a serious nature' including ' "manifest" failure of natural justice …'.[118] The tribunal nevertheless applied this high threshold in a way that it was met by a simple allegation of a potential breach of the Canadian legislation.[119] This was criticized by Professor Donald McRae in his dissenting opinion.[120] All these examples illustrate that the use of evaluative language in CETA provides the tribunal with much discretion so as to decide what state conduct may be in breach of the FET standard at the expense of states' regulatory freedom.

20.37 Besides that, greater specificity in the wording of the FET standard may not necessarily bring more safeguards for states and their regulatory freedom.[121] First, based on past arbitral awards, it appears that the application of FET clauses depends more on how the tribunals perceive parties' conduct rather than on differences of FET language.[122] As pointed out by the *Minnotte* tribunal, '[w]hile the precise formulations of the fair and equitable treatment standard in these, and other, awards differ, they all have in common the notion that the State must be shown to have acted delinquently in some way or other …'.[123] Moreover, the *Saluka* tribunal suggested that different FET formulations, 'when applied to the specific facts of a case, may well be more apparent than real', and that different thresholds 'could be explained by the contextual and factual differences of the cases to which the standards have been applied' rather than by actual differences in FET formulations.[124] Last but not least, in her monographic study on FET, Ioana Tudor rightly pointed out that in the absence of a fixed and unambiguous meaning of fair and equitable treatment, the content and threshold of this standard inevitably depends, at least to a certain degree, on arbitrators' subjective determination of a particular situation.[125] As Tudor puts it, an arbitrator evaluates and balances 'the circumstances of the case in front of him before applying the standard and

---

[116] The tribunal considered *inter alia* that the Canada's conduct was 'driven by the lack of science' and that Canada failed to 'bring clarity to the regulatory uncertainty surrounding the status and the development of the Project'. *Windstream* (n 114) paras 377, 380.
[117] ibid para 379.
[118] *William Ralph Clayton, William Richard Clayton, Douglas Clayton, Daniel Clayton and Bilcoin of Delaware Inc v Government of Canada*, UNCITRAL, PCA Case No 2009-04, Award on Jurisdiction and Liability (17 March 2015) para 443.
[119] ibid para 591.
[120] ibid Dissenting Opinion paras 2, 34.
[121] Zhang (n 8) 6.
[122] Barrera (n 86) 9.
[123] *David Minnotte & Robert Lewis v Republic of Poland*, ICSID Case No ARB(AF)/10/1, Award (16 May 2014) para 198.
[124] *Saluka* (n 103) para 291.
[125] Ioana Tudor, *The Fair and Equitable Treatment Standard in International Foreign Investment Law* (OUP 2008) 120–23.

its sanction ... us[ing] intuition and expertise'.¹²⁶ By analogy, the meaning of the FET standard under CETA may be shaped by specific circumstances of each particular case.¹²⁷ In that regard, CETA does not substantially limit the tribunal's interpretative discretion but merely fixes, for the time being, constitutive elements of the FET standard.

In practice, it therefore seems that in the absence of unambiguous wording, there will always be scope for adjudicative discretion and interpretative uncertainties.¹²⁸ Since the FET standard under CETA reproduces an important degree of vagueness, the tribunal may be free, within the humble limits of applicable law and rules of interpretation as enshrined in Article 8.31 CETA,¹²⁹ to hold the state's conduct in breach of the FET standard as soon as it attains a certain degree of seriousness in the tribunal's eyes. While it is impossible to predict how the CETA tribunal will decide particular cases in practice, the very potential for adjudicative discretion should be approached with caution, and adequately addressed (see section D). 20.38

Pursuant to Article 26.1 CETA, the new CETA Joint Committee, composed of representatives from the Contracting Parties, may adopt interpretations binding upon the tribunal in accordance with Articles 8.31(3) and 26.1 CETA. According to the European Commission, this new feature, inspired by agreements such as NAFTA, should 'permit the Parties to control and influence the interpretation of the agreement', and therefore represents a 'safety valve in the event of errors by the tribunals'.¹³⁰ While this is a praiseworthy attempt to remedy any potential expansive interpretation by the tribunal and therefore thoughtful of the states' right to regulate, it should not be confused with a magical solution. First, in practice, it may be difficult for the contracting parties to reach a consensus on a binding interpretation.¹³¹ For instance, within twenty years of the NAFTA existence, only two such interpretations have been issued.¹³² Second, the *Pope & Talbot* award illustrates that the tribunal may be unwilling to accept a binding interpretation if it in fact resembles an amendment.¹³³ Finally, unless specifically provided for in the Agreement, the Joint Committee cannot bypass the amendment process under Article 30.2 CETA and transform its interpretative function into an amendment power. Therefore, it would not be possible for the Committee to, for instance, 20.39

---

¹²⁶ ibid 120.
¹²⁷ Schreuer (n 61) 364.
¹²⁸ Henckels (n 11) 32–33.
¹²⁹ See Appendix III.
¹³⁰ European Commission, 'Investment provisions in the EU–Canada free trade agreement (CETA)' (n 45) 7.
¹³¹ Eberhardt et al, 'Trading Away Democracy' (n 92) 16.
¹³² ibid.
¹³³ *Pope & Talbot Inc v The Government of Canada*, UNCITRAL, Award in Respect of Damages (31 May 2002) para 47.

remove the controversial element of legitimate expectations or the FET standard as a whole.

20.40 It follows that greater specificity of the new FET standard may fail to guarantee more predictable outcomes for the contracting parties,[134] or to better safeguard states' regulatory freedom. Such a pessimistic conclusion can be anticipated on the basis of the room for discretion under the FET wording on one hand, and the existing body of arbitral awards on the other.

4. The reaffirmation of the right to regulate and the risk of tautologies

20.41 The CETA preamble states that 'the provisions of this Agreement preserve the right of the Parties to regulate … and the Parties' flexibility to achieve legitimate policy objectives … '.[135] Similarly, Article 8.9 CETA underlines that 'the Parties reaffirm their right to regulate within their territories to achieve legitimate policy objective …'.[136] This attempt to safeguard states' regulatory freedom is in line with the Union's desire to restore the balance between private and public interests in the EU investment treaty landscape.[137]

20.42 First, it should be recalled that the right to regulate in the public interest, as one of the states' fundamental functions, appears to be already recognized to a certain extent.[138] Some literature suggests that states are, at least in theory, entitled to regulate in the public interest without being exposed to liability under customary international law.[139] Moreover, arbitral tribunals appeared to be sensitive to the states' right to regulate in the past.[140] For instance, the *Parkerings-Campagniet* tribunal underlined that '(i)t is each State's undeniable right and privilege to exercise its sovereign legislative power. A State has the right to enact, modify or cancel a law at its own discretion.'[141] The *Saluka* tribunal even declared that the states' right to regulate in the public interest 'forms part of customary international law'[142] and that 'States are not liable to pay compensation to a foreign investor when, in the normal exercise of their regulatory powers, they adopt in a non-discriminatory manner bona fide regulations that are aimed to the general welfare'.[143]

---

[134] Zhang (n 8).
[135] See Appendix IV.
[136] See Appendix V.
[137] European Commission, 'Towards a Comprehensive European International Investment Policy' (n 42) 9.
[138] Catharine Titi, *The Right to Regulate in International Investment Law* (Nomos/Hart 2014) 143; Catharine Titi, 'Embedded Liberalism and IIAs: The Future of the Right to Regulate, with Reflections on WTO Law' in Gillian Moon and Lisa Toohey (eds), *20 Years of Domestic Policy Under WTO Law: The Embedded Liberalism Compromise Revisited* (CUP 2017) 2; Tietje and Crow (n 4).
[139] Titi, 'Embedded Liberalism and IIAs' (n 138) 3.
[140] de Brabandere (n 9) 288.
[141] *Parkerings-Compagniet* (n 17) para 332.
[142] *Saluka* (n 103) para 262.
[143] ibid para 255.

Despite a formal acknowledgement of the states' right to regulate, arbitral tribu- **20.43**
nals have been criticized for paying lip service to this right before asking states
to compensate investors.[144] For instance, the *CMS*, *Enron*, and *Impregilo* tribunals acknowledged, as a first step, the existence of a formal right to regulate in
the public interest.[145] While stressing investors' entitlement to a 'stable and predictable legal and business environment' under the FET standard, they clarified
that the stability requirement does not erase states' regulatory power.[146] As the
Enron tribunal puts it, the 'stabilization requirement does not mean the freezing
of the legal system or the disappearance of the regulatory power of the State'.[147]
However, as a second step and despite the right to regulate, the three aforementioned tribunals held that the states had breached their obligations under the
treaty.[148] Since the tribunals are not afraid to condemn national governments despite their acknowledged regulatory freedom, Professor Catharine Titi prefers to
speak about a *legitimate* right rather than a *legal* right. Such terminology implies
the power of the tribunals to decide whether to take into account states' legitimate
interests.[149]

When assessing whether there was a legitimate objective for the contested state **20.44**
regulation, tribunals have recognized that host states enjoy broad regulatory
freedom.[150] For instance, the *Thunderbird* tribunal acknowledged that Mexico
enjoyed 'wide regulatory "space" for regulation', 'can change its regulatory policy
and ... has a wide discretion with respect to how it carries out such policies by
regulation and administrative conduct'.[151] The tribunal then recalled that it would
need to assess whether the Mexican regulation breached the NAFTA obligations.[152] The *SD Myers* tribunal considered that it was a legitimate goal for Canada
to 'ensure the economic strength of the Canadian industry'. However, the tribunal
held that the Canadian measure was not a legitimate way to achieve this goal.[153]
Last but not least, the *Saluka* tribunal underlined that 'the host State's legitimate
right ... to regulate domestic matters in the public interest must be taken into
consideration' when considering a FET claim.[154] Yet again, the aforementioned

---

[144] Titi, *The Right to Regulate in International Investment Law* (n 138) 276.
[145] *CMS Gas Transmission Company v The Republic of Argentina*, ICSID Case NO ARB/01/8, Award (12 May 2005) para 277; *Enron* (n 68) para 261; *Impregilo SpA v Argentine Republic*, ICSID Case No ARB/07/17, Award (21 June 2011) para 290.
[146] ibid.
[147] *Enron* (n 68) para 261.
[148] *CMS* (n 145) para 295; *Enron* (n 68) para 268; *Impregilo* (n 145) para 331.
[149] Titi, 'Embedded Liberalism and IIAs' (n 138) 3.
[150] Roland Kläger, 'Revising Treatment Standards—Fair and Equitable Treatment in Light of Sustainable Development' in Steffen Hindelang and Markus Krajewski (eds), *Shifting Paradigms in International Investment Law: More Balanced, Less Isolated, Increasingly Diversified* (OUP 2016) 76.
[151] *Thunderbird* (n 112) 127.
[152] ibid.
[153] *SD Myers Inc. v Government of Canada*, UNCITRAL, Partial Award (13 November 2000) para 255.
[154] *Saluka* (n 103) para 305.

awards illustrate that the states' right to regulate is often not contested *per se* but has to be balanced against investors' interest in receiving fair and equitable treatment under specific FET clauses.

20.45 When the CETA drafters explicitly mentioned the right to regulate in the Agreement, they adhered to the prevalent view that states do have such a right, without providing guarantees that the *explicit* right would be better protected than the *implicit* right has been. Indeed, the CETA wording on the right to regulate presents several difficulties. The first difficulty corresponds to the vague delimitation of such a right. Pursuant to paragraph 1 of Article 8.9, the right to regulate is reaffirmed 'to achieve legitimate policy objectives, such as the protection of public health, safety, the environment or public morals, social or consumer protection or the promotion and protection of cultural diversity'. First, it is not clear what the five listed categories encompass. In this regard, it will be up to the tribunal's discretion to decide what measures are aimed to achieve 'legitimate policy objectives'. Then, while the wording indicates that the list is non-exhaustive, no guidance is provided as to what other categories such as human rights or protection of cultural heritage could constitute 'legitimate policy objectives'. Most importantly, the wording is silent on how the tribunal should assess the relationship between the contested regulation and its objective.[155] Therefore, it is unclear whether the tribunal should apply a necessity test, a proportionality test or any other technique. The literal meaning of 'to achieve legitimate policy objectives' may suggest that the regulation ought to be shown to in fact achieve the legitimate policy objective.[156] This ambiguity creates further potential for the tribunal's discretion to the detriment of regulatory freedom.

20.46 Moreover, nothing in the text indicates that the right to regulate shall override states' obligations under CETA such as the one to accord fair and equitable treatment. As already highlighted in section C .2. of this chapter, paragraph 2 of Article 8.9 appears to be inapplicable in relation to legitimate expectations based on specific representations under Article 8.10(4). Furthermore, the same paragraph, which specifies that 'the mere fact that a Party regulates … in a manner which negatively affects an investment … does not amount to a breach of an obligation under this Section', seems to state the obvious: a simple interference with the covered investor's investment, through the Parties' right to regulate, does not amount to breaches under CETA. It does not indicate that the interference, which fails to satisfy the FET standard, would also excused by the reason of the states' right to regulate in the public interest. In this vein, CETA seems to reproduce the traditional situation where states' right to regulate is limited, *de jure* and *de facto*, by the FET and other protective standards.[157]

---

[155] Greenpeace (n 15) 9.
[156] ibid.
[157] Giegerich (n 11).

It is also unclear how to balance competing interests, namely investors' interest in being protected under the FET standard, and public interest in ensuring states' right to regulate in the public interest. This task is particularly challenging insofar as states' regulatory freedom is difficult to reconcile with the underlying *raison d'être* of the international investment treaty regime—the promotion of investment through additional protective guarantees to foreign investors.[158] The negotiations with Canada have revealed the irreconcilability of the competing interests when the European institutions called for 'the highest possible level of legal protection and certainty for European investors',[159] and the 'gold standard of investment protection provisions'[160] while emphasizing 'the right of the EU and the Member States to adopt and enforce ... measures necessary to pursue legitimate public policy objectives'.[161] Indeed, high levels of legal protection will necessarily interfere with states' regulatory freedom.

20.47

The CETA text nevertheless fails to provide any guidance on this balancing task. When balancing the FET standard against the Parties' right to regulate, the tribunal will need recourse to the tools of interpretation contained in Article 8.31 CETA, namely the Vienna Convention on the Law of Treaties (VCLT), and 'other rules and principles of international law applicable between the Parties'.[162] First, the reference to international law applicable between the Parties, without clearly defined boundaries, increases the tribunal's discretion in its interpretative task to the detriment of legal certainty, and possibly to regulatory freedom. As for the VCLT, the tribunal will need to apply the conventional principles of treaty interpretation as contained in Articles 31 and 32.[163] In particular, the tribunal will need to look to the 'ordinary meaning to be given to the terms of the treaty in their context and in light of its object and purpose'.[164] In order to ascertain the object and purpose of an agreement, tribunals have often referred to agreements' preambles.[165] The difficulty resides in how to balance different objects and purposes in the absence of an apparent hierarchy between them.[166] As many authors

20.48

---

[158] Tietje and Crow (n 4) 10.
[159] Council (EU) Negotiating directives (Canada, India, Singapore) (12 September 2011) <https://www.bilaterals.org/?eu-negotiating-mandates-on&lang=en> accessed 18 July 2017.
[160] Kriebaum (n 10) 456.
[161] European Commission, Recommendation from the Commission to the Council on the modification of the negotiating directives for an Economic Integration Agreement with Canada in order to authorise the Commission to negotiate, on behalf of the Union, on investment (Brussels, 15 December 2015) 12838/11 <http://data.consilium.europa.eu/doc/document/ST-12838-2011-EXT-2/en/pdf> accessed 23 July 2017, 4
[162] Comprehensive and Economic Trade Agreement (CETA) art 8.31(1); see Appendix III.
[163] VCLT art 31 on General Rule of Interpretation; 32 VCLT art 32 on Supplementary Means of Interpretation.
[164] Vienna Convention on the Law of Treaties (adopted 23 May 1969, entered into force 27 January 1980) 1155 UNTS 331 (VCLT) art 31(1).
[165] See eg *Saluka* (n 103) para 299; *Ioannis Kardassopoulos v The Republic of Georgia*, ICSID Case No ARB/05/18, Award (3 March 2010) paras 432–33.
[166] Spears (n 4) 29.

have pointed out, tribunals may have tended to resolve ambiguities in the preambular language in favour of investors' rights and to the detriment of states' regulatory freedom.[167] For instance, based on the narrow preambular language in Philippines–Swiss BIT, the *SGS* tribunal held that it was 'legitimate to resolve uncertainties in [the treaty's] interpretation so as to favor the protection of covered investments'.[168]

20.49 The CETA preamble is silent, yet again, on both the hierarchy between different interests, and the proper way to balance them. On one hand, it emphasizes the establishment of 'an expanded and sure market ... through the reduction or elimination of barriers to trade and investment', and recognizes that 'the provisions of this Agreement protect investments and investors with respect to their investments, and are intended to stimulate mutually-beneficial business activity'. On the other hand, this protection is to be recognized 'without undermining the right of the Parties to regulate in the public interest within their territories'. It is unclear how the tribunal will reconcile these potentially antithetical aims. Since the articles of the Agreement do not support the view that the FET standard is not applicable by the mere fact of the Parties' right to regulate in the public interest, and since the preambular language does not give rise to binding obligations,[169] the CETA preamble may be read as merely emphasizing Parties' regulatory freedom. The question remains whether the *emphasized* right to regulate in the public interest adds anything to the *non-emphasized* right to regulate, already acknowledged by many arbitral tribunals.[170]

20.50 Given their vagueness, the CETA provisions on the right to regulate are unlikely to represent operable carve-outs, capable of effectively safeguarding states' regulatory freedom. Their wording rather indicates that the provisions are meant to serve as guidance for the tribunal when balancing different interests.[171] The only presumably operable carve-out may be seen in paragraph 3 of Article 8.9, which specifies that a 'Party's decision not to issue, renew, or maintain a subsidy ... does not constitute a breach of the provisions of this Section'. However, this solution is unlikely to go far enough to safeguard states' regulatory freedom. First, paragraph 3 specifies that the carve-out shall not apply in case of 'any specific commitment

---

[167] See eg ibid; Luke Eric Peterson, *Bilateral Investment Treaties and Development Policy-Making* (International Institute for Sustainable Development November 2004) 24; Jose E Alvarez, 'Book Review of Gus Van Harten, Investment Treaty Arbitration and Public Law', 102 American Journal of International Law (2008) 913.

[168] *SGS Société Générale de Surveillance SA v Republic of the Philippines*, ICSID Case No ARB/02/6, Decision of the Tribunal on Objections to Jurisdiction (29 January 2004) para 116.

[169] UNCTAD, Fair and Equitable Treatment: UNCTAD Series on Issues in International Investment Agreements II (2012) <http://unctad.org/en/Docs/unctaddiaeia2011d5_en.pdf>112>

[170] See nn 141, 142, 145.

[171] BEUC et al, 'Joint Analysis of CETA's Investment Court System (ICS): Prioritising Private Investment over Public Interest' <http://epha.org/wp-content/uploads/2016/07/Joint-Analysis-CETA-ICS-1.pdf> accessed 25 July 2017, 2.

under law or contract to issue, renew, or maintain that subsidy'. Under such wording, the carve-out could be neutralized by invoking commitments under general legislation, which were not made in relation to covered investment and not directed to covered investors. Moreover, while this specific carve-out reacts to the infamous *Micula* case,[172] and to the clashes between EU provisions on state aid and EU member states' obligations under BITs, in practice, it may cover an insignificant number of challenged measures.[173]

20.51 In light of this, it is disputable whether the CETA provisions on the right to regulate may better help safeguard states' regulatory freedom. Rather than adding any substantial guarantees to the contracting states, the CETA provisions risk to become a *de facto* tautology to the often acknowledged right.

5. Implications for the balance between private and public interests within the EU investment treaty landscape

20.52 The analysis in section C has revealed that the new formulation of the FET standard, read together with the provisions on the right to regulate, is unlikely to bring substantial improvements for states' regulatory freedom. First, the FET standard under CETA merely mirrors the scope and threshold of other FET clauses as interpreted by arbitral tribunals. Second, by including investors' legitimate expectations in the FET clause, CETA drafters have recognized their relevance in the analysis of FET breaches, which risks to operate as a Pandora's box with a negative effect on the states' right to regulate. Third, rather than providing a clear, and circumscribed definition of the FET standard, the new wording leaves an important room for interpretative discretion and creates new uncertainties. Fourth, instead of guaranteeing additional safeguards for states' regulatory freedom, the reaffirmation of the right to regulate under CETA may become a mere tautology to the often acknowledged right.

20.53 The current wording of the Agreement therefore presents important loopholes that could prove, in practice, ill-tailored to rebalance the competing interests. If the EU fails to further reconsider the role and place of the FET standard within the EU investment treaty landscape, the legitimacy crisis of the European investment regime may keep deepening and putting at risk the existence of future free trade agreements and investment treaties. The following section is aimed at providing ideas about how to further address the current imbalance between investors' overprotection and the states' right to regulate. Even though the actual

---

[172] Tietje and Crow (n 4) 13; see also *Ioana Micula, Viorel Micula, SC European Food SA, SC Starmill SRL and SC Multipack SRL v Romania*, ICSID Case No ARB/05/20, Final Award (11 December 2013).

[173] Zoe Phillips Williams, 'What, When, Where and Why? Patterns in Investor-State Arbitration' in Kavaljit Singh and Burghard Ilge (eds), *Rethinking Bilateral Investment Treaties: Critical Issues and Policy Choices* (Both Ends, Madhyam and SOMO 2016) 35.

re-drafting of CETA appears unthinkable since the Agreement provisionally entered into force on 21 September 2017,[174] the suggested refinements could serve either as a basis for negotiations by the EU for future FTAs or IIAs, or for discussions on binding interpretations by the CETA Joint Committee.

D. A Call for a Further Reconsideration of the Scope and Place of the FET Standard in the European Investment Treaty Practice

20.54 The first subsection will suggest a radical solution that is best suited to safeguard states' regulatory space within the EU, that is removing the FET standard from the European investment treaty practice. In the alternative, a couple of refinements will be outlined that could contribute to the rebalancing of the competing interests.

1. A case for removing the FET standard from the EU investment treaty practice

20.55 The following suggestion to remove the FET standard from the EU investment treaty practice should be read with one caveat in mind. It is tailored to the aim highlighted in the introduction, that is the implementation of changes substantial enough to protect regulatory freedom, and ultimately to remedy the legitimacy crisis of the EU investment regime. Therefore, it may not be adequate to attain other goals of the EU such as providing EU investors with the highest level of protection when investing abroad. The chapter does not attempt to settle what the prevailing goal should be, but rather limits itself to answering the question how to restore the balance between competing interests.

20.56 It is often taken for granted that FTAs and IIAs have to contain the FET standard.[175] For instance, at the start of the process of re-defining the EU investment treaty practice, the European Commission stated that protective standards 'such as "fair and equitable treatment" … should inspire the negotiation of investment agreements at the EU level'.[176] Moreover, some scholars believe that the inclusion of the FET standard into investment treaties is crucial for the protection of foreign investors.[177] However, the FET standard is not always indispensable in guaranteeing fair and equitable treatment for foreign investors. Indeed, in countries such

---

[174] European Commission, 'EU–Canada Comprehensive Economic and Trade Agreement' <http://ec.europa.eu/trade/policy/in-focus/ceta/> accessed 11 October 2017.
[175] Tudor (n 125) 3.
[176] European Commission, 'Towards a Comprehensive European International Investment Policy' (n 42) 8.
[177] Zhang (n 8) 2.

as EU member states and Canada, they can enjoy fundamental rights already guaranteed under both the EU legal system and national constitutions.[178]

Besides this protection, foreign investors are already entitled to the 'minimum standard of treatment of aliens' since this standard is believed to be a part of customary international law.[179] However, the minimum standard may not necessarily be enforceable through the dispute resolution mechanism under the treaty. Indeed, such a mechanism is often limited, as it is the case for CETA,[180] to claims based on breaches of the treaty.[181] The expansion of the dispute resolution clauses to 'any disputes arising out of an investment' in order to encompass claims related to the minimum standard of treatment of aliens is not advisable. It could create new uncertainties detrimental to the states' right to regulate. The contracting parties should rather rely on legal guarantees available under domestic laws. **20.57**

It could be argued that the inclusion of the FET standard would be necessary in situations where host countries treat their own nationals poorly.[182] In such situations, legal guarantees for foreign investors could be insufficient. However, this argument does not stand with respect to highly developed countries such as Canada and the EU member states. Indeed, the Rule of Law Index of the World Justice Project places these countries at the top of the ranking.[183] In any case, large investors, to whom the access to the dispute resolution mechanism under the treaty is *de facto* restricted, are sophisticated enough to assess investment risks in host countries. *Nota bene*, as controversial as it may seem, the non-inclusion of the FET standard is neither innovative nor unheard of. For instance, the FET standard is missing in the FTA between India and Singapore,[184] and in the recently concluded Cooperation and Investment Facilitation Agreements between Brazil and Mozambique, and between Brazil and Angola.[185] **20.58**

The FET provisions under different treaties have the effect to accord greater rights to foreign investors than those available to domestic investors.[186] The elimination of the FET standard would therefore probably lead to the decrease in the level of protection that foreign investors currently enjoy under the FET **20.59**

---

[178] Greenpeace (n 15) 7.
[179] UNCTAD, Fair and Equitable Treatment (n 169) 104; Titi, *The Right to Regulate in International Investment Law* (n 138) 144.
[180] CETA art 8.18(1).
[181] ibid.
[182] Zhang (n 8) 2.
[183] World Justice Project, WJP Rule of Law Index 2016 <https://worldjusticeproject.org/our-work/wjp-rule-law-index/wjp-rule-law-index-2016> accessed 27 July 2017.
[184] Comprehensive Economic Cooperation Agreement between the Republic of India and the Republic of Singapore (India-Singapore CECA) (signed 29 June 2005, entered into force 1 August 2005).
[185] Brazil–Mozambique Cooperation and Investment Facilitation Agreement (CIFA) (2015); Brazil–Angola Cooperation and Investment Facilitation Agreement (CIFA) (2015).
[186] van Harten et al (n 92) 2.

clauses.[187] However, this seems to be a necessary pre-condition for greater regulatory freedom, and therefore for the re-balancing of private and public interests. Moreover, the elimination of the FET standard would be in line with the EU's alleged objective not to grant greater rights to foreign investors as compared to domestic investors.[188]

20.60 Finally, it could be argued that the non-inclusion of the FET standard could scare off foreign investors, and therefore harm the economy of the EU.[189] However, this concern is unsupported by empirical data. For instance, Singapore does not necessarily include the FET clauses in its investment agreements,[190] and is nonetheless the fifth largest recipient of FDI worldwide.[191] Furthermore, despite the fact that no bilateral investment treaty has entered into force in Brazil,[192] the country is the sixth largest recipient of FDI worldwide.[193] This suggests that investment flows are not simply correlative to the applicable protective standards but are subject to a much more complex matrix of factors. Indonesia may serve as yet another example. In 2014, it initiated an open process of revising its investment treaties so as to lower the level of protection accorded to foreign investors and rebalance private and public interests.[194] Despite that, Indonesia attracted the highest inflows of FDI in history in that same year.[195] Many other studies deny, or are at least inconclusive about, any correlation between the level of protection accorded under investment treaties and the level of FDI inflows.[196]

20.61 In light of this, the elimination of the FET standard from the EU investment treaty practice appears to be the preferable remedy to the current imbalance of interests perpetrated through the FET standard. However, given the affirmed support that EU member states[197] and the European

---

[187] Barrera (n 86) 10.
[188] Council of the European Union, Joint Interpretative Instrument (n 58) 5.
[189] Jailani (n 81) 119.
[190] See eg Singapore–Australia Free Trade Agreement (entered into force 28 July 2003); Agreement between New Zealand and Singapore on a Close Economic Partnership (signed November 2000, entered into force January 2001); India-Singapore CECA.
[191] Barrera (n 86) 10–11.
[192] Investment Policy Hub, International Investment Agreements Navigator: Brazil <http://investmentpolicyhub.unctad.org/IIA/CountryBits/27> accessed 12 January 2018.
[193] Barrera (n 86) 10–11.
[194] ibid 113.
[195] ibid119.
[196] See eg Susan Rose-Ackerman and Jennifer Tobin, 'Foreign Direct Investment and the Business Environment in Developing Countries: The Impact of Bilateral Investment Treaties' (2005) Yale Law & Economics Research Paper No 293 <https://ssrn.com/abstract=557121> accessed 19 July 2017; Jason D Yackee, 'Sacrificing Sovereignty: Bilateral Investment Treaties, International Arbitration, and the Quest for Capital (PhD thesis, May 2007) <https://cdr.lib.unc.edu/indexablecontent/uuid:ae712737-245c-462d-a5ba-85b706fa9ee2> accessed 22 July 2017. Lauge N Skovgaard Poulsen, 'The Importance of BITs for Foreign Direct Investment and Political Risk Insurance: Revisiting the Evidence' in Karl Sauvant (ed), *Yearbook on International Investment Law and Policy 2009/2010* (OUP 2010).
[197] Kriebaum (n 10) 455.

Commission[198] accord to the FET standard, it may be politically difficult to implement this solution. The following subsection therefore outlines an alternative approach that could help to better safeguard states' regulatory freedom in relation to the FET standard.

2. An alternative approach: suggestions for further refinements

First, the FET standard should be defined with greater precision. It is desirable to explicitly clarify that the list of constitutive elements of the FET standard is exhaustive. Moreover, the language used in the FET clause should be defined with more precision. Broad categories such as 'due process' and 'abusive treatment' should be circumscribed by dropping the open-ended wording of 'such as'. The evaluative terms, including 'manifest', 'fundamental' and 'rare', should be clarified in order to avoid ambiguities and restrain the Tribunal's discretion.[199] For instance, it should be specified that 'manifest' and 'fundamental' refer to a particularly high degree of severity rather than to the ease to perceive, and to fundamental principles and rules. 20.62

With regard to the content of the FET standard, it is first advisable to eliminate the reference to legitimate expectations as they have proved to be a catch-all element in the past that unnecessarily increases states' obligations and harms their regulatory freedom. The notion of legitimate expectations is *a priori* not a part of the minimum standard of treatment of aliens under customary international law, and therefore overprotects foreign investors. In the alternative, the wording of 'specific representations' that give rise to legitimate expectations should be clarified and restricted. For instance, it could be limited to 'written promises specifically addressed by the host countries to covered investors'. Moreover, if investors' legitimate expectations are indeed included in future EU investment treaties, the EU should consider including the legitimate expectations of the contracting states as well. As suggested by Professors Sauvant and Unuvar, states' expectations, based on investors' commitments and representations, could be taken into account when considering investors' claims.[200] 20.63

Another compromise solution between omitting the FET standard and rending it a binding obligation in the treaty, would be to transform it into a political commitment in the preamble. As such, it would not be an obligation binding upon the contracting states, but could guide the tribunal when interpreting other states' obligations under the treaty.[201] Some countries have already taken this 20.64

---

[198] Reinisch (n 41) 129.
[199] Henckels (n 11) 37.
[200] Karl Sauvant and Gunes Unuvar, 'Can Host Countries Have Legitimate Expectations' (Columbia FDI Perspectives No 183, 26 September 2016) <https://ssrn.com/abstract=2844432> accessed 24 July 2017.
[201] UNCTAD, Investment Policy Framework for Sustainable Development Framework (2015) <http://unctad.org/en/PublicationsLibrary/diaepcb2015d5_en.pdf> 97.

direction.[202]

20.65 With respect to the provisions on the right to regulate, it should be clarified how the relationship between state regulation and 'legitimate public policy objectives' is to be assessed by the tribunal. The use of wording such as 'related to', 'directed to', or 'designed to achieve', as opposed to 'necessary to achieve' are likely to be more deferential to the contracting states.[203] The categories that fall within public policy objectives should be expanded to other areas such as human rights, protection of cultural heritage, essential social services (eg education and power supplies), or 'compliance with laws and regulations that are not inconsistent with the treaty'.[204] Moreover, other operable carve-outs, besides the subsidies under Article 8.9(3) CETA, should be included in the wording of the agreements. Those could include, *inter alia*, sectors such as environment, taxation, defence industry, nuclear energy, or essential social services.[205]

20.66 These refinements could better help safeguard states' regulatory freedom but may not be entirely satisfactory. In the long term, some more far-reaching improvements should be envisaged in order to safeguard states' regulatory space and rebalance private and public interests. It seems inevitable that the EU addresses the asymmetrical structure of the investment regime and assigns to covered investors not only rights but also obligations such as the one to respect Ruggie's Guiding Principles on Business and Human Rights.[206] In this vein, states should be allowed to bring claims against investors in case of breaches of their obligations. The states should be also allowed to invoke such breaches in their defence, as a counter-balancing factor to investors' claims including FET breaches.

20.67 Last but not least, despite these refinements, the tribunal's discretion when balancing the antagonist interests could not be entirely eliminated. It could therefore be useful to develop an interpretative framework that would respond to the imperative of the rebalancing of the competing interests, and would guide the arbitrators' interpretation towards a more pro-state approach. As many scholars suggest, it seems indispensable to liberate the investment treaty regime from a pro-corporate bias by means of a public law logic.[207] For instance, comparative public law, used

---

[202] See eg Agreement between The Republic of Turkey and The United Arab Emirates concerning the Reciprocal Promotion and Protection of Investments (signed 28 September 2005, entered into force 24 July 2011) (Turkey–UAE BIT); Agreement between the Government of the Republic of Azerbaijan and the Government of the Republic of Estonia on the Promotion and Reciprocal Protection of Investments (signed 7 April 2010, not in force) (Azerbaijan–Estonia BIT).
[203] UNCTAD, World Investment Report 2015: Reforming International Investment Governance (2015) <http://unctad.org/en/PublicationsLibrary/wir2015_en.pdf> 141.
[204] UNCTAD, Investment Policy Framework for Sustainable Development Framework (n 201) 103.
[205] ibid 94.
[206] Tietje and Crow (n 4) 26.
[207] van Harten (n 14); Schill and Kingsbury (n 18); Kleinheisterkamp (n 4).

as a proxy to states' sovereignty, could guide the tribunal's interpretation of the FET standard in a way respectful of states' sovereign prerogatives.

In light of the analysis in this chapter, it is suggested that simple redrafting techniques that would reach greater precision of the FET standard and provisions on the right to regulate, while restricting tribunal's discretion, may not be a satisfactory response to the current imbalance perpetrated through the FET standard. More game-changing proposals should enter into the matrix of balancing the states' obligation to provide fair and equitable treatment and the states' right to regulate in the public interest. 20.68

E. Conclusion

While much available literature praises the improvements that the new FET formulation under CETA presumably brings in terms of the rebalancing of the antithetical interests, this chapter casts doubt on such overconfident outlooks. Instead, it suggests that the newly drafted FET standard, read in conjunction with the provisions on the right to regulate, is unlikely to serve as a substantially better safeguard for states' regulatory freedom. 20.69

In order to avoid deepening of the legitimacy crisis of the EU investment regime, the EU is therefore advised to further rethink the scope and place of the FET standard in its investment practice. While the elimination of the FET standard from the wording of EU investment treaties may be politically unfeasible, it would be the most satisfying redress of the current imbalance perpetrated through the FET clauses. Alternatively, this chapter makes proposals for further refinements that could help protect the states' right to regulate in the public interest. 20.70

The redefinition of the new EU investment policy is not a *fait accompli* but a long process of testing new solutions and distilling best practices. Even if the FET standard under CETA may be considered as a missed opportunity to restore the balance between private and public interests in the EU investment treaty landscape, the game is not over. 20.71

Appendices

APPENDIX I:

Examples of FET Clauses in BITs of EU Member States

First type of the FET clause: FET as an autonomous standard

The 2010 Austria-Kazakhstan BIT: Article 3 (Treatment of Investments)

(1) Each Party shall accord to investments by investors of the other Party fair and equitable treatment and full and constant protection and security.

...

Second type of the FET clause: FET standard linked to the 'principles of international law'

The 2007 France-China BIT: Article 3 (Fair and Equitable Treatment)

Chacune des Parties contractantes s'engage à assurer sur son territoire et dans sa zone maritime aux investissements réalisés par les investisseurs de l'autre Partie contractante un traitement juste et equitable, conformément aux principes généralement reconnus du droit international.

...

Third type of the FET clause: FET standard liked to 'customary international law'

The 2009 Canada-Latvia BIT: Article II (Establishment, Acquisition and Protection of Investment)

...

2. (a) Each Contracting Party shall accord investments or returns of investors of the other Contracting Party treatment in accordance with the customary international law minimum standard of treatment of aliens, including fair and equitable treatment and full protection and security. (b) The concepts of "fair and equitable treatment" and "full protection and security" in paragraph (a) do not require treatment in addition to or beyond that which is required by the customary international law minimum standard of treatment of aliens.

(...)

APPENDIX II:

The CETA Article on the FET Obligation

Article 8.10
Treatment of investors and of covered investments
1. Each Party shall accord in its territory to covered investments of the other Party and to investors with respect to their covered investments fair and equitable treatment and full protection and security in accordance with paragraphs 2 through 6.
2. A Party breaches the obligation of fair and equitable treatment referenced in paragraph 1 if a measure or series of measures constitutes:
    (a) denial of justice in criminal, civil or administrative proceedings;
    (b) fundamental breach of due process, including a fundamental breach of transparency, in judicial and administrative proceedings;
    (c) manifest arbitrariness;
    (d) targeted discrimination on manifestly wrongful grounds, such as gender, race or religious belief;

(e) abusive treatment of investors, such as coercion, duress and harassment; or
(f) a breach of any further elements of the fair and equitable treatment obligation adopted by the Parties in accordance with paragraph 3 of this Article.

3. The Parties shall regularly, or upon request of a Party, review the content of the obligation to provide fair and equitable treatment. The Committee on Services and Investment, established under Article 26.2.1(b) (Specialised committees), may develop recommendations in this regard and submit them to the CETA Joint Committee for decision.
4. When applying the above fair and equitable treatment obligation, a Tribunal may take into account whether a Party made a specific representation to an investor to induce a covered investment, that created a legitimate expectation, and upon which the investor relied in deciding to make or maintain the covered investment, but that the Party subsequently frustrated.
5. For greater certainty, "full protection and security" refers to the Party's obligations relating to the physical security of investors and covered investments.

For greater certainty, a breach of another provision of this Agreement, or of a separate international agreement does not establish a breach of this Article.

For greater certainty, the fact that a measure breaches domestic law does not, in and of itself, establish a breach of this Article. In order to ascertain whether the measure breaches this Article, a Tribunal must consider whether a Party has acted inconsistently with the obligations in paragraph 1.

APPENDIX III:

The CETA Article on the Applicable Law and Interpretation

Article 8.31: Applicable law and interpretation
1. When rendering its decision, the Tribunal established under this Section shall apply this Agreement as interpreted in accordance with the Vienna Convention on the Law of Treaties, and other rules and principles of international law applicable between the Parties.
2. The Tribunal shall not have jurisdiction to determine the legality of a measure, alleged to constitute a breach of this Agreement, under the domestic law of the disputing Party. For greater certainty, in determining the consistency of a measure with this Agreement, the Tribunal may consider, as appropriate, the domestic law of the disputing Party as a matter of fact. In doing so, the Tribunal shall follow the prevailing interpretation given to the domestic law by the courts or authorities of that Party and any meaning given to domestic law by the Tribunal shall not be binding upon the courts or the authorities of that Party.
3. Where serious concerns arise as regards matters of interpretation that may affect investment, the Committee on Services and Investment may, pursuant to Article 8.44.3(a), recommend to the CETA Joint Committee the adoption of interpretations of this Agreement. An interpretation adopted by the CETA Joint Committee shall be binding on a Tribunal established under this Section. The CETA Joint Committee may decide that an interpretation shall have binding effect from a specific date.

APPENDIX IV:

Extracts from the CETA Preamble

...

CREATE an expanded and secure market for their goods and services through the reduction or elimination of barriers to trade and investment;

...

RECOGNISING that the provisions of this Agreement preserve the right of the Parties to regulate within their territories and the Parties' flexibility to achieve legitimate policy objectives, such as public health, safety, environment, public morals and the promotion and protection of cultural diversity;

…

RECOGNISING that the provisions of this Agreement protect investments and investors with respect to their investments, and are intended to stimulate mutually-beneficial business activity, without undermining the right of the Parties to regulate in the public interest within their territories;

…

APPENDIX V:
The CETA Article on the Right to Regulate

Article 8.9: Investment and regulatory measures
1. For the purpose of this Chapter, the Parties reaffirm their right to regulate within their territories to achieve legitimate policy objectives, such as the protection of public health, safety, the environment or public morals, social or consumer protection or the promotion and protection of cultural diversity.
2. For greater certainty, the mere fact that a Party regulates, including through a modification to its laws, in a manner which negatively affects an investment or interferes with an investor's expectations, including its expectations of profits, does not amount to a breach of an obligation under this Section.
3. For greater certainty, a Party's decision not to issue, renew or maintain a subsidy:
   (a) in the absence of any specific commitment under law or contract to issue, renew, or maintain that subsidy; or
   (b) in accordance with any terms or conditions attached to the issuance, renewal or maintenance of the subsidy,

   does not constitute a breach of the provisions of this Section.
4. For greater certainty, nothing in this Section shall be construed as preventing a Party from discontinuing the granting of a subsidy or requesting its reimbursement where such measure is necessary in order to comply with international obligations between the Parties or has been ordered by a competent court, administrative tribunal or other competent authority, or requiring that Party to compensate the investor therefor.

21

THE NOTION OF INVESTOR UNDER THE ENERGY CHARTER TREATY
The Latest Developments in the Spanish Solar Disputes

*Crina Baltag**

A. Introduction	21.01	D. The Spanish Solar Disputes and the Notion of 'Investor'		21.24
B. Article 1(7)(a)(ii) of the ECT and the Meaning of 'Investor'	21.06	E. Concluding Remarks		21.35
C. Lifting the Corporate Veil under the Provisions of the ECT	21.19			

A. Introduction

In the past years, Spain faced over forty disputes submitted to arbitration under the Energy Charter Treaty ('ECT' or 'Treaty')[1] as a result of the regulatory measures taken by Spain affecting the feed-in tariff regime for the photovoltaic sector. In most of these cases, referred to as 'Spanish solar disputes', Spain challenged the jurisdiction of arbitral tribunals on the basis of the non-fulfilment of the nationality requirement set forth in Article 1(7)(a)(ii) of the ECT, by asking these tribunals to lift claimants' corporate veil in order to establish their real nationality. However, the arbitral tribunals sitting in the Spanish solar disputes have confirmed the previous practice of ECT tribunals in finding that the only requirement set   **21.01**

---

* The author would like to thank Dr Roberto Castro de Figueiredo and Janice Lee for their valuable input.
[1] Energy Charter Treaty (entered into force 16 April 1998) 2080 UNTS 95; 34 ILM 360 (1995) 373–457.

forth by Article 1(7)(a)(ii) is for a legal entity to be organized in accordance with the applicable law of a Contracting Party to the ECT.[2]

21.02 Investment treaties, including the ECT, link nationality of legal persons to the place of their incorporation.[3] This connecting factor may sometimes be supplemented by additional requirements related to the nationality of the owners or shareholders, or to the activity of the entity. These requirements may be incorporated in a so-called 'control clause', which usually concerns the nationality of the controllers of the entity—owners, shareholders, beneficial owners —or may be included in a 'denial of benefits' clause under which the benefits of the treaty are denied where the investor is a shell structure owned or controlled by nationals of non-signatory states of the treaty in question. These restrictive provisions serve the object and purpose of these treaties and prevent the misuse of their substantive and procedural protection.

21.03 Where investors misuse the provisions of the ECT by ignoring the scope and purpose of the Treaty on long-term cooperation in the energy field, based on complementarities and mutual benefits,[4] a legitimate debate that touches the very essence of the Treaty arises: should investors be allowed to take advantage of the definition in Article 1(7) of the ECT, but in breach of Article 2 of the Treaty? This discussion fundamentally questions *who* is protected by the ECT, *why* this protection is granted and *how* this protection functions. The growing number of investment disputes under Article 26 of the ECT, providing for resolution of investment disputes under the Treaty, as well as the increased sophistication of investors seeking the protection of the Treaty, is, undoubtedly, putting to the test this fragile balance between investors' rights and the object and purpose of the ECT.

21.04 The arbitral tribunals in the Spanish solar disputes suggested that lifting of the corporate veil and establishing the real or effective nationality of an investor should be limited to cases where allegations of fraud directed at jurisdiction are presented.[5] Moreover, in confirming that Article 1(7)(a)(ii) of the ECT only looks at the incorporation test for legal entities, the arbitral tribunals in the Spanish

---

[2] *Isolux Netherlands, BV v Kingdom of Spain*, SCC Case V2013/153, Award (17 July 2016) para 661 *et seq*. The original Award is in Spanish. Any translations from this Award are unofficial translations of the author.

[3] See the Hague Convention concerning the Recognition of Legal Personality of Foreign Companies, Associations and Institutions (signed on 1 June 1956, not in force), art 1.

See also Kenneth Vandevelde, *Bilateral Investment Treaties: History, Policy, and Interpretation* (OUP 2010) 159, referring to the incorporation test as being 'the most easily administered because rarely will there be doubt about the place where the company is organized'.

[4] ECT, art 2.

[5] For example, one arbitral tribunal referred to situations of fraud, where there 'could be an instrumental transfer of the assets of the investment after the emergence of the dispute'. See *Charanne BV and Construction Investments Sàrl v The Kingdom of Spain*, SCC Case No 062/2012, Final Award (21 January 2016) para 415. The original Award is in Spanish. The author relied on an unofficial translation by MENA Chambers.

solar disputes emphasized that 'shell companies' or companies 'which simply [have] stakes or shares in other companies' are not excluded from the protection of the ECT.[6] To balance the interests of investors with those of the Contracting Parties to the ECT and to ensure that the protection offered by the ECT is not abused, the arbitral tribunals referred to Article 17 of the ECT, which provides for the denial of benefits of the Treaty to certain investors and their investments 'if citizens or nationals of a third state own or control such entity and if that entity has no substantial business activities in the Area of the Contracting Party in which it is organised'.[7] The 'denial of benefits' right must be exercised by the host Contracting Party to the ECT. The Decision on Jurisdiction in *Plama* suggests that such exercise must be made publicly and in an effective way so it becomes available to investors,[8] although no requirement of prior notification appears to exist under the denial of benefits clause of the ECT. As such, this denial of benefits clause is a tool that can be used by respondent states in counteracting elements of fraud in the nationality of investor.

21.05 This chapter reviews the notion of 'investor' under the ECT in the light of the new arbitral decisions in the Spanish solar disputes. A general inquiry shall be made into the definition of the term under Article 1(7)(a)(ii) of the ECT, with reference to 'a company or other organisation organised in accordance with the law applicable in that Contracting Party', and whether the rules of treaty interpretation would allow the inference of additional requirements that must be satisfied by a legal entity to qualify as an 'investor', which would justify the lifting of the corporate veil. Focusing on the Spanish solar disputes, this chapter concludes that that there is, indeed, a uniform practice of Article 1(7)(a)(ii) of the ECT that gives preference to the incorporation test for legal entities, to the exclusion of other criteria.

---

[6] *RREEF Infrastructure (GP) Ltd and RREEF Pan-European Infrastructure Two Lux Sàrl v Kingdom of Spain*, ICSID Case No ARB/13/30, Decision on Jurisdiction (6 June 2016) para 142 et seq.

[7] ECT, art 17 refers to the following:

Each Contracting Party reserves the right to deny the advantages of this Part to:

(1) a legal entity if citizens or nationals of a third state own or control such entity and if that entity has no substantial business activities in the Area of the Contracting Party in which it is organised; or
(2) an Investment, if the denying Contracting Party establishes that such Investment is an Investment of an Investor of a third state with or as to which the denying Contracting Party:
   (a) does not maintain a diplomatic relationship; or
   (b) adopts or maintains measures that:
      (i) prohibit transactions with Investors of that state; or
      (ii) would be violated or circumvented if the benefits of this Part were accorded to Investors of that state or to their Investments.

[8] *Plama Consortium Ltd v Republic of Bulgaria*, ICSID Case No ARB/03/24, Decision on Jurisdiction (8 February 2005) para 161.

B. Article 1(7)(a)(ii) of the ECT and the Meaning of 'Investor'

21.06 Article 26 of the ECT provides that disputes between a Contracting Party and an investor of another Contracting Party relating to an investment of the latter in the area of the former, and which concern an alleged breach of a substantive protection of investments under Part III (Investment Promotion and Protection) of the ECT, may be submitted to arbitration (i) at the International Centre for Settlement of Investment Disputes (ICSID), (ii) at the Arbitration Institute of the Stockholm Chamber of Commerce (SCC) or (iii) under the Arbitration Rules of the United Nations Commission on International Trade Law (UNCITRAL Arbitration Rules).[9]

---

[9] ECT, art 26 provides, among others the following:

(1) Disputes between a Contracting Party and an Investor of another Contracting Party relating to an Investment of the latter in the Area of the former, which concern an alleged breach of an obligation of the former under Part III shall, if possible, be settled amicably.

(2) If such disputes cannot be settled according to the provisions of paragraph (1) within a period of three months from the date on which either party to the dispute requested amicable settlement, the Investor party to the dispute may choose to submit it for resolution:

(a) to the courts or administrative tribunals of the Contracting Party party to the dispute;

(b) in accordance with any applicable, previously agreed dispute settlement procedure; or

(c) in accordance with the following paragraphs of this Article.

...

(4) In the event that an Investor chooses to submit the dispute for resolution under subparagraph (2)(c), the Investor shall further provide its consent in writing for the dispute to be submitted to:

(a) (i) The International Centre for Settlement of Investment Disputes, established pursuant to the Convention on the Settlement of Investment Disputes between States and Nationals of other States opened for signature at Washington, 18 March 1965 (hereinafter referred to as the 'ICSID Convention'), if the Contracting Party of the Investor and the Contracting Party party to the dispute are both parties to the ICSID Convention; or

(ii) International Centre for Settlement of Investment Disputes, established pursuant to the Convention referred to in subparagraph (a)(i), under the rules governing the Additional Facility for the Administration of Proceedings by the Secretariat of the Centre (hereinafter referred to as the 'Additional Facility Rules'), if the Contracting Party of the Investor or the Contracting Party party to the dispute, but not both, is a party to the ICSID Convention;

(b) a sole arbitrator or ad hoc arbitration tribunal established under the Arbitration Rules of the United Nations Commission on International Trade Law (hereinafter referred to as 'UNCITRAL'); or

(c) an arbitral proceeding under the Arbitration Institute of the Stockholm Chamber of Commerce.

...

21.07 The investor's nationality is an essential element in establishing the jurisdiction of arbitral tribunals constituted under Article 26 of the ECT. Article 1(7)(a)(ii) of the ECT defines an investor as 'a company or other organisation organised in accordance with the law applicable in that Contracting Party'.[10] This definition encompasses virtually any entity, with or without legal personality, which is organized in accordance with the laws of a Contracting Party to the ECT.[11] It can be a company, as expressly mentioned by the provision, or any kind of organization, including consortiums, joint ventures, and even non-governmental organizations.[12] The plain language of Article 1(7)(a)(ii) appears to suggest that the only test set forth by this provision in determining nationality is for the legal

---

(7) An Investor other than a natural person which has the nationality of a Contracting Party party to the dispute on the date of the consent in writing referred to in paragraph (4) and which, before a dispute between it and that Contracting Party arises, is controlled by Investors of another Contracting Party, shall for the purpose of article 25(2)(b) of the ICSID Convention be treated as a 'national of another Contracting State' and shall for the purpose of article 1(6) of the Additional Facility Rules be treated as a 'national of another State'.

[10] The particularity of the ECT also comes into play in the context of its Contracting Parties: not only states, but also Regional Economic Integration Organisations (REIOs) are Contracting Parties to the Treaty. For example, the European Union and the EURATOM are Contracting Parties to the ECT. As such, the term 'investor' must be read in view of this peculiarity. The case law developed under art 26 of the ECT provides good examples of when this element became relevant in the context of jurisdiction *ratione personae* of arbitral tribunals. For instance, in *Stati v Kazakhstan*, the tribunal held that one of the claimants was a company organized in accordance with the laws of Gibraltar, a territory of the European Union, Contracting Party to the ECT. See *Anatolie Stati, Gabriel Stati, Ascom Group SA and Terra Raf Trans Traiding Ltd v Kazakhstan*, SCC Case No V 116/2010, Award (19 December 2013). In considering whether the claimant Terra Raf, incorporated under the laws of Gibraltar, satisfied the requirements of the ECT, the tribunal held that:

the Tribunal need not consider whether, as Respondent argues, that provisional application of the ECT has ceased or whether the decision of the *Petrobart v Kyrgyzstan* tribunal provides guidance in this respect. For, in any case, the ECT applies to Gibraltar on the basis that Gibraltar is a part of the European Community, which is itself party to the ECT. According to Art. 52 of the Treaty on the European Union and Art. 355 of the Treaty on the Functioning of the European Union, Gibraltar is included in its territory (*Stati*, para 746, emphasis in original).

[11] For a discussion on the nationality tests adopted by different treaties and jurisdictions, see Crina Baltag, *The Energy Charter Treaty. The Notion of Investor* (Wolters Kluwer 2012) 102 *et seq*. See also Chapter 7 in this volume, for a discussion of the definitions of 'investor' in 2017 agreements.

[12] The ECT is silent with respect to the requirement of legal personality of an investor. In the context of bilateral investment treaties (BITs), some specifically include legal entities without legal personality. See for example, art 1(3) of the Germany–Jordan BIT:

The term 'investors' shall mean

a) in respect of the Federal Republic of Germany:
　… – any juridical person as well as any commercial or other company or association with or without legal personality having its seat in the territory of the Federal Republic of Germany, irrespective of whether or not its activities are directed at profit (Agreement between the Federal Republic of Germany and the Hashemite Kingdom of Jordan concerning the Encouragement and Reciprocal (entered into force 28 August 2010) (Germany–Jordan BIT))

entity to be organized in accordance with the laws applicable in that Contracting Party to the ECT.[13]

21.08 ECT arbitral tribunals, established in cases prior to the Spanish solar disputes, unanimously held that the place of incorporation of the legal entity is necessary and sufficient to qualify as an investor under the ECT. In *Nykomb*, the tribunal briefly concluded that '[i]t is not in dispute that Nykomb, being a company organized under the laws of Sweden and having its seat in Sweden is an investor'.[14] Although the arbitral tribunal in *Plama* had to decide on the application of the denial of benefits clause, it concluded, based on Article 1(7)(a)(ii) of the ECT, that '[t]he Claimant is an 'Investor of another Contracting Party' within the definition provided by Article 1(7)(a)(ii) ECT, being a company organized in accordance with the law applicable in Cyprus.'[15] In *Petrobart*, the tribunal concluded that under 'Article 1(7)(a)(ii) of the Treaty, an investor is a company organised in accordance with the law applicable in a state that is a Contracting Party', and since 'Petrobart is a joint stock company incorporated in Gibraltar', 'Petrobart is thus an investor as defined in Article 1(7) of the Treaty.'[16]

21.09 In *Yukos*, the tribunal agreed with the expert opinion of Professor James Crawford and concluded the following:

> On its face, Article 1(7)(a)(ii) of the ECT contains no requirement other than that the claimant company be duly organized in accordance with the law applicable in a Contracting Party. The Tribunal agrees with Professor Crawford that in order to qualify as a protected Investor under Article 1(7) of the ECT, a company is merely required to be organized under the laws of a Contracting Party.[17]

Other BITs explicitly exclude entities without whole or partial legal personality, as art 1 of the Austria–Tajikistan BIT illustrates:
(1) 'investor of a Contracting Party' means:
   … (b) an enterprise constituted or organised under the applicable law of a Contracting Party, making or having made an investment in the other Contracting Party's territory.

(3) 'enterprise' means any entity possessing at least partial legal personality (Agreement for the Promotion and Protection of Investment between the Republic of Austria and the Republic of Tajikistan (entered into force 21 December 2012) (Austria-Tajikistan BIT))

For the requirement of legal personality under the ICSID Convention, see Chester Brown and Ashique Rahman, 'Juridical Personas and the Requirements of the ICSID Convention' in Crina Baltag (ed), *ICSID Convention after 50 Years. Unsettled Issues* (Wolters Kluwer 2017) 163–87, 168.

[13] That is the incorporation test.
For further comments regarding the legal personality of an investor and different types of entities covered by the ECT, see Baltag (n 12) 102 *et seq*. With particular focus on NGOs, see Nick Gallus and Luke Eric Peterson, 'International Investment Treaty Protection of NGOs' (2006) 4 Arbitration International 527.

[14] *Nykomb Synergetics Technology Holding AB v The Republic of Latvia*, SCC Case No [X], Award (16 December 2003) 2.1.

[15] *Plama* (n 9) para 124.

[16] *Petrobart Limited v The Kyrgyz Republic*, SCC Case No 126/2003, Award (29 March 2005) 24.

[17] *Yukos Capital Sàrl v Russian Federation*, PCA Case No AA 227, Interim Award on Jurisdiction and Admissibility (30 November 2009) para 411.

Mindful to the challenges raised by Russia, the tribunal in *Yukos* rightfully concluded that 'assertions concerning ownership and control of Claimant' are properly addressed in the context of 'Article 17 of the Treaty, according to which ownership or control of a claiming party by citizens or nationals of a third State may, if certain other conditions are met, entitle a responding State to deny the benefits of Part III of the Treaty to the claiming party.'[18] The *Yukos* tribunal further stated that:

21.10

> The Tribunal is bound to interpret the terms of the ECT, including Article 1(7), not as they might have been written but as they were actually written.... Claimant was organized 'in accordance with the law applicable' in a Contracting Party. Claimant accordingly qualifies as a company so organized in the instant case. The Tribunal is not entitled, by the terms of the ECT, to find otherwise.[19]

The conclusions of these ECT arbitral tribunals seem to be in line with the decisions of investment arbitral tribunals outside the ECT framework, which often confirm that they cannot read into applicable treaties something that the parties have not intended to include. For instance, in *Saluka,* where the tribunal applied the BIT between the Netherlands and the Czech Republic, the Czech Republic claimed that the investor was a shell company controlled by its Japanese owners, the tribunal positioned itself as follows:

21.11

> ... the predominant factor which must guide the Tribunal's exercise of its functions is the terms in which the parties to the Treaty now in question have agreed to establish the Tribunal's jurisdiction. In the present context, that means the terms in which they have agreed upon who is an investor who may become a claimant entitled to invoke the Treaty's arbitration procedures. The parties had complete freedom of choice in this matter, and they chose to limit entitled 'investors' to those satisfying the definition set out in Article 1 of the Treaty. The Tribunal cannot in effect impose upon the parties a definition of 'investor' other than that which they themselves agreed. That agreed definition required only that the claimant-investor should be constituted under the laws of (in the present case) The Netherlands, and it is not open to the Tribunal to add other requirements which the parties could themselves have added but which they omitted to add.[20]

Furthermore, states have the freedom of drafting the terms of a treaty as they consider appropriate and, consequently, may include any limitations they find adequate in achieving the object and purpose of such treaty. In *Rompetrol*, Romania claimed that while the formal requirements of the applicable BIT were satisfied, the evidence showing the control and ownership of claimant indicated that it was not a national of the Netherlands, but of Romania, the respondent state in the arbitral proceedings.[21] The tribunal stressed that:

21.12

---

[18] ibid para 412.
[19] ibid para 413.
[20] *Saluka Investments BV v The Czech Republic*, UNCITRAL, Partial Award (17 March 2006) para 241.
[21] *Rompetrol Group NV v Romania*, ICSID Case No ARB/06/3, Decision on Respondent's Preliminary Objections on Jurisdiction and Admissibility (18 April 2008) para 78.

within the framework of Article 25(2)(b) of the [ICSID] Convention, it is open to the Contracting Parties to a BIT to adopt incorporation under their own law as a necessary and also sufficient criterion of nationality for purposes of ICSID jurisdiction, without requiring in addition an examination of ownership and control, of the source of investment funds, or of the corporate body's effective seat.[22]

Furthermore, the *Rompetrol* tribunal highlighted that:

… the Tribunal cannot find any trace of justification for an argument that international law deprives the States concluding a particular treaty—whether a multilateral Convention like ICSID or a bilateral arrangement like a BIT—of the power to allow, or indeed to prescribe, the place and law of incorporation as the definitive element in determining corporate nationality for the purposes of their treaty.[23]

21.13 Recently, in *KT Asia*, the arbitral tribunal was called to look into the provisions of Article 25(2)(b) of the ICSID Convention[24] and to determine whether the claimant satisfied the conditions set forth for the jurisdiction of ICSID. Having decided that the ICSID Convention does not impose any particular test for the nationality of juridical persons not having the nationality of the host state, the tribunal concluded that this 'leaves broad discretion to Contracting States to define … corporate nationality, under the relevant BIT'.[25] When considering the provisions of Article 1(b)(ii) of the applicable Kazakhstan–Netherlands BIT referring to 'legal persons constituted under the law of that Contracting Party', the tribunal came to the conclusion that, 'simply reading this provision, a legal entity incorporated in a Contracting State is deemed a national of that State'.[26] The tribunal then considered the objection submitted by Kazakhstan that the principle of effective nationality should apply and the tribunal should look beyond the definition in Article 1(b)(ii) of the BIT. By employing the rules of treaty interpretation under Article 31(1) of the Vienna Convention, the arbitral tribunal reasoned that:

In the present case, the ordinary meaning of the words is clear. In conformity with the general method for determining corporate nationality in international law in Article 1(b)(ii) of the Treaty, the Contracting Parties agreed that the place of

---

[22] ibid para 83.
[23] ibid para 92.
See also Christoph H Schreuer with Loretta Malintoppi, August Reinisch, Anthony Sinclair, *The ICSID Convention: A Commentary* (CUP 2009) 281.
[24] ICSID Convention, art 25(2)(b) provides that a 'national of another Contracting State' is:

any juridical person which had the nationality of a Contracting State other than the State party to the dispute on the date on which the parties consented to submit such dispute to conciliation or arbitration and any juridical person which had the nationality of the Contracting State party to the dispute on that date and which, because of foreign control, the parties have agreed should be treated as a national of another Contracting State for the purposes of this Convention.

[25] *KT Asia Investment Group BV v Republic of Kazakhstan*, ICSID Case No ARB/09/8, Award (17 October 2013) para 113.
[26] ibid para 114.

incorporation would establish the nationality of legal persons. Hence, a legal person constituted under the law of a Contracting Party is a national of that State. KT Asia is a legal person constituted under the law of the Netherlands. As a result, it is a Dutch national under the nationality test of the BIT.[27]

21.14 In *ADC*, the arbitral tribunal stressed that if states choose not to include additional requirements other than the incorporation test, tribunals cannot 'read more into the BIT than one can discern from its plain text'.[28] Consequently, tribunals should not add additional requirements, such as the effective nationality or genuine link with another state, when the applicable treaty does not incorporate them into its text.

21.15 In contrast with the decisions mentioned, the Dissenting Opinion of Prosper Weil in *Tokios Tokelés* prioritized the purpose and object of the ICSID Convention, advising arbitral tribunals to look into the corporate structure if the facts of the case so require in order to establish nationality. In that case, Ukraine argued that while the claimant was duly established under the laws of Lithuania, it was, in fact, owned and controlled by nationals of Ukraine.[29] In addition, Ukraine submitted that the claimant had 'no substantial business activities in Lithuania and maintain[ed] its *siège social*, or administrative headquarters, in Ukraine'.[30] The majority of the arbitral tribunal held that 'under the terms of the Ukraine–Lithuania BIT, interpreted according to their ordinary meaning, in their context, and in light of the object and purpose of the Treaty, the only relevant consideration is whether the Claimant is established under the laws of Lithuania'.[31] The majority of the arbitral tribunal was clear in stating that:

> It is not for tribunals to impose limits on the scope of BITs not found in the text, much less limits nowhere evident from the negotiating history. An international tribunal of defined jurisdiction should not reach out to exercise a jurisdiction beyond the borders of the definition. But equally an international tribunal should exercise, and indeed is bound to exercise, the measure of jurisdiction with which it is endowed.[32]

21.16 In the Dissenting Opinion in *Tokios Tokelés*, Prosper Weil looked at the object and scope of the ICSID Convention, and concluded that:

> The ICSID arbitration mechanism is meant for *international* investment disputes, that is to say, for disputes between States and *foreign* investors. It is because of their international character, and with a view to stimulating private *international*

---

[27] ibid para 116.
[28] *ADC Affiliate Ltd and ADC & ADMC Management Ltd v The Republic of Hungary*, ICSID Case No ARB/03/16, Award (2 October 2006) para 359.
[29] *Tokios Tokelés v Ukraine*, ICSID Case No ARB/02/18, Decision on Jurisdiction (29 April 2004) para 55.
[30] ibid para 21, emphasis in the original.
[31] ibid para 38.
[32] ibid para 36.

investment, that these disputes may be settled, if the parties so desire, by an *international* judicial body. The ICSID mechanism is not meant for investment disputes between States and their own nationals.[33]

21.17 Prosper Weil relied on both the origin of the capital invested by the claimant and on the real and effective nationality of the claimant.[34] At least one author has suggested that the notion of investment under the ICSID Convention is explicitly referring to *international* investment, such that 'the lack of any requirement based on the effective origin of the investment in the nationality criteria of the juridical person' set forth in Article 25(2)(b) of the ICSID Convention does not extend the jurisdiction of the Centre to 'disputes not related to a foreign investment.'[35] The conclusion of Prosper Weil remains isolated and, at least until now, his prophecy regarding the negative consequences of the *Tokios Tokelés* decision on the future of the ICSID Convention by dissuading governments from adhering to the ICSID Convention or, if they have already adhered, from providing for ICSID arbitration in their future BITs or investment contracts, remains unfulfilled.[36]

21.18 Arbitral tribunals are therefore firm in concluding that tribunals may not infer any other requirements in qualifying the nationality of a legal entity and, as such, in establishing the quality of 'investor', other than those found within the clear provisions of a treaty.

---

[33] *Tokios Tokelés*, Dissenting Opinion of Prosper Weil (29 April 2004), para 5, emphasis in original.

[34] ibid para 15 *et seq*.

[35] Roberto Castro de Figueiredo, 'ICSID and Non-Foreign Investment Disputes' (2007) 4(5) TDM, 3 < https://www.transnational-dispute-management.com/article.asp?key=1071#citation > accessed 15 June 2018. Castro de Figueiredo relies instead on the requirement that 'investment' under the ICSID Convention must be of 'international' character. As explained by the author:

> This general purpose is stated in the ICSID Convention's preamble .... The first recital, which recognizes 'the need for international cooperation for economic development, and the role of private *international investment* therein' as the main purpose of the ICSID Convention ... the following recitals cannot be understood without any reference to the first recital and especially to 'international investment.' The second recital refers to 'the possibility that from time to time *disputes may arise in connection with such investment* between Contracting States and nationals of other Contracting States.' It is clear that the reference in the second recital to 'such investment' is a direct allusion to 'international investment' contained in the first recital.... Consequently, it is not difficult to conclude that, although the first recital is the single indication of the foreign character of the notion of investment, the subsequent recitals of the ICSID Convention's preamble are referring to *disputes in connection with international investment* (34–35, emphasis in original).

The author concludes as follows:

> However, the lack of any requirement based on the effective origin of the investment in the nationality criteria of the juridical person set forth in Article 25(2)(b) of the ICSID Convention does not extend the jurisdiction of the Centre to disputes not related to a foreign investment (38).

[36] *Tokios Tokelés* Dissenting Opinion (n 34) para 30.

C. Lifting the Corporate Veil under the Provisions of the ECT

In adopting the incorporation test, arbitral tribunals are prevented from looking **21.19** into the nationality of the owners or shareholders. This would go against the general rule of treaty interpretation with the negative consequence of destabilizing the certainty and predictability of the ECT legal framework. The Vienna Convention on the Law of Treaties, which codifies the customary international law rules in this respect,[37] gives preference to the textual or literal interpretation of a treaty, providing that 'ordinary meaning [is] given to the terms …'.[38]

---

[37] The rules of treaty interpretation of the Vienna Convention on the Law of Treaties (Vienna, 23 May 1969) 1155 UNTS 331 (entered into force 27 January 1980) (Vienna Convention on the Law of Treaties) are recognized as codifying the existing customary international law and, therefore, applicable to the interpretation of the provisions of the ECT. See *Case Concerning Avena and Other Mexican Nationals (Mexico v United States of America)*, Judgment (31 March 2004), ICJ Reports 2004, 12, para 83:

> This phrase therefore requires interpretation according to the customary rules of treaty interpretation reflected in Articles 31 and 32 of the Vienna Convention on the Law of Treaties.

[38] The Vienna Convention on the Law of Treaties provides for the following:

Article 31—General rule of interpretation

1. A treaty shall be interpreted in good faith in accordance with the ordinary meaning to be given to the terms of the treaty in their context and in the light of its object and purpose.
2. The context for the purpose of the interpretation of a treaty shall comprise, in addition to the text, including its preamble and annexes:
   (a) any agreement relating to the treaty which was made between all the parties in connexion with the conclusion of the treaty;
   (b) any instrument which was made by one or more parties in connexion with the conclusion of the treaty and accepted by the other parties as an instrument related to the treaty.
3. There shall be taken into account, together with the context:
   (a) any subsequent agreement between the parties regarding the interpretation of the treaty or the application of its provisions;
   (b) any subsequent practice in the application of the treaty which establishes the agreement of the parties regarding its interpretation;
   (c) any relevant rules of international law applicable in the relations between the parties.
4. A special meaning shall be given to a term if it is established that the parties so intended.

Article 32—Supplementary means of interpretation

Recourse may be had to supplementary means of interpretation, including the preparatory work of the treaty and the circumstances of its conclusion, in order to confirm the meaning resulting from the application of article 31, or to determine the meaning when the interpretation according to article 31:
(a) leaves the meaning ambiguous or obscure; or
(b) leads to a result which is manifestly absurd or unreasonable.

21.20 Nevertheless, arbitral tribunals could be allowed to disregard an economic manifestation of a legal entity and cast doubt on its corporate structure or ownership if exceptional circumstances require so, in order to protect this precise legal framework.

21.21 In the seminal case of *Barcelona Traction*, the International Court of Justice was unequivocal in concluding that the piercing or lifting of the corporate veil in international law is admitted to be 'exceptional' in both national and international law,[39] and it is employed when 'special circumstances' so require.[40] This is done 'to prevent the misuse of the privileges of legal personality, as in certain cases of fraud or malfeasance, to protect third persons such as a creditor or purchaser, or to prevent the evasion of legal requirements or of obligations'.[41] In *Tokios Tokelés*, the majority of the tribunal held that the respondent 'ha[d] not made a prima facie case, much less demonstrated, that the Claimant has engaged in any of the types of conduct described in *Barcelona Traction* that might support a piercing of the Claimant's corporate veil', nor did the respondent show or suggest 'that the Claimant has used its status as a juridical entity of Lithuania to perpetrate fraud or engage in malfeasance' or 'to evade applicable legal requirements or obligations',[42] which would justify the application of this 'equitable doctrine'.[43] In *ADC*, the arbitral tribunal acknowledged the existence of the 'principle of '*piercing the corporate veil*'', but concluded that 'it is rarely and always cautiously applied', only 'to situations where the real beneficiary of the business misused corporate formalities in order to disguise its true identity and therefore to avoid liability'.[44] In *Rumeli*,

---

See also Alexander Orakhelashvili, 'The Recent Practice on the Principles of Treaty Interpretation' in Alexander Orakhelashvili and Sarah Williams (eds), *40 Years of the Vienna Convention on the Law of Treaties* (British Institute of International and Comparative Law 2010) 117–54, 125.

[39] *Barcelona Traction, Light and Power Co, Ltd (Belgium v Spain)*, Judgment (5 February 1970), ICJ Reports 1970, 3, para 58.
[40] ibid para 58.
[41] ibid para 56.
[42] *Tokios Tokelés* (n 30) para 55.
[43] ibid para 53.
[44] *ADC* (n 29) para 358, emphasis in original.

The 'piercing of corporate veil' is often argued in conjunction with the so-called doctrine of 'abuse of rights', as an alternative argument. Arbitral tribunals relied on this 'doctrine' when a claimant, in gaining access to the protection of a treaty, has structured the investment at a time and in a manner which triggered the tribunal to ascertain the existence of an abuse of rights. In *Phoenix Action, Ltd v The Czech Republic*, ICSID Case No ARB/06/5, Award (15 April 2009) , the tribunal concluded that the arbitration was an abuse of the ICSID system, given the fact that 'the Claimant made an 'investment' not for the purpose of engaging in economic activity, but for the sole purpose of bringing international litigation against the Czech Republic.' (ibid para 142 and 144) The tribunal in *Venezuela Holdings, BV, et al (case formerly known as Mobil Corporation, Venezuela Holdings, BV, et al) v Bolivarian Republic of Venezuela*, ICSID Case No ARB/07/27, Decision on Jurisdiction (10 June 2010), followed the reasoning of the *Phoenix* tribunal and held 'that to restructure investments only in order to gain jurisdiction under a BIT for such disputes would constitute … 'an abusive manipulation of the system of international investment protection under the ICSID Convention and the BITs.' (ibid para 205) It is probably useful to emphasize that the argument based on the 'abuse of rights' should be approached with caution by States, given the fact that such a doctrine is not grounded in the text of international investment agreements.

the arbitral tribunal relied on the reasoning of the tribunal in *ADC* and concluded that it 'does not see any reason to "pierce the corporate veil" as requested by Respondent', as 'the principle of piercing the corporate veil only applies to situations where the real beneficiary of the business misused corporate formalities in order to disguise its true identity and therefore to avoid liability'.[45]

The ECT provides, through its provisions under Article 17 on the denial of benefits to investors and investments, an opportunity to preserve the object and scope of the Treaty and to ensure that the provisions of the ECT are not abused. As confirmed by the arbitral tribunal in *Yukos*, the opportunity to lift the corporate veil and prevent the misuse of the provisions of the ECT is to be found in Article 17 of the Treaty, and not in Article 1(7)(a)(ii) of the ECT. Article 17 of the ECT, as indicated, provides that '[e]ach Contracting Party reserves the right to deny the advantages of this Part to … a legal entity if citizens or nationals of a third state own or control such entity and if that entity has no substantial business activities in the Area of the Contracting Party in which it is organised'. Hence, it is under this provision that any concerns as to real and effective nationality should be addressed. The ECT case law is uniform in this sense and, as will be shown, the decisions of arbitral tribunals in the Spanish solar disputes confirm this approach. **21.22**

In addition to Article 17, Article 26(7) of the ECT provides the second instance in which an arbitral tribunal can lift the corporate veil of the investor, but it would not be used to justify reading additional requirements for investors into Article 1(7)(a)(ii). Article 26(7) of the ECT extends the treaty protection to investors that have 'the nationality of a Contracting Party party to the dispute … and which … is controlled by Investors of another Contracting Party'. As such, for the purpose of Article 25(2)(b) of the ICSID Convention, this investor shall be treated as a 'national of another Contracting State'.[46] Unlike Article 17 of the ECT, Article 26(7) is not meant to restrict the jurisdiction *ratione personae* of arbitral tribunals by putting forward the real nationality of the investor. As explained by the tribunal in *Tokios Tokelés*: **21.23**

> The use of a control-test to define the nationality of a corporation to *restrict* the jurisdiction of the Centre would be inconsistent with the object and purpose of Article 25(2)(b). Indeed, as explained by Mr. Broches, the purpose of the control-test in the second portion of Article 25(2)(b) is to *expand* the jurisdiction of the Centre.[47]

---

[45] *Rumeli Telekom AS and Telsim Mobil TelekomunikasyonHizmetleri AS v Republic of Kazakhstan*, ICSID Case No ARB/05/16, Award (29 July 2008) para 328.
    For further discussion on the lifting of corporate veil in the context of investor-state arbitration, see Albert Badia, *Piercing the Veil of State Enterprises in International Arbitration* (Wolters Kluwer 2014) 133–62.
[46] Similar in the context of art 1(6) of the ICSID Additional Facility Rules, ICSID/11/Rev. 1 (January 2003).
[47] *Tokios Tokelés* (n 30) para 46, emphasis in original.
    See also Schreuer (n 24) 283:

D. The Spanish Solar Disputes and the Notion of 'Investor'

21.24 ECT arbitral tribunals established in cases prior to the Spanish solar disputes took the approach that they cannot read into Article 1(7)(a)(ii) of the Treaty requirements in addition to the incorporation test. With over forty cases arising out of the Spanish solar disputes and with Spain constantly challenging the legal standing of the investor in these arbitrations, it is legitimate to take a look at the relevant cases and to determine whether there is a change in respect of the approach of ECT arbitral tribunals regarding the notion of 'investor', which might deviate from the plain language of Article 1(7)(a)(ii).

1. Isolux

21.25 The facts in *Isolux* are similar to the other Spanish solar disputes. Spain attracted investments in the photovoltaic field by granting the feed-in-tariff for the production of energy from these sources, initially under a special regime promoted under Law 54 of 1997. The specific regime under this Law was later developed by the Royal Decree 661 of 2005, which provided, among other things, for 'lesser administrative intervention in fixing the electricity prices as well as a better and more efficient attribution of the costs of the system'.[48] The benefits granted to investors in the photovoltaic sector were later modified, starting with the Royal Decree 1565 of 2010, which eliminated the regulated tariffs for solar photovoltaic facilities and introduced a series of additional technical requirements, and continuing with the Royal Decree Law 14 of 2010, which amended the tariff deficit in the electricity sector.[49] Starting with 2012, Spain introduced additional changes to the regime of energy from photovoltaic sources.[50]

21.26 The claimant in *Isolux* was a Dutch company, Isolux IN, incorporated in 2012. Isolux IN was the majority shareholder of Grupo T-Solar Global SA, T-Solar Global Operating Assets SL, and of Tuin Zonne Origen SLU T-Solar Global Operating Assets SL and Tuin Zonne Origen SLU were, in turn, the majority shareholders of 117 limited responsibility companies which owned photovoltaic power plants in Spain.[51] Isolux IN was established by an investment agreement signed between the Spanish companies Grupo Isolux Corsan Concesiones, SL

The overwhelming weight of the authority points towards the traditional criteria of incorporation or seat for the determination of corporate nationality of claimants under Art. 25(2)(b) [of the ICSID Convention]. It follows that the reference to foreign control in Article 25(2)(b) does not impose a further general requirement upon investors having the requisite foreign nationality in order for them to submit a dispute to ICSID.

[48] *Isolux* (n 3) para 94.
[49] ibid para 112 *et seq*.
[50] ibid para 117 *et seq*.
[51] ibid para 1.

(GIC Concesiones or GICC) and Grupo Isolux Corsan, SA ('GIC') (GICC and GIC are jointly referred to as 'ISOLUX'), on the one hand, and of the Canadian companies Public Sector Pension Investment Board (PSP or PSP Investments) and its subsidiary Infra-PSP Canada Inc (Infra-PSP), on the other hand.[52]

21.27 Spain challenged the jurisdiction *ratione personae* of the tribunal based on the fact that Isolux IN, although a Dutch company, was controlled by PSP, a Canadian investor and by ISOLUX, a Spanish investor.[53] As indicated by Spain, Canada is not a Contracting Party to the ECT, while a Spanish national cannot avail itself of the provisions of the ECT to bring a claim against its own state.[54] As such, the real claimant was ISOLUX, as there was no real connection between Isolux IN and the Netherlands. As explained by Spain, the employees of Isolux IN were all based in Spain, the activities of Isolux IN were also located in Spain and concerned the photovoltaic plants, while the registered office in the Netherlands coincided with the registered office of another company, United Trust.[55] Based on these facts, Spain alleged that the claimant was a mere shell company which, by relying on the formalistic argument and using its place of registration, benefited from the protection of the ECT.[56] These exceptional circumstances justified, according to Spain, the lifting of the corporate veil, without having to prove any case of fraud or intention.[57]

21.28 The arbitral tribunal was firm in dismissing Spain's contentions, by noting that the only criteria employed by the ECT (in Article 1(7)(a)(ii)) to determine who receives its protection is a legal one: 'el criterio es únicamente jurídico: la constitución con arreglo a la legislaciónen la Parte Contratante'.[58] Furthermore, the tribunal highlighted that the ECT contains no express provision which would allow the piercing of the corporate veil, not even in cases of fraud.[59]

---

[52] ibid paras 141 *et seq*.
[53] Ibid para 182.
[54] ibid para 182.
[55] ibid para 185.
[56] ibid para 186.
[57] ibid para 187. The Kingdom of Spain also relied on the reasoning of ICSID tribunals in *Tokios Tokelés* (n 30) and *Venoklim Holding BV v Bolivarian Republic of Venezuela*, ICSID Case No ARB/12/22.

Spain also argued the application of the denial of benefits clause under art 17 of the ECT, stressing the nature of a shell company of the Claimant (*Isolux* (n 3) para 235 *et seq*.), as well as the doctrine of abuse of process in the form of forum shopping (*Isolux* (n 3) para 215 *et seq*.). On the denial of benefits clause, it is interesting to note here that the arbitral tribunal rejected the application of the clause as Spain failed to trigger the applicability of the provision prior to the commencement of the dispute. As such, in the opinion of the tribunal, the clause cannot have retroactive effects (*Isolux* (n 3) para 715).

[58] Translated: 'the only criterion is the legal one: organization in accordance with the laws of a Contracting Party' *Isolux* (n 3) para 667.
[59] ibid para 670.

2. Charanne

21.29 In *Charanne*, the claimants, Charanne BV (Charanne), a Dutch company, and Construction Investments Sàrl (Construction), a Luxembourg company, were initially the direct shareholders of Grupo T-Solar Global SA ('T-Solar'), a limited liability company established in 2007 in Spain, and formerly known as Tuin Zonne SA. The activity of T-Solar consisted in the generation and sale of electricity produced by photovoltaic solar plants. In 2012, Charanne and Construction transferred their shares in T-Solar to Grupo Isolux Corsán SA, as contribution in kind to capital, as well as to acquire a stake in the company and its parent company, Grupo Isolux Corsán SAA.[60] At the time of the dispute, Charanne and Construction maintained interest in T-Solar through their shares in Grupo Isolux Corsán S.A. (2.43 per cent and 52.02 per cent, respectively) and Grupo Isolux Corsán Concesiones SA (1.756 per cent and 0.44765 per cent, respectively).[61] The facts of the case are similar to the *Isolux* case, with the caveat that it concerned the facts up to 2012.

21.30 Spain claimed that behind the corporate veil of Charanne and Construction there were two natural persons of Spanish nationality, Mr José Gomis Cañete and Mr Luis Antonio Delso Heras.[62] As Spain explained, the claimants were nothing but two 'empty shells' through which two individuals of Spanish nationality 'realise their investments', and that in order 'to allow Claimants to benefit from the protections that the ECT offers to foreign investors would amount to overlooking the aim sought by the instrument, that is no other than to protect foreign investors, and not domestic investors that structure their investment in an artificially complex manner.'[63] Spain contended that the ECT was created to encourage foreign investments and not investments of a state's own nationals.[64] Spain stressed that in order to avoid such shortcomings, the 'foreign' requirement of an investor must be an objective condition, which allows tribunals to pierce the corporate veil and to determine the effective nationality of the investor.[65]

---

[60] *Charanne* (n 6) para 8.
[61] Ibid para 8 *et seq*.
It is useful to note here that in both *Isolux* and *Charanne*, the parties nominated the same co-arbitrators to act in both cases, only with the President of the tribunal differing.
[62] ibid para 412.
[63] ibid para 412.
[64] ibid para 225 *et seq*.
[65] ibid para 228.
Spain also submitted that if jurisdiction would be found by the tribunal, the arbitral award would violate the public policy of Spain, the seat of arbitration, as it would provide for a different treatment for Spanish nationals, depending on the vehicle through which they decided to invest (ibid para 230). To this proposition, claimants argued that under no circumstances would this result in a discrimination, but rather, would result in an enlargement of the rights of the disadvantaged individuals, rather than restricting their rights. (ibid para 267).

The arbitral tribunal rejected Spain's arguments by concluding that the protection provided by the ECT applies to investments made by an investor, as defined by Article 1(7) of the ECT, requiring that the entity is organized in accordance with the applicable law in the Contracting Party, and that in this case, The Netherlands and Luxembourg are Contracting Parties to the ECT.[66]

21.31

Spain also relied on Article 26(7) and suggested that this is an indication that an arbitral tribunal may lift the veil and determine the real nationality of the claimants.[67] The tribunal agreed with Spain that it was possible to lift the corporate veil and to ignore the legal personality of an investor, but only in case of fraud directed at jurisdiction, which was not the case of these proceedings.[68] To do otherwise, the tribunal continued, would mean to apply the denial of benefits clause under Article 17 of the ECT to a situation not envisaged by this provision.[69]

21.32

3. RREEF

In *RREEF*, the two claimants, RREEF Infrastructure GP Limited and RREEF Pan-European Infrastructure Two Lux Sàrl, incorporated under the laws of Jersey and Luxembourg, respectively, were entities specialized in infrastructure investments, with extensive experience across different sectors, including the power generation sector.[70] Spain submitted that the claimants were not investors for the purpose of the ECT, relying on an argument similar to the one put forward in *Isolux*. According to Spain, a legal entity would qualify as 'investor' under the ECT if it is a 'company' or 'other organization' which has 'the arrangement of personal resources (subjective element) and material resources (objective element) to achieve a purpose (theological (*sic*) element) which, in this case, must be the rendering of service or the production of goods on the market'.[71] Spain pointed out that claimants lacked most of these elements. In addition, claimants were mere 'shell companies'.[72] As highlighted by Spain, an entity that only sells and buys shares cannot satisfy the threshold set by Article 1(7) of the ECT.[73]

21.33

The arbitral tribunal rejected Spain's arguments. In particular, extensive attention was devoted to the allegations of 'shell companies' concerning both claimants and, thus, their exclusion from the protection of the ECT. As explained by the tribunal, the term 'shell company' is often used to identify entities with 'little or

21.34

---

[66] ibid para 414.
[67] ibid para 226.
[68] ibid para 415.
[69] ibid para 416.
[70] *RREEF* (n 7) para 5. The information regarding the proper facts underlying the dispute is quite limited; nevertheless, the dispute is related to the measures taken by Spain in relation to the photovoltaic energy tariffs.
[71] ibid para 130.
[72] ibid para 134.
[73] ibid para 134.

no activity apart from owning or controlling directly or indirectly assets'.[74] Unless there is a specific provision under the municipal law or under the applicable investment treaty, the tribunal reasoned, there is no reason why a 'shell company' should be excluded from the protection afforded by these instruments, nor did Spain present evidence to the contrary.[75] The ECT does not provide for this exclusion.[76] The arbitral tribunal thus concluded that the requirements *ratione personae* under the ECT were fulfilled and emphasized that:

> while [t]here are examples of investment treaties that include within the definition of investor only commercial entities that can demonstrate certain characteristics or activities[,][t]here is no such limitation in the ECT or the ICSID Convention. It would not be proper to read such an artificial limitation into the plain meaning of the ECT, the ICSID Convention or into international law generally.[77]

E. Concluding Remarks

21.35 The matters raised in *Isolux, Charanne*, and *RREEF* come to reinforce the interpretation of Article 1(7)(a)(ii) of the ECT that a legal entity must only be organized in accordance with the laws of a Contracting Party to the ECT. These tribunals, like the previous ones in *Yukos, Petrobart, Nykomb*, and *Plama*, and in line with other non-ECT investment arbitral tribunals, confirm that a tribunal cannot read into a treaty something that the Contracting Parties did not include. In this sense, an arbitral tribunal is called to interpret the applicable treaty and not to rewrite it.

21.36 It is true that while the incorporation test gives the certainty in and the ease of detecting the nationality of a legal entity, it also comes with its shortcomings, such as failing to show the accurate economic reality beyond this formal requirement of incorporation. This is the reason why states have the opportunity, when entering into international agreements, to tailor the definition or applicable rules, whether in the definition of investor or investment, or by way of other provisions, such as the denial of benefits clause.

21.37 Although the arbitral tribunals in the Spanish solar disputes referred to the possibility of piercing or lifting the corporate veil in cases of abuse of the Treaty's provisions, they could not agree if an arbitral tribunal can do this within the confinement of the denial of benefits clause under Article 17 of the ECT only, or simply as an exception to the provisions of Article 1(7). The tribunal in *Charanne*, in line with the reasoning of the arbitral tribunal in *Yukos*, noted that such inquest

---

[74] ibid para 145.
[75] ibid paras 145–46.
[76] ibid para 145.
[77] ibid para 145.

into the corporate structure or beneficial ownership of an investor must be done only under the provisions of Article 17 of the ECT. As such, Contracting Parties to the ECT[78] have the option to deny the benefits of the Treaty when nationals of a third state own or control the investor legal entity and the entity does not have substantial business activities in a Contracting Party.[79] While Article 17 is silent as to a requirement on timing or process for denying benefits, ECT tribunals have consistently held that a Contracting Party cannot deny the benefits of the ECT after the commencement of a dispute,[80] as this would frustrate the legitimate expectations of the investor.[81] The tribunal in *Plama*, in line with the conclusion of the tribunal in *Isolux*,[82] suggested that such exercise should be made publicly and in an effective way so it becomes available to investors and that, in any case, the denial right may only have prospective effect.[83] The conclusions of the ECT tribunals are quite interesting from this point of view, as Article 17 of the ECT contains no such express requirements. Nevertheless, by looking at the wording of Article 17 of the ECT referring to '[e]ach Contracting Party reserves the right to deny', the tribunal in *Plama* considered Article 17 to be 'at best only half a notice.'[84]

21.38 The arbitral awards rendered in the Spanish solar disputes confirm the strong preference of arbitral tribunals for the plain language of Article 1(7)(a)(ii) of the Treaty. Tribunals are sceptical in reading into the ECT implied requirements for investors,[85] such as the one that the nationality of the real owners or controllers be that of a Contracting Party to the ECT, and in particular, not of the respondent. ECT arbitral tribunals seem to follow the ICJ judgment in *Barcelona Traction* in

---

[78] And, in general, of other international investment agreements. See eg art 1113 of The North American Free Trade Agreement (entered into force 1 January 1994).
[79] As it is, the wording of art 17 of the ECT does not preclude the phenomenon of round-tripping, ie the case where investors choose to incorporate a company in a state with which their home state has an investment treaty and use this vehicle to channel their investments into their home states.
[80] In *Isolux*, the tribunal held that the respondent Contracting Party must avail itself of the denial of benefits clause under Art. 17 of the ECT before the commencement of the dispute. (*Isolux* (n 3) para 715).
For a detailed discussion of art 17 of the ECT, see Loukas A Mistelis and Crina M Baltag, 'Denial of Benefits and Article 17 of the Energy Charter Treaty' in Thomas E Carbonneau and Angelica M Sinopole (eds), *Building Civilization of Arbitration* (Wildy, Simmonds & Hill Publishing 2010) 302–22.
[81] This is in contrast with the conclusions of non-ECT arbitral tribunals dealing with denial of benefits provisions in other international investment agreements. For example, in *Guaracachi America, Inc and Rurelec Plc v The Plurinational State of Bolivia*, UNCITRAL, PCA Case No 2011-17, Award (31 January 2014) paras 378–84, the tribunal held that the respondent Contracting State may deny the benefits of the US–Bolivia BIT after the commencement of arbitration.
[82] *Isolux* (n 3) para 175.
[83] *Plama* (n 9) para 159 *et seq*.
[84] ibid para 157.
[85] Although, interestingly enough, and as mentioned, ECT tribunals tend to read an implied requirement in art 17 of the ECT as to the prior notification of the denial of benefits right.

allowing the lifting of the corporate veil only in exceptional circumstances, that is under the provisions of the denial of benefits clause of the ECT.

21.39 Balancing the interests of the parties to an international investment agreement and those of individuals, natural, and legal persons, who are the beneficiaries of the protection of such instruments, is a complex task. Investors need to be assured that their investments are well protected, while states as parties to a certain treaty must ensure that this instrument is employed properly, in light of its object and purpose. For this reason, states must warrant that their real intention is accurately reflected in a treaty, especially when qualifying the individuals benefiting from the protection of its provisions.

22

POLICY COHERENCE AND THE PROMOTION OF FOREIGN DIRECT INVESTMENT IN THE RENEWABLE ENERGY SECTOR
Lessons from Europe

Avidan Kent

A. Introduction	22.01	C. Home Country Measures (HCMs) and the promotion of RE-related FDI	22.14
B. Policy Coherence for Development: An Emerging Trend	22.07	D. Concluding Remarks	22.113

A. Introduction

Despite significant technological advancements, it is clear that the renewable energy (RE) sector cannot be based on free-market incentives alone. According to the International Energy Agency (IEA), investment in RE remains 'well below' the level necessary for achieving the goals of the Paris Agreement.[1] Achieving the commitments made under the Paris Agreement will require a 'USD 13.5 trillion investment in energy efficiency and low-carbon technologies—40% of total energy sector investment to 2030'.[2] As the current commitments do not even come close to achieving the 1.5°C target aspired by the Paris Agreement, the numbers described are expected to be significantly higher.[3]   **22.01**

On its own, the free market is not expected to deliver the necessary rise in investment. Large-scale RE projects are associated with too many market failures, political uncertainties (eg expropriations and retrospective changes in support   **22.02**

---

[1] International Energy Agency (IEA), *Energy, Climate Change & Environment* (IEA 2016) 13.
[2] ibid 20.
[3] ibid 11.

schemes) and financial risks (eg price volatilit[4]).[5] Indeed many countries are constantly adopting domestic policies that are aimed at intervening in markets and correcting these deficiencies.[6]

22.03 On the international level these problems are amplified. On the one hand, the developing countries' demand for development and increasing hunger for energy present a unique, even historical opportunity for the deployment of RE infrastructure, and base these economies on cleaner foundations. On the other hand, many developing countries suffer from a weak starting point in terms of hosting foreign direct investment (FDI), namely insufficient resources[7] and frail governance which significantly reduces investors' willingness to invest in long term projects.

22.04 This chapter will discuss the legal tools offered by *public international law* that can or potentially could support FDI in the RE sector in the developing world. The focus in this respect will be not on tools that are designed to *attract* FDI, but rather on those far less studied measures that are used by investors' home countries (home country measures, or HCMs) to support *outward* FDI (OFDI);[8] an area described by Sauvant et al as 'unexplored'.[9] In order to concretize the discussion (and due to space limitations), this chapter will focus mostly on the European Union (EU), its international commitments, development policies, and private investors.

22.05 This chapter's main objective is to test the hypothesis that while public international law HCMs indeed offer many tools to support the needs of investors in the RE sector, the current legal framework is fragmented. In other words, this chapter asks whether international law HCMs are being designed in isolation from one another with no coordination or attempts to create synergies and policy coherence. This fragmentation, it will be argued, is damaging as it inhibits the efforts to deploy RE-technologies in the developing world.

---

[4] Souvik Sen et al, 'Opportunities, Barriers and Issues with Renewable Energy Development—a Discussion' (2017) 69 Renewable and Sustainable Energy Review 1170.

[5] According to the IEA, a 'radical near-term reductions in energy sector' is required if the international community is to achieve the 1.5°C goal prescribed by the Paris Agreement. See IEA, *World Energy Outlook: 2016, Executive Summary* (IEA 2016) 5–6.

[6] Please see numbers of states adopting policies such as FIT (110 states) quotas (100 states), and bio-fuel obligations (66 states) in REN21, *Renewables 2017 Global Status Report* (REN21 2017) 21.

[7] This includes high initial capital costs, lack of financing mechanisms, lack of subsidies, lack of consumers' paying capacity, lack of local infrastructure, lack of national infrastructure, and more. See review in Sunil Luthra et al, 'Barriers to Renewable/Sustainable Energy Technologies Adoption: Indian Perspective' (2015) 41 Renewable and Sustainable Energy Reviews 762, 765–69; Mohammed Yaqoot et al, 'Review of Barriers to the Dissemination of Decentralized Renewable Energy Systems' (2016) 58 Renewable and Sustainable Energy Review 477, 478–86.

[8] Karl P Sauvant et al, 'Trends in FDI, Home Country Measures and Competitive Neutrality' in Andrea K Bjorklund (ed), *Yearbook on International Investment Law & Policy 2012–2013* (OUP 2014) 3.

[9] ibid 4.

22.06 This chapter will begin by explaining the guiding concept of Policy Coherence for Development (PCD), which is increasingly recognized as crucial in the context of FDI in the RE sector (section B). It will then define the concept of public international law HCMs and will provide a review of these measures (section C). The purpose of this review is twofold. The first objective of this section is to map and illustrate the universe of RE-related international law HCMs. The second objective of this section is to evaluate whether each of the reviewed HCMs was designed in a manner that is consistent with the notion of PCD, and whether the EU considered the existence of, or potential for, synergies between different HCMs when designing individual HCMs. After performing this HCM review, this chapter comes to the conclusion that the design of existing international law HCMs is relatively fragmented (section D). Such fragmentation is inconsistent with the notion of PCD, inefficient, and to a certain extent even wasteful.[10] It is therefore recommended that a new generation of *sector-specific* investment treaties should be designed, such that will be based on PCD and will rely on a myriad of relevant HCMs (rather than the limited tools offered by BITs). Such instruments, it is argued, will provide foreign investors with a more comprehensive and effective support, and will support the global effort to shift into a greener economy.

B. Policy Coherence for Development: An Emerging Trend

22.07 Before delving into the technical waters of RE-related FDI, it is necessary to explain the conceptual background of this chapter and the current academic debate to which this chapter will contribute.

1. Policy coherence for development: background

22.08 The basic premise that different policies must be harmonious or at least coordinated, has gained ground in recent years.[11] Notably, the Organisation for Economic Co-operation and Development (OECD) has been paying increasing attention to policy coherence in the context of development. A key landmark was the 2008 OECD Ministerial Declaration, in which it was stated *inter alia*:[12]

---

[10] It may seem wasteful eg to provide Official Development Assistance for the establishment of facilities in countries where funds are likely to be misappropriated, or where high trade barriers are still in place that increase the cost of funded projects.

[11] See an historical review in Lauri Siitonen, 'Theorising Politics behind Policy Coherence for Development (PCD)' (2015) 28(1) European Journal of Development Research 1, 7. Although the OECD began their work on Policy Coherence already in 1996, we see the emergence of reports and more practical recommendations only since 2008, following the OECD's Ministerial Declaration. See in OECD, 'Policy Coherence for Inclusive and Sustainable Development' OECD and Post-2015 Reflections <http://www.oecd.org/pcd/POST-2015%20PCD.pdf> accessed 27 June 2018, 3.

[12] OECD, 'Ministerial Declaration on Policy Coherence for Development' (4 June 2008) C/MIN(2008)2/FINAL, <http://www.oecd.org/pcd/ministerialdeclarationonpolicycoherencefordevelopment.htm> accessed 27 June 2018.

WE AGREE on the necessity of greater coherence and better co-ordination between the various international arrangements and institutions in order to help ensure that the benefits of globalisation are realised and broadly shared and to cope with the challenges it brings and maximise its benefits;

The term often used with respect to policy coherence in the context of development is Policy Coherence for Development (PCD), or Policy Coherence for Sustainable Development (PCSD), defined as 'a policy tool to systematically integrate the economic, social, environmental, and governance dimensions of sustainable development into policymaking, and ensuring that they are mutually supportive.[13]

22.09 In the past, most efforts in the context of PCD were focused on how to avoid conflicts between policies and preventing a situation where policy from one area (eg protectionist agriculture policy), frustrates the success of another (eg support of developing countries agricultural sector).[14] In recent years however, the focus has expanded to also include *synergies* between policies, that is the manner in which one policy from one policy area could *promote* the effectiveness of policies from other areas.[15]

2. Development, PCD, and RE-related FDI

22.10 This study places the need to promote RE-related FDI within the context of PCD as a search for *synergetic policies*, that will link the attainment of climate change objectives with the process of development. Today, consideration of RE-related FDI within this context sounds today sensible by most people's standards. However, this was not always the case. As explained by Gupta and van der Grijp, 'the political framing of the climate change problem has changed over time'.[16] During the early 1990s, the problem of climate change 'was seen as an abstract, global, technological and economic challenge' and even 'technocratic in nature'.[17] Climate change was not considered an issue that was strongly linked to developing countries' attempts to make progress, or to the specific challenges that those countries faced in this context.

---

[13] OECD, *Better Policies for Development 2015: Policy Coherence and Green Growth* (OECD 2015) 3.

[14] OECD, 'Policy Coherence for Inclusive and Sustainable Development' (n 11) 5; Maurizio Carbone and Niels Keijzer, 'The European Union and Policy Coherence for Development: Reform, Results, Resistance' (2015) 28(1) European Journal of Development Research 30, 31.

[15] OECD, 'Policy Coherence for Inclusive and Sustainable Development' (n 11) 5; Carbone and Keijzer (n 14) 31. Please also see the work of Thomas Gehring and Sebastian Oberthür, notably *Institutional Interaction in Global Environmental Governance* (MIT 2006).

[16] Joyeeta Gupta and Nicolien van der Grijp, 'Introduction: Mainstreaming Climate Change in Development Cooperation' in Joyeeta Gupta and Nicolien van der Grijp (eds), *Mainstreaming Climate Change in Development Cooperation* (CUP 2010) 8.

[17] ibid 8–9.

However in the past twenty years, a variety of reasons (notably the political shift towards the achievement of the Millennium Development Goals) have led to a shift in the conceptualization of this problem, as development-oriented and development-linked.[18] The links between climate change and development have been explored at length.[19] Such links include *inter alia* the fact that the developing world is highly vulnerable to the adverse effects of climate change on the one hand, and the increasing demand by these countries for energy (and the implications of such demand for climate change) on the other. 22.11

The link between RE-related FDI and development should be understood within this context and the search for *synergetic* policies should be expanded.[20] Any attempt to design synergetic and active interactions between policies requires some level of climate change 'mainstreaming', defined by Gupta as 'a process by which development policies, programmes and projects are (re)designed, (re)organized, and evaluated from the perspective of climate change mitigation and adaptation'.[21] Such a process inevitably requires the re-allocation of resources, notably in the context of financial transfers, from a variety of development-oriented objectives towards development objectives that are related to climate change. This situation unavoidably creates new 'winners and losers'.[22] For example, the channelling of more fixed Official Development Assistance (ODA) resources towards RE-related projects will mean that less of those resources will be available for the achievement of other objectives (eg health and education). 22.12

Understanding this point is crucial in the context of this chapter, for two reasons. First, it is important to realize that there are no 'magic' solutions: the resources invested in supporting RE-related investment may help to mitigate the impacts of climate change, but such benefits will certainly come at a price. Secondly, understanding the 'price' tag of such mainstreaming clarifies the importance of synergies and competing policies, notably in the context of trade and investment rules that do not require the direct allocation of resources but rather are aimed at increasing resources by *reducing costs* and *facilitating* the operation of green industries abroad. The importance of such policies in PCD design therefore is clear as their 'price tag' for other developmental goals is usually very low (if not outright profitable). 22.13

---

[18] ibid 9–10.
[19] See eg World Bank, *World Development Report 2010: Development and Climate Change* (World Bank 2010).
[20] Christopher Flavin and Molly Hull Aeck, *Energy for Development: The Potential Role of Renewable Energy in Meeting the Millennium Development Goals* (REN 21 2001).
[21] Joyeeta Gupta, 'Mainstreaming Climate Change: A Theoretical Exploration' in Joyeeta Gupta and Nicolien van der Grijp (eds) *Mainstreaming Climate Change in Development Cooperation* (CUP 2010) 77.
[22] ibid 90.

C. Home Country Measures (HCMs) and the promotion of RE-related FDI

22.14 Before continuing, clarification concerning this chapter's methodology is necessary. While it is clear that each of the reviewed HCMs deserves an in-depth review of its features and potential, this chapter discusses the issues at hand at a rather high-level of abstraction. This methodological choice is required due to space restrictions, but that is not the only reason. The chapter's objective is to address a *systemic* issue—the existence of a certain fragmentation in the investment environment, a reality in which many HCMs are designed in isolation, with no coordination and with little regard to the concept of PCD. This objective justifies a 'bird's eye view' approach, addressing a number of HCMs and the manner in which they connect (or not), rather than a detailed focus over one HCM or another.

1. HCMs: background

22.15 Most of the literature on investment and climate is concerned with the measures that *host states* may take in order to attract foreign investors.[23] This chapter explores this relationship from a different perspective. More specifically, it considers the policy measures that an investor's *home state* may implement in order to increase outwards RE-related FDI.[24]

22.16 The United Nations Conference on Trade and Development (UNCTAD) defined HCMs as:[25]

> [P]olicy measures taken by the home countries of firms that choose to invest abroad designed to encourage FDI flows to other countries. Their formulation and application may involve both home and host country Government and private sector organizations.
>
> HCMs exist at the national, regional and multilateral levels and involve a broad variety of measures, ranging from information provision, technical assistance and capacity-building, to financial, fiscal and insurance measures, investment-related trade measures, and measures related to the transfer of technology. Given this variety, HCMs have to be adaptable and flexible, since 'no one size fits all'.

---

[23] See eg Marie-Claire Cordonier Segger et al (eds), *Sustainable Development in World Investment Law* (Kluwer 2011); Caroline Henckels, 'Protecting Regulatory Autonomy through Greater Precision in Investment Treaties: The TPP, CETA and TTIP' (2016) 19(1) Journal of International Economic Law 27; Lone Wandahl Mouyal, *International Investment Law and the Right to Regulate* (Routledge 2016); Anthony VanDuzer et al, *Integrating Sustainable Development into International Investment Agreements: A Guide for Developing Country Negotiators* (Commonwealth Secretariat 2013).
[24] Sauvant et al, 'Trends in FDI, Home Country Measures and Competitive Neutrality' (n 8) 4.
[25] UNCTAD, *Home Country Measures* (UNCTAD 2001) 66.

To date, the author is aware of two attempts to map the universe of available HCMs; the aforementioned UNCTAD report (2001) and the work of Sauvant et al (2014).[26] The UNCTAD report identified six major types of HCMs, which are especially useful for the promotion of FDI in developing countries. 22.17

The first type is described as 'policy positions', defined as 'positive in tone but vague in specific commitments ... generalized statements on intentions or goals'.[27] As will be seen, the EU often relies on this type of measure. The second type of HCMs is identified as 'information provision and technical assistance'.[28] This type of HCM refers to the provision of necessary information such as concerning potential risks, sectoral conditions, legal frameworks, etc. The UNCTAD report also included within this group the possibility of providing technical assistance to host states wishing to improve elements related to transparency and the availability of information. 22.18

The third type of HCMs is defined as 'technology transfer facilitation'.[29] This category of measures refers to those which are tailored to support FDI intended to increase technology transfer, for example, by prioritizing grants to such projects, or even through technical assistance to host states in order to strengthen their capacity to host such investments. The fourth type of HCMs is defined as 'financial and fiscal incentives',[30] straightforwardly referring to financial support measures such as grants, loans, equity participation, tax measures, and more. 22.19

A fifth type of HCMs are investment insurance, defined as guarantees and insurance that help to mitigate the costs involved with FDI in developing states. Such measures include *inter alia*, political and non-commercial risks which are traditionally conceived as being higher in developing countries.[31] A sixth type of HCMs are market access regulations.[32] The UNCTAD report refers here mostly to trade related measures and the removal of trade barriers, which may impact the viability and profitability of investments. Sauvant et al address trade-related measures as only 'indirectly' supporting FDI.[33] As will be explained, however, the author believes that certain trade policies should indeed be regarded as 'direct' measures, affecting investment in a manner similar to that of other HCMs. 22.20

Sauvant et al provides an extensive list of more specific HCMs, including a range of financial measures (grants, loans, etc), investment insurance measures, information services, as well as services offered by export credit agencies, trade/investment 22.21

---

[26] Sauvant et al, 'Trends in FDI, Home Country Measures and Competitive Neutrality' (n 8) 3.
[27] UNCTAD (n 25) 8.
[28] ibid 9.
[29] ibid.
[30] ibid 10.
[31] ibid 10.
[32] ibid.
[33] Sauvant et al, 'Trends in FDI, Home Country Measures and Competitive Neutrality' (n 8) 19.

promotion agencies, and lastly, international treaties.[34] Despite the clear relevance of public international law tools and their efficiency in this context, Sauvant et al did not focus on international treaties, and indeed many of these were omitted from their discussion.[35] International treaties will therefore be the focus of this chapter.

2. International law HCMs

22.22 The term 'international law HCMs' is not defined in the literature. A short elaboration is therefore required. International law HCMs are those that were created in a treaty between two (or more) states following negotiations, and are based on the notion of international cooperation. They differ from other HCMs that are offered unilaterally by states to their investors on several levels.[36] Notably, unilateral HCMs incorporate mostly private economic and commercial objectives. They are meant to support local industry in its efforts to increase its wealth through international expansion, and indirectly promote the well-being of the supporting state. International law HCMs on the other hand, are intended to support much wider and more public objectives: notably the well-being of *all involved* states, and in some cases even more (as in the case of climate change which affects the international community as a whole). As such, international law HCMs often include objectives that are related to sustainable development, poverty alleviation, technology transfer, and as discussed in this chapter, also to environmental protection. Increasingly, these HCMs are also designed with careful attention to the host states' right to regulate, which is often regarded as restricted due to the involvement of international law.

22.23 The wider nature of international law HCMs makes them far more challenging to design than regular unilateral HCMs. The objectives of unilateral HCMs are simple and straightforward, and can be achieved through relatively simple tools, based mostly on commercial viability and risks. International law HCMs on the other hand are at least in theory, far more selective and complex, as states will aspire to support only investments that could potentially achieve *a number of goals* (eg investments must be commercially viable, be sustainable in nature, and harmless/supportive to the environment). With the specific nature of RE-related HCMs the challenge is even greater because as explained, investors' needs are unique and require careful long-term design.

---

[34] ibid box 2, 13.
[35] ibid 18–19.
[36] For a list of 'non-international law' mechanisms see: 'Chapter 16: Cross-cutting Investment and Finance Issues' in IPCC, *Climate Change 2014: Mitigation of Climate Change: Contribution of Working Group III to the Fifth Assessment Report of the Intergovernmental Panel on Climate Change* (CUP 2014) 1226–27.

22.24 Moreover, the increasingly 'distributive' nature of certain international law arrangements suggests that the role and the importance of international law HCMs will significantly increase in the near future. Obligations made under international law, whether in the form of ODA (see eg the instruments discussed in section C.2.b) or through the extensive financial pledges made by the members of the United Nations Framework Convention on Climate Change (UNFCCC), imply that much of the resources that will be allocated for climate-related projects will be delivered via international law-based instruments. These large amounts are expected to dwarf equivalent national funds, making international sources much more important. Linking these international law-based tools to the wider effort to increase RE-related investment is therefore expected to be ever more urgent.

22.25 Lastly, at least in theory, international law HCMs could well be much more effective and beneficial than unilateral HCMs. This is due to the fact that both home and host countries are committed to these HCMs (indeed both were involved in their design).

22.26 In the following section, a review and analysis of the HCMs that are provided by public international law, will be presented. This subsection will concentrate on those international treaties through which, at least potentially, states are able to actively promote RE-related FDI. As the focus of this chapter is on EU investors that are operating in developing countries, the emphasis will be on the treaties that are relevant for those specific investors.

22.27 As this chapter examines the existence of policy coherence with respect to development, special attention will be given to the manner in which these HCMs are connected, and coordinated, *if at all*.

a. Official Development Assistance (ODA)

22.28 When discussing PCD, the first type of HCM to consider is development assistance. More specifically, this study will be focused upon ODA as an HCM and the key for increasing RE-related FDI in the developing world. ODA is a clear international law HCM, which can be classified as falling under the *fourth type* of HCMs (financial and fiscal incentives).

22.29 The EU is a fruitful source of ODA. In 2015 it provided a staggering US$68 billion[37] (the US in comparison provided US$31 billion during this year[38]). This

---

[37] See in European Commission, 'EU Official Development Assistance reaches highest-ever share of Gross National Income' (European Commission, 13 April 2016) <http://europa.eu/rapid/press-release_IP-16-1362_en.htm> accessed 27 June 2018.
[38] See data collected by the OECD, 'Table 1: Net Official Development Assistance from DAC and Other Donors in 2015: Preliminary Data for 2015' <http://www.oecd.org/dac/stats/ODA-2015-complete-data-tables.pdf> accessed 27 June 2018.

sum is a combination of ODA originating from the EU's institutions (almost US$14 billion)[39] and from EU member states.[40]

b. ODA and RE-related FDI

22.30 Due to its difficult competitive position vis-à-vis fossil-fuel based energy production, private FDI in RE is often dependant on external financial support. This reality is well understood by decision-makers, and indeed the vast majority of the world's nations have adopted national support schemes in order to promote the RE.[41] Technological improvements imply that, at some point in the future, RE will become commercially viable and RE support schemes will no longer be needed. In most parts of the world, however, this point in time has not yet arrived, and waiting for the free market's invisible hand to simply take its course does not sit well with the urgency of the struggle to overcome the problem of climate change. As stated in the introduction to this chapter, a massive financial effort is still necessary to achieve the commitments undertaken via the Paris Agreement, and an even greater effort is necessary in order to attain the 1.5°C target.[42] The IEA aptly describes the need for 'radical near-term reductions',[43] which even according the more optimistic scenarios will not happen at the desired speed without aggressive policies to support this change.

22.31 Efficient support schemes are a viable alternative only where the state can allocate the necessary funds. As many developing countries have more urgent concerns and far less resources to rely on, investing funds in RE support schemes is not always a priority.[44] Furthermore, many developing countries also resist the idea that they have any obligation to invest precious resources in RE schemes intended

---

[39] ibid.

[40] Denmark's direct contribution for example, played a key role in the establishment of the AfDB's Sustainable Energy Fund for Africa (SEFA). Other states that contributed to SEFA directly include the UK and Italy, see SEFA, *Annual Report* (AfDB 2015) <http://www.afdb.org/fileadmin/uploads/afdb/Documents/Generic-Documents/SEFA_ANNUAL_REPORT_2015.pdf> accessed 27 June 2018, 4–5.

[41] According to the OECD, by 2015, 145 states have adopted national support schemes in order to promote the RE. See OECD, *Overcoming Barriers to International Investment in Clean Energy* (OECD 2015) <http://www.oecd-ilibrary.org/environment/green-finance-and-investment_24090344>, accessed 27 June 2018, 19.

[42] IEA, *Energy, Climate Change & Environment* (n 1).

[43] IEA *World Energy Outlook: 2016* (n 5). The reader should note that the IEA (just like other major energy forecasting agencies such as the US Energy Information Administration) has been criticized in the past for underestimating the future deployment of RE. The reader should therefore proceed with caution. Regardless, the author is unaware of any respectable estimate to the contrary, ie according to which external funding is unnecessary and the 1.5°C target could be achieved without it. This study will therefore accept the uncontroversial assumption that the free market's invisible hand, on its own, will not deliver the 1.5°C target and external intervention, including in the form of subsidization, is necessary.

[44] See data on number states support schemes, according to their levels of income in REN21, *Renewables 2015: Global Status Report* (REN21 2015) Table 3, 99.

to mitigate the effects of a problem they feel has been caused by the developed West.[45]

22.32 The solution for this situation may come in the shape of 'external' financial support from developed counties, which will fund developing countries effort to transit into a greener economy. Such financial support may arrive in the shape of ODA, defined as 'government aid designed to promote the economic development and welfare of developing countries'.[46] According to the OECD's definition, funds transfer for the purpose of supporting local RE investment are most likely to be considered as ODA.[47]

22.33 As for the sums that were transferred in the past via ODA, the Inter-governmental Panel on Climate Change (IPCC) presented (now somewhat dated) data concerning the climate-related ODA's commitments, according to which the seven multilateral development banks distributed US$24.1 billion in 2011, and US$26.8 billion in 2012.[48] A more recent assessment by the OECD estimates bilateral climate-related development finance in 2016 at US$30 billion.[49] Multilateral climate-related development finance is estimated in the same review until 2015, at US$21 billion for that year. The transfer of ODA to support developing countries' transition into a low-carbon economy is also expected to continue into the future as the 2015 UNFCCC Paris agreement instructs the developed world to transfer financial assistance (such as ODA) in order to support developing states' attempt to meet the objectives of the UNFCCC.[50]

22.34 ODA transfers are structured so that they are administered mostly via public international funds. As identified by the IPCC, there are approximately fifty relevant public international funds.[51] One could, therefore, argue that this fact alone is evidence of the fragmentation of international law HCMs. However, when one considers the existence of these funds along with additional sources such as carbon market funds (forty-five according to the IPCC) and the numerous private funds (about 6000) that are available for investors it is difficult to deny the fragmented landscape of international law HCMs.[52]

---

[45] See the meaning, history, and origins of the principle of common but differentiated responsibilities under the climate change regime in Jutta Brunnée and Charlotte Streck, 'The UNFCCC as a Negotiations Forum: towards Common but More Differentiated Responsibilities' (2013) 13(5) Climate Policy 589.
[46] OECD, 'OECD Net ODA' <https://data.oecd.org/oda/net-oda.htm> accessed 27 June 2018.
[47] See OECD, 'Is it ODA?' Factsheet (November 2008) <https://www.oecd.org/dac/stats/34086975.pdf> accessed 27 June 2018.
[48] IPCC, 'Chapter 16: Cross-cutting Investment and Finance Issues' (n 36) 1215.
[49] OECD, *Climate-related Development Finance in 2016* (OECD 2017) <http://www.oecd.org/dac/stats/climate-change.htm> accessed 27 June 2018.
[50] See The Paris Agreement (adopted 12 December 2015, entered into force 4 November 2016) (Paris Agreement) art 9.
[51] IPCC, 'Chapter 16: Cross-cutting Investment and Finance Issues' (n 36) 1228.
[52] ibid.

22.35 Reviewing all the funds and the channels through which ODA is distributed is beyond the scope of this chapter. However, three key actors, namely the UNFCCC's Green Climate Fund (GCF), the Global Environmental Facility, and the World Bank's Climate Investment Funds are worth mentioning.

c. The Green Climate Fund

22.36 The GCF was established under the UNFCCC, and defined as its 'main financial entity'.[53] The GCF was established in 2010 but only became fully operational in 2015.[54] It is managed by an independent board, which receives instructions from the UNFCCC's COP. The GCF's declared objective is 'to support projects, programmes, policies and other activities in developing country Parties'.[55] Around 50 per cent of the fund's resources (currently about US$10 billion) are provided by EU member states.

22.37 One of the GCF's four declared 'mitigation strategic impacts' is 'energy generation and access',[56] making it very relevant for investment in RE. Furthermore, this fund also sets up a 'Private Sector Facility', with the purpose of using its (relatively) scarce resources for scaling up much larger private sector investments. The GCF offers a wide variety of financial tools, including grants, loans, equity investments, and various forms of guarantees.[57] The resources of the GCF are distributed via multilateral development banks (MDBs), as well as through a list of public and private accredited entities.[58]

d. Global Environmental Facility (GEF)

22.38 The Global Environmental Facility (GEF) was established in 1991 in order to support the finance of a variety of international environmental agreements. GEF funds are contributed by a list of donor countries, which include most but not all EU member states.[59] The GEF's role is inherently

---

[53] Green Climate Fund, *Brief on the Green Climate Fund for Climate Change Negotiators* (GCF 2015) 4.

[54] For more details about the fund and its operation see Liana Schalatek et al, 'The Green Climate Fund' (2015) Climate Finance Fundamentals <https://www.odi.org/sites/odi.org.uk/files/odi-assets/publications-opinion-files/10066.pdf> accessed 27 June 2018.

[55] UNFCCC 'Decision 1/CP.16' (2011) UN Doc FCCC/CP/2010/7/Add.1 para 102.

[56] Green Climate Fund, *Investment Opportunities for the Green Climate Fund: GFC's Role and Impact within the Climate Finance Ecosystem* (GCF 2015) 2.

[57] See a review of projects supported by the fund so far in Green Climate Fund, *Project Briefs* (Green Climate Fund 2015) <http://www.greenclimate.fund/documents/20182/194568/GCF_Project_Briefs_2015.pdf/b3cb6cd3-cac4-409f-92e7-028ad2fb902b> accessed 27 June 2018.

[58] List of accredited entities can be found here: <http://www.greenclimate.fund/documents/20182/114261/20160516_-_GCF_List_of_Accredited_Entities.pdf/e09bb9b3-9730-4adc-bca9-ff32739ecae8> accessed 27 June 2018.

[59] See list of donor countries on GEF's website <https://www.thegef.org/partners/participants> accessed 27 June 2018.

linked to development and indeed contributions to GEF are considered as ODA.⁶⁰

According to the GEF, since its inception a total of US$5.2 billion has been invested in 167 countries, for 839 projects related to climate adaptation and mitigation.⁶¹ Much of this finance was invested in order to foster and scale up the private sector via the deployment of a variety of financial instruments.⁶² **22.39**

According to the GEF's most recent programming directions (GEF-6):⁶³ **22.40**

> [GEF's strategy] does not prioritize direct support for large-scale deployment and diffusion of mitigation options with GEF financing only. Rather, GEF-6 resources are utilized to reduce risks and address barriers, so that the results can facilitate additional investments and support by other international financing institutions, private sector, and/or domestic sources. This approach also ensures that the GEF mandate is complementary to those of other climate finance options that aim for scaling-up.

Furthermore, according to the 'Instrument for the Establishment of the Restructured Global Environmental Facility'⁶⁴ the GEF 'shall ensure the cost-effectiveness of its activities'.⁶⁵ These instructions all suggest that the GEF could and should explore policy synergies with other policy areas, which may improve the 'cost-effectiveness' of its investment, as well as the scaling up of the private sector's role. **22.41**

With respect to PCD, the GEF programming directions emphasize the necessity of promoting synergies between policies.⁶⁶ While the GEF activity indeed shows promise with respect to achieving PCD (eg with respect to issues such as gender equality), this institution currently does not explore synergies with international trade and investment laws.⁶⁷ **22.42**

---

⁶⁰ Please see Note prepared by the OECD secretariat which lists GEF as one of the institutions 'core contributions to which may be reported as official development assistance, either in whole or in part.' OECD Secretariat, 'Is it ODA?' Factsheet (May 2007) <https://www.oecd.org/dac/stats/34086975.pdf> accessed 27 June 2018.
⁶¹ GEF, *Report of the Global Environment Facility to the Twenty-first Session of the Conference of the Parties to the United Nations Framework Convention on Climate Change* (GEF 2015) 2.
⁶² See eg the GEF non-grant pilot <https://www.thegef.org/gef/NGI> accessed 27 June 2018.
⁶³ GEF, *GEF-6 Programming Directions* (2014–2018) (GEF 2014) <https://www.thegef.org/gef/sites/thegef.org/files/webpage_attached/GEF6_programming_directions_final_0.pdf> accessed 27 June 2018, 52.
⁶⁴ The 'Instrument' is essentially a treaty between the relevant states, which regulates the GEF's activity, available online: GEF, 'Instrument for the Establishment of the Restructured GEF' (2 March 2015) <https://www.thegef.org/documents/instrument-establishment-restructured-gef> accessed 27 June 2018.
⁶⁵ ibid art I(5).
⁶⁶ GEF, *GEF-6 Programming Directions* (n 63) 52, and 54 (see box 2 in this page).
⁶⁷ Nothing is mentioned with respect to these areas in any of the GEF's leading guidelines or programming directions.

e. Climate Investment Funds (CIF)

22.43 Another key ODA-based instrument is the World Bank-managed multilateral Climate Investment Fund (CIF), and more specifically its Clean Technology Fund (CTF) and the Scaling Up Renewable Energy Program (SREP). The CIF's aim is, among others, to support private investment in RE by 'covering high up-front costs and risks, championing first-movers, stimulating markets, and bridging financing and information gaps'.[68] The funds made available by the CIF for this purpose, are allocated via its partner MDBs, *inter alia* in the form of loans, grants, equity, and guarantees.[69] Examples of the activity of CIF include early finance of large-scale RE projects in Morocco, Thailand, Indonesia, Turkey, and Mexico.[70] According to CIF, its funding in these cases allowed the reduction of financing costs, and of finance risks for lenders. CIF funds further helped to bridge financing gaps between available commercial loans and investors' needs, to reduce interest rates, and more.[71]

22.44 In light of the establishment of the GCF, the future of the CIF is somewhat uncertain as donor states may not be willing to finance 'twin' funds that are largely aimed to achieve the same goal.[72]

f. ODA and PCD

22.45 ODA could play an important role in the efforts to achieve PCD. Notably, it could be useful in addressing *some* of the obstacles faced by RE-related investors, whether through the creation of a better investment environment (eg by investment in infra-structure, or training programmes), the reduction of the cost of investment (eg loans, guarantees, etc), or even through the financing of support schemes and ensuring sufficient levels of returns,[73] or the mitigation of some

---

[68] See CIF's website <http://www-cif.climateinvestmentfunds.org/fund/private-sector> accessed 27 June 2018.
[69] ibid.
[70] See a factsheet issued by CIF, 'Clean Technology Fund' (November 2015) <http://www-cif.climateinvestmentfunds.org/sites/default/files/knowledge-documents/ctf_factsheet_nov2015_web.pdf> accessed 27 June 2018.
[71] ibid. See also CIF, 'De-risking Climate Smart Investment' <http://www-cif.climateinvestmentfunds.org/sites/default/files/knowledge-documents/ps_factsheet_nov2015_web.pdf> accessed 27 June 2018.
[72] Chiara Trabacchi and Jessica Brown, 'Uncertain Future of the Climate Investment Funds makes Achieving Climate Finance Goals Tougher' (Climate Policy Initiative, June 2016) <http://climatepolicyinitiative.org/2016/06/14/uncertain-future-climate-investment-funds-makes-achieving-climate-finance-goals-tougher/> accessed 27 June 2018.
[73] The IPCC 2014 report reviews the rates of return expected by investors in low-carbon sector, and summaries that '[m]any renewable energy projects, especially in developing countries where additional risk margins are added, are struggling to reach returns of this level to satisfy the expectations of financiers of equity and debt.' IPCC, 'Chapter 16: Cross-cutting Investment and Finance Issues' (n 36) 1223.

risks.⁷⁴ In other words, *if targeted and designed properly*, ODA could supplement and enhance other HCMs and improve their effectiveness.

On the other hand, one must also be aware of the dangers of such a possibility. Notably, linking ODA to firmer, stricter international legal obligations, may reduce donor states' willingness to undertake meaningful financial commitments. Perhaps the most striking example in this respect, is the US$100 billion commitment that was accepted via the Copenhagen Accord, which was achieved through a 'soft', non-binding mechanism. It is doubtful whether such commitments would have been made under a more binding mechanism.

22.46

Compared to the rest of the developed world, the EU's commitment to climate-related ODA is indeed impressive. However, the relevant sums *on their own,* are without a doubt insufficient for supporting a genuine transition into a green economy as well as for achieving the objectives of UNFCCC goals, such as those stipulated in the Paris Agreement. Much of the ODA is indeed dedicated to *scaling up* existing funds by creating adequate infrastructure, or through mechanisms such as the Private Sector Facility. In other words, PCD is not only recommended but in fact crucial for the effectiveness of ODA.

22.47

However impressive the EU's ODA-related efforts are, RE-related investors require more than mere financial support; they require *inter alia* a sufficient answer to policy uncertainties and risks, as well as means that will ensure sustainable high returns in the longer run. Other HCMs could be useful in this respect. IIAs for example, could provide an answer for the first requirement, while reduced, bound tariffs on environmental goods could help with the latter. The role of PCD in this respect is far from completed and more policies should be dedicated to the challenge of increasing RE-related FDI. Further international law HCMs that could be engaged to support this process are discussed in the following sections.

22.48

3. International investment agreements (IIA)

Despite the ever-growing critique by certain academics and non-governmental organizations (NGOs) concerning the use of IIAs, and in light of proposals to improve these,⁷⁵ many states are concluding IIAs in order to increase foreign

22.49

---

⁷⁴ Elizabeth Asiedu et al, 'Does Foreign Aid Mitigate the Adverse Effect of Expropriation Risk on Foreign Investment? (2009) 78(2) Journal of International Economics 268.

⁷⁵ See eg Armand de Mestral and Celine Levesque (eds), *Improving International Investment Agreements* (Routledge 2013); Anthony VanDuzer et al, (n 23); Marie-Claire Cordonier Segger and Avidan Kent, 'Promoting sustainable development through international investment law' in Marie-Claire Cordonier Segger, Markus Gehring, and Andrew Newcombe (eds), *Sustainable Development in World Investment Law* (Kluwer 2011); Karl Sauvant and Federico Ortino, *Improving the International Investment Law and Policy Regime: Options for the Future* (Ministry for Foreign Affairs of Finland 2013).

investment. At the time of writing, the UNCTAD estimates that there are 3324 IIAs in force.[76]

22.50 There is a constant debate regarding whether IIAs actually promote foreign investment. While the author is certainly not qualified to judge, a review of the literature suggests that at least to a certain extent and under certain conditions, IIAs do promote investment,[77] including in developing countries.[78] IIAs may include both investment protection provisions and investment promotion provisions; the former are extremely common while the latter can be found only on rare occasions. The following subsection of this chapter presents a review of both types of provisions, however greater emphasis is placed on the far less explored investment promotion provisions.

a. Investment protection under IIAs

22.51 Several authors have addressed the manner in which IIAs are supportive of RE-related investment.[79] Notably, the standard of protection found in IIAs can offer predictability, stability, and a fair business environment for foreign investors. For example, IIAs protect foreign investors from protectionism and the need to deal with corrupt judicial systems. They also often assure foreign investors of Western standards of administrative due process, and provide protection from arbitrary state behaviour, an effective recourse for compensation, and a non-politicized dispute settlement mechanism. Notably the fair and equitable treatment standard of protection (FET) provides guarantees that investors' legitimate expectations at the time of making the investment will be maintained. These measures are important in order to reduce the risk of long-term investment, and to encourage investors to operate abroad. The reduction of the political risks inherent in foreign investment directly diminishes financial risk, and reduces the cost of capital.

22.52 When discussing HCMs, the notion of investment *protection* seems *prima facie* irrelevant as it is the *host* state that is acting in order to promote the investment.

---

[76] UNCTAD, *World Investment Report* (UNCTAD 2017) xii.

[77] See literature review in Roberto Echandi et al, 'The Impact of Investment Policy in a Changing Global Economy: A Review of the Literature' (2015) World Bank Group, Policy Research Working Paper 7437, 22; and a literature review in Zbigniew Zimny et al, 'The Role of International Investment Agreements in Attracting Foreign Direct Investment' (2009) UNCTAD Series on International Investment Policies for Development (UNCTAD 2009) <http://unctad.org/en/Docs/diaeia20095_en.pdf>.

[78] Matthias Busse et al, 'FDI Promotion through Bilateral Investment Treaties: More than a Bit?' (2010) Review of World Economics 147.

[79] See eg Anatole Boute, 'Combating Climate Change through Investment Arbitration' (2012) 35 Fordham International Law Journal 613; Edna Sussman, 'The Energy Charter Treaty's Investor Protection Provisions: Potential to Foster Solutions to Global Warming and Promote Sustainable Development' (2007) 14(2) ILSA Journal of International and Comparative Law 391. More recently the OECD identified the 'insufficient investor protection' as one of the reasons inhibiting a growth in low-carbon investment, see OECD, *Better Policies for Development 2015: Policy Coherence and Green Growth* (OECD 2015) 73.

Despite this initial inclination, this author believes that IIAs should also be seen as HCMs, especially where one of the parties is an investment exporting state (which is almost always the case). In such cases, investment exporting states are actively negotiating a treaty that will be useful for their home investors and will provide them with sufficient guarantees. In other words, investment exporting states are actively preparing and improving the business environment for their own prospective investors.

IIAs' investment protection guarantees fall under the UNCTAD report's *fifth type* of HCMs, as these guarantees operate as a form of investment insurance by reducing some of the risks associated with investing abroad. These types of assurances may be especially useful in the case of RE-related FDI, which are often long-term, and include a significant component of sunk cost.[80] Most RE support schemes, for example, are built on a similar model; the investor invests a substantial amount of money to create the energy production facilities (eg solar farms) and as 'payment' receives some sort of a long term contractual right to profit from these facilities. In other words, once the investment is made, the investor's ability to profit is completely dependent on the host state's intention to respect its part in the deal, a dependency that usually lasts for a very long period. The need for investment protection provisions in the case of RE-related investment is therefore clear.   22.53

Addressing investment risks and policy uncertainties is particularly crucial in the case of climate-friendly investments. For example, investment in climate-friendly technologies is considered to be unusually 'risky',[81] due *inter alia* to the relatively high initial cost of these technologies, and the difficulty in making long-term predictions about profitability of investments in this field. Likewise, other particular factors such as the current lack of long-term climate change policies, the need to engage closely with governments (often susceptible to political 'moods'), and the high upfront expenses on infrastructure, all decrease the attractiveness of these investments. As a result, any form of assurance or guarantee for long-term stability will continue to be important in order to promote RE-related FDI and mitigate the impacts of climate change.   22.54

Such guarantees are particularly important when one considers some of the recent decisions host countries have made to renege on long-term commitments in the RE sector. For example, a number of states recently decided to retroactively change the terms of long-term support schemes such as feed-in tariffs, *de facto*   22.55

---

[80] See IPCC, 'Chapter 16: Cross-cutting Investment and Finance Issues' (n 36) 1227.
[81] For a full review of the risks embedded in RE-related investment: IEA, *Tracking Clean Energy Progress 2015* (IEA 2015); Souvik Sen et al, 'Opportunities, Barriers and Issues with Renewable Energy Development—a Discussion' (2017) 69 Renewable and Sustainable Energy Review 1170; MIGA, *World Investment and Political Risk: World Investment Trends and Corporate Perspectives; The Political Risk Insurance Industry; Breach of Contract* (World Bank 2014); Iordanis M Eleftheriadis, 'Identifying Barriers in the Diffusion of Renewable Energy Sources' (2015) 80 Energy Policy 153.

reducing the returns expected by investors in this sector, at the time of making their investment.[82] The use of IIA protection provisions in these cases, has proven to be popular among investors seeking to recover their promised profits.[83]

22.56 Whether RE investors' rights will be protected by investment tribunals remains an open question.[84] Arbitral awards so far attempt to balance investor rights with the sovereign rights of host states. While certain changes to the regulatory framework protecting RE sector investment are permissible, arbitral tribunals suggest that more drastic regulatory changes would be problematic. In *Charanne v Spain* the tribunal rejected the claim according to which certain retroactive changes made in Spain's support schemes could be protected under IIAs.[85] The following *Eisner v Spain* tribunal however, ruled in favour of foreign investors, justifying the inconsistency with the *Charanne* ruling by explaining that '[t]he measures complained of in *Charanne* had far less dramatic effects than those at issue here.'[86]

22.57 In a different case (*Blusun v Italy*), the foreign investors' claim was rejected *inter alia* as the Italian measure was deemed 'quite substantial, but was not in itself crippling or disabling', and 'the reduction in incentives was proportionately less than the reduction in the cost of photovoltaic technology', and that other important conditions (notably the length of the support scheme) remained intact.[87] In summary, most tribunals have suggested that the state will not be held liable for relevant changes in the legal and fiscal framework. If one may predict, it is somewhat likely that this line will also be adopted in future decisions (at least in cases against Spain) as the disputed measure in these cases[88] are likely to be similar to

---

[82] See description of changes made in Spain in Pablo del Rio and Pere Mir-Artigues, 'A Cautionary Tale: Spain's Solar PV Investment Bubble' (2014) IISD/GSI <https://www.iisd.org/gsi/sites/default/files/rens_ct_spain.pdf> accessed 27 June 2018; see reports about changes made in Greece in Nilima Choudhury, 'Greece Cuts FITs Retroactively' (*PV-TECH*, 14 May 2013) <http://www.pv-tech.org/news/greeks_cuts_fits_retroactively> accessed 27 June 2018; in Italy, see Edgar Meza, 'Italian PV Industry Threatened by Retroactive FIT Cuts' (*PV Magazine*, 19 June 2014) <http://www.pv-magazine.com/news/details/beitrag/italian-pv-industry-threatened-by-retroactive-fit-cuts_100015473/#axzz48ulPwlNK> accessed 27 June 2018; and in the Czech Republic, see Ian Clover, 'Czech PV Industry Denounces Retroactive Measures on Renewable Energy' (*PV Magazine*, 12 June 2014) <http://www.pv-magazine.com/news/details/beitrag/czech-pv-industry-denounces-retroactive-measures-on-renewable-energy_100015395/#axzz48ulPwlNK> accessed 27 June 2018.

[83] According to the UNCTAD, in 2015 the '[s]tate conduct most frequently challenged by investors in 2015 included legislative reforms in the renewable energy sector'. UNCTAD, 'IIA Issues Note No 2' (June 2016) <http://investmentpolicyhub.unctad.org/Upload/ISDS%20Issues%20Note%202016.pdf> accessed 27 June 2018.

[84] The most relevant question was whether retroactive changes in RE support schemes such as FIT could (or could not) be legitimately expected by foreign investors.

[85] *Charanne v Spain*, SCC Case No V062.2012, Award (21 January 2016).

[86] *Eiser v Spain*, ICSID Case No ARB/13/36, Award (4 May 2017) para 368.

[87] *Blusun v Italy*, ICSID Case No ARB/13/3, Award (27 December 2016) para 342.

[88] One can only speculate as to the content of claims in unpublished cases, but the author assumes that these claims will be mostly similar to the (now publicly available) *Eiser, Isolux, and Novenergia* claims in which investors addressed also the recent and more drastic measures that were imposed by the Spanish government.

those discussed in *Eisner* (as well as other publicly available cases such as *Isolux*[89] and *Novenergia*[90]). However, due to the lack of binding precedent in investment arbitration, this prediction should be regarded as speculative.

b. Investment promotion under IIAs

22.58 While the traditional tools available in the majority of the 3000 plus investment treaties can be considered as supportive of RE-related FDI (ie if one is to accept the view that IIAs indeed promote FDI), there is no doubt that more could be done by states wishing to actively support such investment. Notably, while most investment treaties include investment *protection* provisions, only a handful also include investment *promotion* that is measures that provide active support for foreign investment.[91] An UNCTAD report defines investment promotion provisions in the following words:[92]

> Investment promotion provisions stand out as a special category in IIAs since—contrary to the treaty obligations concerning investment protection—they establish a commitment of the contracting parties to do something. While investment protection is geared to prevent contracting parties from taking certain measures—e.g. to discriminate against investors or to expropriate them without proper compensation – investment promotion goes further and demands from contracting parties to become active.

22.59 As stated in the UNCTAD report, investment promotion provisions may arrive in many different shapes and colours.[93] The usefulness of these provisions in the context of RE-related FDI is clear as they could be tailored for the needs of RE-related FDI, or even be used only for RE investors, thereby granting these investors an advantageous competitive position over fossil fuel-based investments. Furthermore, studies have shown in the past that investment promotion policies (although not necessarily policies that were enshrined in treaties) that targeted specific sectors were indeed very efficient in promoting investment.[94]

22.60 As for the types of investment promotion provisions available in IIAs, available surveys of this universe describe measures such as exchange of information on investment opportunities and increased transparency with respect to host state regulatory environment.[95] For example, Schedule II of the Common Market for Eastern and Southern Africa (COMESA) investment agreement (title 'promotion

---

[89] *Isolux Infrastructure Netherlands v Spain*, SCC V2013/153, Award (17 July 2016).
[90] *Novenergia II—Energy & Environment v Spain*, SCC 2015/063, Award (15 February 2018).
[91] UNCTAD, *Investment Promotion Provisions in International Investment Agreements* (UNCTAD 2008) 13.
[92] ibid 6.
[93] ibid 5.
[94] Torfinn Harding and Beata Javorcik, 'Roll Out the Red Carpet and They Will Come: Investment Promotion and FDI Inflows' (2011) 121 The Economic Journal 1445.
[95] See surveys of investment promotion provisions in UNCTAD (n 91) 14; VanDuzer et al (n 23) ch 8.

and awareness programme') instructs member states to organize investment promotion activities such as joint seminars, the organization of investment-related training programmes for civil servants, and the exchange of information.[96] Another example can be found in the investment chapter of the Association of Southeast Asian Nations (ASEAN)–New Zealand—Australia FTA, in which the parties agree to assist certain ASEAN member states, *inter alia* by providing technical assistance to strengthen their capacity to attract investment, indirectly making it easier for their own investors to invest in these countries.[97]

22.61 Other measures that are mentioned at times include the granting of preferential market access by removing trade barriers,[98] which is discussed in more detail under 'trade treaties'.[99] Other activities include the establishment of follow-up, monitoring councils and the organization of joint investment promotion activities, such as workshops, outreach, and education events.[100]

22.62 The most striking example of an investment promotion HCM would be the granting of financial incentives, by home (often rich) countries, for investment in the other (often developing nation) party. Examples of such provisions are naturally very rare, but where they do occur these provisions are drafted in vague and non-obligatory language. For example in Article 34 of the European Free Trade Association (EFTA)–Egypt agreement, EFTA states 'declare their readiness' to provide financial support to Egypt, in order to facilitate investment by EFTA's investors in this country.[101]

22.63 Similar examples can be found in several EU Association Agreements. However, most of these agreements are not considered investment agreements and do not include typical investment protection provisions. The EU–Egypt Association Agreement addresses investment only in a very limited manner and calls for the conclusion of an IIA as a means to create a more 'conducive' legal environment for investors (a call that on its own demonstrates the desire to increase PCD).[102] This very agreement however, also mentions the possibility that investment in Egypt will be promoted *inter alia*, via financial support, fiscal incentives, and investment

---

[96] See Investment Agreement for the COMESA Common Investment Area (signed 23 May 2007), Schedule II. Please also see ASEAN Comprehensive Investment Agreement (signed 26 February 2009, entered into force 24 February 2012), art 24.

[97] See Agreement Establishing the ASEAN-Australia-New Zealand Free Trade Area (signed 27 February 2009, entered into force 10 January 2010), Investment Chapter, art 15. A somewhat similar provision can also be found in the ASEAN Comprehensive Investment Agreement, art 23.

[98] UNCTAD (n 91) 19.

[99] It is important to note that in this respect, to the best of the author's knowledge, no standalone IIA (ie an investment treaty that is not an integral chapter within a FTA) addresses trade barriers.

[100] UNCTAD (n 91) 26.

[101] See Free Trade Agreement between the European Free Trade Association (EFTA) and Egypt (signed 27 January 2007, entered into force 1 September 2008), art 34.

[102] See European Communities (EC)–Egypt Association Agreement (signed 25 June 2001, entered into force 1 June 2004), art 46.

insurance.¹⁰³ It is not clear however, who will be paying for such support and whether it could be considered as a HCM.

A more interesting prospect can be found in the EU–Economic Community of West African States (ECOWAS)/West African Economic and Monetary Union (UEMOA) Economic Partnership Agreement. While this Agreement does not currently include an investment chapter, the 'rendezvous' clause specifies that the parties will be discussing this possibility in the future. Indeed this agreement states that the promotion of investment is one of its objectives,¹⁰⁴ and even targets investment in specific sectors.¹⁰⁵ **22.64**

Interestingly, Article 61 of this Agreement establishes a 'regional fund' as 'the main financing instrument of the EPA Development Programme', which is intended to be the 'preferred instrument for channelling support from the European Union'.¹⁰⁶ The EU committed to transfer 6.5 billion euros through this regional fund. However, for the time being this fund is not operational.¹⁰⁷ Once operated, this fund could benefit from completing legal instruments such as provisions on investment promotion, protection and trade facilitation, in line with the notion of PCD. **22.65**

Investment treaties have the potential to facilitate RE-related FDI but they address only certain type of investors' rights, particularly those that concretize after an investment has been established in a host state. As discussed, there are examples where states have attempted to *supplement* IIAs with other HCMs in order to improve the effectiveness of IIAs in promoting investment and achieve wider goals in line with the notion of PCD. This could be implemented also in the context of RE-related investment. On very few occasions are the possibilities of adding direct financial contributions mentioned, as well as the realization that investment protection tools should be added in order to maximize the efficiency of other HCMs. These examples however are very few in number, often defined in a vague and non-committed manner, and in some cases (eg COMESA) were not followed up by the parties. **22.66**

Similar to the context of investment protection instruments, investment promotion-based HCMs will have to be designed with the utmost sensitivity towards states' right to regulate, with carefully designed exceptions and mechanisms that **22.67**

---

¹⁰³ ibid.
¹⁰⁴ See Economic Partnership Agreement between the West African States, the Economic Community of West African States (ECOWAS) and the West African Economic and Monetary Union (UEMOA) and the EU, Preamble, art 1.2(d), art 56(3)(f).
¹⁰⁵ ibid. Mentioned sectors are Agriculture (see art 48(2)), Fisheries (art 49(1)(c)).
¹⁰⁶ ibid, art 61.
¹⁰⁷ See ECOWAS, 'West Africa–EU prepare for Final Signatures towards Implementation of the EPA' <http://www.ecowas.int/west-africa-eu-prepare-for-final-signatures-towards-implimentation-of-the-epa/> accessed 27 June 2018.

will ensure the price paid to investors is fairly and systematically re-evaluated and indexed in line with the cost of production. A treaty that simply 'locked' the transfer of public funds to private investors without adequate regard being given to public considerations and needs will not, and cannot, be regarded as reflecting the notion of PCD.

4. Trade treaties

22.68 Trade treaties can support RE-investment in several ways, including via the facilitation of trade in services, the adjustment of rules on subsidies and the protection of IP rights. Notably, in several forums states are currently negotiating the liberalization of the international trade in environmental goods and services (EGS), such as those necessary for RE-related investments.

22.69 It is clear that educing the tariffs and non-tariffs[108] trade barriers on EGS will support RE investment.[109] Most green technologies are developed in a very limited number of states.[110] An international dissemination of these products therefore requires international trade. Reduced tariffs will naturally decrease the price of EGS and increase their availability. Reduced tariffs that result in *bound* tariffs (rather than applied tariffs) will also reduce financial uncertainties and increase investor confidence.[111] A UNCTAD report on investment promotion identified the removal of trade barriers as key for encouraging FDI, stating that '[a]long with market size, openness to trade has been identified as one of the most reliable indicators of the attractiveness of a location for foreign investment.'[112]

22.70 Efforts to liberalize the international trade in EGS are being made by a group of World Trade Organization (WTO) member states where a specific WTO Environmental Goods Agreement (EGA) is being negotiated,[113] as well as under

---

[108] According to some, the reduction of non-trade barriers is expected to be much more impactful than the mere reduction of tariffs, see EU Commission, 'Trade Sustainability Impact Assessment on the Environmental Goods Agreement: Inception Report' (European Commission, May 2015) <http://trade.ec.europa.eu/doclib/docs/2015/may/tradoc_153485.pdf> accessed 27 June 2018, 15.

[109] For a review of tariffs/non-tariffs trade barriers, see Heiner Bucher et al, 'Trade in Environmental Goods and Services: Opportunities and Challenges' (2014) International Trade Centre Technical Paper <http://www.intracen.org/uploadedFiles/intracenorg/Content/Publications/AssetPDF/EGS%20Ecosystems%20Brief%20040914%20-%20low%20res.pdf> accessed 27 June 2018.

[110] Antoine Dechezlepretre et al, 'Invention and Transfer of Climate Change–Mitigation Technologies: A Global Analysis' (2011) 5(1) Review of Environmental Economics and Policy 109.

[111] Jaime de Melo and Mariana Vijil, 'Barriers to Trade in Environmental Goods and Environmental Services: How Important Are They? How Much Progress at Reducing Them?' (2014) FEEM Working Paper No 36.2014 <http://papers.ssrn.com/sol3/papers.cfm?abstract_id=2428192> accessed 27 June 2018, 11.

[112] UNCTAD (n 91) 19.

[113] See ICTSD, 'Environmental Goods Agreement Negotiators Discuss Tariff Cut Offers' (ICTSD 28 April 2016) <http://www.ictsd.org/bridges-news/bridges/news/environmental-goods-agreement-negotiators-discuss-tariff-cut-offers> accessed 27 June 2018.

bilateral and regional frameworks.[114] Within the WTO, the negotiations are currently focused on the list of EGS which will be eligible for preferential treatment.[115] As an important hub for the production of RE generation-related EGS, the EU is currently attempting to push for the inclusion of goods such as solar panels and wind turbines in the final list, as well as related services (eg the maintenance of wind farms).[116]

The EGA is expected to be a plurilateral WTO agreement, that is not all members of the WTO will be included. Only WTO members that ratify the agreement will be bound by its provisions. Currently the list of negotiating states is rather short. It includes only the EU and an additional eighteen (mostly) developed states, including China.[117] On the one hand, if successfully concluded, there is no doubt that the RE industry will benefit greatly from the EGA, as the negotiating states include the most developed (and lucrative) markets. On the other hand, the EGA, in its current form, will not solve the problem discussed; green technology does not transfer to the developing parts of the world, where tariffs on EGS on average are much higher than in the developed world.[118] 22.71

Given this reality, it is important to examine bilateral/regional agreements, which include both RE-developers (such as the EU) and developing countries. Gehring et al have surveyed the provisions that are related to climate change within regional trade agreements.[119] These authors identified *inter alia*, several trade agreements which stated environmental protection as a leading principle. One such agreement is the EU–Chile Association Agreement, the Preamble of which states that 'sustainable development and environmental protection' shall be taken into account when interpreting the provisions in the treaty.[120] Similarly, Articles 1 and 3 of The Forum of the Caribbean Group of African, Caribbean and Pacific States (CARIFORUM)–EC Agreement affirms 'sustainable development' as the treaty's objective.[121] Still other agreements incorporate exceptions for measures that are 22.72

---

[114] See eg the list concluded by the member states of the Asia Pacific Economic Cooperation (APEC) Forum, 'Annex C—Trade and Investment in Environmental Goods and Services', <http://egs.apec.org/more-articles/285--annex-c-trade-and-investment-in-environmental-goods-and-services-> accessed 27 June 2018.

[115] See more in EU Commission, 'Report from the 13th Round of Negotiations for an Environmental Goods Agreement (EGA)' (4 May 2016) <http://trade.ec.europa.eu/doclib/docs/2016/may/tradoc_154551.pdf> accessed 27 June 2018.

[116] See European Commission, 'Environmental Goods Agreement: Promoting EU Environmental Objectives through Trade' (22 January 2016) <http://trade.ec.europa.eu/doclib/press/index.cfm?id=1438> accessed 27 June 2018.

[117] ibid.

[118] de Melo and Vijil (n 111) 23.

[119] Markus Gehring et al, *Climate Change and Sustainable Development Measures in Regional Trade Agreements* (ICTSD 2013).

[120] Chile–EC Association Agreement (signed 18 November 2002, entered into force 1 February 2003), Preamble.

[121] CARIFORUM–EC Economic Partnership Agreement (signed 15 October 2008, entered into force 1 January 2009), art 1 and 3.

related to climate change (mostly General Agreement on Tariffs and Trade (GATT) Article XX-like exceptions),[122] or provide specific instructions concerning compliance with environmental agreements.[123] These measurers, it should be stated, are 'defensive' in nature as they are aimed to ensure states' right to regulate, and notably that their climate policies will not conflict with their trade law obligations.[124] As such, these provisions can hardly be considered as HCMs, as they are not aimed at investment promotion (at least not directly).

22.73 With respect to directly and explicitly promoting trade in EGS and climate-related investment, some relevant instructions can be identified within EU FTAs. These instructions, however, are mostly declaratory, vague, and non-committed, and they often build on future arrangements which may or may not be negotiated. As such their usefulness could be doubted. For example, Article 275(4) of the Colombia–Ecuador–EU–Peru FTA states:[125]

> Considering the global objective of a rapid transition to low-carbon economies, the Parties will promote the sustainable use of natural resources and will promote trade and investment measures that promote and facilitate access, dissemination and use of best available technologies for clean energy production and use, and for mitigation of and adaptation to climate change.

22.74 Article 138 of the CARIFORUM–EC agreement (titled: 'Cooperation on eco-innovation and renewable energy') provides somewhat more concrete (but nevertheless non-committed) language according to which 'the Parties agree to cooperate, including by facilitating support, in the following areas ... projects related to energy efficiency and renewable energy'.[126] Article 183(5) of this agreement states with respect to EGS:[127]

> The Parties and the Signatory CARIFORUM States are resolved to make efforts to facilitate trade in goods and services which the Parties consider to be beneficial to the environment. Such products may include environmental technologies, renewable- and energy-efficient goods and services and eco-labelled goods.

22.75 Another similarly worded provision can be found in Article 288 of the Central American Common Market (CACM)–EU Association Agreement (title: 'Trade

---

[122] See eg Colombia–Ecuador–EU–Peru Trade Agreement (signed 26 June 2012, entered into force 1 June 2013), art 106.
[123] See eg Central American Common Market (CACM)–EU Association Agreement (signed 29 June 2012), art 287.
[124] The reader should note that existing exceptions may not always be useful in avoiding conflicts between trade obligations and climate change obligations, and much depends on how such provisions are to be interpreted, the manner in which preambles' statements and treaty objectives are understood by panels, or even whether existing legal exceptions apply (eg most will agree that GATT XX exceptions do not cover the SCM Agreement).
[125] See also Colombia–Ecuador–EU–Peru Trade Agreement (n 122) art 24.12; EU–Canada Comprehensive Economic and Trade Agreement (CETA), art 24.9.
[126] CARIFORUM–EC Agreement (n 121) art 138(b).
[127] ibid art 183(5).

Promotion of FDI in the Renewable Energy Sector

favouring sustainable development'). Pursuant to this clause the parties 'reconfirm that trade should promote sustainable development', 'endeavour' to 'facilitate and promote trade and foreign direct investment in environmental technologies and services, renewable-energy and energy-efficient products and services, including through addressing related non-tariff barriers'.[128] The parties also agree to facilitate and promote trade in EGS.[129] These provisions could, at best, be classified under the first type of HCMs, that is vague, non-committed, and declaratory language, which at least for now does not mean much in practice.

While tariffs are obviously relevant for international trade in EGS, other trade law disciplines should also be considered in the context of climate change mitigation.[130] Notably, the author has claimed in the past that the trade rules on subsidies and anti-dumping (including relevant remedies) can be problematic for international trade in EGS, especially if one is to aspire to the quick and massive dissemination of these technologies.[131] The remedies that states are using in their reaction to the subsidization of EGS production are inhibiting the international trade in EGS. Representatives from the Solar Trade Association commented with respect to the EU's decision to extend the use of countervailing and anti-dumping duties on Chinese solar panels:[132] **22.76**

> These price controls on imports of Chinese solar panels need to be dropped. Europe is currently paying far more than it should for its solar—and that applies both to our homeowners and our governments....

The main issue with these trade rules is that they impose difficulties on the subsidization of EGS (eg it is prohibited to provide export-based subsidies, or subsidies that are dependent on local content), and thus prevents the existence of the fourth type of HCMs, that is direct financial contributions.[133] **22.77**

---

[128] Emphasized by the author, CACM–EU Association Agreement (n 123) art 288(b).
[129] ibid art 288(c)–(d).
[130] An EU Commission impact assessment report on the EGA mentions in this respect barriers such as Accreditation procedures for standards, Government procurement rules, customs and licenCes procedures, and local content requirements. EU Commission, 'Trade Sustainability Impact Assessment on the Environmental Goods Agreement' (n 108) 15–16.
[131] Avidan Kent and Vioma Jha, 'Keeping Up with the Changing Climate: The WTO's Evolutive Approach in Response to the Trade and Climate Conundrum' (2014) 15(1) Journal of World Investment and Trade 245; Avidan Kent, 'WTO Law on Subsidies and Climate Change: Overcoming the Dissonance' (2013) 5 Trade Law and Development 344.
[132] Solar Trade Association, 'European Commission Extends 'Unfair' Import Tariff on Chinese Solar Panels' (Solar Trade Association, 7 December 2015) <http://www.solar-trade.org.uk/european-commie-solar-panels/> accessed 27 June 2018; see also views of STA's representatives in Sonia Dunlop, 'Why EU Tariffs on Solar Panels Need to End' (*The New Economy*, 8 February 2016) <http://www.theneweconomy.com/energy/eu-import-tariffs-on-chinese-solar-panels-need-to-end> accessed 27 June 2018.
[133] See EG the author's criticism of *Canada—Measures Relating to the Feed-in Tariff Program* WT/DS412/AB/R in this respect; Kent, 'WTO Law on Subsidies and Climate Change' (n 131); and Kent and Jha, 'Keeping Up with the Changing Climate' (n 131).

22.78 Questions with respect to the subsidization of the RE industry have been debated to a great extent by many authors,[134] and due to space limitations, these issues will not be discussed in this chapter. It is important nevertheless to mention their relevance to PCD, and to stress that they (as well as other non-tariff trade barriers) should not be ignored in any future attempts to regulate this field.

22.79 The issue of subsidies can also be addressed from a different angle by designing trade rules that will lead to the elimination of fossil-fuels subsidies, considered by most as a significant barrier to the dissemination of RE. Indeed in a recent Ministerial Conference, a group of eleven member states issued a statement on the need for such a reform, recognizing *inter alia*, 'that fossil fuel subsidies encourage wasteful consumption, disadvantage renewable energy, and depress investment in energy efficiency, and that effectively addressing fossil fuel subsidies will deliver trade, economic, social and environmental benefits'.[135] Joel Trachtman has mentioned in this context the possibility of designing a specific agreement for energy subsidies (as was already done in the case of agriculture-related subsidies).[136] Trachtman, as well as others,[137] have made detailed proposals in this respect which could be relied on in the design of new HCMs.

22.80 The previously reviewed is not intended to provide an exhaustive review of the manner in which trade treaties could be used as HCMs, but simply to demonstrate that at least potentially, they can. This brief review also points at the fact that this potential is currently not being fulfilled. While the EU is indeed pushing forward some of these goals, notably the negotiated EGA within the WTO framework, these efforts are limited and will not result in RE-related investment in the majority of the developing world.

---

[134] See EG Aaron Cosbey and Petros Mavroidis, 'A Turquoise Mess: Green Subsidies, Blue Industrial Policy and Renewable Energy: The Case for Redrafting the Subsidies Agreement of the WTO' (2014) 17(1) Journal of International Economic Law 11; Luca Rubini, 'Ain't Wastin' Time No More: Subsidies for Renewable Energy, The SCM Agreement, Policy Space, and Law Reform' (2012) 15(2) Journal of International Economic Law 525; Sadeq Bigdeli, 'Clash of Rationalities: Revisiting the Trade and Environment Debate in Light of WTO Disputes over Green Industrial Policy' (2014) VI(1) Trade Law and Development 177.

[135] WTO, 'Fossil Fuel Subsidies Reform Ministerial Statement' (12 December 2017) WT/MIN(17)/54 <http://fffsr.org/wp-content/uploads/2018/01/ministerial-statement-ffsr-mc11-side-event.pdf > accessed 27 June 2018.

[136] Joel P Trachtman, 'Fossil Fuel Subsidies Reduction and the World Trade Organization' (ICTSD 2017) <https://www.ictsd.org/themes/climate-and-energy/research/fossil-fuel-subsidies-reduction-and-the-world-trade-organization> accessed 27 June 2018; see also Gary Horlick, 'The WTO Subsidies Agreement Can Be Changed to Discipline Fossil Fuel Subsidies' (ICTSD 22 August 2017) <https://www.ictsd.org/opinion/the-wto-subsidies-agreement-can-be-changed-to-discipline-fossil-fuel-subsidies>; Heloisa Pereira, 'How the WTO Can Help Tackle Climate Change through Fossil Fuel Subsidy Reform: Lessons from the Fisheries Negotiations' (ICTSD 2017) <https://www.ictsd.org/themes/climate-and-energy/research/how-the-wto-can-help-tackle-climate-change-through-fossil-fuel> accessed 27 June 2018.

[137] ibid.

Promotion of FDI in the Renewable Energy Sector

When looking at the EU's efforts to connect trade policies with other policies that are aimed at the promotion of RE-related FDI, whether within the WTO or in the EU's bilateral trade agreements, one cannot avoid the conclusion that at least for now, such efforts seem to lack a level of concreteness. While the EU identified the tools by which trade agreements could be useful (eg the facilitation of trade in EGS), its international law commitments include mostly declaratory language and avoid any concrete instructions. This point of departure is not helpful from the perspective of PCD. Not only are trade policies not connected with other types of policies, but for the time being it seems that trade climate policies are not sufficiently concretized such that connection with other international HCMs is difficult. 22.81

5. International cooperation and development agreements

Another interesting type of international law HCMs can be found in international cooperation and development agreements. While trade and investment agreements are mostly under the responsibility of trade ministries (or DG Trade in the case of the EU), these agreements often fall under the responsibility of international development ministries (or DG international cooperation and development, in the case of the EU). 22.82

International cooperation and development agreements can be found in different shapes and under different titles. It is not always easy to classify an agreement as a 'trade' agreement, or a 'development' agreement, especially as many agreements are 'hybrid' in nature and include both aspects. The CARIFORUM–EC Economic Partnership Agreement for example, is focused around both elements and indeed the EU Commission states on its website that 'the Economic Partnership Agreement between the EU and the 15 Caribbean countries is *in part* a free trade agreement', and that this agreement 'comes with substantial EU aid for trade'.[138] Indeed the objectives of this agreement intertwine elements such as poverty reduction and international trade,[139] and Article 3 specifically places the principle of sustainable development as a guiding principle for the implementation of this agreement. 22.83

The CARIFORUM–EC Agreement includes provisions with respect to both trade (discussed previously) and investment.[140] Interestingly in the context of PCD, this agreement states that the parties will 'facilitate support' for projects related to energy efficiency, and more specifically also for FDI established via the Kyoto Protocol's Clean Development Mechanism (CDM); effectively an HCM 22.84

---

[138] See the EU Commission's website <http://ec.europa.eu/trade/policy/countries-and-regions/regions/caribbean/index_en.htm> accessed 27 June 2018.
[139] CARIFORUM–EC Agreement (n 121) art 1.
[140] ibid Title II.

established under a different international regime. While the meaning of such a vague commitment is not yet clear, the mentioning of CDM in this context demonstrates at least an appetite for PCD.

22.85 Another very relevant example where investment promotion provisions are attempted within an economic development agreement, is the Cotonou Agreement between the EU and the African, Caribbean and Pacific Group of States (ACP), entitled 'investment and private sector development support'. Article 75 for example, states that the parties will 'implement measures' to encourage private investors 'who comply with the objectives and priorities of ACP-EC development cooperation',[141] 'support efforts of the ACP States to attract financing, with particular emphasis on private financing, for infrastructure investments and revenue generating infrastructure critical for the private sector',[142] 'disseminate information on investment opportunities and business operating conditions in the ACP States',[143] all of which can be considered as falling within the UNCTAD categories of HCMs.

22.86 Article 76 of this agreement ('investment and financial support') provides for 'long-term financial resources, including risk capital, to assist in promoting growth in the private sector' including grants, technical assistance, 'institutional support related to a specific investment,' 'risk capital for equity or quasi-equity investments, guarantees in support of domestic and foreign private investment and loans or lines of credit on the conditions laid down'.[144]

22.87 Other relevant instructions can be found in Article 77, in which the parties commit to increase the availability of investment guarantees in order to 'boost investor confidence in the ACP States', to 'assist with guarantees funds', including via re-insurance schemes against legal and political uncertainties, guarantees for debt financing, and by supporting 'national and regional guarantee funds'.[145]

22.88 As reviewed, attracting FDI in RE will require a range of interventions. While investment and trade facilitation (and promotion) are indeed a part of development and cooperation agreements, in most countries RE-related FDI will benefit drastically also from some sort of subsidization, whether in a direct form or not as well as from the removal of local fossil-fuel subsidies as discussed. From a PCD perspective, it is imperative that the EU's ODA be linked to such agreements, to ensure their effectiveness. Indeed, the EU does connect some of its financial instruments to these treaties. The Cotonou Agreement for example, is linked to

---

[141] The Cotonou Agreement (signed 23 June 2000) <http://www.europarl.europa.eu/intcoop/acp/03_01/pdf/mn3012634_en.pdf> accessed 27 June 2018, art 75(a).
[142] ibid art 75(f).
[143] ibid art 75(h).
[144] ibid art 76.
[145] ibid art 77(1)–(2).

the European Development Fund (EDF). Annex IA of this Agreement dictates not only that the EU shall maintain its aid efforts, but also that such 'efforts' will remain 'at least the same' as its previous commitments,[146] for a period of five to six years.[147]

22.89 Currently, financial assistance is being provided through the '11th EDF' (years 2014–2020),[148] according to an agreed budget of 29,089 million euro.[149] Annex IC sets the framework for the allocation of this sum. Interestingly, a small part of it will be allocated to the Investment Facility, established in Annex II of this agreement, through which funds will be allocated to 'eligible enterprises' in a variety of forms,[150] and which will be made available to investors in 'all economic sectors'.[151] This language suggests that RE-related investors could potentially enjoy access to this fund.

22.90 From the perspective of PCD, it is interesting to find Chapter 5 of Annex II, which is entitled 'investment protection agreements'. The fact that IIAs are connected to development policies is encouraging as it demonstrates a wider understanding of the environment in which the private sector is operating. This Chapter, however, includes only a vague recognition of the usefulness of IIAs, most of which is seen as redundant. Perhaps the most useful commitment in this Chapter is an obligation to study the main features of IIAs, in order to allow a better fit with the circumstances of FDI flows between the parties.

22.91 Other forms of HCMs that can be found in the Cotonou Agreement include the establishment of the Centre for the Development of Enterprise (CDE), whose role is to provide 'necessary support in the promotion of private sector development activities in ACP countries and regions'.[152] The CDE's role is to provide non-financial support, *inter alia* via the provision of relevant information, facilitating business cooperation, providing technical, professional and managerial training, and more. The CDE is mostly geared towards assisting ACP private investors. Nonetheless, Article 2(f) of Annex III prescribes for example, that the CDE shall 'provide information to European companies and private sector organisations on business opportunities and modalities in ACP countries'.

---

[146] 9th EDF period (2000–2007).
[147] See The Cotonou Agreement (n 141) Annex IA, para 2.
[148] Internal Agreement between the Representatives of the Governments of the Member States of the European Union, meeting within the Council, on the financing of European Union aid under the multiannual financial framework for the period 2014 to 2020, in accordance with the ACP–EU Partnership Agreement, and on the allocation of financial assistance for the Overseas Countries and Territories to which Part Four of the Treaty on the Functioning of the European Union applies [2013] OJ L 210/1.
[149] See The Cotonou Agreement (n 141) , Annex IC, para 2.
[150] ibid Annex II art 2.
[151] ibid Annex II art 3.
[152] The Cotonou Agreement (n 141) Annex III.

22.92 Another promising sign (with respect to PCD) can be found in the latest amendment of The Cotonou Agreement (2010) in which Article 32A (entitled 'climate change') was added. This article states *inter alia*:

> The Parties acknowledge that climate change is a serious global environmental challenge and a threat to the achievement of the Millennium Development Goals requiring adequate, predictable and timely financial support. For these reasons, and in accordance with the provisions of Article 32, and particularly of point (a) of paragraph 2 thereof, cooperation shall: ... (b) strengthen and support policies and programmes to mitigate and adapt to the consequences of, and threat posed by, climate change including through institutional development and capacity building ...
>
> And that cooperation shall be focussed on activities such as:
> (i) integrating climate change into development strategies and poverty reduction efforts; ...
> (vii) promoting renewable energy sources, and low-carbon technologies that enhance sustainable development.

22.93 This reveals positive signals with respect to future linkages between development policies and climate-related policies, and more specifically also for the promotion of RE-related FDI. At the same time, it should be noted that financial support may not always be enough. The Cotonou Agreement for example, does not include necessary trade rules or an investment protection chapter that would undoubtedly add further attractiveness to RE-related FDI. The necessity for an investment protection agreement in the context of EU–ACP countries was stressed already in 2003 by Konrad von Moltke, who stated in this respect:[153]

> A Cotonou Investment Agreement is needed to amplify investment provisions of the CPA to identify the full range of issues that need to be addressed to ensure that a Cotonou Investment Agreement promotes the objectives of the CPA.

22.94 For the time being however, investment protection is mentioned only in Chapter 5 of Annex II ('investment protection agreements'), which states, in essence, that a 'Contracting State may request where appropriate, the negotiation of an investment promotion and protection agreement with another Contracting State'.[154]

22.95 Lastly, it is important to stress that especially in the context of development and cooperation agreements, HCMs will have to be *custom designed*. They should support technologies that are suitable for the host countries circumstances, sophistically financed and reflect the genuine cost of production, provide suitable guarantees for investors, *and states*, and address relevant trade barriers, including fossil-fuel subsidies. There is no 'one size fits all' arrangement, and each development agreement must be designed according to the specific needs of the relevant state.

---

[153] Konrad von Moltke, 'A Cotonou Investment Agreement: Report for the Commonwealth Secretariat' (Commonwealth Secretariat 2003) <http://www.iisd.org/pdf/2003/investment_cotonou.pdf> accessed 27 June 2018.

[154] See The Cotonou Agreement (n 141) Annex II art 15.

6. MIGA

22.96 Another instrument that can be defined as an international law HCM is the World Bank's Multilateral Investment Guarantee Agency (MIGA) Convention, which established MIGA. There are currently 181 member states to the MIGA Convention. The mission of MIGA is the promotion of 'foreign direct investment (FDI) into developing countries to help support economic growth, reduce poverty, and improve people's lives'.[155] MIGA's operation is focused on providing private sector investors with political risk insurance guarantees. The risks that are covered by the MIGA Convention are essentially non-commercial,[156] and include expropriation ('and similar measures'), currency transfer, the breach of contract by host states, and war and civil disturbance.[157] Although MIGA's coverage is currently limited to US$250 million, it can cover higher amounts through reinsurance.[158]

22.97 Being essentially an insurance provider, MIGA falls within UNCTAD's fifth category of HCMs. The distinctiveness of *international law* HCMs from other HCMs is especially striking in this case; unlike private insurance arrangements, MIGA supports only investments that are 'developmentally sound and meet high social and environmental standards.'[159] Indeed the Convention's preamble states that the parties are '[d]esiring to enhance the flow to developing countries of capital and technology for productive purposes under conditions consistent with their development needs, policies and objectives ...'.[160] The commentary on the Convention further states that MIGA 'should satisfy itself that the investment concerned will contribute to the economic and social development of the host country, comply with the laws and regulations of that country, and be consistent with the country's declared development objectives'.[161]

22.98 Political risks are one of the main factors that deter FDI in the RE sector.[162] MIGA's role in reducing these risks (especially in light of its focus on developing

---

[155] See MIGA's website <https://www.miga.org/who-we-are> accessed 27 June 2018. See also The Convention Establishing the Multilateral Investment Guarantee Agency (signed 11 October 1985, entered into force 12 April 1988) (MIGA Convention), Preamble.
[156] MIGA Convention (n 155) art 2(a).
[157] ibid art 11.
[158] MIGA, 'Investment Guarantee Guide' (MIGA 2015) <https://www.miga.org/Documents/IGGenglish.pdf> accessed 27 June 2018.
[159] See MIGA <https://www.miga.org/who-we-are> accessed 27 June 2018.
[160] MIGA Convention (n 155) Preamble.
[161] MIGA, 'Commentary on the Convention establishing the Multilateral Investment Guarantee Agency' (MIGA 2010) <https://www.miga.org/documents/commentary_convention_november_2010.pdf> accessed 27 June 2018 para 21.
[162] See eg Cheuk Wing Lee and Jin Zhong 'Financing and Risk Management of Renewable Energy Projects with a Hybrid Bond' (2015) 75 Renewable Energy 779; Gianleo Frisari and Valerio Micale, *Risk Mitigation Instrument for Renewable Energy in Developing Countries: A Case Study on Hydropower in Africa* (CPI 2015); MIGA, 'Investment in Clean Power MIGA Brief' <https://www.miga.org/documents/cleanpower.pdf> accessed 27 June 2018.

countries) is important. MIGA however is also useful for investment promotion in two other meaningful ways. Notably, the Convention created an *organizational body*—an agency. A large body of academic literature demonstrates that institutions possess autonomous powers, and can in fact impact the activity/behaviour of states.[163] It is interesting to note in this respect that MIGA's affiliation with the World Bank provides it (according to MIGA's secretariat) with an 'umbrella of deterrence against government actions that could disrupt insured investments'.[164] While some research indeed supports MIGA's claim in this respect,[165] admittedly not much information is available on this issue and more research will be required for confirming the credibility of this claim.

22.99 Secondly, MIGA also offers dispute mediation services, for dealing with investor–state disputes. While not much is known about the operation of this mediation service, it seems to be very successful, as according to MIGA's website '[t]o date, MIGA has been able to resolve disputes that would have led to claims in all but two cases.'[166]

22.100 The MIGA Convention was drafted in the early 1980s and does not include specific language with respect to environmental protection. Further developments however, established that MIGA does view environmental protection (and more specifically climate change) as an inherent part of its operation. Notably in 2013, MIGA adopted its environmental and social policy.[167] Furthermore, MIGA's Strategic Directions for the years 2015–2017 also emphasize MIGA's aspiration to promote environmental and social goals, including the need to address climate change through the promotion of energy efficiency and RE projects.[168] Indeed in the past MIGA has insured a list of RE projects.[169]

---

[163] See eg Michael Barnett and Martha Finnemore, 'The Politics, Power, and Pathologies of International Organizations' (1999) 53(4) International Organizations 699; Sikina Jinnah, 'Secretariat Influence on Trade-Environment Politics' (2010) 10(2) Global Environmental Politics 54; Steffen Bauer, 'Does Bureaucracy Really Matter? The Authority of Intergovernmental Treaty Secretariats in Global Environmental Politics' 6(1) Global Environmental Politics 23; Avidan Kent, 'Implementing the Principle of Policy Integration: Institutional Interplay and the Role of International Organizations' (2014) 14(3) International Environmental Agreements: Politics, Law and Economics 203.

[164] MIGA, 'Dispute Resolution' <https://www.miga.org/investment-guarantees/dispute-resolution> accessed 27 June 2018.

[165] Axel Drehel et al, 'Membership has its Privileges—The Effect of Membership in International Organizations on FDI' (2015) 66 World Development 346.

[166] ibid.

[167] MIGA, 'Policy on Environmental and Social Sustainability' (MIGA 2013) <https://www.miga.org/documents/Policy_Environmental_Social_Sustainability.pdf> accessed 27 June 2018, para 1.

[168] MIGA, 'MIGA Strategic Directions FY 15–17'< https://www.miga.org/documents/MIGA_FY15-17_Strategy.pdf> accessed 27 June 2018, paras 13, 62.

[169] See review of certain projects in IEG, *Climate Change and the World Bank Group: Phase II: The Challenge of Low-carbon Development* (World Bank 2010) 21–22.

22.101 MIGA's environmental policy is implemented mostly via the requirement that insured projects comply with a set of environmental and social performance standards.[170] MIGA's performance standards are enforced through its due diligence and monitoring mechanisms,[171] as well as through the independent Office of Compliance Advisor/Ombudsman (CAO), which addresses concerns regarding supported projects' compliance with MIGA's performance standards.

22.102 MIGA's Performance Standards (modified in 2013) contain eight standards, including a variety of environmental and cultural issues. Although low levels of GHG emissions were not defined as a standard by itself, this objective is included within some of MIGA's wider standards. Notably, Standard 3 (entitled 'resource efficiency and pollution prevention') specifically mentions the need to reduce GHG levels[172] and the reduction of 'project-related GHG emissions' is explicitly mentioned as one of this standard's three objectives.

22.103 As for the requirements that projects must abide by in order to comply with Standard 3, Paragraph 7 of this Standard vaguely instructs investors to take certain actions that will reduce their project's emissions. Paragraph 7 of Standard 3 provides an open list of examples of what such action might be, but does not include any mandatory, specific obligations.[173] A more concrete obligation can be found in Paragraph 8, in which large emitters are instructed to quantify their emissions.[174]

22.104 In short, while the idea of using performance standards may be a step in the direction of PCD, the standards themselves are relatively unclear and weak. Indeed nothing in these standards prevents the insurance of extremely polluting projects, as long as the investor has 'implement[ed] technically and *financially feasible* and *cost-effective* options to reduce project-related GHG emissions during the design and operation of the project'.[175] The words 'financially feasible' and 'cost-effective' significantly water down any substance that this vague obligation might have had. In addition, the fact that the obligation to 'reduce' GHG emissions is not quantified reduces its effectiveness.

22.105 A much stronger standard would, for example, dictate that a certain percentage of insured projects' energy demands must be provided from RE sources. Other examples of more meaningful standards are that only projects that rely on certain

---

[170] MIGA, 'Policy on Environmental and Social Sustainability' (n 167).
[171] These include *inter alia* site visits by MIGA staff and a reporting mechanism, see: MIGA, 'Understanding MIGA's Environmental and Social Due Diligence Process' <https://www.miga.org/Documents/Understanding_MIGA_ES_Due_Diligence_Process.pdf> accessed 27 June 2018.
[172] MIGA, *Performance Standards on Environmental and Social Sustainability* (MIGA 2013) Standard 3, para 1.
[173] MIGA (n 172) Standard 3, para 7.
[174] ibid Standard 3, para 8.
[175] Emphasis added. ibid Standard 3, para 7.

technological (green) standards would qualify, or that projects that pollute above a certain level of GHG would be disqualified.[176]

22.106 Another feature that is currently lacking in the MIGA's framework is the active incentivizing of RE-related investment. For example, MIGA could offer significantly cheaper tariffs for such projects, or a much higher coverage than the standard US$250 million. In other words, MIGA could achieve both the fourth and the fifth types of HCMs by providing a competitive commercial advantage for RE investment, as well as insurance against risks. MIGA could look into the experience of national investment promotion agencies (eg the US Overseas Private Investment Corporation (OPIC)), in which far more targeted RE-related products indeed exist.

7. The Kyoto Protocol's flexible mechanisms

22.107 The Kyoto Protocol's (KP) flexible mechanisms provide perhaps the most striking example of an international law instrument that was designed to incentivize RE-related FDI. Briefly put, the KP's Joint Implementation (JI)[177] and Clean Development Mechanism (CDM)[178] allow investors to gain tradable emission reduction units, by investing in projects that result in a reduction of GHG emissions. The additional funds provided by the CDM and JI can increase the competitiveness of RE projects, and *may* be seen as falling under the fourth type of HCMs (financial and fiscal incentives).

22.108 It is not entirely clear whether the CDM and JI should be regarded as HCMs, as the financial contribution element is not necessarily sourced in the investor's home country.[179] One may claim however that investors' home countries are 'paying' for this financial support by agreeing to be included in Annex I, which implies undertaking pricey emission cuts.

22.109 In the context of PCD, the CDM is certainly relevant as unlike the JI, it is directed at investors from developed countries (Annex B countries) who invest in the developing world. The connection between development and climate policies is made explicitly in Article 12 of the Kyoto Protocol, according to which the CDM's 'purpose' 'shall be to assist Parties not included in Annex I in achieving sustainable development'.[180]

---

[176] Such a condition could include exceptions, such as the performance of emission 'offsetting' action (eg purchasing emission trading units under a certain recognizable emission trading schemes).
[177] Kyoto Protocol to the United Nations Framework Convention on Climate Change (signed 11 December 1997, entered into force 16 February 2005) (Kyoto Protocol), art 6.
[178] ibid art 12.
[179] Other states may also purchase European investors' units via the EU ETS.
[180] Kyoto Protocol (n 177), art 12.

22.110 Following the conclusion of the 2015 UNFCCC Paris Agreement, it seems that the Kyoto Protocol will eventually be discontinued. As this international agreement will, likely, eventually expire, an exhaustive review of the CDM mechanism will not be provided. A few issues however, should be highlighted. Notably, it should be stressed that the connection of CDM and development policies has been criticized by authors.[181] The criticism concerns *inter alia*, the allocation of already limited ODA for CDM capacity-building purposes, *de facto* transferring resources from development goals to climate mitigation goals.[182] Others may also criticize the *de facto* transfer of ODA to Western private investors. Scholars have also claimed that the CDM basically allows rich countries to 'buy their way out' from having to reduce their emissions locally.[183]

22.111 Nevertheless, the CDM did support many projects that had positive impact on development goals.[184] Moreover, according to the UNFCCC's secretariat, the CDM contribution was efficient in terms of leveraging finance, as well as in terms of CO2 reductions (1.5 giga-tonnes of CO2 were reduced/avoided, according to the UNFCCC secretariat).[185] It also worth remembering that the CDM is an innovative tool, which requires 'trial and error' refinement and therefore, expecting 'perfection' in this respect may be unreasonable.

22.112 From a PCD perspective, the CDM can be seen as a positive step, as it was explicitly aimed at the incorporation of environmental and development goals, including through the use of ODA. The CDM however, is blind to any existing trade and investment policies which could in theory, maximize its potential. While the CDM provides mostly financial incentives, it could have benefited from additional features such as tax adjustments and investment protection guarantees which are significant for longer term assurances and profitability. Indeed authors have argued in the past in favour of linking the CDM mechanism with IIAs.[186] Supplementing the CDM with relevant trade rules could have also been useful; reduction of tariffs on EGS for CDM-approved projects,[187] would provide additional incentive for foreign investors. Economic treaties however, seem to be 'clinically isolated' from UNFCCC negotiations, despite obvious relevance.

---

[181] See review in Joyeeta Gupta, Harro van Asselt, and Michiel van Drunen, 'Global Governance: Climate Cooperation' in Gupta and van der Grijp (n 16) 155–61.

[182] ibid.

[183] ibid.

[184] See a review of such projects on the UNFCCC's CDM website <http://cdm.unfccc.int/about/ccb/index.html> accessed 27 June 2018.

[185] UNFCCC Secretariat, *CDM Fact Sheet, Leveraging Private Finance, Delivering Verified Results* (UNFCCC 2014).

[186] Edna Sussman, 'The Energy Charter Treaty's Investor Protection Provisions' in Segger, Gehring, and Newcombe (n 75) 524–29.

[187] While EGS negotiations are based on the 'list approach' (described in this chapter), a 'project based' approach was also considered in the past.

D. Concluding Remarks

22.113 The universe of international law is complex and fragmented in nature. The analogy of an ocean, filled with isolated islands is often used to describe the architecture of this world. Addressing this 'fragmentation' requires what may be seen as an oxymoron—on the one hand, a more general and holistic view of international law is essential, one that overviews its entirety and is not restricted to one 'island' or another. Such a 'bird eye-view' approach is necessary in order to understand the different fields of international law, and the manner in which they could potentially complete one another and work in harmony.

22.114 On the other hand, much more concrete specialization (even 'atomization') is needed in order to connect the different spheres of international law. It is not enough to understand 'trade law', or 'environmental law' any more, as this type of specialisation seems too 'general' for dealing with concrete and multifaceted problems. Rather, new specialties such as 'trade and climate' are now required in order to effectively *connect* the different fields.

22.115 The challenge faced by those wishing to design policies with respect to RE-related FDI is therefore highly complex. The EU is indeed trying to address this challenge head on. It appointed a PCD rapporteur in 2015, it established an investment 'blending' mechanism, and it is constantly seeking to improve the efficiency of its policies via improved PCD.

22.116 As reviewed, the EU is attempting to apply a coherent approach also with respect to the issue at hand, namely the promotion of RE-related FDI via international law. But while the EU connects (to a certain extent) between its environmental and development policies, the remit of international economic treaties is mostly being ignored, and attempts to engage instruments such as IIAs, trade treaties and even insurance treaties (MIGA) to this goal are not being seriously made. In light of the amount of both public and private money that is being invested in RE, as well as the economic, social, and environmental benefits that such investments may bring to the European public, the EU's lack of action in this area is questionable.

22.117 The case for an integrated legal framework is clear. A legal framework that will provide RE investors with a complete 'one-stop shop dream package', including *all* mentioned HCMs at once, (eg MIGA's securities and meditation services, ODA grants, the legal protection of IIAs, zero tariffs on imported (and exported) goods, trade facilitation rules, etc) will, without a doubt, provide these investors with a significant competitive advantage, address their needs, and eventually boost RE-related investment. Moreover, the availability of such a comprehensive instrument might even attract investors from other fields to enter this market. Such a legal framework might be especially effective if accompanied with proper technical and legal assistance, that is officials that will inform and direct investors concerning *all* different angles and possibilities that are available to them, and will provide guidance with respect to the utilization of these tools.

Also politically, the wrapping up of the variety of international law HCMs into one package might well be beneficial. Many developing states for example, resist developments *in some* of the aforementioned channels (eg WTO and investment treaties). Linking these 'sticks' with the 'carrots' (ie ODA, MIGA, Kyoto tools) may convince these states to accept more instruments than they currently do, at least with respect to RE-related investment. It is also likely that the re-framing (or re-packaging) of the more contentious elements within new institutions away from their current Bretton-Woods-oriented environment could untangle these issues from other non-related sensitive debates. **22.118**

This all points towards the need to integrate the existing legal frameworks. The need to integrate policies with respect to climate change and development is receiving increasing attention in recent years, notably from the OECD and the European Union. The efforts of these two organizations, so it seems, are in their early stage, and often include mostly vague and declaratory language. **22.119**

Exactly how such a comprehensive package will be designed, whether through a bilateral *ad hoc* RE treaty, the expansion of the Energy Charter Treaty, via a plurilateral WTO agreement or any other possibility, are open questions worthy of attention. It is hoped that this chapter has laid the foundations for proposals and future research on this matter. **22.120**

23

INTEGRATING CIVIL LIABILITY PRINCIPLES INTO INTERNATIONAL INVESTMENT LAW

A Solution to Environmental Damage Caused by Foreign Investors?

Alessandra Mistura

A. Introduction	23.01	C. International Investment Law and Civil Liability Regimes: Options for Reforms	23.101
B. Overview of Civil Liability Regimes	23.09	D. Conclusions	23.149

A. Introduction

23.01 It is known that foreign investments may produce a long-lasting and devastating impact on the environment, often resulting in significant air, water, and soil pollution in the territory of the host state. Adverse environmental effects of investment activities may sometimes be so catastrophic as to extend even beyond the borders of the host state, thus causing transboundary harm to other states or territories beyond national jurisdiction. In all of these instances, it is undisputed that the foreign investor, usually a transnational corporation (TNC),[1] should be held

---

[1] Transnational corporations are traditionally defined as 'economic entities operating in more than one country or a cluster of economic entities operating in two or more countries—whatever their legal form, whether in their home country or country of activity, and whether taken individually or collectively'. See Sub-commission on the Promotion and Protection of Human Rights, *Norms on the Responsibilities of Transnational Corporations and Other Business Enterprises with regard to Human Rights* (2003) UN Doc E/CN.4/Sub.2/2003/12/Rev.2, para 20. Slightly different from transnational corporations are multinational enterprises (MNEs), which have a more defined national base. According to the OECD, MNEs usually comprise 'companies or other entities established more than one country and so linked that they may co-ordinate their operations in

accountable for the environmental damage caused by its investment activities. In practice, however, determining which rules should govern the foreign investor's responsibility for environmental damage is all but straightforward.

The issue of the responsibility of TNCs for environmental damage is, in fact, governed by several different legal norms and systems, each with a specific scope of application. Reference is made, in particular, to the domestic law of the host state and to international law. 23.02

The national law of the host state appears to play a dominant role, often holding TNCs directly liable for the adverse effects of the activities they carried out within the host state's territory.[2] However, leaving the issue of the liability of TNCs for environmental damage entirely to the domestic law of each state is highly undesirable, especially since there might be several instances in which a state is ultimately unwilling or unable to adopt or enforce national laws and regulations designed to protect the victims and the environment.[3] And yet, regardless of the potential shortcomings of domestic law, the role that international law plays in the field is still severely limited, and appears mostly confined to two extremely different and apparently unrelated fields: international civil liability regimes, on the one hand, and international investment law, on the other. 23.03

As to the former, the expression 'international civil liability regimes' refers to a series of international conventions that have been concluded to address the potentially devastating consequences of specific activities dangerous to the environment, with a view to facilitating civil liability claims by the victims of such damage, as well as reparation of the damaged environment.[4] Such conventions create a uniform system of rules on liability,[5] to be adopted and enforced by the 23.04

---

various ways'. However, the degree of influence and autonomy may vary widely from case to case. See OECD, *Annual Report 2001. Guidelines for Multinational Enterprises: Global Instruments for Corporate Responsibility* (Paris 2001). For the purpose of this chapter, TNCs will be used to refer also to MNEs.

[2] See André Nollkaemper, 'Responsibility of Transnational Corporations in International Environmental Law: Three Perspectives' in Gerd Winters (ed), *Multilevel Governance of Global Environmental Change* (CUP 2006) 186.

[3] Reference is made, eg, to phenomena such as the so-called race-to-the-bottom and regulatory chill, the host state's lack of expertise and capacity, and the imbalance of strength between the TNC and the state. In addition, TNCs may take advantage of the corporate law principle of limited liability and corporate veil theory to avoid the application of sanctions and fines and to resist the supervision and control from the host state. See Stavros-Evdokimos Pantazopoulos, 'Towards a Coherent Framework of Transnational Corporations' Responsibility in International Environmental Law' (2014) 24 Yearbook of International Environmental Law 131, 137. All this, obviously, relies on the assumption that domestic law on liability is actually in place, which may not always be the case.

[4] See Robin R Churchill, 'Facilitating (Transnational) Civil Liability Litigation for Environmental Damage by Means of Treaties: Progress, Problems, Proposals' (2001) Yearbook of International Environmental Law 3.

[5] An extensive overview of the principles constituting the international civil liability system will be carried out in this chapter. See section B.2.

states parties to the relevant convention at the national level, through the enactment of the necessary implementing legislation.[6] As such, even though the ultimate source of the private entity's liability is international law, the direct relevance of international civil liability regimes in ensuring that such private entity be held accountable for the consequences of its activity is limited at best. Indeed, not only national law is being delegated the task of implementing and enforcing the international principles governing liability, but such principles have to be adopted only by those states that have ratified the relevant conventions, thus further increasing the risks of creating gaps in the protection of the victims.

23.05 As to international investment law, this is directly relevant to the economic activities carried out by private entities, setting out the treatment to which these should be subjected in the territory of the state in which the activity is performed. However, in its traditional form, international investment law grants to private entities qualifying as 'investors' exclusively rights and/or protections against host state's actions that are detrimental to their investment.[7] Such rights and protections are then directly enforceable by the investor at the international level, due to recourse to the peculiar mechanism of investor–state arbitration.[8] Nevertheless, in recent years, the increasing awareness of the imbalance between the private entity's powers, often a TNC, and the host state's, often a developing country, has led to calls for the reform of the international investment law framework, in order to achieve a more equitable system. Potential avenues of reform include the introduction of mechanisms and remedies, such as investor obligations and counterclaims,[9] directly enforceable by the host state against the foreign investor in the event that the latter's activity causes damages in the territory of the former.[10]

23.06 Thus, we have two different areas of international law with diverging advantages and shortcomings. On one hand, international civil liability regimes provide for a set of principles specifically designed to hold private entities liable for the damage caused in the performance of specific, ultra-hazardous economic activities. However, their reliance on national law severely limits their effectiveness in

---

[6] For example, the ascertainment of the operators' liability, as well as the award of damages, is entrusted to national courts and, in many instances, state parties to civil liability conventions have the authority to derogate from the provisions of the conventions themselves when implementing them at the national level. See section B. See also Nollkaemper (n 2) 188.

[7] See Joost Pauwelyn, 'Rational Design or Accidental Evolution? The Emergence of International Investment Law' in Zachary Douglas, Joost Pauwelyn, and Jorge E Vinuales (eds), *The Foundations of International Investment Law: Bringing Theory into Practice* (OUP 2014) 18.

[8] See Nollkaemper (n 2) 186.

[9] See section C.2.b.

[10] These instruments will be examined in more detail. For more information, see, among others: (i) Karl Sauvant, *The Evolving International Investment Law and Policy Regime: Ways Forward* (The E15 Initiative 2016); (ii) Kavaljit Singh and Burghard Ilge (eds), *Rethinking Bilateral Investment Treaties. Critical Issues and Policy Choices* (SOMO 2016); (iii) J Anthony Van Duzer, Penelope Simons, and Graham Mayeda, *Integrating Sustainable Development into International Investment Agreements* (Commonwealth Secretariat 2012).

all of those instances in which the relevant state is not a party to those regimes or the state does not incorporate similar principles in its own domestic law. On the other hand, international investment law provides private entities qualifying as 'investors' with a set of rights and protections that can be directly enforced against states at the international level, and typically does not impose obligations on the private entities related to their investment activities. It could then be theoretically possible to use the strength of one area of international law to supplement the deficiencies of the other, with a view to establishing the directly enforceable international liability of TNCs for damage caused in the performance of their activities.

23.07 The purpose of this chapter is, therefore, to explore whether and to what extent it is possible to incorporate civil liability principles enshrined in international civil liability conventions into the international investment law framework, and to make them directly enforceable by the host state against TNCs qualifying as investor.

23.08 In this context, section B provides an overview of the main features of civil liability regimes that have been negotiated among states. It begins by briefly reviewing the normative basis for such regimes. Subsequently, it describes their core features, focusing, in particular on: (i) the definition of the types of damage covered; (ii) the channelling of the liability for damage through one specific legal or natural person; (iii) the standard of liability adopted, whether strict and/or fault-based; (iv) the limitations of liability in amount and/or duration; (v) the requirement for insurance or other financial security; (vi) the establishment of additional compensation mechanisms; and (vi) the identification of courts with jurisdiction over compensation claims and the provision for the enforcement and recognition of relevant judgments.

Finally, section C analyses the possibility of incorporating certain solutions and mechanisms developed within the context of civil liability regimes into international investment law with a view to ensuring a more effective protection of the host state's environment and taking an additional step towards the achievement of sustainable development goals. In particular, this section will examine the possibility of classifying TNCs investing in the host state as 'operators' and attaching to them the obligations that are usually imposed under civil liability regimes, in particular, those concerning the adoption of preventive and reinstatement measures and the payment of compensation in case of environmental damage.

B. Overview of Civil Liability Regimes

23.09 Drawing up a list of the major environmental disasters occurred in the past fifty years is not a difficult task. Incidents such as Chernobyl,[11]

---

[11] On 26 April 1986, a combination of human errors and structural inadequacy of the Chernobyl nuclear plant caused a series of explosions in one of the reactors. This, in conjunction with a fire,

Bhopal,[12] the Torrey Canyon[13] and, more recently, the Deepwater Horizon,[14] and Fukushima[15] are widely known for the devastating consequences that they produced on human lives and the environment alike.

23.10 What these incidents have in common is, among other things, the circumstance that they all took place during the performance of lawful but ultra-hazardous activities carried out by private companies: nuclear activities, in case of Chernobyl and Fukushima; oil extraction and transportation, in case of the Torrey Canyon and the Deepwater Horizon; chemical activities, in the case of Bhopal. While all these activities are heavily regulated, both on a national and international level, the existence of rules and due diligence standards does not necessarily erase the inherent risk that incidents will continue to occur in the future. And if incidents do occur, their consequences are usually so grave, serious, and long-lasting that additional sets of rules need to be in place in order to ensure that the victims of those incidents can be promptly and adequately compensated for the damage

---

which burned for more than ten days, caused the release into the air of enormous quantities of radioactive material, first in the surrounding area and, subsequently, throughout Europe. The consequences of the accident on human life and the environment were devastating. However, their actual scope and impact has been impossible to assess. For more information, see IAEA, *Chernobyl's Legacy: Health, Environmental and Socio-Economic Impacts* (The Chernobyl Forum, 2003–2005) <www.iaea.org/sites/default/files/chernobyl.pdf> accessed 3 July 2018.

[12] On 3 December 1984, an accident at Union Carbide pesticide plant in Bhopal, India, lead to the spill of more than 40 tons of methyl isocyianate gas, a highly toxic substance. The immediate death toll was of at least 3,800 people, although estimates indicate that over 500,000 people were exposed to the gas. The disaster, which has risen to fame as the worst industrial incident in history, highlighted the need for enforceable international standards for environmental safety. For more information, see Edward Broughton, 'The Bhopal Disaster and its Aftermath: A Review' (2005) 4 Environmental Health 6.

[13] In 1967, the oil tanker *Torrey Canyon* was shipwrecked off the coast of southwest England, spilling 119,000 tons of crude oil into the sea and causing the death or injury of a large number of animal species. In lack of any international regime on liability for oil pollution damage, victims were forced to have recourse to national liability rules. The incident, therefore, prompted the international community to start negotiating for the development of new international rules for the compensation of oil pollution damage. For more information, see Peter G Wells, 'The Iconic *Torrey Canyon* Oil Spill of 1967. Marking Its Legacy' (2017) 115 Marine Pollution Bulletin 1.

[14] On 20 April 2010, an explosion in the Deepwater Horizon drilling rig, located off the coasts of Louisiana, caused a spill of overall 4.9 million barrels of oil, which flowed incessantly for eighty-seven days. The Deepwater Horizon oil spill is considered the largest marine spill in the petroleum history, causing devastating environmental consequences.

[15] On 11 March 2011, the 9.0 magnitude earthquake that hit the coasts of Japan damaged the cooling mechanisms of the Fukushima Daiichi nuclear reactor, causing the explosion and destruction of three units of the plant. As a consequence, radioactive material was discharged into the surrounding environment through the air and deposited in the soil and water. The Fukushima incident appears to have assumed a limited international relevance, as it has affected mainly the territory of Japan. Indeed, while traces of radioactive material from the incident have been detected in South Korea, Russia, and China, they did so in harmless amount, posing no threat for livestock, people, or the environment. For more information on the subject, see Yeo Hoon Park, 'International Legal Implications of the Fukushima Daiichi Nuclear Power Plant Incident' (2011) 1 Asian Law Journal 2.

suffered. In some cases, the victims' protection might depend exclusively on the availability—and the adequacy—of remedies provided under their own domestic law. But especially in cases involving significant reparation costs, transboundary harm, and/or transnational actors, domestic law remedies may be unduly limited.

The need to fill the gaps of protection left open by domestic laws, coupled with the increased awareness of the potentially devastating cross-border consequences of incidents arising from the performance of lawful, but ultra-hazardous, activities, has led the international community to negotiate and adopt international instruments designed to facilitate the victims' access to compensation. In particular, the second half of the twentieth century was characterized by the negotiation of international civil liability conventions, specifically designed to enhance the protection afforded to the victims of damage caused by ultra-hazardous activities, through the provision of a uniform set of principles to which the domestic laws of the states parties must conform.[16]

23.11

Under such international regimes, the states parties are obliged to establish, through their own national law, the civil liability of natural or legal persons, in accordance with harmonized minimum standards set out in the treaties themselves.[17] Civil liability, therefore, operates at the national level, creating a relationship between the liable person, on one side, and the person injured by the conduct of the former, on the other side.[18] Such direct relationship is also subsequently enforced at the national level, as the victim will be entitled to bring compensation claims directly against the responsible person before national courts.

23.12

The following sections will provide a general overview of the uniform set of principles provided under existing international civil liability regimes. In particular, they will focus on: (i) their legal foundation and the policy objectives commonly associated with their implementation (section B.1); (ii) the elements common to all international civil liability conventions (section B.2); and (iii) the effectiveness of the regime in pursuing the desired objectives (section B.3).

23.13

1. Civil liability regimes: legal foundation and policy objectives

The legal foundation of civil liability regimes lies in the polluter-pays principle, which allocates responsibility for pollution damage among all the different actors

23.14

---

[16] Such principles include, among other things, the channelling of the liability to the operator, the adoption of a strict liability regime, and the provision of compulsory insurance or additional compensation schemes. All of these features will be examined in more detail. See section 2.b.

[17] See Philippe Sands and Jacqueline Peel, *Principles of International Environmental Law* (3rd edn, CUP 2012) 700.

[18] See Luisa Rodriguez-Lucas, 'Compensation for Damage to the Environment per se under International Civil Liability Regimes' in Sandrine Maljean-Dubois and Lavanya Rajamani (eds), *La mise en oeuvre du droit de l'environnement* (Leiden 2011) 420.

involved. In its most general formulation, the principle requires that the costs of pollution be borne by the person responsible for causing it.[19]

23.15 The principle first appeared in the 1972 OECD's Recommendation on the International Economic Aspects of Environmental Policies,[20] as a means of preventing distortions in competition. Indeed, the OECD interpreted the principle as a way to allocate costs of pollution so as to ensure the rational use of scarce environmental resources and to avoid distortions in international trade and investment.[21]

23.16 The meaning of the polluter-pays principle has since evolved. It has gained, for example, a redistributive dimension,[22] inextricably connected to the economic theory of cost-internalization and the notion of externalities. The polluter-pays principle thus also reflects the notion that pollution should be considered as an externality, costs of which must be borne by those who produce them or cause their production, and not pushed on to society as a whole. Externalities are internalized by shifting the costs entailed by pollution from society to the person performing the activity that gives rise to the pollution.[23]

23.17 The economic and redistributive functions of the polluter pays principle are clearly highlighted in Principle 16 of the Rio Declaration on Environment and Development,[24] expressly calling on national authorities to 'promote the internalization of environmental costs … taking into account the approach that the polluter should, in principle, bear the costs of pollution, with due regard to the public interests and without distorting international trade and investment'.[25]

23.18 Over time, the principle has also acquired a curative dimension, meaning that the polluter should be required to bear the costs of losses suffered by those harmed by environmental pollution.[26] In this sense, civil liability regimes can be used to implement the polluter-pays principle in its curative function, aiming to ensure funds are available to promptly and adequately compensate the victims of pollution damage.[27]

---

[19] ibid 228.
[20] OECD, 'Recommendation of the Council Concerning International Economic Aspects of Environmental Policies' C(72)128 (OECD Guiding Principles).
[21] ibid Principle A.a.4.
[22] See Nicolas de Sadeleer, *Environmental Principles. From Political Slogans to Legal Rules* (OUP 2002) 35.
[23] ibid.
[24] See Rio Declaration on Environment and Development (14 June 1992) UN Doc A/Conf.151/26 (Rio Declaration).
[25] See ibid Principle 16.
[26] See Priscilla Schwartz, 'Polluter Pays Principle' in Malgosia Fitzmaurice, David M Ong, and Panos Merkouris (eds), *Research Handbook on International Environmental Law* (Edward Elgar 2010) 251.
[27] For more information, see section 2.b.vi.

23.19 This curative function has been acknowledged in several international instruments. In addition to the civil liability conventions that will be examined, the UN Declaration on Human Environment[28] sets forth the international community's obligation to 'cooperate to develop further the international law regarding liability and compensation for the victims of pollution and other environmental damage' caused by ultra-hazardous activities.[29] The same need is restated in Principle 13 of the Rio Declaration, calling on states to develop 'national law regarding liability and compensation for the victims of pollution and other environmental damage'.[30]

23.20 The polluter-pays principle that forms the legal justification of civil liability regimes heavily influences the identification of the policy objectives that such regimes strive to achieve. While there is no agreement in legal academia on what, exactly, civil liability regimes should attain, the following goals are usually the most widely mentioned.[31]

a. Compensation and victim protection

23.21 The most immediate reason advanced in support of civil liability regimes is that they facilitate claims for compensation of damages resulting from the performance of ultra-hazardous activities.[32] Indeed, by shifting the loss from the victim to the person responsible for it, liability rules allow that the victim be made whole, through the payment, by the liable person, of an amount equal to the loss.[33]

23.22 The need to provide adequate and prompt compensation to victims suffering environmental or pollution damage is the objective most commonly expressed in all main civil liability regimes negotiated to date.[34] Yet as will be discussed, whether they are successful in reaching this goal is still subject to debate.

---

[28] See Declaration of the United Nations Conference on the Human Environment (16 June 1972) UN Doc A/Conf. 48/14 (Stockholm Declaration).
[29] ibid Principle 22.
[30] See Principle 13, Rio Declaration.
[31] In addition to the ones discussed, which are the most commonly cited, there are also other objectives that civil liability regimes may help achieving, such as corrective justice and wealth redistribution. For a comprehensive analysis of the subject, please refer to Lucas Bergkamp, *Liability and the Environment: Private and Public Law Aspects of Civil Liability for Environmental Harm* (Springer 2001) 5.
[32] See Jutta Brunnée, 'Of Sense and Sensibility: Reflections on International Liability Regimes as a Tool for Environmental Protection' (2004) 53 International and Comparative Law Quarterly 351, 357.
[33] See Bergkamp, *Liability and the Environment* (n 31) 70. Whether compensation and victim protection is actually one of the objectives that liability wants to achieve is highly debatable. Indeed, in many instances the victim of pollution damage will not be able to recover the loss in full, either because the person carrying out the dangerous activity is not liable for it or because certain heads of damage are not compensable under the applicable law. As civil liability regimes compensate harm selectively, compensation should be more correctly considered as one of their consequences, but not as one of their objectives. See ibid 71.
[34] See, among others: (i) Convention on Civil Liability for Damage resulting from Activities Dangerous to the Environment (signed 21 June 1993, not yet entered into force), art 1; (ii) Directive

b. Cost-internalization

23.23 Another, frequently quoted argument in support of civil liability regimes is that they help increase efficiency by imposing the environmental costs of pollution on the person responsible for it.[35] Under this reading, pollution is treated as an externality, whose costs will be ultimately borne by society as a whole unless some measures are implemented to shift them on the polluter. Liability, therefore, acts as the instrument to implement cost-internalization and the polluter-pays principle.[36] Cost-internalization is often argued to be beneficial for society as a whole. By increasing the costs for the performance of the ultra-hazardous activity so as to account for the risks of pollution damage, for example, the prices to be paid by consumers may also rise, thus ultimately entailing a drop in the demand.[37]

23.24 Nevertheless, under current civil liability regimes, cost-internalization of pollution damage may be limited, offering only a partial justification for these treaties.[38]

c. Incentives for compliance

23.25 It is also argued that civil liability regimes help create incentives for due diligence and reasonable conduct, thus acting as deterrent for pollution damage.[39] In other words, if the operator is required to bear all costs of pollution damage potentially caused by the performance of an ultra-hazardous activity, it will be induced to use all possible due care and to implement the required preventive measures. Up to a certain point, any investment in preventive measures will be cheaper for the operator than providing compensation for pollution damage.[40] While this theory certainly has merit, it remains largely unverified, as there are no comprehensive studies on the effectiveness of civil liability regimes in influencing behaviour or preventing pollution damage.

2004/35/EC of the European Parliament and Council of 21 April 2004 on Environmental Liability with Regard to the Prevention and Remedying of Environmental Damage (adopted 21 April 2004), art 1; (iii) Paris Convention on Third Party Liability in the Field of Nuclear Energy, Preamble; (iv) Vienna Convention on Civil Liability for Nuclear Damage, Preamble; (v) London Protocol to Amend the International Convention on Civil Liability for Oil Pollution Damage (signed 27 November 1992, entered into force 30 May 1996), Preamble; (vi) International Convention on the Establishment of an International Fund for Compensation for Oil Pollution Damage (signed 27 November 1992, entered into force 30 May 1996), art 2; (vii) Convention on Civil Liability for Bunker Oil Pollution Damage (signed 23 March 2001, not yet entered into force), Preamble; (viii) International Convention on Liability and Compensation for Damage in Connection with the Carriage of Hazardous and Noxious Substances by Sea (signed 3 May 1996, not yet entered into force), Preamble; and (ix) Basel Convention, Preamble and art 1.

[35] See Brunnée (n 32) 358. See also Bergkamp, *Liability and the Environment* (n 31) 73.
[36] Bergkamp, *Liability and the Environment* (n 31) 73. Please note that liability is only one of the many ways in which costs can be internalized. Other ways include direct command by the public authority and the implementation of regulatory measures.
[37] Bergkamp, *Liability and the Environment* (n 31) 74.
[38] See Brunnée (n 32) 366.
[39] ibid. See also Bergkamp, *Liability and the Environment* (n 31) 86.
[40] Bergkamp, *Liability and the Environment* (n 31) 86.

d. Liability as a back-up system

The last main reason advanced in support of civil liability regimes is that, ultimately, they act as a back-up system in the event that environmental damage actually occurs.[41]   23.26

It is possible to identify a wide range of international law rules providing for the state's obligation to adopt measures and behaviours aimed at preventing environmental damage. However, circumstances such as the uncertainties in scientific and technologic knowledge, the general profitability of ultra-hazardous activities, and incentives of and pressures on governments to adopt policies prioritizing economic growth over other, potentially competing, considerations, such as environmental protection, raise risks of environmental harms.   23.27

Civil liability regimes, therefore, help address this reality, establishing rules to be followed and mechanisms to be used when dealing with the consequences of environmental damage, and helping spread relevant losses among different subjects, through recourse to insurance and additional compensation mechanisms.   23.28

2. Common features of civil liability regimes

Civil liability regimes have usually been developed to deal with the consequences of certain specific ultra-hazardous activities, especially activities with potential transboundary effects or impacts on the global commons. Early efforts concerned the negotiation of civil liability conventions for nuclear damage[42] and oil pollution damage.[43] These were soon followed by regimes addressing damage caused by   23.29

---

[41] See Brunnée (n 32) 358. See also Bergkamp, *Liability and the Environment* (n 31) 96.
[42] See, among others: (i) Paris Convention on Nuclear Liability on Third Party Liability in the Field of Nuclear Energy (signed 29 July 1960, entered into force 1 April 1968) (Paris Convention on Nuclear Liability); (ii) Vienna Convention on Civil Liability for Nuclear Damage (signed 21 May 1963, entered into force 12 November 1977) (Vienna Convention on Nuclear Damage); (iii) Joint Protocol on the Application of the Vienna Convention on Nuclear Damage and the Paris Convention on Nuclear Liability (signed 21 September 1988, entered into force on 27 April 1992); (iv) Brussels Convention on Supplementary Compensation for Nuclear Damage (signed on 12 September 1997, entered into force 15 April 2015) (Brussels Supplementary Convention on Nuclear Damage); and (v) Convention on Supplementary Compensation for Nuclear Damage (signed 12 September 1997, entered into force 15 April 2015) (Supplementary Compensation Convention for Nuclear Damage).
[43] See, among others: (i) Brussels International Convention on Civil Liability for Oil Pollution Damage (signed 29 November 1969, entered into force 19 June 1975) (1969 Civil Liability Convention on Oil Pollution Damage), eventually replaced by the London Protocol of 27 November 1992; (ii) Brussels International Convention on the Establishment of an International Fund for Compensation for Oil Pollution Damage (signed 18 December 1971, entered into force 16 October 1978) (1971 Fund Convention for the Compensation of Oil Pollution Damage), eventually replaced by the London Protocol of 27 September 1992; (iii) London Protocol to Amend the International Convention on Civil Liability for Oil Pollution Damage (signed 27 November 1992, entered into force 30 May 1996) (1992 Civil Liability Convention for Oil Pollution Damage); (iv) International Convention on the Establishment of an International Fund for Compensation for Oil Pollution Damage (signed 27 November 1992, entered into force 30 May 1996) (1992 Fund Convention for the Compensation of Oil Pollution Damage); and (v) the Convention on Civil

the movement of hazardous goods and waste,[44] living modified organisms,[45] industrial activities on transboundary waters,[46] and damage caused in the Antarctic region.[47]

23.30 A notable exception to the specific, sector-based approach adopted by most civil liability conventions is represented by the Convention on Civil Liability for Damage resulting from Activities Dangerous to the Environment.[48] This instrument is of general application, providing for civil liability rules addressing any type of environmental damage, regardless of the activity that caused it.[49]

23.31 A related instrument is the Directive 2004/35/EC of the European Parliament and Council of 21 April 2004 on Environmental Liability with Regard to the Prevention and Remedying of Environmental Damage (European Liability Directive).[50] An administrative law instrument and not an international civil

---

Liability for Bunker Oil Pollution Damage (signed 23 March 2001, not yet entered into force) (Bunker Oil Convention).

[44] See, among others: (i) International Convention on Liability and Compensation for Damage in Connection with the Carriage of Hazardous and Noxious Substances by Sea (signed 3 May 1996, not yet entered into force) (HNS Convention); (ii) Convention on Civil Liability for Damage Caused during Carriage of Dangerous Goods by Road, Rail and Inland Navigation Vessels (signed 10 October 1989, not yet entered into force); (iii) Protocol on Liability and Compensation for Damage Resulting from Transboundary Movements to the Convention on the Control of Transboundary Movements of Hazardous Wastes and their Disposal (signed 10 December 1999, not yet entered into force) (Basel Protocol on Damage by Transboundary Movement of Hazardous Wastes).

[45] See Nagoya–Kuala Lumpur Supplementary Liability Protocol to the Biosafety Protocol (signed 15 October 2010, not yet entered into force) (Nagoya–Kuala-Lumpur Protocol).

[46] See Protocol on Civil Liability and Compensation for Damage Caused by the Transboundary Effects of Industrial Accidents on Transboundary Waters (signed 23 May 2003, not yet entered into force) (Transboundary Waters Damage Protocol).

[47] See: (i) Annex VI to the Protocol on Environmental Protection to the Antarctic Treaty on Liability Arising from Environmental Emergencies (signed 14 June 2005, not yet entered into force) (Annex VI to the Antarctic Liability Protocol); and (ii) Convention on the Regulation of Antarctic Mineral Resource Activities (signed 2 June 1988, not yet entered into force) (CRAMRA).

[48] See Convention on Civil Liability for Damage resulting from Activities Dangerous to the Environment (signed 21 June 1993, not yet entered into force) (Lugano Convention on Damage Caused by Dangerous Activities).

[49] The shift to a general approach to liability—as opposed to the sectorial one adopted by the majority of civil liability conventions—can be explained with the increased importance gained by the notion that the environment is a value that must be protected in and of itself, regardless of whether human life or property have also suffered damages. The relevance attributed to the environment *per se* entails the necessity to put in place adequate protective measures for the reparation of environmental damages, regardless of the activity that caused them. See Martin Hedemann-Robinson, *Enforcement of European Union Environmental Law: Legal Issues and Challenges* (Routledge 2007) 594. While the objectives and ideas underlying the Lugano Convention on Damage Caused by Dangerous Activities, and in particular the increased focus on pure environmental damage, were certainly laudable, it does not seem that the Convention was successful in implementing them in practice. See section B.3.a.

[50] See Directive 2004/35/EC of the European Parliament and Council of 21 April 2004 on Environmental Liability with Regard to the Prevention and Remedying of Environmental Damage, adopted 21 April 2004 (European Liability Directive).

liability regime,[51] it focuses on the EU member states' obligation to ensure the adoption by relevant operators of prevention and restoration measures in case of environmental harm.[52] Nevertheless, the European Liability Directive includes several provisions of interest for the purpose of civil liability regimes and, as such, will also be discussed in this chapter.

An analysis of the main provisions of the international civil liability regimes that have been negotiated shows that conventions have all been construed on the basis of the same principles. In particular, these: 23.32

- provide for a definition of the damage covered;
- channel the liability for damage through one specific legal or natural person;
- specify that liability imputed to such specific person is usually strict and subject to specific exemptions;
- limit liability in amount and/or time;
- require the maintenance of adequate insurance or other financial security;
- establish additional compensation mechanisms; and
- identify the courts with jurisdiction over compensation claims and the applicable law and provide for the recognition and enforcement of the relevant judgments.

In the following paragraphs, each of those elements will be examined more closely.

a. Civil liability regimes provide for a definition of the covered damage

As mentioned in the introduction to this section, the type of damage that triggers liability under applicable civil liability conventions is usually limited in scope. Most conventions are focused on damage caused by specific ultra-hazardous activities, thereby necessarily restricting their area of application to, for example, 'nuclear damage'[53] or 'oil pollution damage'.[54] The damage considered by each convention is then further delimited through the identification of its components. 23.33

The relevance attributed to each of these items has evolved over time. The earliest international civil liability conventions provided for compensation only with respect to death, personal injuries, or property damage.[55] Compensation was, 23.34

---

[51] The European Liability Directive follows an administrative law approach as it prioritizes the reparation of pure ecological damage through the action of public authorities, rather than focusing on compensation—as it is typical of civil liability regimes. See Lucas Bergkamp, 'Implementation of the Environmental Liability Directive in EU Member States' (2005) 6 ERA Forum—Journal of the Academy of European Law 389, 390.
[52] See European Liability Directive, arts 5 and 6.
[53] See eg the Vienna Convention on Nuclear Damage and the Paris Convention on Nuclear Liability.
[54] See eg the 1992 Civil Liability Convention for Oil Pollution Damage and related instruments.
[55] See, among others: (i) Vienna Convention on Nuclear Damage, art 1.1.k; (ii) Paris Convention on Nuclear Liability, art 3(a); (iii) 1969 Civil Liability Convention on Oil Pollution Damage, art 1.6; and (iv) Convention on the Liability of Operators of Nuclear Ships (signed 25 May 1962, not yet entered into force) (Nuclear Ships Convention), art 1.7.

23.35 The scope of the damage covered has subsequently been extended so as to also include the recovery of costs sustained for the adoption of preventive measures and remediation.[56] This approach represents a middle ground between the older, more limited approach of restricting compensation to human or societal effects of environmental damage, and a more far-reaching approach to compensation, which can allow recovery for 'pure environmental damage' (or 'ecological damage'), damage suffered by the environment in and of itself.

23.36 While several international instruments have called for the reparation of ecological damage,[57] the international community has long been relatively reluctant to provide for such remedies, in light of the difficulties arising from the evaluation of damage to the environment *per se*.[58] The most recent international instruments on civil liability, however, appear increasingly open to this possibility, as they place direct focus on the restoration of the environment to its original conditions, through the duty to adopt measures of reinstatement or preventive measures.

23.37 For example, the European Liability Directive provides for a comprehensive definition of 'environmental damage' as including all adverse changes produced

---

[56] 'Preventive measures' are usually defined as any reasonable measure taken after the occurrence of an accident to prevent or minimize the damage. 'Measures of reinstatement', instead, are defined as any reasonable measure aimed at reinstating or restoring damaged or destroyed components of the environment or, if restoration is not possible, to introduce equivalent components into the destroyed environment. Such definitions, or similar variations, have been adopted by, among others: (i) Paris Convention on Nuclear Liability as amended by the 2004 Protocol to Amend the Paris Convention on Nuclear Liability (signed 12 February 2004, not yet entered into force) (2004 Protocol), art 1(a)(vii); (ii) Vienna Convention on Nuclear Damage as amended by the 1997 Protocol to Amend the Vienna Convention (signed 12 September 1997, 4 October 2003) (1997 Protocol), art 1.1.k; (iii) 1992 Civil Liability Convention for Oil Pollution Damage art 1.6; (iv) Bunker Oil Convention, art 1.9; (v) HNS Convention, art 1.6; (vi) Basel Protocol on Damage by Transboundary Movement of Hazardous Wastes, art 1.2(c); and (vii) Transboundary Waters Damage Protocol, art 2.2(d).

[57] For example, the Institut de Droit International affirmed: 'environmental regimes should provide for the reparation of damage to the environment as such separately from or in addition to the reparation of damage relating to death, personal injury or loss of property or economic value'. See Institut de Droit International, Responsibility and Liability under International Law for Environmental Damage (1997), art 23 <https://justitiaetpace.org/idiE/resolutionsE/1997_str_03_en.PDF>. Similarly, the International Law Commission stated: 'Environmental damage will often extend beyond that which can be readily quantified in terms of cleanup costs or property devaluation. Damage to such environmental values is, as a matter of principle, no less real and compensable than damage to property, though it may be difficult to quantify'. See International Law Commission, 'Report of the International Law Commission on the work of its fifty-third session' in *Yearbook of the International Law Commission* (2001) Vol II, part 2, 101, para 15.

[58] Indeed, while the traditional components of environmental damage are evaluated through reference to their market value, the recourse to such approach is impossible with respect to ecological damage, as the environment does not have an intrinsic market value. See Rodriguez-Lucas (n 18) 421.

by dangerous activities on protected species and habitats, land, and water.[59] Furthermore, while it still provides that the operator shall reimburse the costs borne by the competent authorities for the adoption of preventive measures or response actions, it focuses on setting forth and establishing the operator's direct obligation to implement such measures, thus placing outmost importance on remediation and restoration of the environment to its original condition.[60] The Nagoya–Kuala Lumpur Protocol,[61] CRAMRA,[62] and, to a lesser extent, the Annex VI to the Antarctic Liability Protocol,[63] adopt a similar approach.

In the most recent instruments, the obligation to adopt adequate response or restoration measures may also be implemented through the introduction of equivalent components into the environment, a possibility that was first provided under the Lugano Convention on Damage Caused by Dangerous Activities (the Lugano Convention).[64] The introduction of equivalent components into the environment is particularly noteworthy, as it could potentially allow addressing the consequences of irreparable damage by achieving an equivalent, instead of an identical, environment.[65]

23.38

b. Civil liability regimes channel liability through one specific person

Civil liability regimes shift the loss caused by the environmental damage from the victim to another person that can be held liable for the loss itself.[66] Liability for environmental damage is often channelled through one person, usually the owner of the installation or ship or the individual otherwise in control of the ultra-hazardous activity. Such choice is justified by the circumstance that these individuals are in the best position to control the performance of those activities and prevent the occurrence of damages, as they have the necessary technical and scientific knowledge required for the performance of the ultra-hazardous activity. In addition, the principle of legal channelling simplifies the bringing of compensation

23.39

---

[59] See European Liability Directive, art 2.1.
[60] ibid arts 4 and 5.
[61] See Nagoya–Kuala Lumpur Protocol, art 5.
[62] See CRAMRA, art 8.
[63] Where it is left to the states parties to ensure that the operator adopts the required preventive and response measures. See Antarctic Liability Protocol, arts 3 and 5, Annex VI.
[64] See Lugano Convention on Damage Caused by Dangerous Activities, art 2.8. The possibility to introduce equivalent components into the damaged environment is provided also under: (i) European Liability Directive; (ii) 2004 Protocols to the Paris Convention on Nuclear Liability and the Brussels Supplementary Convention on Nuclear Damage; (iii) Transboundary Waters Damage Protocol; and (iv) Nagoya–Kuala Lumpur Protocol.
[65] See Explanatory Report to the Convention on Civil Liability for Damage Resulting from Activities Dangerous to the Environment, paraa 40 <http://conventions.coe.int/Treaty/EN/Reports/Html/150.htm>.
[66] See Rudiger Wolfrum, 'Elements of Coherency in the Conception of International Environmental Liability' in Rudiger Wolfrum, Christine Langenfeld, and Petra Minnerop (eds), *Environmental Liability in International Law: Towards a Coherent Conception* (Erich Schmidt Verlag Berlin 2005) 505.

claims by the victims, as it makes it easier to identify the person legally responsible for the damage suffered.[67]

23.40 In this context, therefore, international civil liability conventions usually provide for the exclusive liability of the operator of the dangerous activity[68] or nuclear installation,[69] the owner of the ship causing pollution damage,[70] or the carrier of dangerous goods or wastes.[71] The liability of other defendants who would ordinarily be liable under traditional principles of domestic tort law—such as agents, employees, servants, suppliers, or contractors of the shipowner or operator—is excluded under the relevant convention.[72] However, in the event that more than two operators or shipowners are involved in the incident causing the damage, all of them will be held jointly and severally liable for the arising losses.[73]

23.41 Certain conventions adopt a different approach and extend the definitions of 'operator' and 'shipowner', so as to include other individuals involved in the performance of the dangerous activity and in control of its outcome. For example, the Bunker Oil Convention defines 'shipowner' as 'the owner of the ship, including registered owner, bareboat charterer, manager, and operator of the ship'[74] and provides for the joint and several liability of all of these subjects, should they be involved in the incident causing pollution damage.[75] A similarly broad definition is adopted in the Nagoya–Kuala Lumpur Supplementary Protocol, where

---

[67] See Churchill (n 4) 38. See also Alan Boyle, 'Globalizing Environmental Liability: The Interplay of National and International Law' (2005) 17 Journal of Environmental Law 3, 14.

[68] See Lugano Convention on Damage Caused by Dangerous Activities, arts 2.5 and 6; European Liability Directive, art 2.6; Annex VI to the Antarctic Liability Protocol, arts 2(c) and 6; CRAMRA, arts 1.11 and 8.

[69] See Paris Convention on Nuclear Liability, arts 1(a)(vi) and 3; Vienna Convention on Nuclear Damage, arts 1.1.c and 2; Nuclear Ships Convention, arts 1.4 and 2.

[70] See 1992 Civil Liability Convention for Oil Pollution Damage, arts 1.1.3 and 2; Mineral Resource Convention, arts 1.3 and 3; HNS Convention, art 7.

[71] See Dangerous Goods Convention, arts 1.8 and 8.

[72] While the liability is legally channelled through the operator, this does not mean that agents, employees, suppliers, or contractors will never bear the economic consequences of their actions. For example, in certain limited circumstances, international nuclear liability regimes grant to the operator a direct right of recourse against third parties, either because such third parties have directly caused the nuclear damage through their wilful action or omission or because such right is expressly provided in the contract governing the relationship between the operator and the third party. See (i) Vienna Convention on Nuclear Damage, art 10; (ii) Paris Convention on Nuclear Liability, art 6(f). Other conventions, instead, follow a different approach, by providing that the relevant regime shall not prejudice any right of recourse that the operator/shipowner may have against third parties, for example under domestic law. See, among others: (i) 1992 Civil Liability Convention for Oil Pollution Damage, art 3, para 5; (ii) Bunker Oil Convention, art 3, para 6; and (iii) Lugano Convention on Damage Caused by Dangerous Activities, art 6, para 5.

[73] See, among others: (i) Lugano Convention on Damage Caused by Dangerous Activities, art 9; (ii) Paris Convention on Nuclear Liability, art 5; (iii) Vienna Convention on Nuclear Damage, art 2; (iv) 1992 Civil Liability Convention for Oil Pollution Damage, art 4; and (v) HNS Convention, art 8.

[74] See Bunker Oil Convention, art 3.

[75] ibid.

'operator' is defined as 'any person in direct or indirect control of the living modified organism ... including, *inter alia*, the permit holder, person who placed the living modified organism on the market, developer, purchaser, notifier, exporter, importer, carrier or supplier'.[76]

The Basel Protocol adopts yet another approach, holding generators, exporters, importers, and disposers equally liable for the damage caused during the transboundary movement of hazardous waste, depending on the stage of the waste's journey to its final destination.[77] Also in this case, the spreading of liability to subjects other than the 'operator' is justified by the inherent complexity in the transboundary movement of hazardous wastes, which involves the participation of a plurality of subjects, all exercising different degrees of control on the ultra-hazardous activity. 23.42

Ultimately, therefore, the choice to channel the liability on one or more subject—as well as the choice of the liable subjects—entirely depends on the nature of the activity carried out and the identity of person in the best position to control its outcome. 23.43

c. *The liability is usually strict and subject to exemptions*

Traditionally, liability is imputed to a subject on the basis of three different standards: (i) fault-based liability; (ii) strict liability; and (iii) absolute liability.[78] 23.44

Fault-based liability generally requires the existence of a clearly defined standard of care with which an individual is required to comply in the performance of a given activity. If the relevant person does not comply with the standard, because of either negligence or wilful misconduct, then he will be liable for the damage caused.[79] In this case, the existence of fault justifies shifting the loss from the injured party to the responsible person.[80] 23.45

In strict liability regimes, instead, liability is imposed on the relevant subject regardless of fault, negligence, or wilful misconduct. This means that, even if the operator has complied with all applicable standards of diligence and damage has occurred anyway, the operator will still be held responsible for the loss suffered by the victim. In practice, the adoption of this standard relieves the victims from the burden of proving the fault or negligence of the operator in the context of activities often characterized by high technical complexity. Indeed, for the operator's 23.46

---

[76] See Nagoya–Kuala Lumpur Supplementary Protocol, arts 2.c and 5.
[77] See Basel Protocol on Damage by Transboundary Movement of Hazardous Wastes, art 4.
[78] The structure of absolute liability is identical to strict liability. The only difference is that, as it will be explained in more detail, while strict liability regimes provide for grounds of exemption of liability, absolute liability regimes do not allow such exemptions.
[79] See Wolfrum (n 66) 504.
[80] See Bergkamp, *Liability and the Environment* (n 31) 5.

liability to arise, the victims will be required only to prove that the damage caused by the ultra-hazardous activity caused the losses suffered.[81]

23.47 Strict liability is therefore seen as an exception to the general fault-based approach and is justified on several grounds. The first, most immediate, justification is that certain activities, while not unlawful, pose such dangers for society as a whole that it is only equitable that the risk of loss be shifted from the injured person to the person that created the risk by merely engaging in that activity. This is exactly the case of ultra-hazardous activities, which may entail high costs for society when damages actually occur. Strict liability then represents the price that the operator has to pay to engage in such activities in the first place.[82]

23.48 Strict liability may be also warranted by the polluter-pays principle and the need for cost-internalization that this entails.[83] As the operator benefits from the performance of ultra-hazardous activities, then it should bear both the costs of preventative measures and the costs of the losses suffered by victims in the event that damage occurs, regardless of its fault or negligence.

23.49 Therefore, it should not come as a surprise that most civil liability conventions provide for the strict liability of the operator or shipowner performing the ultra-hazardous activity. Such standard is particularly beneficial not only for the victims, who will be relieved from the burden of proving fault, but also for courts or other adjudicators, as they will not be dragged into the complex task of determining the standard of care with which the operator should have complied.[84] Additionally, some authors have highlighted how strict liability standards create incentives for better risk management and facilitate the out-of-court settlement of claims, thus allowing the victims to save time and money.[85]

23.50 The operator's liability is usually not absolute, as it can be avoided if one of the grounds provided under each convention is applicable. The operator will usually

---

[81] See Louise de la Fayette, 'Environmental Liability for Damage to the Environment' in Malgosia Fitzmaurice, David M Ong, and Panos Merkouris (eds), *Research Handbook on International Environmental Law* (Edward Elgar Publishing 2010) 326. However, proof of causation may still be significantly difficult to provide, in light of the uncertainties surrounding the scope, extent, and consequences of environmental damage. The outcome of the inquiry concerning causation would also vary considerably depending on the test adopted by the courts. Among the various theories on causation, it is possible to remember: (i) foreseeability, whereby the agent is considered liable only for the losses that are reasonably foreseeable; (ii) *causa proxima*, which limits liability to harms that are within the risks that made the injurer's conduct tortious; and (b) probabilistic causation test, which deals with the uncertainties associated with causal relationships through the allocation of only part of the damage to the injurer on the basis of probability. For more information, see Bergkamp, *Liability and the Environment* (n 31) 280 ff.

[82] See Alan Boyle, 'Making the Polluter Pay? Alternatives to State Responsibility in the Allocation of Transboundary Environmental Costs' in F Francioni and T Scovazzi (eds), *International Responsibility for Environmental Harm* (Graham and Trotman 1991) 374.

[83] ibid. See also, section B.1.a.

[84] See Boyle, 'Globalizing Environmental Liability' (n 67) 13.

[85] See Churchill (n 4) 34.

be exempt from liability if the damage is the result of, among others, *force majeure*, war, natural disasters, acts of third parties, actions of public authority, or fault of the victim.[86] Such exemptions are justified on the ground that it would be unfair to make the operator liable for damages caused by events over which it had no control.[87] Such choice, however, also means that, unless the applicable convention provides for additional tiers of compensation[88] or the relevant state independently puts in place alternative compensation mechanisms,[89] the victim may be forced to bear the entirety of the loss suffered.

Lastly, it is interesting to note that certain conventions deviate from the aforementioned approach by adopting a twofold liability system. For example, the Basel Protocol provides for both the strict liability of the person under the duty to notify the movement of hazardous wastes[90] and of the disposer of hazardous wastes[91] as well as the fault-based liability of any person for damages 'caused or contributed to by his lack of compliance with the provisions implementing the [Basel Convention] or by his wrongful, reckless or negligent acts or omission'.[92] The Transboundary Waters Protocol similarly provides for the additional fault-based liability of any person for damage 'caused or contributed to by his or her wrongful, reckless or negligent acts or omission'.[93] Lastly, the European Liability Directive provides that its provisions shall apply in any event in case of environmental damages arising from the performance of certain specific activities listed under its Annex III and to all other non-listed activities only when the operator has been at fault,[94] using wording that parallels the distinction between strict and fault-based liability. 23.51

---

[86] See, among others: (i) Lugano Convention on Damage Caused by Dangerous Activities, art 8; (ii) 1992 Civil Liability Convention for Oil Pollution Damage, art 3; (iii) HNS Convention, art 7; (iv) Bunker Oil Convention, art 3; (v) Transboundary Waters Damage Protocol, art 4; (vi) Environmental Liability Annex, art 8; and (vii) CRAMRA, art 8. It is interesting to note that the grounds of exemptions are usually more limited in nuclear liability regimes, which only exempt the operator from liability if the nuclear damage was caused by act of armed conflict, hostilities, civil war, insurrection. See (i) Paris Convention on Nuclear Liability, art 9; and (ii) Vienna Convention on Nuclear Damage, art 4.

[87] See Churchill (n 4) 34.

[88] See section B.2.f.

[89] This is what happened, eg, in the aftermath of the Fukushima incident, as the Japanese government and the operator responsible for the functioning of the nuclear power plant signed an indemnity agreement whereby the former agreed to cover all those risks, such as earthquakes and tsunamis, that were not insurable with the private sector. For more information, see Ximena Vasquez-Maignan, 'The Japanese Nuclear Liability Regime in the Context of the International Nuclear Liability Principles' in OECD, *Japan's Compensation System for Nuclear Damage* (OECD 2012) 11.

[90] The 'notifier', in the language of the Basel Protocol on Damage by Transboundary Movement of Hazardous Wastes. See Basel Protocol on Damage by Transboundary Movement of Hazardous Wastes, art 4.

[91] ibid.

[92] See Basel Protocol on Damage by Transboundary Movement of Hazardous Wastes, art 5.

[93] Transboundary Waters Damage Protocol, art 5.

[94] See European Liability Directive, art 3.

23.52 In all of these instances of fault-based liability, therefore, the victim shall be required to prove that the relevant individual—not necessarily the operator—breached the due diligence obligations applicable to the performance of the relevant ultra-hazardous activity.

d. The liability is limited in its amount and in time

23.53 The operator's strict liability under civil liability regimes is usually subject to quantitative and temporal limitations. Where a claim exceeds the limits of the operator's liability or when the term to bring a claim against the operator has expired, the victim will not be compensated for the damage suffered, unless additional tiers of compensation have been established under the applicable convention or domestic law.

23.54 Limitation of liability is usually excluded when the damage has been caused by an operator's act or omission committed with fraud or reckless negligence.[95] In addition, in certain instances, the operator is only entitled to limit its liability provided that it has previously established a fund covering the total amount of its limited liability.[96]

23.55 Several justifications are advanced in support of limited liability. For one, it is usually claimed that limited liability represents a *quid pro quo* for strict liability.[97] In addition, limited liability schemes protect the industries concerned from damage awards that are so high that they might prevent the performance of any subsequent ultra-hazardous activity, no matter how useful such activity could be in practice.[98] As it has been noted, an effective civil liability regime must strike a correct balance between the need to facilitate claims of compensation for the victims of pollution damage and the need to shield the operator of ultra-hazardous but beneficial activities from excessive awards of compensation.[99] An additional argument in favour of limited liability provisions is that, in the absence of such limitations, it would be impossible for the operators to get the insurance coverage required under the applicable conventions.[100]

23.56 Limited liability rules can result in recovery that is less than it would be if based solely on victims' needs;[101] nevertheless, with the exception of the Lugano Convention,[102] quantitative limitations to liability represent a constant feature

---

[95] See, among others: (i) 1992 Civil Liability Convention for Oil Pollution Damage, art 5; (ii) Seabed Mineral Resource Convention, art 6; and (iii) HNS Convention, art 9.
[96] See, among others: (i) 1992 Civil Liability Convention for Oil Pollution Damage, art 5; (ii) Seabed Mineral Resource Convention, art 6; and (iii) HNS Convention, art 9.
[97] See Churchill (n 4) 36.
[98] ibid 35. See also Boyle, 'Making the Polluter Pay?' (n 82) 374.
[99] See Brunnée (n 32) 357.
[100] ibid.
[101] See Churchill (n 4) 36.
[102] Under the Lugano Convention on Damage Caused by Dangerous Activities, liability is unlimited. In addition, the 2004 Protocol to Amend the Paris Convention (signed 12 February 2004,

of all civil liability conventions. After all, what arguably is most important is not whether liability is unlimited, but whether the correct balance between the interests of the industry and the need to ensure adequate protection to the victims of environmental damage is reached.[103] Whether this happens in practice, however, is highly debatable.

Indeed, most of the quantitative limitations to liability with respect to nuclear damage[104] and oil pollution damage[105] have been constantly amended and increased over time, usually after incidents highlighting the inadequacy of the applicable limitations. Furthermore, in certain instances, concerns about the amounts provided under the limitations caps—and whether they were high enough to

23.57

---

not yet entered into force) provides for the possibility of the states parties to opt for an unlimited liability regime. In this case, however, they must also introduce a limit to the financial security that the operator is required to provide, equal to the operator's maximum liability under the Paris Convention on Nuclear Liability, as amended. See Paris Convention on Nuclear Liability as amended by the 2004 Protocol, art 7. See also Vienna Convention on Nuclear Damage, as amended by the 1997 Protocol, art 7. The Transboundary Waters Damage Protocol, instead, provides that no limitation shall apply to fault-based liability under art 5. See Transboundary Waters Damage Protocol, art 9.

[103] See Francisco Orrego Vicuna, 'Current Trends in Responsibility and Liability for Environmental Damage under International Law' in Kalliopi Koufa (ed), *Protection of the Environment for the New Millennium* (Sakkoulas Publications 2002) 149.

[104] For example, the quantitative limitations provided under the Paris Convention on Nuclear Liability resulted immediately insufficient to allow adequate protection for nuclear damage, leading the international community to enter into the Brussels Supplementary Convention on Nuclear Damage in 1963, merely three years after the signing of the Paris Convention on Nuclear Liability. Twenty years later, the Chernobyl accident proved that the quantitative limitations provided under the Paris Convention on Nuclear Liability, the Brussels Supplementary Convention on Nuclear Damage, and the Vienna Convention on Nuclear Damage were still insufficient. Negotiations were soon undertaken, leading to the adoption of the 1997 Protocol and the Supplementary Compensation Convention for Nuclear Damage. At the same time, efforts were initiated to increase the quantitative limitations under the Paris Convention on Nuclear Liability and the Brussels Supplementary Convention on Nuclear Damage. On 12 February 2004, two Protocols to amend both conventions were signed. However, none of them has entered into force yet. For more information, see Marco Citelli, 'Questioni di Diritto e Organizzazione Internazionale ai Tempi di Fukushima: Norme e Meccanismi in caso di Incidente Nucleare' (2013) 68 Comunità Internazionale 19. See also Julia Schwartz, 'International Nuclear Third Party Liability Law: The Response to Chernobyl' in OECD/IAEA, *International Nuclear Law in the Post-Chernobyl Period* (OECD, 2006).

[105] Similar to what happened with respect to nuclear damage, the Amoco Cadiz incident of 1978 and the Tanio incident of 1980 showed the inadequacy of the 1969 Civil Liability Convention on Oil Pollution Damage and the 1971 Fund Convention for the Compensation of Oil Pollution Damage in addressing oil pollution damage. The review process lead to the adoption, in 1984, of two Protocols, which, however, never entered into force. Only following the *Exxon Valdez* incident in 1989 both conventions were ultimately replaced with the 1992 Civil Liability Convention for Oil Pollution Damage and the 1992 Fund Convention for the Compensation of Oil Pollution Damage, which provided for increased quantitative limitations to liability. Also these new conventions, however, proved inadequate to provide compensation for the damages caused by the *Nakhodka* incident in 1997, the *Erika* incident in 1999 and the *Prestige* incident in 2000. As such, the 2003 Protocol to the 1992 Fund Convention for the Compensation of Oil Pollution Damage was adopted to create an additional tier of compensation for oil pollution damage. For more information, see Rodriguez-Lucas (n 18).

allow effective compensation for the damage suffered by the victims—have been so severe that they prevented the civil liability convention's entry into force.[106]

23.58 Related to the quantitative limitations on liability is the issue of the 'significance' threshold of environmental damage. Several conventions make reference to the need that the damage be 'significant' in order to be relevant for their application. For example, Annex VI to the Antarctic Treaty Protocol defines an 'environmental emergency' relevant for the purpose of the application of its provisions as 'any accidental event that … results in, or imminently threatens to result in, any *significant* and harmful impact on the Antarctic environment',[107] thus excluding the relevance of all those events that do not meet the stated threshold. The Lugano Convention, instead, follows a different approach, exempting the operator from liability in the event that the damage 'was caused by pollution at tolerable levels under local relevant circumstances'.[108] In other words, the operator will not be liable in the event that the damage caused does not exceed a threshold of tolerability or significance.

23.59 The introduction of a minimum threshold of damage does not appear *per se* unreasonable. Indeed, the lack of such minimum threshold may lead to undesirable results, as it would impose, both on states and on private entities, the obligation to avoid any kind of alteration to the status quo, whether or not harmful to the environment, thus forcing them to abandon all those activities, including lawful and profitable economic activities, that may cause only potential damage to the environment. The main issue that arises from these provisions is, rather, how to determine whether the significance threshold has been met in the first place.

23.60 Some authors have suggested that, as a general rule, the more the effects deviate from the state that would be regarded as being sustainable and the less foreseeable and limited the consequential losses are, the closer the effects come to the threshold of significance.[109] Another approach that has been advanced to evaluate whether the significance threshold has been met is to adopt a case-by-case evaluation, which takes into account all of the circumstance of the case and the time when the accident occurred.[110]

23.61 Guidance may be found also in the works of the International Law Commission (ILC) in the codifications of the rules applicable for the prevention of transboundary harm from lawful but hazardous activities. In setting out the notion of 'significant

---

[106] This has been the case, eg of the Convention on Civil Liability for Oil Pollution Damage Resulting from the Exploration for and Exploitation of Seabed Mineral Resources (signed 1 May 1977, not yet entered into force). For more information on this issue, see section B.3.
[107] See Annex VI to the Antarctic Liability Protocol, art 2.b.
[108] See Lugano Convention on Damage Caused by Dangerous Activities, art 8.
[109] See Wolfrum (n 66) 501.
[110] See Johan G Lammers, *Pollution of International Watercourses: A Search for Substantive Rules and Principles of Law* (The Hague 1984) 346–47.

transboundary harm', the ILC specified that, while a case-by-case determination has to be made in any event, 'significant' must be interpreted as 'something more than "detectable" but need not be at the level of "serious" or "substantial"'.[111] The ILC further stated that the harm must lead to real detrimental effects on human health, industry, property, or the environment, measurable on the basis of factual and objective standards.[112]

The parameters offered by the ILC, however, do not help to identify when, in practice, the threshold of significance is satisfied. In light of the persistent uncertainties surrounding the evaluation of whether such threshold has been met, some newly implemented international instruments have set out specific criteria or factors to determine whether the damage suffered is actually 'significant'.

23.62

In this respect, the European Liability Directive, after having specified that its provisions apply only if the environmental damage produces significant adverse effects on habitat, species, land, and water,[113] sets out the specific criteria to be followed in the assessment of the significance threshold. It refers, among other factors, to: (i) the number of individuals, their density, and the area covered by the damage; (ii) the role of the particular individuals or of the damaged area in relation to the species or to the habitat conservation, the rarity of the species or habitat; and (iii) the species' or habitat's capacity to recover within a short time after the damage.[114] The European Liability Directive also specifies that, when damage has a proven effect on human health, it must be classified as significant.[115]

23.63

Similarly, the Nagoya–Kuala Lumpur Protocol defines 'damage' as a significant adverse effect on the conservation and sustainable use of biological diversity.[116] The Protocol then provides that whether damage is significant must be determined on the basis of different factors, including the long-term or permanent change caused, the extent of the qualitative or quantitative adverse effect produced, the reduction of biological diversity, and the risks for human health.[117]

23.64

e. Civil liability regimes require the maintenance of insurance or other financial security

The majority of civil liability regimes require that operator or shipowner enter into and maintain adequate insurance policy or other financial security,[118] so as

23.65

---

[111] See International Law Commission, 'Commentary to the Draft Articles on Prevention of Transboundary Harm from Hazardous Activities' in *Yearbook of the International Law Commission* (2001) Vol II, part 2, 152, para 4.
[112] ibid.
[113] See European Liability Directive, art 2.1.
[114] See European Liability Directive, Annex 1.
[115] ibid.
[116] See Nagoya–Kuala Lumpur Protocol, art 2.2.b.
[117] ibid.
[118] Such financial securities may consist of, among others: (i) self-insurance or reserves established by the operator; (ii) traditional security interests in property such as mortgages, liens, or

to cover its liability up to the amounts specified under the relevant conventions. Notable exceptions are the Lugano Convention, which only requires states to ensure that operators conducting a dangerous activity in their territory are covered by the necessary insurance, if needed,[119] and the European Liability Directive, whereby member states are only required to adopt measures to encourage the development of financial security instruments and markets.[120]

23.66 The insurance requirement allows spreading the risk of loss among different subjects—that is, the operator/shipowner and the insurer—thus ensuring that future claims of compensation will be effectively paid. This requirement recognizes that the limited nature of operator assets could hinder the effectiveness of liability rules.[121] Indeed, holding the operator/shipowner liable for the damage caused by ultra-hazardous activities would be pointless in the event that it had no assets or resources to pay.

23.67 The existence of an insurance policy or other financial security thus helps ensure that compensation claims will effectively be paid, as the relevant losses are shifted to a third party, which has the resources necessary to bear them, at least within the limits provided by the insurance policy or other relevant agreement.

f. Civil liability regimes may provide for additional compensation mechanisms

23.68 As anticipated in the previous sections, there might well be cases in which the operator either is not liable, because exemptions from liability apply,[122] or is liable but the damage exceeds the limitations of liability provided by the treaty.[123] In these instances, the victims face the risk of bearing all or part of the losses caused by the damage, unless the applicable civil liability convention provides for additional compensation mechanisms.[124]

23.69 It has been argued by some that the provision of additional compensation mechanisms derogates from the polluter pays principle, as such mechanisms can allow liability to be spread across different subjects even if those subjects were not necessarily responsible for or beneficiaries of the activity causing the harm.[125] While arguably a valid concern, in some cases at least, the problem seems less compelling. Indeed, certain compensation schemes are based upon

---

privileges; (iii) deposits, trust funds, and escrow agreements; and (iv) guarantees issued by the parent company, bonds, or other bank guarantees.

[119] See Lugano Convention on Damage Caused by Dangerous Activities, art 12.
[120] See European Liability Directive, art 14.
[121] See Hubert Bocken, 'Alternative Financial Guarantees for Environmental Liabilities under the ELD' (2009) 18 European Energy and Environmental Law Review 146, 146.
[122] See section B.2.c.
[123] See section B.2.d.
[124] It being understood that, of course, similar compensation mechanisms may also be provided unilaterally under the domestic law of the relevant state.
[125] See Boyle, 'Making the Polluter Pay?' (n 82) 374.

contributions by members of the industry engaged in the performance of ultra-hazardous activities, which may well be considered as 'polluters'.[126] Moreover, even when contributions to additional compensation mechanisms are fulfilled by member states (and thus societies as a whole, in the form of taxpayers' money), it might be argued that, while not directly engaged in the ultra-hazardous activity, they may still be held responsible as receivers and ultimate beneficiaries of that activity.[127]

Additional compensation schemes are currently provided in the civil liability regime for nuclear damage, oil pollution damage, and damage caused by the transportation of hazardous and noxious substances.[128] These schemes do not follow a pre-determined approach but, rather, have their own specific rules and funding mechanisms. 23.70

i. **Compensation mechanisms for nuclear damage** Compensation mechanisms under the nuclear liability conventions are based upon contributions from the states parties, which undertake to make public funds available in the event of nuclear accidents. 23.71

In particular, the Brussels Supplementary Convention provides for an additional compensation mechanism that may be used in the event that the damage caused by a nuclear incident exceeds the operator's liability.[129] More specifically, the Convention establishes two additional tiers of compensation, one to be financed through public funds made available by the liable operator's state,[130] and the other financed through public funds made available by the contributions of all states parties to the Convention.[131] In the latter case, the amount of contributions is determined on the basis of a formula that takes into account gross national product of each state party to the Brussels Supplementary Convention and the installed 23.72

---

[126] As in the case of oil pollution damage. See section B.2.f.ii.
[127] See Schwartz, 'Polluter Pays Principle' (n 26) 252.
[128] See HNS Convention, art 14. The HNS Fund, however, is not active as the HNS Convention has yet to enter into force.
[129] Slightly different is the regime provided under the 1997 Protocol to the Vienna Convention on Nuclear Damage. Here, the states parties may provide for the operators' liability up to 300 million SDR. However, if they decide to establish a lower limit, they will have to make available public funds up to that amount. As such, a second tier of compensation may be established depending on the internal choice of each state party. See Vienna Convention on Nuclear Damage as amended by the 1997 Protocol, art 5.
[130] It is interesting to note that the Brussels Supplementary Convention on Nuclear Damage also provides for the possibility for the state party to escape its duty to make available public funds under the second tier of compensation by shifting the relevant burden to the operator. Indeed, the state party may increase the liability of the operator from the maximum amount provided under the first tier of compensation to the maximum amount provided for the second tier of compensation, thus avoiding the duty to provide the relevant public funds to finance the second tier. The state, however, has no way to escape the duty of contribution provided under the third tier of compensation. See Article 3(c)(i), Brussels Supplementary Convention on Nuclear Damage, art 3(c)(i).
[131] See Brussels Supplementary Convention on Nuclear Damage, art 3.

nuclear capacity of the states parties, thus placing a higher burden on power generating states.[132]

23.73 Funds are to be made available only after an accident has occurred and only provided that the operator's insurance is insufficient to cover the amount of the damage. Therefore, the Brussels Supplementary Convention does not create any international fund as such. No rules are provided with respect to how the states parties are supposed to make funds available or who should bear the costs for it. As such, complete freedom is left to each state party, which may decide either to use taxpayer money or set up a mechanism whereby the relevant costs are recovered from members of the industry or other groups.[133]

23.74 The Supplementary Compensation Convention follows a similar approach, requiring the operator's state to make available public funds up to a certain amount. Also in this case, the relevant state is free to determine how these amounts are to be funded.[134] Beyond that, compensation shall be covered through funds provided by all states parties to the Convention in accordance with a pre-determined formula, which takes into account both the installed nuclear capacity of each state party and the contribution of each of them to the United Nations budget.[135]

23.75 **ii. Compensation mechanisms for oil pollution damage** Oil pollution damage conventions follow a different approach from nuclear liability conventions, as they essentially rely on the establishment of international compensation funds financed through contributions of the industry.

23.76 With respect to oil pollution damage, additional compensation mechanisms are provided under the 1992 Fund Convention and its 2003 Protocol, which establish, respectively, the International Fund for Compensation of Oil Pollution Damage (IOPC Fund) and the Supplementary Fund for Compensation of Oil

---

[132] The original text of the Brussels Supplementary Convention on Nuclear Damage provided that the formula should be determined: (i) as to 50 per cent, on the basis of the ratio between the gross national product of each state party and the total of the gross national product of all state parties; and (ii) as to 50 per cent, on the basis of the ratio between the thermal power of the reactors situated in the territory of each state party and the total thermal power of the reactor situated in all states parties. See Brussels Supplementary Convention on Nuclear Damage, art 12. The formula will be modified with the entry into force of the 2004 Protocol. This latter provides that contributions shall be determined: (i) as to 35 per cent, on the basis of the ratio between the gross domestic product of each state party and the total of the gross domestic products of all states parties; and (ii) as to 65 per cent, on the basis of the ratio between the thermal power of the reactors situated in the territory of each state party and the total thermal power of the reactor situated in all states parties. See Brussels Supplementary Convention on Nuclear Damage, as amended by the 2004 Protocol, art 12.

[133] See Tom Vanden Borre, 'Shifts in Governance in Compensation for Nuclear Damage, 20 Years after Chernobyl' in Michael Faure and Albert Verheij (eds), *Shifts in Compensation for Environmental Damage* (Springer 2007) 280.

[134] ibid.

[135] See Supplementary Compensation Convention for Nuclear Damage, art 4.

Pollution Damage (Supplementary Fund and, jointly with the IOPC Fund, the Funds).

Contrary to what happens with respect to nuclear damage, both of the Funds are financed through contributions paid by members of the industry based on the quantity of contributing oil that they have received during a given calendar year.[136] More specifically, each year the states parties to the 1992 Fund Convention and 2003 Protocol must submit to the Secretariat established under the 1992 Fund Convention a report containing the information of all individual contributors and the amounts of oil received that they have received.[137] The Assembly managing the Funds will then use the amounts thus notified as the basis to calculate individual contributions,[138] which will be used to both administer the Funds and to pay claims as approved by the governing bodies. Payments are then made by the individual contributors directly into the Funds.

23.77

In 2016, the Assembly of the IOPC Fund levied contributions for £9.7 million.[139] No additional funds were levied with respect to the Supplementary Fund, as there had been no incidents requiring payments of damages in excess of the limitations of liability provided under the 1992 Fund Convention.[140]

23.78

g. Civil liability regimes identify the courts with jurisdiction over compensation claims and provide for the recognition and enforcement of the relevant judgments

Lastly, all civil liability conventions create a uniform set of rules for the identification of the forum where claims of compensation may be brought, also in order to avoid potential risks in connection with forum shopping.[141] Such forum is usually

23.79

---

[136] For more information on the amounts relevant for the purpose of the contribution, please refer to Annex I.

[137] See 1992 Fund Convention for the Compensation of Oil Pollution Damage, arts 15 and 29; see also 2003 Protocol, arts 12 and 13.

[138] See 1992 Fund Convention for the Compensation of Oil Pollution Damage, art 12.

[139] See IOPC Fund, *Annual Report 2016*, 17 <http://www.iopcfunds.org/publications/>. Additional contributions have been levied in the same year in order to finance specific funds for the compensation of damage caused by specific incidents, such as the *Prestige*, *Volgoneft 139*, and the *Hebei Spirit* incidents. ibid.

[140] ibid 19.

[141] See Churchill (n 4) 37. It is important to remember that states that are parties to international civil liability regimes containing rules on the choice of forum for claims may also fall under the application of private international law conventions or institutional European Union norms that also provide for the jurisdiction of certain forums in the adjudication of a specific set of disputes. It is the case, for example, of the EU Council Regulation (EC) No 44/2001 on jurisdiction and the recognition and enforcement of judgment in civil and commercial matters, as well as of the Lugano Convention on jurisdiction and the recognition and enforcement of judgments in civil and commercial matters (signed 30 October 2007, entered into force 1 January 2010). While the relationship between international civil liability regimes and private international law does not fall under the scope of this chapter, the issues arising from the potential overlapping of these two areas should always be kept in mind. For more information on the subject, See Carmen Otero Garcia-Castrillon, 'International Litigation Trends in Environmental Liability: A European Union-United States Comparative Perspective' (2011) 7 Journal of Private International Law 551.

identified in the courts of the place where the damage occurred,[142] although civil liability regimes for nuclear damage entrust jurisdiction to the courts of the place state where the incident occurred.[143] Other conventions, instead, provide for a choice of forum among the place where the damage occurred, the place where the incident occurred, or the place of habitual residence of the defendant.[144]

23.80 Claimants under the conventions are all natural or legal persons that have suffered damages as a consequence of the ultra-hazardous activity. This broad framing entails that claims can be brought by individuals, companies, private organizations, and public bodies, including states themselves or their local authorities.[145]

23.81 In addition, in order to facilitate the recovery of the loss by the victorious claimant, all civil liability conventions provide for the recognition and enforcement of final judgments issued by the competent courts of the other states parties.[146]

3. Assessment of the Effectiveness of Civil Liability Regimes

23.82 Whether civil liability regimes are actually effective in achieving the objectives set out in the previous section is far from clear. Legal scholars have long engaged in debates over the desirability and usefulness of negotiating civil liability regimes, highlighting in the process a number of concerns regarding civil liability schemes as currently envisaged.[147] Leaving aside the issues that are still not adequately addressed in civil liability conventions,[148] challenges to their effectiveness arise primarily from their low rates of entry into force and from questions about their ability to ensure prompt and adequate compensation for victims.

---

[142] See, among others: (i) 1992 Civil Liability Convention for Oil Pollution Damage, art 9; (ii) 1992 Fund Convention for the Compensation of Oil Pollution Damage, art 7; (iii) Bunker Oil Convention, art 9; and (iv) HNS Convention, art 38.

[143] See Paris Convention on Nuclear Liability, art 13; Vienna Convention on Nuclear Damage, art 11. Exceptions to this general rule are provided in the event that it is impossible to determine where the incident took place or that the incident took place outside the territory of a state party. ibid.

[144] See, among others: (i) Lugano Convention on Damage Caused by Dangerous Activities, art 29; (ii) Basel Protocol on Damage by Transboundary Movement of Hazardous Wastes, art 17; and (iii) Transboundary Waters Damage Protocol, art 13.

[145] States will likely bring claims arising from pure environmental damage on behalf of their citizens, including in particular those claims related to the recovery of costs associated with measures of reinstatement or preventive measures.

[146] See Churchill (n 4) 38.

[147] See, among others, Churchill (n 4); Brunnée (n 32); Tullio Scovazzi, 'State Responsibility for Environmental Harm' in *Yearbook of International Environmental Law* (OUP 2001) 43; Anne Daniel, 'Civil Liability Regimes as a Complement to Multilateral Environmental Agreements: Sound International Policy or False Comfort?' (2003) 12 Review of European Comparative & International Environmental Law 225.

[148] Reference is made, more specifically, to the lack of provisions addressing causation between the incident and the damage suffered (with the only exception of the Lugano Convention on Damage Caused by Dangerous Activities) and what happens in the event that the limitations of liability are exceeded and no additional tiers of compensation are available.

a. Lack of entry into force

23.83 The most immediate weakness of the system is the low rate of entry into force of civil liability conventions. Of all international instruments negotiated, more than one half has not entered into force, a picture that does not appear likely to change.[149] There are several actual and potential reasons for this.

23.84 In some cases, the issue preventing the entry into force of a treaty is merely technical. For example, with decision 2004/294/EC, the European Council has determined that all EU member states should simultaneously deposit their instruments of ratifications or accession to the 2004 Protocols to the Paris Convention and the Brussels Supplementary Convention,[150] thus significantly slowing the process for their entry into force.

23.85 In other instances, states have refused to ratify a treaty because they were not completely satisfied of the regime set out in therein.[151] For example, while the general focus of the Lugano Convention on damages to the environment *per se* was generally welcomed, this Convention will likely never enter into force due to some states' concerns with its specific provisions.[152] In particular, states felt that the specific definitions of 'environment', 'damage', and 'dangerous activities' were so broad and vague that legal certainty in the implementation of the Convention would be prejudiced. In addition, the Convention did not set out the reparatory consequences of environmental damages in a sufficiently defined manner, as it did not provide either for the duty of restoring the environment or for the criteria to be followed in the economic evaluation of environmental damage. And lastly, states were unsatisfied with the Convention's approach to liability, with many rejecting the lack of limitations thereof.[153]

23.86 States have also declined to ratify conventions because they were concerned that limits on liability set out in the relevant treaty were too low to ensure adequate protection to the victims in case of damage.[154] Sometimes, states' objections to the

---

[149] See Daniel (n 147) 236; Brunnée (n 32) 367.
[150] OECD Agreement Supplementary to the Paris Convention of 1960 on Third Party Liability in the Field of Nuclear Energy (signed 31 January 1693, entered into force 4 December 1974) 1041 UNTS 358 (as amended by 1964 Protocol).
[151] In certain limited instances, states may not ratify the relevant treaty because, at some point, the relevant ultra-hazardous activities became obsolete, removing the need for a civil liability convention to address their potential harms. This is the case, for example, of the Nuclear Ships Convention, which was signed in 1962 and never entered into force. Given that nuclear ships have now ceased to operate, there is no need for a convention regulating the consequences of a potential accident in this area. See Churchill (n 4) 15.
[152] ibid 28. See also Daniel (n 147) 227; Scovazzi, 'State Responsibility' (n 147) 59.
[153] See Hedemann-Robinson (n 49) 594. See also European Commission, 'White Paper on Environmental Liability' COMM(2000)/66.
[154] For example, the Seabed Mineral Resource Convention has not received a single ratification, as many states perceived that the limits of liability it established were too low and others were unhappy with the possibility that such limits vary from state to state. See Churchill (n 4) 23. The entry into force of CRAMRA was also prevented by the belief of many states that the Convention did

relevant treaty have prompted amendments (or attempts to secure amendments). For example, the 1996 version of the International Convention on Liability and Compensation for Damage in Connection with the Carriage of Hazardous and Noxious Substances by Sea (HNS Convention) was drastically amended by means of a 2010 Protocol, which removed the most controversial provisions of the original version.[155] However, as of 2017, the 2010 Protocol has received only a single ratification.

23.87 A similar uncertainty surrounds the entry into force of the Basel Protocol, which has received only eleven ratifications out of the twenty needed to enter into force.[156] With respect to this Protocol, the main obstacle to the entry into force seems to be, among other things, the lack of an autonomous compensation fund for cases in which the operator's liability is not sufficient to grant adequate victim protection.[157]

23.88 Currently, the only regimes in force are the ones concerning liability for nuclear damage and oil pollution damage. This disappointing result has thus led many authors to question whether it still makes sense to dedicate time, resources, and energy in the negotiation of additional civil liability treaties or, rather, whether it would be better to develop alternative or complementary approaches,[158] such as the strengthening of national laws on the prevention and punishment of environmental harm or the recourse to international funds and principles of corporate and social responsibility.[159]

b. Successful claims of compensation under applicable civil liability regimes

23.89 Even if a civil liability convention has entered into force, this does not necessarily mean that it will be effective in addressing the consequences of damage caused by ultra-hazardous activities, as the level of state participation to a civil liability convention impacts its effectiveness.

23.90 Nuclear conventions, in particular, are characterized by their limited participation,[160] as well as the absence, among their parties, of states with significant

---

not go far enough to ensure effective protection of the Antarctic environment, so that, eventually, CRAMRA was ultimately superseded by Annex VI to the Antarctic Liability Protocol. See Sands (n 17) 582.

[155] Including the states parties' obligation to report to the IMO the quantities of HNS substances that they had received. See Sands (n 17) 760.

[156] The Convention on Civil Liability for Damage Caused during Carriage of Dangerous Goods by Road, Rail and Inland Navigation Vessels (signed 10 October 1989, not yet entered into force) has also received only one ratification since its adoption. While negotiations were undertaken in 2003 to remove the obstacles surrounding the entry into force, it appears that no significant advancement has been reached so far, leaving the fate of the convention extremely uncertain.

[157] See Jan Albers, *Responsibility and Liability in the Context of Transboundary Movement of Hazardous Wastes by Sea* (Springer 2015) 301.

[158] See Churchill (n 4) 32. See also Daniel (n 147) 236.

[159] Daniel (n 147) 239–40.

[160] The Vienna Convention on Nuclear Damage currently has thirty-three parties. Out of these, thirteen signed the 1997 Protocol, which significantly extends the scope of protection for the

nuclear generating capacity.¹⁶¹ With respect to such non-states parties, therefore, the issue of compensation for nuclear damage will be governed largely by their national legislation, with radically different outcomes. This is particularly evident with respect to Russia and Japan, each home of one of the two most devastating nuclear incidents in recent history: respectively, Chernobyl and Fukushima.

In relation to the former, it is widely known that the Chernobyl incident provoked devastating and long-lasting consequences on a great part of the European continent.¹⁶² However, neither the USSR nor, following its dissolution, Russia were ever part of either the Paris Convention or the Vienna Convention on Nuclear Damage. When, after the incident, the Soviet Union refused to pay compensation to foreign victims, many individuals suffering the consequences were left devoid of protection.¹⁶³ If compensation was paid, it was on the basis of the victims' own national law. For example, on the basis of its Atomic Energy Act, since 1986 Germany has been paying compensation to victims of nuclear damage caused by the Chernobyl incident in the event that those victims were unable to obtain compensation under the law of the incident state.¹⁶⁴ Similarly, the Swedish government decided to award funds for compensation of those nationals that suffered nuclear damage, even if no international regime for the compensation of nuclear damage was applicable to Sweden at the time.¹⁶⁵ 23.91

The situation is different with respect to the Fukushima incident. Japan is not a party to either the Vienna Convention on Nuclear Damage or the Paris Convention. However, given that the consequences of the incident manifested exclusively on a domestic level,¹⁶⁶ and in light of the highly favourable national 23.92

---

victims of nuclear damage, and only five actually ratified it. See Schwartz, 'International Nuclear Third Party Liability Law' (n 104) 48. Similarly, both the Paris Convention on Nuclear Liability and the Brussels Supplementary Convention on Nuclear Damage account for only eighteen signatories, while their 2004 Protocols are still not into force, although it appears that entry into force will occur in the near future. See ibid 57. See also Sara Poli, *La Responsabilità per Danni da Inquinamento Transfrontaliero nel Diritto Comunitario e Internazionale* (Giuffré 2006) 254.

¹⁶¹ The states with major nuclear generating capacity are currently the United States, Russia, Canada, France, Japan, and South Korea. See Nuclear Energy Agency, *NEA Annual Report 2016* (2017) <https://www.oecd-nea.org/pub/activities/ar2016/ar2016.pdf> accessed 3 July 2018. Out of these, only France has joined the nuclear liability regime set out in the Paris Convention on Nuclear Liability, while the United States, India and Japan have either signed or are party to the Supplementary Compensation Convention for Nuclear Damage. None of these states is party to the regime set out under the Vienna Convention on Nuclear Damage.

¹⁶² See n 11.

¹⁶³ See Vanda Lamm, 'The Protocol Amending the 1963 Vienna Convention' in OECD/IAEA, *International Nuclear Law in the Post-Chernobyl Period* (OECD 2006) 170.

¹⁶⁴ See Werner Eich, 'The Compensation of Damage in Germany Following the Chernobyl Accident' in OECD, *Indemnification of Damage in the Event of a Nuclear Accident. Workshop Proceedings 26–28 November 2001* (OECD 2001) 94.

¹⁶⁵ ibid 95.

¹⁶⁶ See n 15.

laws governing compensation for nuclear damage,[167] it appears safe to say that the lack of participation to international civil liability regimes on nuclear damage has not prejudiced the level of protection afforded to the victims.

23.93 In practice, the effectiveness of nuclear liability regimes in ensuring prompt and adequate compensation to the victims has still not yet been fully tested and is therefore difficult to evaluate. However, given that several states have implemented the principles enshrined in nuclear liability conventions in their domestic legislation even without being parties to the same, it seems that such principles are, at least in theory, deemed sufficient and effective to ensure adequate protection to the victims.[168]

23.94 In contrast, international civil liability regimes seem to play a bigger role with respect to compensation for oil pollution damage. There are currently 138 state parties to the 1992 Civil Liability Convention and 114 parties to the 1992 Fund Convention. Out of these 114, 31 also participate to the IOPC Supplementary Fund. Widespread participation in these conventions is essential to create a uniform and effective system for the compensation of oil pollution damage. Indeed, victims belonging to any of the state parties will be able to benefit from the same procedure for compensation and to avail themselves of the financial resources made available by all states parties through the IOPC Fund and the Supplementary Fund.

23.95 In this respect, since its establishment in October 1978, the IOPC Fund has been involved in 150 incidents and has paid an overall amount of £600 million in compensation claims.[169] In 2016, the IOPC Fund and the Supplementary Fund paid overall £36,620,860 in compensation for damages caused by oil spills.[170] The Funds are currently managing compensation claims with respect to twelve incidents, the last of which involved the oil spill caused by the *Trident Star* tanker in Malaysia in 2016.[171] Claims are mainly settled out of court, with the victims issuing specific requests for compensation directly to the Funds and to the insurer liable under the first tier of compensation provided under the 1992 Civil Liability Convention.[172]

---

[167] It suffices to say here that, under Japanese law, TEPCO, the operator of the Fukushima Daiichi power plant, is strictly and exclusively liable for nuclear damage, its liability is unlimited and the victims may refer compensation claims directly to the operator concerned, to a local court or to a special committee for nuclear damage compensation. For more information, See Vasquez-Maignan (n 89) 11.

[168] For example, states such as United States and Japan have already put in place national legislation implementing the fundamental principles of the international civil liability regime for nuclear damage, in certain instances even improving it. This is the case of Japan, whose national legislation outright rejects the notion of 'limited liability', instead providing for the unlimited liability of the operator. See Schwartz, 'International Nuclear Third Party Liability Law' (n 104).

[169] See IOPC Fund, *Annual Report 2016* (n 139) 14–15.

[170] ibid 41.

[171] ibid 15.

[172] ibid 13.

It appears, therefore, that the international scheme for compensation of oil pollution damage has been the most successful among the civil liability regimes currently into force, a result that may be explained, at least in part, by the immediate and well-defined effects of oil pollution damage, and the ease of identifying the responsible party.[173]

23.96

4. TNCs and international civil liability

The analysis carried out in the previous sections shows that international civil liability regimes are built upon a common set of generally accepted principles designed to hold private entities accountable for damage caused in the performance of an ultra-hazardous activity and facilitate the bringing of claims by the victims.

23.97

In particular, a TNC performing one of the specific ultra-hazardous activities falling under the scope of an international liability convention will qualify under such convention as the entity through which liability for the damage suffered will be channelled, to the exclusion of other subjects.[174] As a consequence of this channelling, the TNCs will have to pay prompt and adequate compensation to the victims—both private natural or legal persons and states—as well as to undertake and implement measures for the prevention or restoration of environmental damage, if so required under the applicable convention.[175] The TNC will not be able to avoid liability by claiming that it had complied with all applicable due diligence rules and that, as such it was not at fault in the performance of the activity.[176] However, its liability will be limited in amount and in time.[177] Lastly, the TNC will be required to provide adequate insurance or other financial guarantee,[178] and to make contributions to additional compensation mechanisms, if established under the convention.[179]

23.98

While, as also noted, international civil liability conventions have generally had limited success in terms of ratifications and entry into force, the lack of participation seems due mainly to the dissatisfaction of states with respect to certain specific elements of the conventions, rather than with the principles governing liability themselves.[180] This is even more true if considering that, when such regimes have entered into force and have been applied in practice, they have been particularly successful in ensuring prompt and adequate compensation to the victims, thus reinforcing the idea that the principles enshrined in international civil

23.99

---

[173] See Brunnée (n 32) 367.
[174] See section B.2.b.
[175] See section B.2.a.
[176] See section B.2.c.
[177] See section B.2.d.
[178] See section B.2.e.
[179] See section B.2.f.
[180] This is particularly true with respect to the quantitative limitations to liability, which were perceived as too low by the international community. See section B.3.1.

liability conventions may play a key role in holding TNCs liable for the reparation of environmental damage.

23.100 It follows, therefore, that what is needed at this stage is to develop a new way to make such principles immediately and effectively enforceable against TNCs. It is at this stage, then, that international investment law comes into play.

C. International Investment Law and Civil Liability Regimes: Options for Reforms

23.101 International investment law has become subject of increased attention in recent years, especially in light of questions regarding its compliance with sustainable development objectives. The following subsections will provide: (i) a brief overview of the main criticisms of the international investment law framework and consequent calls reform (section 3.a), and (ii) the analysis of one option of reform through linking international investment law with international civil liability principles (section 3.b).

1. The limitations of international investment law and the need for reform

23.102 As briefly anticipated at the very beginning of the analysis, international investment law is traditionally concerned with the treatment to be accorded to private entities, including TNCs, qualifying as investors, and conducting investment activities in a foreign state.[181]

23.103 The international investment law framework is particularly fragmented, with rules and principles deriving both from customary international law and the multitude of international investment agreements (IIAs) that have been negotiated since the 1980s.[182] In general, IIAs provide to investors of one state party undertaking investments in the territory of the other state party a series of protections, including guarantees of fair and equitable treatment, protections in case of expropriation, and guarantees of national treatment. Such protections can typically then be enforced directly by the investor against the host state through the recourse to investor–state arbitration.

23.104 One explanation for the high number of in-force IIAs is that states (typically capital-exporting states) have concluded these agreements to protect their

---

[181] See section A.
[182] For an overview of the numbers of IIAs that have been negotiated in recent years, See United Nation Commission on Trade and Development (UNCTAD), *World Investment Report. Investor Nationality: Policy Challenges* (2016) 101 <http://unctad.org/en/PublicationsLibrary/wir2016_en.pdf> accessed 3 July 2018.

own nationals in the performance of investment activities in foreign countries. Additionally, states (typically capital-importing states) have apparently considered IIAs as important tools for encouraging, promoting, and attracting foreign direct investment, and that such foreign investment will bolster the economic and social development of the country.[183]

Over time, however, these assumptions have been increasingly subject to critique.[184] There is, in particular, a heightened level of concern about the asymmetrical nature of IIAs.[185] Those treaties, as they have been designed and adopted in recent decades, establish rules that enable capital to be more mobile, enabling TNCs to, for instance, move to jurisdictions with lower labour and environmental standards, or structure their operations so as to judgment-proof their assets if subject to civil or criminal suits. Additionally, IIAs grant TNCs significant power to challenge adverse government laws, regulations, investigations, court decisions, and penalties, even when such government decisions are measures are adopted in good faith to address environmental (or other) issues and concerns.[186] 23.105

Thus, there is the increasing awareness that, should such treaties grant investors the powerful benefits highlighted, they should also be accompanied by relevant obligations, including those designed specifically to combat some of the problems that can be generated by the increased power, mobility, and activities of TNCs due to IIAs' provisions. In this context, calls for reform of the current international investment law framework have led to the slow incorporation in new generation IIAs of provisions designed to protect public interest concerns, including environmental concerns, of the host state.[187] None of the recent developments, however, addresses the issue of the liability of TNCs qualifying as investors for damages, and in particular environmental damages, caused in the performance of an investment activity protected under an applicable IIA. 23.106

---

[183] See, among others, M Sornarajah, *The International Law on Foreign Investment* (CUP 2010) 48.

[184] See, among others, UNCTAD, *The Role of International Investment Agreements in Attracting Foreign Direct Investment to Developing Countries* (UNCTAD Series on International Investment Policies for Development, 2009). See also Emma Aisbett, 'Foreign Direct Investment: Correlation versus Causation' in Karl Sauvant and Lisa Sachs (eds), *The Effects of Treaties on Foreign Direct Investment* (OUP 2009).

[185] See Pauwelyn (n 7) 16. See also Gus Van Harten, *Investment Treaty Arbitration and Public Law* (OUP 2007).

[186] The chilling effects produced by the threat of arbitration on the powers of the host state to adopt laws and regulations designed to protect human, social, and environmental interest are now widely known. See, among others, Jorge E Vinuales, *Foreign Investment and the Environment in International Law* (CUP 2012) 342; Kyla Tienhaara, 'Regulatory Chill and the Threat of Arbitration: A View from Political Science' in Chester Brown and Kate Miles (eds), *Evolution in Investment Treaty Law and Arbitration* (CUP 2011).

[187] For an overview of how environmental concerns are incorporated and dealt with in IIAs, see Kathryn Gordon and Joaquim Pohl, 'Environmental Concerns in International Investment Agreements: A Survey' (OECD Working Papers on International Investment, 2011).

23.107 This issue is not merely theoretical, as evidenced, among other things, by recent environmental counterclaims filed by host states within the context of investor–state arbitration.[188] More generally, it is undeniable that, while IIAs are often adopted as means of supporting TNCs' international investments and expanding their global reach, these outcomes can easily increase those TNCs' environmental footprints. Moreover, while the activities of such TNCs can produce positive environmental outcomes, for example by enabling the transfer of clean technologies across borders, they can also result in significant environmental harms, especially if the relevant activities are ultra-hazardous.[189] And lastly, even in the context of foreign investment, victims of environmental harm often face daunting challenges in securing remedies.[190]

23.108 In light of these issues, one potentially promising avenue for reform is the option of using IIAs to expand civil liability regimes, so as to hold TNCs qualifying as 'investor' liable for environmental damage caused in the territory of the host state and arising from the performance of ultra-hazardous activities.

2. The integration between international investment law and international civil liability

23.109 At first, international investment law and international civil liability regimes appear to be two independent and completely unrelated fields. Indeed, one is concerned with the protections applicable to foreign investments in host countries, while the other deals with the liability of private individuals arising from the performance of ultra-hazardous activities. International investment law grants to natural and legal persons qualifying as 'investors' protections directly arising under international law and enforceable against states; international civil liability regimes, in contrast, provide for the obligations of natural and legal persons qualifying as 'operators' when their liability arises.

23.110 However, there might well be instances in which both areas of law are relevant and applicable. Indeed, a TNC may sometimes qualify both as an 'investor', thus benefitting from the protections of applicable IIAs, and as an 'operator', thus being subject to the liability provisions of applicable civil liability conventions. A textbook example would be that of a TNC whose investment in a host state is represented by the construction and operation of a nuclear installation. In the

---

[188] See *Perenco Ecuador Ltd v The Republic of Ecuador and Empresa Estatal Petróleos del Ecuador (Petroecuador)*, ICSID Case No ARB/08/6, Interim Decision on Environmental Counterclaim (11 August 2015). See also *Burlington Resources Inc v Republic of Ecuador*, ICSID Case No ARB/08/5, Decision on Ecuador's Counterclaim (7 February 2017).

[189] In addition to nuclear and oil transportation activities traditionally considered by civil liability regimes, other activities, such as the extractive industries, may be qualified as ultra-hazardous.

[190] TNCs' international structures can exacerbate those challenges, making it exceedingly difficult for victims of environmental harms to sue those TNCs for harms and/or actually recover any compensation, if and when their suits are successful.

event that an ultra-hazardous activity is implemented as a foreign investment in a host country, the same concerns that justify the adoption of a civil liability regime will arise.

Incorporating civil liability principles into IIAs could grant the host state and its citizens an important safeguard against potential damage caused by foreign investors.[191] Most importantly, the incorporation could grant such principles direct effectiveness and application under international law, as they would no longer depend on the ratification of the relevant civil liability convention and their subsequent implementation at the national level. By doing so, civil liability principles could achieve a broader reach, thus overcoming some of the challenges that international civil liability conventions have faced in terms of participation and effectiveness.

23.111

As for why states should be willing to include provisions on civil liability regimes in their IIAs, one incentive could be that such provisions would be a condition of securing the treaty (and other associated benefits expected to arise therefrom). Thus, a negotiating state could potentially seek to include such civil liability provisions in exchange for agreeing to the disciplines an investment treaty imposes or the market access commitments it includes.

23.112

Such a liability system within IIAs would serve at least two essential purposes: (i) ensuring adequate protection to the victims of environmental damage caused by the investment; and (ii) restoring the affected environment to its original conditions, insofar as possible. Drawing from the examples discussed, the system could establish a basic strict liability regime for 'operators' of ultra-hazardous activities, which could be defined as such in the relevant IIA. In this respect, the activities for which the investor would be liable need not be limited to the traditional ultra-hazardous activities considered by civil liability regimes, such as transport and handling of hazardous wastes, but could be extended to all activities that, in practice, have the potential to produce significant adverse environmental impact, as it is the case of mining and other extractive industries. The new system could also potentially include a broader range of provisions designed to prevent and remedy fault-based harm. These and other issues and options are discussed further in following sections.

23.113

a. Investor as operator

The first step to ensure that the host state and its population receive adequate protection from environmental damage caused by the foreign investor is to specifically provide in the applicable IIA that the investor will be liable for such damage. TNCs that own or control covered 'investments' or enterprises, therefore, could be treated akin to 'operators' under civil liability conventions and assigned a range

23.114

---

[191] See section C.1.

of obligations aimed at preventing, restoring, and compensating the environmental damage caused by their activities in the host state.[192]

23.115 With respect to the definition of 'investment' relevant for the purpose of attaching liability to the investor/operator, this should be defined in broad terms so as to include any possible activity of the investor in the host state. It is obvious that the primary focus of liability rules is on investments in all those operational activities whose performance entails a risk of environmental damage (eg mining, oil and gas extraction, operation of chemical plants etc). However, in order to avoid the risks arising from an enumerative listing of covered investment activities—thus restricting liability to investments in certain activities with the danger of omitting certain equally dangerous activities—the best approach would be to provide only for a general definition.[193]

23.116 If a restriction to the scope of liability must be introduced, an intermediate position could be to attach liability only to direct investments,[194] over which the investor exercises a significant degree of control. In such cases the investor can effectively decide and implement business and strategic decisions, including those relevant to compliance with environmental standards and regulations.

b. Environmental investor obligations

23.117 Partly in response to concerns about the asymmetrical nature of investment treaties, investor obligations have become increasingly common in new-generation IIAs, binding the investor to comply with host state's laws[195] and meet specific human rights and social standards,[196] and preventing it from engaging in bribery and corruption.[197] Some approaches also require investors to comply with environmental

---

[192] See section C.3.b.
[193] A general approach would allow focusing on the reparation of environmental damage, thus following the approach of the Lugano Convention on Damage Caused by Dangerous Activities. In this case, however, particular attention should be placed on the drafting of the relevant definitions of 'dangerous activity', 'damage', and 'environment' in a sufficiently specific manner as to avoid risks of vagueness that would prejudice the implementation of the relevant provisions. It was exactly this circumstance that, jointly with others, ultimately doomed the Lugano Convention on Damage Caused by Dangerous Activities and prevented its entry into force. See section B.3.a.
[194] Direct investment may be defined as 'a category of investment that reflects the objective of establishing a lasting interest by a resident enterprise in one economy (*direct investor*) in an enterprise (*direct investment enterprise*) that is resident in an economy other than that of the investor'. The characterizing feature of foreign direct investment is, therefore, the establishment of a long-lasting relationship between the direct investor and the direct investing enterprise, manifesting itself through the management and control of the former over the latter. Evidence of the exercise of such control is the direct or indirect ownership by the direct investor of a stake representing at least 10 per cent of the voting rights in the direct investment enterprise. This is in contrast to portfolio investment, where such long-lasting relationship and control over the investment are missing See OECD, *OECD Benchmark Definition of Foreign Direct Investment* (2008) 234.
[195] See, among others, 2015 India Model BIT, art 12; 2012 SADC Model BIT, art 11; Investment Agreement for the COMESA Common Investment Area (signed 23 May 2007), art 13.
[196] See 2012 SADC Model BIT, art 12.
[197] See, among others, 2015 India Model BIT, art 9; 2012 SADC Model BIT, art 10.

and social impact assessment rules of the host state,[198] thus granting additional, though arguably limited, consideration to environmental concerns. However, the scope of the protection afforded to the environment could be extended by introducing additional investor obligations that do not merely require the investor to comply with the domestic law of the host state but, rather, impose direct obligations on the investor under the treaty.

Such a proposal could find support in two developments that are currently under way within the international community. First of all, the traditional approach whereby international law is considered to not directly impose rights and obligations on private actors is slowly being abandoned.[199] It has increasingly been recognized, for instance, that individuals may be held accountable for their actions when they constitute a crime under international criminal law.[200] The development of international investment law—which grants protections to private actors (ie the investor) and is slowly starting to impose obligations on them—further indicates that there is no necessary impediment to the development of environmental investor obligations directly binding the investor. 23.118

Environmental investor obligations that could be included in new generation IIAs are examined in following subsections. The provision of similar obligations in IIAs might arguably be redundant in the event that the host state's domestic law already provides for the investor's obligation to adopt preventive and reinstatement measures, and the IIA requires the investor to comply with the law of the host state. Nevertheless, their direct inclusion into IIAs could be extremely useful in those instances in which the applicable national law does not provide for these kind of measures or is not effectively implemented and enforced, or in which the transboundary nature of the TNC's activities or structure make securing environmental remedies more difficult. 23.119

i. **Adoption of preventive and reinstatement measures** Following the approach adopted by the European Liability Directive and civil liability regimes, new generation IIAs could require investors to take all necessary preventive measures to avoid grave and imminent threats of environmental damage caused by their investment activities.[201] Preventive measures could also follow the general definition provided under civil liability regimes, which identifies them as any reasonable measures taken in response to an act or omission that has created a grave and imminent threat of environmental damage with the purpose of preventing or minimizing such threat.[202] 23.120

---

[198] See SADC Model BIT, art 13.
[199] As it occurred, eg, in the field of human rights law.
[200] See Rome Statute of the International Criminal Court (UNGA, 17 July 1998).
[201] See European Liability Directive, art 5.
[202] See section B.2.a.

23.121 In the event that an environmental damage has already occurred, IIAs could require investors to take all practicable and necessary steps to reduce, contain, or manage the damage and to adopt the required remedial or reinstatement measures. Also in this case, the definition of remedial measures could match the one provided under the most recent civil liability convention, constituting 'any reasonable measure aiming to reinstate or restore damaged or destroyed components of the environment', including the introduction of equivalent components into the environment.

23.122 The obligation to adopt preventive or reinstatement measures is of outmost importance, as it is the main instrument to achieve the second objective of a liability system within IIAs—namely, the protection, and restoration of the environment. In this context, it has to be noted that the foreign direct investor is often the entity with the best understanding of the risks arising from—as well as the technical and scientific knowledge required for—the performance of the investment activity.[203] As such, it is in the best position to implement measures aimed at both preventing and removing the risk of environmental damage and, in the event that such measures should fail, removing and restoring the environment of the host state to its original condition.

23.123 In light thereof, IIAs could provide for the investors' obligations to put in place the relevant preventive measures and, if necessary, additional measures of reinstatement, so as to ensure an adequate protection of the environment.[204]

23.124 The imposition of these obligations is justified by the circumstances that (i) it is the same investor that, by performing its activity in the host state, creates the risk of environmental damage and (ii) it is the investor's transnational structure that often renders investor accountability elusive. It is, therefore, only equitable that, during all of the phases of its investment, the investor should bear primary responsibility for implementing all of the measures required to protect the environment.

23.125 This does not mean, however, that the investor should in all cases be the sole entity responsible for the adoption of such measures. Indeed, in the event that the damage was entirely caused by a wilful action or omission of a third party, the investor should have a right of recourse against it. In addition, in the adoption of both preventive and reinstatement measures, the intervention of the competent authorities of the host state should always be envisaged, both with respect to a procedural perspective (eg issuance of permits, authorizations, and approvals) and from a financial perspective, in the event the financial capacity of the investor is not sufficient to sustain the adoption of the necessary measures.

---

[203] See section B.2.b.
[204] See n 78.

ii. Compensation It has been already remarked that, with respect to several **23.126** ultra-hazardous activities, the risk of environmental damage cannot be completely erased, even if the operator complies with all applicable standards of care.[205] While investor obligations to adopt preventive measures and measures of reinstatement could act as safeguards against such risks and harms, they might not be enough to prevent environmental damage or to contain its effects.

New generation IIAs can address this by also establishing obligations on investors **23.127** to provide prompt and adequate compensation for the environmental damage caused by their investments in the host state. The definition of environmental damage covered should follow the approach of the most recent civil liability regimes,[206] thus allowing for the reparation of pure environmental damage, through either the recovery of the costs associated with the adoption of preventive and reinstatement measures or the introduction of equivalent components into the damaged environment.

Liability should, therefore, cover damages relating to: (i) loss of life and personal **23.128** injury; (ii) property damage; (iii) economic loss arising from personal and property damage; (iv) loss of income deriving from a direct economic interest in any use or enjoyment of the environment; and (v) the reimbursement of the costs for the adoption of preventive measures and measures of reinstatement, including the introduction of equivalent components.

While the investor should be liable for the environmental damage regardless of **23.129** whether it was at fault, in accordance with a strict liability standard,[207] the host state (or others with a right of standing under the treaty) will still be required to prove the existence of a causal link between the investment's activities and the damage suffered. In order to facilitate such proof, new generation IIAs should provide for rules on the basis of which to ascertain the proof of causation. A possible solution would consist of following the approach set out under the Lugano Convention, which requires that, in ascertaining the existence of causation, the court must take 'due account of the increased danger of causing such damage inherent in the dangerous activity'.[208]

As with civil liability regimes, and to counterbalance the strict liability standard, **23.130** the investor's liability for compensation of environmental damage could be

---

[205] See section B.
[206] See section B.2.a.
[207] See section B.2.c.
[208] See Lugano Convention on Damage Caused by Dangerous Activities, art 10. The provision, however, is still very vague, as it does not provide any particular indication on how the causal nexus should be determined in practice. A better solution would be to specify in the provision the criteria to be followed in the ascertainment of the causal link. However, this approach would require choosing among several theories of causation, all equally valid and bearer of legal difficulties. For more information on causation, see n 81.

limited and subject to exemptions.[209] Therefore, the investor might not be liable when the occurrence of the environmental damage was completely outside its control, as it was due to events such as war, terrorism, act of God, or act of third parties. Similarly, if the damage was caused with the contributory fault of the host state, the investor could be entitled to benefit from a reduction in the amount of compensation due. As for quantitative limitations of liability, however, given the range of ultra-hazardous activities that might be covered by an IIA, it would be impossible to determine them *a priori*, at the time of the negotiation of the IIA. The treaty could, instead, establish a standing, multi-stakeholder body capable of establishing such limits and reviewing and revising them over time so as to ensure they advance identified objectives and comply with relevant policies and principles.

23.131 In all cases in which liability is limited or excluded, however, additional tiers of compensation should be provided—either under the applicable IIA or under a separate agreement—in order to cover the outstanding amount of damage and not leave the victims devoid of protection.[210]

23.132 **iii. Insurance** Lastly, the IIAs could establish mechanisms requiring investors in relevant activities to obtain insurance or other financial security covering damages arising from its investment in the host state. The provision of insurance or other financial security is justified by the need to spread any potential damages and losses among different subjects, so as to facilitate the payment of compensation to the victims. Following the approach of civil liability regimes, IIAs could frame this obligation in broad terms, leaving the investor and the host state free to determine relevant details at a later stage, when more information on the investment become available.

23.133 Such choice might concern, for example, the type of insurance required. For example, the host state could require the investor to secure environmental liability insurance, whereby the insurer will cover the risk that his insured/responsible party will have to compensate third parties for environmental damage.[211] Environmental liability insurance, however, may be hard to obtain, in light of the lack of data that makes it hard for the insurer to determine the frequency of the insured risk or the exact scope of environmental liabilities covered, especially in case of damages that gradually accumulate over time.[212]

---

[209] See section B.2.c.
[210] See section C.2.d.
[211] See Michael Faure, 'Alternative Compensation Mechanisms as Remedies for Uninsurability of Liability' (2004) 29 The Geneva Papers on Risk and Insurance 455, 462 .
[212] In addition to lack of information concerning the risk and the exact scope of the liability, insurability of environmental liability is rendered more difficult also by the danger that the insurer lacks the necessary financial resources to cover all liabilities caused, especially in the event of catastrophic damage, and the uncertainties surrounding the ascertainment of the causal link between the damaging event and the losses justifying the request for compensation. In addition, traditional insurance issues such as moral hazard (ie an increase in the exposure to risks when protection against

23.134 As an alternative to environmental liability insurance, environmental damage insurance could also be considered. In this case, the risk covered is not a potential request of compensation for environmental damage but, rather, the occurrence of environmental damage.[213] With this type of insurance, the insurer pays as soon as the damage occurs, provided that it can be proven that such damage has been caused by the insured risk, and irrespective of whether there is liability.[214] Hence, proof that the insured damage has occurred should suffice to recover.[215] However, it will still be necessary to specifically describe the type of insured risk and, in any event, coverage should be provided for all the components of the environmental damage—that is, death and personal injury, property damage, and the recovery of costs for the adoption of measures of reinstatement and preventive measures.

23.135 Another issue left to the parties' decision concerns the establishment of the maximum amount covered by the insurance. It is reasonable to believe that such amounts will vary depending on the different type of investment undertaken and that, as such, it will be impossible to determine them *a priori*, at the time of the signing of the relevant IIA. Moreover, the insurer will also need to be involved in such determination, making any prior decision extremely difficult to make.

23.136 Lastly, the parties should be free to determine whether the investor should provide an insurance policy, or a different form of financial security, such as a parent company guarantee, or both, depending on the circumstance of each case.

c. Jurisdictional provisions

23.137 Assuming that the investor obligations examined in the previous subsection were introduced in new IIAs, they would be completely ineffective if there was no way available to enforce them. IIAs, however, could be revised to enable state claims against investors, and even to allow non-parties to bring cases against investors. This could be done through provisions requiring host states to adopt relevant laws setting forth substantive obligations and granting rights of standing to private citizens or government entities to enforce those obligations.[216] The IIA could also

---

the potential consequences is available) and adverse selection (ie the demand of insurance is positively correlated to the risk that the loss may occur) are also applicable in this case. See Michael Faure, 'A Shift Towards Alternative Compensation Mechanisms For Environmental Damage?' in Michael Faure and Albert Verheij (eds), *Shifts in Compensation for Environmental Damage* (Springer 2007) 75.

[213] Environmental damage insurance can be structured both as a first-party insurance (whereby the insured/operator seeks coverage directly from the insurer for damages occurring on the insured site) or as a direct insurance (where damages suffered by third parties are also covered). See Faure, 'Alternative Compensation Mechanisms' (n 211) 463.

[214] ibid 462.

[215] ibid 464.

[216] See SADC Model BIT, art 17. See also Howard Mann, Konrad von Moltke, Luke Peterson, and Aaron Cosbey, *IISD Model International Investment Agreement for Sustainable Development: Negotiator's Handbook* (IISD 2005) 17.

contain provisions aimed at ensuring that resulting court judgments would be enforceable in the courts of the parties to the IIA.

23.138 The IIA could also provide for arbitration of these claims brought by states (or other stakeholders given standing), though the investor, as a respondent, would have to provide its consent to arbitrate those disputes. Such consent could potentially be secured from the investors as a condition of acquiring the relevant permits or authorizations to operate an ultra-hazardous activity, or establishing or acquiring an investment engaged in the relevant activity. The IIA could also indicate that if the investor were to bring a claim against the host state based on any issue, it would be deemed to consent to arbitrate disputes arising out of environmental (and potentially other) harms.

23.139 As in civil liability conventions, the possibility to bring claims against the investor could be subject to time limitations. Thus, IIAs could include: (i) a provision whereby the host state's claim needs be brought within a specified period of time; as well as (ii) a period of extinction or prescription accruing from the date when the host state knew or should reasonably have known about the occurrence of the environmental damage.[217] The issue in this case would be to determine general time limits applicable to the different types of environmental damage that could arise from the covered ultra-hazardous activities, an exercise that may be difficult for circumstances when consequences can be perceived only a significant time after the accident.

23.140 In addition, the possibility to bring claims of compensation for environmental damage could be precluded in the event that the damage has been already covered through the available insurance policies or financial securities. That is, the existence and enforcement of insurance should preclude liability claims from the victims against the investor, up to the maximum amount of the insurance.[218]

23.141 Lastly, in light of the high specificity and technicality of environmental disputes, IIAs could expressly provide for the participation of environmental experts in the arbitration proceedings. This solution is not new to international investment law practice, as some IIAs, including the North American Free Trade Agreement (NAFTA), expressly provide for the possibility of the tribunal to appoint one or more environmental experts to report on any factual issue raised by the parties during the proceeding.[219]

---

[217] See, among others: (i) Vienna Convention on Nuclear Damage, art 6; (ii) 1992 Civil Liability Convention for Oil Pollution Damage, art 37; and (iii) Basel Protocol on Damage by Transboundary Movement of Hazardous Wastes, art 13.

[218] It is understood that, in this case, the insurer will still maintain its right to be subrogated in the victims' claims against the investor.

[219] See, among others: (i) NAFTA (signed 17 December 1992, entered into force 1 January 1994), art 1133; (ii) Canada–Jordan BIT (2009); (iii) Canada–Peru BIT (2006); (iv) Mexico–United Kingdom BIT (2006); (v) United States–Rwanda BIT (2008). For more information, see Gordon, 'Environmental Concerns' (n 187) 20.

d. Additional tiers of compensation

23.142 Limitations to—or exemptions from—liability create a need for additional tiers of compensation, so as to ensure full protection to the victims of environmental damage.[220] Incorporating mechanisms for additional compensation into IIAs, however, might be particularly troublesome, especially if they were to take the form of compensation funds.[221]

23.143 Civil liability regimes have introduced two different approaches to compensation funds: the one followed by the nuclear liability conventions, requiring state parties to make available public funds in the event of nuclear accidents;[222] and the oil pollution conventions, which established international funds financed through contributions of the industry.[223]

23.144 The first option might be easier to incorporate, as the IIA could simply provide that states parties (potentially on a special and differential treatment basis, shared between home and host governments) be required to make available public funds to cover environmental damage caused by investments of their nationals in the territory of the other party. States would then remain free to determine how such funds could be gathered, either by sharing the burden on the taxpayers or recovering the relevant amounts from the industry—although, ideally, they should try to impose the burden on the industry, following the oil pollution conventions' approach, so as to ensure compliance with the polluter-pays principle.

23.145 The implementation of this option would, however, require resolution of several difficult issues. First of all, it would be necessary to determine the maximum amount for which each state party would be liable, an operation that may be difficult, if not impossible, to perform *a priori*. Second, and most importantly, it may be extremely difficult to determine how to allocate payment among the states parties, each of which likely benefits from the investment, and has some power to regulate it (whether at the investor or investment level).

23.146 As for the approach adopted by oil pollution conventions, the establishment of an international fund for the reparation and compensation of environmental damage could benefit from establishment of a separate multilateral convention, as it may be difficult to deal with the complexity of setting up the institutional framework for such a fund within the context of individual IIAs.[224] If that approach

---

[220] See section B.2.f.
[221] The term 'compensation fund' is inherently misleading, since it may refer to a plurality of financial arrangements with different purposes and structure. See Faure, 'Alternative Compensation Mechanisms' (n 211) 480.
[222] See section B.2.f.i.
[223] See section B.2.f.ii.
[224] It is important to highlight that the compensation fund is not designed to replace insurance coverage and other financial guarantees, but rather to supplement them in the event that they cannot perform their institutional purpose (eg in case exemptions from liability are applicable).

were pursued, however, an issue that might arise is whether enough states would willing to negotiate and enter into the relevant treaty, especially if its conclusion were not a condition of negotiating and ratification specific IIAs.

23.147 It would also be necessary to determine the exact purpose of the fund. Practice has given rise to several different models of 'compensation funds', each with its own specific rules, principles, and objectives.[225] One challenge, for example, will be identifying the damage covered by the international fund, that is whether it will cover environmental damage caused by any activity whatsoever or only damage caused by specific activities.[226] The choice will have an impact, in addition to the scope of victims entitled to compensation, on the costs and fees for the management and administration of the fund, as costs of bureaucracy will increase the wider the scope is of the damages covered.[227]

23.148 Lastly, the parties will need to determine how the fund will be financed. Options include financing through taxation of TNCs, and/or through sector-based contributions, which would be more in line with the polluter-pays principle.[228]

D. Conclusions

23.149 There is no general, inherent incompatibility between the principles governing civil liability regimes and international investment law; and current reform initiatives could be used to incorporate the former into the latter, thus achieving an equitable balance between investor protection and environmental concerns of the host state. The incorporation of civil liability principles could also be easily implemented by means of an extension in the scope of investor obligations, as well as in the scope of the arbitral tribunal's jurisdiction to hear claims arising from the IIA. The provision of additional tiers of compensation would however be more

---

[225] It is possible to identify, among others: (i) guarantee funds, to be used in the event that the insured party is insolvent; (ii) advancement funds, which grant prepayments to the victims of certain kind of damage when the ascertainment of responsibility would take too long, rendering the protection afforded ineffective (eg as in case of asbestos claims); (iii) restoration funds, which operate in the event that no one can be identified as liable party for the environmental damage caused; and (iv) limitation funds, whereby the operator is entitled to limit its liability up to the amounts paid to the fund itself. Many of these solutions have been developed within the context of national legislations and have not yet been transposed at the international level. See Faure, 'Alternative Compensation Mechanisms' (n 211) 480.

[226] The division into specific funds (concerning, eg, offshore drilling damage, damage caused by chemical substances, damages caused by mining activities etc) would be particularly useful if the participating state decided to impose the costs of contribution to the members of the industry, which would be specifically identified on the basis of the dangerous activities identified by each special fund.

[227] Faure, 'Alternative Compensation Mechanisms' (n 211) 484.

[228] See section B.1.

complex to implement, as it would require the setting up of an independent institutional framework.

23.150 Ultimately, however, the proposals advanced still remain at a highly theoretical stage. Whether or not it will be possible to implement them will depend heavily on both the developments to which international investment law will be subject in the future as well as, most importantly, the actual willingness of states to pursue and implement such changes.

24

UNANTICIPATED CONSEQUENCES

The Human Rights Implications of Bringing Sovereign Debt Disputes within Investment Treaty Arbitration

Juan Pablo Bohoslavksy and Edward Guntrip[*]

A. Introduction	24.01	C. Sovereign Debt Disputes in Investment Treaty Arbitration	24.25
B. The Definition of 'Investment' and Sovereign Debt	24.10	D. Human Rights Implications	24.46
		E. Conclusion	24.63

A. Introduction

24.01 The use of investment treaty arbitration (ITA) as a forum for resolving sovereign debt disputes is contentious. The controversy arises because sovereign debt displays different attributes to those classically associated with foreign direct investment (FDI).[1] Despite its different characteristics, creditors have argued that sovereign debt is protected by international investment law (IIL) based on the generic term 'investment' in the ICSID Convention[2] and the use of non-exhaustive,

---

[*] This chapter is based on the report prepared by the United Nations Independent Expert on Foreign Debt and Human Rights, for the United Nations General Assembly in 2017, available at <http://undocs.org/A/72/153> accessed 21 September 2018. The authors wish to extend their gratitude for the comments, insights, critiques, and questions received from Moshe Hirsch, David Kinley, Stephan Schill, Celine Tan, and Michael Waibel on the research paper on which this chapter is based. The authors would also like to thank Chris Henderson for his comments on a draft version of this chapter.

[1] See Michael Waibel, *Sovereign Defaults before International Courts and Tribunals* (CUP 2011) 230–51; Josef Ostřanský, 'Sovereign Debt Defaults in Investment Treaty Arbitration: Jurisdictional Considerations and Policy Implications' (2015) 3 Groningen Journal of International Law 27, 44–52.

[2] Convention on the Settlement of Investment Disputes Between States and Nationals of Other States (entered into force 14 October 1966), art 25(1) (ICSID Convention).

asset-based lists to define investments in international investment agreements (IIAs).[3] Some investment arbitrators have accepted these arguments and interpreted 'investment' in a manner to include sovereign debt instruments within the scope of IIL.[4] This interpretation allows creditors to rely on investment protection standards in IIAs and assert that an investment tribunal has subject-matter jurisdiction over sovereign debt disputes.[5] A finding of jurisdiction entitles creditors to seek full repayment of the debt and can significantly impact how a state manages its financial crisis.[6] If an insolvent sovereign must pay its debt in full, funds will need to be diverted from essential state services, such as health and education,[7] which will already be suffering from the effects of the financial crisis. Thus, using ITA to resolve sovereign debt disputes can negatively impact the human rights[8] of the local population.

When defining the term investment in the ICSID Convention, and in their IIAs, many states did not focus their full attention on whether sovereign debt would be protected by IIL.[9] Similarly, when interpreting the term 'investment', it is improbable that investment arbitrators have focused on how their determination might affect a state's ability to undertake sovereign debt restructuring (SDR).[10] On this basis, it is unlikely that states, and investment arbitrators, have been conscious of the human rights implications of their decisions.[11] This chapter traces 24.02

---

[3] See generally, Pietro Ortolani, 'Are Bondholders Investors? Sovereign Debt and Investment Arbitration after *Poštová*' (2017) 30 Leiden Journal of International Law 383.

[4] See *Abaclat and others (formerly Giovanna a Beccara and others) v Argentine Republic*, ICSID Case No ARB/07/5, Decision on Jurisdiction and Admissibility (4 August 2011) (*Abaclat*); *Ambiente Ufficio S.P.A and others (formerly Giordano Alpi and others) v Argentine Republic*, ICSID Case No ARB/08/9, Decision on Jurisdiction and Admissibility (8 February 2013) (*Ambiente*); *Giovanni Alemanni and others v Argentine Republic*, (ICSID Case No ARB/07/8, Decision on Jurisdiction and Admissibility (7 November 2014) (*Alemanni*).

[5] See Andrew Newcombe and Lluís Paradell, *Law and Practice of Investment Treaties: Standards of Treatment* (Kluwer Law International 2009) 65; Zachary Douglas, 'Property, Investment and the Scope of Investment Protection Obligations' in Zachary Douglas, Joost Pauwelyn, and Jorge E Viñuales (eds), *The Foundations of International Investment Law: Bringing Theory into Practice* (OUP 2014) 363–406, 365; Gus van Harten and Martin Loughlin, 'Investment Treaty Arbitration as a Species of Global Administrative Law' (2006) 17 European Journal of International Law 212, 230.

[6] Matthias Goldmann, 'Foreign Investment, Sovereign Debt and Human Rights' in Ilias Bantekas and Cephas Lumina (eds), *Sovereign Debt and Human Rights* (OUP forthcoming 2018) 5 <https://papers.ssrn.com/sol3/papers.cfm?abstract_id=3103632> accessed 21 September 2018.

[7] Celine Tan, 'Life, Debt and Human Rights: Contextualizing the International Regime for Sovereign Debt Relief' in Krista Nadakavukaren Schefer (ed), *Poverty and the International Economic Legal System: Duties to the World's Poor* (CUP 2013) 307–24, 311; Cephas Lumina, 'Sovereign Debt and Human Rights: The United Nations Approach' in Juan Pablo Bohoslavsky and Jernej Letnar Černič (eds), *Making Sovereign Financing and Human Rights Work* (Hart Publishing 2014) 251–68, 252.

[8] Given that sovereign debt can negatively impact upon the human rights of a host state population in a multitude of ways, the term 'human rights' is used in a generic sense in this chapter to capture human rights obligations that are legally binding under international law.

[9] See section B.

[10] See section C.

[11] See section D.

these unanticipated consequences to better understand how the actions of numerous states, and some investment arbitrators, have given rise to detrimental human rights implications and identifies what action can be taken to prevent human rights obligations from being breached in this context.

24.03 Merton's 1936 article entitled 'The Unanticipated Consequences of Purposive Social Action'[12] explains why action intended to achieve a particular purpose can result in unanticipated consequences.[13] Purposive action describes motivated acts that result in a choice between alternative courses of action.[14] Purposive acts may generate positive and negative consequences,[15] some of which will be anticipated, whilst others will be unanticipated.[16] Merton identifies five attributes associated with purposive action that result in unanticipated consequences: first, an actor's ignorance of the potential consequences that may flow from an act;[17] second, actors make errors when attempting to accurately predict the consequences of their actions;[18] third, the actor becomes focused on the immediate, foreseen consequence and excludes the possibility of any other consequences;[19] fourth, the actor does not take into account the action's further consequences because the action aligns with the actor's fundamental values;[20] fifth, the actors take into account predictions regarding the consequences of actions, and by so doing, alter the consequences of their actions. Merton stresses that the unanticipated consequences that may arise from an action are not restricted to the specific area in which the action was focused because action ramifies across interrelated fields.[21]

24.04 Whilst Merton's article focuses on the impact of unanticipated consequences for formulating social policy,[22] the principles Merton identifies can be equally applied to how international law functions.[23] This can be illustrated with reference to the processes of treaty drafting and treaty interpretation. States negotiate treaties in order to, amongst other things, ensure that international law addresses new

---

[12] Robert K Merton, 'The Unanticipated Consequences of Purposive Social Action' (1936) 6 American Sociological Review 894.
[13] ibid 898.
[14] ibid 895.
[15] ibid.
[16] As to the distinction between unanticipated consequences and unintended consequences, see Frank de Zwart, 'Unintended but not Unanticipated Consequences' (2015) 44 Theory and Society 283.
[17] Merton (n 12) 901.
[18] ibid.
[19] ibid 903.
[20] ibid 903–04.
[21] ibid 903.
[22] ibid 904.
[23] See eg Jack Goldsmith, 'The Self-defeating International Criminal Court' (2003) 70 University of Chicago Law Review 89, 100. The factors identified by Merton are being indirectly introduced into studies of international law through the adoption of behaviourism as a theoretical and methodological framework. See Jeffrey Dunoff and Mark Pollack, 'Experimenting with International Law' (2017) 28 European Journal of International Law 1317, 1318–34.

circumstances.[24] Hence, a treaty will reflect the international setting in which it is negotiated and its provisions will endeavour to respond to the challenges faced by the international community at that time. However, the treaty-drafting process inevitably results in linguistic uncertainty.[25] Decision-makers play a key role in resolving disputes over the meaning of treaty provisions by interpreting treaties, but they often do so in a different international context to the one in which the treaty was drafted. The interpretative process, although governed by the Vienna Convention on the Law of Treaties (VCLT),[26] may give rise to a range of valid interpretations.[27] Given the different global environment in which the decision-maker is operating, the interpretations given to the treaty provisions may not align with the subjective intentions of the treaty drafters. Therefore, through the process of interpreting the treaty, decision-makers may create unanticipated consequences by applying the treaty in unexpected conditions or to new forms of conduct. As a result, treaty provisions may not fulfil their intended purpose or inadvertently capture conduct that was not envisaged at the time of drafting. Hence, both the treaty drafting process, which creates linguistic uncertainty, and the subsequent interpretation of the treaty provisions, may give rise to unanticipated consequences.

The unanticipated consequences are generated because the actions of both states and decision-makers will be influenced by any, or all, of the five factors identified by Merton: ignorance; error; focusing on the foreseeable; aligning their conduct with specific values; or creating self-defeating prophesies.[28] For example, states cannot anticipate every development within the international community that may alter how the treaty provision is understood. Therefore, when states focus on the foreseeable consequences of their act, and ignore or miscalculate other potential consequences, it may influence whether treaty terms perform their desired function. Decision-makers may not fully consider the wider consequences of their interpretations because they function as part of epistemic and interpretative communities.[29] Consequently, the subject-matter expertise of the decision-maker, combined with the forum in which they operate, will emphasize the importance of certain results based on the specific values of the legal regime that generates

24.05

---

[24] Andrew Clapham, *Brierly's Law of Nations* (OUP 2012) 56.
[25] See James Crawford, *Chance, Order, Change: The Course of International Law* (Hague Academy of International Law 2014) 150–57; Jörg Kammerhofer, *Uncertainty in International Law: A Kelsenian perspective* (Routledge 2011) 119.
[26] Vienna Convention on the Law of Treaties (entered into force 27 January 1980), arts 31–33.
[27] Ervin P Hexner, 'Teleological Interpretation of Basic Instruments of Public International Organizations' in Salo Engel (ed), *Law, State, and International Legal Order: Essays in Honor of Hans Kelsen* (University of Tennessee Press 1964) 119–38, 123.
[28] Merton (n 12) 898–904.
[29] Jason Webb Yackee, 'Controlling the International Investment Law Agency' (2012) 53 Harvard International Law Journal 391, 404–06; on interpretative communities, see Ian Johnstone, 'Treaty Interpretation: The Authority of Interpretative Communities' (1991) 12 Michigan Journal of International Law 371.

their authority.³⁰ These values will vary between different communities of decision-makers³¹ and may lead to divergent results. The unanticipated consequences that arise from the actions of states and decision-makers have the potential to extend to other regimes of international law, resulting in new dilemmas that international law must resolve. This is evident from the variety of intersections that have arisen between regimes in public international law, for example, between international trade law and international environmental law,³² international human rights law and international humanitarian law,³³ and international investment law and international human rights law.³⁴

24.06 By adopting the framework set out by Merton, this chapter provides an original perspective on the intersection between sovereign debt, investment arbitration, and human rights. The chapter argues that a large number of states, and several investment arbitrators, when dealing with the term 'investment', have acted in a manner that generates unanticipated consequences. When applied to sovereign debt disputes, the cumulative effect of these unanticipated consequences can reduce a debtor state's ability to comply with its human rights obligations. Thus, the chapter argues that ITA should not be used as a forum to resolve sovereign debt disputes. Whilst this chapter cannot impute a definite motivation for each action that has generated unanticipated consequences,³⁵ or evidence a causative relationship between the factors identified,³⁶ it can demonstrate the degree to which the actions of states and decision-makers in IIL have generated uncertainty, creating the opportunity for unanticipated consequences to arise. By identifying the process that has permitted unanticipated consequences to arise, the chapter is able to make pragmatic suggestions to potentially prevent sovereign debt disputes in ITA from giving rise to negative human rights consequences in the future. It is acknowledged that each set of recommendations will be subject to further

---

³⁰ John Ruggie, 'International Responses to Technology' (1975) 29 International Organization 557, 569–70; Peter M Haas, 'Introduction: Epistemic Communities and International Policy Coordination' (1992) 46 International Organization 1, 20.

³¹ See Jean D'Aspremont, *Epistemic Forces in International Law: Foundational Doctrines and Techniques of International Legal Argumentation* (Edward Elgar Publishing 2015); Martti Koskenniemmi, 'The Fate of Public International Law: between Technique And Politics' (2007) 70 Modern Law Review 1.

³² For example, see Brian R Copeland and M Scott Taylor, *Trade and the Environment: Theory and Evidence* (Princeton University Press 2003); Edith Brown Weiss, John Jackson, and Nathalie Bernasconi-Osterwalder (eds), *Reconciling Environment and Trade* (Brill 2008).

³³ For example, see Roberta Arnold and Noëlle N R. Quénivet (eds), *International Humanitarian Law and Human Rights Law: Towards a New Merger in International Law* (Brill 2008); René Provost, *International Human Rights and Humanitarian Law* (CUP 2014).

³⁴ For example, see Pierre-Marie Dupuy, Francesco Francioni, and Ernst-Ulrich Petersmann (eds), *Human Rights in International Investment Law and Arbitration* (OUP 2009); Heejin Kim, *Regime Accommodation in International Law: Human Rights in International Economic Law and Policy* (Brill 2016); Filip Balcerzak, *Investor-State Arbitration and Human Rights* (Brill 2017).

³⁵ Merton (n 12) 897.

³⁶ ibid.

unanticipated consequences. However, as Merton indicates, this dilemma is impossible to resolve because actors are highly unlikely to be able to control all five factors that give rise to unanticipated consequences. Nonetheless, by curtailing the unanticipated consequences of past actions, the recommendations can result in insolvent states being able to maximize their compliance with international human rights law. Additionally, based on this underlying dynamic, the chapter is able to identify broader actions that states and decision-makers in international law can take more generally to prevent unanticipated consequences in the future.

To achieve these aims, this chapter addresses each action and consequence in turn. Initially, the chapter examines how FDI was understood at the time the modern IIL regime was developed to identify if the intention of states was to encompass sovereign debt instruments. This section finds that the majority of states did not actively consider whether sovereign debt would amount to an investment for the purposes of IIL. By focusing on the foreseeable consequences of decolonization, most states failed to expressly exclude this possibility. On the basis of this discussion, the section proceeds to suggest how states can limit the unanticipated consequences of their approach with reference to the treaty-drafting process. **24.07**

The chapter then analyses how investment arbitrators have defined the term investment in sovereign debt disputes against the backdrop of how sovereign debt disputes have usually been resolved. It submits that interpretations of the term 'investment' in these awards may reflect value-based judgments of investment arbitrators. Given their expertise, and the environment in which they operate, investment arbitrators are more likely to prioritize IIL and ITA above state insolvency in the decision-making process. In this instance, further unanticipated consequences arise from the finding that ITA can, in some circumstances, exercise jurisdiction over sovereign debt disputes. In particular, if ITA operates as an alternative forum to resolve sovereign debt disputes, it undermines the effectiveness of mechanisms designed specifically to encourage collective SDR. Recommendations are made regarding how states can seek to minimize the negative aspects of sovereign debt disputes being resolved through ITA. **24.08**

Finally, the chapter considers the human rights implications of permitting sovereign debt disputes to be heard before ITA. It discusses how using ITA to resolve sovereign debt disputes affects states' ability to comply with human rights obligations and identifies the lack of international forums that can simultaneously address sovereign debt disputes and human rights. Further recommendations are made that could minimize the human rights implications of sovereign debt disputes being resolved by way of ITA. Given the cumulative effect of these unanticipated consequences, the chapter concludes that ITA should not be used as a forum to resolve sovereign debt disputes. Based on this example, the chapter then outlines, in more general terms, how actors in international law can amend their actions to minimize the negative effects of unanticipated consequences. **24.09**

B. The Definition of 'Investment' and Sovereign Debt

24.10 The term 'investment' plays a pivotal role in the functioning of the IIL regime. The definition of investment dictates whether the activities of a foreign investor are covered by investment protection standards[37] and determines the availability of ITA as a dispute resolution forum.[38] Consequently, how 'investment' is understood dictates IIL's scope of application. Hence, any linguistic uncertainty generated by the term 'investment' may give rise to unanticipated consequences by enlarging (or narrowing) IIL's scope beyond what states foresaw when assenting to the legal regime.

1. The foundations of IIL

24.11 When the modern IIL regime was formed during the 1960s and 1970s, the ongoing process of decolonization influenced how IIL was to operate. Many newly decolonized states[39] were dissatisfied with the manner in which they had been economically exploited during the colonial period, and objected to the continuation of pre-existing concession agreements with, what were now, foreign investors.[40] To assert their economic independence (in addition to their political independence) newly decolonized states started to expropriate foreign-owned investments.[41] These large-scale expropriations highlighted the shortcomings of the international regime, as foreign investors had to rely on the customary international minimum standard of treatment of aliens,[42] which set a high threshold for violations[43] and could only be enforced at the international level through diplomatic

---

[37] Newcombe and Paradell (n 5) 65; Douglas (n 5) 365.
[38] Douglas (n 5) 365; van Harten and Loughlin (n 5) 230.
[39] Although these states were diverse, they used their common experience of decolonization to form the Group of 77.
[40] Kenneth Vandevelde, 'A Brief History of International Investment Agreements' (2005) 12 UC Davis Journal of International Law and Policy 157, 166; Kate Miles, *The Origins of International Investment Law: Empire, Environment and the Safeguarding of Capital* (CUP 2013) 78; Edward Guntrip, 'Self-determination and Foreign Direct Investment: Re-imagining Sovereignty in International Investment Law' (2016) 65 International and Comparative Law Quarterly 829, 839.
[41] Muthucumaraswamy Sornarajah, *The International Law on Foreign Investment* (CUP 2017) 26; Vandevelde, 'A Brief History of International Investment Agreements' (n 40) 166; Samuel Asante, 'International Law and Foreign Investment: A Reappraisal' (1988) 37 International and Comparative Law Quarterly 588, 594; Guntrip, 'Self-determination and Foreign Direct Investment' (n 40) 839.
[42] Rudolf Dolzer and Christophe Schreuer, *Principles of International Investment Law* (OUP 2012) 3.
[43] The test was espoused in *L F H Neer & Pauline Neer v United Mexican States* IV RIAA 60 (1951) as 'the treatment of an alien, in order to constitute an international delinquency, should amount to an outrage, to bad faith, to wilful neglect of duty, or to an insufficiency of governmental action so far short of international standards that every reasonable and impartial man would readily recognize its insufficiency' (at 61–62).

protection.⁴⁴ To further their position, newly decolonized states asserted the legality of their stance before the international community as part of the New International Economic Order in both the Sixth Special Session and Twenty-Ninth Regular Session of General Assembly of the United Nations.⁴⁵ Developed states, including those whose investors were the subject of the expropriations, rejected the legal foundations of the approach put forward by their former colonies.⁴⁶ In the wake of the large-scale expropriations, and the legal uncertainty generated by debates in the United Nations regarding the legal rights of foreign investors, treaties were introduced to provide legal certainty.⁴⁷ International investment agreements (IIAs) in the form of bilateral investment treaties (BITs) were drafted to provide for more comprehensive investment protection standards, whilst the ICSID Convention was drafted to create dispute resolution procedures specifically tailored to investment disputes. By drafting IIAs and the ICSID Convention, states, as actors, made decisions that amount to purposive actions, thereby potentially generating unanticipated consequences.

At the time of drafting the early BITs and the ICSID Convention, states generated the risk that unanticipated consequences might arise in the context of FDI by focusing on the foreseeable consequences of decolonization. Discussions regarding how FDI should be protected centred, for newly decolonized states, on issues of independence, sovereignty, and territorial control.⁴⁸ This position reflected the anticipated consequence that foreign investors from developed states would seek to continue to exploit the natural resources of their former colonies, and in effect, 24.12

---

⁴⁴ Francesco Francioni, 'Access to Justice, Denial of Justice and International Investment Law' (2009) 20 European Journal of International Law 729, 731; Antonio R Parra, *The History of ICSID* (OUP 2017) 16.

⁴⁵ This resulted in the following resolutions: Declaration on the Establishment of a New International Economic Order, UNGA Res 3201 (S-VI) (1 May 1974) UN Doc A/RES/S-6/3201 (Declaration); Programme of Action on the Establishment of a New International Economic Order, UNGA Res 3202 (S-VI) (1 May 1974) UN Doc A/RES/S-6/3202 (Programme); Charter of Economic Rights and Duties of States, UNGA Res 3281 (XXIX) (12 December 1974) UN Doc A/RES/29/3281 (Charter).

⁴⁶ For example, regarding the Sixth Special Session see Canada (United Nations, General Assembly Sixth Special Session Official Records, 2229th Plenary Meeting, 1974 (A/PV.2229) para 146); New Zealand (United Nations, General Assembly Sixth Special Session Official Records, 2230th Plenary Meeting, 1974 (A/PV.2230) para 69); Norway (United Nations, General Assembly Sixth Special Session Official Records, 2230th Plenary Meeting, 1974 (A/PV.2230) para 82) and the United Kingdom (United Nations, General Assembly Sixth Special Session Official Records, 2231st Plenary Meeting, 1974 (A/PV.2231) para 34). Regarding the 29th Regular Session of the General Assembly, see Finland (United Nations, General Assembly Twenty-Ninth Session Second Committee Economic and Financial Questions, Summary Records of Meetings, 1649th Meeting (A/C.2/SR.1649) para 18) and Italy (United Nations, General Assembly Twenty-Ninth Session Second Committee Economic and Financial Questions, Summary Records of Meetings, 1650th Meeting (A/C.2/SR.1650) para 10), United Nations, General Assembly Twenty-Ninth Session Second Committee Economic and Financial Questions, Summary Records of Meetings, 1650th Meeting (A/C.2/SR.1650) para 46).

⁴⁷ Miles (n 40) 84.

⁴⁸ Sornarajah, *The International Law on Foreign Investment* (n 41) 27.

deny them economic independence.[49] In contrast, for developed states, the protection of investors, and the economic benefits that flowed from relatively unrestricted access to natural resources, remained paramount. Thus, developed states sought to maintain unhindered access to the large quantities of natural resources located in former colonies.[50] As a result, discussions regarding IIL were framed by opposing political perspectives that directly correlated with the anticipated consequences of decolonization.

24.13 What states anticipated would arise from the decolonization process influenced what activities they deemed to amount to FDI. At the time that the ICSID Convention was proposed, the World Bank intended that ICSID would be able to resolve a variety of investment disputes, including sovereign debt disputes.[51] In 1960, prior to the establishment of ICSID, the World Bank resolved a sovereign debt dispute by facilitating a settlement between the City of Tokyo and French holders of city bonds who had been negatively impacted by the restructuring of Japan's debt following the Second World War.[52] This case was cited as an example of the type of dispute that could be addressed by ICSID.[53] Hence, states were initially aware that disputes over sovereign bonds could amount to investment disputes. However, debates between state delegates during the creation of ICSID focused on investments in the form of concessions that former colonial powers had granted to their nationals, as this form of investment had been the subject of widespread expropriations by newly independent states.[54] Therefore, the decolonization process altered the initial focus of what conduct would amount to an investment dispute for the purposes of ICSID. The emphasis states placed on concessions could also be attributed to the framing of ICSID as a forum to decide contractual disputes, rather than treaty-based claims.[55] As concession

---

[49] Developing states had pre-empted this during the New International Economic Order by relying on the concept of Permanent Sovereignty over Natural Resources (UNGA Resolution 1803 (XVII) (14 December 1962) UN Doc A/5217). See Declaration (n 45) art 4(e); Programme (n 45) s VIII; Charter (n 45) art 2(2).

[50] Celine Tan and Julio Foundez, 'Introduction' in Celine Tan and Julio Foundez (eds), *Natural Resources and Sustainable Development: International Economic Law Perspectives* (Edward Elgar Publishing 2017) 1–7, 1; Surya P Subedi, 'Reassessing and Redefining the Principle of Economic Sovereignty of States' in Duncan French (ed), *Global Justice and Sustainable Development* (Martinus Nijhoff Publishers 2010) 401–10, 405, n 1.

[51] Michael D Nolan, Frédéric G Sourgens, and Hugh Carlson, 'Leviathan on Life Support? Restructuring Sovereign Debt and International Investment Protection after *Abaclat*' in Karl P Sauvant (ed), *Yearbook of International Investment Law and Policy 2011–2012* (OUP 2013) 485–538, 495.

[52] ibid 495–96; Waibel, *Sovereign Defaults before International Courts and Tribunals* (n 1) 83.

[53] Nolan, Sourgens, and Carlson (n 51) 495.

[54] Kenneth Vandevelde, *US International Investment Agreements* (OUP 2009) 21; Surya P Subedi, *International Investment Law: Reconciling Policy and Principle* (Hart Publishing 2008) 114–15; Mavluda Sattorova, 'Defining Investment under the ICSID Convention and BITs: of Ordinary Meaning, Telos, and Beyond' (2012) 2 Asian Journal of International Law 267, 283.

[55] Sergio Puig, 'Emergence & Dynamism in International Organizations: ICSID, Investor-State Arbitration & International Investment Law' (2013) 44 Georgetown Journal of International Law 531, 541, n 30.

agreements clearly fell within the class of contractual disputes, many states are likely to have directed their attention to how ICSID would address this type of dispute. Therefore, the majority of states approached the negotiation of both BITs and the ICSID Convention based on what was immediately foreseeable in light of the investment environment at the time. Accordingly, the foundations of IIL were premised on what most states understood to amount to FDI in the context of decolonization.

2. The definition of 'investment'

24.14 The background of decolonization played a fundamental role in the drafting of the definition of investment in the ICSID Convention. Discussions surrounding what would amount to an investment for the purposes of ICSID arbitration evidence that states were keen to protect their immediately threatened interests. Throughout the negotiations, developed states sought to adopt an open-ended definition of investment to provide flexibility.[56] The definitions proposed by developed states were characterized by unlimited subject matter jurisdiction for ICSID arbitration to ensure that a wide range of disputes would be governed by ICSID.[57] A broad definition of investment would ensure that developed states' nationals would be able to access ITA. In contrast, other states comprised mainly, but not exclusively, of developing states wanted to formulate a definition that generated clear jurisdictional limits on ICSID arbitration.[58] In trying to delimit 'investment', definitions based on generalized characteristics of FDI were rejected by these states.[59] However, this group of states could not reach agreement on an alternative definition.[60] The compromise reached was that the ICSID Convention would not define the term investment.[61] Based on this outcome, Article 25(1) ICSID Convention provides that the jurisdiction of ICSID extends 'to any dispute of a legal character, arising directly out of an investment'.

---

[56] Julian Davis Mortenson, 'The Meaning of "investment": ICSID's *Travaux* and the Domain of International Investment Law' (2010) 51 Harvard International Law Journal 257, 280.

[57] For example, the United Kingdom thought that the definition of investment definition 'ought to be simple and should say as little as possible in the interests of devising a convention that could serve as a practical instrument for the settlement of as wide a range of disputes as possible'. International Centre for the Settlement of Investment Disputes, *History of the ICSID Convention: Volume II-1* (International Centre for the Settlement of Investment Disputes 2009) 450.

[58] Mortenson (n 56) 284.

[59] ibid 286, 287–89.

[60] Tarcisio Gazzini, *Interpretation of International Investment Treaties* (Hart Publishing 2016) 114; Mortenson (n 56) 287–88.

[61] Report of the Executive Directors on the Convention on the Settlement of Investment Disputes Between States and Nationals of Other States, para 27 <http://icsidfiles.worldbank.org/icsid/ICSID/StaticFiles/basicdoc/partB.htm> accessed 21 September 2018; Gazzini (n 60) 114; Mortenson (n 56) 290–91; Rudolf Dolzer, 'The Notion of Investment in Recent Practice' in Steve Charnovitz, Debra P Steger, and Pert Van den Bossche (eds), *Law in the Service of Human Dignity: Essays in Honour of Florentino Feliciano* (CUP 2005) 261–75, 266.

24.15 To delimit the jurisdiction of ICSID arbitration, states could impute 'investment' with content in two ways. First, in accordance with Article 25(4) ICSID Convention, states are permitted to notify other states of any subject matter that they did not consider to be within the jurisdiction of ICSID. Although this procedure puts other states on notice, its legal impact may be restricted because the effect of a notification on the jurisdiction of an ICSID arbitral tribunal remains unclear.[62] Second, states could limit the scope of the term 'investment' more definitively in their BITs, which sets out the state's agreement to arbitrate. By restricting the terms of their consent to ICSID arbitration in their BITs,[63] states could limit the class of disputes permitted to go to ICSID arbitration. Thus, whilst Article 25(1) ICSID sets out the jurisdictional limits of ICSID in general terms, states can specifically limit what amounts to an investment in their BITs, and in so doing, restrict the jurisdiction of an ICSID arbitral tribunal.

24.16 Whilst reaching a suitable compromise for the purposes of establishing ICSID arbitration, leaving investment undefined in the ICSID Convention created the potential for unanticipated consequences to arise. At this time, many states understood investment to primarily involve concession contracts based on their experience of decolonization. However, this understanding was not reflected in the wide definitions of investment subsequently adopted in IIAs. Developed states initiated most IIA negotiations based on model treaties,[64] which captured a variety of economic activity. As a result, many states' subjective understandings of what constituted an investment, which would limit the jurisdiction of all forms of ITA, was not mirrored by the actual terms used in IIAs. Therefore, most states focused on the foreseeable consequences of their actions and failed to take into account how other commercial activities could fall within either definition of investment. A few states have made express reference to sovereign debt in definitions of investment contained in their IIAs, indicating that they consented to the use of ITA to resolve sovereign debt disputes. However, those states that did not are bound by IIAs that are either silent on this point, or merely refer to terms such as 'bonds' or 'financial obligations'. It is the latter group of IIAs that have generated debate over whether sovereign debt amounts to an investment.

3. Sovereign debt as an investment

24.17 Broadly understood, sovereign debt is a type of government borrowing that provides additional liquidity to state economies. In return for the injection of capital, states pay interest on the loan at a pre-determined interest rate and make a

---

[62] Mortenson (n 56) 294–95; see Tony Cole and Kumar Vaksha, 'Power-conferring Treaties: the Meaning of "Investment" in the ICSID Convention' (2011) 24 Leiden Journal of International Law 305, 318–22.
[63] Mortenson (n 56) 293.
[64] Jeswald Salacuse, *The Law of Investment Treaties* (OUP 2009) 92.

repayment of capital when the debt matures.[65] Sovereign debt instruments are contractual in nature[66] (in most jurisdictions) and since the late 1980s, have been readily transferrable on the secondary market.[67] Sovereign debt can be external (paid in a foreign currency, governed by foreign law and under the jurisdiction of foreign courts) or domestic (paid in the domestic currency, governed by domestic law and under the jurisdiction of domestic courts).[68] Based on these characteristics, sovereign debt may more accurately be described as a portfolio investment rather than FDI.[69]

24.18 Although the attributes of sovereign debt may be indicative of how it functions, whether or not it amounts to an investment for the purposes of ITA is a matter of treaty interpretation. Investment tribunals have recognized the customary status of the rules of treaty interpretation[70] (which are reflected in Articles 31–33 VCLT).[71] These principles apply to the interpretation of IIAs and provide a coherent and structured means by which to ascertain the meaning of the provisions set out in the applicable IIA.[72] When interpreting the term 'investment' in IIL, the treaty interpreter must examine the definition section of the applicable IIA.

---

[65] Felipe Suescun de Roa, 'Investor-State Arbitration in Sovereign Debt Restructuring: the Role of Holdouts' (2013) 30 Journal of International Arbitration 131, 134–35; Michael Waibel, 'Opening Pandora's Box: Sovereign Bonds in International Arbitration' (2007) 101 American Journal of International Law 711, 719.

[66] As to the significance of sovereign debt's contractual nature, see Mitu Gulati, Christoph Trebesch, and Jeromin Zettelmeyer, 'International Finance and Sovereign Debt' in Francesco Parisi (ed), *The Oxford Handbook on Law and Economics: Volume 3: Public Law and Institutions* (OUP 2017) 482–500.

[67] In 1989, under the Brady Plan, banks were permitted to transfer bad debt in the form of sovereign bonds, which were transferable on the secondary market.

[68] International Law Association, Sovereign Insolvency Study Group, 'State Insolvency: Options for the Way Forward' Interim Report Presented at the Hague Conference 2010, 9 <http://www.ila-hq.org/index.php/study-groups?study-groupsID=44> accessed 21 September 2018.

[69] See Muthucumaraswamy Sornarajah, 'Portfolio Investments and the Definition of Investment' (2009) 24 ICSID Review—Foreign Investment Law Journal 516.

[70] See eg *Asian Agricultural Products LTD (AAPL) v Republic of Sri Lanka*, ICSID Case No ARB/87/3, Final Award (27 June 1990) para 38; *Salini Costruttori SPA and Italstrade SPA v Kingdom of Morocco*, ICSID Case No ARB/00/4, Decision on Jurisdiction (16 July 2001) para 75; *Muhammet Çap & Sehil Insaat Endustri ve Ticaret Ltd. Sti v Turkmenistan*, ICSID Case No ARB/12/6, Decision on Jurisdiction (13 February 2015) para 93.

[71] See Reports of the Commission to the General Assembly, *Yearbook of International Law Commission Volume 2 1966* (United Nations 1967) 187–274, 218–19. This view has been adopted by investment tribunals. See *Bureau Veritas, Inspection, Valuation, Assessment and Control, BIVAC BV v Republic of Paraguay*, ICSID Case No ARB/07/9, Decision on Jurisdiction (29 May 2009) para 59; *Romak SA v Republic of Uzbekistan*, UNCITRAL, Award (26 November 2009) para 169.

[72] J Romesh Weeramantry, *Treaty Interpretation in Investment Arbitration* (OUP 2012) 38; Michael Waibel, 'International Investment Law and Treaty Interpretation' in Rainer Hofmann and Christian Tams (eds), *International Investment Law and General International Law—From Clinical Isolation to Systemic Integration?* (Nomos 2011) 29–30; Andrea Saldarriaga, 'Investment Awards and the Rules of Interpretation in the Vienna Convention: Making Room for Improvement' (2013) 28 ICSID Review—Foreign Investment Law Journal 197, 197.

When the parties select ICSID arbitration, the treaty interpreter must additionally consider Article 25 ICSID Convention.

24.19 Investment is usually defined in the applicable IIA by referring to a non-exhaustive, asset-based list of legal interests that are indicative of an investment.[73] These definitions are vague and open to interpretation. The non-inclusion of an asset within the definition does not preclude it from being an investment.[74] Consequently, the nature of sovereign debt must be interpreted in light of whether it meets the attributes of the definition of investment set out in the applicable BIT.[75] Given that all treaty drafting is subject to linguistic uncertainty,[76] BIT definitions of investment that include generic terms such as 'bonds' and 'financial obligations' could generate arguments that, by analogy, sovereign debt can be classified as an investment. However, given their focus on decolonization, many states intended IIAs to protect FDI,[77] rather than portfolio investments. Therefore, sovereign debt was not what these states originally contemplated when drafting definitions of investment in their IIAs. Although states repeatedly adopted broad definitions of investment in their IIAs, it was not clear that these definitions could encompass sovereign debt until recent ITA awards addressing sovereign debt disputes. Given this, the potential inclusion of sovereign debt within asset-based definitions of investments in BITs that do not explicitly refer to sovereign bonds is an unanticipated consequence for many states, despite the existence of the Tokyo bonds dispute and the inclusion of more general indicators such as 'bonds' and 'financial obligations' within these definitions. The potential inclusion of sovereign debt within the definition of investment is particularly problematic if the parties do not select ICSID arbitration. This is because, if the ICSID Convention is not applicable, the definition of investment in the IIA is determinative of whether the arbitral tribunal has subject-matter jurisdiction.

24.20 Should the disputing parties select ICSID arbitration, when the tribunal determines if it has subject-matter jurisdiction, it must take into account the term 'investment' in Article 25(1) ICSID Convention alongside the definition in the applicable IIA. The failure of states to define the term investment in Article 25(1)

---

[73] Gazzini (n 60) 110; Ostřanský (n 1) 50; Dolzer (n 61) 263–64; Barton Legum and Caline Mouawad, 'The Meaning of "Investment" in the ICSID Convention' in Pieter H F Bekker, Rudolf Dolzer, and Michael Waibel (eds), *Making Transnational Law Work in the Global Economy* (CUP, 2010) 326–56, 331.

[74] See eg *Azurix Corp v Argentine Republic*, ICSID Case No. ARB/01/12, Award on Jurisdiction (8 December 2003) para 63; *Mytilineos Holdings SA v The State Union of Serbia & Montenegro and Republic of Serbia*, UNCITRAL, Partial Award on Jurisdiction (8 September 2006) paras 101–06; *Romak* (n 71) paras 180, 188.

[75] Gazzini (n 60) 113.

[76] See Crawford, *Chance, Order, Change: The Course of International Law* (n 25) 150–57; Kammerhofer (n 25) 119.

[77] Vandevelde, *US International Investment Agreements* (n 54) 21; Subedi, *International Investment Law: Reconciling Policy and Principle* (n 54) 114–15; Sattorova (n 54) 283.

ICSID Convention has also given rise to the unanticipated consequence for many states that sovereign debt could be understood to fall within the jurisdiction of ICSID. The inability of the parties to the ICSID Convention to define investment requires that investment tribunals confer it with meaning.[78] As a result, to try and give content to 'investment', both objective and subjective interpretative tools have been used.[79] For ICSID arbitrations, definitions of investment in BITs initially guided investment tribunals when determining whether they had jurisdiction over a claim.[80] Thus, the interpretation given to the definition of investment in the BIT (which mirrors the subjective intention of the state parties) determines whether the tribunal possessed the jurisdiction to hear the claim.[81] This practice continues. Therefore, if the definition of investment in a BIT is interpreted to encompass sovereign debt, even though it is not a form of FDI, this will satisfy the jurisdictional requirements of Article 25(1) ICSID Convention. However, an alternative approach has developed.

24.21 To provide greater clarification regarding what conduct amounts to an investment, some ICSID arbitral tribunals sought to identify objective characteristics associated with an investment. The *Salini v Kingdom of Morocco* tribunal relied on those characteristics identified in previous decisions and academic commentary to formulate a test to determine whether an activity amounted to an investment.[82] Subject to some variations,[83] the *Salini* test has been adopted within a stream of ITA jurisprudence.[84] The elements of the test include that an investment must: involve a contribution of money or assets; exist over a certain duration of time; contribute to the economic development of the host state; and involve the foreign investor participating in the risks of the transaction (usually through the management of the investment).[85] A further element is often added

---

[78] Tony Cole, *The Structure of Investment Arbitration* (Routledge 2013) 21.
[79] Gazzini (n 60) 114; Legum and Mouawad (n 73) 329; Brigitte Stern, 'The Contours of the Notion of Protected Investment' (2009) 24 ICSID Review—Foreign Investment Law Journal 534, 535; Laurens JE Timmer, 'The Meaning of "Investment" as a Requirement for Jurisdiction Ratione Materiae of the ICSID Centre' (2012) 29 Journal of International Arbitration 363, 365; cf Emmanuel Gaillard, 'Identify or Define? Reflections on the Evolution of the Concept of Investment in ICSID Practice' in Christina Binder, Ursula Kriebaum, August Reinisch, and Stephan Wittich (eds), *International Investment Law for the 21st Century: Essays in Honour of Christoph Schreuer* (OUP 2009) 403–16 (who classifies these approaches as the deductive and intuitive methods).
[80] Mortenson (n 56) 269–70.
[81] Gazzini (n 60) 114–15; Legum and Mouawad (n 73) 330–31; Stern (n 79) 538.
[82] Although this task had been undertaken by the *Fedax* tribunal earlier. *Salini* (n 70) para 52.
[83] Gazzini (n 60) 120; Stern (n 79) 536; Timmer (n 79) 367.
[84] See eg *Bayindir Insaat Turizm Ticaret Ve Sanayi AS v Islamic Republic of Pakistan*, ICSID Case No ARB/03/29, Decision on Jurisdiction (14 November 2005) paras 130–38; *Saipem SpA v People's Republic of Bangladesh*, ICSID Case No. ARB/05/07, Decision on Jurisdiction and Recommendation on Provisional Measures (21 March 2007) para 99; *Grupo Francisco Hernando Contreras SL v Republic of Equatorial Guinea*, ICSID Case No. ARB(AF)/12/2, Award on Jurisdiction (5 December 2015) paras 139–40.
[85] *Salini* (n 70) para 52.

requiring a territorial nexus between the investment and the host state.[86] If an investment is established under the *Salini* test, the subjective definition of the investment in the BIT is then considered to determine the limits of party consent. Although the use of the *Salini* test may be problematic in terms of the drafting history of Article 25 ICSID (similar characteristics were discussed and rejected by the drafters)[87] these characteristics of FDI were likely to have been contemplated by states at the time they sought to define an investment for the purposes of the ICSID Convention.

24.22 Sovereign debt is less likely to align with the characteristics identified in the *Salini* test as financial obligations are akin to portfolio investments. In particular, academics have suggested that sovereign debt fails to meet the *Salini* test on two fundamental bases. First, it has been argued that sovereign debt does not clearly possess a territorial nexus to the host state,[88] and, second, if recently purchased, the investor is unlikely to be able to claim that is a long-term investment.[89] The use of the *Salini* test to identify whether an investment exists is controversial.[90] Whether the test is accepted as appropriate or otherwise, it highlights the distinction that can be drawn between the characteristics of an investment understood by many states based on their experiences in the 1960s and 1970s, that are mirrored in the *Salini* test, and sovereign debt instruments. The differences reinforce that the potential inclusion of sovereign debt within the term 'investment' is an unanticipated consequence of states leaving investment undefined in the ICSID Convention.

4. Excluding sovereign debt from the definition of investment

24.23 Many states did not turn their full attention to whether portfolio investments such as sovereign debt fell within the definition of investment in IIAs or the ICSID Convention when creating the IIL regime. However, depending on the approach taken by the treaty interpreter, sovereign debt could be included in the definition of investment due to the inclusion of broadly constructed asset lists in IIAs. Therefore, it is necessary to examine how states might definitively exclude the possibility that sovereign debt constitutes an investment. The drafting history of Article 25 ICSID Convention illustrates that states are able to control the definition of investment by delimiting its scope. One means of limiting the definition of investment is by reference to Article 25(4) ICSID

---

[86] Waibel, 'Opening Pandora's Box: Sovereign Bonds in International Arbitration' (n 65) 723.
[87] Mortenson (n 56) 280–81.
[88] See Ostřanský (n 1) 44–48; Waibel, 'Opening Pandora's Box: Sovereign Bonds in International Arbitration' (n 65) 727; Caroline Kleiner and Francesco Costamagna, 'Territoriality in Investment Arbitration: the Case of Financial Instruments' (2018) 9 Journal of International Dispute Settlement 315.
[89] Sornarajah, 'Portfolio Investments and the Definition of Investment' (n 69) 519.
[90] Sattorova (n 54) 269.

Convention, but this method may not be determinative, as it can be understood as being indicative, rather than legally binding.[91] Further, using this mechanism only applies to ICSID arbitrations. On this basis, it is better for states to control how investment is understood through the terms of consent to investment arbitration offered in BITs.[92] This approach enables states to exclude sovereign debt disputes from all forms of investment arbitration. Hence, states that want to exclude investment claims related to sovereign debt disputes should expressly state this in their IIAs and BITs. Some states already follow this practice. For example, recent Colombian IIAs provide that investment does not include 'public debt operations'[93] and does not extend investment protections to state 'bonds, debentures, loans and other forms of debt'.[94] Other states have used similar tactics.[95] This practice is available to all states. It can either be implemented when new IIAs are drafted, or could potentially form the basis of joint interpretations between the contracting states to an existing IIA.[96] Both processes will inform the interpretation of the IIA and delimit the scope of how investment can be interpreted.[97] By excluding sovereign debt from the definition of investment in an IIA, and delimiting the terms of state consent to ITA, states can address the unanticipated consequence of sovereign debt being included in the definition of investment.

---

[91] Mortenson (n 56) 294–95; see Cole and Vaksha (n 62) 318–22.

[92] Karen Halverson Cross, 'Sovereign Debt' in Rosa M Lastra and Lee Buchheit (eds), *Sovereign Debt Management* (OUP 2014) 151–73, 166.

[93] See eg Agreement for the Promotion and Protection of Investments between the Republic of Colombia and the Republic of India BIT (entered into force 2 July 2012), art 1(2.1) and the Bilateral Agreement for the Promotion and Protection of Investments between the Government of the United Kingdom of Great Britain and Northern Ireland and the Republic of Colombia (entered into force 17 March 2010), art 1(2)(b)(i).

[94] See eg Agreement between the Government of the Republic of Peru and the Government of the Republic of Colombia on the Promotion and Reciprocal Protection of Investments (entered into force 30 December 2007), art 42.

[95] See eg Mexico (eg Agreement between the Government of the Republic of France and the Government of the United Mexican States on the Reciprocal Promotion and Protection of Investments (entered into force 12 October 2000), art 1(1)) and Peru (eg Agreement between Japan and the Republic of Peru for the Promotion, Protection and Liberalisation of Investment (entered into force 10 December 2009), art 1(a)(c)).

[96] See Anthea Roberts, 'Power and Persuasion in Investment Treaty Interpretation: the Dual Role of States' (2010) 104 American Journal of International Law 179–225; David Gaukrodger, 'The Legal Framework Applicable to Joint Interpretive Agreements of Investment Treaties' OECD Working Papers on International Investment, 2016/01 (OECD Publishing 2016) <http://dx.doi.org/10.1787/5jm3xgt6f29w-en> accessed 21 September 2018; Geoffrey Gertz and Taylor St John, 'State Interpretations of Investment Treaties: Feasible Strategies for Developing Countries' Global Economic Governance and Blavatnik School of Government Policy Brief June 2015 <http://www.geg-test.nsms.ox.ac.uk/policy-brief-state-interpretations-investment-treaties-feasible-strategies-developing-countries> accessed 21 September 2018. This option could also be available under ICSID Convention (n 2) art 64. See Cole and Vaksha (n 62) 322–26.

[97] See Lise Johnson and Merim Razbaeva, 'State control over interpretation of investment treaties' (2014) <http://ccsi.columbia.edu/files/2014/04/State_control_over_treaty_interpretation_FINAL-April-5_2014.pdf> accessed 21 September 2018.

5. Preliminary conclusions

24.24 In summary, whether sovereign debt amounts to an investment depends on the definition of 'investment'. Given the backdrop of decolonization, states were not able to agree on a definition for the purposes of the ICSID Convention, preferring to leave this decision to states when consenting to investment arbitration. The process of decolonization also meant that states were focused on concessions as a form of investment and failed to anticipate that portfolio investments, such as sovereign debt, might fall within the definition of investment. The uncertainty over the term 'investment' has resulted in two unanticipated consequences for states. First, BITs that include asset-based lists to define investment have the potential to include portfolio investments. Numerous states did not foresee this possibility. Further, should the term investment include portfolio investments, sovereign debt disputes can fall within the jurisdiction of ICSID arbitration given the generic nature of the term 'investment' in the ICSID Convention. Consequently, sovereign debt disputes are capable of falling within the jurisdiction of all forms of ITA. Therefore, if states wish to avoid using ITA as a forum to resolve sovereign debt disputes, states must expressly exclude sovereign debt from the scope of their BITs. If this approach is not taken, the term investment might be interpreted to encompass sovereign debts even though this outcome was not foreseeable to many states at the time the modern IIL regime was created.

C. Sovereign Debt Disputes in Investment Treaty Arbitration

24.25 Whilst the treaty drafting process was conducted by states with a view to protecting FDI, it is how decision-makers interpret the term 'investment' that is decisive as to whether sovereign debt disputes fall within the jurisdiction of ITA. As a result, the linguistic uncertainty surrounding the term 'investment' that was generated by states becomes subject to the purposive actions of a new set of actors—decision-makers. In the case of ITA, these decision-makers are investment arbitrators.

1. Investment arbitrators as epistemic and interpretative communities

24.26 Given that a small number of elite investment arbitrators conduct the majority of investment arbitrations,[98] investment arbitrators are often recognized as being part of an epistemic community.[99] Epistemic communities consist of individuals with

---

[98] See Sergio Puig, 'Social Capital in the Arbitration Market' (2014) 25 European Journal of International Law 387.
[99] See Yackee (n 29) 404–06.

a specific expertise in a field combined with 'an authoritative claim to policy-relevant knowledge'.[100] Members of epistemic communities seek to achieve common goals based on their training in a particular field, which is reinforced by being surrounded by like-minded individuals and forming part of a profession with shared understandings.[101] Although traditionally linked to policy formation,[102] the idea of epistemic communities has been applied to international law.[103] In this context, epistemic communities are said to have resulted from the fragmentation of international law[104] because the creation of regimes within public international law has resulted in actors with expertise in specialist areas. Actors within each sub-field of international law seek to promote the regime's specific interests and goals.[105] Thus, decision-makers within each regime prioritize the objectives of their regimes when they make decisions,[106] often to the exclusion of other factors.[107] Although investment arbitrators are subject to the professional standards of independence and impartiality,[108] the training of an investment arbitrator, and the environment in which they function, may influence what they understand the role of IIL to be, and based on this, how ITA should function.[109] These perspectives may dominate the decision-making process to the detriment of other factors, including the application of other sub-fields of international law that pursue different agendas.[110] The like-mindedness of members of an epistemic community will result in a certain degree of collective decision-making. However, this is not to suggest that investment arbitrators are homogenous in their outlook. Investment arbitrators

---

[100] Haas, 'Introduction: Epistemic Communities and International Policy Coordination' (n 30) 3.
[101] ibid.
[102] See Peter M Haas, 'International Environmental Law: Epistemic Communities' in Daniel Bodansky, Jutta Brunnée, and Ellen Hey (eds), *The Oxford Handbook on International Environmental Law* (OUP 2007) 791–806, 795 (the idea of an epistemic community stems from the transfer of scientific knowledge, but it can apply to economists and engineers).
[103] See D'Aspremont (n 31); David J Galbreath and Joanne McEvoy, 'How Epistemic Communities Drive International Regimes: the Case of Minority Rights in Europe' (2013) 35 Journal of European Integration 169, 170; Lisa Toohey, 'Accession as Dialogue: Epistemic Communities and the World Trade Organization' (2014) 27 Leiden Journal of International Law 397, 407.
[104] Koskenniemi (n 31) 4.
[105] ibid 6.
[106] ibid 7–8.
[107] ibid. See Haas, 'Introduction: Epistemic Communities and International Policy Coordination' (n 30) 20.
[108] See Loretta Malintoppi, 'Independence, Impartiality, and Duty of Disclosure of Arbitrators' in Peter Muchlinski, Federico Ortino, and Christoph Schreuer (eds), *The Oxford Handbook of International Investment Law* (OUP 2008) 789–829.
[109] See D'Aspremont (n 31) 11; Puig, 'Social Capital in the Arbitration Market' (n 98) 422; Michael Waibel and Yanhui Wu, 'Are Arbitrators Political? Evidence from International Investment Arbitration' (2017) <http://www.bcf.usc.edu/~yanhuiwu/arbitrator.pdf> accessed 21 September 2018.
[110] See Moshe Hirsch, *Invitation to the Sociology of International Law* (OUP 2015) 129–56.

are usually experienced legal practitioners[111] that have specialized in international commercial arbitration or public international law.[112] Therefore, within this epistemic community, the goals that are being promoted may shift between those that prioritize commercial considerations and those that emphasize IIL's public international law aspects.[113] However, epistemic communities tend to generate a dominant approach.[114] Hence, whether individual arbitrators view sovereign debt disputes as capable of falling within the jurisdiction of ITA may depend on their professional outlook, which may be influenced by the values that are present within the epistemic community.

24.27 Decision-makers in IIL exercise their expertise and authority by resolving disputes, which require that they conduct treaty interpretation.[115] As part of an epistemic community, it is highly likely that an investment arbitrator's viewpoint will inform the interpretations given to key terms of IIAs and the ICSID Convention, such as 'investment'. This process additionally creates an interpretative community. An interpretative community constrains the possibility of certain interpretations as it is predisposed to understandings that are mutually acceptable to members of that community.[116] What influences generate the limits of acceptable interpretations remains contentious.[117] Nonetheless, it is possible that how investment arbitrators define investment will be influenced by whether they view IIL as performing a commercial function, or whether IIL is situated in public international law. Merton identifies this type of value-based decision-making as being a contributing factor to the creation of unanticipated consequences.[118] Unanticipated consequences arise because the actor (in this case the decision-maker) does not take into account the further consequences of their action because it aligns with the actor's fundamental values.[119] Consequently, investment arbitrators from both

---

[111] Karl-Heinz Böckstiegel, 'Commercial and Investment Arbitration: How Different are they Today? The Lalive Lecture 2012' (2012) 28 Arbitration International 577, 581–83.

[112] ibid.

[113] These are not definitive classifications, but indicative identifiers of what aspects of international investment law investment arbitrators prioritize within the regime. See Stephan W Schill, 'Crafting the International Economic Order: the Public Function of Investment Treaty Arbitration and its Significance for the Role of the Arbitrator' (2010) 23 Leiden Journal of International Law 401; Alex Mills, 'Antinomies of Public and Private at the Foundations of international Investment Law and Arbitration' (2011) 14 Journal of International Economic Law 469.

[114] See Toohey (n 103) 407.

[115] Andreas Kulick, 'Reassertion of Control: an Introduction' in Andreas Kulick (ed), *Reassertion of Control over the Investment Treaty Regime* (CUP 2017) 3–29, 19.

[116] D'Aspremont (n 31) 18; Johnstone (n 29) 387. As to how this relates to constructivism, see Peter M Haas, 'Ideas, Experts and Governance' in Monika Ambrus, Karin Arts, Ellen Hey, and Helena Raulus (eds), in The Role of 'Experts' in *International and European Decision-Making Processes: Advisors, Decision Makers or Irrelevant Actors?* (CUP 2014) 19–43.

[117] See Owen Fiss, 'Objectivity and Interpretation' (1982) 34 Stanford Law Review 739; Stanley Fish, 'Fish v Fiss' (1984) 36 Stanford Law Review 1325; Owen Fiss, 'The Jurisprudence [?] of Stanley Fish' 1985 80 ADE Bulletin 1.

[118] Merton (n 12) 903–04.

[119] ibid.

2. Investment awards addressing sovereign debt

The investment awards that address whether sovereign debt falls within the jurisdiction of ITA support the view that investment arbitrators undertake value-based decision-making. Two approaches can be discerned in the jurisprudence that align with the professional values associated with investment arbitrators. One approach views sovereign debt primarily as a form of contractual obligation, which is associated with an understanding that portfolio investments can constitute an investment for the purposes of IIL. The other perspective distinguishes sovereign debt from FDI and reflects a public international law view that prioritizes state consent over an expansive remit for IIL.

24.28

The view that sovereign debt is a contractual obligation is evident in a series of investment awards stemming from the Argentinian financial crisis of 2001–2002: *Abaclat v Argentina*,[120] *Ambiente Ufficio v Argentina*,[121] and *Alemanni v Argentina*.[122] Each claim was based on the same factual scenario and raised similar legal issues. The claims were made by three separate groups of Italian creditors who held sovereign bonds issued in a foreign currency by Argentina during the preceding decade that they had purchased through secondary market transactions. They argued that Argentina's attempts to amend the terms of the sovereign bonds to restructure its debt[123] violated the Italy–Argentina BIT.[124] The analysis of these awards is limited to those points of law that relate to whether portfolio investments should be included in the definition of investment. That is, how investment should be defined for the purposes of Article 25(1) ICSID Convention and whether the investment needs to be in the physical territory of the host state. The additional issue of whether the claims were treaty or contract based will also be taken into account.

24.29

The first issue for the tribunal was whether investment in Article 25(1) ICSID Convention should be interpreted subjectively, relying the definition of investment in the BIT, or with reference to objective criteria (the *Salini* test). When addressing the relationship between Article 25 ICSID Convention and the Argentina–Italy BIT, the arbitrators in the majority in each tribunal minimized

24.30

---

[120] *Abaclat* (n 4).
[121] *Ambiente* (n 4).
[122] *Alemanni* (n 4).
[123] Argentina made an exchanges offer in 2005 before passing Law 26,017 in 2005 that prevented the government from re-opening the exchange process or entering into other exchange transactions. A further exchange offer was made in 2010.
[124] Fra La Repubblica Italiana e La Repubblica Argentina Sulla Promozione e Protezione degli Investimenti (entered into force 14 October 1993).

the importance of Article 25(1) ICSID Convention as a delimiting factor on the jurisdiction of the tribunal.[125] Instead, each tribunal emphasized the definition of investment in the Argentina–Italy BIT. The tribunals referred to Article 1(1)(c) of the Argentina–Italy BIT that defines investment as encompassing '*obbligazioni*', which is Italian for 'bonds'. All three tribunals used principles of treaty interpretation to find that the term 'obbligazioni' includes sovereign bonds.[126] The tribunal in *Ambiente* went further to elaborate on the role, and interpretation, of Article 25(1) ICSID Convention. The tribunal rejected the application of the *Salini* criteria as a strict means of finding jurisdiction, preferring to use the characteristics set out in the *Salini* test as indicators of an investment, together with the definition of investment in the BIT.[127] This finding was despite Argentina's argument that the term investment in Article 25(1) ICSID Convention possessed an objective meaning.[128] Contrary to Argentina's submissions, the tribunal considered that the meaning of investment in the ICSID Convention was capable of evolving to encompass 'non-standard and atypical investments'.[129] By minimizing the significance of the *Salini* test, the investment arbitrators favoured a more expansive definition of investment that was capable of capturing portfolio investments. This type of interpretation increases the chances that sovereign debt would fall within the jurisdiction of the tribunal.

24.31 Article 1(1) of the Argentina–Italy BIT requires that the investment be in the territory of the host state. This provision mirrors one of the key attributes of FDI identified in early definitions of investment. At issue was whether there was a sufficient territorial nexus between the host state and the creditor given that the debt instruments had been traded on the secondary market. The majority in *Abaclat* held that, despite the sovereign bonds being purchased on the secondary market, a territorial connection was established because, for financial instruments to be present in the territory, the funds only have to be made available to the host state.[130] The majority justified this stance by understanding that the issuance of bonds, which are sold on the primary market, were always intended to be divided into smaller securities for sale on the secondary market.[131] Whilst the bonds and securities are technically different, the tribunal viewed this as one economic process,[132] which although involving two different forms of payment from different parties, conferred Argentina with the ultimate benefit of receiving the funds.[133] A similar logic underpinned the reasoning in *Ambiente*, where the majority established a

---

[125] *Abaclat* (n 4) paras 362–64; *Ambiente* (n 4) paras 470–71; *Alemanni* (n 4) para 296.
[126] *Abaclat* (n 4) para 352–56; *Ambiente* (n 4) paras 490–95; *Alemanni* (n 4) para 296.
[127] *Ambiente* (n 4) paras 475–81.
[128] ibid paras 364–71.
[129] ibid para 481.
[130] *Abaclat* (n 4) para 374.
[131] ibid para 358.
[132] ibid paras 358–59.
[133] ibid paras 377–78.

territorial link to Argentina based on the capital being used by Argentina to assist with its economic development.[134] The approach in *Alemanni* differed, as it postponed a final determination to the merits stage.[135] The position taken by the majority investment arbitrators in the *Abaclat* and *Ambiente* awards minimized the need for a territorial connection and did not require the physical presence of the investment in the territory of the host state.[136] This differs to what states anticipated when the modern IIL regime was created and reflects an understanding that the jurisdiction of ITA can extend beyond traditional forms of FDI to portfolio investments.

To establish that the claims were treaty-based rather than purely contractual in nature, each tribunal emphasized that the restructuring of the bonds were sovereign acts of Argentina. It was held in *Abaclat* that the claim was not purely contractual in nature on the basis that the restructuring was based on legislation, which 'derives from Argentina's exercise of sovereign power'.[137] A similar view was taken in *Ambiente*. The tribunal emphasized that it was Argentina's sovereign 'prerogatives when restructuring its debt' that was at issue.[138] Whilst the tribunal acknowledged that Argentina could not alter the law governing the debt instruments, it could influence the entitlements of the claimants within its territory.[139] This view was mirrored in *Alemanni*.[140] Each tribunal characterized sovereign debt as contractual for the purposes of the definition of investment, but emphasized the sovereign element when determining the nature of the claim. Again, this aspect of the awards reflects the perspective of the investment arbitrators that the scope of IIL is capable of being extended to address sovereign acts that affect portfolio investments. 24.32

The approach taken by the majority in these awards evidences how these investment arbitrators understand IIL to function, which reflects the values that dominate their epistemic community. When these investment arbitrators consider the nature of sovereign debt, and how state conduct affects sovereign debt instruments, it is clear that they view IIL as having a wide scope. The creation of an expansive interpretation of investment that includes both portfolio investments and FDI is indicative of how epistemic and interpretative communities' function. Actors within an epistemic community in international law seek to promote and apply the aims of their specific legal regime across a wide range of subject matter. This is achieved by interpreting key components of the regime in a manner that reinforces the shared understandings of that community. The investment arbitrators 24.33

---

[134] *Ambiente* (n 4) para 508.
[135] *Alemanni* (n 4) para 297.
[136] See Kleiner and Costamagna (n 88).
[137] *Abaclat* (n 4) para 323.
[138] *Ambiente* (n 4) para 543.
[139] ibid para 547.
[140] *Alemanni* (n 4) para 300.

in the majority in these awards sought to include portfolio investments within the scope of investment, despite numerous states believing that IIL was limited to FDI. They extended the original application of IIL beyond FDI by incorporating sovereign debt into the definition of the term 'investment' based on the existence of the generic term '*obbligazioni*'. This reasoning suggests that these investment arbitrators support a commercial view of the term investment, which enables IIL to apply to any commercial conduct. By adopting this stance, each tribunal found that it possessed subject-matter jurisdiction to hear the claim.

24.34 The approach just outlined can be contrasted to the view of IIL that more closely reflects how numerous states understood IIL to operate during the 1960s and 1970s. Whilst the IIA in these awards was concluded during the 1990s, it defined investment by reference to an asset-based list that continued to reflect the linguistic uncertainty that was prevalent when early BITs were drafted. Given the existence of uncertainty, investment arbitrators are also able to interpret this IIA by emphasizing the significance of state consent, as evidenced in the dissenting awards in *Abaclat* and *Ambiente*. In his dissenting award in *Abaclat*,[141] Professor Abi-Saab emphasized that the term investment in Article 25(1) ICSID Convention 'is not infinitely elastic'.[142] Whilst the definition of investment in Article 1(1) of the Argentina–Italy BIT was capable of including sovereign debt,[143] his opinion was that portfolio investment should not automatically be included within the jurisdiction of ICSID given that ITA was intended to protect FDI.[144] He further held that security entitlements do not satisfy the territorial nexus by reference to the characteristics of the investment.[145] In relation to both points, Professor Abi-Saab focused on what Argentina had explicitly consented to in these treaties. Arbitrator Bernárdez in the *Ambiente* decision[146] disagreed with the majority arbitrators' understanding of Article 25(1) ICSID Convention and the term '*obbligazioni*' in Article 1(1)(c) of the Argentina–Italy BIT. He critiqued the treaty interpretation process applied by the majority and concluded that 'investment' in Article 25(1) ICSID Convention has an objective meaning.[147] Having considered how the majority investment arbitrators had interpreted Article 1(1)(c) of the Argentina–Italy BIT, he asserted that the majority had created a new definition of investment, rather than adhering to the definition in the BIT.[148] In taking these positions, both

---

[141] *Abaclat v Argentina*, ICSID Case No ARB/07/5, Dissenting Opinion, Georges Abi-Saab (28 October 2011).
[142] ibid para 46.
[143] ibid para 68.
[144] ibid paras 53–57.
[145] ibid paras 73–119.
[146] *Ambiente Ufficio v Argentina*, (ICSID Case No ARB/08/9, Dissenting Opinion of Santiago Torres Bernárdez (2 May 2013) (*Ambiente* dissent).
[147] ibid paras 190–209.
[148] ibid para 297.

dissenting arbitrators focused on understanding 'investment' in the ITA based on state consent, which aligns with a public international law ideology.

24.35 A different interpretation was evident in the *Poštová Banka v Greece* award.[149] In 2013, a claim was brought against Greece by Poštová banka, a.s under the Slovakia–Greece BIT based on Greece's restructuring of their sovereign debt. Poštová banka had purchased Greek bonds on the secondary market. In *Poštová Banka v Greece* the tribunal distinguished sovereign debt from private debt[150] and noted the absence of the term sovereign bonds in the definition of investment in the BIT.[151] Given the special nature of sovereign debt, it was distinguishable from 'loans'[152] and 'claims to money', which were deemed to be limited to private obligations.[153] This meant that sovereign bonds were not within the scope of the Slovakia–Greece BIT. As a result, the tribunal did not have jurisdiction to hear the claim.[154] The terms of the definition of the Slovakia–Greece BIT made it easier for this tribunal to reach this conclusion.

24.36 The dissenting investment arbitrators in the Argentina cases, and the *Poštová Banka* award, evidence a different view of investment. Although the investment arbitrators apply different reasoning in each case, they all focus on whether sovereign debt possesses the characteristics of FDI. The differences in reasoning can, in part, can be attributed to the variation in the definitions of investment between the Argentina–Italy BIT and the Slovakia–Greece BIT. It was much easier for the *Poštová Banka* tribunal to exclude sovereign debt from the scope of coverage from the Slovakia–Greece BIT. Nonetheless, the overall stance taken in this award, and the dissents in the Argentina awards, align with what states foresaw when IIL was created and the terms of consent set out in the applicable BITs. The centrality of the treaty and state consent underpinning this approach is indicative of a public international law understanding of IIL. Therefore, the minority view that sovereign debt does not amount to an investment demonstrates that different values underpin the decision-making process of these investment arbitrators.

24.37 The varied reasoning of investment arbitrators in these awards illustrate that decision-making in ITA can be reflective of how decision-makers understand the regime to function. Both the contractual and sovereign approaches identified rely on value-based decision-making, which can give rise to unanticipated consequences.

---

[149] *Poštová Banka v Greece*, ICSID Case No ARB/13/8, Award (9 April 2015).
[150] ibid paras 318–24.
[151] ibid para 332.
[152] ibid paras 337–39.
[153] ibid paras 341–47.
[154] ibid para 350.

3. Sovereign debt restructuring

24.38 As the contractual understanding of sovereign debt has been the most successful in terms of establishing jurisdiction (and based on the limited number of awards to date, appears to be the dominant understanding) the unanticipated consequences of this approach will be examined. For those investment arbitrators involved in the decision-making process, it is not an unanticipated consequence that the awards resulted in a finding of jurisdiction in the Argentina awards. The purpose of the acts was to make a finding on this precise point of law. However, by failing to take into account the further effects of this decision, unanticipated consequences arise for the majority investment arbitrators. Unanticipated consequences arise because the awards undermine the pre-existing legal mechanisms that exist to resolve sovereign debt disputes, which enable SDR to occur.

24.39 Should a state default on its debts, it can undertake a SDR. Every SDR differs depending on the circumstances. Broadly construed, SDR involves collectively renegotiating the contractual terms of the debt instrument.[155] This usually requires 'haircuts' for the creditors in the form of deferred interest payments, reductions in the rate of interest, and a loss in the face value of the debt.[156] The restructuring process is market driven,[157] and as a result of political interests and the differing legal frameworks that govern sovereign bonds,[158] can be disorderly.[159] 'Hold-out' creditors often reject proposed SDR terms and try to secure a more beneficial outcome in the future.[160] The risks involved in holding out has created a market for those who seek to exploit the debt restructuring process by purchasing outstanding debt at a considerable discount before trying to enforce the terms of the instrument to maximize their return (so-called 'vulture funds').[161] In an attempt

---

[155] UNCTAD, 'Sovereign Debt Restructuring and International Investment Agreements' (2011) IIA Issues Note, 2; Youngjin Jung and Sanwook Daniel Han, 'Sovereign Debt Restructuring under the Investor-State Dispute Regime' (2014) 31 Journal of International Arbitration 75, 76; Ostřanský (n 1) 29; Stephen Kim Park and Tim R Samples, 'Tribunalizing Sovereign Debt: Argentina's Experience with Investor-State Dispute Settlement' (2017) 50 Vanderbilt Journal of Transnational Law 1033, 1035.

[156] UNCTAD (n 155) 2; Alison Wirtz, 'Bilateral Investment Treaties, Holdout Investors, and their Impact on Grenada's Sovereign Debt Crisis' (2015) 16 Chicago Journal of International Law 249, 254. See also Rachel D Thrasher and Kevin P Gallagher, 'Mission Creep: the Emerging Role of International Investment Agreements in Sovereign Debt Restructuring' (2015) 6 Journal of Globalization and Development 257, 261; Ostřanský (n 1) 29.

[157] Alice de Jonge, 'Returning to Fundamentals: Principles of International Law Applicable to the Resolution of Sovereign Debt Crises' (2013) 36 Suffolk Transnational Law Review 1, 15.

[158] Juan Pablo Bohoslavsky and Kunibert Raffer (eds), *Sovereign Debt Crises: What Have We Learned?* (CUP 2017); Martin Guzman and Joseph E Stiglitz, 'Creating a Framework for Sovereign Debt Restructuring that Works' in Martin Guzman, José Antonio Ocampo, and Joseph E. Stiglitz (eds), *Too Little Too Late: The Quest to Resolve Sovereign Debt Crises* (Columbia University Press 2016) 3–32, 4.

[159] Tan (n 7) 319.

[160] Suescun de Roa (n 65) 132; Jung and Han (n 155) 77; Wirtz (n 156) 254; Ostřanský (n 1) 36; Waibel, 'Opening Pandora's Box: Sovereign Bonds in International Arbitration' (n 65) 713.

[161] UNCTAD (n 155) 2; Guzman and Stiglitz (n 158) 5, 10.

to resolve the negative impact of hold-out creditors and vulture funds, collective action clauses (CACs) have been introduced into some sovereign debt instruments.[162] CACs prevent a minority of bondholders from holding out by permitting a specified supermajority to accept changes to bondholder terms, which bind all bondholders.[163] However, many sovereign debt instruments do not have CACs[164] and vulture funds can purchase the minimum percentage required to block the operation of CACs.[165] To enforce the original terms of the sovereign debt instrument, hold-out creditors and vulture funds can commence claims in domestic courts (either in the debtor state or overseas, depending on whether the debt is internal or external), which have jurisdiction to hear disputes.[166] Vulture funds and hold-outs have achieved a relatively high level of success using domestic legal forums, in spite of CACs.[167] However, enforcement can be difficult for successful creditors as there may be a limited pool of attachable assets from which to recover their debt.[168] Consequently, when investment arbitrators permit claims relating to sovereign debt in ITA, they may provide creditors with a further opportunity to enforce the entirety of the debt.[169] This undermines the attractiveness of CACs, exacerbates problems coordinating SDR and increases the corresponding chances of hold-outs and vulture funds seeking to minimize their loss using ITA.[170] If investment arbitrators do not take these considerations into account, unanticipated consequences may arise.

24.40 Given that each SDR varies, investment arbitrators need to understand how states and creditors might seek to use the legal framework governing SDR to manage sovereign debt defaults. Argentina and Greece had very different experiences within this framework. For example, Argentina enacted legislation that had the effect of swapping existing bonds for new debt instruments without negotiating directly with creditors.[171] The sovereign bonds Argentina sought to swap are

---

[162] Jung and Han (n 155) 78.
[163] International Law Association (n 68) 37–38; Christian Hofmann, 'Sovereign-Debt Restructuring in Europe under the New Model Collective Action Clauses' (2014) 49 Texas International Law Journal 385, 397; de Jonge (n 157) 23; Tomoko Ishikawa, 'Collective Action Clauses in Sovereign Bond Contracts and Investment Treaty Arbitration—an Approach to Reconcile the Irreconcilable' (2014) 4 AEL: A Convivium 63, 66; Jung and Han (n 155) 78; Ostřanský (n 1) 40.
[164] Guzman and Stiglitz (n 158) 16; Suescun de Roa (n 65) 150; Park and Samples (n 155) 1040.
[165] Guzman and Stiglitz (n 158) 11; Jung and Han (n 155) 79.
[166] Ostřanský (n 1) 37; Park and Samples (n 155) 1038.
[167] See Julian Schumacher, Christoph Trebesch, and Henrik Enderlein, 'Sovereign Defaults in Courts' <https://ssrn.com/abstract=2189997> or 36 accessed 21 September 2018.
[168] Wirtz (n 156) 255; Ostřanský (n 1) 37; Park and Samples (n 155) 1035; Suescun de Roa (n 65) 136, 138.
[169] Waibel, 'Opening Pandora's Box: Sovereign Bonds in International Arbitration' (n 65) 715; Cross (n 92) 152.
[170] Waibel, 'Opening Pandora's Box: Sovereign Bonds in International Arbitration' (n 65) 715.
[171] See Shaina Potts, 'Deep Finance: Sovereign Debt Crises and the Secondary Market "Fix"' (2017) 46 Economy and Society 452, 453.

governed by the law of New York and do not contain CACs.[172] Hold-out creditors sought to enforce the terms of the original bonds against Argentina in the courts of New York.[173] Argentina has been involved in prolonged litigation that resulted in the Supreme Court of the United States of America finding that Argentina cannot make issue payments under its restructured debt plan without making proportionate payments to its hold-out creditors based on a *pari passu* clause in the bond contract.[174] An injunction was issued that, whilst protecting the hold-out creditors, in effect, also prevented Argentina from operating in the capital markets.[175] Domestic legal proceedings can permit hold-out creditors to use the terms of sovereign bonds to gain benefits over majority creditors, which can simultaneously influence the ongoing solvency of a debtor state. Greece's experience was less problematic for the state. As domestic law primarily governed Greece's privately held sovereign bonds, Greece was able to retroactively insert CACs into the terms of the bonds.[176] By using domestic law in this way, Greece was able to use the legal framework governing SDR to impose haircuts.[177] Although creditors sought to challenge Greece's approach in the domestic courts of Germany and Austria, these claims were unsuccessful.[178] However, Greece paid out sovereign bonds governed by English law that already had CACs to avoid litigation with hold-out creditors as the threshold to establish a binding majority was not reached for around half of these bonds.[179] These examples illustrate how hold-out creditors, CACs, and domestic litigation have the potential to interact in varied ways when insolvent states are undertaking complex negotiations with creditors. Investment arbitrators should be aware of these interactions, together with the potential consequences of permitting ITA to be used as an additional forum for hold-out creditors to enforce sovereign debt.

24.41 The use of ITA to resolve sovereign debt disputes to the advantage of a few hold-out creditors is likely to be detrimental to states experiencing a financial crisis.

---

[172] Anna Gelpern, Ben Heller, and Brad Setser, 'Count the Limbs: Designing Robust Aggregation Clauses in Sovereign Bonds' in Martin Guzman, José Antonio Ocampo, and Joseph E Stiglitz, (eds) *Too Little, Too Late: The Quest to Resolve Sovereign Debt Crises* (Columbia University Press 2016) 109–143, 117.

[173] For discussions on this litigation, see Tomás M Araya, 'A Decade of Sovereign Debt Litigation: Lessons from the NML v Argentina Case and the Road Ahead' (2016) 17 Business Law International 83; Anna Gelpern, 'Contract Hope and Sovereign Redemption' (2013) 8 Capital Markets Law Journal 132; Lee C Buchheit and Mitu Gulati, 'Restructuring Sovereign Debt after *NML v Argentina*' (2017) 12 Capital Markets Law Journal 224.

[174] See *NML Capital, Ltd v Republic of Argentina*, No. 08 Civ. 6978 (TPG), 2012 WL 5895784 (S.D.N.Y. Nov. 21, 2012), which established the injunction.

[175] Buchheit and Gulati (n 173) 228.

[176] Sebastian Grund, 'Enforcing Sovereign Debt in Court—a Comparative Analysis of Litigation and Arbitration following the Greek Debt Restructuring of 2012' (2017) 1 University of Vienna Law Review 34, 41.

[177] ibid 42.

[178] ibid 44–60.

[179] ibid 42–43; Gelpern, Heller, and Setser (n 172) 119.

An award on the merits in ITA may permit a creditor to enforce its rights under the terms of the original sovereign debt instrument.[180] This will inevitably lead to some states being placed under increased fiscal pressure whilst already managing a financial crisis. Investment arbitrators are unlikely to have anticipated this consequence of establishing jurisdiction over sovereign debt disputes in ITA. As part of an epistemic and interpretative community, the focus of investment arbitrators would have been on the implications of the decision for IIL and ITA, rather than on the wider implications of their decision for the insolvent state. Although subject to limitations, SDR has some benefits. SDR gives parties time to negotiate,[181] states can seek to prevent hold-outs and vulture funds,[182] and states can agree terms that they can comply with, which increases their chances of repaying the debt; all of which are in the majority of creditors' best interests.[183] It also protects state sovereignty by allowing states to respond appropriately to the financial crisis, in a manner that is most beneficial to its interests and population.[184] These benefits are removed if ITA becomes a forum in which sovereign debt can be individually and separately enforced. If investment arbitrators do not take these considerations into account, it is probable that using ITA to resolve sovereign debt disputes will be counterproductive for states attempting SDR. Therefore, ITA should not be used as a forum for this type of dispute.

4. Reforming investment treaty arbitration to reflect the nature of sovereign debt

24.42 To prevent these risks from arising, the first option is to exclude sovereign debt from the scope of BITs by excluding them from the definition of investment. However, if this is not possible, a second option is to reform the manner in which ITA is conducted. This option requires that investment arbitrators take the wider consequences of establishing jurisdiction over sovereign debt disputes in ITA into account.[185] A final option is to remove sovereign debt restructuring from the scope of ITA through the use of carve-out provisions that are independent of the definition of investment in the applicable IIA.

24.43 As value-based decision-making can generate unanticipated consequences, IIAs should include rules that require appointed arbitrators to be independent. Whilst decision-makers can never be entirely neutral, procedures need to be available to ensure that investment arbitrators with vested interests can be challenged, and if necessary, removed from this role. From the perspective of ensuring that

---

[180] Goldmann, 'Foreign Investment, Sovereign Debt and Human Rights' (n 6) 5.
[181] International Law Association (n 68) 38.
[182] ibid.
[183] ibid.
[184] ibid.
[185] See *Ambiente* dissent (n 146) para 330.

investment arbitrators understand how sovereign debt operates, they should also possess knowledge of both international investment law and international law standards in the fields of finance, human rights, labour, and the environment. If investment arbitrators possess these attributes, value-based decision-making should be less focused on a specific type of value, and could result in more nuanced and balanced awards that take into account both the financial and sovereign aspects of sovereign debt, together with the implications of a finding of jurisdiction over sovereign debt disputes. Very few investment arbitrators will meet this requirement. Consequently, if investment arbitrators do not possess this expertise, ideally, they should consult with independent experts in these fields. A global understanding of the implications of their decision-making may limit the risk that sovereign debt will be viewed as an investment. If investment arbitrators do assert jurisdiction to solve debt disputes, then they should incorporate, and apply, existing principles of financial and bankruptcy law as part of their reasoning at the merits stage. In particular, investment arbitrators should contemplate the implications of their awards for the economy of the debtor state, the rights of the affected population, and the rights of all creditors. If there are implications that arise in other fields of international law, such as human rights, applicable law from these regimes should also be taken into account. It is acknowledged that this proposal would fundamentally alter how ITA currently functions and will be difficult to implement. As an alternative, it is also possible for states to pre-empt the need for investment arbitrators to do this by ensuring that IIAs contain clauses in relation to the right to regulate economic activities, especially during times of economic or financial collapse. By taking this action, states would preclude investment arbitrators from addressing their conduct when undertaking SDR as part of ITA. To be effective, this right should extend to include debt agreements reached in a non-discriminatory manner with supermajorities of creditors under CACs. This will permit states sufficient flexibility to reach negotiated settlements and to deprive hold-out creditors and vulture funds of alternative avenues to enforce their obligations. This recommendation would address the unanticipated consequences that have arisen, but would not require such wide-ranging reforms, as it does not seek to alter the values of the epistemic community.

5. Preliminary conclusions

24.44 In conclusion, investment arbitrators are part of epistemic and interpretative communities, and as such, interpret terms in IIL to give effect to the IIL regime as understood by their community. This has resulted in two divergent interpretations of the term investment and, specifically, whether it encompasses sovereign debt. The majority decisions in the Argentina awards focus on the commercial aspects of sovereign debt. They emphasize the contractual aspects of the obligation and minimize the significance of the state as a party to the debt instrument. In so doing, this approach diminishes how states understood investment at the time early BITs and the ICSID Convention were drafted. In contrast, the minority approach takes into account the sovereign nature of the state and emphasizes an interpretation of investments that would have been familiar to states during the 1960s and 1970s. In part, this is because the *Poštová Banka v Greece* award reflects a different definition of investment in the applicable BIT. Nonetheless, the polarized interpretations of investment suggest that arbitrators prioritize different factors when interpreting this term.

Merton points to values, like those that are pre-eminent within the relevant epistemic community, as a potential cause of unanticipated consequences. The adoption of a commercial rather than a public international law understanding of IIL, based on the preferences of investment arbitrators, explains why contractual factors have been prioritized above the ability of the state to effectively address a financial crisis. The finding that some investment tribunals have jurisdiction over sovereign debt disputes leads to unanticipated consequences. By providing an alternative forum for sovereign debt disputes, with greater prospects of recovery and enforcement against a debtor state than in the majority of domestic forums,[186] decision-makers in IIL have encouraged hold-out creditors and vulture funds to resist state efforts to restructure sovereign debts in times of financial crisis. In order to ensure that investment arbitrators are able to anticipate the consequences of their decisions, states should attempt to appoint arbitrators with broader expertise than just IIL. In the context of sovereign debt where an investment tribunal may have jurisdiction, this should include knowledge of finance and bankruptcy law, in addition to other relevant fields of public international law that can be applied at the merits stage of a dispute. This should enable investment arbitrators to be fully aware of the implications of their decisions and counter value-based decision-making. Finally, states should protect their regulatory autonomy in relation to financial crises. This can be achieved by a carve-out in IIAs allowing states to restructure sovereign debt without risking claims before investment tribunals. **24.45**

D. Human Rights Implications

The combination of states failing to define investment, and decision-makers enabling sovereign debt disputes to be heard before ITA, has resulted in ITA providing an alternative forum in which creditors can pursue their debts without entering into collective SDR. ITA potentially entitles a creditor to enforce the entirety of its debt. For a state experiencing a financial crisis, compliance with the original terms of a sovereign debt instrument can divert funds away from fundamental services **24.46**

---

[186] New York courts have exercised wide jurisdiction over sovereign debt disputes. However, as discussed above, the enforceability of domestic decisions creates an additional barrier for creditors.

in the state, such as health and education.[187] This gives rise to a final unanticipated consequence for both states and investment arbitrators—using ITA to resolve sovereign debt disputes has implications for the debtor state's ability to comply with human rights law. This section highlights that, by permitting creditors access to ITA, states and investment arbitrators have enabled the human rights obligations of the insolvent state to be overlooked in sovereign debt disputes.

1. Sovereign debt and human rights

24.47 Financial crises have immediate economic implications for states,[188] such as currency collapses, spikes in inflation, and the economy can shrink in size.[189] The economic changes impact the local population through rises in unemployment,[190] reduced spending power as a result of wage reduction and increases in the price of imported goods.[191] The decrease in expenditure detrimentally affects state revenue, and as a result, public services may cease to function[192] and people may become impoverished.[193] Despite the economic impact of financial crises, states continue to be under a duty to protect fundamental human rights,[194] and, specifically, must be able to provide a minimum standard of basic public services such as education, health, and security.[195] Thus, states must preserve these standards within the framework of SDR.[196]

24.48 Whilst the funds made available from sovereign bonds may enable a state to fund services that give effect to human rights, SDR requires a debtor state to divert

---

[187] Tan (n 7) 311; Lumina, 'Sovereign Debt and Human Rights: The United Nations Approach' (n 7) 252.
[188] Juan Pablo Bohoslavsky, 'Economic Inequality, Debt Crises and Human Rights' (2016) 41 The Yale Journal of International Law Online 177, 189.
[189] International Law Association (n 68) 6.
[190] Bohoslavsky, 'Economic Inequality, Debt Crises and Human Rights' (n 188) 190.
[191] ibid.
[192] International Law Association (n 68) 6.
[193] ibid; Bohoslavsky, 'Economic Inequality, Debt Crises and Human Rights' (n 188) 190; Lumina, 'Sovereign Debt and Human Rights: The United Nations Approach' (n 7) 252.
[194] Committee on Economic Social and Cultural Rights, *Public debt, austerity measures and the International Covenant on Economic, Social and Cultural Rights* (22 July 2016) E/C.12/2016/1 para 4; Armin von Bogdandy and Matthias Goldmann, 'Sovereign Debt Restructurings as Exercises of International Public Authority: towards a Decentralized Sovereign Insolvency Law' in Carlos Espósito, Yuefen Li, and Juan Pablo Bohoslavsky (eds), *Sovereign Financing and International Law* (OUP 2013) 39–70, 61; Daniel Bradlow, 'Can Parallel Lines ever Meet? The Strange Case of the International Standards on Sovereign Debt and Business and Human Rights' (2016) 41 The Yale Journal Of International Law Online 201, 227.
[195] von Bogdandy and Goldmann (n 194) 61.
[196] Guiding Principles on Foreign Debt and Human Rights (10 April 2011) A/HRC/20/23 paras 48–54; von Bogdandy and Goldmann (n 194) 61; Bradlow (n 194) 227; Robert Howse, 'Toward a Framework for Sovereign Debt Restructuring: What Can Public International Law Contribute?' in Martin Guzman, José Antonio Ocampo, and Joseph E Stiglitz (eds), *Too Little Too Late: The Quest to Resolve Sovereign Debt Crises* (Columbia University Press 2016) 241–52, 243; Margot E Salomon and Robert Howse, 'Odious Debt, Adverse Creditor, and the Democratic Ideal' in Ilias Bantekas and Cephas Lumina (eds), *Sovereign Debt and Human Rights* (forthcoming OUP 2018).

national income from social and economic expenditure to debt servicing.[197] Therefore, SDR inevitably affects the degree to which states are able comply with their human rights obligations. The human rights affected tend to be economic, social, and cultural rights including the right to health, the right to education, the right to adequate housing, and the right to work.[198] However, SDR can also impact democratic governance.[199] As a result, it is imperative that a states' human rights obligations are taken into account when the extent of SDR and haircuts are determined.[200] In order to facilitate the protection of human rights during SDR, it is necessary to consider whether SDR will undermine compliance with human rights obligations and how human rights impacts are likely to interact with each other.[201] In order to achieve a human rights compliant SDR, ideally, a human rights impact assessment will be conducted followed by the creation of monitoring mechanisms to ensure that the human rights impact is as expected.[202] The ability of a state to undertake a human rights compliant SDR will be impeded if hold-out creditors and vulture funds are able to use ITA to seek repayment of their entire debt, as funds that are payable to hold-out creditors and vulture funds are likely to be diverted from human rights compliance.

24.49 In extreme cases, instruments such as the Heavily Indebted Poor Countries (HIPC) Initiative[203] will apply. Provided that states meet the requisite criteria,[204] the HIPC (together with the Multilateral Debt Relief Initiative (MDRI))[205] attempts to link debt relief to poverty reduction, macroeconomic stability, and structural reform[206] by reducing unsustainable debt burdens. Once the state has

---

[197] Tan (n 7) 311; Lumina, 'Sovereign Debt and Human Rights: The United Nations Approach' (n 7) 252.

[198] Cephas Lumina, 'Sovereign Debt and Human Rights' in United Nations Human Rights Office of the High Commissioner, *Realizing the Right to Development: Essays in the Commemoration of 25 Years of the United Nations Declaration on the Right to Development* (United Nations 2013) 289–301, 293; Michael Riegner, 'Legal Frameworks and General Principles for Indicators in Sovereign Debt Restructuring' (2016) 41 The Yale Journal Of International Law Online 141, 168–69.

[199] Salomon and Howse (n 196); Matthias Goldmann, 'Human Rights and Sovereign Debt Workouts' in Juan Pablo Bohoslavksy and Jernej Letnar Černič (eds), *Making Sovereign Financing and Human Rights Work* (Hart Publishing 2014) 79–100, 84–85.

[200] Riegner (n 198) 170; Lumina, 'Sovereign Debt and Human Rights' (n 198) 299.

[201] Bradlow (n 194) 227.

[202] Juan Pablo Bohoslavsky, 'Guiding Principles to Assess the Human Rights Impact of Economic Reforms? Yes' in Ilias Bantekas and Cephas Lumina (eds), *Sovereign Debt and Human Rights* (OUP forthcoming 2018); Goldmann, 'Human Rights and Sovereign Debt Workouts' (n 199) 99–100.

[203] See The World Bank, *Heavily Indebted Poor Country (HIPC) Initiative* <http://www.worldbank.org/en/topic/debt/brief/hipc> (HIPC) accessed 21 September 2018.

[204] Conditions are imposed in two separate stages: eligibility and completion. See The International Monetary Fund, *Debt Relief Under the Heavily Indebted Poor Countries (HIPC) Initiative* <https://www.imf.org/en/About/Factsheets/Sheets/2016/08/01/16/11/Debt-Relief-Under-the-Heavily-Indebted-Poor-Countries-Initiative> accessed 21 September 2018.

[205] There are currently no debts eligible for the MDRI. See The International Monetary Fund, *The Multilateral Debt Relief Initiative* <https://www.imf.org/external/np/exr/facts/mdri.htm> accessed 21 September 2018.

[206] Lumina, 'Sovereign Debt and Human Rights' (n 198) 297; de Jonge (n 157) 18.

implemented prescribed policy reforms, debt relief is granted to the state based on a model of burden sharing between all creditors.[207] Thus, the HIPC and MDRI recognize the need to balance human rights with SDR. Whilst this is a positive development, in so far as HIPC and MDRI depart from the pre-existing system that did not recognize these aims,[208] the programme does not cancel debt. Further, creditors control the programme,[209] and as not all creditors participate, the scheme can still be vulnerable to vulture funds and hold-outs.[210] If ITA is available as an alternative forum to seek full repayment of sovereign debt, initiatives such as the HIPC and MDRI are weakened because there is a reduced incentive for creditors to agree to debt relief.

24.50 The ability of creditors to use ITA to enforce sovereign debt repayments undermines the effectiveness of human rights compliant SDR and the aims of HIPC and MDRI. First, in instances where measures to encourage collective SDR are not in place, or fail, ITA permits creditors to circumvent the collective SDR process. If creditors can recover their debt through ITA, it is unlikely that they will be willing to engage with collective SDR (or HIPC and MDRI). Therefore, an unanticipated consequence of including sovereign debt within the definition of investment is to discourage creditors from engaging in SDR processes intended to achieve a sustainable, human rights compliant, debt recovery.

2. International investment law and human rights

24.51 ITA does not provide an alternative forum in which sovereign debt and human rights can be jointly addressed because human rights have not been fully integrated into the IIL regime.[211] Although IIL and international human rights law are both sourced in public international law, there has been little interaction between the two regimes. Rather, the primary actors in ITA (states, foreign investors, and investment arbitrators) tend to disregard international human rights law.[212] The narrow view that human rights are not relevant in the context of investment disputes can, at least in part, be attributed to the lack of express human rights provisions in IIAs.[213] The introduction of express human rights provisions

---

[207] Mark A Walker and Barthélemy Faye, 'Sovereign Debt Renegotiation: Restructuring the Commercial Debt of HIPC Debtor Countries' (2010) 73 Law and Contemporary Problems 317, 319.
[208] Tan (n 7) 314.
[209] Lumina, 'Sovereign Debt and Human Rights' (n 198) 298.
[210] ibid.
[211] Luis Gonzales Garcia, 'The Role of Human Rights in International Investment Law' in N Jansen Calamita, David Earnest, and Markus Burgstaller (eds), *The Future of ICSID and the Place of Investment Treaties in International Law* (BIICL 2013) 29–43, 29.
[212] See Silvia Steininger, 'What's Human Rights Got to Do With It? An Empirical Analysis of Human Rights References in Investment Arbitration' (2018) 31 Leiden Journal of International Law 33.
[213] Garcia (n 211) 29–30.

into BITs has historically been problematic. For example, in late 2007, Norway circulated a Draft Model BIT that made reference to international human rights law in its preamble,[214] but did not contain any substantive human rights obligations.[215] Nonetheless, businesses were troubled by the inclusion of human rights in this instrument.[216] Those who advocated for human rights in BITs were not content with the exclusion of human rights from ITA.[217] As a result of this experience, Norway temporarily abandoned its BIT programme.[218] It took until 2015 for Norway to release another Draft Model BIT, which contains several references to human rights both in the preamble and its substantive articles.[219] South Africa has also struggled to strike an appropriate balance between human rights and investment protection. In 2007, the *Piero Foresti v Republic of South Africa* claim challenged the implementation of South Africa's anti-apartheid Black Economic Empowerment programme.[220] The claim highlights the conflict between redress for racial inequality on human rights grounds and the protections offered to foreign investors in IIAs.[221] Rather than continue its BIT programme, South Africa has introduced investment protection standards through domestic legislation.[222] By taking this approach, South Africa can ensure that, amongst other policy considerations, its investment programme is consistent with its racial equality laws.[223]

24.52 Despite these initial experiences, states have begun to introduce more flexible investment protection standards into their IIAs that refer to human rights. The 2018 Netherlands Draft Model BIT,[224] for example, includes provisions that seek to protect human rights.[225] It additionally permits tribunals to take into account when a foreign investor does not comply with specific soft law human rights instruments when calculating compensation.[226] As the current draft is still open for

---

[214] 2007 Draft Norway Model BIT <http://investmentpolicyhub.unctad.org/Download/TreatyFile/2873> accessed 21 September 2018.

[215] Preambles may be used to determine the object and purpose of the BIT. See Federico Ortino, 'The Social Dimension of International Investment Agreements: Drafting a new BIT/MIT Model?' (2005) 7 International Law Forum du droit international 243, 246.

[216] Peter Muchlinski, 'Trends in International Investment Agreements 2008/2009: Review of the Model Bilateral Investment Treaties of Norway, South Africa and the United States' in Karl P Sauvant (ed.), *Yearbook on International Investment Law and Policy 2009—2010* (OUP 2010) 41–86, 59.

[217] ibid.

[218] ibid.

[219] 2015 Draft Norway Model BIT <https://www.regjeringen.no/contentassets/e47326b61f424d4c9c3d470896492623/draft-model-agreement-english.pdf> accessed 21 September 2018.

[220] *Piero Foresti, Laura de Carli and others v Republic of South Africa* ICSID Case No ARB(AF)/07/1.

[221] Engela C Schlemmer, 'An Overview of South Africa's Investment Treaties and Investment Policy' (2016) 31 ICSID Review—Foreign Investment Law Journal 168, 173.

[222] The Protection of Investment Act, Act 22 (2015).

[223] Schlemmer (n 221) 173.

[224] 2018 Netherlands Draft Model BIT <https://www.internetconsultatie.nl/investeringsakkoorden/document/3586> accessed 21 September 2018 .

[225] ibid, eg, arts 6(5) and 7.

[226] ibid art 23.

consultation, it is yet to be seen how other states will receive this Model BIT. The Morocco–Nigeria BIT also includes human rights obligations that seek to bind foreign investors.[227] Despite these developments, existing BITs that do not reference human rights will continue to bind states for a significant period of time and, as a result of sunset clauses, will continue to apply even when states withdraw from some BITs.[228] Therefore, the vast majority of future investment disputes will have no textual foundation in BITs that will enable an investment tribunal to discuss relevant human rights obligations.

24.53 Nonetheless, the lack of express human rights provisions IIAs should not preclude the application of human rights in ITA. International human rights law forms part of the corpus of public international law and international human rights law instruments have been widely ratified.[229] Many human rights obligations are also considered to be binding as customary international law (although fewer economic, social, and cultural rights).[230] Consequently, it cannot be presumed that a state entering into an IIA has willingly placed itself in violation of its human rights obligations. Further, the applicable law of an investment tribunal will often include reference to public international law,[231] which includes international human rights law. Obligations sourced from IIL and international human rights law can interact without conflicting. However, to enable this interaction, investment arbitrators must interpret public international law in a coherent manner to reduce the impact of fragmentation.

24.54 Several procedural mechanisms have been identified that might enable investment tribunals to incorporate human rights into investment arbitration, including: treaty interpretation and systemic integration;[232] the use of proportionality

---

[227] Reciprocal Investment Promotion and Protection Agreement between the Government of the Kingdom of Morocco and the Government of the Federal Republic of Nigeria (signed 3 December 2016, not yet entered into force), arts 15, 18(2), and 18(4) (Morocco–Nigeria BIT).

[228] This is the case for states such as Poland. See Agnieska Zarowna, 'Termination of BITs and Sunset Clauses—What can Investors in Poland Expect?' (*Kluwer Arbitration Blog*, 2017) <http://arbitrationblog.kluwerarbitration.com/2017/02/28/booked-22-february-polish-bits/> accessed 21 September 2018.

[229] The International Covenant on Civil and Political Rights (entered into force 23 March 1976) has 170 state parties. The International Covenant on Economic, Social and Cultural Rights (entered into force 3 January 1976) has 167 state parties. These are the most widely ratified human rights treaties.

[230] The process for establishing a customary human rights obligation has been debated, however, many of the rights set out in the Universal Declaration of Human Rights are considered to amount to customary international law. See Hurst Hannum, 'The Status of the Universal Declaration of Human Rights in National and International Law' (1996) 25 Georgia Journal of International and Comparative Law 287.

[231] This may be in accordance with ICSID Convention, art 42 or at the disputing parties' request. International law would primarily be used to inform the interpretation of the IIA, but is not necessarily limited to principles of treaty interpretation or IIL.

[232] Campbell McLachlan, 'Investment Treaties and General International Law' (2008) 57 International and Comparative Law Quarterly 361; Rumiana Yotova, 'Systemic Integration: an Instrument for Reasserting the State's Control in Investment Arbitration?' in Andreas Kulick (ed), *Reassertion of Control over the Investment Treaty Regime* (CUP 2017) 182–208, 182.

analysis and balancing from domestic constitutional settings and the European Court of Human Rights;[233] and conflicts of law approaches.[234] Nonetheless, investment arbitrators do not systematically utilize these tools and investment tribunals frequently fail to recognize the significance of human rights, or downplay the potential for treaty conflicts to arise between obligations sourced in BITs and human rights instruments.[235] Investment tribunals have addressed international human rights law when the disputing parties have directly raised it. However, even in these instances, tribunals have applied human rights inconsistently. For example, in *von Pezold v Zimbabwe*, the tribunal rejected *amicus curiae* submissions based on indigenous rights as irrelevant to the claim, before relying on the prohibition of racial discrimination in favour of the foreign investor.[236] In *Urbaser v Argentina*,[237] the state relied on human rights arguments in its counterclaim. This decision evidences that some investment arbitrators are open to arguments based on human rights as the investment tribunal integrated human rights into the fair and equitable treatment standard,[238] the defence of necessity[239] and found jurisdiction over a human rights based counterclaim.[240] However, the *Urbaser* award is problematic because the tribunal sought to confer human rights obligations directly on the foreign investor, contrary to the accepted position that human rights confer obligations only on states.[241] Following *Urbaser*, in *Bear Creek v Peru*,[242] a partial dissent considered the impact of the foreign investor's mining activities on indigenous communities, and the law that protects their rights.[243] However,

---

[233] Gebhard Bücheler, *Proportionality Analysis in Investor-State Arbitration* (OUP 2015); Caroline Henckels, *Proportionality and Deference in Investor-State Arbitration: Balancing Investment Protection and Regulatory Autonomy* (CUP 2015); Benedict Kingsbury and Stephan W Schill, 'Public Law Concepts to Balance Investor's Rights with State Regulatory Actions in the Public Interest—the Concept of Proportionality' in Stephan W Schill (ed), *International Investment Law and Comparative Public Law* (OUP 2010) 75–104.

[234] Ralf Michaels and Joost Pauwelyn, 'Conflict of Norms or Conflict of Laws?: Different Techniques in the Fragmentation of Public International Law' (2012) 22 Duke Journal of Comparative and International Law 349; Henning Grosse Ruse-Kahn, 'A Conflict-of-laws Approach to Competing Rationalities in International Law: the Case of Plain Packaging between Intellectual Property, Trade, Investment and Health' (2013) 9 Journal of Private International Law 309.

[235] For example, *CMS Gas Transmission Company v Argentine Republic*, ICSID Case No ARB/01/8, Award (12 May 2005) para 121.

[236] *Bernhard von Pezold and others v Republic of Zimbabwe*, ICSID Case No ARB/10/15, Award (28 July 2015).

[237] *Urbaser SA and Consorcio de Aguas Bilbao Biskaia, Bilbao Biskaia Ur Partzuergoa v Argentine Republic*, ICSID Case No ARB/07/26, Award (8 December 2016).

[238] ibid paras 621–25.

[239] ibid paras 707–32.

[240] ibid paras 1182–221.

[241] See Edward Guntrip, '*Urbaser v Argentina*: The Origins of a Host State Human Rights Counterclaim in ICSID Arbitration?' *EJIL: Talk!* (2017) <https://www.ejiltalk.org/urbaser-v-argentina-the-origins-of-a-host-state-human-rights-counterclaim-in-icsid-arbitration/> accessed 21 September 2018.

[242] *Bear Creek Mining Corporation v Republic of Peru*, ICSID Case No. ARB/14/21, Partial Dissenting Opinion of Professor Philippe Sands QC (30 November 2017) (*Bear Creek* partial dissent).

[243] ibid paras 7–36.

these awards remain isolated instances. Thus, whilst human rights' relevance to BITs and investment arbitration are beginning to be recognized, they are a long way from being entrenched. As a result, the use of human rights in IIL remains on the periphery of the legal regime and is likely to be reflective of IIL's dominant epistemic community.

24.55 An alternative means of introducing human rights into ITA is for the state to rely on defences sourced from the law of state responsibility. Defences, such as a state of necessity or *force majeure*, could potentially be used to justify state measures on human rights grounds.[244] However, for either defence to be successful, specific requirements for each standard must be met. In accordance with Article 23 of the ILC Articles on State Responsibility (ARSIWA),[245] *force majeure* only applies to circumstances that do not relate to the conduct of the state.[246] Further, the commentary to Article 23 excludes the application of the principle in situations where the performance of obligations is made more difficult due to 'some political or economic crisis'.[247] Similarly, the defence of necessity based on Article 25 of ARSIWA cannot be invoked if the state has contributed to the situation or the conduct of the state was not the only way for the state to safeguard its essential interest.[248] Consequently, creditors can argue that the state could have handled the economic crisis (and the associated SDR) differently or at a different point in time. Given the strict conditions, states will be unable to avoid liability in ITA relating to sovereign debt claims on the basis that a state of necessity or *force majeure* existed, even if these arguments are framed in terms of human rights compliance. This has the potential to result in the state's concurrent liability for the breach of investment protection standards and human rights obligations.

24.56 It is possible to mitigate the impact of SDR on the human rights obligations of states through human rights impact assessments and the establishment of monitoring mechanisms. This aim can partly be achieved, in certain circumstances, through mechanisms such as the HIPC and MDRI. However, if hold-out creditors and vulture funds can access ITA to enforce the terms of their sovereign bonds, then this human rights framework is likely to be undermined. IIAs rarely contemplate human rights and investment arbitrators are unlikely to permit the human rights aspects of SDR to influence their decision-making. This can be

---

[244] As was used in *Case Concerning the Payment of Various Serbian Loans Issued in France (France v Serbia)* (Judgment) PCIJ Rep Series A No 20. Howse (n 196) 243; Cross (n 92) 155. See August Reinisch and Christina Binder, 'Debts and State of Necessity' in Juan Pablo Bohoslavksy and Jernej Letnar Černič (eds), *Making Sovereign Financing and Human Rights Work* (Hart Publishing 2014) 115–28.

[245] See International Law Commission Articles on State Responsibility for Internationally Wrongful Acts in James Crawford, *The International law Commission's Articles on State Responsibility: Introduction, Text and Commentaries* (CUP 2002) 170–73.

[246] ibid 170.

[247] ibid 171.

[248] ibid 184.

attributed to how the investment arbitrators' epistemic community understands of the goals of IIL. Therefore, creditors can seek full repayment of sovereign bonds without reference to the debtor state's human rights obligations. Thus, ITA remains an inappropriate forum for the resolution of sovereign debt disputes.

3. Ensuring human rights compliance during sovereign debt restructuring

The cumulative effect of the unanticipated consequences identified in this chapter has resulted in sovereign debt disputes being able to be heard in a forum that does not take into account the human rights obligations of the insolvent state. Although it is suggested that ITA is an inappropriate forum to hear sovereign debt disputes, as ITA is being used for this type of dispute, it must acknowledge the human rights implications of sovereign debt disputes. Therefore, ITA must be reformed to accommodate human rights. Both states and investment arbitrators can amend their practices in order to incorporate human rights within ITA. Given the wide-ranging human rights implications of SDR, the necessary reforms outlined in this section are likely to be longer term and require structural change. As a result, these recommendations are aimed at changing state practice with regard to IIL and human rights more generally. Nonetheless, these recommendations would still improve the implementation of human rights law in sovereign debt disputes that fall within the scope of IIL. 24.57

Until recently, human rights have not been addressed in IIAs. States should conduct human rights impact assessments prior to the conclusion of IIAs to ensure that the human rights implications are clear and to pre-empt the unanticipated consequences of entering into IIAs. The Guiding principles on human rights impact assessments of trade and investment agreements,[249] as well as the recent General Comment No 24 of the UN Committee on Economic, Social and Cultural Rights on State obligations under the International Covenant on Economic, Social and Cultural Rights in the context of business activities,[250] provide guidance to states on how best to ensure that trade and investment agreements are consistent with their obligations under human rights law. This approach may highlight specific problems within individual IIAs and, thereby, permit states to avoid the unanticipated consequences identified on a case-by-case basis. By taking this approach, states can be made aware of the human rights implications of IIAs and include provisions to counter any harmful human rights consequences, including those that relate to sovereign debt disputes. 24.58

---

[249] The Guiding principles on human rights impact assessments of trade and investment agreements (19 December 2011) A/HRC/19/59/Add.5.
[250] Committee on Economic, Social and Cultural Rights, General Comment No 24 (2017) on State obligations under the International Covenant on Economic, Social and Cultural Rights in the context of business activities, E/C.12/GC/2 (10 August 2017) paras 13, 25, 29.

24.59 When states experience financial crises, it is the state's population that suffers. At present, there are limited forums for the population to raise concerns regarding how ITA might affect their human rights in the event of a sovereign default. Appropriate consultation procedures and mechanisms should be developed at the time of the creation of IIAs to ensure that the right to participate in the drafting, negotiation, and approval of IIAs is guaranteed.[251] Specifically, states should ensure that negotiations of IIAs are conducted in an open and transparent manner, allowing parliamentarians, affected communities, and other stakeholders (such as taxpayers) access to all relevant documentation. This will facilitate an informed debate regarding the nature of the obligations being considered and the consequences that may eventuate. Although this would be particularly beneficial in relation to the issues raised regarding sovereign debt in this chapter, it can also be considered to be a good practice in relation to IIAs more generally.

24.60 States should integrate investor obligations into IIAs to ensure that creditors cannot avoid considering human rights should they seek to enforce sovereign bonds using ITA. When negotiating or revising IIAs, states should ensure that they include explicit provisions that refer to the human rights obligations of investors and host and home states. Recent BITs have started to move towards this approach.[252] IIAs should include provisions explicitly reaffirming that investors should respect human rights, as set out in international human rights treaties, the Guiding principles on business and human rights[253] and in the ILO Declaration on Fundamental Principles and Rights at Work.[254] IIAs should specify that bona fide measures aimed at protecting the human rights of the population and ensuring debt sustainability do not constitute a breach of the agreement and are non-compensable. This includes offering debt-restructuring terms that allow states to ensure basic human rights and safeguard that debt is sustainable from a financial and budgetary perspective. By expressly addressing the relationship between human rights and investment that extends to portfolio investments, states can avoid many of the problems identified in this chapter.

24.61 In addition to state action, arbitration tribunals must consider human rights law as applicable law for the interpretation of investment treaties. Whilst two recent tribunals have made reference to human rights,[255] this practice needs to become more widespread and coherent. It is important that the mechanisms adopted to facilitate this are sound so as to avoid questionable awards that have the potential

---

[251] See Lorenzo Cotula, 'Democracy and International Investment Law' (2017) 30 Leiden Journal of International Law 351.

[252] See the Morocco–Nigeria BIT and the 2018 Netherlands Draft Model BIT discussed above.

[253] See The Guiding principles on human rights impact assessments of trade and investment agreements (n 249).

[254] Declaration on Fundamental Principles and Rights at Work (concluded 18 June 1998) 37 ILM 1233.

[255] *Urbaser* (n 237); *Bear Creek* partial dissent (n 242).

undermine investment tribunals' continued engagement with human rights. ITA's transparency should also be increased by publishing all details of disputes, and in general, holding hearings in public.[256] Non-parties to the dispute should have a right to attend arbitration proceedings and affected communities and public interest organizations should have a right to make written presentations and *amicus curiae* submissions.[257] These recommendations are likely to expose investment arbitrators to perspectives beyond those present in their epistemic community. By adopting this approach, the wider implications of the decision-making process may be taken into account to a greater degree. This will reduce the risk of value-based decision-making that only focuses on commercial aspects of sovereign debt.

4. Preliminary conclusions

For a state suffering from a financial crisis, the diversion of funds from essential services has human rights implications for their population. States have a continuing duty to comply with human rights, even during SDR. Collective SDR can permit states to manage the human rights implications of sovereign debt by giving them flexibility as to how they manage their debt and human rights obligations. However, their ability to minimize the impact on human rights is curtailed when investment arbitrators provide creditors with the ability to fully enforce sovereign debt in ITA. This issue is exacerbated because IIL has not robustly integrated human rights considerations in IIAs or through arbitrator practice. As a result, it is unlikely that ITA will take into account the broader human rights implications of sovereign debt restructuring. To counteract the unanticipated consequences of including sovereign debt within interpretations of investment, wide-ranging structural reform is required to resolve these difficulties. States need to actively scrutinize the human rights impacts of IIAs, make drafting processes transparent and open to multiple stakeholders, and include express human rights provisions within IIAs. Investment arbitrators should recognize the human rights implications of their decision-making and permit those affected by their awards to have access to the dispute resolution process, and where appropriate, make submissions. These steps can offset the unanticipated consequences that result from wide definitions of investment, and investment arbitrator practice that only focuses on the commercial aspects of sovereign debt, which have enabled ITA to become a forum for sovereign debt disputes to the detriment of human rights.

24.62

---

[256] The United Nations Convention on Transparency in Treaty-based Investor-State Arbitration (entered into force 18 October 2017) and the UNCITRAL Rules on Transparency in Treaty-based Investor-State Arbitration seek to increase the transparency of ITA.

[257] See eg Christina Knahr, 'Transparency, Third Party Participation and Access to Documents in International Investment Arbitration' (2007) 23 Arbitration International 327; Maciej Zachariasiewicz, 'Amicus Curiae in International Investment Arbitration: Can it enhance the Transparency of Investment Dispute Resolution?' (2012) 29 Journal of International Arbitration 205. See generally, Astrid Wiik, *Amicus Curiae Before International Courts and Tribunals* (Hart Publishing 2018).

E. Conclusion

24.63 The use of ITA to resolve sovereign debt disputes gives rise to potential human rights implications. This outcome was unanticipated by both states and investment arbitrators during IIL's evolution. Merton's account of how purposive actions can generate unanticipated consequences provides an explanation as to how these human rights implications might have arisen.[258] Merton describes how unanticipated consequences arise when actors are ignorant; make errors; focus on the foreseeable; align their conduct with specific values; or create self-defeating prophesies.[259] Some of these factors are present when the actions of states and investment arbitrators are reviewed in the context of sovereign debt.

24.64 The failure of states to define investment in the ICSID Convention when the modern IIL regime was created can be attributed to the focus on the foreseeable consequences of decolonization for FDI. As states failed to look beyond the near future, wide definitions of investment were adopted in their BITs. This resulted in the unanticipated consequence that sovereign debt instruments have been recognized to fall within the term 'investment', in some instances. Investment arbitrators have interpreted this term differently depending on the text of the applicable BIT. However, by drawing analogies with commercial obligations, several tribunals have found that they possess jurisdiction to hear claims in ITA regarding sovereign debt. While investment arbitrators clearly anticipated that this analysis would result in a finding of jurisdiction, it is unclear whether they were aware that this would undermine the desirability of other forms of SDR for hold-out creditors and vulture funds. The epistemic and interpretative preferences of investment arbitrators may have prevented them from fully realizing all of the implications of this approach. A final unanticipated consequence is that by providing an alternative forum for creditors, states and investment arbitrators have reduced the ability of states suffering the effects of financial crises to comply with human rights obligations and reach sustainable SDR agreements with all creditors. Whilst human rights based approaches can be applied to SDR, ITA is unlikely to recognize the role of human rights in SDR at the present time. Given the cumulative effect of the conduct of states and investment arbitrators, and their failure to fully anticipate the consequences of this conduct, it is suggested that ITA should not be able to hear sovereign debt disputes.

24.65 Although it is impossible to control all unanticipated consequences of actions, it is possible to limit the human rights implications of using ITA to resolve sovereign debt disputes. This chapter has made recommendations that have the potential

---

[258] See Merton (n 12).
[259] ibid 898–904.

to limit the effects of these unanticipated consequences. The implementation of these recommendations varies in difficulty, ranging from amending the definition of investment in IIAs to exclude sovereign debt instruments from the scope of ITA, to requiring structural change to the way in which ITA functions to enable human rights and financial law to be considered during the decision-making process. These recommendations may address the identified problems generated by using ITA to resolve sovereign debt disputes. However, they also have the potential to lead to new unanticipated consequences, given that the wider implications of these changes cannot be entirely foreseen. As a result, it is necessary to consider how actors in international law might need to alter their practices more generally to better respond to unanticipated consequences as they arise.

The practices evident in IIL are indicative of wider issues regarding how states and decision-makers act in international law. First, there appears to be a tendency for states to focus on the immediately foreseeable consequences of their actions. This is demonstrated by the failure of states to delimit the term investment. This is also evidenced by more recent practice. Following investment awards that have found that they have jurisdiction over sovereign debt disputes, states have omitted to include standards or guidelines in recent BITs that will enable SDR to be addressed holistically,[260] or to deal with the collective action problems that lie at the heart of any bankruptcy process. On the contrary, creditors are incentivized to withhold their contribution to any collective SDR, while enjoying the benefits that result from the efforts of all the other creditors. States need to recognize the limitations of existing practices sooner, and use foresight and political will to resolve detrimental unanticipated consequences, either before, or as they arise. The potential consequences of using ITA to resolve sovereign debt disputes have become clear, however, states have not fully embraced the actions that can ameliorate the negative human rights implications outlined in this chapter.

24.66

A second issue is that decision-makers may not always take a holistic view of a legal problem. This in part may be a result of the fragmentation of public international law, which has led to the creation of multiple dispute resolution forums, each with specific jurisdictional limits. However, it can also potentially be attributed to the existence of epistemic and interpretative communities of decision-makers that, through training and experience, seek to promote the aims and purposes of particular legal regimes. While these reasons may partially justify investment arbitrator conduct, investment arbitrators have provided a route by which creditors can deliberately disrupt collective SDR, in spite of broader efforts by states (and

24.67

---

[260] Recent IIAs, such as the EU–Canada Comprehensive Economic Trade Agreement (entered into force provisionally 21 September 2017), provide more scope for states to regulate (see art 8.9) but do not make any express provision regarding sovereign debt.

the wider international community) to prevent or minimize vulture and hold-out litigation.[261] The focus of investment arbitrators becomes less justifiable when it is clear that neither financial law nor human rights law play a meaningful role in ITA. Consequently, decision-makers, such as investment arbitrators, need to be cognizant of the wider implications of their conduct, and how this might affect state compliance with other international obligations when making decisions and writing awards. This position may be unrealistic. While in theory, IIAs can be interpreted in a manner that takes into account the need for financial stability and broader macroeconomic and social goals, in practice, investment arbitrators will be constrained by the limitations present in BITs. Consequently, investment arbitrators may be prevented from adequately addressing the complex and comprehensive questions that debt restructuring entails, including finding human rights-compliant solutions to financial crises.

24.68 Both trends additionally highlight that there is a clear need for better, well-coordinated responses from states and global institutions regarding how international law should address new problems.[262] For example, an institutional forum that solves sovereign debt disputes needs to be based on a broad international consensus. It is not clear whether states wish to permit creditors to access ITA: their BITs do not suggest that this was their intention; and almost all sovereign bonds issued provide for dispute resolution by way of litigation rather than arbitration.[263] However, by failing to expressly respond to developments in IIL relating to sovereign debt, states have tacitly permitted ITA to perform a function that appears to be contrary to their intentions, and enabled ITA to potentially generate detrimental human rights implications. A unified and strategic response is required to alter the current practice.

24.69 The use of ITA to resolve sovereign debt disputes creates negative human rights implications. Whilst this might have been an unanticipated consequence for both states and investment arbitrators, there are ways in which the identified problems can be mitigated. However, by examining the process underlying these

---

[261] See eg, Effects of foreign debt and other related international financial obligations of States on the full enjoyment of all human rights, particularly economic, social and cultural rights: the activities of vulture funds (3 October 2014) A/HRC/RES/27/30. This conduct is declared to be abusive in the UNCTAD, 'Principles on Promoting Responsible Sovereign Lending and Borrowing' (10 January 2012) <http://unctad.org/en/PublicationsLibrary/gdsddf2012misc1_en.pdf> Principle 7 accessed 21 September 2018.

[262] On how an underlying deliberative approach of those norms requires an openness towards interpreting 'different rationalities of various segments of financial regulation', as monetary, fiscal, banking, and development policies are intrinsically interlinked, see Matthias Goldmann, 'International Investment Law and Financial Regulation: towards a Deliberative Approach' in Christian J Tams, Stephan W Schill, and Rainer Hofmann (eds), *International Investment Law and the Global Financial Architecture* (Edward Elgar Publishing 2017) 57–85.

[263] See eg Stephen J Choi and Mitu Gulati, 'An Empirical Study of Securities Disclosure Practice' (2006) 80 Tulane Law Review 1023; Park and Samples (n 155) 1041.

problems, it is evident that the actions behind these consequences are indicative of larger problems in international law. Thus, there is a need for more integrated thinking regarding how to address the unanticipated consequences of actions taken by actors in the international community. Any purposive actions by actors in international law should be monitored to determine their wider effects. As unanticipated consequences arise, actors need to alter their conduct to avoid further detrimental and unanticipated outcomes. Had this position been adopted at the outset, the negative repercussions of using ITA as a forum for sovereign debt disputes might have been minimized.

25

HAS ISDS GONE ROGUE FOR AUSTRALIA AND NEW ZEALAND? CPTPP (C-3PO), RCEP (R2-D2), and Beyond

Amokura Kawharu and Luke Nottage[*]

A. Introduction	25.01	D. Low-profile Treaty	
B. Dual-Track ISDS Reforms	25.04	(Re)Negotiations	25.28
C. New Zealand's Renunciation of		E. Conclusions: C-3PO, R2-D2,	
ISDS: Déjà Vu	25.16	and Beyond	25.58

A. Introduction

25.01 This chapter considers the prospects for Australia and New Zealand to help lead 'bottom up' reform of investor–state dispute settlement (ISDS) in their current and planned investment treaty negotiations. Against a backdrop of increasing concern about ISDS, Australia briefly renounced ISDS between 2011 and 2013. In late 2017, New Zealand renounced ISDS for future treaties, creating a sense of déjà vu. This followed a period of intense public and political debate about New Zealand's participation in free trade agreements (FTAs), such as the Trans-Pacific Partnership (TPP), where much of that debate was focused on ISDS. Yet, despite New Zealand changing its position regarding ISDS, both it and Australia recently re-signed the TPP (re-named the Comprehensive and Progressive Trans-Pacific Partnership or CPTPP), which includes ISDS. Both are also participating in the negotiations for the Regional Comprehensive Economic Partnership (RCEP), which has been expected to include ISDS, as well as negotiations for other agreements and upgrades to existing ones. Thus, despite persistent concerns that ISDS

---

[*] For helpful information and/or feedback on earlier draft material, but without attributing any responsibility for the views expressed in this chapter, we thank Jonathan Bonnitcha, Amanda Murphy, two anonymous reviewers, and this *Yearbook*'s editorial team.

has gone 'rogue', rejection of ISDS is unlikely to be sustainable for either country. Instead, both should develop a joint reform agenda and pursue an investment court mechanism alternative to traditional ISDS, or some variant of it, in their ongoing treaty (re)negotiations. Path dependency and domestic political considerations may hamper these efforts. Nonetheless, and adopting a Star Wars movie theme,[1] we find that the CPTPP or 'C-3PO' is serviceable yet awkward, RCEP or 'R2-D2' has the potential to be more streamlined, while their treaties beyond both (rather like the 'BB8' droid) may turn out quite different again.

25.02 Overall, this chapter is mainly descriptive, outlining recent treaty (re)negotiations in both countries in complex and evolving (geo-)political contexts. However, section B introduces the idea of dual-track reforms, and argues that Australia and New Zealand should adopt a joint reform agenda in their treaty (re)negotiations while also participating in wider, multilateral reform initiatives. Section C then examines New Zealand's recent renunciation of ISDS for future treaties such as RCEP, yet its signature of the CPTPP with only minor amendments. Section D outlines lower-profile treaty (re)negotiations by New Zealand and Australia (eg with Singapore, Uruguay, Indonesia, India, and the EU).

25.03 The concluding section E comes back to a more normative argument. In a 2015 article in *The Guardian* newspaper, Foley Hoag lawyer Luis Parada considered the state of affairs regarding ISDS, and concluded: 'I think the investor-state arbitration system was created with good intentions, but in practice it has gone completely rogue'.[2] New Zealand's recent rejection of ISDS, following Australia's earlier example, underscores that the system continues to face demands for further reflection and reform. Thus, in the concluding section E, we reiterate our earlier arguments that an investment court mechanism is a promising way forward for Australia as well as New Zealand. Both countries' commonalities, particularly regarding contemporary investment treaty negotiations and drafting, create a platform for more concerted and pro-active contributions towards redesigning aspects of international investment dispute resolution. Both countries should therefore work together in promoting an investment court mechanism or some hybrid in their ongoing treaty (re)negotiations, given their many shared interests and particularly close economic, legal and geopolitical connections.[3]

---

[1] Jonathan Roberts, 'Star Wars: These Could be the Droids We're Looking for in Real Life' *The Conversation* (18 December 2015) <https://theconversation.com/star-wars-these-could-be-the-droids-were-looking-for-in-real-life-52285>. For further information about the droids in the *Star Wars* universe, see Daniel Wallace, *Star Wars: The New Essential Guide to Droids* (2nd edn, Del Rey 2006).

[2] Claire Provost and Matt Kennard, 'The Obscure Legal System That Lets Corporations Sue Countries' *The Guardian* (online), 10 June 2015 <https://www.theguardian.com/business/2015/jun/10/obscure-legal-system-lets-corportations-sue-states-ttip-icsid>. We thank Amanda Murphy for drawing our attention to this article.

[3] Amokura Kawharu and Luke Nottage, 'Models for Investment Treaties in the Asian Region: An Underview' (2017) 34 Arizona Journal of International and Comparative Law 461, Part 1B.

B. Dual-Track ISDS Reforms

25.04 The number of known treaty-based investor–state dispute settlement (ISDS) claims reached 855 by the end of 2017 (including 65 in that year),[4] mostly brought since the early 1990s.[5] Almost all host states have experienced at least one ISDS claim, even developed countries such as Australia. The 2011 Phillip Morris challenge to tobacco plain packaging laws drew much public attention in Australia until it was dismissed on jurisdictional grounds in late 2015,[6] as indicated in Figure 25.1.

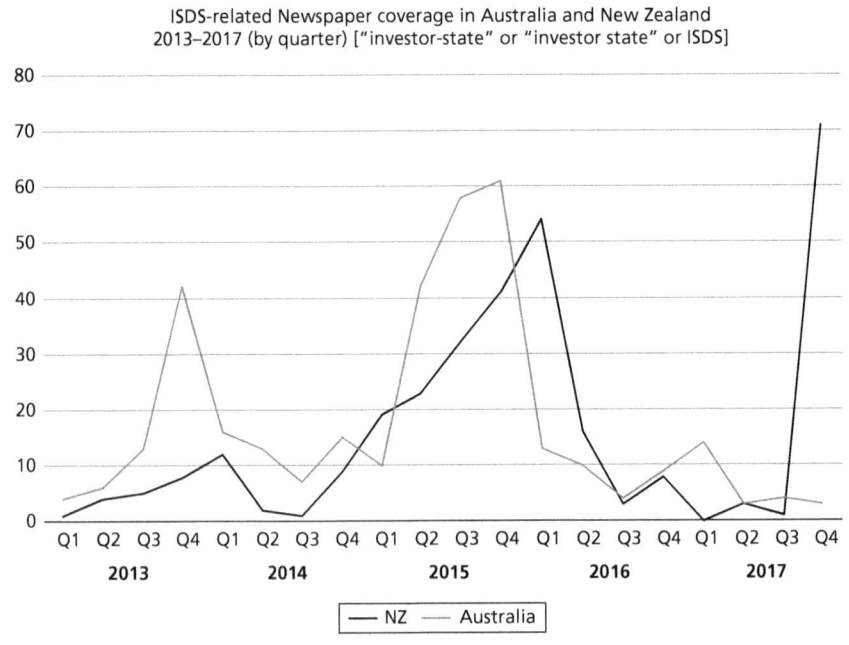

Figure 25.1 ISDS-related Newspaper Coverage in Australia and New Zealand (2013–17, by quarter)[a]

[a] Newspaper records were retrieved from the Factiva database using the expression ['investor-state' or 'investor state' or ISDS]: Australian print newspapers selected for analysis were *The Australian*, *Australian Financial Review*, the *Daily Telegraph*, the *Sydney Morning Herald*, *The Age*, the *Herald Sun*, the *Courier-Mail*, the *Adelaide Advertiser*, and the *West Australian*. New Zealand print newspaper selected for analysis were the *New Zealand Herald*, the *Dominion Post*, *The Press*, *Waikato Times*, *Otago Daily Times*, *The Southland Times*, *Hawke's Bay Today*, *Taranaki Daily News*, and *Bay of Plenty Times*.

---

[4] United Nations Conference on Trade and Development, *Investment Dispute Settlement Navigator* <http://investmentpolicyhub.unctad.org/ISDS>.

[5] This compares with 542 mostly trade-related inter-state claims brought before the World Trade Organization (WTO) since it became operational in 1995. WTO, 'Dispute Settlement: The Disputes' <https://www.wto.org/english/tratop_e/dispu_e/find_dispu_cases_e.htm>.

[6] Jarrod Hepburn and Luke Nottage, 'A Procedural Win for Public Health Measures' (2017) 18 Journal of World Investment and Trade 307, updated and expanded in Anselmo Reyes (ed), *Hochelaga Lectures 2017* (University of Hong Kong, forthcoming).

New Zealand has not yet been subjected to a treaty-based ISDS claim, only an early contract-based claim where consent had been given to arbitration before the International Centre for Settlement of Investment Disputes (ICSID).[7] But Figure 25.1 indicates the sharp increase in newspaper coverage of ISDS in New Zealand in 2015 and in 2017, which is all the more remarkable given that the population and newspaper circulation is much smaller than in Australia. The upsurge in 2015 was partly because ISDS became a matter of public and parliamentary debate as New Zealand concluded and brought into force a free trade agreement (FTA) with South Korea, a debate that was influenced by the Phillip Morris claim against Australia. But the main reason for the increase was that the then national government was pressing for conclusion of the Trans-Pacific Partnership (TPP) FTA including the United States (US).[8] This stoked public fears, as in Australia and other TPP negotiating partners like Japan,[9] about New Zealand potentially being sued by supposedly litigious Americans.[10]

25.05

In response to growing concerns about ISDS in some developed as well as developing countries, reform initiatives are now proceeding in multilateral fora. Notably, in late 2017 the United Nations Commission on International Trade Law (UNCITRAL) began a project to investigate possible ISDS reforms.[11] This project will build on ongoing research from the United Nations Conference on Trade and Development (UNCTAD), which had moved from being a strong

25.06

---

[7] *Mobil Oil Corp v Her Majesty the Queen in Right of New Zealand*, , ICSID ARB/87/2, Findings on Liability, Interpretation and Allied Issues (4 May 1989); (1997) 4 ICSID Reports 140 <https://icsid.worldbank.org/en/Pages/cases/casedetail.aspx?CaseNo=ARB%2f87%2f2> (and related litigation proceedings, *Attorney-General v Mobil Oil NZ Ltd* [1989] 2 NZLR 649).

[8] Amokura Kawharu, 'Process, Politics and the Politics of Process: The Trans-Pacific Partnership in New Zealand' (2016) 17 Melbourne Journal of International Law 286, 297–99.

[9] Luke Nottage, 'Investor-State Arbitration Policy and Practice in Australia' in Armand de Mestral (ed), *Second Thoughts: Investor-State Arbitration Between Developed Democracies* (Centre for International Governance Innovation 2017); Shotaro Hamamoto, 'Recent Anti-ISDS Discourse in the Japanese Diet: A Dressed-Up But Glaring Hypocrisy' (2015) 16 Journal of World Investment and Trade 931.

[10] See eg the comments in relation to the New Zealand–Korea FTA of Hon Phil Goff, then an opposition Labour MP: 'I want to touch on the investor-State dispute settlement, because that was the area in the treaty examination that really drew the flak. It was not about Korea.... The concern that people had, and I think it is a genuine concern, was that the United States is a litigious country' (NZPD vol 706/4401, 16 June 2015). See also Chris Bramwell, 'Will the TPP undermine NZ's sovereignty?' *Radio New Zealand* (3 February 2016) <https://www.radionz.co.nz/news/political/295605/will-tpp-undermine-nz%27s-sovereignty> (quoting prominent ISDS critic, Professor Jane Kelsey: 'You're looking at empowering more than 1000 US corporations that are notoriously litigious'). In fact, eg, Canadian investors are more likely to file ISDS claims on a per capita basis than US investors. See Luke Nottage, 'Are US Investors Exceptionally Litigious with ISDS Claims?' (*Kluwer Arbitration Blog*, 14 November 2016) <http://kluwerarbitrationblog.com/2016/11/14/are-us-investors-exceptionally-litigious-with-isds-claims/>.

[11] UNCITRAL, Working Group III, '2017 to Present: Investor-State Dispute Settlement Reform' <http://www.uncitral.org/uncitral/en/commission/working_groups/3Investor_State.html>. This initiative follows the publication of a paper by the UNCITRAL Secretariat, *Possible Reform of Investor-State Dispute Settlement (ISDS)*, 34th session (18 September 2017) UN Doc A/CN.9/WG.III/WP.142.

advocate of pro-investor bilateral investment treaties (BITs) until the early 2000s, to advocating for reforming ISDS and the investment treaty framework more broadly in favour of host state interests.[12] Even the Organisation for Economic Co-operation and Development (OECD), whose membership is comprised of developed economies, has shifted away from promoting ISDS, as it did in negotiations for the Multilateral Agreement on Investment, which stalled in the late 1990s. For example, a recent OECD report casts doubt on the empirical evidence for the rationales conventionally given for providing for ISDS in investment treaties, including fostering more cross-border foreign direct investment (FDI) and respect for the rule of law, particularly in developing countries.[13]

25.07 However, given the inevitably slow pace of UNCITRAL deliberations as well as the decentralized nature of the investment treaty system,[14] there is also much scope for 'bottom-up' reforms to be promoted through innovations in bilateral and regional BIT and FTA (re)negotiations. For example, in late 2017, New Zealand's newly elected Labour-led coalition government declared that it would no longer agree to ISDS provisions in future treaties—reversing the country's longstanding treaty practice, especially for FTAs. This explains the upsurge in New Zealand newspaper discussions of ISDS, as shown in Figure 25.1. As will be explained, there is a strong sense of 'déjà vu' with Australia's renunciation of ISDS under the centre-left Gillard government from 2011 until it lost power in 2013, and Australia reverted to its longstanding practice of mostly including ISDS but sometimes omitting provisions on a case-by-case basis.

25.08 New Zealand's new government also declared that it would seek amendments to the ISDS provisions in the TPP signed by its predecessor and eleven other states on 5 February 2016 in Auckland, in the context of President Donald Trump's withdrawal of the US in January 2017. Section C below shows, however, that minimal amendments were made to the TPP text when it was re-signed by New Zealand and ten other states on 8 March 2018.[15] The re-signed agreement was re-named as the 'Comprehensive and Progressive Trans-Pacific Partnership' (CPTPP),

---

[12] Nicolás M Perrone, 'UNCTAD's World Investment Reports 1991–2015: 25 Years of Narratives Justifying and Balancing Foreign Investor Rights' (2018) 19(1) Journal of World Investment and Trade 7.

[13] Joachim Pohl, 'Societal Benefits and Costs of International Investment Agreements: A Critical Review of Aspects and Available Empirical Evidence' (OECD Working Papers on International Investment 2018/01, Organisation for Economic Co-operation and Development, 2018) <http://www.oecd-ilibrary.org/finance-and-investment/societal-benefits-and-costs-of-international-investment-agreements_e5f85c3d-en> 16–31.

[14] Joost Pauwelyn, 'At the Edge of Chaos? Foreign Investment Law as a Complex Adaptive System, How It Emerged And How It Can Be Reformed' (2014) 29 ICSID Review 372.

[15] The CPTPP will enter into force from 31 December 2018 as at least six (or at least 50 per cent of the signatories, whichever is the smaller number) have ratified it (art 3), including Australia and New Zealand. For its text and updates, see <https://dfat.gov.au/TRADE/AGREEMENTS/NOT-YET-IN-FORCE/TPP-11/Pages/trans-pacific-partnership-agreement-tpp.aspx>.

likely in an effort to suggest to observers that the changes were more substantial. However, in our view, the name change is rather meaningless. (Accordingly, partly to make some fun of the attempt to convince observers that the CPTPP is more 'progressive' than the TPP, we sometimes instead abbreviate this treaty simply as 'C-3PO', the clunky but serviceable droid from the blockbuster *Star Wars* movies.[16]) Additionally, New Zealand signed bilateral side-letters, excluding ISDS altogether, with Australia (consistent with their past treaties, including the original TPP), Peru, Brunei, Malaysia, and Vietnam. Yet this exclusion under the CPTPP is symbolic for the latter three, both because ISDS-based protections and liberalization commitments remain under the 2009 ASEAN–Australia–New Zealand FTA (AANZFTA), and because investment to and from those countries is minimal anyway.

25.09 Thirdly, when signing the CPTPP, New Zealand issued a Joint Declaration with Canada and Chile stating that they 'intend to work together on matters relating to the evolving practice' of ISDS, 'including as part of the ongoing review and implementation' of the CPTPP.[17] Most of their guiding principles for this joint project, as stated in the Joint Declaration, are aspirational (reaffirming the right to regulate and strong safeguards for host states, input from civil society and others, consideration of multilateral initiatives), but may appeal to domestic constituencies, especially in New Zealand. But the Joint Declaration also highlights that New Zealand, Canada, and Chile wish to focus on vexed issues such as 'double-hatting' (ISDS arbitrators still acting as counsel in other cases, possibly addressing similar issues) and costs of proceedings especially for smaller investors.[18]

25.10 Interestingly, however, Australia was not prepared to join in the Joint Declaration with New Zealand and its two partners, including Canada which has already

---

[16] See n 1.
[17] Ministry of Foreign Affairs and Trade, *CPTPP Joint Declaration* <https://www.mfat.govt.nz/assets/CPTPP/CPTPP-Joint-Declaration-ISDS-Final.pdf>. We thank Murray Griffin for bringing this document to our attention. It is not listed among the CPTPP texts (including side instruments) online (see n 16) perhaps because the three states do not intend to be bound under international law by this joint statement of intent.
[18] Specifically, the three parties to the Joint Declaration state (ibid) that they:

- 'Intend to promote transparent conduct rules on the ethical responsibilities of arbitrators in ISDS procedures, including conflict of interest rules that prevent arbitrators from acting, for the duration of their appointment, as counsel or party appointed expert or witness in other proceedings, pursuant to Article 9.22.6 of the CPTPP [requiring guidance or a code of ethics for ISDS arbitrators before the treaty comes into force]; and
- Recognise the need to ensure that small and medium-sized enterprises (SMEs) are able to fully benefit from the protections of the investment chapter, and intend to promote rules that reduce the costs of dispute settlement for SMEs.'

agreed to a permanent court alternative in its FTA with the European Union (EU) that expressly prohibits double-hatting for court members. This is despite empirical evidence that the double-hatting problem perceived in ISDS has not been 'working itself clean' world-wide,[19] and emerging criticism of this phenomenon from Australian commentators.[20]

25.11 Such conservatism may reflect Australia's greater path-dependence on contemporary US treaty practice recently, as compared to New Zealand's. This is despite previous studies showing weaker path dependency through at least some willingness particularly on Australia's part to experiment in some respects.[21] Until recently such path-dependence on US treaty practice had been pervasive among many Asia-Pacific states, and epitomized by the TPP (and even still the CPTPP).[22] As we show, Australia still seems to be (re)negotiating treaties following the TPP template, although these developments are much more low profile and have attracted little media attention. Nonetheless, Australia may be jolted out of this path if the current government loses power (with the next election due by April 2019), as the Labor opposition maintains its opposition in principle to ISDS provisions. Since it has only a knife-edge majority in the lower House of Representatives and no majority in the Senate, the government may also need to find a compromise approach to be able to negotiate and then ratify the Regional Comprehensive Economic Partnership (RCEP), which we sometimes dub 'R2-D2' (the droid in *Star Wars* who accompanies C3PO but with a significantly different design).[23] Australia will also need to be open to a new design in the FTA it is negotiating with the EU. The EU has already signalled that it has abandoned conventional ISDS, achieving instead a permanent investment court mechanism in FTAs with Canada, Vietnam, Singapore, and Mexico (all signatories to the CPTPP or C-3PO) and is now pressing for a multilateral investment court solution within the UNCITRAL reform project.[24] Core features of the permanent investment court mechanism include:

---

[19] Malcolm Langford, Daniel Behn, and Runar Hilleren Lie, 'The Revolving Door in International Investment Arbitration' (2017) 20 Journal of International Economic Law 301.

[20] Andrew Mitchell, Elizabeth Sheargold, and Tania Voon, *Regulatory Autonomy in International Economic Law: The Evolution of Australian Policy on Trade and Investment* (Elgar 2018) 195; Murray Griffin, 'Pacific Pact Could Limit Who Sits on Investor Dispute Panels' Bloomberg BNA's *International Trade Daily* (29 March 2018).

[21] Examples include the insertion of WTO-like general exception clauses, the unique 'public welfare notice' provision in 2015 Australia's FTA with China, and Australia's willingness to exclude ISDS altogether in some FTAs (although including one with the US signed in 2004). See generally Nottage (n 10); Mitchell, Sheargold, and Voon (n 21) 121–62.

[22] Wolfgang Alschner and Dmitriy Skougarevskiy, 'The New Gold Standard? Empirically Situating the Trans-Pacific Partnership in the Investment Treaty Universe' (2016) 17 Journal of World Investment & Trade 339.

[23] See references cited, n 1.

[24] Council of the European Union, Negotiating directives for a Convention establishing a multilateral court for the settlement of investment disputes, 12981/17 ADD 1 DCL 1 (1 March 2018).

- the member states (not individual investors) pre-selecting arbitrators;
- outright prohibition of double-hatting (rather than relying on general requirements for arbitrator independence and impartiality); and
- an appellate review mechanism (envisaged only as a topic for future discussion in the TPP, Article 9.23(11)).

25.12 Such a joint initiative is particularly important given that both countries have focused on FTAs in Asia. It is the most dynamic region in the world economy, where some states (like Indonesia and especially India) are also having second thoughts about ISDS and investment treaties, or are increasingly becoming 'rule makers' rather than 'rule takers' in international investment law.[25] Australia and New Zealand cannot afford to wait and see whether UNCITRAL comes up with a concrete *multilateral* reform proposal, and then whether other countries adopt it. That will take many years and adoption will be less likely unless examples can be given where innovations such as an investment court, or at least some of its core features, can be shown to have been acceptable and effective at *bilateral and regional* levels. In other words, we urge both countries to collaborate in pursuing *dual-track* reforms to the international investment dispute resolution system. The outcome of such a joint initiative may contribute to further innovations in design—analogous to 'BB8', a completely different model of droid that appears in the most recent *Star Wars* movies.[26] Further creative thinking and flexibility will be needed to address concerns that the traditional ISDS mechanism (or its C-3PO variant) has gone rogue—a view that brings to mind the recent 'Rogue One' spin-off movie.[27] Australia and New Zealand cannot afford to be complacent, given the additional risk that the increasingly negative public image of investment treaty arbitration will spread into the field of commercial arbitration.[28]

---

[25] Luke Nottage, Julien Chaisse, and Sakda Thanitcul, 'International Investment Treaties and Arbitration Across Asia: A Bird's Eye View' in Julien Chaisse and Luke Nottage (eds), *International Investment Treaties and Arbitration Across Asia* (Brill 2017).

[26] Namely, JJ Abrams, 'Star Wars: Episode VII—The Force Awakens' (Lucasfilm Ltd, Bad Robot Productions, Walt Disney Studios, 2015) and Rian Johnson, 'Star Wars: Episode VIII—The Last Jedi' (Lucasfilm Ltd, Walt Disney Studios, Ram Bergman Productions, 2017).

[27] Gareth Edwards, 'Rogue One: A Star Wars Story' (Lucasfilm, Allison Shearmur Productions, Black Hangar Studios, Truenorth Productions, Walt Disney Pictures, 2016).

[28] Luke Nottage, 'International Arbitration and Society at Large' in Andrea K Björklund, Franco Ferrari, and Stefan Kröll (eds), *The Cambridge Compendium on International Arbitration* (forthcoming), with a manuscript version available at <https://papers.ssrn.com/sol3/papers.cfm?abstract_id=3116528> and James Allsop, Chief Justice of the Federal Court of Australia, 'Commercial and Investor-State Arbitration: The Importance of Recognising Their Differences' (Opening Keynote Address delivered at ICCA Congress, Sydney, 16 April 2018) <http://www.fedcourt.gov.au/digital-law-library/judges-speeches/chief-justice-allsop/allsop-cj-20180416>.

C. New Zealand's Renunciation of ISDS: Déjà Vu

25.13 New Zealand's acceptance of the 'rogue' status of ISDS was made clear following the election of a new centre-left Labour-led coalition government that took office in October 2017. In a post-Cabinet press conference on 31 October, Prime Minister Jacinda Ardern announced that: 'We remain determined to do our utmost to amend the ISDS provisions of TPP. In addition, Cabinet has today instructed trade negotiation officials to oppose ISDS in any future free trade agreements.'[29] (Ardern is also reported to have described ISDS as a 'dog'.[30]) The announcement followed the unexpected electoral victory over the more centre-right National Party, which had governed for three terms. The National Party had actively promoted FTAs, including ISDS-backed commitments. Earlier Labour governments had also promoted FTAs, notably with China (in force from 2008, and also containing ISDS provisions). While correlation does not necessarily mean causation, it is noteworthy that the FTA with China has been accompanied by a four-fold increase in goods exports from New Zealand to China, while China has risen to become New Zealand's ninth largest source of foreign investment.[31] Overall, China now ranks as New Zealand's second-largest trading partner.[32]

25.14 However, bipartisan support over FTAs and foreign investment had begun to fray when the national government signed the South Korea FTA in 2015 and the TPP in February 2016. During inquiries into ratification, Labour parliamentarians raised concerns about whether these agreements allowed sufficient host state regulatory space.[33] A key concern was whether they allowed New Zealand to introduce new types of restrictions over purchases by foreigners of residential property, the market for which had been booming. Some questions were also raised about ISDS, reflecting increasing awareness of and generally negative public sentiment towards ISDS, as evidenced in the analysis of New Zealand newspaper reports,[34] and Figure 25.1. Also in 2015, and shortly after the parliamentary select

---

[29] Derek Cheng, 'Ban on Foreign House Buyers by Early 2018—But Aussie Buyers Exempt' *New Zealand Herald* (online) (31 October 2017) <http://www.nzherald.co.nz/business/news/article.cfm?c_id=3&objectid=11939067>.

[30] Vernon Small, 'Jacinda Ardern Seeking TPP Concessions at First Appearance on International Stage' *stuff.co.nz* (online) (6 November 2017) <https://www.stuff.co.nz/national/politics/98605976/jacinda-ardern-seeking-tpp-concessions-at-first-appearance-on-international-stage>.

[31] New Zealand Ministry of Foreign Affairs and Trade, 'NZ-China FTA Upgrade' <https://www.mfat.govt.nz/en/trade/free-trade-agreements/free-trade-agreements-in-force/nz-china-free-trade-agreement>.

[32] Australia has also seen an upsurge since it signed an FTA in 2015: Kirsty Needham, 'China Trade with Australia Soars, Along with War of Words' *Sydney Morning Herald* (online) (12 January 2018) <http://www.smh.com.au/world/china-trade-with-australia-soars-along-with-war-of-words-20180112-h0hfkq.html>.

[33] See further Kawharu (n 9) Oliver Hailes and Andrew Geddis, 'The Trans-Pacific Partnership in New Zealand's Constitution' (2016) 27(2) New Zealand Universities Law Review 226.

[34] Kawharu and Nottage (n 3).

committee report on the South Korea FTA was issued, the populist New Zealand First party tabled the 'Fighting Foreign Corporate Control Bill'[35] which would have precluded governments from agreeing to ISDS provisions in future treaties. At the time, the Labour Opposition was prepared to support the Bill through to the select committee stage so as to enable focused scrutiny of ISDS. It was unlikely to have backed the legislation any further since it was contrary to Labour's view of the Executive's prerogative to negotiate treaties, yet the Bill was anyway defeated at its first reading.

25.15 As in countries like Japan[36] and Korea,[37] the recent public concerns over ISDS may in part have reflected New Zealand's love-hate relationship with the US, and the purported litigiousness of its businesspeople.[38] The US was a driving force behind the TPP negotiations, but also a major attraction for New Zealand since an FTA with the US had long been a top trade priority. Concerns also arose in response to the lack of time allowed for proper parliamentary scrutiny and the lack of independent reporting on the agreement, which gave rise to the impression that it was being rushed through the ratification process without sufficient opportunity for informed public discussion.[39]

25.16 In the October 2017 general election, Labour took 46 out of 120 seats in Parliament, while National took 56. Since neither party had an overall majority, New Zealand First entered into negotiations with each of them with a view to forming a coalition government.[40] New Zealand First eventually decided to join with Labour, citing closer alignment with Labour on the role of capitalism in society, and perhaps sensing a mood for change. Policy-wise, there is reasonable alignment between New Zealand First and Labour on controls over foreign investment and immigration.

25.17 Against this political backdrop, it is unsurprising that the new Labour-led government declared soon after taking office that it would legislate stricter controls over foreign investment in residential land. Specifically, the new government introduced a bill that will subject the acquisition by foreigners of residential (including

---

[35] New Zealand Parliament, 'Fighting Foreign Corporate Control Bill' <https://www.parliament.nz/en/pb/bills-and-laws/bills-proposed-laws/document/00DBHOH_BILL62503_1/fighting-foreign-corporate-control-bill>.

[36] Shotaro Hamomoto, 'Debates in Japan over Investor-State Arbitration with Developed States' in Armand deMestral (ed), *Second Thoughts: Investor-State Arbitration Between Developed Democracies* (Centre for International Governance Innovation 2017).

[37] Younsik Kim, 'Investor-State Arbitration in South Korean International Trade Policies: An Uncertain Future, Trapped by the Past' in Armand deMestral (ed), *Second Thoughts: Investor-State Arbitration Between Developed Democracies* (Centre for International Governance Innovation 2017).

[38] See n 11.

[39] See Kawharu (n 9).

[40] New Zealand First has been led since its establishment in 1993 by former National Party politician Winston Peters, while its current deputy is former Labour Party politician Shane Jones. It has formed governments with both National and Labour.

lifestyle) land to new consent pathways, effectively adding residential housing to New Zealand's foreign investment screening regime.[41] Presumably, it is treating residential housing as a new class of 'sensitive land', and will rely on an exemption in New Zealand's FTAs that allows New Zealand to maintain its screening regime with respect to the current categories of screened investment (which include sensitive land). The one exception is its FTA with Singapore (in force since 2001), which expressly confines sensitive land to non-urban land.[42] The government accepts it will need to negotiate a solution with Singapore, while Australian investors will be excluded from the new measure.[43]

25.18 It is also unsurprising that the new government made the announcement regarding ISDS on 31 October 2017. What is rather more surprising was the New Zealand government's reaching an agreement in principle for the CPTPP at the APEC Leaders' meeting on 11 November in Vietnam, with a few more changes (reportedly unrelated to investment chapter) agreed on 23 January 2018 in Tokyo.[44] As signed on 8 March 2018, the CPTPP will commit New Zealand and the remaining ten other signatories, including Japan (with which it still has no bilateral FTA), to ISDS provisions, but their application to investment agreements and investment authorizations will be suspended.[45] In New Zealand's case however, investment authorizations were already excluded from ISDS by virtue

---

[41] Overseas Investment Amendment Act 2018. Lifestyle land is defined in s 4 of the Act as land which is classified as lifestyle land in valuation rolls for rating purposes. It generally covers land in rural areas that is used for residential purposes.

[42] Agreement Between New Zealand and Singapore on a Closer Economic Partnership (opened for signature 14 November 2000, entered into force 1 January 2001), Annex 3.1.A.

[43] Henry Cooke, 'Labour will Make all Existing Homes "Sensitive," Effectively Banning Foreign Buyers' *stuff.co.nz* (online) (31 October 2017) <https://www.stuff.co.nz/national/politics/98417459/labour-will-make-all-existing-homes-sensitive-effectively-banning-foreign-buyers>.

[44] Vernon Small, 'Trans-Pacific Partnership: 11 Trade Ministers Reach Deal to Keep Deal Alive' *stuff.co.nz* (online) (11 November 2017) <https://www.stuff.co.nz/business/98790099/transpacific-partnership-11-trade-ministers-reach-deal-to-keep-deal-alive>. After Prime Minister Justin Trudeau did not attend a final meeting in Vietnam, it was unclear whether Canada would sign up to the Vietnam agreement in principle or some variant: Rosie Lewis, 'Terror, Trade and North Korea Top Turnbull's Tokyo Agenda' *The Australian* (online) (18 January 2018) <http://www.theaustralian.com.au/national-affairs/foreign-affairs/terror-trade-and-north-korea-top-turnbulls-tokyo-agenda/news-story/364422cef06bfd5476df7d4a185264e4>. One Australian news report even implied that this upset might have been linked to Australia notifying a WTO dispute against Canada over wine, its first claim since 2003: 'Trade Row Escalates After Trudeau Snub at Vietnam Summit' *The Australian* (online) (18 January 2018). But agreement on C-3PO was then reached by all eleven original signatories other than the US: Josh Wingrove et al, 'Pacific Nations Agree to Save TPP Trade Pact After Trump Quit' *Bloomsberg* (23 January 2018) <https://www.bloomberg.com/news/articles/2018-01-23/tpp-members-complete-text-seek-to-sign-by-march-singapore-says>.

[45] CPTPP Annex, para 2. ASEAN, Australia (except for its FTA with Korea) and New Zealand had not agreed in previous FTAs or 'ASEAN+' investment treaties to extend ISDS procedures to investment agreements or authorizations, but only to violations of substantive treaty commitments. See Luke Nottage, 'The Investment Chapter and ISDS in the CPTPP: Lessons from and for Southeast Asia' in Cassey Lee (eds), *The CPTPP: Implications for Southeast Asia* (Institute for Southeast Asian Studies, Singapore, forthcoming).

of Annex 9-H of the original TPP text.[46] A further change from the original TPP is that the minimum standard of treatment protection has been suspended with respect to ISDS for investments in the financial services sector.[47] However, ISDS-backed protections for fair and equitable treatment or other violations may also remain under any pre-existing bilateral or regional treaties, such as AANZFTA.[48]

25.19 As noted, New Zealand also exchanged bilateral side letters excluding ISDS with Australia (consistent with their past practice) and Peru, as well as (more symbolically) with Brunei, Malaysia, and Vietnam, and issued a Joint Declaration on ISDS reforms with Canada and Chile. Despite these efforts, it seems that New Zealand has proven agreeable to quite limited actual changes to the TPP provisions on ISDS. Those were not renegotiated, for example, to add an appellate review mechanism. This is even though future agreement on such a mechanism is envisaged in TPP Article 9.23(11), and despite some form of appellate review being increasingly advocated by those unhappy about inconsistencies in rulings from traditionally structured one-tier ISDS tribunals.[49] Looking also at the other outcomes from the renegotiated TPP and adopting a wider perspective, an acute observer of New Zealand's international trade policy has suggested that the new government's bark may prove worse than its bite.[50]

25.20 Given these developments with the TPP, what will happen now with the ongoing 'ASEAN+6' negotiations for RCEP? ISDS was included in a leaked 2015 draft RCEP investment chapter that the authors of this chapter analysed in a separate paper.[51] The danger for New Zealand is that if it insists on removing ISDS in this proposed regional FTA, counterparties insistent on ISDS commitments may force New Zealand to leave the pact. Those counterparties may hope that the National Party will return to power so that New Zealand can then sign the treaty, including ISDS commitments. Another option would be for New Zealand to exclude the application of ISDS to New Zealand, via bilateral side letters exchanged with RCEP counterparties. In light of the CPTPP experience (in which New Zealand only secured side letters with Australia, Peru, Brunei, Malaysia, and

---

[46] The same is true for Australia, Canada, and Mexico, which were also covered by TPP, Annex 9-H.

[47] CPTPP Annex, para 4. For further discussion of the changes between the TPP and CPTPP with respect to investment, see Jarrod Hepburn, 'Revived Trans-Pacific Partnership (TPP) Treaty Text is Released, with a Few Tweaks to the Previously Negotiated Investment Chapter; Australia and New Zealand Continue to Disapply ISDS between them' *Investment Arbitration Reporter* (21 February 2018).

[48] Most foreign investment in the New Zealand financial services sector is by Australian investors, who do not enjoy ISDS-backed protections.

[49] See generally eg Jaemin Lee, 'Taming Investor-State Arbitration? Joint Committees and Binding Interpretations' in Julien Chaisse and Tsai-yu Lin (ed), *International Law and Government: Essays in Honour of Mitsuo Matsushita* (OUP 2016).

[50] Gary Hawke, 'New Zealand Trading Policy for Fig Leaves' *East Asian Forum* (23 November 2017) <http://www.eastasiaforum.org/2017/11/23/new-zealand-trading-policy-for-fig-leaves/>.

[51] Kawharu and Nottage (n 3).

Vietnam), it seems unlikely that the government will be able to fulfil its policy promise of opposing ISDS in future agreements.

25.21 As mentioned, there are clear parallels with the situation in Australia over 2011–2013.[52] The centre-left Gillard Labor government was in coalition with the more leftist Greens, which later proposed an anti-ISDS Bill in 2014 (eventually voted down by both the new Liberal coalition government and the by-then Labor opposition).[53] The Gillard government adopted a recommendation (by majority) from the Australian government's Productivity Commission 2010 trade policy review report to eschew ISDS in future FTAs.[54] Consequently, until it lost power in 2013, the Gillard government was unable to conclude major FTAs with countries like China and Korea that had strongly pressed for ISDS. The Australian experience reinforces our view that New Zealand risks its participation in treaty negotiations if it maintains a hard opposition to ISDS.

25.22 There are however differences in the circumstances leading to the Australian and New Zealand positions against ISDS, and these differences should also sound caution for New Zealand. A first difference was that by 2011 Australia had already been notified of its first treaty-based ISDS claim, whereas New Zealand has still not been subject to any. In other words, there was no single controversial issue directly affecting New Zealand that might warrant a dramatic policy decision. Secondly and relatedly, New Zealand's Labour Party announced its anti-ISDS policy without the benefit of a cost-benefit analysis such as that produced by the Australian Productivity Commission.[55] A practical difference for New Zealand is

---

[52] Nottage (n 10).

[53] Luke Nottage, 'The 'Anti-ISDS Bill' Before the Senate: What Future for Investor-State Arbitration in Australia?' (2015) XVIII International Trade and Business Law Review 245.

[54] For early academic critiques of the Commission's report, see eg Luke Nottage, 'The Rise and Possible Fall of Investor-State Arbitration in Asia: A Skeptic's View of Australia's "Gillard Government Trade Policy Statement"' (2011) 5 Transnational Dispute Management Journal <https://ssrn.com/abstract=1860505>; Jurgen Kurtz, 'Australia's Rejection of Investor-State Arbitration: Causation, Omission and Implication' (2012) 27 ICSID Review 65; Leon Trakman, 'Choosing Domestic Courts over Investor-State Arbitration: Australia's Repudiation of the Status Quo' (2012) 35 University of New South Wales Law Journal 979. These authors subsequently were awarded an Australian Research Council grant (DP140102526, 2014-7), along with Shiro Armstrong, to investigate international investment dispute management from an Australian perspective with a focus on the Asia-Pacific region. For a summary and outputs, see Luke Nottage, 'Publications Listing' on *Japanese Law and the Asia-Pacific* (19 February 2016) <http://blogs.usyd.edu.au/japaneselaw/2016/02/publications_listing_arc2.html>. For a very recent critique of the Productivity Commission's approach and the 2011 Trade Policy Statement, see Kyle Dickson-Smith and Bryan Mercurio, 'Australia's Position on Investor-State Dispute Settlement: Fruit of a Poisonous Tree or a Few Rotten Apples?' (2018) 40 Sydney Law Review 213.

[55] It appears to be common for policymakers to determine policy with respect to investment treaties without the benefit of cost-benefit analyses. See Jonathan Bonnitcha, Lauge Poulsen, and Michael Waibel, *The Political Economy of the Investment Treaty Regime* (OUP 2017) at 202, 206, and 223–26, describing the historical lack of debate and awareness of the implications of investment treaties by policymakers, as well as the lack of expertise within developing countries during negotiations. Others have pointed out that developed countries (such as Australia) also appear to have lacked expertise in negotiating and drafting (early) BITs, but that some developing countries

that major FDI exporting countries negotiating RCEP, which have strong interests in ISDS protections, already have access to those ISDS protections through existing FTAs with New Zealand (namely with China, Korea, and Singapore via earlier FTAs as well as AANZFTA) or will obtain ISDS if CPTPP comes into force (namely Japan). Australia is the other big FDI exporter into New Zealand, but their particularly closely linked economies, polities, and legal systems arguably make this a special case for excluding ISDS protections anyway. New Zealand does not have an FTA with India, but while India may push for ISDS in RCEP based on its Model BIT finalized and publicized in January 2016,[56] ISDS is heavily circumscribed in the Indian Model through a lengthy exhaustion of local remedies requirement (as will be discussed further). India apparently agreed to omit ISDS altogether in its recent investment facilitation agreement with Brazil (which has a longer-standing aversion to ISDS).[57] As for the Southeast Asian countries negotiating RCEP, most states are comfortable with ISDS but are not strong proponents (except perhaps Singapore),[58] while Indonesia is reconsidering its position in light of some recent high-profile claims (as will be mentioned further).

25.23 Given the complex domestic situation in New Zealand and for RCEP negotiations, it is time for New Zealand—and indeed Australia, where the current coalition government struggles to retain a bare majority[59]—to rethink its approach more generally towards investment treaties. After all, the month before Australia's general election in July 2016, the opposition's deputy leader had also declared that a new Labor government 'will not accept [ISDS] provisions in new trade agreements'. She also announced that it would 'develop a negotiating plan to remove ISDS provisions in [older agreements]. Where this is not possible we will seek to update the provisions with modern safeguards.'[60] So far, the New

---

(notably Thailand) have displayed more expertise than posited by Poulsen. See Luke Nottage, 'Rebalancing Investment Treaties: Two Approaches' (2016) 17 Journal of World Investment and Trade 1015 (adapted in Mahdev Mohan and Chester Brown (eds), *Regulation and Investment Disputes: Asian Perspectives* (CUP 2019), forthcoming) and more generally Nottage, Chaisse, and Thanitcul (n 26).

[56] Prabhash Ranjan and Pushkar Anand, 'Investor State Dispute Settlement in the 2016 Indian Model Bilateral Investment Treaty: Does it Go Too Far?' in Julien Chaisse and Luke Nottage (eds), *International Investment Treaties and Arbitration Across Asia* (Brill 2017).

[57] Joel Dahlquist, 'Brazil and India Conclude Bilateral Investment Treaty' *Investment Arbitration Reporter* (28 November 2016) <https://www.iareporter.com/articles/brazil-and-india-conclude-bilateral-investment-treaty/>.

[58] See generally Luke Nottage and Sakda Thanitcul, 'Special Issue: International Investment Arbitration in Southeast Asia' (2017) 18(5–6) *Journal of World Investment and Trade* 767.

[59] Bevan Shields and James Massola, 'Citizenship Crisis: Turnbull Government Reduced to Minority after John Alexander Resignation' *Sydney Morning Herald* (online) (11 November 2017) <http://www.smh.com.au/federal-politics/political-news/citizenship-crisis-turnbull-government-reduced-to-minority-after-john-alexander-resignation-20171111-gzjch0.html>.

[60] Senator Penny Wong, 'Speech to the Export Council of Australia, Australian Chamber of Commerce and Industry Trade Forum' (Sydney, 7 June 2016) <http://www.pennywong.com.au/speeches/export-council-of-australia-australian-chamber-of-commerce-and-industry-trade-forum-sydney/>.

Zealand government has not fully clarified its approach to pre-existing FTAs or BITs. Anyway, New Zealand has very few standalone BITs compared to Australia, which signed twenty-one between 1998 and 2005.[61]

25.24 Accordingly, in November 2017 the authors of this chapter wrote to leaders in both New Zealand and Australia, recommending a shift towards introducing a two-tier investment court model along the lines proposed by the EU, as one compromise way forward among other 'half-way houses' for reform.[62] We highlighted recent econometric research suggesting that ISDS commitments had contributed significantly to cross-border FDI flows world-wide, especially in promptly ratified treaties and into non-OECD countries, but that positive effects were also very evident with scaled-back ISDS commitments.[63]

25.25 New Zealand's Minister for Trade and Export Growth was first to respond, in December 2017. In his reply,[64] the minister noted his government's concerns with the current form of ISDS in respect of issues such as arbitrator appointments. He also confirmed that the government is actively considering recent policy developments, including the investment court model, and expressed a hope that there would be further engagement 'with all interested stakeholders on New Zealand's approach to trade policy including ISDS clauses' in the near future. The latter is consistent with statements made during the 2017 election campaign, when Labour proposed a Trade Advisory Commission, to be comprised of academics, representatives of business and union interests and others, to advise on the broad

---

[61] Nottage (n 10). This number includes Australia's BIT with India, terminated last year by India.
[62] See Kawharu and Nottage (n 3) Part 6B.
[63] Shiro Armstrong and Luke Nottage, 'The Impact of Investment Treaties and ISDS Provisions on Foreign Direct Investment: A Baseline Econometric Analysis' (2016) 16/74 Sydney Law School Research Paper. Similar results were found focusing on FDI with respect to 'ASEAN+3' economies: Shiro Armstrong, 'The Impact of Investment Treaties and ISDS Provisions on FDI in Asia and Globally' in Julien Chaisse and Luke Nottage (eds), *International Investment Treaties and Arbitration Across Asia* (Brill 2017). However, a stronger result for ISDS overall was found by a later study measuring FDI differently, for intra- and extra-Asian investment treaties coded for strength of investor protections ('BITSel') over 2000–16. There was a significant positive impact on the cumulative number of FDI projects not only with respect to such investment treaties overall, but also with respect to their ISDS provisions. In fact, when the *marginal* effects on FDI were analysed, ISDS was the *only* provision having a significant positive influence from among the five components of the BITSel index, meaning that 'the most important provision in BITs is access to international arbitration'. See also Asian Development Bank, *ASEAN Economic Integration Report 2016*, 163 (with reference to Tables 6.28 and 6.29). For a critical review of further studies into the impact of investment treaties on FDI, see Joachim Pohl, 'Societal Benefits and Costs of International Investment Agreements: A Critical Review of Aspects and Available Empirical Evidence' (OECD Working Papers on International Investment 2018/01, Organisation for Economic Co-operation and Development, 2018) <http://www.oecd-ilibrary.org/finance-and-investment/societal-benefits-and-costs-of-international-investment-agreements_e5f85c3d-en> 16–31; and Bonnitcha, Poulsen and Waibel (n 56) ch 6 (detailing some of the methodological challenges in designing econometric studies of the relationship between investment treaties and levels of FDI).
[64] Letter from Hon David Parker to the authors (11 December 2017) on file with the authors.

implications of FTA negotiations.⁶⁵ However, as yet, further details of its proposed Commission have not been made public and it remains unclear how and to what extent the new government will review New Zealand's policy.

We received a response on behalf Australia's Trade Minister in March 2018. It briefly reaffirmed the country's existing policy, which is to consider ISDS on a case-by-case basis.⁶⁶ This contrasts with his New Zealand counterpart's desire to consider new approaches, and indeed to some extent with earlier responses from his predecessor after being urged to undertake public consultations to develop a model investment treaty or provisions for Australia.⁶⁷ Perhaps the current minister did not wish to show political weakness, by suggesting that the ISDS mechanism and US-style treaty drafting more generally may not have been optimal.⁶⁸ It may also have been seen as potentially complicating Australian parliamentary inquiries into ratifying the CPTPP, retaining ISDS provisions, although legislation allowing that treaty to be ratified scraped through the lower House of Representatives in September 2018.⁶⁹ Or perhaps Australia's minister did not think that the government could lose its slim majority, so did not see any benefits of exploring a compromise with the opposition as proposed in our November 2017 letter.⁷⁰ 25.26

Unfortunately, this suggests that polarization between both major parties in foreign investment policy is now well entrenched in Australia, in contrast to many decades of common interests.⁷¹ That may also not augur well for New Zealand. A similar political polarization appears to be developing following the pressure 25.27

---

⁶⁵ See Sam Sachdeva, 'David Parker Plots a New Approach to Trade' *newsroom.co.nz* (online) (8 November 2017) <https://www.newsroom.co.nz/2017/11/07/58682/david-parker-plots-a-new-approach-to-trade>. In mid-2018, the government announced a 'Trade for All' consultation process to review and modernize New Zealand's trade policy. The appointment of a Trade for All Advisory Board is part of this process, but as at October 2018, its membership had not been announced.
⁶⁶ Letter to the authors from Alistair Mitchell on behalf of Steven Ciobo MP (2 March 2018) on file with the authors.
⁶⁷ Luke Nottage, 'Investment Treaty Arbitration Policy in Australia, New Zealand and Korea' (2015) 25(3) Journal of Arbitration Studies 185 (citing correspondence with Andrew Robb MP). For similar calls for better public consultation and even a Model BIT for Australia, see also eg Mitchell, Sheargold, and Voon (n 21) 252–56.
⁶⁸ This is a dilemma also facing Korea, for example: see Kim (n 38).
⁶⁹ For Nottage's brief Submission to parallel inquiries, with further references (including to one parliamentary committee's Report in July 2018 recommending ratification), see http://blogs.usyd.edu.au/erga-omnes/2018/04/the_tpp_is_back_submission_to.html. See also Rebecca Gredley, 'TPP Passes First Hurdle in Parliament' *Australian Associated Press* (online) (17 September 2018) <https://www.news.com.au/national/breaking-news/tpp-deal-passes-first-hurdle-in-parliament/news-story/82764e76993d86f26aadbf8c04189c05>.
⁷⁰ More surprisingly, no response to our letter has been forthcoming from the Australian Labor opposition trade spokesperson. Perhaps he too does not wish to be seen as open to compromise either, with a general election approaching.
⁷¹ See generally David Uren, *Takeover: Foreign Investment and the Australian Psyche* (Black Inc 2015), summarized in Luke Nottage, 'The Evolution of Foreign Investment Regulation, Treaties and Investor-State Arbitration in Australia' (2015) 21 New Zealand Business Law Quarterly 266.

already placed on FTA bipartisanship between National and Labour by the New Zealand–Korea FTA and then the TPP.[72]

D. Low-profile Treaty (Re)Negotiations

25.28 Meanwhile, however, both countries continue to (re)negotiate investment treaties. We outline next the current state of play in the most interesting (rather than all) recently concluded or ongoing treaty negotiations:

- a joint agreement signed with Pacific Island nations in 2017 (section D.1);
- New Zealand's treaty renegotiations with Singapore and China (section D.2);
- Australia's treaty renegotiations with Singapore and Uruguay (section D.3) and
- FTA negotiations with the EU and (for Australia) other Asian economies such as India and Indonesia (section D.4).

1. PACER-Plus

25.29 The previous New Zealand government and the current Australian government signed on 14 June 2017 a regional FTA with an investment chapter omitting ISDS: the Pacific Agreement on Closer Economic Relations (PACER) Plus.[73] That the agreement omitted ISDS was not mentioned in any of the twenty-one newspaper articles referring to PACER-Plus over 2015–2017 in both countries.[74]

25.30 PACER-Plus takes its name from the original PACER Agreement (2001) and also builds on the even earlier South Pacific Regional Trade and Economic Cooperation Agreement (SPARTECA, 1980). Although these earlier trade agreements have been in place for many years, PACER-Plus is the first agreement in which Pacific Island countries have agreed to include commitments on trade in services and foreign investment with Australia and New Zealand. The stated intention behind the addition of these commitments is that they will improve confidence for Australian and New Zealand investors, while also helping to address, through improved conditions for foreign investment, some of the particular development challenges that Pacific Island countries face,

---

[72] Kawharu (n 9). New Zealand Parliament, Foreign Affairs, Defence and Trade Committee, 'International treaty examination of the Comprehensive and Progressive Agreement for Trans-Pacific Partnership' <https://www.parliament.nz/en/pb/sc/business-before-committees/document/ITE_76583/international-treaty-examination-of-the-comprehensive-and>.

[73] Australia and New Zealand signed on that date with eight small Pacific Island states; Vanuatu followed on 7 September 2017. See Department of Foreign Affairs and Trade, Australian Government, 'Pacific Agreement on Closer Economic Relations (PACER) Plus' <http://dfat.gov.au/trade/agreements/pacer/pages/pacific-agreement-on-closer-economic-relations-pacer-plus.aspx>.

[74] Results retrieved from the Factiva database from selected print media sources, listed n 7, using the search terms 'PACER Plus' or 'Pacific Agreement on Closer Economic Relations'.

such as limited productive capacity, distant markets, and high infrastructure costs.⁷⁵ To these ends, the investment chapter includes the standard suite of investor protections such as national treatment, most favoured nation (MFN), the guarantee of the minimum standard of treatment under customary international law, and compensation for expropriation, but these are all quite pared-back compared, for instance, to the standard of the 2012 US Model Bilateral Investment Treaty. For example, national treatment is provided on a positive list basis (applicable only to specified sectors), while non-discriminatory public welfare regulation is deemed not to constitute expropriation (with no allowance for 'rare circumstances', as per the US Model). As noted, ISDS is omitted altogether.

In the context of PACER-Plus, a moderate approach to investor protections and the exclusion of ISDS make sense for several reasons relating to the size of the island countries involved and their relationships with Australia and New Zealand. With respect to investor protections, there is limited need for them. The economically larger Pacific countries, Papua New Guinea and Fiji, have thus far elected not to participate. Therefore, as indicated by Table 25.1, and apart from Australia and New Zealand, many of the signatories to the agreement are micro-states. Any positive impact of the agreement in terms of increased investment into these countries is likely to be marginal; as one commentator has observed, PACER-Plus cannot by itself address issues such as the absence of economies of scale, given the very small populations involved, and limited access to land, in these countries.⁷⁶ As for ISDS, several of the signatories are not members of the WTO, and have limited or no experience in obligations covering trade in services and foreign investment, or in enforcing them through trade disputes, let alone ISDS. They have much smaller populations than other 'small' developing states such as Laos (which have been able to defend vigorously the occasional ISDS claim),⁷⁷ and far fewer resources available to participate in dispute settlement as compared to other nearby small states like oil-rich Brunei (which has a population of less than half a million, but few bilateral investment treaties and so far no inbound ISDS claims).⁷⁸

25.31

---

⁷⁵ New Zealand Ministry of Foreign Affairs and Trade, 'The Pacific Agreement on Closer Economic Relations Plus—Overview: Purpose and Benefits' <https://www.mfat.govt.nz/assets/Uploads/PACER-Plus-factsheet-overview.pdf> 1. For further discussion of investment policy making in the Pacific, see Daniel Kalderimis and Kate Yesberg 'Investment Policy-Making in its Broader Context' (2015) 21 New Zealand Business Law Quarterly 253, 262–64.
⁷⁶ Matthew Dornan, 'PACER Plus is Not Much to Celebrate' *East Asia Forum* (2 June 2017) <http://www.eastasiaforum.org/2017/06/02/pacer-plus-is-not-much-to-celebrate/>.
⁷⁷ See Romesh Weeramantry and Mahdev Mohan, 'International Investment Arbitration in Laos: Large Issues for a Small State' (2017) 18 Journal of World Investment and Trade 1001.
⁷⁸ Bruno Jetin and Julien Chaisse, 'International Investment Policy of Small States: The Case of Brunei' in Julien Chaisse and Luke Nottage (eds), *International Investment Treaties and Arbitration Across Asia* (Brill 2017).

Table 25.1 PACER-Plus FTA Demographics Table[a]

Country	Population	GDP ($US)	GDP per capita ($US)	WTO membership / accession[b]	Number of investment treaties signed[c]
Australia	24.6 million	1,359.7 billion	55,215.3	1 January 1995	36
New Zealand	4.7 million	200.8 billion	41,629.3	1 January 1995	19
Cook Islands	11,700	288 million	24,614.5	N/A	3
Kiribati	112,000	186 million	1,625.2	N/A	3
Nauru	13,000	114 million	8,574.7	N/A	3
Niue	1,500	20.4 million (2012)	12,945.0	N/A	3
Samoa	195,000	844.0 million	4,283.1	10 May 2012	3
Solomon Islands	601,000	1.3 billion	2,074.2	26 July 1996	3
Tonga	104,000	437.0 million	4,176.7	27 July 2007	4
Tuvalu	11,000	40.0 million	3,618.9	N/A	3
Vanuatu	275,000	837.0 million	2,976.2	24 August 2012	4

[a] Data for the 'Population', 'GDP ($US)', and 'GDP per capita ($US)' columns in this table was retrieved from the Australian Government's Department of Foreign Affairs and Trade factsheets, available at <http://dfat.gov.au/trade/resources/pages/trade-and-economic-fact-sheets-for-countries-and-regions.aspx>. GDP per capita for the Cook Islands (as with some other states) is bolstered by remittances from the (much larger) population living outside the islands, especially in New Zealand. Its economy has also grown significantly from tourism and fisheries in recent years, threatening its eligibility for aid: Eleanor Ainge Roy, 'Cook Islands faces its "Worst Case Scenario"' *The Guardian—Australian Edition* (online) (8 October 2017) <https://www.theguardian.com/world/2017/oct/08/cook-islands-faces-its-worst-case-scenario-being-granted-developed-country-status>.
[b] WTO, 'Members and Observers' <https://www.wto.org/english/thewto_e/whatis_e/tif_e/org6_e.htm#collapseA>.
[c] UNCTAD, Investment Policy Hub, *International Investment Agreements Navigator* <http://investmentpolicyhub.unctad.org/IIA/IiasByCountry#iiaInnerMenu>.

25.32 Apart from these factors, the relationships between the countries also weighs against ISDS. For one, ISDS claims by Australian or New Zealand investors might lead to allegations of neo-colonialism and bullying.[79] Moreover, both countries have a history of supporting the development of judicial systems in Pacific countries and judges from Australia and New Zealand are regularly appointed to their courts. In this respect, it would be awkward for Australia and New Zealand to argue, in favour of ISDS, that those Pacific judicial systems are unreliable.

---

[79] See further Jenny Bryant-Tokalau and Ian Frazer, 'Introduction: The Uncertain Future of Pacific Regionalism' in Jenny Bryant-Tokalau and Ian Frazer (eds), *Redefining the Pacific?: Regionalism Past, Present and Future* (Ashgate 2006), referring to the deep-seated tension over the terms of co-operation between Pacific states on the one hand and Australia and New Zealand on the other; Jane Kelsey, *Big Brothers Behaving Badly: The Implications for the Pacific Islands of the Pacific Agreement on Closer Economic Relations (PACER)* (Report Commissioned by the Pacific Network on Globalisation, 2004).

The Asian Development Bank is currently funding a legal assistance project in co-operation with UNCITRAL to encourage reform of commercial arbitration laws in the Pacific. One of the ultimate objectives of the project is to promote cross-border trade and foreign investment into the region.[80] This raises the possibility that, at least insofar as state contracts are involved in an investment, Australian and New Zealand investors could conclude such contracts and resolve disputes arising under them through private arbitration, and then enforce awards in reliance on the New York Convention (if implemented effectively into domestic law as part of the reform agenda). Problems could arise as individually negotiated contracts can be more oppressive for host states than investment treaties, especially in their more contemporary forms.[81]

2. New Zealand's renegotiations with Singapore and China

As discussed, the current New Zealand policy position on ISDS is potentially unstable and it is uncertain whether the policy will be reviewed. The uncertainty also extends to whether the change in government will have an impact on scheduled reviews or 'upgrades' of New Zealand's existing FTAs, most notably the one with China. Discussions on the upgrade of the China FTA began in November 2016. ISDS was not then part of the upgrade agenda, which initially had a focus instead on trade in goods, and maintaining a degree of parity with China's FTA with Australia, although other issues such as investment have been discussed in the negotiations.[82]

New Zealand's earlier FTA with Singapore is also now the subject of upgrade negotiations, which were launched in April 2017, to ensure the FTA keeps pace with the changing trade and investment environment. The New Zealand–Singapore FTA's provisions on investment are relatively skeletal, covering only national treatment, MFN treatment, and currency transfers, with no ISDS. But again, as with the negotiations to upgrade the New Zealand–China FTA, the focus of this upgrade currently appears to be on trade in goods.[83] It may be that the parties are content to leave ISDS to the CPTPP. Unlike the case with Australia's bilateral FTA with Singapore, there are no ISDS provisions that would benefit from

---

[80] See Asian Development Bank, 'Project Overview: Promotion of International Arbitration Reform for Better Investment Climate in the South Pacific' <https://www.adb.org/projects/50114-001/main>.

[81] See eg Antony Crockett, 'Stabilisation Clauses and Sustainable Development: Drafting for the Future' in Chester Brown and Kate Miles (eds), *Evolution in Investment Treaty Law and Arbitration* (CUP 2011).

[82] New Zealand Ministry of Foreign Affairs and Trade, 'NZ-China FTA Upgrade' <https://www.mfat.govt.nz/en/trade/free-trade-agreements/free-trade-agreements-in-force/nz-china-free-trade-agreement/>.

[83] New Zealand Ministry of Foreign Affairs and Trade, 'CEP Upgrade Negotiations' <https://www.mfat.govt.nz/en/trade/free-trade-agreements/free-trade-agreements-in-force/singapore/>.

3. Australia's renegotiations with Singapore and Uruguay

25.36 Another treaty where (re)negotiations have been completed is the Singapore–Australia FTA (SAFTA). SAFTA was Australia's first FTA, signed in 2003. The states have made several subsequent amendments, including adding Fair and Equitable Treatment (FET) protections in 2011—consistent with Australia's other FTA and earlier BIT practice.[84] The latest amendments retrofit many provisions of the TPP, which was signed between Australia, Singapore, and ten other Asia-Pacific states in February 2016, and were agreed for SAFTA in October 2016. However, these amendments only came into force on 1 December 2017, after ratification by both Singapore and Australia.

25.37 Ratification was preceded by parliamentary scrutiny by the Commonwealth Parliament.[85] The Joint Standing Committee on Treaties (JSCOT) inquiry attracted only nineteen submissions, which is fewer than those for Australia's recent FTAs, such as those with Korea or China as well as the TPP, but still quite a few for a treaty amendment. Several focused on the Investment Chapter, notably raising concerns about the specific exclusion of tobacco control measures from ISDS, which was given as only an option for signatories to the TPP in 2016 (but which Australia as well as New Zealand had indicated they would take). The primary objection was that discriminating against a particular product or sector that can still legally be supplied under national laws sets a dangerous precedent for WTO and other treaty negotiations. Objectors preferred generic public health exceptions, which they argued were anyway reflected in Australia's recent investment treaties, including indeed the TPP.[86] By contrast, other submissions favoured adding the express exclusion for tobacco control measures, notably those by the Australian Fair Trade and Investment Network (AFTINET, Submission No 13) and the Public Health Association (PHA, No 15). That stance is quite understandable given the fact that tobacco is subject to a separate multilateral instrument (the WHO Framework Convention on Tobacco Control), and also given the history

---

[84] cf Singapore's investment treaty practice: Jean Ho, 'Singapore' in Chester Brown (ed), *Commentaries on Selected Model Investment Treaties* (OUP 2013); and Mahdev Mohan, 'Singapore and Its Free Trade Agreement with the European Union: Rationality "Unbound"' (2017) 18 Journal of World Investment and Trade 858, reproduced as 'The European Union's Free Trade Agreement with Singapore—One Step Forward, 28 Steps Back?' in Julien Chaisse and Luke Nottage (eds), *International Investment Treaties and Arbitration Across Asia* (Brill 2017).

[85] Parliament of Australia, Joint Standing Committee on Treaties (JSCOT), 'Singapore Free Trade Agreement—Amendment' <https://www.aph.gov.au/Parliamentary_Business/Committees/Joint/Treaties/SingaporeFTA-Amendment>.

[86] See eg submissions from tobacco companies (Nos 5 and 7) and an association (No 3), as well as the pro-choice Australian Taxpayers Alliance (No 10), as well as former UNSW Law Professor Bryan Mercurio (No 4). cf also generally Mitchell, Sheargold, and Voon (n 21) 192.

of tobacco companies vigorously using national and international dispute resolution processes to protect their interests.[87]

However, both AFTINET and PHA went further by repeating their longstanding objections to ISDS more generally. A submission by Nottage[88] included several responses to the PHA[89] regarding issues that persistently recur in parliamentary (and many other public) debates in Australia regarding investment treaties and ISDS.[90] **25.38**

The PHA further noted that SAFTA amendments included more legal safeguards than in the TPP, intended to favour states faced by claims over public health or environmental protection, but the PHA suggested that experts viewed such safeguards as insufficient to prevent investors from bringing ISDS claims. Nottage's Submission pointed out that there is a big difference between being able to bring a claim, and succeeding. It suggested that the procedural and substantive provisions of the TPP, reflecting a general trend in Asia-Pacific treaty drafting,[91] include numerous express provisions that should make claimants less likely to prevail in inappropriate cases,[92] as well as streamlining proceedings.[93] As such, it was argued that organizations and individuals interested in advancing public health should **25.39**

---

[87] WHO Framework Convention on Tobacco Control (opened for signature on 16–22 June 2004) 2302 UNTS 166 (entered into force 27 February 2005); and Tania Voon, Andrew D Mitchell, and Jonathan Liberman with Glyn Aryes, *Public Health and Plain Packaging of Cigarettes: Legal Issues* (Elgar 2012).

[88] No 18, dated 25 July 2017, available at <https://www.aph.gov.au/DocumentStore.ashx?id=939d3a5a-a824-4c3c-8c48-6385606bb74a&subId=514167>.

[89] Submission No 15, available at <https://www.aph.gov.au/DocumentStore.ashx?id=c9aa5de1-506e-4b32-8c2c-bfbeed0554d3&subId=511132>.

[90] These issues include assertions about 'litigiousness', especially from US investors (cf Nottage (n 11), comparing per capita ISDS rates); general examples of foreign investors contesting public health or environment protection measures (two cases cited by the PHA are old ones under the North American FTA. By contrast, tribunal rulings have gone distinctly more in favour of host states even under old treaties over the last decade: Malcolm Langford and Daniel Behn, 'Managing Backlash: The Evolving Investment Treaty Arbitrator?' (2018) 29 European Journal of International Law 551). The third claim was recently rejected: *Eli Lilly and Company v Canada*, ICSID Case No UNCT/14/2 <http://www.international.gc.ca/trade-agreements-accords-commerciaux/topics-domaines/disp-diff/eli.aspx?lang=eng>); and the specific example of the Philip Morris claim against Australia. Although the PHA's Submission noted that Philip Morris lost, it observed that the jurisdictional ruling does not clarify the implications of ISDS for health policymaking. Nottage's Submission responded that the ruling should be supplemented by the decision on the merits favouring Uruguay (Nottage and Hepburn, forthcoming (n 6)). That arguably demonstrates how contemporary investment treaty tribunals are able to use even older treaties, albeit supplemented by general public international law principles, to reach decisions allowing appropriate deference to host state regulatory space for genuine and proportionate public health measures.

[91] Tomer Broude, Yoram Z Haftel, and Alexander Thompson, 'The Trans-Pacific Partnership and Regulatory Space: A Comparison of Treaty Texts' (2017) 20 Journal of International Economic Law 391. Focusing on the evolution of Australia's investment treaty provisions, see also Mitchell, Sheargold, and Voon (n 21) 122–62 and 181–95.

[92] Luke Nottage, 'The TPP Investment Chapter and Investor-State Arbitration in Asia and Oceania: Assessing Prospects for Ratification' (2016) 17 Melbourne Journal of International Law 1.

[93] Kawharu and Nottage (n 3). Kawharu's separate work is cited in the PHA Submission.

welcome retrofits to older treaties like SAFTA, rather than complaining about them, despite Australia's political polarization over ISDS.

25.40 Other TPP-like features included in the SAFTA amendments, which should favour or at least entrench host state interests, include:[94]

- Disclosure in principle of ISDS-related documents and open hearings, a sixty-day comment period on draft awards (as in the Korea–Australia FTA signed in 2015), and a code of conduct for arbitrators similar to that found in the original investment chapter in the Singapore–EU FTA (albeit lacking an express prohibition on double-hatting);[95]
- Clarifications on FET and indirect expropriation;
- Annex 4-II precluding ISDS claims against Australia over performance requirements and discrimination in 'social services established for a public purpose', creative arts, 'indigenous traditional cultural expressions', and other cultural heritage (as well as complete preclusion of ISDS claims against Australia regarding specified public health regimes[96]).

25.41 In August 2017, JSCOT issued its Report 172 recommending ratification, after concluding that 'the proposed Agreement will amend SAFTA to include some of the most useful aspects of the TPP, in particular an improved protection for government regulation on public interest grounds'.[97]

25.42 However, the minority Labor (opposition) members of the Committee, while not dissenting with respect to ratification, remarked that:[98]

> Labor remains concerned that the ISDS provisions within SAFTA leaves [sic] Australia vulnerable to lengthy legal disputes with foreign-owned corporations. What is evident is that ISDS poses a significant threat to Australia's sovereignty and could stop future governments from pursuing legitimate public policy goals.

---

[94] See further Jarrod Hepburn, 'Singapore and Australia Agree a Raft of Changes' (4 December 2017) <https://www.iareporter.com/articles/singapore-and-australia-agree-a-raft-of-changes-to-investment-chapter-of-2003-free-trade-agreement-including-with-respect-to-tobacco-transparency-and-social-and-health-exclusions/>.

[95] See generally Mohan (n 85) 879. Neither the Singapore–EU FTA (concluded in 2014) nor the amended SAFTA Code of Conduct expressly prohibits arbitrators serving elsewhere as counsel. This contrasted with the Investment Court judges under the EU-Canada Comprehensive Economic and Trade Agreement (CETA), art 8.30(1) signed in October 2016: European Commission, 'EU-Canada Comprehensive Economic and Trade Agreement (CETA)' <http://ec.europa.eu/trade/policy/in-focus/ceta/>.

[96] Specifically, n 18 to Section B (ISDS) of the amended SAFTA's Investment chapter precludes any ISDS claim regarding 'measures comprising or related to the Pharmaceutical Benefits Scheme, Medicare Benefits Scheme, Therapeutic Goods Administration and Office of the Gene Technology Regulator'.

[97] Joint Standing Committee on Treaties, Parliament of Australia, *Report 172: Singapore Free Trade Agreement—Amendment; Defence Supplies and Services—Japan* (2017) 14, para 2.62.

[98] ibid 40, paras 1.6–1.7.

This was the concern of many submissions to the Committee is indicative of community sentiment [sic]. Labor acknowledges that a large proportion of the Australian community are either extremely sceptical or directly oppose ISDS provisions in trade agreements.

25.43 Notably, in April 2018, Singapore agreed with the EU to substitute the investment chapter of their FTA, containing ISDS, with a separate investment treaty including an EU-style investment court and expressly prohibiting double-hatting.[99] This was likely driven primarily from the EU side, given the latter's strong policy preference for a court model, which is also found in the investment chapter agreed between the EU and Mexico in 2018.[100]

25.44 Australia has also recently commenced treaty renegotiation with Uruguay, namely over their 2001 BIT. Part of the impetus for the renegotiation comes from the shared experience of both Uruguay and Australia in each successfully defending claims brought by Philip Morris.[101] The TPP appears to be the template being proposed by Australia to frame renegotiations. As in SAFTA, the states may also be considering an outright exclusion from ISDS regarding claims over tobacco measures.

25.45 However, it seems there has been no move yet to include the distinctive 'public welfare notice' procedure added to the China–Australia FTA signed in 2015. This omission indicates again the significant 'path dependence' in Australia's investment treaty practice over the last fifteen years, heavily influenced by the US Model BIT of 2004 and the investment chapter of the North American FTA,[102] with reform away from that US-style approach being ad hoc rather than sustained. Yet the unique public welfare notice procedure adds useful and original safeguards for host states regarding public health and other community concerns more generally.[103] Under Article 9.11 of the Investment Chapter (with no

---

[99] Investment Protection Agreement Between the EU and Singapore (agreed in April 2018, not yet in force), ch 3, Dispute Settlement, art 3.11(1) <http://trade.ec.europa.eu/doclib/docs/2018/april/tradoc_156731.pdf> (upon appointment as investment court judges, 'they shall refrain from acting as counsel, party-appointed expert or party-appointed witness in any pending or new investment protection dispute under this or any other agreement or domestic law').

[100] Damien Charlotin and Jarrod Hepburn, 'Analysis: EU-Mexico Investment Text Is Released, Allowing For Comparison With Other Agreements; Permanent Two-Tier System Of Adjudication Is Envisioned' *Investment Arbitration Reporter* (2 May 2018) <https://www.iareporter.com/articles/analysis-eu-mexico-investment-text-is-released-allowing-for-comparison-with-other-agreements-permanent-two-tier-system-of-adjudication-is-envisioned/>.

[101] *Philip Morris Brands Sàrl, Philip Morris Products SA and Abal Hermanos SA v Oriental Republic of Uruguay*, ICSID Case No ARB/10/7, Award (8 July 2016) <https://www.italaw.com/sites/default/files/case-documents/italaw7417.pdf>. See also Hepburn and Nottage (n 6).

[102] See generally the more qualitative study by Mitchell, Sheargold, and Voon (n 21) as well as the quantitative comparisons by Alschner and Skougarevskiy (n 23) and Broude, Haftel, and Thompson (n 95).

[103] The following points about the China—Australia FTA are adapted from Nottage (n 68). More recently regarding the attraction of the public welfare notice mechanism, see also Anthea Roberts and Richard Braddock, 'Protecting Public Welfare Regulation Through Joint Treaty Party

counterpart in any other Australian treaty), within Section B related specifically to ISDS:[104]

> 4. Measures of a Party that are non-discriminatory and for the legitimate public welfare objectives of public health, safety, the environment, public morals or public order shall not be the subject of a claim under this Section.
> 5. The respondent may, within 30 days of the date on which it receives a request for consultations (as provided for in paragraph 1), state that it considers that a measure alleged to be in breach of an obligation under Section A is of the kind described in paragraph 4, by delivering to the claimant and to the non-disputing Party a notice specifying the basis for its position (a 'public welfare notice').
> 6. The issuance of a public welfare notice shall trigger a 90 day period during which the respondent and the non-disputing Party shall consult. The dispute resolution procedure contemplated by this Section shall be automatically suspended for this 90 day period.
> 7. The issuance of a public welfare notice is without prejudice to the respondent's right to invoke the procedures described in Article 9.16.5 or Article 9.16.6.[105] The respondent shall promptly inform the claimant, and make available to the public, the outcome of any consultations.
> 8. In any proceeding brought pursuant to this Section, the tribunal shall not draw any adverse inference from the non-issuance of a public welfare notice by the respondent, or from the absence of any decision between the respondent and the non-disputing Party as to whether a measure is of a kind described in paragraph 4.

In addition, Article 9.18 of the China–Australia FTA later states (emphasis added):

> ... 2. A joint decision of the Parties, acting through the Committee on Investment, declaring their interpretation of a provision of this Agreement shall be binding on a tribunal *of any ongoing or subsequent dispute*, and any decision or award issued by such a tribunal must be consistent with that joint decision.
> 3. A decision between the respondent and the non-disputing Party that a measure is of the kind described in Article 9.11.4 shall be binding on a tribunal and any decision or award issued by a tribunal must be consistent with that decision.

25.46 The italicized wording in Article 9.18(2) clearly indicates that the joint Committee, comprising representatives of both states, can agree on how to interpret any uncertainty in the provisions of this FTA even with respect to ISDS proceedings already filed by the home state's investor. If they declare that the scope of the

---

Control: A ChAFTA Innovation' (Columbia FDI Perspectives No 176, Columbia Center on Sustainable Investment, 20 June 2016); Mitchell, Sheargold, and Voon (n 21) 190–91.

[104] Department of Foreign Affairs and Trade, Australian Government, 'China-Australia Free Trade Agreement FTA Text and Tariff Schedules' <http://dfat.gov.au/trade/agreements/chafta/official-documents/Pages/official-documents.aspx>.

[105] Those provisions deal with expedited objections regarding matters of law or jurisdiction of the tribunal, and track Korea–Australia FTA, art 11.20(5)–(6).

protection is not as alleged by the investor, the latter's claim should not succeed before the tribunal. This mechanism, helping primarily to safeguard host state interests, is broader than the innovative 'public welfare notice' mechanism added in Article 9.11 and Article 9.18(3). Article 9.18(2) on joint decisions does have parallels with provisions contained in earlier Australian FTAs (including Article 11.22(3) of the Korea FTA), in turn influenced by US treaty practice. But those provisions lacked the italicized wording and therefore can give rise to the question of whether the Joint Committee's interpretation can bind presently constituted tribunals dealing with pending disputes, or instead only future tribunals.[106]

25.47 Hopefully, Australia will seek to incorporate such 'TPP-Plus' clarifications or safeguards when renegotiating its Uruguay BIT, leading also to a broader programme of review and renegotiation of Australia's older BITs. Such a broader review, including more structured public consultation about the features to guide BIT renegotiations, was recommended by Nottage and others during a 2015 parliamentary inquiry into Australia's treaty-making, with the inquiry report (by majority) adopting this recommendation.[107] However, the present Australian government has not expressly declared any policy about reviewing or renegotiating older treaties. By contrast, as mentioned, the Labor opposition in 2016 had announced it would seek to remove ISDS altogether from older treaties lacking sufficient deference to host state interests.

4. Negotiations with the EU, India, Indonesia, and others

25.48 The EU and New Zealand announced an agreement to start the process for FTA negotiations in late 2016, which was then followed by scoping discussions between them with respect to their proposed FTA. According to a report on those discussions, New Zealand adopted an open mind to the EU's initiatives for ISDS reform, including the possibility of an investment court.[108] That said, the EU's negotiating mandate (submitted for approval to the European Council in September 2017, and approved in May 2018)[109] is confined to matters within the

---

[106] cf also the more open-ended TPP art 9.25(3) (joint decisions 'shall be binding on a tribunal, and any decision or award issued by a tribunal must be consistent with that decision') and generally Tomoko Ishikawa, 'Keeping Interpretation in Investment Treaty Arbitration "On Track": The Role of States Parties' (2014) 1 Transnational Dispute Management <http://www.transnational-dispute-management.com/article.asp?key=2048>.

[107] Nottage (n 68).

[108] New Zealand Ministry of Foreign Affairs and Trade, 'European Union—New Zealand Free Trade Agreement: Outline of Ambition and Scope of Future Negotiations' (11 June 2017) <https://www.mfat.govt.nz/assets/FTA-Publications/EU-FTA/EU-NZ-FTA-Scoping-Summary-and-Q-A-May-2017.pdf>.

[109] See European Commission Recommendation for a Council Decision Authorising the Opening of Negotiations for a Free Trade Agreement with New Zealand, COM/2017/0469 (13 September 2017) <http://eur-lex.europa.eu/legal-content/EN/TXT/?uri=COM:2017:469:FIN> and European Council Outcome of the Council Meeting 9102/18 (22 May 2018) <http://www.consilium.europa.eu/media/34837/st09102-en18.pdf>.

EU's exclusive competence and does not cover ISDS nor portfolio investment.[110] For political rather than legal reasons, the mandate does not cover investor protections either, but is instead limited to investment liberalization.[111] The negotiating mandate for the proposed FTA with Australia is similarly limited.[112]

25.49 Meanwhile, the EU is pressing ahead for negotiations on a multilateral investment court, outside of the bilateral setting of its FTA negotiations.[113]

25.50 The EU's apparent emphasis on investment liberalization in the bilateral negotiations raises an interesting dilemma for New Zealand and Australia. After all, it leaves these already open trading economies with less to bargain with, in exchange for better market access for agricultural products during the FTA negotiations.

25.51 A further complication is the recent suggestion by the European Commission that the EU should adopt an investment screening system to address concerns about investments by state-owned enterprises in strategic sectors, especially state-backed investors from China.[114] It may well take some time for a comprehensive EU-wide screening system to be designed, let alone approved. If such a system is seriously proposed, then the FTAs with New Zealand and Australia will need to accommodate it—and this may be easier said than done. As noted earlier, in New Zealand's experience, the problematic drafting of its FTA exemption for investment screening (and specifically, the lack of express flexibility to add new categories of land-based investments) has been the subject of political controversy. The drafting of Australia's exemptions for its screening mechanism has also been criticized as inadequate.[115] In any event, the EU will expect the same treatment with regard to exemptions for investment screening, and want to retain the ability in the proposed FTAs to screen investors before entry into the EU. The parties may also wish to exclude their respective screening regimes from ISDS, following

---

[110] The limitations on EU competence were addressed by the Court of Justice of the European Union in C-2/15 Opinion 2/15 of the Court (16 May 2017).

[111] The draft mandate states generally that 'The Agreement should provide for the progressive and reciprocal liberalisation of trade in goods, services and foreign direct investment. It will include rules on other trade-related areas in order to promote, facilitate or govern such trade and foreign direct investment.' (see Annex to the Recommendation for a Council Decision authorising the opening of negotiations for a Free Trade Agreement with New Zealand, para A.)

[112] See European Commission Recommendation for a Council Decision Authorising the Opening of Negotiations for a Free Trade Agreement with Australia, COM/2017/0472 (13 September 2017) <http://eur-lex.europa.eu/legal-content/EN/TXT/?uri=COM:2017:472:FIN>; also Council directives (n 25).

[113] See Recommendation for a Council Decision Authorising the Opening of Negotiations for a Convention Establishing a Multilateral Court for the Settlement of Investment Disputes, COM/2017/0493 final (13 September 2017) <http://eur-lex.europa.eu/legal-content/EN/TXT/?uri=COM:2017:493:FIN>.

[114] See Nikos Lavranos, 'Some Critical Observations on the EU's Foreign Investment Screening Proposal' (*Kluwer Arbitration Blog*, 2 January 2018) <http://arbitrationblog.kluwerarbitration.com/2018/01/02/critical-observations-eus-foreign-investment-screening-proposal/>.

[115] Vivienne Bath, 'Australia and the Asia-Pacific' in Fabio Morosini and Michelle Ratton Sanchez Badin (eds), *Reconceptualizing International Investment Law from the Global South* (CUP 2017).

the precedent set by the TPP and as carried forward into the CPTPP.[116] All this being said, at this stage and despite positive rhetoric, it remains unclear what priority the EU will give to the negotiations with either New Zealand or Australia.

25.52 Next is India, now a significant player in international investment law and policy-making. After earlier settling a dispute over the Daphol power plant project, it decided to contest the claim brought by White Industries under the 2000 Australia–India BIT[117]—but the tribunal found against India in 2010 under UNCITRAL Rules.[118] Although mounting a mostly successful defence, India was found liable for not providing 'effective means' for White Industries to enforce an international commercial arbitration award against an Indian state-owned enterprise. This was a protection provided in the 2001 India–Kuwait BIT that the tribunal held to be incorporated into the Australia–India BIT under the latter's MFN provision.

25.53 This reasoning highlighted significant potential extra liability under India's many BITs containing MFN clauses, as well as the extent of the Indian court system's lengthy delays generally as well as for enforcing arbitral awards. The award consequently triggered extensive public and political discussion and consultations resulting in a new Model BIT finalized in January 2016 that extensively restricted protections offered to foreign investors, including a complete omission of MFN protections. ISDS provisions were still retained, but subject to a minimum five years' 'exhaustion of local remedies' provision and then a narrow window to file ISDS proceedings before a limitation period applies.

25.54 The Indian government then approached its BIT treaty counterparts, first notifying them of unilateral termination if allowed under the relevant treaty (eg due to the expiry of its original term), although pre-existing investments would then be protected under any 'sunset' clauses. On this basis, with no media coverage in Australia, its BIT with India was terminated on 23 March 2017. For other treaties not yet open to unilateral termination, India approached counterparties seeking an agreed joint interpretation on sensitive provisions, based partly on its Model BIT. Additionally, India is using its new Model BIT when embarking on treaty negotiations with new countries, notably managing to get Cambodia apparently

---

[116] TPP / CPTPP, ch 9, Annex 9-H; CPTPP Annex, para 2.
[117] Ranjan and Anand (n 57).
[118] cf eg Vietnam, which also settled early claims but has contested—so far successfully—several subsequent ISDS claims: Dzung Manh Nguyen and Trang Thi Thu Nguyen, 'International Investment Dispute Resolution in Vietnam: Opportunities and Challenges' (2017) 18 Journal of World Investment and Trade 918, reproduced in Chaisse and Nottage (n 26). This pattern of initially settling, then gaining confidence to contest cases in arbitration proceedings, may be quite common or at least quite rational particularly for developing countries. cf generally eg Lauge Poulsen, *Bounded Rationality and Economic Diplomacy: The Politics of Investment Treaties in Developing Countries* (CUP 2015).

to agree to its almost whole-scale adoption in a BIT approved by the Indian Cabinet on 27 July 2017.[119]

25.55 Despite termination of the Australia–India BIT, limited progress has been made in negotiating a bilateral FTA.[120] Presumably, Indian officials are proposing provisions based substantially on their new Model BIT. On the one hand, Australia might be quite happy to adopt many of its features. Such provisions would allow much more extensive room to manoeuvre if and when the already politically controversial Adani coal mine investment near the Great Barrier Reef were to go ahead,[121] and later prompt regulatory interventions on environmental or public health grounds. On the other hand, the White Industries saga and the many other subsequent ISDS claims brought against India under other BITs have highlighted the very great difficulties faced by foreign investors in that large developing country. An investment chapter with extensive carve-outs and other limitations on investor protections, coupled with a very restrictive ISDS enforcement mechanism, will provide little comfort and incentive for Australia's outbound investments interested in expanding and diversifying economic relations with the rapidly growing Indian economy.

25.56 The Australian government may therefore be calculating that it is likely to obtain a more balanced outcome with India by concluding instead negotiations for RCEP commenced in late 2012. That involves more FDI exporting states, as mentioned in section C, but its future is also unclear now that New Zealand has declared that it is unwilling to agree to any form of ISDS in new treaties.

25.57 Similar considerations as those for Australia's negotiations with India apply with respect to its similarly long-running negotiations with Indonesia.[122] However,

---

[119] Romesh Weeramantry, 'International Investment Law and Practice in the Kingdom of Cambodia: An Evolving "Rule Taker"?' (2017) 18 Journal of World Investment and Trade 942, reproduced in Chaisse and Nottage (n 26).

[120] Stephen Dziedzic, 'New Trade Deal with India Could be Years Away, Malcolm Turnbull says' *ABC News* (online) (10 April 2017) <http://www.abc.net.au/news/2017-04-10/new-trade-deal-with-india-could-be-years-away-turnbull/8432130>. Negotiations to conclude a new agreement between Australia and India commenced in May 2011, and there have been nine rounds of negotiations up to September 2015: see further Department of Foreign Affairs and Trade, Australian Government, 'Australia-India Comprehensive Economic Cooperation Agreement' <http://dfat.gov.au/trade/agreements/aifta/Pages/australia-india-comprehensive-economic-cooperation-agreement.aspx>. Negotiations to create a free trade agreement between New Zealand and India commenced in April 2010 and, like Australia, have similarly stalled, with the most recent round of negotiations occurring in February 2015. A joint statement between former New Zealand Prime Minister John Key and Indian Prime Minister Nerendra Modi was issued in October 2016 reaffirming commitment to the negotiation process, but tangible progress has not yet materialized: see eg New Zealand Ministry of Foreign Affairs and Trade, 'New Zealand-India FTA' <https://www.mfat.govt.nz/en/trade/free-trade-agreements/agreements-under-negotiation/india/>.

[121] Julien Vincent, 'Adani's Mega Mine: It's Not Over Yet' *Sydney Morning Herald* (online) (10 January 2018) <http://www.smh.com.au/business/mining-and-resources/adanis-mega-mine-its-not-over-yet-20180109-h0fh1q.html>.

[122] Jewel Topsfield, 'Australian-Indonesia Free Trade Talks Going Round in Circles' *Sydney Morning Herald* (online) (20 September 2017) <http://www.smh.com.au/business/the-economy/

there is less pressure on Australia to resolve them. Its 1992 BIT with Indonesia is not one that Indonesia can quickly terminate unilaterally, as it has been doing with its treaty partners since 2014. As with India, this policy shift followed a high-profile ISDS claim brought by Australian—and British—investors[123] as well as several other arbitration filings including even one by Indian mining investors.[124] Anyway, the ASEAN–Australia–New Zealand FTA signed in 2009 (AANZFTA, in force for Indonesia since January 2010) would remain in effect, including an investment chapter containing ISDS protections. The Indonesian government also has not yet finalized or at least disclosed a new Model BIT, and domestic law initiatives seem to envisage ongoing scope for ISDS provisions in new treaties. This therefore evidences a more sophisticated and flexible approach towards investment treaty negotiations,[125] despite some resurgent economic nationalism, especially resource nationalism, in recent years.[126]

E. Conclusions: C-3PO, R2-D2, and Beyond

25.58 The Asian region has generally become more embedded in and quite comfortable with ISDS-backed investment treaties, but there remain some longstanding concerns over foreign investment and ISDS. These are illustrated, for example, by the non-ratification of the ICSID Convention by major economies such as India, Thailand, and Vietnam. In more recent times, India settled on a pro-state model

---

australiaindonesia-free-trade-talks-going-round-in-circles-20170920-gylbqi.html>. Negotiations initially commenced in 2011, but were 'reactivated' in March 2016: see also Department of Foreign Affairs and Trade, Australian Government, 'Indonesia-Australia Comprehensive Partnership Agreement' <http://dfat.gov.au/trade/agreements/iacepa/Pages/indonesia-australia-comprehensive-economic-partnership-agreement.aspx>.

[123] The convoluted procedural history and the final Award are available via ICSID, 'Case Details: Churchill Mining Plc and Planet Mining Pty Ltd, formerly ARB/12/40 v Republic of Indonesia, ICSID Case No. ARB/12/40 and 12/14' <https://icsid.worldbank.org/en/Pages/cases/casedetail.aspx?CaseNo=ARB/12/40%20and%2012/14>.

[124] Luke Eric Peterson, 'Indonesia Ramps Up Termination of BITs—And Kills Survival Clause in One Such Treaty—But Faces New $600 Mil. Claim From Indian Mining Investor' *Investment Arbitration Reporter* (20 November 2015) <https://www.iareporter.com/articles/indonesia-ramps-up-termination-of-bits-and-kills-survival-clause-in-one-such-treaty-but-faces-new-600-mil-claim-from-indian-mining-investor/>.

[125] Antony Crockett, 'The Termination of Indonesia's BITs: Changing the Bathwater, But Keeping the Baby?' (2017) 18 Journal of World Investment and Trade 836, reproduced in Chaisse and Nottage (n 26).

[126] See Luke Nottage and Simon Butt, 'Recent International Commercial Arbitration and Investor-State Arbitration Developments Impacting on Australia's Investments in the Resources Sector' in Philip Evans and Gabriel Moens (eds), *Arbitration and Dispute Resolution in the Resources Sector: An Australian Perspective* (Springer 2015) 153; Fifi Junita, 'The Foreign Mining Investment Regime in Indonesia: Regulatory Risk Under Resource Nationalism Policy and How International Investment Treaties Provide Protection' (2015) 33 Journal of Energy and Natural Resources Law 241; and generally Edward Aspinall, 'The New Nationalism in Indonesia' (2016) 3 Asia and the Pacific Policy Studies 72.

investment treaty finalized in January 2016, while Indonesia has been allowing BITs to lapse and has plans to replace them with its own (possibly incomplete, and certainly as yet undisclosed) model. Ongoing ISDS claims against these and other countries in the region, under old treaties with outdated procedures, sustain the pressure for reform.[127]

25.59 In this complex regional environment, and given their common interests, Australia and New Zealand should work together to influence the future trajectory of international investment law, through the CPTPP (eg through a Code of Conduct for ISDS arbitrators),[128] but especially in RCEP. This joint effort should also guide each country's approach to (re)negotiating significant treaties, sometimes with the same counterparties.[129] In their negotiations and treaty drafting, they should also learn from the issues faced by Australia as host state, especially the delays and problems regarding a lack of transparency highlighted by the *Phillip Morris* case.[130] In addition, both countries can draw lessons from the growing number of claims by Australia's outbound investors.[131]

25.60 Yet the ability of Australia and New Zealand to influence the path of international investment law, by working more closely together in the region, may be dampened by two factors. The first is that both countries have demonstrated considerable path-dependence in their recent FTA practice, although with some ad hoc variations in a few Australian treaties (notably the omission of ISDS in FTAs with the US, Japan, and New Zealand; and the additional public welfare notice

---

[127] Nottage, Chaisse, and Thanitcul (n 26).

[128] For both countries' parliamentary inquiries into ratifying CPTPP, see Luke Nottage, 'The TPP is Back: Submission to Australian Parliamentary Inquiries' *Japanese Law and the Asia-Pacific* (13 April 2018) <http://blogs.usyd.edu.au/japaneselaw/2018/04/the_tpp_is_back_submissions_to.html>; and <https://www.parliament.nz/en/pb/sc/make-a-submission/document/52SCFD_SCF_ITE_76583/international-treaty-examination-of-the-comprehensive-and>.

[129] See also eg each country's negotiations for a 'Pacific Alliance' FTA with Chile, Colombia, Mexico, and Peru; and further bilateral, regional and multilateral investment treaties being negotiated by Australia and New Zealand, see respectively <http://dfat.gov.au/trade/agreements/Pages/status-of-fta-negotiations.aspx> and <https://www.mfat.govt.nz/en/trade/free-trade-agreements/agreements-under-negotiation/>. Australia may also be negotiating changes to its 2015 China FTA investment chapter, pursuant to its Article 9.9 'work program': see generally Tania Voon and Elizabeth Sheargold, 'Australia, China and the Coexistence of Successive International Investment Agreements' in Colin Picker, Heng Wang and Weihuan Zhou (eds), *The China-Australia Free Trade Agreement: A 21st-Century Model* (Hart 2017).

[130] On 18 July 2017, Australia did become the first Asia-Pacific state to sign the 2014 (Mauritius) United Nations Convention on Transparency in Treaty-based Investor-State Arbitration (at <http://www.uncitral.org/uncitral/uncitral_texts/arbitration/2014Transparency_Convention.html>), which helps retrofit broader transparency provisions onto pre-existing treaties. But Australia has not yet ratified this treaty and a related Bill has not yet passed the Senate: see Luke Nottage and James Morrison, 'Accessing and Assessing Australia's International Arbitration Act' (2017) 34(6) Journal of International Arbitration 963, 969–71.

[131] Amokura Kawharu and Luke Nottage, 'Renouncing Investor-State Dispute Settlement in Australia, then New Zealand: Déjà vu' (2018) Sydney Law School Research Paper No 18/03 <https://papers.ssrn.com/sol3/papers.cfm?abstract_id=3116526>.

procedure found only in the China–Australia FTA).[132] Investment treaty practice over the last fifteen years has been clearly inspired by the US Model BIT, epitomized by the TPP (and still CPTPP) but also other agreements including both countries' recent FTAs with Korea. At least in the initial stages of the RCEP negotiations, Australia also appeared to pursue US-style commitments, as did New Zealand—albeit to a lesser extent.[133] We see such path-dependence again for example in Australia's latest bilateral FTA amendments with Singapore, as well as its FTA signed with Peru (another CPTPP partner) on 12 February 2018,[134] and its decision not to join with New Zealand, Canada and Chile in their Joint Declaration in March 2018. Given this history, Australia unfortunately still seems unlikely to respond—at least on its own—to a recent call by commentators for the nation to be 'pursuing an ambitious reform agenda with respect to the investment regime in general and ISDS in particular'.[135]

25.61 The second factor impeding joint initiatives relates to domestic political considerations. In Australia, ISDS was temporarily off the table following the Gillard government's decision to eschew ISDS in future FTAs, and it seems like a déjà-vu in New Zealand, after the newly elected Labour-led government in New Zealand similarly renounced ISDS in late 2017. It is an open question however whether New Zealand's current stance is sustainable. It was not so for Australia (and the recent outbound cases illustrate some practical utility of ISDS for Australian investors), and New Zealand similarly may risk its participation in the important RCEP and other negotiations if it does not seek to compromise.

25.62 In this respect, we reiterate the view expressed (even before the current New Zealand policy shift away from ISDS) that an EU-style investment court proposal—or some variant or half-way house—is a plausible model for both countries to adopt and promote, even perhaps in their treaty negotiations with other developed countries.[136] Much of the domestic opposition to, and criticism of, ISDS remains centred on the arbitration model of dispute resolution, rather than

---

[132] n 22 (and references cited therein).
[133] Kawharu and Nottage (n 3) (based an investment chapter draft leaked in late 2015).
[134] See generally Department of Foreign Affairs and Trade, Australian Government, Peru–Australia Free Trade Agreement <http://dfat.gov.au/trade/agreements/pafta/Pages/peru-australia-fta.aspx>.
[135] Mitchell, Sheargold, and Voon (n 21) 197.
[136] US shareholders in NuCoal are pressing a claim for compensation from the Australian government following the cancellation of NuCoal's mining licence. The licence was cancelled because the previous holder had obtained it through corruption. (For details, see Kawharu and Nottage, 'Renouncing Investor-State Dispute Settlement in Australia, then New Zealand: Déjà vu' (n 135).) The NuCoal dispute illustrates how even a developed country like Australia can experience corruption at the highest levels of government, and then arguably over-react if and when a new government comes into power, with domestic constitutional law protections being lower than international law standards even for some types of direct expropriations. However, the more obvious benefits from an investment court system (or ISDS) should arise in treaties concluded instead with developing countries.

on the resolution of investment disputes per se.[137] The idea of an investment court can be seen as a maturing of the system for resolving these disputes, from an ad hoc to more institutionalized approach. Issues such as arbitrator conflicts of interest (such as double-hatting) that have plagued ISDS would be minimized, if not avoided, by the appointment of permanent judges. Other improvements to the usual ad hoc form of ISDS would include agreement on a mechanism for appellate review of awards, and/or the creation of a standing panel of arbitrators pre-selected by the states parties and subject to an agreed code of conduct. Yet these options may not achieve the distance from ISDS that the New Zealand government, at least, is now seeking.

25.63 A further issue that may weigh in on policy-making in Australia and New Zealand relates to the wider discussions taking place on ISDS reform. Although these discussions have been underway for years, notably within UNCTAD, they have garnered greater attention from government officials now that UNCITRAL has joined in the efforts. Australia and New Zealand may be tempted to allow the debate over whether to improve the ad hoc arbitration process, or institutionalize ISDS through a standing investment court, to be resolved within the UNCITRAL forum. However, that will take a very long time, and neither country really has that luxury. Meanwhile, jointly leading initiatives within current and foreseeable bilateral and regional FTA negotiations has many attractions. It may allow Australia and New Zealand to achieve more balanced individual FTA outcomes, influence those outcomes more than they may be able to through a multilateral process (assuming an agreement is even able to be reached),[138] and demonstrate to other countries that a new approach is feasible.

25.64 To sum up in a rather a tongue-in-cheek manner, especially for *Star Wars* movie tragics,[139] if the recently re-signed CPTPP is dubbed instead 'C3PO', its core features can be seen as quite serviceable but rather awkward. In contrast to its US-style approach to investment treaty drafting, RCEP or 'R2D2' could end up with a significantly different and somewhat more streamlined model. It may well be influenced by contemporary EU-style FTA drafting as a compromise way forward, for substantive provisions and/or dispute settlement procedures, especially

---

[137] Compare Martti Koskenniemi, 'It's not the Cases, It's the System' (2017) 18 Journal of World Investment and Trade 343, 352 (arguing that the focus on technical aspects of ISDS and investor protection obscures the overall significance of the investment system, and that the EU's investment court idea has 'monopolised' creative thinking).

[138] cf generally Anthea Roberts, 'UNCITRAL and ISDS Reform: Not Business as Usual' *EJIL: Talk* (11 December 2017) <https://www.ejiltalk.org/uncitral-and-isds-reform-not-business-as-usual/>; and Anne-Karin Grill (Schoenherr), 'Mind the Label: Loyalists and Reformists and ISDS' (*Kluwer Arbitration Blog*, 29 December 2017) <http://arbitrationblog.kluwerarbitration.com/2017/12/29/uncitral-isds-working-group-vienna-11-12-2017/>.

[139] Miles Surrey, 'Ranking the Delightfully Sassy Droids in 'Star Wars' *mic.com* (24 December 2016) <https://mic.com/articles/163277/ranking-the-delightfully-sassy-droids-in-star-wars#.BkNxDFcO5>.

if Australia and New Zealand join forces to promote innovations. But future treaties in the Asian region might even end up looking like the skittish but loyal 'BB8', a completely different model of droid that appears in the most recent *Star Wars* movies. There are exciting times ahead. Yet it could be premature to write off conventional ISDS, or C3PO as a variant. Although some argue that ISDS has gone 'rogue',[140] it is worth remembering that in the 'Rogue One' spin-off movie, that eponymous spaceship ends up being on the good side.

---

[140] n 2. That statement by the Foley Hoag lawyer was made before his firm prevailed in the defence of Uruguay against Philip Morris' challenge of tobacco regulations: see <www.foleyhoag.com/news-and-events/news/2016/july/foley-hoag-helps-uruguay-secure-landmark-victory-over-philip-morris>.

26

INDIA'S 2015 MODEL BIT AGAINST THE BACKDROP OF GLOBAL ISDS REFORMS

Aveek Chakravarty

A. Introduction	26.01	C. ISDS in India's BITs	26.13
B. ISDS Reform and the Role of States	26.07	D. India's 2015 Model BIT	26.33
		E. Conclusions	26.81

A. Introduction

26.01 The proliferation of investment treaties in the form of bilateral investment treaties (BITs) and other international investment agreements (IIAs) in the last three decades has been accompanied by a rising number of investor claims under the investor–state dispute settlement (ISDS) system. The number of such treaty-based ISDS claims grew rapidly during the late 1990s, and since the early 2000s has maintained a general upward trajectory.[1] In fact, the highest number of known ISDS cases ever filed in a single year was in 2015, with seventy new disputes raised against states by foreign investors.[2] While the number of known disputes instituted in 2016 dropped slightly to sixty-two,[3] the ISDS system continues to be widely employed as the primary mechanism for resolution of investor-state disputes.[4] However, along with the growing corpus of cases filed under the ISDS system, the criticism arising from the perceived deficiencies in the system has led

---

[1] UNCTAD, *World Investment Report 2016* (United Nations 2016) <https://unctad.org/en/PublicationsLibrary/wir2016_en.pdf> accessed 10 March 2017.

[2] ibid.

[3] UNCTAD, 'Arbitrations Initiated in 2016' <http://investmentpolicyhub.unctad.org/ISDS/FilterByYear> accessed 30 March 2017.

[4] Stephen M Schwebel, 'The Outlook for the Continued Vitality, or Lack thereof, of Investor–State Arbitration' (2016) 32 Arbitration International 1, 1–6.

to calls for major reform from a wide spectrum of stakeholders, observers, and practitioners. Some of these critiques have highlighted the lack of uniformity in arbitral jurisprudence, the opaque nature of investment arbitration that restricts public access and participation, wide interpretative and jurisdictional authority that is frequently exercised by arbitral tribunals, the lack of facilities for appeal or review of arbitral awards, and other issues as the major faults in the present ISDS framework. The substantive and procedural laws that govern ISDS proceedings are contained in the IIAs entered into by states. Therefore, the process of reshaping ISDS provisions in investment agreements is seen as an essential requirement for reforming the ISDS system.

26.02 The role of states is central to the institution of reforms in ISDS as the processes of negotiating, drafting, finalizing, and subsequently adopting investment treaties are sovereign functions of states alone. In the past decade, there has been a significant shift in the position of several states with respect to investment treaties. These countries have seemingly woken up to the need for reforms, especially when faced with a series of high value investment suits. Perhaps no country is a better example of this trend than India, which, in 2012, initiated major reforms to its investment treaty policy as well as its existing BIT framework. The result of such processes has been the abandonment of its 1993 model BIT in favour of a new model text that not only incorporates India's varied experiences with investment disputes, but also brings together various streams of contemporary state practices in ISDS reform. Therefore, this chapter attempts to analyse India's approach to ISDS reform through its new Model BIT within the context of changing state practices around the world.

26.03 Although the focus of this chapter is on India's BIT policy and the changes proposed by the new model text with specific context to ISDS, the dispute settlement provisions contained in India's four free trade agreements (FTAs)[5] have also been taken into account. For the sake of convenience and ease of reference, the standalone BITs and FTAs will be collectively referred to as BITs. It should also be noted that until the notification of the new model text, most BITs and FTAs signed by India contained largely identical ISDS provisions, even though the substantive investment protection provisions varied. Therefore, this chapter analyses both BITs and FTAs collectively. The 2015 Model BIT and the ISDS chapter contained therein, as notified by the Indian government on 28 December 2015,[6]

---

[5] India currently has four FTAs in force that were signed with Singapore (2005), South Korea (2009), Japan (2011), and Malaysia (2011). India also signed an FTA with the Association of South East Asian Nations (ASEAN) in 2014 that is yet to enter into force.

[6] It is notable that although the new Model BIT was notified on 28 December 2015 via office memorandum F. No 26/5/2013-IC, it was made public on 14 January 2016. Based on the date

marks a paradigm shift in Indian BIT policy and practice, and it is the aim of this chapter to gauge this marked change with a specific focus on ISDS.

26.04 The chapter has been structured as follows. The first section, titled 'ISDS Reform and the Role of States', builds the background for the case study by providing a brief description of the criticism of ISDS, the calls for reform of ISDS and the role that has been played by states in initiating such reform.

26.05 The second section is titled 'ISDS in India's BITs', which delves into the case study with an overview of the nature of ISDS provisions in India's existing BITs. It seeks to identify the general structure of the ISDS system as developed over the years and the mechanisms through which it regulates the admission and conduct of investment treaty-based disputes.

26.06 The third and final section, titled 'The 2015 Model BIT', analyses some of the key features contained in the ISDS chapter of the 2015 Model BIT. The new provisions are also compared with similar drafting practices of other states in order to place India's ISDS reforms within the larger global context.

B. ISDS Reform and the Role of States

1. Criticism and calls for reform of ISDS

26.07 Though ISDS chapters have been a part of several generations of BITs, they came under greater academic and public scrutiny from the early 2000s, a period that saw an exponential rise in the number of claims filed by investors against host states. Though on an average, fewer than ten new cases were being filed per year during the 1990s, this figure shot up to over thirty-five new cases per year in the early 2000s.[7] As per the latest available figures with the United Nations Conference for Trade and Development (UNCTAD), the cumulative number of known treaty-based arbitration cases stands at 767, with over 107 countries having been respondent states to investors' claims.[8] Considering the fact that not all investment arbitrations are publicly reported, the actual number of cases is certainly higher.

26.08 A recurring criticism of ISDS has been with regard to the functioning and the decision-making processes of arbitral tribunals appointed under relevant BITs and other IIAs. The interpretation of IIAs by arbitral tribunals with insufficient regard

---

of notification, this chapter has referred to the new model text as the '2015 Model BIT', '2015 Model', etc.

[7] UNCTAD, *World Investment Report 2016* (n 1).
[8] ibid.

to the state's right to regulate, inconsistencies in the decision-making process, concerns regarding the impartiality and independence of arbitrators, accusations of bias in favour of investors, lack of transparency in the arbitral proceedings, lack of options for review or appeal against arbitral decisions, increasing costs of arbitration of investment disputes, among other factors,[9] have contributed to the present backlash against the ISDS system.[10] At the same time, ISDS also faces a crisis of legitimacy from the perspective of public law.[11] The central question that has been raised in this context is whether the private adjudication of essentially public disputes as characterized by arbitration violates the fundamental features of public law adjudication, including judicial accountability and right to appeal.[12] Thus, the unique ecosystem in which ISDS operates is also a major cause of criticism against it.

As a response to the varied criticisms regarding the operation of ISDS, measures for comprehensive review of the existing ISDS framework and practices have been initiated at several levels. At the international organizational level, the UNCTAD and the Organisation for Economic Co-operation and Development (OECD) have from time to time organized meetings and produced studies with regard to ISDS reform. The UNCTAD, for example, has produced information on ISDS and IIA reform based on its Investment Policy Framework for Sustainable Development (IPFSD), which seeks to place the objectives of inclusive growth and sustainable development at the core of national and international investment policies.[13] The UNCTAD has proposed five pathways for states towards achieving ISDS reform:[14] (i) promoting alternative dispute resolution (or ADR); (ii) tailoring the existing system through individual IIAs; (iii) limiting investor access to ISDS; (iv) introducing an appeals facility; and (v) creating a standing international investment court. Beyond international organizations, efforts at reforming ISDS have received support at multiple

26.09

---

[9] Stephan W Schill, 'Reforming Investor-State Dispute Settlement (ISDS): Conceptual Framework and Options for the Way Forward' (International Centre for Trade and Sustainable Development/World Economic Forum 2015) 5–6 <http://hdl.handle.net/11245/1.483161> accessed 1 March 2017.

[10] For a detailed study of the rising opposition to investment arbitration and ISDS, see Michael Waibel, Asha Kaushal, Kyo-Hwa Chung, and Claire Balchin (eds), *The Backlash Against Investment Arbitration* (Kluwer Law International 2010).

[11] See generallySusan D Franck, 'The Legitimacy Crisis in Investment Treaty Arbitration: Privatizing Public International Law Through Inconsistent Decisions' (2005) 73 Fordham Law Review 1521.

[12] Gus Van Harten, *Investment Treaty Arbitration and Public Law* (OUP 2007)

[13] UNCTAD, 'Investment Policy Framework for Sustainable Development' (UNCTAD 2015) <http://unctad.org/en/PublicationsLibrary/diaepcb2015d5_en.pdf> accessed 10 March 2017.

[14] UNCTAD, 'Reform of Investor-State Dispute Settlement: In Search of a Roadmap' (UNCTAD 2013) <http://unctad.org/en/PublicationsLibrary/webdiaepcb2013d4_en.pdf> accessed 10 March 2017.

levels, including academia,[15] practitioners,[16] and public and non-governmental organizations.[17]

2. State responses towards ISDS reform

26.10 The interaction of states with the ISDS reform process has been complex and multi-faceted. While some states have espoused their faith in the system by continuing to incorporate standardized ISDS clauses imported from older investment treaties into new IIAs, others have adopted reforms that range from minor tweaks to relatively major changes. In recent years, some states have withdrawn themselves from ISDS mechanisms altogether. Bolivia, Ecuador, and Venezuela were three Latin American countries that withdrew from the Convention on the Settlement of Investment Disputes between States and Nationals of Other States (ICSID Convention) in 2007, 2009, and 2012, respectively.[18] Australia followed a similar path in 2011 by announcing that it would no longer pursue ISDS provisions in its future international economic agreements with developing states,[19] although ISDS has found its way back into Australia's treaty negotiations in recent years.[20] Indonesia notably terminated

---

[15] See Van Harten (n 12) for a public law critique of investment arbitration. See also Jose E Alvarez et al (eds), *The Evolving International Investment Regime: Expectations, Realities, Options* (OUP 2011); Stefan Hindelang and Markus Krajewski, *Shifting Paradigms in International Investment Law* (OUP 2016); M Sornarajah, *Resistance and Change in International Law on Foreign Investment* (CUP 2015).

[16] Jean E Kalicki and Anna Joubin-Bret (eds), *Reshaping the Investor-State Dispute Settlement System* (Brill/Nijhoff 2015) (the collection makes a rich contribution to legal scholarship on investor–state dispute settlement, providing multiple perspectives on the reshaping process of ISDS); Jonathan Ketcheson, 'Investment Arbitration: Learning from Experience' in Steffen Hindelang and Markus Krajewski (eds), *Shifting Paradigms in International Investment Law: More Balanced, Less Isolated, Increasingly Diversified* (OUP 2016); Joshua D H Karton, 'Reform of Investor-State Dispute Settlement: Lessons from International Uniform Law' (2014) Queen's University Faculty of Law Research Paper Series 2015-019 <https://papers.ssrn.com/sol3/papers.cfm?abstract_id=2383516> accessed 10 October 2016; David W Rivkin, 'Towards a New Paradigm in International Arbitration: The Elder Town Model Revisited' (2008) 24 Arbitration International 375.

[17] See generally Nathalie Bernasconi-Osterwalder and Diana Rosert, 'Investment Treaty Arbitration: Opportunities to Reform Arbitral Rules and Processes' (2014) IISD Report <http://www.iisd.org/pdf/2014/investment_treaty_arbitration.pdf> accessed 10 October 2016; IISD Investment and Sustainable Development Program, 'IISD Investment and Sustainable Development Program Investment Related Dispute Settlement: Reflections on a New Beginning' (2015) <http://www.iisd.org/sites/default/files/publications/investment-related-dispute-settlement-expert-meeting-report.pdf> accessed 10 March 2017; Simon Lester, 'Liberalization or litigation? Time to Rethink the International Investment Regime' (Cato Institute 2013) <http://www.cato.org/publications/policy-analysis/liberalization-or-litigation-time-rethink-international-investment> accessed 10 March 2017.

[18] Nicolas Boeglin, 'ICSID and Latin America: Criticisms, Withdrawals and Regional Alternatives' (2013) <http://www.bilaterals.org/?icsid-and-latin-america-criticisms> accessed 10 October 2016.

[19] Department of Foreign Affairs and Trade of the Government of Australia, 'Gillard Government Trade Policy Statement: Trading our Way to More Jobs and Prosperity' (2011) <http://blogs.usyd.edu.au/japaneselaw/2011_Gillard%20Govt%20Trade%20Policy%20Statement.pdf> accessed 10 March 2017.

[20] For example, the Australia–China FTA signed by the two countries in 2015 contains provisions for investment arbitration. The Comprehensive and Progressive Agreement for Trans Pacific Partnership to which Australia is a party, also contains similar provisions.

several existing BITs with developed and developing economies[21] and conveyed its intention to develop a new Model BIT for future negotiations.[22] Similarly, South Africa terminated several BITs and implemented an act in December 2015 titled 'Protection of Investment Act 2015', which would replace the terminated and otherwise lapsed investment treaties.[23] In the instance of Brazil, which had not ratified any of the traditional investment treaties that it had negotiated with other states, it moved forward with new investment-related instruments known as 'Cooperation and Facilitation Investment Agreements' (CFIAs) that do not incorporate any ISDS provisions.[24]

26.11 Perhaps a more measured approach by states in this regard has been the recasting of their respective BIT programmes and incorporating substantial changes in the ISDS provisions. In effect, states have attempted to re-work the structure of ISDS in order to address its systemic deficiencies. This has been sought to be achieved through the incorporation of measures limiting investor access to ISDS,[25] ensuring a greater degree of fairness and transparency in arbitral proceedings,[26] restricting the scope of interpretation of treaty provisions by arbitral tribunals,[27] and the provision of an appeals and/or review facility for arbitral awards.[28] Some examples of these changes have found their way into Model BITs of several of states, and in this regard, they have been useful indicators of ongoing changes in state practice. However, implementing changes through treaty drafting is an inherently slow process.[29] BIT negotiations between states can last several years and may be shaped by larger economic and political considerations as well as the leverage available to a state during negotiations. Therefore, the shifts in a state's position with respect to

---

[21] Ben Bland and Shawn Donnan, 'Indonesia to Terminate More than 60 Bilateral Investment Treaties' *Financial Times* (London, 16 March 2014) <https://www.ft.com/content/3755c1b2-b4e2-11e3-af92-00144feabdc0> accessed 10 March 2017.

[22] Global Business Guide, 'What is Going on with Indonesia's Model Bilateral Investment Treaties?' (13 June 2016) <http://www.gbgindonesia.com/en/main/legal_updates/what_is_going_on_with_indonesia_s_bilateral_investment_treaties.php> accessed 8 March 2018.

[23] UNCTAD, 'Protection of Investment Act Approved' (13 December 2015) <http://investmentpolicyhub.unctad.org/IPM/MeasureDetails?id=2828&rgn=&grp=&t=&s=&pg=&c=&dt=&df=&isSearch=false> accessed 8 March 2018.

[24] Pedro Martini, 'Brazil's New Investment Treaties: Outside Looking Out?' (2015) <http://kluwerarbitrationblog.com/2015/06/16/brazils-new-investment-treaties-outside-looking-out-2/> accessed 10 March 2017.

[25] Pohl, J K Mashigo and A Nohen, 'Dispute Settlement Provisions in International Investment Agreements: A Large Sample Survey' (2012) OECD Working Papers on International Investment, 2012/02 < https://www.oecd.org/investment/investment-policy/WP-2012_2.pdf >. In this research document, OECD sampled over 1,660 BITs and other IIAs and mapped trends in the drafting of ISDS clauses.

[26] ibid.

[27] August Reinisch, 'The Scope of Investor-State Dispute Settlement in International Investment Agreements' (2013) 12 Asia Pacific Law Review 1.

[28] For instance, see the provision for review and appeal in the 2012 US Model BIT. A copy of the treaty text is available at <https://ustr.gov/sites/default/files/BIT%20text%20for%20ACIEP%20Meeting.pdf> accessed 10 April 2018.

[29] Liang-Ying Tan and Amal Bouchenaki, 'Limiting Investor Access to Investment Arbitration: A Solution without a Problem?' in Kalicki and Joubin-Bret (n16) 290–95.

BIT practice may be better appreciated over a longer timeframe. This is reflected in the fact that variations in BITs are usually categorized as different generations.[30]

26.12 Through the introduction of its new model text, India seems to have journeyed into a new generation of its BIT policy, and has emerged as an important voice in the global narrative of IIA and ISDS reforms initiated by states. The country has entrenched itself in the ongoing debate over the reform of the international investment regime. The changes envisaged by India in the way it engages with ISDS can prove to be an important addition to the larger roadmap for investment treaty reform.

C. ISDS in India's BITs

1. Overview of India's BIT programme

26.13 India's BIT programme began with the signing of the India–UK BIT in 1994. As a part of major economic reforms that were initiated in 1991, India's economic policy shifted towards increased facilitation of foreign trade and investment. Bilateral Investment Promotion and Protection Agreements (BIPAs), the official terminology used for BITs in India, were perceived as valuable tools for building investor confidence that would accelerate foreign investment. The number of India's BITs grew rapidly, with thirty-five BITs signed by the year 2000. Between 2000 and 2011, another forty-four BITs were concluded. Over eighty-three BITs were signed by India in total, out of which seventy-three entered into force.[31] Additionally, India is a party to four FTAs[32] in force that contain chapters on investment and ISDS.

26.14 In recent years, India has been one of the top foreign direct investment (FDI) destinations in the world. Since April 2000, the country has received over US$ 450 billion in FDI, including equity inflows, reinvested inflows, and other capital.[33] In 2016, FDI inflows into India totalled over US$ 43 billion, marking a 24 per cent rise over the previous year.[34] This continues a series of years marking tremendous growth in

---

[30] Kenneth J Vandevelde, 'Model Bilateral Investment Treaties: the Way Forward' (2011) 18 Southwestern Journal of International Law 307.

[31] For the full list of India's BITs, see Government of India, Ministry of Finance, Bilateral Investment Promotion and Protection Agreements <https://dea.gov.in/bipa> accessed 10 April 2018. As part of ongoing reform, the government of India sent out termination notices for fifty-eight of these seventy-three BITs in force in 2017. For a discussion on the issuance of termination notices, see Prabhash Ranjan, 'As India's New Bilateral Investment Strategy Sputters out, the Secrecy and Opaqueness Must Go' (*The Wire*, 1 May 2017) accessed 10 April 2018.

[32] Free trade agreements in India are officially denoted as Comprehensive Economic Cooperation Agreements (CECA) or Comprehensive Economic Partnership Agreements (CEPA). For full texts of the FTAs, see UNCTAD, 'Indian Treaties with Investment Provisions' <http://investmentpolicyhub.unctad.org/IIA/CountryOtherIias/96#iiaInnerMenu> accessed 10 March 2017.

[33] Department of Industrial Policy & Promotion, 'Annual Report 2016–17' (2017) <http://dipp.nic.in/English/Publications/Annual_Reports/AnnualReport_Eng_2016-17.pdf> accessed 10 March 2017.

[34] ibid.

investment in the country and has highlighted its comparative stability amidst a turbulent period in the global economy. However, a series of well publicized BIT-based disputes that were initiated since 2012 began to place increasing international focus on India's legal and regulatory system for protection of foreign investments that marked a significant turn for the country's investment treaty system.

In 2012, the government of India initiated a review of its extant law and policy with respect to investment treaties following an adverse arbitral award that it received under the India–Australia BIT. The *White Industries Ltd v Republic of India*[35] arbitration of 2011 can be considered a watershed moment in India's relationship with investment treaties in general and investment treaty arbitration in particular, which prompted a dramatic shift in the country's approach to investment treaties. While the award drew criticism from certain quarters with regard to the interpretation of several provisions such as the most favoured nation (MFN) clause by the arbitral tribunal,[36] more importantly, it became a catalyst for the government's decision to initiate reforms in its BIT policy. Other BIT-based claims were subsequently filed against India by foreign investors. There are currently almost a dozen known investment treaty-based claims pending against India that have been filed since 2012.[37]

26.15

Following the official public notification of the text of the 2015 Model BIT, the Indian government initiated several steps with regard to its existing BIT framework. In July 2016, the government sent out notices to fifty-eight countries seeking termination of respective BITs whose initial duration had either expired or would be expiring by the end of the year.[38] Further, the government notified

26.16

---

[35] *White Industries Australia Ltd v Republic of India*, UNCITRAL, Final Award (30 November 2011). White Industries Ltd, an Australian company, brought a claim against India due to 'inordinate delay' by Indian courts in hearing an application for enforcement of an International Chamber of Commerce (ICC) arbitral award that the company had won against Coal India, an Indian company. White Industries proceeded with investment arbitration under the ISDS system provided in the India–Australia BIT. The arbitral tribunal for the dispute held that India had not provided 'effective means' to White Industries for enforcing its rights against Coal India with respect to the enforcement of the ICC award. Though the 'effective means' provision was not contained in the India–Australia BIT, the arbitral tribunal borrowed the provision from the India–Kuwait BIT using the MFN provision of the India–Australia BIT. The arbitral tribunal justified this by stating that the MFN provision allowed an Australian investor to avail all of the protections extended by India to investors of its other BIT partner states, such as Kuwait in the present case.

[36] For a critical analysis of the interpretation of the arbitral tribunal's findings, see Sumeet Kachwaha, 'The White Industries Australia Limited—India BIT Award: A Critical Assessment' (2013) 29 Arbitration International 275; For a more general analysis of the award, see Manu Sanan, 'The White Industries award- Shades of Grey' (2012) 12 Journal of World Investment and Trade 661.

[37] For a full list of investment disputes pending against India, see UNCTAD, 'India as Respondent State' <http://investmentpolicyhub.unctad.org/ISDS/CountryCases/96?partyRole=2> accessed 10 March 2017.

[38] Kavaljit Singh and Burghard Ilge, 'India Overhauls its Investment Treaty Programme' *Financial Times* (London, 15 July 2016) <http://blogs.ft.com/beyond-brics/2016/07/15/india-overhauls-its-investment-treaty-regime/> accessed 10 March 2017.

twenty-five other countries with whom its BITs would expire after July 2017, seeking to issue joint interpretative statements that would clarify ambiguities in treaty texts and possibly reduce the scope for interpretation by arbitral tribunals.[39] India also reportedly concluded negotiations with Brazil at the end of 2016 for a new investment treaty, which combines elements from both India's Model BIT as well as Brazil's CFIA[40] and marks the first reported instance where the new model text has been used in concluding an investment treaty.

26.17 Another major reform has been in the government strategy towards negotiation of IIAs. Until the notification of the 2015 Model BIT, different government bodies independently undertook the negotiation of India's BITs and FTAs. While the Ministry of Commerce and Industry handled FTA negotiations, including investment chapters, all BIT-based negotiations were handled by the Ministry of Finance. This has been a cause for concern for the government as different negotiation strategies of the two ministries resulted in significant differences between investment protection provisions contained in BITs and FTAs.[41] Therefore, while publishing the text of the 2015 Model BIT, the Ministry of Finance also announced that the power to conduct negotiations regarding investment-related provisions, regardless of the type of IIAs in question, would lie exclusively within its authority.[42]

26.18 In order to appreciate the changes brought in by the 2015 Model BIT, it is important to understand the nature of ISDS clauses in Indian BITs, as they have existed. The next subsection deals with this and other related aspects.

2. Features of ISDS provisions in existing BITs

26.19 Provisions for ISDS are present in every BIT that India has concluded up to the most recent BIT entered into with United Arab Emirates (UAE) in 2013.[43] On

---

[39] Kavaljit Singh, 'Remodeling India's Investment Treaty Regime' (Madhyam 2016) <http://www.madhyam.org.in/remodeling-indias-investment-treaty-regime-ii/> accessed 10 March 2017.

[40] IISD, 'Brazil and India Initial Bilateral Investment Treaty (BIT); Text yet to Be Published' <https://www.iisd.org/itn/2016/12/12/brazil-and-india-initial-bilateral-investment-treaty-bit-text-yet-to-be-published/> accessed 10 March 2017.

[41] Prabhash Ranjan, 'India and Bilateral Investment Treaties—A Changing Landscape' (2014) 29 ICSID Review 420. Ranjan opines that the dichotomy between India's BITs and FTAs on investment protection provisions is largely due to the fact that both ministries employ different approaches and negotiators for treaty negotiation, with an evident lack of cooperation between them. Resultantly, the Ministry of Commerce, with its superior experience in trade negotiations at the WTO, has negotiated investment provisions that are strict and precise, as opposed to several Indian BITs that contain vague and loosely drafted provisions.

[42] Ministry of Finance of the Government of India, 'Office Memorandum' (28 December 2015) F. No 26/5/2013-IC <http://finmin.nic.in/reports/ModelTextIndia_BIT.pdf> accessed 10 March 2017.

[43] Until the present date, no new BITs were entered into by India following the UAE BIT. An exception to this would be the Investment Cooperation and Facilitation Treaty signed with Brazil in 2016, which has neither been ratified nor made public. This chapter analyses the treaty texts of all seventy-three BITs that are currently in force between India and other states, as well as the texts

the basis of an analysis of ISDS chapters contained in all publicly available Indian BIT texts, the following subsection presents an overview of the broad characteristics of the ISDS system contained within these treaties.[44]

a. Limitation on the types of disputes

26.20 ISDS clauses in BITs generally contain provisions that define or limit the type of disputes that can be settled using the ISDS mechanism. In sixty-four BITs, the ISDS clauses provide that any dispute in relation to an investment made by the investor of one contracting state in the other contracting state and arising under the terms of the applicable BIT is eligible for settlement under the ISDS mechanism.[45] The texts of most BITs specify that 'any dispute' between the investor and the host state arising under the terms of an applicable BIT can be brought for settlement under ISDS as long as the incorporated pre-conditions are satisfied. The term 'any dispute' provides a wide scope for interpretation regarding the types of investment-related disputes that can be brought for settlement under the ISDS mechanism. As a result, the discretion of the adjudicatory body or arbitral tribunal assumes great importance in this regard, raising the possibility for interpretation that may go beyond the intention of the contracting states. In seven other BITs[46] the term 'disputes' has been used instead of 'any disputes', but whether this would in any way limit the admissibility of disputes remains an open question.

26.21 Only certain Indian BITs contain ISDS provisions that define the types of disputes that can be submitted under ISDS. By defining the applicable scope of ISDS clauses, these BITs more clearly establish what can and cannot constitute a 'dispute'. For example, the India–Mexico BIT limits the types of disputes only to cases of breach of Chapter II of the BIT, which contains substantive provisions for investment protection.[47] Thus, an investor cannot assail other BIT provisions that are not under Chapter II. The India–Bulgaria BIT provides a definition of what constitutes an investment dispute.[48] It states that only those disputes that involve (i) interpretation or application of an investment agreement between the

---

of BITs that have been signed but are not yet enforced, excluding those not available in the public domain.

[44] References to BITs from hereon will also include the FTAs in force, unless specifically differentiated.

[45] For example, see BITs that India has entered into with the UK, Sri Lanka, Italy, the Netherlands, France, and Switzerland, among others.

[46] See BITs that India has entered into with Spain, Morocco, Philippines, Portugal, Kuwait, Mexico, and Saudi Arabia.

[47] Agreement between the Government of the Republic of India and the Government of the United Mexican States on the Promotion and Protection of Investments (signed 21 May 2007, entered into force 23 February 2008) arts 11.1 and 12.1.

[48] Agreement between the Government of the Republic of India and the Government of the Republic of Bulgaria for the Promotion and Protection of Investments (signed 26 October 1998, entered into force 23 September 1999) art 9.3.

investor and host state, or (ii) an alleged breach of any right conferred with respect to an investment under the BIT, are defined as investment disputes.[49] In the India–Slovakia BIT, the treaty specifically excludes any pre-establishment dispute or those arising out of application of national laws of the host state on the investor's investment, including measures taken for protection of security interests or in circumstances of extreme emergency.[50]

b. Multi-tier system

26.22 In general international practice, BITs and other investment agreements typically contain dispute settlement clauses that provide a 'multi-tier' system for dispute resolution. Under such clauses, disputing investors can choose from among several available mechanisms of dispute resolution. However, they must first fulfil the necessary pre-conditions as stated in the treaty text in order to access each mechanism.[51] The *first tier* is a requirement for the investor and state to engage in negotiations or attempts to amicably resolve the dispute for a minimum of six months.[52]

26.23 If a dispute between the investor and host state has not been resolved after that process, Indian BITs generally provide two routes for settlement under the *second tier* that is through international conciliation or through the initiation of proceedings before arbitral, judicial, or administrative bodies of the host state. In fact as many as fifty-seven Indian BITs contain a provision for international conciliation based on the Conciliation Rules of the United Nations Commission on International Trade Law (UNCITRAL Conciliation Rules) that can be exercised at the option of the investor.[53] Similarly, clauses providing the option to resolve disputes through domestic arbitral, judicial or administrative bodies are present in as many as sixty-seven BITs.[54]

26.24 The *third tier* of the ISDS system provides for international arbitration. However, access to arbitration is made available only when certain pre-conditions are fulfilled: (i) the parties fail to agree on a dispute settlement procedure or reach a settlement under the second tier of ISDS; or (ii) by the termination of the

---

[49] ibid.
[50] Agreement between the Government of the Republic of India and the Slovak Republic on the Promotion and Reciprocal Protection of Investments (signed 25 September 2006, entered into force 16 June 2007) art 8.4.
[51] Reinisch, 'The Scope of Investor-State Dispute Settlement in International Investment Agreements' (n 27).
[52] For instance, see art 9.2 of the Agreement between the Government of India and the Government of the Italian Republic for the Promotion and Protection of Investments (signed 23 November 1995, entered into force 26 March 1998).
[53] For example, see BITs entered into by India with Germany, Netherlands, Denmark, Sri Lanka, Vietnam, Switzerland, Mexico, and Bangladesh, among others.
[54] For example, see BITs entered into by India with Czech Republic, Kazakhstan, Sri Lanka, Kuwait, Finland, Hungary, and China, among others.

conciliation proceedings in cases where they have been initiated. For example, the India–Sri Lanka BIT states as follows:[55]

> Should the Parties fail to agree on a dispute settlement procedure provided under paragraph (2) of this Article or where a dispute is referred to conciliation but conciliation proceedings are terminated other than by signing of a settlement agreement, the dispute may be referred to Arbitration.

A question here arises as to whether an investor who has opted to seek local remedies instead of conciliation retains the right to initiate international arbitration proceedings against the host state, either during the pendency of its claims before local bodies or after having received a decision from them. Most Indian BITs are silent on this point. The ambiguity in the text can be problematic as a foreign investor can misuse it to launch parallel proceedings before local courts and arbitral tribunals. Some Indian BITs have sought to specifically address this problem through the incorporation of fork-in-the-road provisions in the treaty text. 26.25

c. Fork-in-the-road (FITR) provisions

FITR clauses can be found in ISDS provisions of a number of Indian BITs. Like a literal fork in the road, these provisions establish distinct 'paths' or dispute settlement mechanisms from which the investor must choose. Once such a choice is made, it is to be final. For example, once the investor has decided to pursue international arbitration as opposed to relief before domestic courts, the FITR clause may prevent the investor from subsequently turning back to domestic courts. Only twelve out of seventy-three Indian BITs in force contain FITR provisions.[56] 26.26

The first Indian BIT with a FITR clause was signed with Romania in 1998. The ISDS clause in this BIT provides the investor a choice between two options for dispute resolution: (i) domestic adjudicatory or arbitral proceedings and (ii) international arbitration. However, the FITR provision in this BIT states that: 26.27

> 'Provided that where the investor has submitted the dispute to the competent judicial or arbitral bodies of the Contracting Party in whose territory the investment has been made, the choice once exercised shall be final.[57]

According to this FITR provision, an investor who chooses to submit the dispute to a domestic judicial or arbitral proceeding at the first instance will be barred from 26.28

---

[55] Agreement between the Government of the Republic of India and the Government of the Democratic Socialist Republic of Sri Lanka for the Promotion and Protection of Investments (signed 22 January 1997, entered into force 13 February 1998) art 9.3. Similar provisions can be found in India's BITs with Myanmar, Israel, Germany, and China.
[56] These clauses are present in Indian BITs with the following countries: Romania, Mauritius, Morocco, Indonesia, Qatar, Argentina, Saudi Arabia, Mexico, Syria, Latvia, Lithuania, and United Arab Emirates.
[57] Agreement between the Government of the Republic of India and the Government of Romania for the Promotion and Reciprocal Protection of Investments (signed 17 December 1997, entered into force 9 December 1999) art 9.2.

filing a claim under international arbitration under the said BIT. However, if the investor instead opts for international arbitration in the first place, no provision bars it from pursuing domestic proceedings at a later stage. That type of provision can be contrasted with the India–UAE BIT of 2014, which provides that once the investor has decided a specific proceeding among the choices of International Centre for Settlement of Investment Disputes (ICSID) arbitration, UNCITRAL arbitration or the host state's domestic courts, the choice will be final and binding on the investor.[58] Such an absolute bar on the choice of forum once the choice has been made is also referred to as a 'no U-turn' clause. The India–Lithuania BIT of 2011 operates similarly to the India–UAE BIT with regard to FITR provisions, providing a non-reversible choice between domestic courts, international conciliation, and international arbitration.[59]

26.29 It is interesting to differentiate India's FTAs in this regard. While the FTAs entered into with Malaysia, Japan, and South Korea contain FITR provisions, the same is not present in the India–Singapore FTA. The language of the FITR provisions also differs in the three FTAs. The Malaysia FTA makes it mandatory for the investor to issue a written waiver of the right to initiate or continue international arbitration or conciliation proceedings, once a domestic adjudicatory mechanism has been selected, thereby discouraging attempts of investors to exhaust all available fora for dispute settlement.[60] The India–Japan FTA allows a party to initiate international proceedings, provided that the disputing party has withdrawn its domestic proceeding within thirty days of filing of an international proceeding.[61] Because of this feature, the clause cannot be said to be a 'no U-turn' clause as it allows a fixed timeframe within which an investor can change his forum of dispute. The India–South Korea FTA, however, is a perfect example of such a clause as it makes any choice of forum once made, be it domestic or international, final and binding on the investor.[62] From these FTAs as well as BITs, it is apparent that FITR provisions exist in India's investment treaties in the following forms: (i) where an investor has to make a non-rescindable choice between domestic and international forum (ie a 'no U-turn' clause is present), (ii) where an investor is allowed to change his choice of forum within a limited time period (ie a limited 'no

---

[58] Agreement between the Government of the Republic of India and the Government of the United Arab Emirates on the Promotion and Protection of Investments (signed 12 December 2013, entered into force 14 August 2014) art 10.5.

[59] Agreement between the Government of the Republic of India and the Government of the Republic of Lithuania for the Promotion and Reciprocal Protection of Investments (signed 31 March 2011, entered into force 1 December 2011) art 9.3.

[60] Comprehensive Economic Cooperation Agreement between the Government of Malaysia and Government of Republic of India (signed 18 February 2011, entered into force 1 July 2011) art 8.

[61] Comprehensive Economic Partnership Agreement between Japan and the Republic of India (signed 16 February 2011, entered into force 1 August 2011) art 96.6.

[62] Comprehensive Economic Partnership Agreement between the Republic of Korea and the Republic of India (signed 7 August 2009, entered into force 1 January 2010) art 10.21.4.

U-turn' clause), and (iii) where investors are precluded from exhausting all available remedies by issuing a mandatory waiver. It should be noted here that arbitral tribunals have (barring a few cases) largely relied on the triple identity test—identity of party, cause of action, and object of dispute—in instances of parallel proceedings, and as such, such FITR provisions are often not very helpful or useful.[63]

d. Procedural rules for arbitration

26.30 A common feature in all Indian BITs is the presence of certain rules governing the procedural aspects of investment treaty arbitration. All Indian BITs (except two)[64] provide the option of conducting arbitration at the ICSID as provided under the ICSID Convention. However, as India is not yet a signatory to the ICSID Convention, an investment treaty-based claim cannot be brought against the country under the ICSID Convention.[65] Parties have the option of submitting a dispute under the Additional Facility for the Administration of Conciliation, Arbitration and Fact-Finding Proceedings of ICSID (ICSID Additional Facility), which is available in sixty-seven out of seventy-three Indian BITs.[66] Investment treaty arbitrations involving India or Indian parties have largely been ad hoc, conducted under the Arbitration Rules of the United Nations Commission on International Trade Law, 1976 (UNCITRAL Arbitration Rules).

26.31 Overall, India's practice with respect to drafting ISDS chapters has been consistent and predictable, characterized by a multi-tier dispute resolution system with certain pre-conditions or restrictions. It is only in a relatively small number of BITs where treaty-making has deviated from the common framework. For example, out of seventy-three BITs in existence, only the India–Cyprus BIT of 2002 provides for arbitral tribunals to be constituted under the rules of the ICC and the Stockholm Chamber of Commerce (SCC) for resolution of investor-state disputes.[67] Though there are certain provisions in the form of temporal restrictions or FITR clauses to avoid a proliferation of disputes or initiation of parallel

---

[63] Jurisprudence on the triple identity test has been developed by a number of arbitral tribunals, including in *Occidental Exploration and Production Company v Ecuador*, LCIA Case No UN3467, Final Award (1 July 2004); *CMS Gas Transmission Company v Argentina*, ICSID Case No ARB/01/08, Decision on Objections to Jurisdiction (17 July 2003) para 80; *Azurix Corp v Argentina*, ICSID Case No ARB/01/12, Decision on Objections to Jurisdiction (8 December 2003) para 89; *Enron Corporation and Ponderosa Assets, LP v Argentina*, ICSID Case No ARB/01/3, Decision on Jurisdiction (14 January 2004) para 98.

[64] India's BITs with Russia and Germany do not contain provisions for arbitration under the ICSID Convention.

[65] Convention on the Settlement of Investment Disputes Between States and Nationals of Other States (adopted 18 March 1965, entered into force 14 October 1966) 575 UNTS 159 (ICSID Convention) art 25.

[66] ICSID Additional Facility is not available only under BITs signed with Russia, Germany, Hungary, Macedonia, Jordan, and Slovak Republic.

[67] Agreement between the Government of the Republic of India and the Government of the Republic of Cyprus for the Mutual Promotion and Protection of Investments (signed 9 April 2002, entered into force 12 January 2004) arts 9.3(d) and 9.3(e).

proceedings, they are present in a small number of BITs that significantly depart from established practice, which is likely a product of negotiations rather than a step towards reform.

26.32 The 1994 India–UK BIT[68] and the similarly drafted 2003 Model BIT have been the primary guidance texts for BIT negotiation by the Indian government. They are almost identical in terms of the ISDS clauses provided in them. Resultantly, the ISDS provisions in Indian BITs have largely been structured identically, leaving aside certain exceptions as discussed earlier. This can largely be attributed to the fact that the Model Indian BIT of 2003 was more of a re-statement of past BIT practice rather than marking any distinct shift in practice. India's limited experience with investment disputes and the absence of any periodic review by the Indian government of its BITs contributed to the stagnation of India's BIT practice and policy.[69]

D. India's 2015 Model BIT

26.33 As discussed previously, the government of India announced the 2015 Model BIT as a part of an extensive review of its existing BIT framework. Among the goals of the review process, the need for balancing investment protection with India's regulatory power was perhaps most urgent. In March 2015, the Indian government made public a new draft Model BIT to 'provide appropriate protection to foreign investors in India and Indian investors in the foreign country, in the light of the relevant international precedents and practices, while maintaining a balance between the investor's rights and the government's obligations'.[70]

1. Background

26.34 The BIT policy review undertaken by the government of India between 2012 and 2015 can be seen as part of a wave of IIA reviews taking place in over 50 countries since 2008.[71] The countries involved in the reform process are not just from a single economic or regional group; they represent diverse interests across Asia, Africa, Europe, and North and Latin America.[72] India's approach to its BIT

---

[68] Agreement between the Government of the Republic of India and the Government of the United Kingdom of Great Britain and Northern Ireland for Promotion and Protection of Investments (signed 14 March 1994, entered into force 6 January 1995) art 9(1).

[69] Ranjan, 'India and Bilateral Investment Treaties—A Changing Landscape' (n 41) 444.

[70] Government of India, 'Call for Comments on the Draft 2015 Model BIT' <https://www.mygov.in/sites/default/files/master_image/Model%20Text%20for%20the%20Indian%20Bilateral%20Investment%20Treaty.pdf> accessed 10 March 2017.

[71] UNCTAD, *World Investment Report 2015* (United Nations 2015) 108 <https://unctad.org/en/PublicationsLibrary/wir2015_en.pdf> accessed 10 March 2017.

[72] ibid.

review was highlighted as one of the three distinct approaches[73] to BIT reform at the UNCTAD's Expert Meeting on the Transformation of the IIA Regime, held in February 2015.[74]

India's BIT review process began in July 2012 with the institution of a Central Government Working Group.[75] It involved close coordination among several ministries of the government of India, with a diverse range of viewpoints put forward regarding India's plan for the future of its BIT system. From several sceptics of the international investment regime from within the government, there was support in favour of termination of India's BIT programme altogether.[76] On the other hand, several stakeholders argued that a sudden radical change in India's BIT policy would significantly affect the status of existing foreign investments and possibly reduce the inflow of investments in the future. They favoured a 'hands off' approach, where the structure and core provisions of BITs would remain untouched.[77] 26.35

The question of substantial importance before the Working Group was regarding the ISDS mechanism itself. The *White Industries* arbitration, followed by the large number of notices filed by companies, made the drafters aware of the dangers of loosely worded treaty provisions and unrestricted access to ISDS.[78] At the same time, there were concerns that the abandonment of ISDS could prove to be highly detrimental to India's investment goals, not only for incoming foreign investment but also for outward Indian investment.[79] Therefore, there was a consensus among the drafters in favour of continuing India's long-standing commitment to the ISDS system. 26.36

Several changes were proposed to the existing system in order to overcome past deficiencies and bring it up to date with modern practice, while still retaining the 26.37

---

[73] The other approaches to BIT reform were those of Brazil and Indonesia.
[74] UNCTAD 'Report of the Expert Meeting on the Transformation of the International Investment Agreement Regime: The Path Ahead' (2015) UN Doc TD/B/C.II/EM.4/3.
[75] Saurabh Garg, Ishita G Tripathy, and Sudhanshu Roy, 'The Indian Model Bilateral Investment Treaty: Continuity and Change' in Kavaljit Singh and Burghad Ilge (eds), *Rethinking Bilateral Investment Treaties: Critical Issues and Policy Choices* (Both ENDS, Madhyam and SOMO 2016) 70–85.
[76] Scepticism against undertaking international obligations and an unwillingness to submit to international law over national law has pervaded Indian political thinking for decades since India's independence. The idea of providing only national treatment to foreign investments and investors has continued from the days of India's leadership in forming the New International Economic Order (NIEO) in the 1970s. One of the foundational ideas behind the NIEO had been on the primacy of national law over international law, in addition to the assertion of state sovereignty.
[77] Garg, Tripathy, and Roy (n 75) 72.
[78] ibid.
[79] India's outward FDI has steadily increased since economic liberalization policies were instituted in 1992, with Indian companies rapidly expanding their areas of operation in the developing and developed markets. For a detailed analysis, see David Collins, *The BRICS States and Outward Foreign Direct Investment* (OUP 2013).

a. Draft Model BIT and the Law Commission report

26.38 Until the publication and subsequent call for comments on the draft model BIT in March 2015, public access had not been granted to the model BIT drafting process. However, once the draft text was made public, the Law Commission of India[80] *suo moto* prepared a detailed report containing an article-by-article analysis of the text.[81] The Commission constituted various sub-committees comprising retired judges, practicing advocates, law professors, researchers, and government officers for the purpose of discussion and debate over the draft text. In its final report,[82] the Law Commission suggested several changes to existing provisions of the draft text.

26.39 On the aspect of ISDS, the primary concerns expressed by the Law Commission were the issues of lack of neutrality among arbitrators and the lack of provisions for appellate scrutiny.[83] The suggestions forwarded by the Law Commission were primarily aimed at some of the highly restrictive provisions of the draft model text, with the aim of balancing the interests of both investors and states.[84] Due to the *suo moto* nature of the Law Commission's review, as well as the lack of legislative or judicial mandate on the government to apply the Commission's suggestions, many of these suggestions were not accepted or even considered. The Ministry of Finance deliberated on the draft text until a revised final model BIT was eventually issued on 28 December 2015. The Law Commission's suggestions did seem to have a limited effect in the end, as several changes addressing the more restrictive provisions in the draft text found their way in the final model text.[85] The changes to the ISDS provisions that became a part of the model text shall be analysed in the next section.

---

[80] The Law Commission of India is an agency of the government of India, which primarily functions as an advisory body to the government with focus on legal reforms. Law Commissions are appointed for fixed tenures and are comprised of legal researchers and scholars and led by chairpersons who are retired judges of the Supreme Court. The Law Commission's recommendations are usually in the form of issued reports.

[81] Law Commission of India, 'Analysis of the 2015 Draft Model Indian Bilateral Investment Treaty' (2015) Report No 260 <http://lawcommissionofindia.nic.in/reports/Report260.pdf> accessed 10 March 2017.

[82] ibid.

[83] ibid.

[84] Anirudh Krishnan, 'A Bit for the State, a Bit for the Investor' *The Hindu* (Chennai, 8 September 2015)<http://www.thehindu.com/opinion/op-ed/a-bit-for-the-state-a-bit-for-the-investor/article7625893.ece> accessed 10 March 2017.

[85] For a detailed comparative study of the draft and final texts of the model BIT, see Grant Hanessian and Kabir Duggal, 'The Final 2015 Indian Model BIT: Is This the Change the World Wishes to See?' (2017) 32 ICSID Review 1.

2. ISDS under the 2015 Model BIT

26.40 The provisions relating to ISDS are provided under Chapter IV (ISDS Chapter) of the 2015 Model BIT. Perhaps the most noticeable change from past practice is the arrangement and breadth of the ISDS Chapter itself, comprising of eighteen articles that can be categorized as follows: (i) Scope and Definitions (Article 13); (ii) Proceedings under different International Agreements (Article 14); (iii) Conditions Precedent to and Submission of a Claim to Arbitration (Article 15 and 16); (iv) Consent to Arbitration (Article 17); (v) Provisions regarding Arbitral Proceedings (Articles 18 to 22); (vi) Burden of Proof and Governing Law (Article 23); (vii) Joint Interpretations (Article 24); (viii) Expert Reports (Article 25); (ix) Provisions on Awards (Article 25 and 26); (x) Costs (Article 28); (xi) Appeals Facility (Article 29); and (xii) Diplomatic Exchange Between Parties (Article 30). The present research will not analyse each and every provision, instead choosing to provide a thematic understanding of the substantial changes in ISDS compared to past practice.

26.41 A basic comparison of the ISDS Chapter of the 2015 Model BIT with provisions of past BITs and the 2003 Model BIT reveals the significant structural and substantive changes that have taken place. While previous Indian BITs had generally contained short and simplistic ISDS provisions that state the framework for dispute settlement, the 2015 Model BIT provides a comprehensive procedural blueprint that incorporates several key features of ISDS reform that other states have begun to incorporate. The following subsections will describe the changes in India's BIT practice with regard to ISDS clauses and how the 2015 Model BIT has tackled inconsistencies in ISDS clauses of Indian BITs. The analysis will also compare these provisions with contemporary BITs and Model BITs developed by other states to see how they have approached the ISDS reform process.

a. Limitations to the scope of ISDS

26.42 It is clear from a careful reading of the scope and definitions provision (Article 13) of the 2015 Model BIT that it seeks to significantly limit access to ISDS by investors as well as the jurisdiction of the arbitral tribunal. First, it restricts the types of disputes that can be brought under the ISDS mechanism only to those which arise out of an alleged breach by a host state of its obligations under Chapter II of the 2015 Model BIT.[86] Second, the Model BIT specifically excludes disputes arising out of alleged breach of contract between a host state and an investor from being brought under ISDS.[87] Third, it excludes all forms of disputes regarding investments that are held to be illegal. This refers to investments made through fraudulent misrepresentation, concealment, corruption, money laundering, or

---

[86] 2015 Indian Model BIT (notified 28 December 2015) (copy of the treaty text is available at <https://dea.gov.in/sites/default/files/ModelBIT_Annex_0.pdf > accessed 10 April 2018 art 13.2.
[87] ibid art 13.3.

conduct amounting to abuse of process.[88] Fourth, an arbitral tribunal is expressly barred from reviewing the merits of a decision made by a judicial authority or over a claim that is or has been arbitrated under the state-state dispute settlement mechanism.[89]

26.43 These provisions are in sharp contrast with previous Indian BITs, where, in general, the only explicit requirement for a 'dispute' to be brought under the ISDS mechanism was that it must be related to an investment made in the territory of the host state.[90] A notable exception in this regard is the India–Mexico BIT, where the ISDS chapter provides that only disputes arising out of breach of obligations under Chapter II (Protection of Investments) can be resolved using the ISDS mechanism.[91] It is also interesting to note how the 2015 Model BIT has carved out certain actions from the scope of ISDS, such as breach of contract between investor and the host state, illegal investments, and decisions of the host state's judicial authorities. However, placing such specific limitations is not new to state practice. For example, Article 9 (4) of the 2009 Turkey Model BIT excludes disputes concerning real estate from the scope of ISDS. The Malaysia–Pakistan Comprehensive Economic Partnership Agreement (CEPA) also excludes all disputes concerning national treatment and performance requirements.[92] The recent Canada–Hong Kong BIT states that claims against certain state obligations cannot be submitted to arbitration.[93]

26.44 State practice has also varied on the issue of jurisdiction of arbitral tribunals on disputes arising out of breach of contracts between investors and host states. Such jurisdiction is generally conferred through specific provisions incorporated into the BIT text. For example, the 2012 US Model BIT permits claims of investors arising out of breach of certain 'investment agreements' to be submitted to arbitration. Sometimes, such disputes may also be raised in the presence of umbrella clauses in BITs.[94] The use of umbrella clauses, however, has significantly declined

---

[88] ibid art 13.4.
[89] ibid art 13.5.
[90] 2003 Indian Model BIT (copy of the treaty text is available at <https://www.italaw.com/sites/default/files/archive/ita1026.pdf> accessed 10 April 2018 art 2.
[91] Agreement Between the Government of the United Mexican States and the Government of the Republic of India on Promotion and Protection of Investments (signed 21 May 2007, entered into force 23 February 2008) art 12.2.
[92] Malaysia–Pakistan Closer Economic Partnership Agreement (signed 8 November 2007, entered into force 1 January 2008) art 98.13.
[93] Agreement Between the Government of Canada and the Government of the Hong Kong Special Administrative Region of the People's Republic of China for the Promotion and Protection of Investments (signed 10 February 2016) art 20.1.
[94] An umbrella clause requires a host state to respect any obligation assumed by it with regard to a specific investment (eg in an investment contract). The clause thus brings contractual and, in some cases, other individual obligations of the host state under the 'umbrella' of the IIA, making them potentially enforceable through ISDS. For a discussion on their interpretation in IIAs, see Katia Yannaca-Small, 'Interpretation of the Umbrella Clause in Investment Agreements' (2006) OECD Working Papers on International Investment <http://dx.doi.org/10.1787/415453814578> accessed 10 August 2016.

in recent years, due to receding state interest in providing the broad protections under such clauses and arising from instances of inconsistent interpretation of these clauses by arbitral tribunals.[95] Provisions that more specifically state when ISDS is available for resolution of disputes arising under investor-state contracts have appeared, at least for some states, to have replaced those more general umbrella clauses.

26.45 In the Indian context, it is noted that most of the early Indian BITs contained umbrella clauses that would bind the parties to observe obligations made with investors. For example, the BITs with UK, Austria, and the Netherlands contain identical provisions as follows:

> Each Contracting Party shall observe any obligation it may have entered into with regard to investments of investors of the other Contracting Party. Provided that dispute resolution under Article 9 of this Agreement shall only be applicable in the absence of a normal, local, judicial remedy being available.[96]

26.46 It is interesting to note that such clauses specifically excluded the operation of ISDS over umbrella clause claims when domestic remedies were available. Such umbrella clause provisions are more commonly found in BITs signed in the 1990s but are virtually absent in BITs signed during the late 2000s and after.

26.47 The 2015 Model Text does away with any doubt regarding umbrella clauses by specifically excluding them from the treaty, and further providing that only domestic courts will resolve contract disputes. India's model thus makes clear that ISDS is not available for breach of contract claims, or for claims that the state has breached other non-treaty-based obligations, such as obligations arising solely under domestic law. The Model text further provides that such disputes will be resolved only by domestic courts or according to procedure provided in the contract,[97] making it apparent that India does not wish to take any liabilities beyond the limited investment protection obligations.

26.48 The bar on arbitral tribunals from reviewing the merits of a decision made by the judicial authority of a state is another limitation provision in the 2015 Model BIT. The genesis of this provision can be attributed to a major financial scandal that erupted in India in 2011, with the revelation that several telecom companies had been previously granted telecommunication licences by the Indian government through a rigged auction process.[98] Consequently, in 2012, the Supreme Court

---

[95] Raul Pereira de Souza Fleury, 'Umbrella Clauses: a Trend towards its Elimination' (2015) 31 Arbitration International 679.
[96] Agreement between the Republic of India and the Kingdom of the Netherlands for the Promotion and Protection of Investments (signed 6 November 1995, entered into force 1 December 1996) art 4(5).
[97] 2015 Model BIT (n 86) art 13.3.
[98] For a detailed account of the financial scandal dubbed as the '2G Spectrum scam', see Bhupesh Bhandari, *Spectrum Grab: Inside the 2G Spectrum Scam* (BS Books 2012).

of India cancelled the licences that had been granted to several of these telecom companies,[99] many of which were backed by foreign investors. In response, foreign investors filed a number of arbitration notices under various BITs, citing the Supreme Court's cancellation order as a basis for their claim.[100] Therefore, the present limitation to the scope of arbitral tribunal's jurisdiction is seen as a measure to defend the judiciary's decision making from scrutiny by foreign tribunals, which is a contentious issue that has been discussed earlier.[101] Such a provision can also be located in the more recent India–UAE BIT,[102] which was interestingly concluded at the time when India was reviewing its BIT system. The said provision limits the scope of ISDS to disputes regarding measures taken by the central or state governments in exercise of their executive functions, but excludes judicial decisions from being challenged on their merits.

26.49 However, it should be noted that both India–UAE BIT and the 2015 Model BIT provide for claims of investors regarding 'denial of justice' in judicial or administrative proceedings. The investor's substantive right to seek remedy for denial of justice is not affected by such limitations to the scope of ISDS. By limiting the arbitral tribunal from reviewing the merits of a judicial decision, the 2015 Model BIT has sought to prevent it from effectively acting as a court of appeal against decisions passed by domestic courts. Even though claims based on denial of justice caused by judicial impropriety can be brought before an arbitral tribunal, such a tribunal is barred from reviewing the merits of such a decision.

b. Conditions precedent to submission of claim to arbitration

26.50 **i. Exhaustion of local remedies** A significant shift in 2015 Model BIT from past practice has been in the procedure for access to international arbitration for a foreign investor. The dispute resolution mechanism had earlier functioned as a multi-tier system in which an investor could access a certain form of dispute settlement after fulfilling the associated pre-conditions. The 2015 Model BIT restructures this system by creating a mandatory obligation on a disputing investor to first exhaust the available domestic adjudication procedures, that is the local remedies of the host state.[103] While customary international law requires an injured foreign person to exhaust domestic remedies before his/her claim becomes admissible at the international level,[104] arbitral tribunals have generally not interpreted IIAs as including those exhaustion requirements.

---

[99] For the Supreme Court judgement, see *Centre for Public Interest Litigation and others v Union of India and others*. WP (Civil) No 423 of 2012.
[100] See, for instance, *Khaitan Holdings Mauritius Ltd v India* (2013, currently pending) that was filed under the India–Mauritius BIT of 1998.
[101] Prabhash Ranjan and Deepak Raju, 'Bilateral Investment Treaties and the Indian Judiciary' (2014) 46 The George Washington International Law Review 809.
[102] India–UAE BIT (n 58) art 10.2.
[103] 2015 Model BIT (n 86) art 15.1.
[104] Christopher Dugan et al, *Investor-state Arbitration* (OUP 2011).

Under the exhaustion of local remedies requirement,[105] the disputing investor must ensure that: 26.51

i. A claim before the relevant domestic authority must be with respect to the *same* measure or *similar factual matters* for which the breach of the relevant BIT is claimed.
ii. A claim must be submitted to the relevant domestic authority within *one year* from the date on which the investor acquired or should have acquired knowledge regarding the State's measure and that the investor had suffered damage or loss as a result of such a measure.

Further, an express provision bars the investor from claiming fulfilment of the exhaustion requirement by attributing its claims to its subsidiaries or to third parties.[106] The only available exemption from the exhaustion requirement can be availed when the investor can demonstrate that there are no available domestic remedies capable of providing relief with respect to the breach of the relevant BIT obligations.[107] Thus, under the 2015 Model BIT, engagement with domestic adjudication procedures is mandatory for an investor bringing a BIT-based claim. This is a clear departure from past practice of providing means of domestic adjudication as an available option that could be exercised by the investor. It should also be noted that submission of a claim to domestic adjudication has replaced negotiation as the first step in the ISDS mechanism.

In comparative international practice, provisions requiring the investor to first seek local remedies are not new, although they are found more commonly in BITs of older vintage and have a broader conception of the 'local remedies' requirement.[108] In fact, the first BIT to contain such a provision was the Netherlands–Malaysia BIT of 1971, which contained a requirement to 'exhaust all local administrative and judicial remedies' before submitting a dispute to arbitration or conciliation.[109] Similar provisions can be found in BITs signed during the 1970s and 1980s. A variation of such a provision was of the form contained in the Germany–Argentina BIT of 1991, which did not make exhaustion of local remedies mandatory, but required the investor to resort to local remedies before submitting the dispute to international arbitration.[110] The contracting states during 26.52

---

[105] 2015 Model BIT (n 86) art 15.1.
[106] ibid.
[107] See proviso to art 15.1, 2015 Model BIT (n 86).
[108] Christoph Schreuer, 'Calvo's Grandchildren: The Return of Local Remedies in Investment Arbitration' (2005) 4 The Law & Practice of International Courts and Tribunals 1.
[109] Agreement on Economic Co-operation between the Kingdom of the Netherlands and Malaysia (signed 15 June 1971, entered into force 13 September 1972) art 12.
[110] Tratado entre la Republica Federal de Alemania y la Republica Argentina sobre Promoción y Proteccion Reciproca de Inversiones / Vertrag zwischen der Bundesrepublik Deutschland und der Argentinischen Republik Über die Förderung und den gegenseitigen Schutz von Kapitalanlagen (signed 9 April 1991, entered into force 8 November 1993) art 10.

this period may have considered exhaustion to be a requirement under customary international law, and therefore they may not have believed it necessary to place a *mandatory* requirement on the investor. The distinction between the requirements between 'exhaustion' of local remedies and 'resorting' to local remedies should be noted here, as 'exhaustion' implies a stricter obligation on the investor to systematically exhaust all opportunities to avail all accessible means of judicial or administrative remedies in the host state, whereas 'resorting' to local remedies may be interpreted as simply engaging with a domestic adjudication process for a period of time, without any requirement to conclude the same.[111]

26.53 The conception of 'exhaustion of local remedies' in contemporary BITs varies significantly from how it was conceived in older BITs, and there are now a number of ways in which these clauses are constructed. For example, the Egypt–Switzerland BIT of 2010 requires the investor to submit the dispute to domestic administrative proceedings of the host state in addition to procedures for amicable settlement of the dispute.[112] Both of these procedures may run parallel to each other and need not exceed a time limit of six months. If there is no settlement within the six-month period, the investor may proceed with international arbitration or submit the dispute to the domestic courts of the host state. Another variation in the local remedies requirement can be seen in the Bangladesh–UAE BIT of 2011, where an investor must submit the dispute to 'competent authorities or arbitration centres' of the host state for at least six months, with no mandatory requirement of exhaustion.[113] UAE also entered into a BIT with the Netherlands in 2013, which takes a different approach to the local remedies requirement. Here, though the investor is required to submit the dispute to the competent court of the host state after three months of consultations, the duration of such a proceeding varies according to the host state. In case of an investment made in the UAE, the foreign investor must first submit the dispute to a competent UAE court, and if the court is unable to provide a resolution to the investor's satisfaction, then arbitration under ICSID may be initiated.[114] However, there is no time limit provided on the court's proceedings, which creates an uncertainty over whether the investor must wait until the court proceedings are concluded. On the other hand, where the Netherlands is the host state, the investor can proceed with arbitration after six

---

[111] Ursula Kriebaum, 'Local Remedies and Standards for the Protection of Foreign Investment' in Christina Binder et al (eds), *International Investment Law for the 21st Century: Essays in Honour of Christoph Schreuer* (OUP 2009).

[112] Agreement between The Swiss Confederation and The Arab Republic of Egypt on the Promotion and Reciprocal Protection of Investments (signed 7 June 2010, entered into force 15 May 2012) art 12.2.

[113] Agreement between the Government of the United Arab Emirates and the Government of the People's Republic of Bangladesh for the Promotion and Reciprocal Protection of Investment (signed 7 January 2011) art 9.3.

[114] Agreement on Encouragement and Reciprocal Protection of Investments between the Kingdom of the Netherlands and the United Arab Emirates (signed 26 November 2013) art 9.3.

months from the date of request for consultations, regardless of the status of the proceedings before the competent domestic court.[115]

26.54 In its 2015 Model BIT, India has adopted a strict approach to the requirement regarding exhaustion of local remedies that is closely aligned with the 'contemporary' approach to construction of exhaustion clauses, as discussed. It is interesting to note that in the text of the draft model that was released earlier by the government of India the same provision for exhaustion was fairly more flexible. As per the draft text, an investor could also claim exemption if it could demonstrate that an available domestic remedy could not be obtained within a 'reasonable period of time'.[116] Perhaps the flexible manner in which the term 'reasonable period of time' could be construed by an arbitral tribunal led the government to remove this provision altogether while preparing the final model text. The requirement on the investor to first seek local remedies is, however, not indefinite. The model text provides that the disputing investor must exhaust the available administrative and judicial remedies for 'at least a period of five years from the date on which the investor first acquired knowledge of the measure'.[117] If the investor has not received a satisfactory resolution to the dispute within this period, it can proceed further with the ISDS mechanism by transmitting a 'notice of dispute' to the host state.[118]

26.55 After fulfilling the 'five-year exhaustion' period and having intimated a notice of dispute, the investor is faced with a minimum 'waiting period' of six months.[119] A fairly common strategy implemented by states in order to provide both parties an opportunity to find solutions through alternative means, waiting periods of variable lengths are found across most BITs.[120] 'Cooling-off period' is another term used for such waiting periods at the pre-arbitral stage. This is because such clauses act more as a breathing space and an opportunity to the investor to settle the dispute with the disputing state without having to resort to arbitration.[121]

26.56 As with the 2015 Model BIT, contemporary BITs and Model BITs usually incorporate waiting periods in mandatory 'local remedies' requirements and at the pre-arbitral stage. As seen earlier, recent investment treaties such as the

---

[115] ibid.
[116] Draft Indian Model BIT (copy of the draft treaty text is available at < https://www.mygov.in/sites/default/files/master_image/Model%20Text%20for%20the%20Indian%20Bilateral%20Investment%20Treaty.pdf > accessed 10 April 2018) art 14.3(b).
[117] 2015 Model BIT (n 86) art 15.2.
[118] ibid.
[119] 2015 Model BIT (n 86) art 15.4.
[120] Christoph Schreuer, 'Travelling the BIT Route: Of Waiting Periods, Umbrella Clauses and Forks in the Road' (2004) 5 Journal of World Investment and Trade 231.
[121] UNCTAD, *Investor State Dispute Settlement: UNCTAD Series on Issues in International Investment Agreements II* (United Nations 2014) <http://unctad.org/en/pages/PublicationWebflyer.aspx?publicationid=958> accessed 10 October 2016.

UAE–Bangladesh BIT and Egypt–Switzerland BIT require investors to seek local remedies for at least six months. Similarly, the Japan–Iran BIT provides for a waiting period of six months at the pre-arbitral stage, during which parties shall endeavour to resolve their disputes amicably.[122] The 2012 US Model BIT adopts a different approach in this regard by requiring the investor to allow the passage of at least six months since the occurrence of events that gave rise to a claim. A cooling-off period of three months is also embedded between the notice of intent and the notice of arbitration. Similarly, the Canadian Model BIT of 2004 also provides a six-month waiting period before submission of a claim to arbitration. At the same time, some states have significantly reformed their waiting period requirements from their treaty practice. For example, the 2008 Austrian Model BIT does not provide for any significant waiting period other than requiring sixty days to elapse after the investor has transmitted a notice of intent to the host state,[123] whereas in previous BITs, the time period used to be on an average of three months after the notice of claims was filed.[124]

26.57 An important consideration for states while incorporating waiting periods in BITs is the existing arbitral jurisprudence on such requirements. There has been a significant divergence in the opinion of arbitral tribunals regarding the nature of waiting period requirements and whether non-observance of such requirements creates a jurisdictional bar to arbitration. Arbitral Tribunals in *Biwater v Tanzania*[125] (waiting period of six months), *SGS v Pakistan*[126] (consultative period of twelve months), and *Occidental v Ecuador*[127] (waiting period of six months) allowed the investors to bring claims notwithstanding the host state's claim that the waiting periods as provided in the underlying BITs had not been completed. Arbitral tribunals in these cases held that waiting periods were procedural and directory in nature, rather than jurisdictional and mandatory.[128] They were regarded as 'mere procedural rules', having no effect on the arbitral tribunal's jurisdiction.[129] However, there has been a significant shift in the position of arbitral tribunals with regard to waiting periods in recent years. The tribunals in *Burlington*

---

[122] Agreement between Japan and the Islamic Republic of Iran on Reciprocal Promotion and Protection of Investment (signed 5 February 2016) art 18.1.

[123] Austria Model BIT 2008 (copy of the treaty text is available at <http://investmentpolicyhub.unctad.org/Download/TreatyFile/4770> accessed 10 April 2018) art 21.

[124] For instance, see Agreement between the Government of the Republic of Austria and the Government of the Arab Republic of Egypt for the Promotion and Protection of Investments (signed 12 April 2001, entered into force 29 April 2002) art 9(2).

[125] *Biwater Gauff (Tanzania) Ltd v United Republic of Tanzania*, ICSID Case No ARB/05/22, Final Award (24 July 2008).

[126] *SGS Société Générale de Surveillance SA v Islamic Republic of Pakistan*, ICSID Case No ARB/01/13, Decision on Objections to Jurisdiction (6 August 2003).

[127] *Occidental Petroleum Corporation and Occidental Exploration and Production Company v The Republic of Ecuador*, ICSID Case No ARB/06/11, Decision on Jurisdiction (9 September 2008).

[128] *Biwater Gauff v Tanzania* (n 125) para 343.

[129] *SGS v Pakistan* (n 126) para 184.

*v Ecuador*¹³⁰ and *Murphy v Ecuador*¹³¹ found that non-compliance by an investor with the waiting period requirements would constitute a jurisdictional defect, not merely a procedural or admissibility defect. Further, waiting period requirements were termed as 'fundamental requirements' to which a disputing investor must comply.¹³² This position was also supported in *Enron v Argentina*,¹³³ where it was found that with respect to a six-month waiting period requiring parties to seek a resolution of the dispute through consultation and negotiation, a 'failure to comply with the requirement would result in a determined lack of jurisdiction'.

Arbitral tribunals have questioned the usefulness of waiting period requirements in states that are unable to provide effective means for dispute settlement.¹³⁴ This might be of concern for India, where the overburdened judicial system is mired with delays and an immense backlog of cases.¹³⁵ The requirement placed on an investor to exhaust local remedies for a minimum period of five years thus seeks to create a balance with investor interests and ensures that the investor does not have to wait for an unduly long amount of time, while at the same time providing enough time for domestic dispute settlement bodies to provide satisfactory adjudication over the dispute. The *White Industries* arbitration itself arose as consequence of the long delays in India's judicial system, which was accepted by the arbitral tribunal as a lack of 'effective means' for the investor.¹³⁶ The exhaustion requirement over a five-year period may therefore provide a much needed balance between the interests of an investor as well as of the state. Additionally, it is proposed that a fast-track system for the resolution of BIT-based disputes within the national legal framework would also ensure that the purpose of local remedies and waiting period provisions is not frustrated by inordinate delays in courts. 26.58

ii. Additional conditions The 2015 Model BIT specifies certain additional conditions that must be fulfilled by the investor when the six-month waiting period following the transmission of the notice of dispute has elapsed without any fruitful settlement reached between the disputing parties. First, a claim to arbitration must be submitted within six years of the investor attaining knowledge 26.59

---

¹³⁰ *Burlington Resources Inc v Republic of Ecuador* (formerly *Burlington Resources Inc and others v Republic of Ecuador and Empresa Estatal Petróleos del Ecuador*), ICSID Case No ARB/08/5, Decision on Jurisdiction (2 June 2010).
¹³¹ *Murphy Exploration and Production Company International v Republic of Ecuador*, ICSID Case No ARB/08/4, Award on Jurisdiction (15 December 2010).
¹³² ibid para 149.
¹³³ *Enron Corp and Ponderosa Assets v The Argentine Republic*, ICSID Case No ARB/01/3, Decision on Jurisdiction (14 January 2004) para 88.
¹³⁴ Tan and Bouchenaki (n 29) 291.
¹³⁵ Krishnadas Rajagopal, 'The "Impossible Burden" of Indian Judiciary: Growth of Litigation Versus Pendency' *The Hindu* (Chennai, 24 April 2016) <http://www.thehindu.com/news/national/indian-judiciary-growth-of-litigation-versus-pendency/article8516458.ece> accessed 25 September 2016.
¹³⁶ Kachwaha (n 36) 278.

about the host state's measure that led to the dispute, as well as the loss or damage incurred consequently.[137] Second, if the dispute was submitted for domestic adjudication, then the claim to arbitration must be submitted within twelve months of the conclusion of such proceedings.[138] The investor is additionally required to waive its right to initiate or continue any administrative or court proceedings in either of the Contracting Parties to the BIT, or from engaging with other dispute settlement procedures.[139] Such a waiver must also be issued by an enterprise owned or controlled by the disputing investor, where damage or loss is caused to the investor's interest in such an enterprise.[140] Finally, the investor must serve a written notice of arbitration to the host state at least ninety days before submitting the claim to arbitration.[141] The Model text states that an investor can submit a claim to arbitration only if these additional conditions are satisfied.[142]

26.60 The limitation periods limit the time frame within which an investor can bring a dispute against the host state. This reduces the liability period for the host state regarding measures that were undertaken or initiated by it beyond a stated period of time in the past. Limitation period provisions are not commonly found in older BITs, which significantly increases the state's exposure to investor claims.[143] Most contemporary BITs, however, contain variable limitation periods. For example, Japan signed three BITs in 2015 with Oman, Ukraine, and Uruguay, all of which contain a limitations period of three years for arbitration.[144] Similarly, Canada signed BITs with three African states in 2014—Senegal, Mali, and Côte d'Ivoire—containing limitation periods of three years. In India's case, most BITs entered by it do not contain limitation period clauses. Though such provisions are present in several FTAs entered into by India,[145] the India–Mexico BIT is the only standalone BIT that contains a three-year limitation period.[146] The longer limitation period of six years, as provided in the 2015 Model BIT, includes the five-year period during which a disputing investor is required to seek local remedies.

26.61 The waiver requirement on the investor along with a notice of arbitration to the host state is a form of 'no U-turn' clauses that are found in contemporary BITs.

---

[137] 2015 Model BIT (n 86) art 15.5(i).
[138] ibid art 15.5(ii).
[139] ibid art 15.5(iii).
[140] ibid art 15.5(iv).
[141] ibid art 15.5(v).
[142] ibid art 15.5.
[143] UNCTAD, *Investor State Dispute Settlement* (n 121) 49.
[144] For example, see Agreement between Japan and the Oriental Republic of Uruguay for the Liberalization, Promotion and Protection of Investment (signed 26 January 2015) art 21.10.
[145] For example, see art 10.4.9 of the Comprehensive Economic Cooperation Agreement between the Government of Malaysia and the Government of the Republic of India (signed 18 February 2011, entered into force 1 July 2011) that provides for a three-year limitation period for claims.
[146] India–Mexico BIT (n 91) art 12.4(c).

c. *Transparency in arbitral proceedings*

26.62 The provisions for transparency in arbitral proceedings mark a significant shift in India's BIT practice. Provisions on transparency are found in only three Indian BITs, which are largely limited to transparency requirements in relation to state obligations. The provisions in BITs signed by India with Australia,[147] Iceland,[148] and Slovenia[149] require the Contracting Parties to publish and make available their domestic laws and judicial decisions to the public. However, there were no specific transparency provisions governing the arbitral process. The new Model text foresees significant changes in this regard. First, the Model text requires that the notices of dispute and arbitration, written submissions on jurisdiction and merits, transcripts of hearings, and other procedural details of the arbitration tribunal must be made available to the public.[150] Second, hearings before the arbitral tribunal must also be made open to the public, subject to the grounds of safety, confidentiality, or logistics as determined by the tribunal.[151] Third, the arbitral award and related documents issued by the tribunal shall also be made publicly available, subject to the redaction of confidential information.[152]

26.63 It is relevant to note here that issues of transparency with regard to arbitration proceedings are a part of a larger discussion on transparency in international investment agreements.[153] Due to rising public concern regarding the secretive nature of arbitral proceedings, there has been a larger push to make investment arbitration transparent and accessible.[154] At the same time, the challenge of reconciling essential private-law features of arbitration such as confidentiality with transparency requirements has also been commented upon.[155] Perhaps the most significant development in this regard has been the introduction of the UNCITRAL Rules on

---

[147] Agreement between the Government of the Republic of India and the Government of Australia on the Promotion and Protection of Investments (signed 26 February 1999, entered into force 4 May 2000) art 6.

[148] Agreement between the Government of the Republic of India and the Government of the Republic of Iceland for the Promotion and Protection of Investments (signed 29 June 2007, entered into force 16 December 2008) art 13.

[149] Agreement between the Government of the Republic of India and the Government of the Republic of Slovenia for the Mutual Promotion and Protection of Investments (signed 14 June 2011, not yet in force) art 5.

[150] 2015 Model BIT (n 86) art 22.1.

[151] ibid art 22.2.

[152] ibid art 22.3.

[153] For a detailed discussion on transparency in IIAs, see UNCTAD, *Transparency: UNCTAD Series on Issues in International Investment Agreements II* (United Nations 2012) <http://unctad.org/en/PublicationsLibrary/unctaddiaeia2011d6_en.pdf> accessed 10 August 2016.

[154] ibid 8.

[155] Julie A Maupin, 'Transparency in International Investment Law: The Good, the Bad, and the Murky' in Andrea Bianchi and Anne Peters (eds), *Transparency in International Law* (CUP 2013). See also Christina Knahr and August Reinisch, 'Transparency Versus Confidentiality in International Investment Arbitration—The Biwater Gauff Compromise' (2007) 6 The Law and Practice of International Courts and Tribunals 1.

Transparency in Treaty-based Investor-state Arbitration (Transparency Rules).[156] The Transparency Rules comprise of a set of procedural rules that provide for transparency and accessibility to the public for treaty-based investor-state arbitrations for UNCITRAL arbitrations in investment agreements that have been concluded on or after 1 April 2014. For treaties concluded after 1 April 2014, the Transparency Rules are deemed to be a part of the UNCITRAL Arbitration Rules as amended in 2010 or thereafter, and will apply any time those UNCITRAL Arbitration Rules govern the dispute.[157] The Transparency Rules are further supplemented by the United Nations Convention on Transparency in Treaty-based Investor-State Arbitration[158] (Transparency Convention), also known as the Mauritius Convention on Transparency. This Convention acts as a formal instrument through which parties to investment treaties can express their consent to apply the Transparency Rules to disputes arising under treaties concluded before 1 April 2014.[159] After the Transparency Rules were adopted, a number of investment treaties expressly incorporated them or provisions modelled on them.[160] The transparency provisions in India's 2015 Model BIT are largely modelled on the Transparency Rules. Some examples include the provisions for the publication of documents related to arbitral proceedings under Article 3 of the Transparency Rules and the requirement to conduct hearings in public under Article 6, along with their associated exceptions. At the same time, certain provisions such as those governing submissions made by third persons under Article 4 of the Transparency Rules are absent from the 2015 Model BIT. The selective incorporation of clauses derived from the Transparency Rules seems to be based on suggestions of the Law Commission of India, which has questioned the administrative capacity of ad hoc arbitral tribunals to fulfil all of the requirements provided in the Transparency Rules.[161] However, the selection of UNCITRAL Arbitral Rules as procedural rules for an arbitration proceeding automatically attracts the full suite of provisions under the Transparency Rules, unless the states that are parties to the BIT/IIA in

---

[156] With effect from 1 April 2014.

[157] UNGA, 'UNCITRAL Rules on Transparency in Treaty-based Investor-State Arbitration and Arbitration Rules (as revised in 2010, with new article 1, paragraph 4, as adopted in 2013)' (16 December 2013) UN Doc A/RES/68/109.

[158] UNGA, 'United Nations Convention on Transparency in Treaty-based Investor-State Arbitration' (10 December 2014) UN Doc A/RES/69/116.

[159] Presently, twenty-two states are signatories to the Transparency Convention, with Cameroon, Mauritius, and Syria being the only three states that have ratified it. See UNCTAD, Status of United Nations Convention on Transparency in Treaty-based Investor-State Arbitration (New York, 2014) <http://www.uncitral.org/uncitral/en/uncitral_texts/arbitration/2014Transparency_Convention_status.html> accessed 8 March 2018.

[160] UNCITRAL's database currently lists seventeen investment agreements signed after 1 April 2014 that incorporate the Transparency Rules or contain provisions modelled on these Rules. See UNCITRAL, Status of UNCITRAL Rules on Transparency in Treaty-based Investor-State Arbitration <http://www.uncitral.org/uncitral/en/uncitral_texts/arbitration/2014Transparency_Rules_status.html> accessed 10 October 2016.

[161] Law Commission of India (n 81).

question agree otherwise.¹⁶² Therefore, in order to maintain only selective rules on transparency, India would have to make specific agreements with its treaty partners, or perhaps agree not to make applicable the Transparency Rules at all.

Prior to the introduction of the Transparency Rules and the revised UNCITRAL Arbitration Rules, most states did not incorporate transparency clauses for arbitration proceedings in their BITs or Model BITs. Interestingly, confidentiality was not a requirement contained in most investment agreements, and the idea of confidentiality of proceedings in investment arbitration is most likely borrowed from commercial arbitration.¹⁶³ However, it was only in 2005 when the United States and Canada pioneered the practice of including provisions for transparency. The 2004 US Model BIT was the first of its kind to provide for transparency provisions in arbitral proceedings.¹⁶⁴ It required the public disclosure of documents related to the arbitration proceedings,¹⁶⁵ and instructed the arbitral tribunal, to the extent possible, to conduct public hearings.¹⁶⁶ At the same time, the disputing investor is also given significant powers to designate certain information as protected information that will not be disclosed publicly.¹⁶⁷ Similarly, the 2004 Canadian Model BIT requires public access to be made available to hearings and production of documents.¹⁶⁸ A notable difference between the US and Canadian Models lies in their handling of confidential information. While the US Model provides greater power to the disputing investor to decide upon the information that will be made public, the Canadian Model provides greater power of determination to the arbitral tribunal. Both of these Model texts have had a significant influence in the BITs entered into by both countries. Canada for instance has incorporated transparency clauses in several BITs that are based on its 2004 Model text. The country has entered into fourteen BITs since 2010, all of which contain provisions for public access to hearings and documents related to arbitral proceedings, although there are several caveats and limitations to these transparency provisions varying across the treaty texts.¹⁶⁹ The more recent 2012 US Model BIT also retains the features on transparency that were introduced in 2004. In BITs involving parties other than the US or Canada, a larger number

26.64

---

¹⁶² UNCITRAL Rules on Transparency in Treaty-based Investor-State Arbitration (n 157) art 1.1.
¹⁶³ A Behlolavek, 'Confidentiality and Publicity in investment arbitration, Public Interest and Scope of Powers vested in Arbitral Tribunals' in A. Belohlavek and N. Rozehnalova (eds), *Czech Yearbook of International Law: Rights of the Host states within the System of International Investment Protection* (vol 2, Juris Publishing Inc 2011).
¹⁶⁴ 2004 US Model BIT (copy of the treaty text is available at <https://www.state.gov/documents/organization/117601.pdf> last accessed on 10 April 2018) art 29.
¹⁶⁵ ibid art 29.1.
¹⁶⁶ ibid art 29.2.
¹⁶⁷ ibid arts 29.3 and 29.4.
¹⁶⁸ 2004 Canada Model BIT (copy of the treaty text is available at <https://www.italaw.com/documents/Canadian2004-FIPA-model-en.pdf> accessed 10 April 2018) art 38.
¹⁶⁹ For example, compare the provisions on public access to hearings and documents in Canada's BITs with Senegal (2014), Hong Kong (2016), and Serbia (2014).

of states began to formally incorporate transparency provisions with respect to ISDS after the Transparency Rules were introduced in 2014. Japan, for example, incorporated modified provisions from the Transparency Rules in its BITs with Uruguay,[170] Ukraine,[171] and Oman[172] in 2015.

26.65 An important aspect in the discussion on transparency in arbitral proceedings is regarding the submission of *amicus curiae* briefs (or *amicus* briefs), that is briefs written by entities that are not parties to the dispute. The role of *amicus* briefs in bringing greater transparency and public access to investment arbitration has been widely discussed[173] ever since the first arbitral award was delivered on this issue in *Methanex Corporation v United States*[174] under the North American Free Trade Agreement (NAFTA). The arbitral tribunal in this case admitted the amicus briefs submitted by several NGOs on the basis that nothing under the NAFTA or UNCITRAL Arbitration Rules prevented amicus briefs from being admitted.[175] It also referred to the wide discretionary powers to conduct arbitral proceedings given under Article 15 of the UNCITRAL Arbitration Rules to support its decision.[176] US and Canada's support in favour of admissibility of *amicus* briefs in arbitrations subsequently provided provisions for the same under their respective Model BITs. The Transparency Rules also incorporate provisions for submissions to be made by a third person[177] and non-disputing Party to the investment treaty.[178]

26.66 However, the 2015 Model BIT does not incorporate provisions for *amicus* briefs or third party participation into its text. It only provides for oral and written submissions to be made by the non-disputing Party regarding the interpretation of the relevant BIT.[179] This raises an important question regarding the admissibility of *amicus* briefs under future BITs based on the Model text, although provisions for this can be imported indirectly from UNCITRAL Transparency Rules when a disputing investor and India agree to apply the UNCITRAL Arbitration Rules for an arbitral proceeding. The absence of

---

[170] Japan–Uruguay BIT (n 144).
[171] Agreement between Japan and Ukraine for the Promotion and Protection of Investments (signed 5 February 2015) art 18.4(c).
[172] Agreement between Japan and the Sultanate of Oman for the Reciprocal Promotion and Protection of Investment (signed 19 June 2015, entered into force 21 July 2017) art 15.4(c).
[173] Brigitte Stern, 'Civil Society's Voice in the Settlement of Investment Disputes' (2007) 22 ICSID Review 280; Eugenia Levine, 'Amicus Curiae in International Investment Arbitration: The Implications of an Increase in Third-Party Participation' (2011) 29 Berkeley Journal of International Law 200.
[174] *Methanex Corp v United States*, UNCITRAL, Decision on Petitions from Third Persons to Intervene as 'Amici Curiae' (15 January 2001).
[175] ibid para 24.
[176] ibid para 30.
[177] Transparency Rules (n 156) art 4.
[178] ibid art 5.
[179] 2015 Model BIT (n 86) art 22.4.

such a provision leaves open the scope for interpretation by the arbitral tribunal, as seen in the *Methanex* arbitration. It would therefore be advisable to incorporate express provisions governing submissions by third persons in the Model text. Although India is not yet a signatory to the Transparency Convention, the incorporation of transparency provisions in the 2015 Model BIT shows the country's intention to bring its BIT practice in line with the global standards. *Amicus curie* briefs are important tools in the facilitation of public access and participation in investment disputes, and several states in recent years have recognised this by incorporating enabling provisions in their investment treaties.[180] Therefore, if it aims to enhance public participation with respect to its investment disputes, providing procedural guidance for third-party submissions in the 2015 Model BIT may be an advantageous proposition for India.

d. Provisions on arbitral awards

Indian BITs generally contain brief and standardized provisions regarding arbitral awards under ISDS. The provisions on awards that are most commonly found in Indian BITs are as follows: (i) the arbitral award must be made in accordance to the relevant BIT and shall be binding on the parties to the dispute; (ii) the arbitral tribunal shall reach its decision by a majority of votes; and (iii) the arbitral tribunal shall state the basis of its decision and give reasons upon the request of either disputing party. The 2015 Model BIT foresees a shift in this practice through the incorporation of detailed provisions on the nature of arbitral award issued by a tribunal[181] as well as the enforcement procedures for the same.[182] The Model text states that an arbitral tribunal can only award monetary compensation for a breach of obligations under Chapter II (Obligations of Parties).[183] It further prohibits the arbitral tribunal from awarding punitive and moral damages or injunctive relief against the host state. While awarding damages, the arbitral tribunal must reduce any prior damages or compensation already provided to the investor by the host state. The arbitral tribunal shall also reduce the damages by taking into account any restitution of property, repeal/modification of the relevant state measure, or other mitigating factors.[184] The Model text explains the term 'mitigating factors' as including usage of the investment, compensation received by the investor from other sources, harm caused by the investor to the environment or local community as well as to balance public interest and the investor's interest.[185]

26.67

---

[180] Stern (n 173) 280.
[181] 2015 Model BIT (n 86) art 26.
[182] ibid art 27.
[183] ibid art 27.3.
[184] ibid.
[185] ibid.

26.68 The provisions as stated place significant restrictions on the kind of awards that can be issued by an arbitral tribunal. While there were no limitations set on the nature of awards that could be issued by arbitral tribunals under Indian BITs, the new Model text makes it clear that such awards must be limited only to monetary compensation. Although IIAs do not generally prohibit non-pecuniary remedies, there are very few publicly available cases where such remedies have been imposed (especially outside of the context of interim measures of injunctive relief). Cases dealing with such damages under ICSID and non-ICSID arbitrations are sparse.[186] However, arbitral tribunals are given some authority to adjudge over claims of restitution of property. For example, the 2012 US Model BIT permits a tribunal to issue awards for restitution of property, or for monetary compensation in lieu of the same.[187] The same feature may also be found in Canada's 2004 Model BIT.[188] The 2008 Austrian Model BIT goes even further by allowing restitution in kind in appropriate cases or other forms of relief that may be agreed to by the disputing parties.[189] The practice of states in contemporary BITs has also shown similar variations.

26.69 A mixed approach in this regard can also be seen in some recent treaties, such as the Iran–Slovakia BIT of 2016. This BIT takes an approach similar to the Indian Model text by expressly excluding punitive and moral damages. Additionally, it specifies that the arbitral tribunal shall consider deductions on quantum of damages awarded, based on balance of interests of both parties to the dispute.[190] At the same time, the BIT also permits the arbitral tribunal to issue awards in the form of monetary compensation as well as the restitution of property, depending on the type of the case.[191] By incorporating a stricter approach on the nature of awards, India may have sought to ensure that the arbitral tribunal does not overturn state actions or measures. At the same time, the arbitral tribunal must consider any restitution of property done voluntarily by the state in favour of the disputing investor while calculating the quantum of compensation to be awarded.[192]

26.70 It is quite pertinent to note at this point that India's FTAs diverge significantly on the provisions for arbitral awards from the 2015 Model BIT. In this regard, they seem to be modelled along the provisions of the US and Canada Model BITs. For example, in the recently signed ASEAN–India Investment Agreement, the

---

[186] Michelle Bradfield and JC Thomas, 'Non-Pecuniary Remedies: A Missed Opportunity?' (2015) 30 ICSID Review 635.
[187] 2012 US Model BIT (copy of the treaty text is available at <https://ustr.gov/sites/default/files/BIT%20text%20for%20ACIEP%20Meeting.pdf> accessed 10 April 2018) art 34.1(b).
[188] 2004 Canada Model BIT (n 168) art 44.1(b).
[189] 2008 Austrian Model BIT (n 123) art 19.1.
[190] Agreement between the Slovak Republic and the Islamic Republic of Iran for the Promotion and Reciprocal Protection of Investments (signed 19 January 2016) art 21.2.
[191] ibid art 21.3.
[192] 2015 Model BIT (n 86) art 26.3.

arbitral awards provisions allow for monetary compensation as well as restitution of property, in which case monetary compensation and applicable interest may be paid in lieu of restitution.[193] Only punitive damages are specifically barred, leaving the scope for interpretation open regarding moral damages or injunctive relief.[194] Older Indian FTAs such as those signed with Malaysia[195] and Japan[196] in 2011 contain similar provisions. However, considering that the 2015 Model BIT will be used for all future BIT as well as FTA negotiations, this divergence will likely be eliminated.

The provisions for enforcement of arbitral awards contained in the 2015 Model BIT are substantially similar to the US and Canadian Model BITs with minor differences in the text. These provisions limit the binding nature of the arbitral award exclusively to the disputing parties and for the particular case. The Model text provides separate pre-requisites for the enforcement of awards made under the ICSID Convention or the UNCITRAL Arbitration Rules.[197] Finally, the Model text provides that any claims arising out of the provisions on enforcement of arbitral awards will be considered as arising out of a commercial relationship or transaction under Article I of the Convention on the Recognition and Enforcement of Foreign Arbitral Awards 1958 (New York Convention)[198] to which India is a signatory. Here, the Model text implies that the provisions of the New York Convention are binding on such arbitrations. This is a re-working of the past practice of Indian BITs, which would simply state the applicability of the New York Convention on arbitral awards rendered by arbitral tribunals appointed under the provisions of the BIT. This is due to the fact that many states, such as India, declare that they will apply the New York Convention only to legal relationships deemed to be 'commercial'.[199] The 2004 Canada Model BIT also contains a similar provision.[200] An important factor regarding enforcement of awards with respect to India is that the country recognizes only one-third of the 156 current signatories to the New York Convention. India's Arbitration and Conciliation Act 1996 provides that the government must declare the recognition of such New York Convention signatory states in its official gazette.[201] For

26.71

---

[193] Agreement on Investment under the Framework Agreement on Comprehensive Economic Cooperation between the Association of Southeast Asian Nations and the Republic of India (signed 12 November 2014) art 20.21.
[194] ibid art 22.22.
[195] Malaysia–India FTA (n 60) art 10.41.21.
[196] Japan–India FTA (n 61) art 96.18(b).
[197] 2015 Model BIT (n 86) art 27.3.
[198] ibid.
[199] See UNCITRAL, Convention on the Recognition and Enforcement of Foreign Arbitral Awards (New York, 1958): Declarations or other Notifications Pursuant to Article I (3) and Article X (1) <http://www.uncitral.org/uncitral/en/uncitral_texts/arbitration/NYConvention_status.html> accessed 10 October 2016.
[200] 2004 Canada Model BIT (n 168) art 45.7.
[201] Arbitration and Conciliation Act 1996 (No 26 of 1996) s 44(b).

example, arbitral awards issued in China and Hong Kong became enforceable in India only in 2012, after official notification by the government of India.[202] Several developing countries in Africa and Latin America are yet to be recognized by India. Therefore, to ensure the effective enforcement of investment arbitral awards, the seat of arbitration should be in a state that is a signatory to the New York Convention and has also been recognized by the government of India.

e. Appeals facility

26.72 Perhaps one of the most innovative features of the 2015 Model BIT is that it foresees the development of an appellate body or a similar mechanism for the review of arbitral awards issued under the relevant BIT. The Model text provides the Contracting Parties with an option to establish an institutional mechanism for the development of such an appellate body.[203] Beyond reviewing awards for correctness, the appellate body may also provide coherence to interpretation of the relevant treaty provisions.[204] The Model text highlights certain factors that the Contracting Parties may consider while developing this mechanism, such as: (i) the nature and composition of the appellate body; (ii) the scope and standard of review; (iii) transparency of proceedings; (iv) effects of its decision-making and its relationship vis-à-vis other arbitral rules; as well as (v) issues of enforcement of the appellate body's decision-making. As no further details are provided in the Model text, it may be assumed that Contracting Parties are expected to use this basic framework to establish an appellate mechanism with a well-defined set of rules and regulations. The 2015 Model BIT also foresees such an appellate mechanism to be used under a multilateral agreement in the future.[205]

26.73 The possibility for an appellate mechanism within the ISDS system has already been widely discussed,[206] with the primary arguments of consistency and error reduction in favour of such an establishment. Contemporary FTAs such as the Comprehensive Economic and Trade Agreement (CETA) contain specific provisions for an appellate tribunal to review the awards issued by an arbitral tribunal.[207] Similarly, the text of the European Union's proposal for the Transatlantic

---

[202] Ministry of Law and Justice of the Government of India, Notification No F. No 12(164)/2012-Judl, *Gazette of India* (19 March 2012).
[203] 2015 Model BIT (n 86) art 29.
[204] ibid.
[205] ibid.
[206] Christian J Tams, 'An Appealing Option? The Debate About an ICSID Appellate Structure' (2006) 57 Beitrage Zum Transnationalen Wirtschaftsrecht 5 (discussing whether 'accuracy' serves as a value that favours the creation of an appellate mechanism within ICSID); Irene M Ten Cate, 'International Arbitration and the Ends of Appellate Review' (2012) 44 New York University Journal of International Law and Politics 1109 (discussing the 'lawmaking' value that an appellate mechanism may serve in investment arbitration); August Reinisch, 'The Future of Investment Arbitration' in Binder et al (eds) (n 111); Ketcheson (n 16).
[207] Comprehensive Economic and Trade Agreement (CETA) between Canada and the European Union and its Member States (signed 30 October 2016) art 8.28.

Trade and Investment Partnership (TTIP) Agreement under negotiation with the United States envisages a permanent appellate tribunal, although bilateral in nature.[208] Presently, there is no IIA-based appeals tribunal in existence with clear powers to review awards for errors of law and fact. Within the BIT regime, provisions on appellate bodies or mechanisms are still rare. The 2012 US Model BIT and some US agreements, for example, contain provisions foreseeing the development of an appellate body within the ISDS system.[209]

It must additionally be noted that although appellate systems established under standalone BITs may lead to greater consistency with respect to interpretation of the specific BIT's provisions, this may not necessarily translate into greater convergence among BITs overall. This is because each appellate system may operate independently within the framework of its relevant BIT, even though it is apparent that most BITs and IIAs adopt similar or even identical terminologies and provisions with respect to investment protection standards and ISDS. For the sake of greater consistency, an appellate facility established under a multilateral agreement among states may prove to be more suitable, but depends upon the creation of a legal and procedural framework for the functioning of such an appellate facility. UNCTAD's World Investment Report 2015 comments on the introduction of appeals facility as a 'new element' in the ISDS system.[210] At the same time, it highlights several issues similar to those provided in the 2015 Model BIT that must be resolved before an effective appeals mechanism can be incorporated. These include issues regarding the structure of such a body, its temporal nature, institutional setup, added time and costs of appeal as well as questions on competence. It is clear that Contracting Parties to a BIT must develop a framework that addresses these issues when incorporating provisions for appellate mechanisms. 26.74

f. Arbitrators and arbitral proceedings

Indian BITs have generally contained rudimentary provisions regarding the appointment of arbitrators and the process of establishment of an ad hoc arbitral tribunal under the UNCITRAL Rules. None of the BITs have ever had any specific provisions with regard to the arbitrator(s). However, with a growing trend among parties to challenge the appointment of arbitrators,[211] the need for establishment of clear rules that safeguard the rights of parties and reduce the probabilities of 26.75

---

[208] Trans-Atlantic Trade and Investment Partnership (US–EU) (not signed) art 10, ch II; European Union's proposal for Investment Protection and Resolution of Investment Disputes (November 2015) <http://trade.ec.europa.eu/doclib/docs/2015/november/tradoc_153955.pdf> accessed 10 October 2016.
[209] 2012 US Model BIT (n 187) art 28.10.
[210] UNCTAD, *World Investment Report 2015* (n 71) 149.
[211] Lars Markert, 'Challenging Arbitrators in Investment Arbitration: The Challenging Search for Relevant Standards and Ethical Guidelines' (2010) 3 Contemporary Asia Arbitration Journal 237; Chiara Giorgetti 'Challenges of International Investment Arbitrators: How Does It Work and Does It Work?' (2010) 7 World Arbitration and Mediation Review 303.

bias on the part of arbitrators have been rightly felt. In fact, case authorities with respect to challenges to the appointment of arbitrators have come up rapidly in the past two decades.[212] In fact, India had also filed a challenge in 2013 to the appointment of an arbitrator in its arbitration with Devas (Mauritius) Pvt Ltd.[213] In this case, India had challenged the appointment of two arbitrators by the Permanent Court of Arbitration on the ground that the arbitrators served together on two tribunals, which took a position on a legal issue that was expected to arise in the proceedings against India. Despite the rise of challenges to arbitrator appointment or arbitral proceedings, only recent investment treaties have adopted provisions governing the independence and impartiality of arbitrators.[214]

26.76 The 2015 Model BIT contains detailed provisions governing the processes of appointment of arbitrators (Article 18), prevention of conflict of interest of arbitrators and challenges (Article 19), conduct of arbitral proceedings (Article 20), and dismissal of frivolous claims (Article 21).

26.77 The challenge to the appointment of arbitrators in the *Devas* case was also an important lesson for Indian drafters, as the issue of impartiality of arbitrators became a major point of contention for the first time for the country in an investment dispute.[215] In this dispute conducted by the Permanent Court of Arbitration, India challenged the appointment of the Presiding Arbitrator and the arbitrator appointed by the claimant-investors[216] primarily on the ground that the two arbitrators had served together on two tribunals that took a position on a legal issue that was expected to arise in the dispute at hand. India contended that the strongly held and articulated positions by two of three arbitrators in the case on the legal standard of 'essential security interests' gave rise to 'justifiable doubts' as to their impartiality and constituted a valid reason for concern for the country.[217] Consequently, the challenge to the appointment of Professor Francisco Orrego Vicuña (the arbitrator appointed by the claimant-investors) was upheld by the President of the International Court of Justice (ICJ). This was on the grounds that Professor Vicuña's public position on the legal standard of 'essential security interests', as demonstrated in his writings, clearly showed that he had a fixed position on the subject and would not be able to preside with an 'open-mind'

---

[212] Sam Luttrell, 'Testing the ICSID Framework for Arbitrator Challenges' (2016) 31 ICSID Review 597.

[213] *CC/Devas (Mauritius) Ltd, Devas Employees Mauritius Private Limited and Telecom Devas Mauritius Limited v Republic of India*, Permanent Court of Arbitration Case No 2013-09, Decision on the Respondent's Challenge to the Hon Marc Lalonde as Presiding Arbitrator and Prof Francisco Orrego Vicuna as Co-Arbitrator (30 September 2013).

[214] UNCTAD, 'Reform of Investor-State' (n 14).

[215] Garg, Tripathy, and Roy (n 75) 96.

[216] Decision on the Respondent's Challenge to the Hon Marc Lalonde as Presiding Arbitrator and Prof Franciso Orrego Vicuna as Co-Arbitrator (n 213).

[217] ibid para 17.

on this issue.²¹⁸ This challenge by India was brought under Article 10(1) of the UNCITRAL Arbitration Rules, which allows for challenge to appointment of arbitrators on grounds of justifiable doubts regarding the arbitrator's independence and impartiality. However, there were no treaty provisions under the India–Mauritius BIT or other Indian BITs governing such instances of challenge to arbitrator appointment. The *Devas* experience therefore translated into detailed treaty-specific provisions under Article 19 of the 2015 Model BIT.²¹⁹ In fact, Article 19.10(h) provides a very specific ground for challenge, where 'the arbitrator has publicly advocated a fixed position regarding an issue on the case that is being arbitrated'—clearly influenced from the challenge raised in the *Devas* case.

26.78 Another likely source for the design of these provisions may be the amendment introduced in 2015 to the Arbitration and Conciliation Act 1996, India's primary piece of legislation governing domestic and international arbitration.²²⁰ The amendment incorporated substantial changes to India's arbitration law, including extensive disclosure requirements on the part of the arbitrator and allowing parties to challenge appointments on grounds of justifiable doubts regarding the arbitrators' independence and impartiality, or based on concerns that the arbitrators lack the necessary qualifications agreed to by the parties to the dispute.²²¹ An example of the close proximities between the provisions of the 2015 Model BIT and the amended Arbitration Act is with regard to the specific factors that can lead to 'justifiable doubt' regarding the independence and impartiality of an arbitrator, on the basis of which their appointment can be challenged. The 2015 Model BIT provides a non-exhaustive list of eight such grounds for challenge under Article 19.10, such as instances of personal and professional conflicts of interest, direct or indirect financial interests, and as discussed earlier, prior advocacy of a fixed position regarding an issue on the case that is being arbitrated.²²² A largely identical list of such grounds can be found under the Seventh Schedule of the Arbitration Act, which was introduced by the 2015 amendment.²²³ Similarly, the Model BIT provides for mandatory disclosure requirements ²²⁴ by the arbitrator, which are quite similar to corresponding provisions of the Amendment Act 2015.²²⁵

---

²¹⁸ ibid para 64.
²¹⁹ Garg, Tripathy, and Roy (n 75) 96.
²²⁰ Arbitration and Conciliation (Amendment) Act 2015 (No 3 of 2016).
²²¹ See specifically, Arbitration and Conciliation (Amendment) Act 2015, s 12 and the Sixth and Seventh Schedules attached therein, which provide for grounds for challenge to the appointment of arbitrators. For a detailed discussion, see Anurag K Agarwal, 'Arbitration and Conciliation (Amendment) Act, 2015: Arbitrators and Conflict of Interest' (2016) 2 NLS Business Law Review 87.
²²² 2015 Model BIT (n 86) art 19.10.
²²³ Arbitration and Conciliation (Amendment) Act 2015, sch 7.
²²⁴ 2015 Model BIT (n 86) art 19.2.
²²⁵ Arbitration and Conciliation (Amendment) Act 2015, s 12.2.

26.79 Beyond the aspect of appointment of arbitrators and the challenges against them, the Model BIT also addresses the issue of frivolous claims.[226] It provides an expedited process for dismissal of frivolous claims by an investor against a defending party on the grounds of (i) being outside the arbitral tribunal's scope of adjudication, or (ii) manifestly without legal merit or unfounded as a matter of law. Article 21.4 also mandates that the arbitral tribunal shall issue an award on such matters no later than 150 days after the date of the receipt of the request. The provisions again seem to have been largely borrowed from the 2012 US Model BIT,[227] which also provides for a similar expedited facility for the same. The objective of the expedited procedure is for the avoidance of time and resources on full proceedings for claims that can be dismissed at an early stage, and is important when accounting the high amount of costs involved in fully arbitrating the disputes. However, the tribunal is also provided the flexibility to decide that it cannot rule on the matter summarily or, when the issues are inextricably intertwined with the merits, it may decide that a hearing of the full case is warranted.[228]

26.80 Such provisions for addressing frivolous complaints are especially important for ad hoc arbitrations outside the ICSID's purview. ICSID amended its arbitration rules in 2006 to provide for an expedited decision on an objection that a claim is 'manifestly without legal merit' under Rule 41. However, the UNCITRAL Rules do not yet contain a similar expedited mechanism. Such a provision in the treaty text itself may therefore prove to be an important measure for states mired in numerous arbitrations that they deem to be frivolous.

E. Conclusions

26.81 For states that have initiated ISDS reform through the process of tailoring their existing BIT framework, a uniform approach is not always discernible, although many common elements and pathways for reforms have been identified. Many states have displayed understanding of the common set of measures that need to be implemented, such as limiting investor access to ISDS, narrowing substantive standards, bringing greater transparency and public access to arbitrations and providing for appellate facilities. In many instances, states have 'borrowed' provisions from the BITs of other states, indicating that significant interrelationships exist among BIT and ISDS systems of contracting as well as non-contracting states.

26.82 While trying to address and resolve the inconsistencies and structural weaknesses in its IIA policy, India has made an important contribution to the global discussion on ISDS reform by way of its Model BIT. While retaining arbitration at the

---

[226] 2015 Model BIT (n 86) art 21.
[227] 2012 US Model BIT (n 187) arts 28.4–28.5.
[228] UNCTAD, 'Reform of Investor-State' (n 14) 101–02.

heart of its system, the model text significantly enhances the state's control over the ISDS mechanism as opposed to past practice. Although the disputing investor is not deprived of legal remedies, it has to strictly follow a stringent set of rules, procedures, and time limitations, which will certainly have an impact upon the choice of investors to pursue such procedures. The focus on improving transparency and accountability of the arbitral process is clearly visible, and quite critically so with respect to arbitrators, who play a central role in the dispute settlement system. Here the Model BIT recognizes the importance of an impartial and independent arbitrator, and the procedures implemented should significantly enhance the perception of ISDS as a viable method for dispute settlement.

26.83 Situating the 2015 Indian Model BIT in the context of global ISDS reform, it is apparent that the Indian model text has drawn significantly from recent treaty practices of other states, most notably the United States and Canada, while at the same time responding to its recent experiences with investor claims and disputes as well as to reforms in its domestic arbitration law. It may be argued that the changes instituted in the ISDS Chapter as well as other parts of the Model text, while continuing the faith placed by the country on arbitration as a system of resolving investment-related disputes, also adopts a system which is more guarded and protective of state interests.

26.84 While it is difficult to fully gauge the impact of the Model BIT, considering the fact that no investment agreement has yet been finalized or made public by India since the adoption of the new text, it has drawn reactions across several quarters that may provide useful guidance on how the Model BIT may be perceived among stakeholders and participants. India's decision to terminate its old BITs that were close to expiry and move to renegotiate other texts indicates the seriousness with which the country is proceeding with its investment treaty reforms. Capital exporting economies such as the United States and EU have been critical of the more restrictive provisions of the Model text,[229] as well as India's decision to abandon its existing agreements.[230] The ongoing negotiations for the multilateral Regional Comprehensive Economic Partnership (RCEP) are indicative of a more guarded stance with respect to ISDS, where India has been significantly more deliberative and careful of state interests while considering the width and application of ISDS.[231] At the same time, as India shifts towards an increasingly

---

[229] Prabhash Ranjan, 'Bit of a Bumpy Ride' *The Hindu* (Chennai, 2 June 2016) < http://www.thehindu.com/opinion/op-ed/Bit-of-a-bumpy-ride/article14378406.ece> accessed 10 March 2017.

[230] For instance, see the European Commissioner for Trade Cecilia Malmstrom's letter to the Indian government dated 25 May .2016 urging the government not to abandon its existing BITs with European nations and its possible negative impact on future investments if a new investment agreement was not negotiated in an expedited manner (Ref Ares(2016)2423246—25/05/2016).

[231] Shalini Bhutani, 'RCEP Meet: Focus on Investor-State disputes' *Deccan Herald* (Bengaluru, 3 August 2016) <http://www.deccanherald.com/content/561863/rcep-meet-focus-investor-state.html> accessed 10 March 2017.

capital exporting model in the future and its investors begin to look abroad for investment, India may also negotiate to dilute some of the more stringent requirements provided in the Model BIT, such as the minimum period of five years for exhaustion of local remedies, in order for Indian investors to have easier access to arbitration proceedings.

26.85 Implementing these substantial amendments in future investment agreements may prove to be a far more difficult process, especially in situations where politically the outcome (finalizing an investment treaty) may seemingly outweigh the costs (conceding on key provisions). With respect to ISDS, it is very likely that states that generally provide far more flexible access to investment arbitration in their treaty practice may resist the inclusion of some of the more restrictive provisions of the Model BIT, not just with respect to ISDS but also extending into crucial aspects, such as the mutually agreed standards of investment protection. One of India's most radical policy decisions in drafting the 2015 Model BIT was to altogether exclude MFN as an investment protection standard. It will be interesting to see whether India's treaty partners will also agree to adopt such changes. As noted earlier, there is no general consensus among states regarding the modalities of ISDS reform, with several states adopting distinct paths to reform. Nevertheless, India stands to benefit from cooperation with like-minded states that are pushing for increased protection of state interests and also considering improvements or alternatives to the arbitration-based model of investment dispute settlement, such as a multilateral investment court system.[232] While India has chosen not to abandon investment arbitration altogether, some of the country's recent practices[233] suggests that it is willing to adopt a flexible and interest-based approach in its negotiations.

---

[232] For instance, the EU Commission has proposed to develop its Investment Court System that was formulated in its TTIP proposals into a multilateral system. The Commission recently released a recommendation in this regard. See Commission, 'Recommendation for a Council Decision authorising the opening of negotiations for a Convention establishing a multilateral court for the settlement of investment disputes' COM(2017) 493 final. This may play a crucial role in the negotiation of a long awaited EU–India FTA that has been in negotiation since 2007.

[233] The conclusion of the negotiations between India and Brazil on a CFIA in November 2016, which reportedly does not include ISDS, seems to suggest that India is willing to be far more flexible than the stance adopted in the Model BIT. See Joel Dahlquist, 'Brazil and India Conclude Bilateral Investment Treaty' *Investment Arbitration Reporter* (2016) <http://www.iareporter.com/articles/brazil-and-india-conclude-bilateral-investment-treaty/>. However, the results of the ongoing negotiations for the mega-regional RCEP Agreement (which is reported to contain ISDS), may prove to be a key indicator of Indian government's position viz-a-viz ISDS.